T0134778

Lecture Notes in Computer Science   13972

Founding Editors

Gerhard Goos
Juris Hartmanis

Editorial Board Members

The series Lecture Notes in Computer Science (LNCS), including its subseries Lecture Notes in Artificial Intelligence (LNAI) and Lecture Notes in Bioinformatics (LNBI), has established itself as a medium for the publication of new developments in computer science and information technology research, teaching, and education.

LNCS enjoys close cooperation with the computer science R & D community, the series counts many renowned academics among its volume editors and paper authors, and collaborates with prestigious societies. Its mission is to serve this international community by providing an invaluable service, mainly focused on the publication of conference and workshop proceedings and postproceedings. LNCS commenced publication in 1973.

Isaac Sserwanga · Anne Goulding ·
Heather Moulaison-Sandy · Jia Tina Du ·
António Lucas Soares · Viviane Hessami ·
Rebecca D. Frank
Editors

Information for a Better World: Normality, Virtuality, Physicality, Inclusivity

18th International Conference, iConference 2023
Virtual Event, March 13–17, 2023
Proceedings, Part II

Springer

Editors
Isaac Sserwanga
iSchool Organization
Berlin, Germany

Anne Goulding ⓘ
Victoria University of Wellington
Wellington, New Zealand

Heather Moulaison-Sandy ⓘ
University of Missouri
Chicago, IL, USA

Jia Tina Du ⓘ
University of South Australia
Adelaide, SA, Australia

António Lucas Soares ⓘ
University of Porto
Porto, Portugal

Viviane Hessami ⓘ
Monash University
Clayton, VIC, Australia

Rebecca D. Frank ⓘ
University of Tennessee at Knoxville
Knoxville, TN, USA

ISSN 0302-9743   ISSN 1611-3349 (electronic)
Lecture Notes in Computer Science
ISBN 978-3-031-28031-3   ISBN 978-3-031-28032-0 (eBook)
https://doi.org/10.1007/978-3-031-28032-0

This Springer imprint is published by the registered company Springer Nature Switzerland AG
The registered company address is: Gewerbestrasse 11, 6330 Cham, Switzerland

Preface

The first wave of COVID-19 disrupted normality and changed the course of the last two years. People became more restricted to their homes. These became times of reflection with the positive effect of more scientific research and more contributions in diverse fields. The Information Sciences played a pivotal role in sustaining our engagement. Working from home became the new normal. Over time, hybrid work became preferable to in-office work as restrictions were eased. The waves of COVID-19 led to new variants, which caused more specific restrictions, but effective vaccine rollouts reduced the threat until once again borders were opened for business.

The existing and demand-driven platforms opened diverse networking opportunities. This brings us to the hybrid iConference 2023 and its virtual and physical components.

As the academic world still explored the virtual, the organizers of the 18th iConference used remote networking to complement outreach and participation globally. This was inherent in the theme of *Normality, Virtuality, Physicality, and Inclusivity.*

The virtual iConference 2023 took place 10 days before the physical conference in Barcelona, Spain. Its hosts included the Universitat Oberta de Catalunya, Monash University, and University of Illinois at Urbana-Champaign. Physical meetings took place at Casa Convalescència on the historical site of the Hospital de la Santa Creu i Sant Pau.

The conference theme attracted a total of 197 submissions with 98 Full Research Papers, 96 Short Research Papers and 3 Information Sustainability Research Papers.

In a double-blind review process by 346 internationally renowned experts, 85 entries were approved, including 36 Full Research Papers and 46 Short Research Papers. The approval rate was 37% for the Full Research Papers and 48% for the Short Research Papers. Additional submissions were selected for the Workshops and Panels, the Doctoral Colloquium, the Early Career Colloquium, the Student Symposium, the Poster session, and the Spanish-Portuguese and Chinese language paper sessions.

The Full, Short and Information Sustainability Research papers are published for the eighth time in Springer's *Lecture Notes in Computer Science* (LNCS). These proceedings are sorted into the following fourteen categories, reflecting the diversity of the information research areas: Archives and Records, Behavioral Research, Information Governance and Ethics, AI and Machine Learning, Data Science, Information and Digital Literacy, Cultural Perspectives, Knowledge Management and Intellectual Capital, Social Media and Digital Networks, Libraries, Human-Computer Interaction and Technology, Information Retrieval, Community Informatics, and Digital Information Infrastructure.

We greatly appreciate the reviewers for their expertise and valuable review work and the track chairs for their relentless effort and vast expert knowledge. We wish to extend our gratitude to the chairs and volume editors; Full Research Papers chairs, Anne Goulding from Victoria University of Wellington, and Heather Moulaison-Sandy from University of Missouri; Short Research Paper chairs, Jia Tina Du from University of

South Australia, and António Lucas Soares from Universidade do Porto; and Information Sustainability Papers chairs, Viviane Hessami from Monash University and Rebecca D. Frank from University of Tennessee.

The iConference lived up to its global representation of iSchools to harness the synergy of research and teaching in the field of information and complementary areas of sustainability.

January 2023

Isaac Sserwanga
Anne Goulding
Heather Moulaison-Sandy
Jia Tina Du
António Lucas Soares
Viviane Hessami
Rebecca D. Frank

Organization

Organizer

Universitat Oberta de Catalunya, Spain

Conference Chairs

Josep Cobarsí Morales	Universitat Oberta de Catalunya, Spain
Gillian Oliver	Monash University, Australia
J. Stephen Downie	University of Illinois at Urbana-Champaign, USA

Program Chairs

Local Arrangements Chair

Jordi Conesa   Universitat Oberta de Catalunya, Spain

Proceedings Chair

Isaac Sserwanga   Humboldt-Universität zu Berlin (iSchools.Inc), Germany

Full Research Paper Chairs

Anne Goulding	Victoria University of Wellington, New Zealand
Heather Moulaison-Sandy	University of Missouri, USA

Short Research Paper Chairs

Jia Tina Du	University of South Australia, Australia
António Lucas Soares	Universidade do Porto, Portugal

Poster Chairs

Caddie Gao   Monash University, Australia
Fredrik Hanell   Linnaeus University, Sweden

Information Sustainability Chairs

Viviane Hessami   Monash University, Australia
Rebecca D. Frank   University of Tennessee, USA

Spanish - Portuguese Papers Chairs

Sara Martínez Cardama   Universidad Carlos III de Madrid, Spain
Marta Ligia Pomim Valentim   Universidade Estadual Paulista, Brazil
Diana Lucio Arias   Pontificia Universidad Javeriana, Colombia

Chinese Paper Chairs

Lihong Zhou   Wuhan University, China
Lei Pei   Nanjing University, China
Hui Yan   Renmin University of China, China

Chinese Event Co-chairs

Di Wang   Wuhan University, China
Yuehua Zhao   Nanjing University, China
Zekun Yang   Renmin University of China, China

Workshops and Panel Chairs

Misita Anwar   Monash University, Australia
Antoni Pérez-Navarro   Universitat Oberta de Catalunya, Spain
Virginia Ortíz-Repiso   Universidad Carlos III de Madrid, Spain

Student Symposium Chairs

Emi Ishita   Kyushu University, Japan
Peter Organisciak   University of Denver, USA
Romain Herault   Linnaeus University, Sweden

Early Career Colloquium Chairs

Mary Grace Golfo-Barcelona	University of the Philippines, The Philippines
Stefanie Havelka	University College Dublin, Ireland
Kate McDowell	University of Illinois at Urbana-Champaign, USA
J. Stephen Downie	University of Illinois at Urbana-Champaign, USA

Doctoral Colloquium Chairs

Joanne Evans	Monash University, Australia
Peter Darch	University of Illinois at Urbana-Champaign, USA
Kirsten Schlebbe	Humboldt-Universität zu Berlin, Germany

Doctoral Dissertation Award Chair

Sandy Hirsh	San José State University, USA

Conference Coordinators

Michael Seadle	iSchools Organization
Slava Sterzer	iSchools Organization
Katharina Gudat	iSchools Organization

Reviewers Full and Short Papers iConference 2023 (346)

Jacob Abbott	Alex Ball
Waseem Afzal	Jessica Kristen Barfield
Noa Aharony	Sarah Barriage
Shameem Ahmed	Zoe Bartliff
Isola Ajiferuke	Gabrielle Baumert
Bader Albahlal	John Robert Bautista
Nicole D. Alemanne	Nanyi Bi
Daniel Alemneh	Bradley Wade Bishop
Hamed Alhoori	Monisa Biswas
Lilach Alon	Maria Bonn
Xiaomi An	Christine L. Borgman
Karen Ann Subin	Theo J. D. Bothma
Misita Anwar	Guillaume Boutard
Muhamammad Naveed	Leane Bowler
Tatjana Aparac-Jelusic	Sarah Bratt
Rhea Rowena Ubana	Paulina Bressel
Hanimm Maria Astuti	Jenny Bronstein

Jo Ann Brooks
Sarah A. Buchanan
Julia Bullard
Mimi Byun
Jennifer Campbell-Meier
Yu Cao
Zhe Cao
Sunandan Chakraborty
Wayland Chang
Yu-Wei Chang
Yun-Chi Chang
Tiffany Chao
Catherine Chavula
Hadyn Chen
Hsin-liang Chen
Hsuanwei Chen
Hui Chen
Jiangping Chen
Minghong Chen
Xiaoyu Chen
Chola Chhetri
Alfred Chikomba
Inkyung Choi
Wonchan Choi
Yunseon Choi
Steven Siu Fung Chong
Anthony Shong-yu Chow
Alton Y. K. Chua
Eunkyung Chung
Mónica Colón-Aguirre
Andrea Copeland
Chris Coward
Andrew Cox
Peter Cruickshank
Sally Jo Cunningham
Amber L. Cushing
Mats Dahlstrom
Gabriel David
Rebecca Davis
Mozhden Dehghani
Shengli Deng
Tom Denison
Brian Dobreski
Güleda Doğan
Karsten Donnay

Caifan Du
Yunfei Du
Yiran Duan
Kedma Duarte
Avsalom Elmalech
Aems Emswiler
Kristin Eschenfelder
Tao Fan
Bruce Ferwerda
Rachek Fleming-May
Fred Fonseca
Ina Fourie
Rebecca D. Frank
Darin Freeburg
Hengyi Fu
Yaming Fu
Maria Gäde
Abdullah Gadi
Chunmei Gan
Zheng Gao
Emmanouel Garoufallou
Yegin Genc
Diane Gill
Dion Goh
Melissa Gross
Michael Gryk
Ece Gumusel
Qiuyan Guo
Kailash Gupta
Neslihan Gurol
Ayse Gursoy
Hazel Hall
Ariel Hammond
Ruohua Han
Kun Hang
Yue Hao
Bruce Hartpence
Stefanie Havelka
Suliman Hawamdeh
Anisah Herdiyanti
Viviane Hessami
Alison Hicks
Simon Hodson
Darra Lynn Hofman
Chris Holstrom

Liang Hong
Lingzi Hong
Md Khalid Hossain
Wenjun Hou
Tsung-Ming Hsiao
Yuerong Hu
Liuyu Huang
Qian Huang
Ruhua Huang
Yun Huang
Yuting Huang
Isto Huvila
Charles Inskip
Yvette Iribe Ramirez
Vanessa Irvin
Emi Ishita
Jonathan Isip
Hiroyoshi Ito
Fariha Tasmin Jaigirdar
Sabrina Olivia Jeffcoat
Wei Jeng
Michael Jones
Heidi Julien
Jaap Kamps
Jai Kang
Ijay Kaz-Onyeakazi
Mat Kelly
Rebecca Kelly
Heikki Keskustalo
Jigya Khabar
Saurabh Khanna
Mahmood Khosrowjerdi
Jeonghyun Kim
Soo Hyeon Kim
Vanessa Kitzie
Bart Knijnenburg
Kyungwon Koh
Masanori Koizumi
Rebecca Koskela
Adam Kriesberg
Mucahid Kutlu
Sara Lafia
Sucheta Lahiri
Deborah Lee
Jian-Sin Lee

Jin Ha Lee
Jou Lee
Kijung Lee
Lo Lee
Alyssa Lees
Guangjian Li
Ying Li
Yingya Li
Lizhen Liang
Louise Limberg
Chi-Shiou Lin
Chiao Min Lin
Jenny Lindberg
Henry Linger
Zack Lischer-Katz
Ping Liu
Yuyang Liu
Jean D. Louis
Kun Lu
Ana Lucic
Xiao Luo
Lai Ma
Rongqian Ma
Kate Marek
Shutian Ma
Simon Mahony
Krista-Lee Meghan Malone
Jin Mao
Kathryn Masten
Machdel Catharina Matthee
Matthew S. Mayernik
Kate McDowell
Claire McGuinness
Pamela Ann McKinney
David McMenemy
Humphrey Mensah
Shuyuan Metcalfe
Selina Meyer
Shawne Miksa
J. Elizabeth Mills
Stasa Milojevic
Marina Milosheva
Chao Min
Yue Ming
Lorri Mon

Jennifer Moore
Atsuyuki Morishima
Lidia Morris
Angela Murillo
Karim Nader
Jessica Navedo
Leila Nemati-Anaraki
David M. Nichols
Melissa G. Ocepek
Lydia Ladi Ogbadu-Oladapo
Erezi Ruth Ogbo
Gillian Oliver
Peter Organisciak
Felipe Ortega
Abraham Oshni Alvandi
Giulia Osti
Guiyan Ou
Yohanan Ouaknine
Murat Ozer
Kathleen Padova
Shreya Paithankar
Velian Pandeliev
Hyoungjoo Park
Min Sook Park
SoHyun Park
Olivia Pestana
Bobby Phuritsabam
Mary Pietrowicz
Ola Pilerot
Alex Poole
Xin Qian
Redoan Rahman
Diane Rasmussen Pennington
Christopher B. Rauch
Alexandria Rayburn
Ariel Rosenfeld
Vassilis Routsis
Alan Rubel
Sarah Elizabeth Ryan
Jumana Salem
Rachel Salzano
Madelyn Rose Sanfilippo
Vitor Santos
Moritz Schubotz
Charles Senteio

Elizabeth Shaffer
Kalpana Shankar
Ryan Shaw
Kristina Shiroma
T. S. Paumunmuang Simte
Luanne Sinnamon
Stephen Slota
Alexander Smith
Catharine Smith
Sheetal Sonawane
Shijie Song
Clay Spinuzzi
Beth St. Jean
Gretchen Renee Stahlman
Hrvoje Stancic
Owen Stewart-Robertson
Caroline Stratton
Jacob Striebel
Besiki Stvilia
Shigeo Sugimoto
Ran Sun
Sebastian Sünkler
Tanja Svarre
Sue Yeon Syn
Andrea Karoline Thomer
Janet Toland
Chunhua Tsai
Tien-I Tsai
Alissa Tudor
Pertti Vakkari
Lulian Vamanu
Frans van der Sluis
Martie van Deventer
Nicholas Vanderschantz
Nitin Verma
Travis Wagner
Jan Philip Wahle
Di Wang
Hao Wang
Jieyu Wang
Lin Wang
Shengang Wang
Yanyan Wang
Ian Robert Watson
Seren Elisabeth Wendelken

Muhamad Prabu Wibowo
Rachel D. Williams
Steven John Wright
Dan Wu
I-Chin Wu
Peng Wu
Ting Xiao
Jian Xu
Lifang Xu
Shenmeng Xu
Xiao Xue
Hui Yan
Lijun Yang
Yu-Ju Yang
Ayoung Yoon
JungWon Yoon
Sarah Young
Bei Yu

Fei Yu
Xiaojun Yuan
Xianjin Zha
Yujia Zhai
Bin Zhang
Chengzhi Zhang
Chenwei Zhang
Pengyi Zhang
Xiaojuan Zhang
Xinyu Zhang
Ziming Zhang
Yiming Zhao
Yuxiang (Chris) Zhao
Jing Zhou
Lihong Zhou
Qinghua Zhu
Han Zhuang

Contents – Part II

Human-Computer Interaction and Technology

Information Retrieval

Community Informatics

Digital Information Infrastructures

Contents – Part I

Information Governance and Ethics

AI and Machine Learning

Data Science

Information and Digital Literacy

Cultural Perspectives

Knowledge Management
and Intellectual Capital

Enabling Knowledge Management Practices in Museums: The Benefits of and Barriers to Achieving Public Value

Neville Vakharia[1]([⊠]) [iD] and Alex H. Poole[2] [iD]

[1] Department of Arts and Entertainment Enterprise, College of Media Arts and Design, Drexel University, Philadelphia, PA 19104, USA
nkv22@drexel.edu
[2] Department of Information Science, College of Computing and Informatics, Drexel University, Philadelphia, PA 19104, USA

Abstract. This qualitative case study explores a new approach to understanding knowledge management in a specific type of information organization: museums. We adapt the broader constructs of knowledge management enablers (KMEs) and a knowledge management orientation (KMO) to study how museums augment their public value through inclusive and equitable community engagement. Semistructured interviews with 45 senior leaders of art and science museums teased out 26 beneficial practices and barriers related to knowledge management enablers and a knowledge management orientation. We found that museums who exhibited these beneficial practices were more successful in creating public value than those who faced barriers in doing so. This critical link between enabling knowledge management practices and public value both opens new research opportunities and suggests practical implications.

Keywords: Knowledge management · Museums · Public value

1 Introduction

Facing the dual challenges of providing increased public value to justify public funding and of grappling with the effects of a global pandemic, museums are at a crucial juncture. As institutions that accumulate, analyze, and distribute knowledge, museums have long provided fertile ground for information science research [1]. Much of this research focuses on information organization and classification related to objects and collections [2–6], or on the role of information professionals who adapt new technologies that foster information organization [7, 8]. While such research helps illuminate museums' core stewardship functions, museums also face ever-increasing pressure to improve their organizational performance and demonstrate their public value to local communities and to society more broadly [9, 10], areas where significant research gaps exist [11].

Understanding the role of knowledge management, specifically its enabling factors and practices, empowers museums to thrive in a uniquely challenging environment.

I. Sserwanga et al. (Eds.): iConference 2023, LNCS 13972, pp. 3–15, 2023.
https://doi.org/10.1007/978-3-031-28032-0_1

Insight into the benefits of and challenges to knowledge management enabling practices provides a holistic view of how museums can remove barriers, implement effective strategies, and augment their public value.

This paper addresses two research questions. First, what benefits and challenges do museums experience in managing organizational knowledge? Second, how do these benefits and challenges affect these museums' ability to provide public value to diverse and often underserved communities? Understanding how leaders of museums facilitate practices that enhance public value opens a vital stream of research with broad implications not only for the study of museums as information organizations, but for their day-to-day practice.

2   Literature Review

Knowledge management is a capacious term [12–16]; scholars have defined and employed it as a theory, a construct, a practice, and a field of study [16–19]. That said, most perspectives on knowledge management frame it as a constellation of socio-technical organizational approaches and practices that embraces knowledge, people, processes, and technology [20]. The conceptual lens of knowledge management offers timely insights into the enabling factors and practices of museums' leaders as they face the exigent challenge of demonstrating public value. Leadership, scholars argue, must intentionally and strategically create the systems and processes that emphasize creating, managing, and sharing museums' organizational knowledge both internally and externally [9, 21, 22].

Since organizational knowledge management scholarship spans multiple concepts and literatures, it can be studied effectively through its enabling factors, termed knowledge management enablers (KMEs), and through the activities that foster it, known as a knowledge management orientation (KMO).

2.1   Knowledge Management Enablers (KMEs)

KMEs initiate knowledge creation and sharing [23–25]. They comprise four dimensions as identified by Lee and Choi [26]: (1) an organizational culture of collaboration and trust; (2) decentralized and non-hierarchical organizational structures; (3) T-shaped worker skills (workers have deep knowledge in their own areas and broad knowledge of what their colleagues do); and (4) well-used and well-supported information technology [see also 27–30].

While scholars have studied KMEs in multiple industries and organization types [28, 31, 32], they have yet to do so in the museum sector—much to the latter's detriment. Museum-oriented scholarship on knowledge management, in fact, has primarily focused on the latter's relationship to museum collections, curatorial processes, and the use of emerging technologies [33–35]. Adapting and assessing KMEs to museums permits a more holistic and rigorous view not only of how museums foster knowledge creation and sharing, but also how they can augment their public value.

2.2 Knowledge Management Orientation (KMO)

An organization's strategic orientation guides its internal and external practices [36–38]. This orientation helps understand an organization's actions and provides a broader view of its goal-oriented practices [39, 40]. A KMO represents one such strategic orientation; a KMO organization effectively leverages knowledge management activities to meet its objectives [41, 42]. Darroch [41], for example, identified and validated three dimensions of KMO activities—(1) knowledge acquisition, (2) knowledge dissemination, and (3) responsiveness to knowledge—that are useful in studying KMO [43, 44].

As with KMEs, scholars have yet to study KMO in museums. Some studies hint at how such an orientation could be developed, however. For one, Fuller [45] urged museums to stimulate knowledge management by improving their training, mentorship, and professional development practices. Understanding museums' strategies to harness knowledge management through a KMO provides insights into how museums strategically acquire, disseminate, and profit from organizational knowledge, and how these activities channel into their ability to enhance their public value.

2.3 Museums and Public Value

Public value denotes the ways in which public and publicly supported institutions can benefit multiple stakeholders, including those served by the organization and those it seeks to serve [46, 47]. To increase its public value, an organization must muster the operational capacity necessary to effectively use its resources [48]. Thus, creating public value represents a strategic management function; it is, more precisely, a key component of overall organizational performance [49]. In museums, Scott [9, 50] found that public value centers on promoting social cohesion, effecting positive social change, and extending their reach into communities, even as museums steward public investment. Given museums' responsibility to promote organizational capacity and management expertise, their senior leadership remains responsible for achieving high levels of organizational performance and thus public value [49, 51].

3 Method

Our qualitative case study [52] centers on semistructured interviews [53] with senior leaders of United States-based museums. Questions adapted Lee and Choi's [29] four dimensions of KMEs and Darroch's [41, 43] three dimensions of KMO. We assessed public value based on elements of Scott's [9, 49] model; we homed in on inclusivity and community engagement approaches.

To obtain a broad perspective, we concentrated on small and mid-sized museums because they comprise the majority of museums in the United States [54]. Further, we focused on art museums and science museums since each embraces a distinct role and mission. While art museums tend to be more collections-focused, science museums tend to focus on education and public programs [54]. Assessing these two types of museums provided the ability to determine if our constructs varied by museum type.

Using the most comprehensive database of museums in the United States [55], we cross-tabulated the data by size (income) and by discipline, identifying a total population of 1,116 small and mid-sized art and science museums (780 art museums and 336 science museums). We then invited the senior leaders from a random sample of these museums to participate in an interview. We interviewed 45 senior museum leaders (25 art museums and 20 science museums; we identify these interviewees as P1-P45). At that point we achieved thematic saturation. We recorded, transcribed, and coded our interviews. A two-stage coding process was undertaken, using *a priori* provisional coding of each construct dimension as the first stage and pattern coding as the second stage, a preferred approach when assessing these types of extant constructs [56].

4 Findings

Provisional coding identified 1,109 references to beneficial practices and barriers as filtered through each dimension of the study's three constructs (KMEs, KMO, and public value). Second-stage pattern coding on the provisional coding references subsequently identified the most common beneficial practices (16; Table 1) and barriers (14; Table 2) that emerged as museum leaders described how they addressed KMEs, KMO, and public value. (Definitions of each pattern code are in the Appendix).

4.1 KMEs: Analyzing Beneficial Practices and Barriers

Pattern coding of the four KMEs' dimensions elicited 16 themes that adumbrated the benefits and challenges leaders faced. The most frequent beneficial practice interviewees reported was their intentional effort to create a collaborative organizational culture that both supported effective knowledge management and helped to foster new ideas and innovation. P8 explained, "I am, by nature, extremely collaborative...I want a bunch of smart people sitting around a table thinking out loud together." In similar spirit, P31 predicted, "the work that we're doing to be collaborative will push us towards innovation."

Conversely, many interviewees struggled to cultivate a collaborative culture. They underscored staff burnout and workload issues; these impeded museums' ability to instantiate knowledge management practices. "I see that people are working more hours than they should be expected to. They are asked to do so many other things that are not within the scope of their job function, which is problematic," explained P4. Two interviewees confessed that burnout had compelled them to leave their museums.

Beneficial practices noted by museum leaders who successfully implemented KMEs included distributed decision making, effective documentation that supported increased knowledge sharing, cross-training of staff, and the use of integrated IT systems scaled to fit the museum and prioritized by leadership. Exemplifying these responses, P14 described his approach to distributed decision making. He stated, "there's a lot of decision making that our staff is doing, and I don't need to know about it, and we're not unnecessarily hampering them in making the decisions that they need to make."

By contrast, challenges interviewees cited with practicing KMEs included a rigid hierarchy, a lack of policies and procedures, a lack of resources to provide effective training, and IT systems that are either unsupported or utilized ineffectively. P45 described a situation that epitomized these challenges: "there was no process in place for how we

Table 1. Provisional codes and associated pattern codes of beneficial practices

Provisional code	Pattern code (Beneficial practices)
KME - Culture	Leader empowerment
	New ideas and thinking
KME - Structure	Delegation with clarity
	Effective documentation and usage
KME - Skills	Cross-training
KME - IT and support	Integrated systems
	Leader prioritization
	Scale matches need
KMO - Acquisition	Continuous professional development
	Knowledge networks
KMO - Dissemination	Structured interpersonal knowledge sharing
	Systems of knowledge sharing
KMO - Responsiveness	Market and stakeholder insights
	Learning from failure
Public value	Museum beyond its walls
	Linking to communities

captured information, where information was stored, and how decisions needed to be made."

4.2 KMO: Analyzing Beneficial Practices and Barriers

Pattern coding of the three dimensions of KMO teased out 10 themes that depict the beneficial practices and the obdurate barriers museum leaders faced. The most frequently cited beneficial KMO practices included professional development for staff, first, and leveraging knowledge networks, second. It was not enough to simply allow staff to engage in professional development, interviewees suggested; organizations intentionally created opportunities for both formal and informal professional development—and materially supported these opportunities. P10 emphasized how her institution incorporated formal professional development into every staff member's role: "We have a robust professional development program and budget. It's built around performance planning, so at the start of the year you would identify opportunities or skill sets and we talk about how we can work on those."

Table 2. Provisional codes and associated pattern codes of barriers

Provisional code	Pattern code (Barriers)
KME - Culture	Burnout/workload
	Silos as barriers to knowledge sharing
KME - Structure	Lack of policies/procedures
	Rigid hierarchy
KME - Skills	Lack of resources
KME - IT and support	Lack of support
	Resistance to use
	Lack of skills
KMO - Acquisition	Lack of resources
	Lack of prioritization
KMO - Dissemination	Lack of knowledge repositories
KMO - Responsiveness	Lack of evaluation
Public value	Representation
	Geographic context

Both formal and informal knowledge sharing networks played important roles in securing the benefits of KMO. Museums that successfully disseminated knowledge created both formalized and interpersonal means of sharing important information broadly—even as they incorporated technical systems that shared information tailored to specific designated stakeholders. Museum leaders described various staff and departmental meetings that focused on sharing knowledge broadly. These meetings ranged from small, daily briefings to larger all-staff affairs that intentionally encouraged sharing. Other interviewees described their success with less formal modes of interpersonal knowledge sharing. Ultimately, beneficial KMO practices coalesced around the combined use of formal and informal knowledge sharing networks.

Museum leaders who successfully implemented the dimensions of KMO reported other beneficial practices. These included technology-centered knowledge sharing, using market and stakeholder data to inform decisions, and learning from failure. While these KMO practices provided significant benefits to museums that exhibited them, museums that did not encountered significant difficulties. P12 confessed that "people really, really, want to have data-informed decisions. None of us know what we're doing is the best way I can put it."

The main challenges museum leaders cited in undertaking KMO practices included a lack of their ability to prioritize knowledge sharing, a lack of knowledge repositories, and a lack of evaluation of their efforts. P35 described resistance to evaluation because "there's a fear with any kind of evaluation that we're going to hear what we don't want to hear." Thus, these challenges hinder knowledge sharing and dissemination and create significant barriers to museums achieving a KMO.

4.3 KMEs and KMO's Impact on Public Value

We conducted pattern coding of the public value provisional codes, identifying four themes, to understand if the beneficial practices of and barriers to KMEs and KMO relate directly to a museum's ability to provide public value. Looking at interviewees who exhibited the beneficial practices of KMEs and KMO, we found a clear link to their ability to achieve the benefits of public value. Put another way, museum leaders that described effective approaches to achieving public value delivered relevant programs to diverse communities outside of their physical spaces rather than expecting them to come into their museums. These leaders additionally understood that reaching diverse communities required collaboration with other trusted organizations that also serve these communities. Museum leaders who prioritized bringing their programs into diverse communities and described it as central to their museum's role. "We pop up at things like big community festivals, but then we've also been doing things like popping up at Walmart," explained P20. P20's approach drove the museum's overarching efforts to serve diverse populations. Understanding the needs of a museum's community, in other words, steers efforts outside of the museum. "We have a lot of programs that we take to schools because a lot of times the schools just can't afford the busing," affirmed P13. Those museums that enabled and practiced effective dimensions of knowledge management, in sum, were more likely to undertake practices that helped them to increase their public value.

Museums that identified barriers to KMEs and KMO also identified challenges in achieving public value. These challenges stemmed first from a gap in representation between the museum's staff, programs, and practices and the communities they sought to serve. A second challenge related to museums' inability to reach diverse communities because of their physical location. P17 tackled the issue of representation bluntly, stating "the biggest disappointment that I have, is that we haven't been able to make sure the people we employ and the people that volunteer with us match my community." Many museum leaders likewise characterized their museum's location as a barrier to achieve public value. P26 observed, "we're located in an area that is not walkable and not served by public transportation, so it's a huge challenge for us." However, she and other interviewees facing this challenge did not describe efforts to bring their programming directly to the community outside the museum, as some others did.

Our findings identified the beneficial practices that museums used to enable, utilize, and capitalize on knowledge management approaches. These practices not only improved museums' ability to create, manage, and share knowledge, but helped them effectively achieve or augment public value. A similar link exists between those museums that struggled with barriers to knowledge management approaches; these barriers hindered these museums' ability to enable knowledge management practices and militated against them achieving appreciable public value.

Parsing these findings by museum type, we found that science museums exhibited more beneficial practices than art museums in achieving public value (85% and 68%, respectively). Pattern coding showed that science museums were more likely to engage diverse communities and provide offerings that were relevant to those communities outside of the museum.

5 Discussion

This exploratory study enriches the information science literature on museums. It bridges a gap between scholars who have studied knowledge management through information science approaches and those who have studied museums through information science approaches. Bringing these two strands of research together by studying museums through a knowledge management approach provides a new means to understand museums more holistically from organizational and public value perspectives. Further, we extend the literature, specifically empirical studies of KMEs and KMO, by identifying the combination of benefits and barriers that are unique to museums, particularly their efforts to increase public value.

Our findings show how museums that enable, and practice knowledge management can create public value and more effectively serve diverse communities. Understanding the specific beneficial practices museums experience through KMEs and KMO elucidates the importance of their relationship to a museum's ability to achieve increased public value. Although certain beneficial practices predominated, only those museums that encompassed the full range of these practices successfully undertook initiatives that generated public value. Similarly, museums that experienced multiple challenges in these practices struggled to create, much less augment, public value. Findings therefore indicate a clear link between museums that effectively leverage the practices of KMEs and KMO, on the one hand, and their ability to undertake practices that generate public value, on the other. By focusing on implementing beneficial practices while addressing these challenges, museums can create more public value, improving their position as thriving community anchors.

6 Conclusion

As museums strive to become more inclusive spaces that serve diverse populations and provide increased public value, understanding how knowledge management is enabled and practiced sheds new light on how public value is achieved—and potentially augmented. We identified a critical link between museums whose leaders actively pursue the beneficial practices of KMEs and KMO and their museums' ability to achieve public value through inclusivity and community engagement approaches. We have also identified a series of specific challenges facing museums that hinder their ability to achieve public value. This study provides both practical implications for museum leaders to leverage benefits and overcome barriers while also providing fertile research pathways for continued study. This study was limited to interviews with senior leaders of 45 small and mid-size art museums and science museums. Future research might focus on three questions. First, how might including a broader range of museum types extend or complicate our findings? Second, how might we develop conceptual models to analyze quantitative associations between KMEs, KMO, and public value? Finally, can museums implement KMEs and KMO to create public value online in addition to in communities? Our holistic approach to understanding knowledge management in museums opens new information science approaches to the study of these vital public institutions.

Appendix

Descriptions of pattern codes that emerged from provisional codes

Provisional code	
Pattern code	Pattern code description
KME - Culture benefits	
Leader empowerment	Museum leaders pro-actively and deliberatively foster a culture of collaboration and trust
New ideas and thinking	Museum leaders see the link between a culture of collaboration and trust and its effect on new ideas and approaches
KME - Culture challenges	
Burnout/workload	Museum leaders and staff experience burnout due to excessive workload
Silos as barriers to knowledge sharing	Museum departments are kept siloed, inhibiting collaboration
KME - Structure benefits	
Delegation with clarity	Museum leaders not only enable delegation but provide clarity on decision-making processes
Effective documentation and usage	Museum leaders ensure that important information and knowledge is documented and used by all staff
KME - Structure challenges	
Lack of policies/procedures	Museum has minimal standardized policies and procedures to codify organizational knowledge
Rigid hierarchy	Museum's senior leaders make all decisions even when others are more capable and knowledgeable
KME - Skills benefits	
Cross-training	Staff are pro-actively trained to understand the work of other departments and roles
KME - Skills challenges	
Lack of resources	Lack of time and money prohibit museum leaders from ensuring broad and deep training of their staff
KME - IT and support benefits	

(*continued*)

(*continued*)

Provisional code	
Pattern code	Pattern code description
Integrated systems	IT systems are integrated and communicate with each other to maximize knowledge sharing
Leader prioritization	Senior leadership prioritizes and invests in IT that is continually current and effective, while ensuring all staff have effective training in its use
Scale matches need	The IT systems and support in place aligns with the scope and needs of the museum
KME - IT and support challenges	
Lack of support	Little to no dedicated support technical staff or resources for IT systems and their usage
Resistance to use	Staff resist using IT systems to their fullest and do not see the benefits of doing so
Lack of skills	Staff are not properly trained to use IT systems, resulting in ineffective use and inability to access necessary information
KMO - Acquisition benefits	
Continuous professional development	Leadership fosters formal and informal professional development occurring inside and outside of the museum
Knowledge networks	Active involvement in professional information-sharing networks regionally and nationally
KMO - Acquisition challenges	
Lack of resources	Museum leaders do not allocate the staff time and funds to acquire new knowledge or skills
Lack of prioritization	Senior leadership does not prioritize data and information gathering
KM0 - Dissemination benefits	
Structured interpersonal knowledge sharing	Museum leaders create structured opportunities for all staff to disseminate knowledge broadly
Systems of knowledge sharing	Data and information are shared in the contexts necessary for broad usage within the museum
KMO - Dissemination challenges	
Lack of Knowledge Repositories	Museums do not have appropriate means to store and share critical data and information
KMO - Responsiveness benefits	
Market and stakeholder insights	Museums prioritize gaining new insights into their markets, communities, and competitors

(*continued*)

(*continued*)

Provisional code	
Pattern code	Pattern code description
Learning from failure	Museum leaders encourage new ideas and use failure as a learning and growth opportunity
KMO - Responsiveness challenges	
Lack of evaluation	Museums are not evaluating their work or ensuring that programs respond to community interests and needs
Public value - Benefits	
Museum beyond its walls	Museums offer programs relevant to diverse communities outside of their own physical spaces
Linking to communities	Museums are integrated within their communities through collaborations and alliances with entities serving diverse communities
Public value - Challenges	
Representation	Museum's staff, programs, and practices are not representative of the communities they seek to serve
Geographic context	Museum's location and surrounding demographics limit broader diversity efforts

References

1. Marty, P.F.: Museum informatics and collaborative technologies: the emerging socio-technological dimension of information science in museum environments. J. Am. Soc. Inf. Sci. **50**(12), 1083–1091 (1999)
2. Chaudhry, A.S., Jiun, T.P.: Enhancing access to digital information resources on heritage: a case of development of a taxonomy at the Integrated Museum and Archives System in Singapore. J. Doc. **61**(6), 751–776 (2005)
3. Jörgensen, C.: Unlocking the museum: a manifesto. J. Am. Soc. Inform. Sci. Technol. **55**(5), 462–464 (2004)
4. Latham, K.F.: Museum object as document. J. Doc. **68**(1), 45–71 (2012)
5. Marty, P.F., Rayward, W.B., Twidale, M.B.: (2005) Museum informatics. Annu. Rev. Inf. Sci. Technol. **37**(1), 259–294 (2005)
6. Marty, P.F.: Changing Role of the Museum Webmaster (n.d.), Museums and the Web 2004 (2004). https://www.archimuse.com/mw2004/papers/marty/marty.html. Accessed 25 July 2022
7. Huvila, I.: How a museum knows? Structures, work roles, and infrastructures of information work. J. Am. Soc. Inf. Sci. Technol. **64**(7), 1375–1387 (2013)
8. Marty, P.F.: The changing nature of information work in museums. J. Am. Soc. Inform. Sci. Technol. **58**(1), 97–107 (2007)

9. Scott, C.: Museums and Public Value: Creating Sustainable Futures. Ashgate, Farnham (2013)
10. Turkel, G., Turkel, E.: Public value theory: reconciling public interests administrative autonomy and efficiency. Rev. Public Adm. Manag. 4(2), 1–7 (2016)
11. Vårheim, A., Skare, R.: Mapping the research on museums and the public sphere: a scoping review. J. Doc. 78(3), 631–650 (2022)
12. Blair, D.C.: Knowledge management: hype, hope, or help? J. Am. Soc. Inf. Sci. Technol. 53(12), 1019–1028 (2002)
13. Faucher, J.P.L., Everett, A.M., Lawson, R.: Reconstituting knowledge management. J. Knowl. Manag. 12(3), 3–16 (2008)
14. Gourlay, S., Nurse, A.: Flaws in the "engine" of knowledge creation. In: Buono, A., Poulfelt, F. (eds.) Challenges and Issues in Knowledge Management, pp. 293–315. Information Age, Greenwich (2005)
15. MacMorrow, N.: Knowledge management: an introduction. Annu. Rev. Inf. Sci. Technol. 35, 381–422 (2001)
16. Wallace, D.P.: Knowledge Management: Historical and Cross-Disciplinary Themes. Libraries Unlimited, Westport (2007)
17. Alavi, M., Leidner, D.E.: Review: knowledge management and knowledge management systems: conceptual foundations and research issues. MIS Q. 25(1), 107–136 (2001)
18. Dalkir, K., Liebowitz, J.: Knowledge Management in Theory and Practice. MIT Press, Cambridge (2011)
19. McInerney, C.: Hot topics: knowledge management – a practice still defining itself. Bull. Am. Soc. Inf. Sci. Technol. 28(3), 14–15 (2002)
20. Desouza, K., Paquette, S.: Knowledge Management: An Introduction. Neal-Schuman Publishers, Inc., Vancouver (2011)
21. Christensen, C.M.: The Innovator's Dilemma: When New Technologies Cause Great Firms to Fail. Harvard Business Review Press, Boston (2013)
22. Koenig, M.E.D.: KM moves beyond the organization: the opportunity for librarians. Inf. Serv. Use 25(2), 87–93 (2005)
23. Ichijo, K., von Krogh, G., Nonaka, I.: Knowledge enablers. In: von Krogh, G., Kleine, D., Roos, J. (eds.) Knowing in Firms: Understanding, Managing and Measuring Knowledge, pp. 173–203. Sage, London (1998)
24. Stonehouse, G.H., Pemberton, J.D.: Learning and knowledge management in the intelligent organisation. Particip. Empower. Int. J. 7(5), 131–144 (1999)
25. Marqués, D.P., Simón, F.J.G.: The effect of knowledge management practices on firm performance. J. Knowl. Manag. 10(3), 143–156 (2006)
26. Leonard, D.: Wellsprings of Knowledge. Harvard Business School Press, Boston (1995)
27. Appleyard, M.M.: How does knowledge flow? Interfirm patterns in the semiconductor industry. Strateg. Manag. J. 17(S2), 137–154 (1996)
28. Bennett, R., Gabriel, H.: Organisational factors and knowledge management within large marketing departments: an empirical study. J. Knowl. Manag. 3(3), 212–225 (1999)
29. Lee, H., Choi, B.: Knowledge management enablers, processes, and organizational performance: an integrative view and empirical examination. J. Manag. Inf. Syst. 20(1), 179–228 (2003)
30. Kogut, B., Zander, U.: Knowledge of the firm, combinative capabilities, and the replication of technology. Organ. Sci. 3(3), 383–397 (1992)
31. Bierly, P., Chakrabarti, A.: Generic knowledge strategies in the US pharmaceutical industry. In: Zack, M.H. (ed.) Knowledge and Strategy, pp. 231–250. Routledge, London (1999)
32. Gupta, A.K., Govindarajan, V.: Knowledge flows within multinational corporations. Strateg. Manag. J. 21(4), 473–496 (2000)
33. Hess, M., Colson, A., Hindmarch, J.: Capacity building and knowledge exchange of digital technologies in cultural heritage institutions. Mus. Int. 70(1–2), 48–61 (2018)

34. Ignjatovic, D.: Knowledge management systems in museums: the next generation for assimilating museum information resources in an electronic environment. Master's thesis, Seton Hall (2004)
35. Moussouri, T.: Knowledge management for collaborative exhibition development. Mus. Manag. Curatorship **27**(3), 253–272 (2012)
36. Day, G.S.: Market-Driven Strategy. The Free Press, New York (1990)
37. Kohli, A.K., Jaworski, B.J.: Market orientation: the construct, research propositions, and managerial implications. J. Mark. **54**(2), 1–18 (1990)
38. Kotler, P.: Marketing Management. Prentice Hall, Upper Saddle River (2000)
39. Hakala, H.: Strategic orientations in management literature: three approaches to understanding the interaction between market, technology, entrepreneurial and learning orientations. Int. J. Manag. Rev. **13**(2), 199–217 (2011)
40. Narver, J.C., Slater, S.F.: The effect of a market orientation on business profitability. J. Mark. **54**(4), 20–35 (1990)
41. Darroch, J.: Developing a measure of knowledge management behaviors and practices. J. Knowl. Manag. **7**(5), 41–54 (2003)
42. Darroch, J., McNaughton, R.: Beyond market orientation: knowledge management and the innovativeness of New Zealand firms. Eur. J. Mark. **37**(3/4), 572–593 (2003)
43. Darroch, J.: Knowledge management, innovation and firm performance. J. Knowl. Manag. **9**(3), 101–115 (2005)
44. Wang, C.L., Hult, G.T.M., Ketchen, D.J., Ahmed, P.K.: Knowledge management orientation, market orientation, and firm performance: an integration and empirical examination. J. Strateg. Mark. **17**(2), 99–122 (2009)
45. Fuller, N.J.: Recognizing and responding to the knowledge needs of museums. Mus. Manag. Curatorship **20**(3), 272–276 (2005)
46. Moore, M.H.: Creating Public Value: Strategic Management in Government. Harvard University Press, Boston (1995)
47. Bennington, J., Moore, M.H.: Public value in complex and changing times. In: Bennington, J., Moore, M.H. (eds.) Public Value. Theory & Practice, pp. 1–30. Palgrave Macmillan, Basingstoke (2011)
48. Spano, A.: Public value creation and management control systems. Int. J. Public Adm. **32**(3–4), 328–348 (2009)
49. Weinberg, M.L., Lewis, M.S.: The public value approach to strategic management. Mus. Manag. Curatorship **24**(3), 253–269 (2009)
50. Scott, C.: Museums: impact and value. Cult. Trends **15**(1), 45–75 (2006)
51. Williams, I., Shearer, H.: Appraising public value: past, present and futures. Public Adm. **89**(4), 1367–1384 (2011)
52. Yin, R.: Case Study Research: Design and Methods. Sage, Thousand Oaks (2008)
53. Weiss, R.S.: Learning from Strangers: The Art and Method of Qualitative Interview Studies. Simon and Schuster, New York (1995)
54. Almeida, A.M.: The personal context of a museum experience: similarities and differences between science and art museums. Historia, Ciencias, Saude-Manguinhos **12**, 31–53 (2005)
55. Institute of Museum and Library Services: Museum Universe Data File [Full data file] (2018). https://data.imls.gov
56. Miles, M.B., Huberman, A.M., Saldaña, J.: Qualitative Data Analysis: A Methods Sourcebook. Sage, Thousand Oaks (2018)

How Much Context Do Users Provide in App Reviews? Implications for Requirements Elicitation

Rob Grace[1](✉)[iD], Kenyan Burnham[1][iD], and Hyeong Suk Na[1,2][iD]

[1] Texas Tech University, Lubbock, TX 79406, USA
{rob.grace,kenyan.burnham}@ttu.edu, hyeongsuk.na@sdsmt.edu
[2] South Dakota School of Mines and Technology, Rapid City, SD 57701, USA

Abstract. People post millions of app reviews on Google Play and Apple's App Store, but developers can struggle to incorporate this feedback in human-centered design processes. Although researchers have developed automated techniques to gather requirement information, including bug reports and feature requests, for developers tasked with app updates, these methods overlook contextual details in app reviews that explain why users encounter problems and offer insight into new design possibilities. However, prior research has not described the relative availability and characteristics of requirement and context information provided by users in app reviews. To address this gap in the literature, this study performs a content analysis of reviews of *Citizen,* a personal safety app, to show that users often include rich, contextual details about where, why, and how they use *Citizen,* but rarely discuss explicit requirements that most automated requirements elicitation techniques attempt to gather from app reviews. These findings suggest opportunities to scale human-centered design processes by collecting and classifying contextual details in app reviews to summarize use case scenarios that can provide rationales for app updates and inspire ideas for the design of new features and products.

Keywords: Scenario-based design · Content analysis · Requirements elicitation

1 Introduction

People have posted hundreds of millions of app reviews for the estimated 5 million apps available on Google Play and Apple's App Store. For app developers, these reviews provide an invaluable source of user-submitted feedback to identify software bugs, requests for new features and content, and assess users' satisfaction with app services [1, 2]. Consequently, attempts have been made to develop natural language processing (NLP) and machine learning techniques to elicit requirements for developers engaged in iterative, development processes [3, 4]. To date, however, this research focuses on classifying, identifying candidate features, and eliciting requirement information, especially bug reports and feature requests, which offer software developers explicit guidance for app updates [5].

I. Sserwanga et al. (Eds.): iConference 2023, LNCS 13972, pp. 16–25, 2023.
https://doi.org/10.1007/978-3-031-28032-0_2

However, studies suggest that people often post reviews that describe rich contexts of use [6, 7]. Raharja et al. [8], for instance, provides an NLP approach to extract "who," "what," and "why" elements of user stories but do not address the extent to which these elements are available in app reviews. For designers and software engineers, the ability to understand the contexts of use described in app reviews stands to offer greater insight into why people are reporting bugs and requesting new features than analyses focused solely on explicit requirement information.

Despite this, systematic reviews note that efforts to develop automated requirements elicitation techniques have largely overlooked context information in app reviews [1, 5, 9]. Instead, studies focus on identifying reports of software bugs, feature requests, and various functional requirements [10–12]. Studies link this feedback to users' experiences by analyzing app ratings and review sentiment [13, 14]. For example, in a content analysis of 3,279 reviews for 161 different apps on the Google Play store, Iacob et al. [15] finds a positive correlation between review sentiment and mention of a feature request.

Furthermore, prior studies speculate that the context in which people post reviews influences the nature and quality of the feedback they provide to app developers [9, 15]. The widespread adoption of Agile development processes creates the challenge of gathering user feedback following regular software updates. Alternatively, the launch of location-based services in new geographic areas creates the need to gather feedback that can explain local adoption behaviors among new users. However, the relationship between the reviewing context and review information remains unexamined [1].

To address these gaps in the literature, we perform an in-depth content analysis of requirement information (i.e., feature requests and bug reports) and—informed by scenario-based design [16]—context information (i.e., activities, actors, events, goals, and settings) included in reviews of *Citizen*, a personal safety app which notifies users if 911 dispatchers report an emergency in their vicinity (https://citizen.com/). Furthermore, we examine if the reviewing context influences requirement and context information in app reviews by analyzing the content of reviews posted during weeks when *Citizen* was updated or launched in a new city.

Our findings show that users frequently post reviews that include rich, contextual details about where, why, and how they use *Citizen*, but infrequently discuss explicit design requirements that most studies attempt to capture through automated requirements elicitation techniques. Furthermore, we find no significant relationship between review content and update and launch weeks, but find a significant, positive relationship between review length and mention of requirement (feature requests) and context information. These findings offer design implications for automated approaches that can identify and describe the use contexts conveyed in app reviews to scale requirements gathering for human-centered design processes.

2 Research Design

The following research questions guide our study: 1) To what extent do app reviews contain requirement and context information? 2) What is the relationship between requirement and context information included in app reviews? 3) What is the relationship between the review context, i.e., weeks following the release of updates or launch in new service areas, and information included in app reviews? Below we describe our research design, findings, and their implications for future research and practice.

To address RQ1, we performed a content analysis of requirement and context information included in app reviews for *Citizen*, a personal-safety application that notifies users when an emergency has been reported in their vicinity. *Citizen* provides users with real-time, location-based safety notifications by scanning radio traffic between 911 dispatchers and first responders in their vicinity. *Citizen* app reviews thus offer an opportunity to examine the relationship between context and requirement information people provide when discussing how they use the app to stay aware of and manage risks in their communities. Beginning with the first review posted for *Citizen* on the Google Play store in 2017, we collected 16,506 reviews posted between January 2017 and May 2021. We then followed a date-stratified, random sampling procedure to select 1703 reviews (>10% of the dataset) for in-depth, manual coding.

Following content analysis procedures for a priori design and intercoder reliability testing [17], we first developed a framework of seven variables based on requirements elicitation and scenario-based design research (Table 1). These include requirement information—software bug reports and feature requests—that remain the focus of studies developing requirements elicitation techniques, and context information based on Carroll's five elements of use case scenarios: activities, actors, events, goals, and settings [16].

Table 1. Content variables analyzed in *Citizen* app reviews

Category	Variable	Description	*Example*
Requirement	
Bug report	Report of software bugs that require fixing. E.g., *"I was really looking forward to using this app for my job and recommending to my co-workers, but I'm extremely disappointed. I downloaded the app & put in my code & my email, but I can't get past the username, it won't allow me to go any further."*
Feature request	Request to add a feature to the app. E.g., *"The app is okay, but it's really annoying that you can't pull down to expand the map at all. A simple pull down so you can expand to pan and zoom would really be a giant improvement."*
Context	
Actions	Mentions a use of the app by an actor in a setting. E.g., *"Well for one, they had a shooting on election day in the project* [Event], *my coworker lives on the same street they was shooting by me* [Actor]. *Having the citizen app, I was able to tell her* [Action]*! Thank you!!"*
Actors	Mentions a person or group. E.g., *"One day next to my dad* [Actor] *we smelt something burning… I went to my citizen app and it said something like a car fire was happening* [Action, Event]*"*

(continued)

Table 1. (*continued*)

Category	Variable	Description	*Example*
Events	Mentions something that happens to an actor in a setting. E.g., *"Sirens all over. Police helicopters flying over my house. No report on the app* [Event]. *Waste of time."*
Goals	Mentions an objective motivating use of the app. E.g., *"This helps me know what's going on...I'm only 13 years old, like, I wanna know what's happening around my school* [SETTING] *and if I should take more caution* [GOAL]."
Setting	Mentions a time and/or place. E.g., *"As someone from Detroit who recently started going out to bars* [Setting]... *this has been super useful. I was always concerned to go out because I knew I would be alone in an area where I'm highly unsure if I'm safe or not* [GOAL]."

The first and second authors independently coded a random sample of 171 app reviews (>10% of the sampled dataset) and performed a pilot reliability test to identify patterns of coding disagreement. After refining the coding scheme and further training, we conducted another round of coding and performed a final intercoder reliability test using Krippendorf's Alpha (α)–a statistic appropriate for calculating coding performed by two coders for nominal variables that considers the possibility for chance agreement. Simple agreement and Krippendorf's Alpha statistics were calculated using ReCal2 software [18]. Table 2 displays the α coefficients for seven content analysis variables, ranging from $\alpha = 0.971$ to 1.00. As a coefficient of > 0.80 indicates high intercoder reliability, we determined that most of the variables have strong agreement in the application of our coding scheme and coded the rest of the sampled app reviews. To address RQ2, UCINET was used to analyze co-occurrences of requirement and context variables in the sampled reviews [19].

Table 2. Intercoder reliability for content analysis of *Citizen* app reviews

Variable	Agreements	Disagreements	Simple agreement	Krippendorf's Alpha
Bug Report	171	0	1.000	1.000
Feature Request	171	0	1.000	1.000
Actions	166	5	0.971	0.823
Actors	168	3	0.982	0.944
Events	166	5	0.971	0.881
Goals	166	5	0.971	0.916
Setting	167	4	0.977	0.939

Lastly, to address RQ3, we collected version history data for *Citizen* to identify the release dates of major software updates and reviewed *Citizen's* blog (https://medium.com/citizen/tagged/citizen-app) to identify the dates when new cities were added to *Citizen's* service areas. We then performed multiple logistic regression analyses to examine the relationships between *Launch Week* (review was posted in the week following the launch of the app in a new city/service area) and *Update Week* (review was posted in the week following a major software update) and the seven requirement and context variables. We did not find any overdispersion in the analyses. To examine the relationship between the length of reviews and mention of requirement or context information, we then conducted full factorial experiments supported by statistical measures such as adjusted R^2 and C_P. The results are presented below.

3   Results

In answer to RQ1, our results show that users frequently write app reviews that include rich, contextual details about where, why, and how they use *Citizen*, but rarely discuss explicit requirements that most studies attempt to capture through automated requirements elicitation techniques (Table 3). *Citizen* app reviews include requirement information in 9.1% (n = 156) of the sampled reviews but include context information in 38.1% (n = 649) of the 1703 reviews sampled for analysis.

Table 3. Requirement information conveyed in *Citizen* app reviews.

Requirement variable	Count	% Sample
Bug report	115	6.8
Feature request	42	2.5
Actors	172	10
Actions	131	8
Events	136	8
Goals	322	19

Although *Citizen* users rarely write reviews that include requirement information, these reviews identify usability issues that developers can fix in future updates: "Doesn't work well with Android 'gestures' as there is no back button [*bug report*]. Had to turn off gestures just so I can use this app! [*action*]." Requirement information also includes requests for features that developers can use to improve the app's utility and perceived value among users: "Would be nice if I could monitor my son's [*actor*] neighborhood [*setting*]…but it wants to use my location, which is not yet covered [*feature request*]." Importantly, as illustrated by these examples, users convey explicit requirement information while also describing the technical (e.g., Android gesture navigation) and social use contexts (e.g., family member co-monitoring of safety notifications) in which the requirements emerge with respect to users' motivations, behaviors, and needs.

In answer to RQ2, we find that *Citizen* users rarely write reviews describing multiple requirements but often provide multiple contextual details in their reviews. Only one review reports a software bug and requests a new feature. In contrast, 56.1% (n = 364) of reviews that mention context include multiple context variables. Table 4 describes the co-occurrences of requirement and context variables in the sampled reviews. Cells highlighted in green identify co-occurrences between variables that represent >20% of reviews that include the column variable. For instance, 38 reviews mention software bugs and actions, and these 38 reviews represent 29% of all reviews that mention actions.

Table 4. Co-occurrences of content variables in *Citizen* app reviews

	Bugs	Features	Actions	Actors	Events	Goals	Settings
Bugs	115	1	38*	9	57	13	24
Features	1	42	8	10	4	14	16
Actions	38	8	131	39	49	29	43
Actors	9	10	39	172	48	68	64
Events	57	4	49	48	136	19	45
Goals	13	14	29	68	19	322	228
Settings	24	16	43	64	45	228	374

*Green cells indicate co-occurrences >20% of app reviews including the column variable.

As the top-left quadrant shows, only one review includes both a bug report and feature request. In contrast, the bottom-right quadrant shows that reviews frequently include multiple context variables. For example, 228 reviews describe both a setting in which *Citizen* was used and a goal motivating use of the app, representing 61% and 71% of reviews mentioning settings and goals, respectively.

However, as the bottom-left quadrant of Table 4 shows, users often contextualize requirement information, i.e., bug reports and feature requests often co-occur with context variables. For example, 59.6% (n = 57) of reviews reporting software bugs also mention events. Conversely, the top-right quadrant shows that users write many reviews including contextual information that do not mention requirements. The exception are reviews that describe user interactions and events when reporting software bugs. For instance, 29% (n = 38) of reviews mentioning user (inter)actions with the app also report a bug. Overall, reviews that mention requirements often include contextual details, but many more reviews describe the use contexts of *Citizen* without conveying explicit requirements.

Lastly, in answer to RQ3, we find no significant relationships between reviews posted in the week after *Citizen* was updated and requirement or context variables (Table 5). Similarly, we find no significant relationship between reviews posted in the week following *Citizen's* launch in a new city and mention of either requirement or context variables.

However, we do observe significant, positive relationships between review length and mention of feature requests and all five context variables.

Table 5. Requirement information conveyed in *Citizen* app reviews

Variable	Significant variables[a]
Update week	–
Launch week	–
Character count	Feature request (+), Actors (+), Setting (+), Actions (+), Events (+), Goals (+)

[a] Ordered by significance level, i.e., from most significant variable to least significant variable

4   Discussion

Our study represents the first attempt to systematically describe the relative availability of requirement and context information in app reviews and the influence of the review context on information people post in app reviews. Below we summarize our findings and outline the limitations of this study and opportunities for future work.

4.1   Summary of Findings and Implications for Requirements Elicitation

App Reviews Include More Context than Requirement Information. The immediate implication of the results is the opportunity to extract rich contextual details from app reviews submitted to Google Play and Apple's App Store. Although prior research suggests these opportunities [6, 7], this study is the first to empirically explore the relative availability of requirement and context information in app reviews. If the basic finding of this study—that people convey more context than requirement information in app reviews—extends to apps other than *Citizen*, than existing efforts to automatically extract and classify only explicit requirements, including bug reports and feature requests, are missing opportunities to understand the use contexts people describe when relating routine and novel user experiences in their reviews. This is significant as understanding context allows designers and software engineers to understand why users are communicating explicit requirements captured by existing automated methods. Although approaches will vary and can make use of existing NLP and machine learning models, future studies need to focus on the automated collection and classification of both requirement and context information included in app reviews.

App Reviews Include Rich Contextual Details. This study also highlights the diversity of contextual details observed across *Citizen* app reviews. These reviews often contain multiple details when, for instance, users write reviews that describe where (i.e., setting) and why (i.e., goal) they use the app. However, while *Citizen* reviews often contain some contextual details, they rarely contain all. Consequently, understanding context requires analyzing the frequency and distribution of contextual details present in thousands of reviews to generate summaries of routine and novel user experiences.

Although studies have used NLP approaches to extract the who, what, and why elements of user stories [8], and evaluated extractive methods to summarize numerous app reviews [20], our study suggests the need to generate summaries of multiple use contexts using the variety of contextual details that users communicate in app reviews. In this regard, these summaries might resemble use case scenarios [16] or user story maps [21], which are more detailed and complex than user stories characterizing functionality in Agile development processes [8]. Future studies can generate summaries that reveal the multiple observed relationships among context information in app reviews and explore visualizations that help designers understand these relationships to generate summaries that target user experiences relevant to specific requirements gathering and ideation activities performed during design and development processes.

App Reviews May Not Provide Timely Usability Feedback. This study examined the relationship between the review context, when users submitted app reviews, and the information they included in these reviews. However, we failed to find a strong relationship between update weeks, launch weeks, and requirement and context information people post in app reviews. These findings suggest that developers launch updates and users post reviews along different timelines. Moreover, as users more often discuss contexts of use than bug reports or feature requests, the findings suggest that app reviews may be more suitable for understanding diverse user experiences than timely usability feedback. As prior studies note, information requested by developers and provided by users are often incongruent [9]. The findings thus highlight challenges for using app reviews for timely, targeted feedback desired by developers.

In contrast, we do find a strong relationship between the length of reviews and the presence of feature requests and contextual details. This finding suggests the commonsensical utility of filtering reviews by length to focus analyses on app reviews that provide the richest feedback.

4.2   Limitations and Future Work

The findings reached in this study are provisional: we analyzed reviews for one app, *Citizen*, such that further research is required to validate the results. Future work can use the content variables introduced in this study to examine the relative availability of context and requirement information in the reviews of multiple apps. Such studies can also examine if user reviews for different kinds of apps include different kinds of context and requirement information. In this study, we examined *Citizen*, a personal safety app that notifies users of dangers reported in their vicinity. Users will likely include different feedback for apps with different functionality and use contexts. Lastly, studies might examine the kinds of information users, rather than developers, find helpful and how users share this information with others in app review forums [22].

5   Conclusion

Findings from a content analysis of *Citizen* reviews show that users often include rich, contextual details about where, why, and how they use the app, but rarely discuss explicit requirements that most automated requirements elicitation techniques attempt to gather from app reviews. These findings suggest opportunities to scale human-centered design processes by collecting and classifying contextual details in thousands of app reviews to summarize use case scenarios that can provide rationales for app updates and inspire ideas for the design of new features and products.

References

1. Dąbrowski, J., Letier, E., Perini, A., Susi, A.: Analysing app reviews for software engineering: a systematic literature review. Empir. Softw. Eng. **27**(2), 1–63 (2022)
2. Panichella, S., Di Sorbo, A., Guzman, E., Visaggio, C.A., Canfora, G., Gall, H.C.: How can I improve my app? Classifying user reviews for software maintenance and evolution. In: IEEE International Conference on Software Maintenance and Evolution (ICSME 2015), pp. 281–290. IEEE (2015)
3. Aslam, N., Ramay, W.Y., Xia, K., Sarwar, N.: Convolutional neural network-based classification of app reviews. IEEE Access **8**, 185619–185628 (2020)
4. Phong, M.V., Nguyen, T.T., Pham, H.V., Nguyen, T.T.: Mining user opinions in mobile app reviews: a keyword-based approach. In: IEEE/ACM International Conference on Automated Software Engineering (ASE 2015), pp. 749–759. IEEE (2015)
5. Lim, S., Henriksson, A., Zdravkovic, J.: Data-driven requirements elicitation: a systematic literature review. SN Comput. Sci. **2**(1), 1–35 (2021)
6. Guo, H., Singh, M.P.: Caspar: extracting and synthesizing user stories of problems from app reviews. In: IEEE/ACM International Conference on Software Engineering (ICSE 2010), pp. 628–640. IEEE (2020)
7. Minen, M.T., Gumpel, T., Ali, S., Sow, F., Toy, K.: What are headache smartphone application (app) users actually looking for in apps: a qualitative analysis of app reviews to determine a patient-centered approach to headache smartphone apps. Headache J. Head Face Pain **60**(7), 1392–1401 (2020)
8. Raharjana, I.K., Siahaan, D., Fatichah, C.: User story extraction from online news for software requirements elicitation: A conceptual model. In: International Joint Conference on Computer Science and Software Engineering (JCSSE 2016), pp. 342–347. IEEE (2019)
9. Genc-Nayebi, N., Abran, A.: A systematic literature review: opinion mining studies from mobile app store user reviews. J. Syst. Softw. **125**, 207–219 (2017)
10. McIlroy, S., Ali, N., Khalid, H., Hassan, A.E.: Analyzing and automatically labelling the types of user issues that are raised in mobile app reviews. Empir. Softw. Eng. **21**(3), 1067–1106 (2016)
11. Khalid, H.: On identifying user complaints of iOS apps. In: International Conference on Software Engineering (ICSE 2013), pp. 1474–1476. IEEE (2013)
12. Khalid, H., Shihab, E., Nagappan, M., Hassan, A.E.: What do mobile app users complain about? IEEE Softw. **32**(3), 70–77 (2014)
13. Pagano, D., Maalej, W.: User feedback in the App Store: an empirical study. In: IEEE International Requirements Engineering Conference (RE 2013), pp. 125–134. IEEE (2013)
14. McIlroy, S., Shang, W., Ali, N., Hassan, A.E.: Is it worth responding to reviews? Studying the top free apps in google play. IEEE Softw. **34**(3), 64–71 (2015)
15. Iacob, C., Veerappa, V., Harrison, R.: What are you complaining about?: a study of online reviews of mobile applications. In: International BCS Human Computer Interaction Conference 2013, pp. 1–6 (2013)
16. Carroll, J.M.: Making use: Scenario-Based Design of Human-Computer Interactions. MIT Press, Cambridge (2003)

17. Neuendorf, K.A.: The Content Analysis Guidebook. Sage, Thousand Oaks (2017)
18. Freelon, D.: ReCal: Intercoder reliability calculation as a web service. Int. J. Internet Sci. **5**(1), 20–33 (2010)
19. Borgatti, S.P., Everett, M.G., Freeman, L.C.: UCINET for Windows: Software for Social Network Analysis. Analytic Technologies (2002)
20. Jha, N., Mahmoud, A.: Using frame semantics for classifying and summarizing application store reviews. Empir. Softw. Eng. **23**(6), 3734–3767 (2018). https://doi.org/10.1007/s10664-018-9605-x
21. Patton, J., Economy, P.: User Story Mapping: Discover the Whole Story, Build the Right Product. O'Reilly Media, Inc., Sebastopol (2014)
22. Grace, R., Fonseca, F.: Participatory asymmetry: theorizing media objects and media flows in a framework of participatory production. First Monday **24**(10) (2019)

Evaluating Tools for Data Management Plans: A Comparative Study of the DART Rubric and the Belmont Scorecard

Sarika Sharma[1]([⊠]), Arlo Obregon[1], Zahir Shaikh[1], Yubing Tian[2], Megan Finn[2], and Amelia Acker[1]

[1] University of Texas-Austin, Austin, TX 78712, USA
sksharma2@utexas.edu
[2] University of Washington, Seattle, WA 98195, USA

Abstract. Data management plans (DMPs) are required from researchers seeking funding from federal agencies in the United States. Ideally, DMPs disclose how research outputs will be managed and shared. How well DMPs communicate those plans is less understood. Evaluation tools such as the DART rubric and the Belmont scorecard assess the completeness of DMPs and offer one view into what DMPs communicate. This paper compares the evaluation criteria of the two tools by applying them to the same corpus of 150 DMPs from five different NSF programs. Findings suggest that the DART rubric and the Belmont score overlap significantly, but the Belmont scorecard provides a better method to assess completeness. We find that most DMPs fail to address many of the best practices that are articulated by librarians and information professionals in the different evaluation tools. However, the evaluation methodology of both tools relies on a rating scale that does not account for the interaction of key areas of data management. This work contributes to the improvement of evaluation tools for data management planning.

Keywords: Scientific data management · Evaluation tools · Assessment

1 Introduction

The management of research data impacts the trust in and efficacy of science. The management of research data also creates possibilities and limitations for data futures. The perceived importance of research data management is embedded into science policy. Over the last decade, federal funding agencies in the United States, such as the National Science Foundation (NSF) and the National Institute of Health (NIH), have required research proposals to include data management plans (DMPs). A DMP states how data will be managed from federally funded grant projects. The DMP requirement by federal agencies aims to make outputs (whether data or publications) from taxpayer funded research openly available and accessible. But how effectively DMPs enact this vision of science is less understood by information scientists, scholarly communication researchers, and policymakers alike.

I. Sserwanga et al. (Eds.): iConference 2023, LNCS 13972, pp. 26–46, 2023.
https://doi.org/10.1007/978-3-031-28032-0_3

To address this gap, librarians and information professionals have developed evaluation tools to assess DMPs. The Data Management Plan as a Research Tool (hereafter the "DART rubric") and the Belmont Scorecard (hereafter "the Belmont score") are two tools that assess the "completeness" of data management. The DART rubric was developed in 2016 by professional librarians funded through a National Leadership Grant LG-07-13-0328 by the Institute of Museum and Library Science (IMLS) [8]. The Belmont score was formed two years later by the Belmont Forum with the goal to improve DMPs of funded projects around climate change [1].

Both tools provide an assessment of the technical aspects of data, management, access, and preservation in a DMP. Each tool assesses statements in DMPs by examining how well those statements reflect best practices for data management. Best practices from the LIS community address the key activities that determine the access to data and enables the interpretation of data. Thus, assessment tools examine DMPs for evidence of activities that enhance data access such as formatting, versioning, documentation such as metadata and data provenance, and technical systems for storage [2]. Assessing DMPs using existing, well-researched, best practices can provide insights into whether a DMP shows that a proposed science project can enable data to move from one evidentiary context to another – a shared interest across science funding agencies, scholars, and library professionals who want to promote open science.

Evaluation tools are vital for understanding whether DMPs can help funding agencies achieve their goals of promoting open science. This paper contributes to the small body of knowledge about DMP evaluation tools. Previous research has been published by researchers who developed the evaluation tools, providing vital insights into the formation of the metrics of analysis that constitute the rubric [1, 3, 10] The growing body of knowledge also informs the quality of DMPs. Studies about the DART rubric analyzes data management practices in a specific NSF program by researchers within the same universities [10] and compare DMPs across NSF programs and across different universities [1]. To date, no studies have drawn on a longitudinal corpus of DMPs; evaluated the Belmont Score; or conducted a comparative study of the tools and their underlying mechanisms of evaluation. Such an interest is motivated by practical matters of data management and the social studies of data. Evaluation tools are reflections of the organizational goals, best practices, and the current state of data management cultures. The purpose of this paper is to interrogate the tools to examine the possible outcomes of evaluation. This research is motivated by two big questions: What is the best tool to evaluate DMPs with? And what can evaluation tools tell us about DMPs? In order to speak to these broad, contextually specific questions, we have broken the question into two research questions: RQ1) What criteria are part of the DART rubric and the Belmont Score to assess DMP statements? RQ2) How do the DART rubric and the Belmont Score assess the same statements made in 150 DMPs from five programs at the NSF?

We specifically respond to the extant literature by reporting: the criteria of evaluation from the two tools; how they overlap and how each tool evaluated the same 150 DMPs; the methods we used to explore the comparisons between the DART Rubric and Belmont Score; and the results of the comparison. Results suggest that the content of the DART rubric and the Belmont score are similar. However, the evaluation of the 150 DMPs scored better in the DART rubric compared to the evaluation of DMPs by the Belmont score. We end the paper with a discussion on the strengths and weaknesses of each tool; the pros and cons of specific evaluation techniques; a recommendation on which tool is ideal for assessment; and lastly data management practices across five NSF programs.

The contributions of this work are three-fold. First, this work provides a methodological contribution to assess evaluation tools to improve the criteria for evaluating DMPs. Second, it provides a guidance to policymakers and other evaluators of which tool (s) may be most efficacious to adopt for evaluating DMPs. Third, it provides insights into the data cultures across five NSF programs that represent different scientific fields. The contributions provide future follow-up work, specifically the question of how evaluation tools can better assess data cultures. In future work, we plan to qualitatively assess DMPs to examine data cultures.

2 Literature and Background

Increasingly federal agencies that fund academic science are focused on open science, or the processes to make science outputs available. The DMP is one way that the NSF has enacted open science. Beginning in 2011 the NSF required that all grant proposals include a DMP. This federal policy introduced data management planning to researchers. How effective this policy is for open science is still a question that looms today. Evaluation tools have provided one path to examine and analyze effectiveness of open science by focusing on the ways data are made mobile through data management planning in science.

DMPs were not always about open science. Since the 1960s, DMPs were used by researchers in technically complex projects to ensure the analysis of data generated from research projects [4]. Today DMPs are required by funding agencies (like the NSF and the National Institutes of Health (NIH)) to provide details of how data and other research outputs will be managed during the lifecycle of a project.

A typical DMP is a two-page document affixed to a grant proposal that outlines how an individual researcher or research team will collect, manage, and preserve research project data. The DMP ideally communicates a researcher's plans to manage scientific data, and other research outputs as part of the proposed research project. However, a DMP is not a blueprint for data management practices during the project. Such a document contains anticipated plans for research outputs. It signifies the aspirations for data management project goals. Plans communicated by a DMP are not always reflective of the actual practices that take place once a project is funded and underway [4].

Several attributes make a DMP an interesting object of study for information scholars concerned with access, institutions, and knowledge commons [5].

Similar to scientific documents such as laboratory notebooks and fieldnotes, DMPs are a genre for science communication that covers core research data management topics in information science including data documentation; data standards; metadata; preservation; cost; roles; intellectual property; and data access. A DMP can signify readiness for data management and insights into the resources scientists draw on to assist in their data management at their home institution.

Several issues have been identified in regard to the DMPs and their effectiveness for data management. First, data management planning varies across disciplines. DMPs are shaped by epistemic differences, the organizational aspects of research projects and collaboration structures, and data documentation standards across research domains. Disciplines show varying philosophies and cultures around the dissemination of research outputs [3, 8–10]. In some cases, despite its importance, researchers often perceive data management planning as a time-consuming administrative task, rather than a central aspect of current research practices [11]. Federal level DMP guideline are often vague leaving it up to researchers to decide what to include in their plans [5, 12]. A look at the NSF DMP guidelines show that policies and recommendations differ across NSF programs [12]. Further, DMP requirements do not consider how data management may change over the course of a project (specifically in the humanities) [13]. Together these findings suggest that data management planning is still not regularized within academic science research.

Regardless of disciplinary differences, data management planning is considered to be vital to the futures of data. Upstream practices around data determine the paths or futures of data. Planning is considered an antecedent step to data management practices because it takes into consideration the technical and social aspects of data management before data are even created. It invokes a time for researchers to think about the formats of data, the ways they will be stored, and the means to share those data across time and space.

2.1 Evaluation Tools

To augment the writing of DMPs and assess how well DMPs capture the key activities for DMPs, information professionals (librarians, research data managers and others) have developed tools to help researchers write DMPs that comply with DMP guidelines and tools to evaluate the completeness of DMPs. For example, the DMPTool was developed by librarians across eight institutions with NSF funding in 2011 and has been periodically updated. The tool guides researchers across data storage, formatting, sharing and long-term storage and provides NSF program and program specific templates for researchers to use during while drafting DMPs.

Given that DMPs provide important documentation to how data will be managed, a set of evaluation tools have emerged in the last decade to assess how well DMPs address management criteria or how well plans cover certain topics areas deemed to be essential for short-term and long-term stewardship of data. The DART rubric and the Belmont Score are two evaluation tools for the assessment of data management plans.

Following the DMP requirements, researchers started developing DMP evaluation tools. The tools provide a means for many stakeholders to evaluate data management planning by providing systematic ways to do so. Such tools contain different areas of measurement that guide the evaluation. Assessments from evaluation can provide information that guides librarians, funding agencies, and researchers. Assessments provide valuable information on whether DMPs meet best practice standards or require improvements. They can also be used by funding agencies to reveal the shortcomings of data management planning.

The DART rubric was the outcome of a two-year National Leadership Grant Libraries Demonstration Project led by research librarians across multiple universities. The DART rubric is available on the Open Science Forum (OSF) and includes several research instruments including the scorecard, and a 33-page guideline that explains how to use the tool to score DMPs [15]. The rubric aims to provide data librarians and other information managers with a standardized analysis tool to evaluate content in DMPs. The framework is based on the generic DMP guidance in the Proposal and Award Procedures and Policies (PAPPG) (specifically Chapter II.C.2.j at the NSF – updated every year). Five key areas of research data management are assessed in the DART rubric using a Likert scale (addressed, addressed but incomplete, not addressed). Those topics include the types of data produced; standards and metadata for data; security, data protection policies for access and sharing; and plans for archiving data. The DART rubric provides stakeholders a way to assess local research data management services including gaps in expertise and training programs [15]. This rubric was in response to the NSF program. It centers its evaluation criteria drawing on policies at NSF directorates. The DART rubric does not provide a score, but it acts as a guide to assess where DMPs can be improved.

The DART rubric has been used in an empirical study of DMPs within universities and across universities [8, 14]. Studies show that DMP evaluation tools can provide insights into the completeness of data management planning and data management practices in domains [6, 8]. What is learned from these studies is that there is a relationship between the completeness DMPs and domain-level efforts to build data infrastructure. For instance, DMPs from the NSF program biology specify the exact metadata standard, a reflection of ongoing efforts in the domain to build repositories [8]. Across different fields of science, DMPs did not have adequate information about data sharing and archiving [8].

The Belmont Score is another tool that was developed by librarians and information professionals to evaluate DMPs [1]. The tool was developed in 2019 by the Belmont Forum, a multi-institutional and international collaboration committed to transdisciplinary global climate change science. The Belmont score was the outcome of the Belmont Forum workshop on e-infrastructures and data management (e-IDM) to make the forum's Open Data Policy and Principles operational. The group took ideas from the DART rubric and incorporated them into the Belmont score. The Belmont score evaluates the Belmont forum's Data and Digital Objects Management Plan (DDOMP), a similar document to the DMP. In contrast to the DMP by the NSF, the DDOMP is a live document that is revisited during the lifecycle of the project. The tool quantitatively analyzes the DDOMPs associated with Belmont Forum proposals by scoring data management topics via a Likert scale. Likert scale responses are given a numerical score. Scores are added up and divided by the number of questions to provide an overall average score. An average closer to 2 signifies a DMP that has attended to all of the requirements of the rubric. A score close to 1 indicates that a DMP has met the minimum standards. A score closer to 0 implies a DMP is missing key areas of data management planning. The scoring framework is based on a combination of existing institutional policies and evaluation tools including the Belmont Forum Grant Operations (BFGO) process, the DART project rubric, the Open Data Policy and Principles, and FAIR Data Principles. The score is also intended to aid in the development of DMPs throughout the lifecycle of a project. The Belmont Score is published in Zenodo. The publication includes a ten-page document with instructions that explains how to use the Belmont score [1]. To date, no studies have applied the Belmont score to the analysis of DMPs until our comparative analysis presented below.

Given the decade long implementation of the DMP requirement policy and the importance of the DMP in shaping futures of data, evaluation tools provide a means to assess DMPs. However, very little is known about the criteria for evaluation and the how the different criteria are similar or different when applied to the evaluation of DMPs. What are the key areas of data management evaluation? How to these key areas get evaluated to assess completeness?

This study examines the two evaluation tools and their criteria for evaluation. It focuses on the key areas of data management planning included in the evaluation tools; how those areas are measured; and the outcomes of evaluation given the criteria from each tool. To do that, we examine the tools and apply them to the same 150 corpus of DMPs. Doing so controls for variation and provides means to examine the two tools including their strengths and weaknesses. The next section provides a detailed discussion of the approach we took to compare the DART rubric and the Belmont score.

3   Method

To carry out our comparative analysis, we began by soliciting DMPs from scientists to create a corpus and then we evaluated the DMPs using both evaluation tools. The first part of this section describes the email study to collect DMPs and the second part discussed the evaluation of the 150 DMPs (see Fig. 1 for workflow that shows the process).

To create the corpus of DMPs, we gathered a comprehensive list of projects awarded since the policy was implemented in 2011 using the NSF's Awards Database. This database allows for program-level queries and the search results can be exported in CSV format. There were several pieces of relevant and administrative metadata in the awards database that were subsequently used in our email campaign for DMP collection, including PI names, email addresses, institutions, dates of awards, award numbers, project titles, and abstracts. From January 2011 to June 2021, awards from five NSF programs were gathered into a spreadsheet: Division of Biological Infrastructure (DBI); Civil, Mechanical, Manufacturing Innovation (CMMI); Secure and Trustworthy Cyberspace (SATC); Science and Technology Studies (STS); and Oceanography (OCE); and the Science, Engineering, and Education for Sustainability (SEES). The SEES program is an NSF wide program that incorporates the other directorates. Grants from SEES can be from the five other directorates.

Once relevant awards were identified, special kinds of awards for student education, early career researchers, or field-building work that were not likely to generate research data were removed. Specifically, the following types of awards were removed: Rapid Response Research (RAPID), Early Concept for Exploratory Research (EAGER), Faculty Early Career Development Grant (CAREER), Education (EDU), Research Coordination Network Grant (RCN), Workshop, Symposium, Research and Curriculum Unit (RCU), and all grants under $100,000. Though RAPID, EAGER, and CAREER Awards require DMPs and generate research data, they were removed as EAGER and RAPID grants are typically short proposals for shorter projects that are more experimental in nature. Meanwhile, CAREER grants are awarded to early career researchers who are generally untenured and less experienced. These types of projects, we reasoned, were not necessary to our inquiry, and we didn't want to overburden PIs. If there were multiple awards for one PI, newer awarded projects were removed from our list, in order to avoid solicitation fatigue from multiple requests and try to obtain DMPs from older projects.

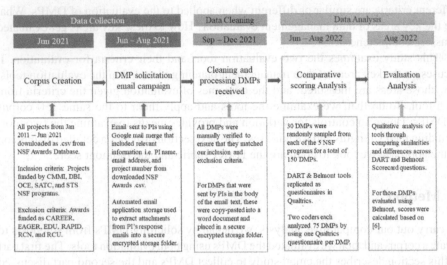

Fig. 1. Workflow

The email campaign was conducted from June through August 2021. Google's developer mail merge template was used to pull relevant data columns from our NSF awards spreadsheet including, PI name, email address, project name, and unique project number. A template email was created that requested PI's participation in our research project and included information about how their DMPs would be used. The mail merge template allowed each email request to be tailored to individual PIs, including their specific award titles and numbers in the email's subject line and message. Participants were asked to respond to the email by attaching their two-page DMP from the specific project we requested. An automated email storage application was used to collect email attachments sent by respondents that deposited them to a secure, encrypted storage folder. Some PIs responded by copying and pasting their DMP prose directly in the email's body without sending an attachment. In these instances, the relevant sections of the email were saved in a word document, .docx. Further document analysis was conducted to confirm that the DMPs received fit our inclusion criteria (e.g., occasionally PIs submitted another DMP or other proposal documents that were not relevant). An email archive was used to collect email responses from PIs for further analysis.

In total 1014 DMP submissions were received for a 18.38% average response rate across all programs (see Fig. 2). For this study, the 150 DMPs were retrieved from the corpus of 1,014.

NSF Program	# Of Emails Sent	# Of DMPs Received	Response Rate %
OCE	1689	395	23.39
DBI	1245	239	19.2
CMMI	1429	204	14.28
STS	221	48	21.72
SATC	915	122	13.33
SEES	40	6	15
Totals	**5339**	**1014**	

Fig. 2. DMPs per program

The comparative scoring analysis was conducted on a longitudinal sample of 150 DMPs from five NSF programs. 30 DMPs were selected from each of the five NSF programs from 2011–2021.

Prior to the comparative DART and Belmont analysis, research team members read all of the available documentation about DART and Belmont scoring processes available on OSF and Zenodo. DART and Belmont scorecards were subsequently recreated in Qualtrics. Scoring was conducted collaboratively by two team members (called "coders"). Each coder analyzed 15 DMPs for each NSF program for a total of 75 DMPs. Intercoder reliability ensured that coders scored DMPs in a consistent manner. For each scoring tool, each coder individually scored two DMPs and then discussed each answer with the team. Scoring discrepancies amongst the coders were settled through discussion and workflows. All DMPs were scored twice, once with the DART rubric and a second time with the Belmont score system. A detailed approach is discussed below.

3.1 Evaluation Tool 1: The DART Rubric

The corpus of 150 DMPs was evaluated using the DART score. The DART survey instrument was accessed from the OSF website and replicated verbatim in a Qualtrics survey. 26 questions had multiple choice responses; 13 questions consisted of both multiple choice and free responses. Following DART's instrument, each multiple-choice question included the following response options: (a) complete and addressed; (b) addressed but incomplete; and (c) did not address. Additional free responses and rotating dial questions were added to the beginning of the survey to keep track of the DMP. This included a free response to write in the PI's name associated with the DMP; a rotating dial to select the NSF program associated with the DMP, and a rotating dial to select the date associated with the DMP. Page breaks were incorporated to separate different sections. The team tested the Qualtrics survey twice for usability and accuracy.

Scoring DMPs required some familiarity with the DMPs' research domains, so the team spent one week learning about the rubric (including topics around outputs, concepts such as metadata and licensing), the rubric's evaluation criteria and reading current and old NSF program specific DMP guidelines as well as a few DMPs to acclimate to the genre.

Whilst scoring, coders kept a lab notebook open during the process to record insights or observations. Coders also kept the DART score rubric open to refer to examples. The coders evaluated the DMP by answering the Qualtrics survey questions. Each DMP was evaluated using this survey and coders answered each question one at a time. Over two weeks, this process was repeated for all 150 DMPs. Qualtrics survey results were retrieved via excel files.

3.2 Evaluation Tool 2: The Belmont Scorecard

After DART scoring was completed, the same corpus of 150 DMPs was evaluated using the Belmont Score. A similar approach to DART scoring was taken. The scorecard was downloaded from Zenodo. Sixteen questions were replicated verbatim to a Qualtrics survey. Each question was given a multiple-choice answer of (a) complete and addressed (b) incomplete response or a (c) no response. Following the Belmont Scorecard guidance, each response was given a weighted score. Responses that were scored complete and addressed received 2 points, responses scored incomplete received 1 point and a response that scored no response received 0 points. Additional free questions were added to connect the DMP including a free response to write the name associated with the DMP; a rotating dial to select the NSF program associated with the DMP, and a rotating dial to select the date associated with the DMP. The Qualtrics survey was tested for usability by the team. Once the instrument was ready, the team read the Belmont scorecard and its evaluation criteria. Due to the similarities across the tools, key concepts were familiar to the coders.

The same 150 DMPs were scored in two weeks. Coders accessed the DMPs in the google doc folders. Coders cross-checked the DMP with an excel file (that documents the DMPs context including the PI who submitted the DMP, the NSF program, and program, the project's proposal) to make sure the correct DMP was accessed. Whilst scoring, coders kept a lab notebook open to record any insights or observations. Coders also kept the Belmont score rubric open to refer to examples. A new survey was created for each DMP. The coders evaluated the DMPs by first reading each DMP. Then coders answered survey questions by reading line by line. Coders answered each question one at a time. Data from Qualtrics was retrieved via excel files.

3.3 Evaluation Analysis

Two methods were applied to conduct the evaluation. First, a qualitative approach was taken to assess the tools. Questions were extracted from both tools and were analyzed by comparing them for similarities and differences. Each question from both rubrics was placed into a category of data management planning. This approach was paired with the coding results in Qualtrics. Data from coding using the DART rubric and the Belmont score in Qualtrics was downloaded in an excel file. Response types were examined across the categories of data management planning. For Belmont, scores were calculated based on the method provided in [1]. The unit of analysis was the statement text at the sentence and paragraph level. The following reports on the comparison of the tools using the response types coded to the data management planning statements.

4 Findings

This section presents results from the comparative analysis of 150 DMPs using the DART rubric and the Belmont score. The findings are presented in two sections. The first section provides a comparison of the total responses that were collected by evaluating 150 DMPs by the DART rubric and the Belmont score. In the next section, comparisons are presented from five topic areas: scientific outputs produced from research grants; roles and responsibilities for data management planning; metadata planning; and planning for cost and volume of scientific data. For each specific topic area, the importance of the area is discussed in relation to data management planning, how each tool evaluates this area, the criteria for evaluation, and findings from using each tool to evaluate 150 DMPs. For each evaluation tool, the metric is presented in parenthesis. For instance, DART rubric (1.1) refers to question 1.1 in the rubric. Similarly, Belmont score (2.1) refers to questions 2.1 in the score.

4.1 Completeness of DMPs

Both the DART rubric and the Belmont score contain similar evaluation features and metrics. Both use the Likert scale model to assess DMPs and both evaluate key areas of data management planning evaluation including: defining outputs; roles and responsibilities; metadata; and cost and volume; security; and data protection.

To begin to understand the similarities and differences across the evaluation of the tools, response types at the statement level were collected from the analysis of 150 DMPs to see how many statements were complete, addressed but incomplete, or incomplete across both tools.

A larger proportion of DMPs evaluated from the DART received a higher complete response type for statements related to data management planning compared statements evaluated by the Belmont Score (Fig. 2 and Fig. 3). The finding is consistent regardless of the NSF program. DMPs in the five NSF programs evaluated by the DART rubric had a higher portion of "complete and addressed" response type. Further, both rubrics show that statements from DMPs across all five NSF programs did not meet the expectations of data management planning. Almost half of the responses by the DART rubric and Belmont score indicate that statements were incomplete (Fig. 3 and Fig. 4).

A Belmont score was calculated to see how each program compared in regard to completeness of data management. We found that DMPs from CMMI received a score of .85. DMPs from DBI received a score of .76. DMPs from OCE received a score of .70. DMPs from SATC received a score of .64. DMPs from STS received a score of .81. All five directorates received a score below one. This indicates that the DMPs across all five programs did not meet the minimum standards for data management planning according to the Belmont score.

To further investigate the differences in the evaluation tools particularly why statements in DMPs evaluated by the Belmont score scored lower, response types were collected by particular areas of evaluation across the two tools including four key criteria research outputs; roles and responsibilities; metadata; and cost and volume.

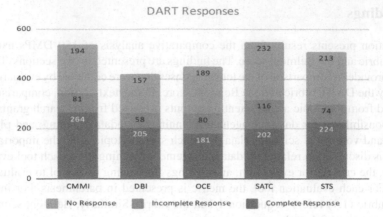

Fig. 3. The number of responses collected by the DART analysis

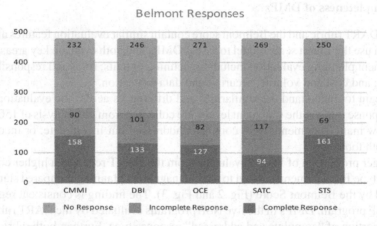

Fig. 4. The number of responses collected by the Belmont analysis

4.2 Research Outputs

Descriptions of research outputs signify what exactly is planned to be managed during the lifecycle of the project – an important statement to include in the DMP because it specifies the meaning of "data" to be managed by researchers. Data included many different objects. For instance, DMPs stated that numerical, media, text data and digital artifacts such as code, software, and databases were all described as the output from the project to be shared or archived.

Both tools evaluate statements of research outputs in DMPs. Evaluation questions include (a) what research output is defined in the DMPs (DART rubric 1.1 and Belmont score 1.1) and (b) how the research output will be generated (DART rubric 1.2 and Belmont score 1.2). However, the tools take different approaches to assess statements of outputs in DMPs. The DART score (1.1) emphasizes research data as a scientific output, and it leaves the definition of data up to a specific research agency or program.

In contrast, the Belmont score (1.1) defines a research output as any scientific object including software, code, or other outputs such as a database. To receive a complete response type, the statement also has to include the format of the data. The Belmont scores couples together the actual data and the format as important factor to data management. The DART rubric 1.2 specifies that the question only applies to specific NSF programs. Also, the Belmont score draws attention to the long-term output, not just any output for management during the project.

Statements about the research outputs and formation of research outputs were evaluated using both tools. The DART rubric 1.1 was applied to the 150 DMPs but not the DART rubric 1.2 (our sample did not have any DMPs from the suggested NSF programs). Both the Belmont 1.1 and 1.2 were applied to the corpus. A direct comparison was made of the DART rubrics 1.1 to the Belmont score 1.1 but a direct comparison of DART rubric 1.2 and Belmont score 1.2 was not conducted.

A comparison of DART rubric 1.1 and Belmont score 1.1 shows that a majority of DMPs are able to identify the outputs from research projects but the majority of DMPs scored higher when using DART as compared to the Belmont (Fig. 5). The higher scores in the DART may be due to the looser criteria for statements. The Belmont score evaluates a DMP to be complete if the output is described along with the format of the research output. The key differences here is that the Belmont score accounts the connection between the output and the format.

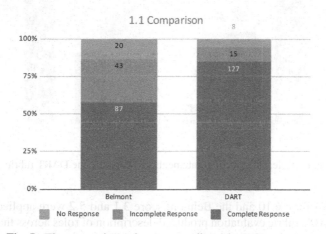

Fig. 5. The comparison of statements discussing research outputs

4.3 Roles and Responsibilities

The second area of overlap between the two tools is the evaluation of roles and responsibilities. The presence of statements that specify roles and responsibilities in data management planning outline the roles of individuals that will be responsible for the day-to-day data management activities. Anticipating the roles and responsibilities of data management is vital to planning because data management takes significant labor. Research outputs have to be cleaned, documented, stored, and licensed for sharing.

The DART rubric (6.10) evaluates roles and responsibilities in a free response question (this dimension is not evaluated from a Likert scale). The rubric provides a list of roles (PI; Co-PI; graduate student; post-doc; other/ N/A) for a coder to capture the roles in statements. The metric can capture specific roles and provide the coder more contextual information associated with the roles during the lifecycle of the project DMP.

In contrast, the Belmont contains a two-tier evaluation of roles and responsibilities compared to the DART rubric. The Belmont score (3.1) assesses whether the DMP defines the member of the team that will be responsible for developing, implementing, and overseeing the data management plan. In addition, the Belmont score (5.2) also assesses who will be responsible for managing the data after the project ends to ensure long-term accessibility. Criteria for a complete response entails statements that provide an exact description of the role during the project and after the project.

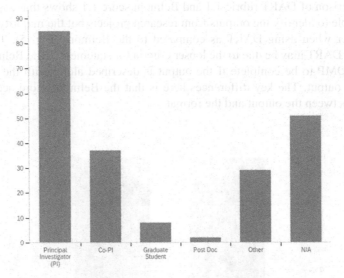

Fig. 6. Roles described in statements evaluated by the DART rubric

The DART rubric 6.10 and the Belmont score 3.1 and 5.2 were applied to the 150 DMPs. The DART rubric evaluation produced description of roles across the 150 DMPs (Fig. 6). The majority of DMPs stated that a PI would be in charge of data management planning. The Belmont score evaluation (3.1 and 5.2) provided an overview of the assessment of statements of roles and responsibilities but could not provide an in-depth look into the exact roles and responsibilities. The majority of DMPs scored low on both questions related to roles and responsibilities. Only one-third of the DMPs had text pertaining to the roles (Fig. 7).

We made qualitative observations about the differences between the NSF programs STS and OCE. When looking closely across NSF program, the DMPs from the STS had a very large number of DMPs that addressed the roles for long-term management of outputs. The coders attribute the high complete statements of roles and responsibilities in STS to the fact that the DMPs also state that sensitive data is a part of the project including clear descriptions of how the data would be used in the project and outside the project. There was an overlap between sensitive data and descriptions for roles. Coders also noted that OCE had a very high number of DMPs that did not state roles and responsibilities but that this was related to the significant number of DMPs that stated a data repository for access. Oceanography researchers receiving grants from the OCE program could be signifying roles and responsibilities by stating the repository. Statements about roles and responsibilities overlap with statements made about data repositories and security of data.

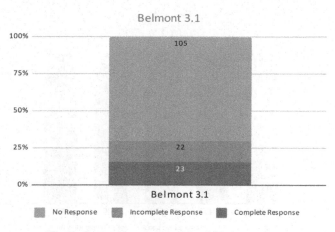

Fig. 7. Response types for roles in Belmont Score

4.4 Metadata

Metadata is vital to data management as it provides the necessary documentation for the data to be stored and reused. Metadata can provide the minimum descriptive documentation for data to be used in different settings.

Both tools evaluate metadata standards as part of data management planning. Two questions evaluate metadata in DART rubric (2.1 and 6.1). Question 2.1 evaluates the presence of a metadata standard and/or a format and question 6.1 qualitatively captures the exact standard that is described. In contrast, the Belmont score only includes one evaluation question for metadata (2.1). The Belmont score 2.1 evaluates metadata presence and kind of metadata. To be considered complete, both the presence and the specific kind of metadata need to be described (statements are not complete if they specify a workflow or an ad hoc standard). This is a much stricter criteria of evaluation compared to the DART rubric.

Comparison of the results show that statements in the DMPs scored by the Belmont score showed that statements scored lower compared to the DART rubric evaluation of statements pertaining to metadata. This is in part because the Belmont score asks for a specific standard as part of evaluation. The comparison of statements in DMPs across the five programs evaluated by the DART rubric (2.1) and the Belmont score (2.1) show that the DART rubric 2.1 had more incomplete and no response types (shown in Fig. 8 and Fig. 9).

The high scores from the DBI program corroborates empirical work on data practices related to metadata standards in biology and the life sciences more broadly [16]. DMPs from this area described many different standards (such as Ecological Metadata Language and Darwin Core). In contrast, a majority of DMPs from all programs scored an incomplete in this area. For example, coders found that the DMPs from the SATC program did not list any metadata standards – an outlier from the other four NSF programs.

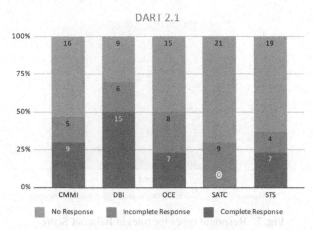

Fig. 8. Response types for metadata statements evaluated by the DART rubric

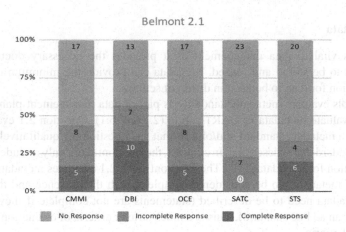

Fig. 9. Response Types for metadata statements evaluated by the Belmont score

4.5 Storage and Labor Costs

The next evaluation metric compared across the two tool was the cost of data management. This criterion involves the social and the technical costs of managing data. The costs associated with data management include infrastructure costs (university or external resources); preservation costs (archiving data for the longterm); time scales of management costs; and labor costs such as staff salaries and/or project-based fees. The DART and Belmont evaluation tools both address the cost of data management but in different ways.

The DART rubric (1.3) evaluates whether DMPs describe the amount of storage necessary, but the rubric does not evaluate cost. In contrast, the Belmont score evaluates both volume (1.3) and cost (9.1). Volume is assessed by the quantity of data that is stated in the DMP. Cost is analyzed in terms of the presence of a statement for the costs associated with long-term data management or costs associated with an assigned data manager. The metric does not specify whether to evaluate labor costs OR technical costs OR both.

The evaluation of volume and cost could not be compared across the tools. The differences between the two tools in regard to cost and volume create a gap in the comparison of the evaluation area.

According to the responses from the Belmont score (1.3), NSF programs across the board received low scores when it came to describing volume (Fig. 10). The majority of DMPs did not anticipate volume of data at all (Fig. 11). The DMPs from OCE had more complete statements about volume whereas the DMPs from SATC had the most DMPs with no response. As is shown though, across the programs a majority did not address the amount of data that the project would produce.

When analyzing how DMPs did on the question of cost, the numbers were striking. Of the 150 DMPs, only 18 addressed the cost of data management plans. Across all programs DMPs did not address cost (Fig. 11).

In summary, the comparison of evaluation tools drawing on the same corpus of 150 DMPs provided insights into differences, similarities and overlaps among criteria.

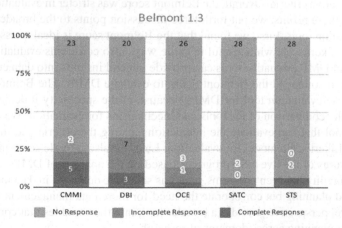

Fig. 10. Response types for storage evaluated by the Belmont score

However, it is unclear whether these scores are statistically different from each other. Qualitatively, the scores across the NSF programs are within a small range. This suggests that not one NSF program did better than the others. These findings though to do pose some interesting points about the state of evaluation.

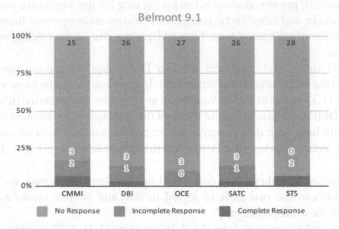

Fig. 11. Response types for cost evaluated by the Belmont score

5   Discussion

The findings above have implications to how we understand the state of evaluation of DMPs. Tools such as the DART rubric and Belmont score are the only tools currently available to assess DMPs. We compared the two to understand their similarities and compare their performance. We found that the 150 DMPs scored better with the DART rubric compared to the Belmont score. We found significant overlaps amongst the two tools but varying evaluative criteria. Overall, the Belmont score was stricter in evaluation criteria. Drawing on these results, we put forth three discussion points to the broader literature on the evaluation tools. First, we found that the Belmont score is ideal to assess DMPs. Second, the Likert scale while useful in some ways also constrains evaluation. Lastly, we found that DMP evaluative tools can provide general insights into data cultures.

First, we recommend the Belmont Score to evaluate DMPs. The Belmont score is a more precise evaluation tool for DMPs because of the specificity it demands. Next, we discuss the comparison of the tools and mechanisms for evaluation. We discuss the need for a tool that can evaluate the interactions among the criteria and the pros and cons of the Likert scale model for evaluation. Last, we also provide some insights into the data cultures of the five NSF programs based on the analysis of DMPs. The results indicate variability between programs, and thus scientific domains, in data management practices and planning but corroborate the need for more data management training. A program level perspective provides a broader look into the variables that constrain data management planning across domains of research.

5.1 Comparison of DMP Assessment Tools

The DART rubric and the Belmont score overlap in many ways. We presented several overlaps in our results: completeness; roles and responsibilities; metadata; storage and labor costs. In addition, both rubrics utilize a Likert scale model to assess evaluation with a set of criteria to evaluate complete, incomplete, or not present. This was expected given the fact that the Belmont score developed by drawing on criteria from the DART rubric.

The two rubrics also differ in unique ways. The DART rubric has many flexible criteria. For example, the DART rubric accepts any form of metadata as long as it documents data. The DART rubric also has a qualitative section that is not part of the Likert evaluation scale which does not cohere with the rest of the rubric but is useful to gain some qualitative text from the DMP. While it does provide a way to capture statements metadata standards, roles, and storage sites data it does not provide a standardized way of doing so for all DMPs. As noted by its developers [15] and confirmed here, it is an excellent tool for librarians and information professionals to identify areas that require attention and the resources that can be developed for data management planning. The downside of this approach though is that it is not a robust tool that can provide a full assessment of the whole document.

On the other hand, the Belmont Score's evaluation criteria are not flexible and requires a stricter interpretation of the criteria for DMPs to achieve a complete score. By stricter we refer to the guidelines for evaluation using a Likert scale. The comparison of the two tools across 150 DMPs shows that the Belmont score requires more detailed responses to data management planning areas compared to the DART in order for the text to be rated as complete. This is reflective of the fact that the Belmont score was developed to assess DMPs during and after the project. Most importantly the Belmont score takes into consideration interactions across data management topics. The Belmont score weights all of its criteria and provides a scoring mechanism to evaluate a DMP. This scoring mechanism provides evaluators with a quick way to score DMPs and compare them across grants.

Based on our comparative study, we recommend the Belmont Score for the assessment of DMPs. The purpose of the Belmont Score numeric score is to evaluate whether DMPs meet or exceed guidelines. This score can be calculated for each DMP. An average score can be calculated for a specific research domain. This score provides evaluators with a standardized method to examine many different kinds of DMPs within and across specific research domains.

5.2 Likert Scale: Pros and Cons

Both tools evaluate data management topics from a Likert scale. A Likert scale is an easy evaluative mechanism to use but it fails to capture the true quality of DMP content. For example, a DMP may specify a metadata standard and the tool would evaluate it as complete, but it does not tell us if this is a good choice for ensuring that future scientists can make use of the data. Future evaluation tools might need to be research field specific in order to evaluate quality of data management, access, and preservation.

We also recommend that evaluation tools need to be reexamined to assess not just key topics of data management but the relationships amongst those key areas. As the study has shown, data management planning provides a window into the intricacies of how data management topics interact. For instance, the technical qualities of data (including volume and format) are relational to its storage and access. Likewise, technical qualities of data are related to cost and labor associated with its management, curation, and preservation. Evaluation tools treat these topics are separate when in practice those topics must overlap. Further, the description of a data repository may cover metadata standards, access, and preservation all at once. Further work could be done to build evaluation tools that takes into consideration the maturation of the institution of data management.

5.3 DMPs Vary Based on Research Program

The comparative assessment of DMPs by tools also provided some insights into the DMPs by program. When statements of practices reoccur across individuals and groups, we say that researchers are drawing on similar norms for data management planning. The recurrence of statements across DMPs across five programs can be a proxy for how researchers across domains approach data management criteria. For instance, DMPs from DBI and OCE programs had higher rates specific statements that contained metadata standards. This is not surprising given the formalized guidelines and requirements of data repositories around metadata in the domain of biology and oceanography [16, 17]. We found that DMPs mostly lacked statements about volume of data and data management costs. This raises questions as to how storage and cost can be anticipated given the abstract nature of the volume of data. Finally, a majority of DMPs fail to define the roles and responsibilities associated with day-to-day management and long-term management. This is not surprising given the fact that data management planning is a form of invisible labor. How this particular area and other areas can be reassessed by exploring DMPs templates at federal funding agencies.

One takeaway from the study is that a majority of DMPs had no responses across the criteria described by librarian professionals as essential for data management planning. This points to a continued need to understand how and why DMPs fail to plan for topics around basic data management planning.

Future research could conduct a comparative analysis of the DART and Belmont rubrics using a larger sample of DMPs in order to investigate longitudinal trends in DMPs. Another takeaway is that assessing best practices provide great insights into how DMPs in NSF programs follow best practices, but we think there could more to examine here from a qualitative perspective. This kind of analysis would be useful to see how researchers theorize about planning and the ways in which they organize their futures for data mobility.

6 Conclusion

Over the last decade, funding agencies have required that researchers submit DMPs with their grant proposals to pursue federally funded science. However, it remains somewhat unclear what sufficient DMPs should address, partly due to abstract guidelines provided by funding agencies [13]. As a result, data managers and librarians have developed rubrics for assessing the content within DMPs. Unlike research about data management policy and guidelines, which is at least a decade old, empirical research about evaluation tools of DMPs is a relatively new [7]. In part, this may be because DMPs are typically not published or public, and represent occluded documents often hidden but essential to the planning and practice of scientific research. Thus, our comparative study contributes directly to empirical research on DMPs by both reporting on the results of scoring a sample of 150 as well as assessing two types of evaluation tools.

In our study, we found that the DART rubric and the Belmont score use the same topics of evaluation but contain different criteria for completeness. Second, we found that the Belmont score takes into consideration overlap of criteria. Third, we found that evaluation tools provide insights into program specific trends around data management. Findings from the study fill several gaps. First, as of writing, this is the first study that applied the Belmont score to the assessment of DMPs. Second, this study uses the same corpus of DMPs to compare different DMP evaluation tools. Furthermore, our corpus of DMPs is unique. Previous studies that have assessed DMPs, collected their DMPs from a single institution. The DMPs used in this study range from multiple US institutions spanning over a decade from the beginning of the NSF DMP mandate in 2011 to 2021. Third, it provides a summary of the evaluation of the tools. It assesses the underlying mechanisms of each tool and how it shapes the analysis of DMPs. Further research should extend this analysis to DMPs for other funding agencies, particularly outside of the US.

References

1. Bishop, B.W., Ungvari, J., Gunderman, H., Moulaison-Sandy, H.: Data management plan scorecard. Proc. Assoc. Inf. Sci. Technol. 57(1), o325 (2020)
2. Kowalczyk, S., Shankar, K.: Data sharing in the sciences. Ann. Rev. Inf. Sci. Technol. 45(1), 247–294 (2011)
3. Bishoff, C., Johnston, L.: Approaches to data sharing: an analysis of NSF data management plans from a large research university. J. Librariansh. Sch. Commun. 3(2), eP1231 (2015)
4. Smale, N., Unsworth, K., Denyer, G., Magatova, E., Barr, D.: A review of the history, advocacy and efficacy of data management plans. Int. J. Digital Curation 15(1), 1–29 (2020)
5. Borgman, C.L.: The conundrum of sharing research data. J. Am. Soc. Inf. Sci. Technol. 63(6), 1059–1078 (2012)
6. Mannheimer, S.: Toward a better data management plan: the impact of DMPs on grant funded research practices. J. eSci. Librariansh. 7(3), e1155 (2018)
7. Hudson-Vitale, C., Moulaison-Sandy, H.: Data management plans: a review. DESIDOC J. Libr. Inf. Technol. 39(6), 322–328 (2019)
8. Whitmire, A.L., Carlson, J., Westra, B., Hswe, P., Parham, S.W.: The DART project: using data management plans as a research tool (23 August 2021)
9. Tian, Y., et al.: An analysis of NSF data management plan guidelines. In: Proceedings of the 16th International Conference iConference (2021)
10. Carlson, J.: An Analysis of Data Management Plans from the University of Michigan. University of Michigan Library (2017)

11. Reichmann, S., Klebel, T., Hasani-Mavriqi, I., Ross-Hellauer, T.: Between administration and research: understanding data management practices in an institutional context. J. Am. Soc. Inf. Sci. **72**(11), 1415–1431 (2021)

12. Pasek, J.E.: Historical development and key issues of data management plan requirements for National Science Foundation grants: a review. Issues Sci. Technol. Librariansh. **87**, 1 (2017)

13. Poole, A.H., Garwood, D.A.: Digging into data management in public funded, international research in digital humanities. J. Am. Soc. Inf. Sci. **71**(1), 84–97 (2020)

14. Rolando, L., Carlson, J., Hswe, P., Parham, S.W., Westra, B., Whitmire, A.L.: Data management plans as a research tool. Bull. Assoc. Inf. Sci. Technol. **41**(5), 43–45 (2015)

15. Parham, S.W., Carlson, J., Hswe, P., Westra, B., Whitmire, A.: Using data management plans to explore variability in research data management practices across domains. Int. J. Digital Curation **11**(1) (2016)

16. Kim, Y., Burns, C.S.: Norms of data sharing in biological sciences: the roles of metadata, data repository, and journal and funding requirements. J. Inf. Sci. **42**(2), 230–245 (2016)

17. Chandler, C.L., Groman, R.C., Allison, M.D., Wiebe, P.H., Glover, D.M., Gegg, S.R.: Effective management of ocean biogeochemistry and ecological data: the BCO-DMO story. In: EGU General Assembly Conference Abstracts, p. 1258 (April 2012)

Topic Evolution Analysis Based on Optimized Combined Topic Model: Illustrated as CRISPR Technology

Yuanda Zhang[1], Shihuan Xu[1], Yan Yang[1], and Ying Huang[1,2]($\boxtimes$)

[1] School of Information Management, Wuhan University, Wuhan 430072, China
ying.huang@kuleuven.be
[2] Centre for R&D Monitoring (ECOOM), Department of MSI, KU Leuven, 3000 Leuven, Belgium

Abstract. Identifying the evolution trend of advanced technology-related topics has become an essential strategic issue affecting the industrial development of all countries in the world. In this paper, based on multiple data sources, we proposed a research framework that integrates the topic model and social network perspective to analyze the topic evolution of a specific technology field. First, we introduced the best-performing BERT pre-trained model in the given field and the Bayesian Optimization method to improve the Combined Topic Model, which achieved the best result in promoting topic coherence so far. Then we used the Optimized Combined Topic Model (OCTM) to complete topic recognition. Second, we constructed the co-occurrence network among topics in the same time window with the topics as the nodes and calculated the co-occurrence coefficient of all topic pairs. Afterward, we combined the co-occurrence coefficient between topics in the same time window and the similarity between topics in the adjacent time window to determine the topic evolution type and identify the path. Third, we utilized the characteristics of the nodes in the network, such as harmonic closeness centrality and weighting degree, completed the weighting by the Criteria Importance Though Intercriteria Correlation (CRITIC) method, and defined the importance index of each node in the undirected weighted network. Finally, according to the importance of nodes, the critical topic evolution paths were selected for specific analysis. We chose CRISPR technology as the empirical research field to preliminarily verify the operability and rationality of the method.

Keywords: Advanced technology · Topic evolution · BERT · Topic modeling · Co-occurrence network

1 Introduction

Amid the COVID-19 recession, the eyes of government officials, scientific researchers, and industry experts worldwide were upon the various emerging technologies to find new growth engines. The identification and evolution analysis results of technology topics are essential for people to make decisions in investment, scientific research, and

I. Sserwanga et al. (Eds.): iConference 2023, LNCS 13972, pp. 47–64, 2023.
https://doi.org/10.1007/978-3-031-28032-0_4

policy making. Among them, the Clustered Regularly Interspaced Short Palindromic Repeats (CRISPR), the hallmark of a bacterial defense system that forms the basis for CRISPR-Cas9 genome editing technology, has carried out much-applied research in the fields of aquaculture, crop cultivation, disease diagnosis, and treatment, and achieved rich results. In particular, during the pandemic, where COVID-19 continues to mutate and the emerging monkeypox virus gradually enters the community transmission stage, CRISPR-related technologies have been used in point-of-care testing (POCT). The rapid development of its applications in POCT has attracted significant attention from the public and academic circles. Therefore, taking CRISPR technology as the empirical research object of the evolution analysis method, its achievements will provide critical decision-making support for individuals, enterprises, and countries, which has both theoretical value and practical significance.

To explore the evolution law and trend of technical topics in the CRISPR field, based on the current best-performing topic model, the Combined Topic Model (CTM)[1], we introduced the PubMedBERT pre-trained model, which achieves state-of-the-art performance on many biomedical NLP tasks in the biomedical field [2], to accomplish the word vector embedding and used Bayesian optimization to adjust the hyperparameters of the model. Then we got an improved version of the CTM, the Optimized Combined Topic Model (OCTM). The OCTM was used to identify technical topics on CRISPR-related scientific and technological literature datasets fused with Web of Science (WoS), Derwent Innovation Index (DII), and Dimensions data sources. In the aspect of topic evolution, a new idea of topic evolution analysis is proposed. For evolutionary relationships involving more than two topics, we should consider both the similarity of topics between adjacent time windows and the co-occurrence coefficient of topics within the same time window to determine comprehensively. Therefore, we built a topic co-occurrence network with topics as nodes to thoroughly explore the association between topics. Then, the importance of the evolution paths was calculated by the node importance, and we selected some critical pathways for analysis.

2   Literature Review

Topic evolution analysis can be divided into two parts: topic recognition and evolution path mining. There are currently two mainstream research ideas in the field of topic evolution. One is completing topic mining by topic model and then set a threshold by calculating the similarity between topics in different time windows to judge the related topics and their evolution states. The other is based on text clustering or the community detection of keyword co-occurrence networks to discover the topics and then calculate the internal centrality, density, and other indicators of different networks to judge the evolution state and analyze the relationship between various networks [3].

For the first idea, some scholars still choose to use the LDA model proposed by Blei et al. [4] to complete the topic recognition. Compared with clustering, community detection, and other methods, the LDA model can better quantify the relationship between documents and topics and reduce the tedious manual processing steps such as adjusting the threshold of network indicators. Compared with the older methods, such as LSA [5] and NMF [6], LDA also shows better results. However, after the Word2Vec [7] method was proposed in 2013, many researchers combined the word embedding method with traditional topic recognition methods such as LDA and LSA to create topic models such as Word2Vec-LDA and GloVe-LDA, which improved the effect of topic recognition by optimizing text representation methods [8]. Some scholars proposed a Word2Vec-LSA [9] method and applied it to the research of blockchain technology trends. The final effect exceeded the PLSA [10] model in many indicators. In 2018, many of the NLP tasks' best records were broken by the emergence of BERT [11]. However, the BERT method is still rarely used in the field of topic recognition and evolution currently. Most of the studies using the BERT model combine BERT with some basic clustering algorithms (e.g., BERT-HDBSCAN) or traditional topic models (e.g., BERT-LDA, BERT-LSA) [12]. In 2020, an advanced topic model -- Combined Topic Model (CTM) was constructed by combining ProdLDA [13], an improved LDA model based on neural networks, and the BERT method. This model can effectively utilize context and other semantic information to accomplish topic recognition, filling the defects of various classic topic models [1]. Therefore, the model can achieve the best recognition effect in multiple datasets. There is currently no research on using novel and complex BERT-related topic models in the field of topic evolution. We believe topic recognition is a vital prerequisite for topic evolution, and its effect will impact the final state of topic evolution and the analysis results of topic association. Therefore, this paper chose the CTM as the basis of topic recognition and used the Bayesian Optimization method [14] to optimize the CTM model by combining the pre-trained model in the application domain to obtain the best topic recognition results.

For the second idea, we consider completing the identification of the topic evolution path combined with this network science perspective. The characteristics of the network determine that it is more suitable for dynamic evolution, association computing, and other fields. However, it needs to be more comprehensive to quantify the relationship between topics in different time windows only from the perspective of similarity, especially for the relationship between topics in the same time window. Liu et al. proposed the idea of mining future associations of topics by constructing a topic co-occurrence network and using a link prediction method [15]. Since the topic co-occurrence network can predict possible future associations between topics, it should also be used to discover existing associations between current topics. In this paper, we proposed enriching the mining of the existing evolutionary relationships by constructing the topic co-occurrence network. With the help of it and the similarity algorithm, we can well explore the relationship of topics in the same time window and determine evolutionary types, such as splitting and merging between topics of different time windows.

3   Dataset and Methodology

3.1   Data Preparation

This study selected three text data types, namely literature, patent, and fund, and adopted three authoritative databases (WoS, DII, Dimensions) as data sources, respectively. A total of 50,524 valid data pieces were obtained, as shown in Table 1. We found that the structure of the abstract part of the three types of data is the same. Therefore, we used the abstract of these three data sources as the original corpus in this study.

Table 1. Search strategy

Data type	Data source	Search strategy	Records
Literature	WoS	TS = ("Clustered Regularly Interspaced Short Palindromic Repeat*" OR CRISPR*) AND PY >= (2002) AND PY <= (2021)	29877
Patent	DII	ABD = ("Clustered Regularly Interspaced Short Palindromic Repeat*" OR CRISPR) OR TID = ("Clustered Regularly Interspaced Short Palindromic Repeat*" OR CRISPR*) AND PY >= (2002) AND PY <= (2021)	7544
Fund	Dimensions	"Clustered Regularly Interspaced Short Palindromic Repeat*" OR CRISPR*' in the Title and Abstract	13103

The specific process of data preprocessing is as follows: the abstract text is cleaned to remove missing errors and duplicate data; To ensure that the text is not too long or too short to affect the model effect, we screened out the abstract text with a length of 100–400 words, obtaining a total of 33165 valid data. The other steps include: Performing the word segmentation and special character filtering; Completing the lowercase conversion, spell check and correction, word form reduction, synonym merging, and removal of stop words, academic words (e.g., 'method', 'survey', 'project', etc.), low-frequency words, and high-frequency interference words.

After data preprocessing, we divided the time window according to the quantity distribution of scientific documents each year. The original dataset is divided into three parts according to the time window.

3.2 Topic Recognition

Through literature research, we know that the CTM model is one of the most compelling topic models. Therefore, based on CTM, this paper combined the PubMedBERT pre-trained model with the best effect in the biomedical field [2] and used the Bayesian optimization method to optimize the model to improve the result of topic recognition. To finally complete the evolution path identification, the total dataset was divided into multiple time window datasets according to the temporal relationship. Regarding the optimal number of topics, we decided on the final number by setting a range of different topics and calculating the coherence of their results.

In evaluating model results, we considered two perspectives: the coherence within topics and the diversity between topics and selected an index to assess the effect of different topic models. Compared with past topic coherence indicators such as NMPI, UCI, and Umass, the C_V index proposed by Röder et al. in 2015 has achieved the performance of reaching the closest score to the human rating and has good interpretability [16]. Therefore, we chose this index to determine the optimal number of topics and evaluate the model. Because the calculation method of the C_V index is complicated, it is not mentioned here. In addition, the C_V metric has been encapsulated in the Gensim library and can be called directly [17]. In terms of topic diversity, the index of "Topic

Diversity" proposed by Dieng et al. is more understandable than others [18], which is calculated using formula (1):

$$T_d = \frac{N \ (unique\_words)}{K * N \ (topics)} \tag{1}$$

where "unique_words" is the non-repeated collection of feature words extracted from all topics. $N \ (unique\_words)$ is the number of removed words. K is the k of "topk", representing the number of the most common words of each topic we selected. In this paper, k = 10. $N \ (topics)$ is the number of topics.

3.3 Topic Co-occurrence Network Construction

According to the results calculated by the topic model, we could obtain the probability of each topic in each document, that is, the "document-topic" probability distribution matrix. The co-occurrence of topics can reflect the degree of association between topics to a certain extent. Since the occurrence of topics in each text is independently distributed, the probability of two topics appearing in the same document is equal to the multiplication of the likelihood of two topics appearing alone, defined as the topic co-occurrence coefficient between a pair of topics. The calculation method is shown in formula (2):

$$C_{T_i T_j} = \sum_{d=1}^{n} P(T_{d_i}) \times P(T_{d_j}) \tag{2}$$

where $C_{T_i T_j}$ is the co-occurrence intensity of topic i and topic j, T_{d_i} is the probability that topic i appears in the d published papers, T_{d_j} is the possibility that topic j appears in the d published documents.

According to the definition, the level of topic co-occurrence coefficient can reflect the degree of association between two topics. To better present the co-occurring pairs of topics with a strong association in the topic co-occurrence network, this paper selected the topic association combinations with co-occurrence coefficient in the top 20% of all edges according to the Pareto Principle. Then, all the topics were taken as nodes, the edges with solid co-occurrence relationships were selected, and their co-occurrence coefficient was taken as edge weight to construct the topic co-occurrence network under each time window. After filtering the pairs of topics with low co-occurrence coefficients, the remaining edges can be regarded as having a robust internal association and have the prerequisite to be judged as merging, splitting, and other evolutionary types. We could obtain the association between topics in different time windows through the finally got topic co-occurrence network, which helped mine the evolutionary relationship.

3.4 Topic Evolution Association Mining

The topic co-occurrence network constructed above can show the co-occurrence relationship between topics in the same time window. The co-occurrence coefficient mentioned above can be used to determine the degree of association of topics in each time window. The similarity algorithm can obtain the association between topics in different time windows. Ten feature words are under each topic; the whole can be regarded as a short text with word segmentation completed. Therefore, the Doc2Bow method and TF-IDF, which are suitable for short texts, are chosen to be combined for similarity calculation in this paper. We accomplished it by the Gensim library in Python. First, the dictionary and corpus were extracted, and the Bow vector of each text was calculated. Then, the IDF values of each feature in the corpus were counted, and the TF-IDF model was established. Finally, we used the trained model to get the TF-IDF value as the similarity between topics.

TF-IDF can be used for calculating the importance of each keyword to the corpus, and its calculation formula is as follow:

$$w_{x,y} = tf_{x,y} \times log\left(\frac{N}{df_x}\right) \tag{3}$$

where $tf_{x,y}$ is the frequency of x in y, df_x is the number of documents containing x, N is the total number of documents.

The similarity between topics in different periods is calculated by the similarity algorithm above to determine whether topics are related. Multiple related pairs of topics can be obtained in every two adjacent time windows. There is a topic evolution relationship between the topics with high similarity.

3.5 Topic Evolutionary Type Analysis and Path Identification

Based on the calculated similarity and co-occurrence coefficient, combined with Pallag et al.'s six network evolution forms of "birth, death, merger, split, growth, and contraction" [19], we integrated the index of topic popularity based on the evolution analysis of topic content. It is because the two evolution forms of topic growth and contraction can be classified as a kind of "inheritance" relationship in essence. For the evolution of the inheritance class, we need to measure the volatility in the process of topic evolution by topic popularity. Considering that the topic not only has volatility but also has specific stability, adding the evolutionary relationship of "continue" can further improve the evolutionary type of "inheritance" topic. Topic popularity usually means the degree of attention to a research topic. A topic with high popularity will attract more scholars to the research of this topic, so more scientific research results related to this research topic will be generated than the general topic. This paper took the mean sum of the probabilities of each topic appearing in each document as the popularity in that dataset. Because the number of topics in different time windows is different, the distribution of topics is diverse. Therefore, the topic popularity value should be aligned with the ratio of the number of topics when comparing topics in adjacent time windows. The formula is as follow:

$$r = \frac{\frac{\sum_{d^{t+1}=1}^{n} T_i^{t+1}}{n}}{\frac{\sum_{d^t=1}^{m} Tj^t}{m}} \cdot \frac{N^{t+1}}{N^t} - 1 \tag{4}$$

where d^{t+1} is the total number of texts in time window (t + 1), d^t is the total number of texts in time window (t), T_i^{t+1} is any topic i in time window (t + 1), Tj^t is any topic j in time window (t), N^{t+1}, N^t is the total number of topics in t respectively.

As for the evolutionary types of topics, merging and splitting are defined based on the co-occurrence of topics from the perspective of social network analysis. Above the threshold, that is, the association coefficient of the involved pair of topics is in the top 20% in the same time slice, which can be defined as a pair of topics with solid association relationship. By setting the threshold, the edges that are not closely related within the network can be excluded, and the complex topic association evolution, such as many-to-one, one-to-many, and many-to-many among the remaining adjacent window topics, can be ensured. So that the definition of complex topic evolutionary types such as merging, and splitting was improved.

Table 2. Criteria for determining the evolutionary type of topic

Evolutionary type	Explanation	Decision condition
Grow	Topic research is gaining traction	The corresponding co-occurrence edge does not exist; $\rho_1 \leq sim\,(T_i^{t-1}, T_j^t) \leq \rho_2$; $\gamma \geq 0$
Continue	The composition of the topic content did not change significantly and remained stable	$sim\,(T_i^{t-1}, T_j^t) \geq \rho_2$
Contract	The popularity of topical research has declined	The corresponding co-occurrence edge does not exist; $\rho_1 \leq sim\,(T_i^{t-1}, T_j^t) \leq \rho_2$; $\gamma < 0$
Merge	The current topic is generated by merging multiple topics from the previous time window	In the last time window, all the related co-occurrence edges exist; $\rho_1 \leq sim\,(T_i^{t-1}, T_j^t) \leq \rho_2$
Split	The multiple current topics are created by splitting a topic in a previous window	In the present time window, all related co-occurrence edges exist; $\rho_1 \leq sim\,(T_i^{t-1}, T_j^t) \leq \rho_2$
Born	The current topic does not exist in the previous window	The topic set of the previous time window is S^{t-1}, $sim\,(T_i^{t-1}, T_j^t) \leq \rho_1$; As well, $T_j^t \notin S^{t-1}$
Disappear	A topic in the previous window disappears in the current window	The topic set of the current time window is S^t, $sim\,(T_i^{t-1}, T_j^t) \leq \rho_1$; As well, $T_i^{t-1} \notin S^t$

To eliminate the interference of the non-core topic evolution path to the final result, a threshold should be set to filter weakly related topics. In the Table 2, $sim\,(T_i^{t-1}, T_j^t)$ represents the similarity between topic j within the time window (t) and the topic i within the time window $(t - 1)$. ρ_1, ρ_2 are all related to similarity threshold: ρ_1 said in adjacent windows topic association mining minimum threshold, below this value about the topic will be filtered; ρ_2 indicates the topic of the show "continue" evolution relationship corresponding similarity threshold to be met, the pair of topics whose similarity is more significant than the ρ_2 will be regarded as a relationship of "continue". γ is the volatility rate in topic popularity. Whether γ is positive or negative indicates whether the topic is growing or contracting. To determine the threshold, first set the initial threshold manually and then adjust it by grid search. When it achieves the best visualization effect, $\rho_1 = 0.15$ and $\rho_2 = 0.54$.

According to the topic evolutionary type defined above, we can comprehensively judge the evolution state of each pair of related topics in the adjacent time window based on the co-occurrence coefficient within the topic, the external similarity between topics, and the topic popularity. Then the topic evolution path drawing is completed by visualization technique.

In terms of topic evolution path recognition, Hui et al. proposed a topic evolution pathway generation algorithm and calculated the importance of each path [3]. To have a more precise and intuitive understanding of the crucial development and changes in technology-related topics, we proposed a method to calculate the importance of the topic evolution path. Firstly, Gephi generated a topic co-occurrence network based on the topic edges with greater co-occurrence intensity within three stages. Then, the importance of each node was calculated based on the harmonic closeness centrality index and its weighted degree in Gephi. Finally, the importance of the nodes on each evolution pathway was summed to obtain the path importance.

The Harmonic Closeness Centrality is a modified measure of so-called centrality, which is a good measure of whether or not a node is in the center of a network or how close it is to the center. For the undirected weighted network, the weighted degree can intuitively reflect the node's frequency of occurrence and its influence in the co-occurrence network. Therefore, considering centrality and power, the importance of a node in the network can be measured well with the help of these two indexes.

Since the weighted degree of the node is affected by the number of topics and documents, it is necessary to normalize the weighted degree of three co-occurrence networks first and then according to the normalized degree of all nodes and the harmonic closeness centrality value calculated by Gephi, use the CRITIC method to calculate the weight of these two indicators. The CRITIC method can be applied to weight comprehensively considering data correlation and fluctuation, and the weight is obtained from the objective calculation, which excludes the subjectivity of artificial weighting [20]. Finally, the node importance of each topic is calculated by weighting the two values according to their weights:

$$K_{T_i} = w_1 * H_{T_i} + w_2 * NW_{T_i} \tag{5}$$

where H_{T_i} represents the harmonic closeness centrality of topic i, NW_{T_i} is the normalized weighted degree of topic i. While the w_1, w_2 are the weights of the former two.

After calculation, we obtained that $w_1 = 0.283$, $w_2 = 0.713$. After weighted analysis, the importance value of each node is received, and then the importance of each evolutionary path is accumulated.

4 Result

4.1 Time Window Division

To study the evolutionary path of the topic in the temporal correlation, it is necessary to divide the data according to the time interval first. The distribution of text quantity over time is shown in Fig. 1.

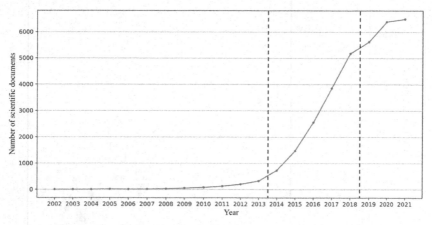

Fig. 1. The distribution of scientific documents quantity over time

Based on the literature growth theory and the quantity distribution of scientific documents [21], this paper divides the whole period into three intervals: preliminary explo ration period (2002–2013), rapid growth period (2014–2018), and stable development period (2019–2021), as follows: (1) The number of documents from 2002 to 2013 is small, and the overall trend of a slight increase indicates that CRISPR-related research at this stage has not been paid attention to and is still in the exploration period. (2) The growth rate of documents from 2014 to 2018 was significantly higher than that of the previous period. The number of documents showed exponential growth, indicating that CRISPR-related research was rapidly growing. (3) Compared with the previous period, the growth rate of the number of documents decreased from 2019 to 2021, and the growth tended to be stable, indicating that the research was in the stage of stable development. Data from each time window will be used for topic identification respectively.

4.2 Topic Recognition

In this study, the time windows' data were labeled as 1) dataset A – 2002–2013; 2) Dataset B – 2014–2018; 3) Dataset C – 2019–2021. Dataset A was used as an example for presenting the subsequent results.

Due to the random initialization of model parameters in the training of the neural network model, the results of each training are different, so the average value of multiple training is needed to determine the optimal number of topics. When choosing the optimal number of topics, the number of topics needs to be set as 1–40 for training in each round of testing, which takes a long time. Therefore, we repeated five rounds of tests and averaged them for comparison.

As shown in Fig. 2, when the number of topics was 9, the average coherence score reached the highest value. After calculating, the optimal number of topics for datasets A, B, and C were 9, 14, 14, respectively.

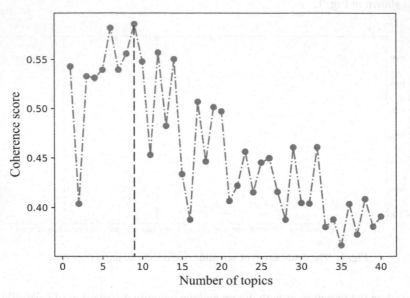

Fig. 2. The average coherence score for different number of topics (dataset A)

The empirical research field selected in this study is CRISPR-related technology. As a critical technology in the biomedical field, its related texts consist of many technical terms. Therefore, the pre-trained model directly using general texts may have a poor effect. So, we chose PubMedBERT, the most influential biomedical text pre-trained model, to accomplish the BERT vector embedding of the corpus. PubMedBERT is a domain-specific language pre-trained model developed by Microsoft researchers for biomedical NLP tasks. The researchers chose PubMed, the authoritative biomedical literature database, as their data source and constructed a pre-trained corpus of 14 million abstracts and 3 billion words. In multiple NLP tasks, PubMedBERT performs significantly better than other biomedical pre-trained models such as BioBERT, BlueBERT, and ClinicalBERT [2].

In the relevant models involving neural networks, the setting of hyperparameters generally significantly influences the final operation results. However, because the mechanism of this effect is somewhat unexplainable, people typically need to manually adjust and constantly try to improve the model's effectiveness. We chose Bayesian optimization to solve the problem of hyperparameter setting. The Bayesian optimization method uses Gaussian process regression to add the new hyperparameter setting information to the prior knowledge of the sampled points. We selected three hyperparameters of the model for optimization, namely dropout, number of network layers, and number of neurons.

After 50 iterations of calculation, as seen in Fig. 3, the output result of iteration 34 (as well as the 35th iteration) achieved the highest coherence value. Then we selected the hyperparameter of it as the best choice.

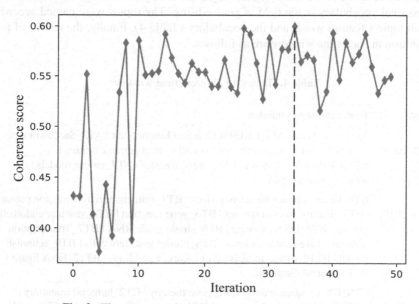

Fig. 3. The average coherence score per iteration (dataset A)

Under the premise of unifying the number of topics, several models, including OCTM, CTM, BERT-LDA, and some classic topic models, were trained and tested for several rounds. Due to the random sampling and parameter initialization in the training process, this paper takes the average effect of 10 times tests for each of the following models as its score to reinforce the reliability of the experimental results. The topic coherence and diversity values of the topic recognition results of each model are shown in Table 3. Through optimization, OCTM performs better than the original CTM and

Table 3. Effect evaluation of each model (Best results are marked in bold)

Model	Coherence	Diversity
LDA	0.448	0.242
NMF	0.422	0.494
ProdLDA	0.563	**0.956**
BERT-LDA	0.531	0.902
CTM	0.570	0.918
OCTM	**0.600**	0.949

topic models proposed by other researchers. It achieved the highest coherence score and the second-highest diversity score.

Using datasets, A, B, and C as a corpus, the topic recognition is completed by using the optimized CTM (OCTM). By consulting experts in gene editing, we summarized a professional vocabulary in the field of gene editing. The topics were named according to each topic's feature words and the vocabulary (Table 4). Finally, the results of topic recognition in each time window are as follows.

Table 4. Topics for different time windows

Dataset	Topics and topics number
A (2002–2013)	AT0_Cas6 gene I AT1_CRISPR Genome Engineering I AT2_Saccharomyces cerevisiae I AT3_breast cancer cells I AT4_viral genome editing I AT5_CRISPR/Cas9 system I AT6_gene transfer I AT7_mouse models I AT8_ribosomal DNA
B (2014–2018)	BT0_human immunodeficiency virus I BT1_mitochondrial membrane potential I BT2_reactive oxygen species I BT3_gene function I BT4_vascular endothelial growth I BT5_DNA cleavage I BT6_single guide RNA I BT7_Transcription Activator-Like Effector Genes I BT8_pluripotent stem cells I BT9_zebrafish model I BT10_mouse models I BT11_cancer cell lines I BT12_DNA ligase I BT13_mental disorders
C (2019–2021)	CT0_DNA sequence data I CT1_gene therapy I CT2_humoral immunity I CT3_antibiotic resistance genes I CT4_human genetic diseases I CT5_AAV delivery I CT6_cell membrane I CT7_model plant Arabidopsis I CT8_cell proliferation I CT9_gene editing I CT10_DNA breaks I CT11_DNA cleavage I CT12_mouse models I CT13_zebrafish model

4.3 Co-occurrence Network

Take dataset C as an example; there are 14 CRISPR domain topics in 2019–2021 and 91 pairs of topics. The maximum co-occurrence intensity among topics is 107.7, the minimum value is 36.2, and the average co-occurrence intensity is 52.8. According to Pareto Principle, we take 18 pairs of topics (20%) with high co-occurrence intensity as the topics with "internal association". Similarly, we took 7 and 18 pairs of topics in datasets A and B, respectively. Then, according to the selected strongly associated topic co-occurrence edges and all topic nodes, the topic co-occurrence networks of the three stages were constructed (Fig. 4).

4.4 Analysis of Topic Evolution

By combining the three indicators of topic popularity, topic similarity, and topic co-occurrence coefficient, and with the help of the topic evolutionary type judgment table mentioned above, we can obtain the evolutionary types of all topics after linking the topics of adjacent windows according to their degree of association.

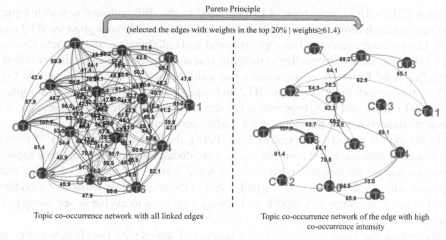

Fig. 4. Two forms of co-occurrence network of topics (dataset C)

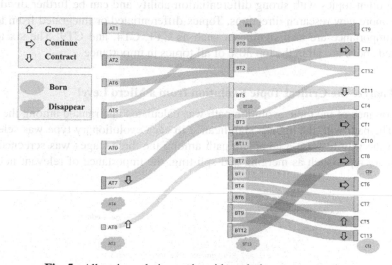

Fig. 5. All topic evolution paths with evolutionary type markers

Figure 5 shows the evolution path of research topics in the CRISPR technology field in three stages in the past 20 years. Longitudinally, each topic in the same period constitutes a node, showing the difference in the distribution of the number of topics in different time windows. Horizontally, the lines between topics in other time windows represent the topic association, showing a variety of complex evolution forms such as splitting and merging.

4.4.1 Analyze the Difference in Topic Evolution from a Macro Level

As seen in Fig. 5, there are considerable differences in the evolutionary types of research topics in different periods in the CRISPR technology field. In the early stage of the research (2002–2013), only topic AT5 belonged to the differentiated research topic. Two new research directions were differentiated in the development process: BT0 and BT5. The research content of this topic is broad and enlightening, and it could also be regarded as the most "prospective" emerging research trend within this time window. Regarding topic fusion, there are mainly two pairs of topics, AT2 + AT6 and AT1 + AT5, in this period, producing topic BT2 and topic BT0, respectively. Several topics, such as BT1, BT4, and BT8, appeared in the second period for the first time and had no apparent connection with the topics in the earlier period of the study.

In the middle period of the study (2014–2018), the differentiation ability of topics was generally enhanced, and multiple topics were divided to produce more new topics. However, due to the frequent occurrence of topic fusion, the number of topics that appeared in the third time window is equal to that of the second time window. As evident from the graph, research on CRISPR technology continues to evolve to see many new topics born and discover more complex topics.

By linking the macroscopic evolution process of topics with the characteristics of topics themselves, we found that topics with high importance, such as AT5, BT0, and BT3, are often topics with strong differentiation ability and can be further divided to generate more new research directions. Topics differentiated or integrated from topics of high importance are also significant such as CT1, CT4, and CT9. The six topics mentioned above are all in the top 30% of all topics in importance.

4.4.2 Analyze the Critical Topic Evolution from a Micro Level

The importance of the topic evolution path was calculated and ranked among the three stages. The path with the highest significance in each evolutionary type was selected, and then the way to form a complete path among the three stages was screened. For evolutionary types such as merging and splitting, the importance of relevant nodes is

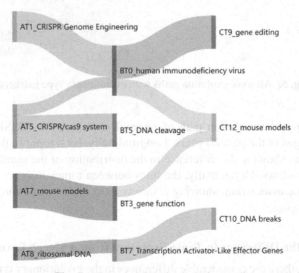

Fig. 6. The crucial topic evolution paths

calculated according to the mean value of the importance of multiple topics involved in the same window. Finally, the critical topic evolution pathways can be obtained, as shown in the figure below.

As can be seen from the figure, there are three main topic evolution paths:

1. *(Inheritance) AT8 → BT7 → CT10*

The first evolutionary path in Fig. 6 is a DNA-related topic, and the primary evolutionary type of this path is the inheritance class. Specifically, it is reflected in two "growing" evolution from AT8 to BT7 and BT7 to CT10, respectively. To a certain extent, this demonstrates the stability of the research topics related to DNA. From ribosomal DNA, it evolved into TALE and its closely related TALENs technology. TALENs were popularized around 2014 and replaced the traditional ZFNs gene editing technology with its unique advantages. Then, within the time window of CT10, CRISPR replaced TALENs, so the topic evolved into DNA breakage-related research related to gene therapy.

2. *(Fusion) AT1 → BT0, AT7 → BT3, BT0 + BT3 → CT12*

This path demonstrates the tenacious vitality of the topic of mouse models. Mouse models have been proposed since the first-time window, and after complex evolution and fusion, they can finally be included in the latest time window. It shows that the mouse model has survived, and the combination with CRISPR-related technology has produced new changes. From the changes of the features under the topic, the connotation of the mouse model has experienced a remarkable development: from the core of "in vivo", "disease" and other broad words to focus on "virus", "infection", and even the research scope gradually extended to "in vitro", "paralysis" and other more diverse and specific research fields.

3. *(Merging & Splitting)AT5 + AT1 → BT0 → CT9 + CT12*

This path first reflects the pivotal position of HIV in CRISPR technology research as scientists strive to overcome the AIDS epidemic that has plagued modern humankind through CRISPR-related gene-editing tools such as Cas9. The following topic-splitting process further confirms the above analysis of the evolution of the mouse model. The emergence of such a grand and broad research topic as "gene editing" also reflects the close relationship between HIV and various gene editing technologies and people's high expectations of using gene editing technologies and methods to solve major diseases.

4.4.3 The Comprehensive Topic Content Evolution

The global evolution of CRISPR-related topics content over the past 20 years is shown in the Fig. 7.

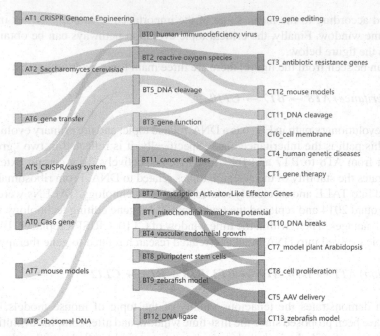

Fig. 7. The global evolution pathway of CRISPR-related topics (2002–2021)

5 Conclusions and Discussion

In this study, we started from the perspective of multi-source data fusion and introduced and optimized the Combined Topic Model (CTM). We obtained excellent topic recognition results based on the Optimized CTM, which performed great in both topic coherence and diversity. After that, we accomplished the topic evolution path identification by similarity, co-occurrence coefficient, and popularity. In addition, we proposed a method of calculating the importance of nodes in the undirected weighted network. According to it, some pivotal evolution paths were selected for specific analysis. Ultimately, we analyzed the evolution of CRISPR-related research topics from macro and micro perspectives.

Overall, our main contribution is to provide a research framework that integrates the topic model and social network perspective to analyze the evolution of a specific technology field. When we determine complex evolutionary relationships, such as merging and splitting, it is more rigorous to consider whether the association between topics exists within and outside the time window.

In the future, we will adopt more heterogeneous data, such as social media data, government documents, and technology-related stock market information, to enrich the diversity of data sources and improve the universality of the method. We used mixing type data for topic modeling, but the topic modeling result may also depend on the text type. So, we plan to verify it by experimenting separately with different kinds of text data. The method we proposed seems to be more complicated than several classic methods. To make our findings more credible, we will further explore differences between our method and other methods regarding feasibility and research efficiency. In addition, we will consider dividing the dataset into more time windows to show specific and detailed CRISPR-related topic evolution paths and use time-series linked data to predict the future development and evolution of the technology.

References

1. Bianchi, F., Terragni, S., Hovy, D.: Pre-training is a hot topic: contextualized document embeddings improve topic coherence. arXiv Preprint, arXiv:2004.03974 (2020)
2. Gu, Y., et al.: Domain-specific language model pretraining for biomedical natural language processing. ACM Trans. Comput. Healthc. Health. **3**, 1–23 (2021)
3. Hui, L., Jixia, H., Zhiying, T.: Subject topic mining and evolution analysis with multi-source data. Data Anal. Knowl. Discov. **6**, 44–55 (2022)
4. Blei, D.M., Ng, A.Y., Jordan, M.I.: Latent Dirichlet allocation. J. Mach. Learn. Res. **3**, 993–1022 (2003)
5. Landauer, T.K., Foltz, P.W., Laham, D.: An introduction to latent semantic analysis. Discourse Process. **25**, 259–284 (1998)
6. Lee, D.D., Seung, H.S.: Learning the parts of objects by non-negative matrix factorization. Nature **401**, 788–791 (1999)
7. Mikolov, T., Sutskever, I., Chen, K., Corrado, G.S., Dean, J.: Distributed representations of words and phrases and their compositionality. In: Advances in Neural Information Processing Systems 26 (2013)
8. Wang, Z., Ma, L., Zhang, Y.: A hybrid document feature extraction method using latent Dirichlet allocation and Word2Vec. In: 2016 IEEE First International Conference on Data Science in Cyberspace (DSC), pp. 98–103. IEEE (2016)
9. Kim, S., Park, H., Lee, J.: Word2Vec-based latent semantic analysis (W2V-LSA) for topic modeling: a study on blockchain technology trend analysis. Expert Syst. Appl. **152**, 113401 (2020). https://doi.org/10.1016/j.eswa.2020.113401
10. Hofmann, T.: Probabilistic latent semantic analysis. arXiv Preprint, arXiv:1301.6705 (2013)
11. Devlin, J., Chang, M.-W., Lee, K., Toutanova, K.: BERT: pre-training of deep bidirectional transformers for language understanding. arXiv Preprint, arXiv:1810.04805 (2018)
12. Cheng, Q., et al.: Bert-based latent semantic analysis (Bert-LSA): a case study on geospatial data technology and application trend analysis. Appl. Sci. **11**, 11897 (2021). https://doi.org/10.3390/app112411897
13. Srivastava, A., Sutton, C.: Autoencoding variational inference for topic models (2017). http://arxiv.org/abs/1703.01488
14. Snoek, J., Larochelle, H., Adams, R.P.: Practical Bayesian optimization of machine learning algorithms. In: Advances in Neural Information Processing Systems 25 (2012)
15. Liu, J., Long, Z., Wang, F.: Finding collaboration opportunities from emerging issues with LDA topic model and link prediction. Data Anal. Knowl. Discov. **3**, 104–117 (2019)
16. Röder, M., Both, A., Hinneburg, A.: Exploring the space of topic coherence measures. In: Proceedings of the Eighth ACM International Conference on Web Search and Data Mining, pp. 399–408 (2015)
17. Rehurek, R., Sojka, P.: Software framework for topic modelling with large corpora. In: Proceedings of the LREC 2010 Workshop on New Challenges for NLP Frameworks. Citeseer (2010)
18. Dieng, A.B., Ruiz, F.J.R., Blei, D.M.: Topic modeling in embedding spaces. Trans. Assoc. Comput. Linguist. **8**, 439–453 (2020). https://doi.org/10.1162/tacl_a_00325

19. Palla, G., Barabási, A.-L., Vicsek, T.: Quantifying social group evolution. Nature **446**, 664–667 (2007)

20. Diakoulaki, D., Mavrotas, G., Papayannakis, L.: Determining objective weights in multiple criteria problems: the critic method. Comput. Oper. Res. **22**, 763–770 (1995)

21. Zhu, G., Pan, G., Li, F.: The topic evolution of information privacy from the perspective of temporal correlation and structural representation. Inf. Sci. **40**, 127–137 (2022). https://doi.org/10.13833/j.issn.1007-7634.2022.04.016

"Design, Design, and Design Again": An Information-Architecture Redesign Workflow from Case Studies of a Government Portal and a Learning-Management System

Yu-Ju Yang[1], Li-Fei Kung[2], and Wei Jeng[2]([⊠]) [iD]

[1] Carnegie Mellon University, Pittsburgh, PA 15213, USA
[2] National Taiwan University, Taipei, Taiwan
wjeng@ntu.edu.tw

Abstract. While heuristics are useful resources for designing the web's information architecture (IA) from scratch today, IA practitioners occasionally receive requests to redesign established products, and guidelines are also needed to address such "redesign" requests. Past studies on IA design tend to focus on prototyping and how iterations contribute to final products, but such iterations have more to do with how users interact with the prototype than with its IA per se. This commentary paper reports a workflow for re-designing and optimizing two websites' information architecture (IA). Based on two case studies, we explored a redesigned workflow of IA, which contains five stages: 1) screening, 2) synergizing, 3) synchronizing, 4) IA development 5) evaluation & execution. Compared to designing an IA from scratch, a team who redesigns an IA may communicate with more stakeholders and consider internal politics' impact. Our proposed IA redesign workflow helps web designers allocate resources and prioritize work when given redesign tasks.

Keywords: Web information architecture · Government Information · Government website · Learning management system

1 Introduction

Information architecture (IA) is the art and science of structuring information products' content through different systems e.g., organization, labeling, and the design of effective navigation tools according to Rosenfeld and Morville [7]. A well-crafted information architecture of a website provides a clear path and speeds up the wayfinding process. It also improves the findability and usability of web content to provide users with an intuitive and efficient experience [9]. In fact, in an information-resilience society, acquiring quality and correct information can help people conduct proper decisions in an era bombarded with overwhelming information.

I. Sserwanga et al. (Eds.): iConference 2023, LNCS 13972, pp. 65–73, 2023.
https://doi.org/10.1007/978-3-031-28032-0_5

However, in the fast-changing information era, several out-of-date websites' IA cannot endure the massive change of intensive information, causing worse accessibility. Redesigning information-oriented websites has thus become a common task for many Web IA or UX designers. While textbooks and heuristics are useful resources when designing IA from scratch, IA practitioners (i.e., information architects) occasionally receive requests to redesign established products, and the same instructions would not be applicable. Unlike the design process that can be followed from scratch, the workflow of such redesign activity is seldom documented, archived, or examined by third parties. Even though several researchers share their experience in optimizing different scenario websites' IA [6, 8], little is known regarding an IA redesigned workflow.

Past studies on IA design tend to focus on prototyping and how iterations contribute to final products, but such iterations have more to do with how users interact with the prototype than with its IA per se. Indeed, in most of the redesign work that we are familiar with, content (e.g., each label of hyperlinks) has not been considered, leading to gaps between final products and users' expectations of "how they should really look" despite numerous iterations. Without consciously examining the websites' information structure, the experience of visiting an information space may be frustrating and unpleasant for its users [1].

Despite the lack of specific protocols when redesigning a web page's IA, several web design guidelines have been developed to foster effective design decisions and checklists set to serve as a mechanism of reminders in redesigning [3]. While the Content strategy guide designed by the department of Digital Profession of the Australian Government provides a series of building new content or redesigning existing content using checklists (e.g., "Is there a metadata strategy?" "What are the relationships among various information"), these listed items notably lack time sequences. These recommendations apply to a process but lack the overall implementation work that should be done in each stage. Therefore, the work can be expanded to introduce a timeline, which could aggregate the appropriate to-do in each stage following a time sequence.

This commentary paper documents a project in which the authors constructed a workflow to enhance two websites' respective IA. Beyond its relevance to the two projects in question, this workflow can also serve as a basis for IA professionals' construction of new IA or whole new websites. It comprises five stages: 1) screening, 2) synergizing, 3) synchronizing, 4) developing IA, and 5) evaluation and execution.

Each of these steps in redesigning an IA contains several distinct tasks and we would have these tasks followed by a time sequence to curate a workflow. To better elaborate the workflow, we extracted objects involved in these tasks and sorted them into two categories: *artifacts* and *stakeholders*. Artifacts are the products we interacted with, including the target website to be improved and exemplar websites whose IA we would like to refer to or adopt. Stakeholders include clients (i.e., redesign sponsors) and users (i.e., website visitors).

The overview of two IA redesign cases is shown in Table 1, namely the city-government portal as well as the learning managing system. During the first redesign case, as several rounds of context were executed within, it generated a "blueprint" of how the process could be, providing the inspiration to apply the approach from the previous to the next. Upon running down the process over again, we were able to adapt the experience to the other and examine the feasibility as a whole.

Table 1. Overview of two IA redesign cases

#	Case	Description
Case 1	City-government portal	A city-government portal for City K (with a population of 370,000, equivalent to Tampa, Florida), which provides services and offers information mainly to its residents and tourists
Case 2	Learning managing system	A research university's learning managing system (LMS), which supports nearly thousands of courses

2 IA Redesign Workflow

In this section, we walk through the redesigned workflow broken down by screening, synergizing, synchronizing, developing IA, evaluation, and execution.

2.1 Stage I: Screening

The goal of environmental screening aims to comprehend the focal websites in their existing forms and identify sets of improvement targets for each of them. This stage began with preliminary interviews with our stakeholders to gather more context for the redesign and its rationale and to consider more weeding and keeping operations.

City-Government Portal. In the case of the city portal redesign, these preliminary interviews with stakeholders included two of the clients – i.e., executives of City K, one from its IT department and the other, an administrator – and users, who were mostly residents of the city (n = 3) or people who commuted to work there (n = 2).

Learning Managing System. For the LMS redesign, we also conducted interviews with the clients, i.e., the team operating the LMS, and the system's users, including faculty (n = 1) and students (n = 11). Additionally, we collected user behavioral data backstage, covering their most commonly used services/functions and their visiting logs.

In both cases, these interviews helped us to considerably clarify our redesign goals, thus reducing labor and other costs, as more fully explained below.

2.2 Stage II: Synergizing

A deep dive into the website's contents, functions, and features is processed to enhance its capability and ensure it can provide its audiences with essential information. The city-government portal has a redesign goal to *enhance the accessibility of content*. As for the learning managing system, its goal is to *make learning tasks easier and more organized* by providing a more efficient access to information. To strengthen these goals, we inspected its existing items and explored new ones through reference work.

Services for City-Government Portal. Apart from delivering timely information and news related to the county or city that we expected to see on the city government portal; the city government portal, in fact plays a crucial role in providing services (e.g., "jobs and employment" and "medical and health care") to its citizens. To enhance the content being delivered, we looked into the service it provides.

To better understand what services should be taken into account for the city portal, we gathered detailed information on the services offered via the web portals of nine other cities of similar scales, listed in Appendix 1 (available at: https://osf.io/e2a3y/). It is worth noting that some of the service items had different granularity levels (e.g., "work" vs. "recruitment information" vs. "government vacancy"), but at this stage, we simply collected all of them.

By labeling the collected service items with various marks or colors, we were able to eliminate duplicates and then sort the unique ones into a finalized list, including 1) arts and cultural, 2) business and investment, 3) covid-19 relief and economic stimulus package, 4) disasters and emergencies, 5) economic development, 6) education, 7) employment/get a job, 8) entertainment/ recreation, 9) environmental protection, 10) fertility/ childcare subsidies, 11) general affairs, 12) household affairs, 13) housing, 14) labor rights, 15) land affairs, 16) medical and health care, 17) opinion mailbox, 18) safety and health, 19) social aid, 20) social assistance, 21) social allowance, 22) social care, 23) tax, 24) tourism, 25) transport infrastructure. This process, which was very similar to card-sorting techniques, was to ensure that we had as broad a coverage as possible among the examined portals, which could later serve as a potential list of services for use when designing and redesigning websites.

Web Components for City-Government Portal. While we can easily come up with several web components that a city-government portal may contain, including announcements, contact us, footers, etc., there was just time that we could nowhere spot specific components that we consider friendly to have. To ensure users can fulfill their requests upon reach, we looked into the components that it provides.

In this process, different web components of the cities were collected. The exact process was undergone in nine other city websites. The list of the compiled components is shown in Appendix 2. In addition to considering which components were present vs. absent from each of the ten cities' portals, we also considered their many different forms. Since the visual designs of these components might affect users' preferences [4], we asked our participants to choose which component(s) they most wanted to see, along with their aesthetic forms. Based on our experience, design teams should avoid putting off potential users with visual design elements, even when no specific negative comments about such components are received. For example, a potential user might vote against a web component because s/he finds its colors disharmonious rather than lacking functionality. The full list of web components after a competitive analysis of nine other city Web portals includes: 1) announcements, 2) annual highlights, 3) awards, 4) city image, 5) city issue, 6) city marketing, 7) contact us, 8) dashboard, 9) external links, 10) float buttons, 11) footer, 12) hamburger menu, 13) header menu, 14) latest news & features, 15) map, 16) services, 17) site search, 18) statistics, 19) tourist calendar, 20) transparency in government, 21) upcoming events, 22) video clip, 23) specialized services. These unique components are readily for-use upon future redesigning.

Functions for Learning Managing System. Since the learning managing system's content is usually specific to individual students and entering them requires identity verification, it was less straightforward to identify websites that were directly comparable but not private and highly secure. Thus, we turned to non-LMS online learning platforms such as Coursera, which have broadly similar content but are more accessible than Moodle, Canvas, etc.

We also looked into other heterogeneous types of websites for other functions that might inspire the redesign of the focal LMS. For example, we identified a project-management system with what we considered an exceptionally well-designed progress bar, and given that the LMS functioned in part as a platform for students to hand in assignments – which could be conceived of as a task resolved – we adopted it. Other web gadgets like weekly screen time recording/display were also incorporated as a possible means of helping LMS users keep better track of their learning behavior.

2.3 Stage III: Synchronizing

This stage began with stakeholders' reviews of the entity components deduced from the previous stages' analysis and compilation work. Specifically, we conducted in-depth interviews with the clients (city government for Case 1; the university for Case 2) and users to ensure that the results of our competitive analysis were legitimate and realistic. Based on our experience, we recommend that IA professionals conduct interviews before and after the synergy stage. The preliminary stakeholder interviews, described above as part of Stage I, can equip the design team with concrete requirements and specific redesign goals. For example, in the Stage I interviews, users' actual logged data can be collected to help shape the team's understanding of a website's most commonly used functions and services. In contrast, in the in-depth interviews after Stage II, stakeholders can be shown the designers' list of derived components, which will likely help them be explicit about needs that might otherwise be difficult to articulate by providing a "big picture" to refer to. In addition, data from the latter set of interviews can help ensure that the results of competitive analysis concretely align with their imagination.

2.4 Stage IV: Developing IA

After completing the first three stages, we commenced building up the IA blueprints. Based on the Stage III data, we prioritized website entity components before adjusting the websites' components according to the insights gathered from our clients and potential users, to improve such sites' IA structures and their navigation tools in particular. Specifically, we applied the "broad and shallow" pattern of IA, as named by Rosenfeld [7], over unorganized services to reduce obstacles that users might encounter when seeking them. We also applied the suggestion by the Australian Taxation Office [2], which claims that the larger and deeper the IA becomes, the more difficult it is for users to navigate, resulting in important search issues as relevant services are buried deep in the site. We applied the suggested categorization rule to ensure each label was hierarchical and logically understandable, and crucially, we confirmed that the IA headings did not contain any overlapping labels. The outcome of this process was the final IA for adoption.

On the other hand, we included a user-type-based IA design mentioned in the Strategy guideline provided by the Australian Government [2]. In this content group by user type, we searched for terms that could be applicable, and we retrieved government, business, residents, and visitors from Hawaii.gov. As a result, at the beginning of the navigation process, users categorize themselves as travelers/ visitors, residents, and business-purpose travelers and thereafter are presented with services accordingly. We expected that this iteration could markedly improve user experience for those who enter a city-government portal without specific needs in mind.

2.5 Stage V: Evaluation and Execution

Finally, we tested the usability of the final products by observing how each user interacted with the newly added features. Specifically, we asked them to perform basic searching and browsing tasks with the think-out-loud approach as they interact with the web, as suggested by Nielsen [5]. And within this stage, unlike user-centered design that has the proximity to change accords to all suggestions, under this scene, we suggest that the clients should be again involved to reach a decision and ensure the improved contents and information architecture that can be aligned with their redesign goal.

As a result, the user interview feedback was actually "pre-prepared" and facilitated the discussion about whether various user-recommended improvements should be carried out. Each improvement that the clients broadly agreed was desirable was then ranked in light of their budgetary and human-resources constraints, and the final products were adjusted accordingly.

2.6 The Five-Stage Redesign Workflow for Website IA

The outcome of the five-stage redesign process for website IA we have described above is the heuristics-based workflow presented in Tables 2 and 3.

Table 2. The overall redesign workflow for IA artifacts

		The website to be improved	Exemplar websites	To-be-adopted IA
Stage I. Screening		§ Comprehend the website § Identify improvement targets		
Stage II. Synergizing	Sub-stage 1	§ Inventory its website entity components	§ Gather and inventory exemplar websites' entity components	§ Gather and inventory exemplar websites' entity components
	Sub-stage 2	§ Sort all website entity components § Prepare list of unique entity components for further use		
Stage III. Synchronizing				
Stage IV. IA development				§ Adjust the website's entity components according to insights collected from stakeholders § Derive IA for use § Improve the website's IA structure and navigation
Stage V. Evaluation & execution				V-1. Conduct usability test of product V-4. Adjust the IA

Table 3. The overall redesign workflow for IA stakeholders

		Clients	Users
Stage I. Screening		§ Conduct preliminary interviews § Collect backstage information on user behavior	§ Conduct preliminary interviews
Stage II. Synergizing	Sub-stage I		
	Sub-stage II		
Stage III. Synchronizing		§ Confirm whether the results of competitive analysis are realistic § Ensure that the goals and results of competitive analysis are aligned	§ Confirm whether the results of competitive analysis are realistic § Ensure that the goals and results of competitive analysis are aligned
Stage IV. IA development		§ Prioritize the website entity components	§ Prioritize the website entity components
Stage V. Evaluation & execution		V-3. Execute the web improvement with clients' further input	V-2. Conduct further user interviews

3   Concluding Remarks

We hope that the five-stage redesign process for website IA can and will be applied to many different products in various contexts, saving IA professionals time and labor. Though its order is fixed, the workflow is also flexible in the sense that if clients articulate additional needs, those needs can be added to it, or, in circumstances where time or other resources are exceptionally constrained, eliminating some tasks would also be acceptable.

It is worth noting that the process in Stage II would be applicable to all entity components. In general, the process would be to inventory entity components of the to-be redesigned websites and the exemplar websites, extract elements that could be applicable within heterogeneous websites, and collect and record them in a spreadsheet. Finally, after aggregating and merging each website's entity components, eliminating duplicates, and filing and renaming similar ones would then result in a list of unique components for use.

It is hoped that this commentary paper's practical experience and workflow could be applied and followed in different practices. With the enrichment of cases, we anticipate that a steadier framework could eventually become a protocol that will be widely circulated in the IA community, both by those engaged in redesign tasks and by those designing websites from the ground up, to considerably streamline their processes.

References

1. Burford, S.: Web information architecture – a very inclusive practice. J. Inf. Archit. **03**(01), 21–44 (2011). http://journalofia.org/volume3/issue1/03-burford/
2. Commonwealth of Australia: Better practice checklist – 15. Information architecture for websites. Department of Finance and Deregulation, Australian Government Information Management Office (2008). http://www.finance.gov.au/e-government/better-practice-and-col laboration/better-practice-checklists/information-architecture.html
3. Downey, L., Banerjee, S.: Building an information architecture checklist. J. Inf. Archit. **02**(02), 25–42 (2010)
4. Lee, S., Koubek, R.J.: Understanding user preferences based on usability and aesthetics before and after actual use. Interact. Comput. **22**, 530–543 (2010)
5. Nielsen, J.: Evaluating the thinking aloud technique for use by computer scientists. In: Advances in Human-computer Interaction (1992)
6. Parandjuk, J.C.: Using information architecture to evaluate digital libraries. Ref. Libr. **51**(2), 124–134 (2010)
7. Rosenfeld, L., Morville, P., Arango, J.: Information Architecture for the World Wide Web. O'Reilly, Farnham (2015)
8. Sood, S., Gilligan, R., Chandler, C., Slack, S.: Disneyworld.com redesign. In: CHI 2004 Extended Abstracts on Human Factors in Computing Systems, pp. 869–884 (2004)
9. Tang, G.-M., Hu, H.-Y., Chen, S.-Y., Jeng, W.: A cross-cultural study on information architecture: culture differences on attention allocation to web components. In: Sundqvist, A., Berget, G., Nolin, J., Skjerdingstad, K.I. (eds.) iConference 2020. LNCS, vol. 12051, pp. 391–408. Springer, Cham (2020). https://doi.org/10.1007/978-3-030-43687-2_31

What Does Provenance LACK: How Retrospective and Prospective Met the Subjunctive

Rhiannon Bettivia[1] , Yi-Yun Cheng[2(✉)] , and Michael Gryk[3,4]

[1] Simmons University, Boston, MA, USA
bettivia@simmons.edu
[2] Rutgers University, New Brunswick, NJ, USA
yiyun.cheng@rutgers.edu
[3] University of Illionis at Urbana-Champaign, Champaign, IL, USA
gryk2@illinois.edu
[4] UCONN Health, Farmington, CT, USA
gryk@uchc.edu

Abstract. Provenance is the story of objects: how they have come to be, what they could have been, what they will be. This paper explores the temporal complexity of provenance and suggests the need for the concept of *subjunctive provenance*. Using the example of building an IKEA LACK table, the authors explore the concepts of retrospective and prospective provenance to highlight gaps and the potential for subjunctive provenance.

Keywords: Provenance · Temporality · Pan-disciplinary · Workflows · Recipes

1 Introduction

Documenting provenance is a core concern in information science. In archives, functional provenance documents the origins of materials [15]. In metadata, provenance elements and properties document process information about digital objects to ensure long-term accessibility [5]. In data curation, provenance helps establish trust in data as it is (re)used [13]. This wide-ranging body of information science research has yielded several provenance documentation models. An OCLC/RLG working group developed PREMIS, metadata for digital preservation. The eScience community developed various provenance-related models, namely PROV and its subsequent *PROVlets*.

Different subfields center different temporal aspects of provenance. History-oriented subfields like archives and museum studies focus on reconstructing the story of how an object came to be (or *retrospective provenance* [6]). In such cases, provenance describes how an object was created and how the object has traveled through space and time to the present. Showing unbroken chains of custody from an artist's hands to a museum curator's, for example, helps establish that a painting is real rather than a forgery. In curation and e-science, models and tools foreground a set of stories about what can or will happen (or *prospective provenance* [6]). Here, provenance documentation speaks to potential futures, what steps could be taken to rerun, recreate or extend upon an experiment. The relationship between retrospective and prospective provenance is a complicated one: provenance documentation travels backward and forward in time. This paper was inspired by the following provocations:

- When do the links between prospective and retrospective provenance break? What can be done to prevent/identify such separation?
- How can retrospective and prospective provenance be distinguished and applied to different areas?

We argue that these two tenses, the retrospective and prospective, are not sufficient to describe the temporal richness of provenance. We propose the term *subjunctive provenance* to speak about non-actual events that are contingent and dependent. This study addresses these questions using the all-too-common challenge of building IKEA furniture as a toy model for exploration and analysis.

2 Context

2.1 Retrospective Provenance

Retrospective provenance is the story of how an object has come to be– its history in the world. In art history, researchers are tasked with constructing a narrative about what happened to artworks in the past, sometimes stretching back hundreds of years [9]. In archives, retrospective provenance operates in relation to concepts like the 19th century French principle of *respect des fonds*. Because many archival records derive from quotidian practices of institutions, in many cases the need to find ownership traces is less relevant than in art history. In its earliest iterations, provenance in archives was tied to the standardization of organization in European archives that privileged original order, as opposed to a library-like organization that sorts materials according to external categories like Dewey and LCSH designations [7]. Challenges in documenting provenance arise where original order is disturbed, when changes to the organizational structure of the institution means the order of the archives also must change, or when provenance documentation for an object is missing.

Cook argues that we need to know about the creator of the archival records; the creation of the record itself becomes bound up with the larger provenance story of an object [3]. Archives scholars introduced secondary provenance to expand the definition of provenance further, to encompass layers of context surrounding objects [2,16]. Nordland [16] examines how archival records change over time as they are reinterpreted, and Conway employs secondary provenance to address the need to re-imagine provenance in a world of digital surrogates where the original objects might no longer be present. Conway's work [2] also invokes the work of digital humanists such as Kirschenbaum and Drucker who raise concerns about digital materiality [8,12]. Kirschenbaum's work [12] on digital traces brings retrospective provenance into conversation with e-materials: the speed of creation and volume of e-materials pose a challenge to older archival approaches to provenance based on *fonds*. Digital humanities work also shares concerns with media history and media archaeology work. While this field rarely labels their work as provenance work, the construction of the context in which media objects are made and deployed, such as Robertson's [17] work on filing cabinets and Sterne's work [18] on MP3s combine the contextual approaches of archives, the material traces of digital humanities, and the historical research of art history.

Yet while most of the literature about retrospective provenance comes from history domains, the germinal literature in these areas rarely uses the *retrospective* qualifier. Provenance in its original use cases is, by dictionary definition, retrospective. This terminological distinction originates with scholars in the e-sciences in particular, who need to differentiate between the recipe (prospective provenance) and the runtime (retrospective provenance) in scientific workflows [14].

2.2 Prospective Provenance

While retrospective provenance is about what happened, prospective provenance can be thought of as a recipe for how to make something happen, or how an object will come to be. Formal recipes, in the form of cookbooks, date back to 1700 B.C.; formalizing recipes into workflows became popular in the computer age, stemming from punch cards in the 1700s s and expanding into computational sciences in the twentieth century. The advent of scientific workflow management systems gave rise to a need to standardize workflow specifications. The Open Provenance Model for Workflows (OPMW) and ProvONE were responses to this need [4,10]. These models allow for the descriptions of the data, processes, and agents that will be used to perform computations.

Computational models link prospective and retrospective provenance. The workflow specification is a description of how a computation can be performed in the future. Retrospective provenance is the description of how a particular computation has actually been performed. The PROV and ProvONE standards center the importance of maintaining connections between these tenses, and each standard has elements for expressing both retrospective and prospective concepts [4,11].

Prospective provenance refers to workflows, plans, or recipes [4,10]. In doing so, it sometimes elides the space between what will happen and what could happen. Some recipes include a finite set of linear steps: in this case, barring equipment failure, the workflow documents what *will* happen. Prospective provenance is also used to refer to situations with branching steps: workflows where agents, human or otherwise, can choose Path A, leading to one set of steps, or Path B, leading to a separate set of steps. These branches might be formalized: a program can include two protocols and it might run each a number of times to generate data for comparison. This process is a simplification of what happens frequently in computational or laboratory experiments. In everyday examples, like cookery recipes, written instructions might not present multiple optional protocols, but people cooking in a kitchen informally add steps, diversions that *could* happen. These conditional changes to the plan occur when, for example, substituting gluten-free flour for wheat because of an allergy or forgetting to add fresh parsley at the end.

While computational sciences tend to combine the *could happens* with the *will happens*, we argue that these two tenses, the conditional and the future, merit separation. If prospective provenance, by definition, is about what will happen in the future, then we propose the term *subjunctive provenance* to speak about what could happen. In the following section, we explore this full temporal spectrum of past, conditional, and future using a simple toy model: building an IKEA table.

3 Use Case: IKEA as a Microcosm

"I'm supposed to attach a brackety thing to the side things using a bunch of these little worm guys. I have no brackety thing. I see no worm guys whatsoever. And I cannot feel my legs."
–Ross Geller in the pilot of *Friends*, building IKEA furniture

Provenance concerns abound in many disciplines, and part of what impacts the diversity of definitions and approaches is the objects to which these provenance stories attach. The provenance of wine may look quite different to the provenance of seeds or the provenance of a nuclear magnetic resonance spectroscopy analysis process, even while we argue that all these conceptions share a foundational definition. provenance is a story of how objects come to be [1].

We offer a tangible example for exploring the temporality of provenance: building IKEA's LACK coffee table. The scenario is derived from the sitcom *How I Met Your Mother* (*HIMYM*), when the characters Marshall and Ted duel with swords to determine who gets to keep tenancy of their shared apartment (Fig. 1). Marshall hops onto a coffee table to gain an advantage. A flashback interrupts, showing the characters building the coffee table when they first moved in. Unable to locate the final support screws, they used wood glue to complete the table's construction. Post flashback, the improperly constructed table collapses under Marshall's weight. He falls as his partner, Lily, walks in and she is stabbed by the sword.

Through this scenario, we will explore retrospective and prospective provenance. By digging into the flashbacks and flash-forwards in *HIMYM*, we will begin to unpack the full temporal spectrum of provenance.

3.1 Retrospective Provenance

The retrospective provenance of an IKEA table is an account of the steps taken when assembling it. Whether the suggested instructions were followed does not

Fig. 1. Marshall and Ted's sword fight in season 1 episode 8 of *How I Met Your Mother: The Duel*. Retrospective provenance documents that they did not precisely follow the prospective instructions for assembling the table. Exploring the consequences of deviations between prospective and retrospective provenance is the realm of subjunctive provenance.

matter: the task is to adequately document what actually happened. If the builder follows each step in the manual without deviation, documenting provenance is likely informal. It might include ticking off steps on the manual or posting an online review stating that the table was successfully built as instructed.

In *HIMYM*, the retrospective provenance story is recounted in the flashback: Marshall followed the written instructions up until the last step, whereupon he used wood glue in place of the final screw. However, much like reconstructing the history of a mysterious painting, if we had to tell this story in the absence of the flashback, it would take some detective work. In this scenario, asking Marshall how he built the table might elicit a response much like the flashback: Marshall would explain about the manual, the screw, and the glue. However, the remembrance of the wood glue was predicated on exceptional circumstances that occurred when the table collapsed: the structural failure of the table and resulting stabbing brought to mind the table's history. Had the table held Marshall's weight or had the sword fight not occurred, the fact that the table was short one screw might have been forgotten in time (Fig. 1). Marshall might tell a friend that he built the table in accordance with the manual; in the absence of a memorably difficult journey building the table, like Ross's negative experience from *Friends*, it's entirely possible that the glue might be left out of the provenance story. The hypothetical is an important one in the realm of retrospective provenance: when reconstructing the past, even the relatively recent past, small details that might later become important can be overlooked, intentionally or unintentionally.

3.2 Prospective Provenance

Prospective provenance deals with how things will come to be. In the *HIMYM* scenario, we can flash even further back to when Marshall and Ted begin to build the coffee table. They use a manual like that of the IKEA LACK table (Fig. 2). There are eight steps involved. Each step demonstrates which furniture pieces are involved, the literal nuts and bolts to complete that step, and the actions required (e.g. rotate the dowels). The steps to building are a simple form of *prospective provenance*.

Yet what seems simple rarely is: what happens when everything doesn't go to plan? A common example is the "tools not included" problem, in which someone doesn't have a Phillips-head screwdriver and so uses a flat-head, or even a butter knife. These deviations to the prospective provenance impact the retrospective provenance: the original prospective provenance in the form of the manual was not inclusive of everything in the real-life workflow. Without documentation, these deviations can be forgotten in the retrospective provenance. Replacing the screwdriver is a process alteration. It is also common to alter underlying materials. Ross lacks brackety things and worm guys; Marshall cannot find screws. Lost screws are omitted; replaced with spare screws or entirely different screws; or replaced by another fastener like wood glue.

Recording real world provenance like this gets messy. PROV has Prov:activities with associated plans, but how do we document deviations to the plan at all the various levels of abstraction between entities (objects), agents (builders), and activities (events)? Is there a mechanism for crafting and future-proofing prospective provenance to allow for common variations, like the simple culinary case of roasting time being proportional to turkey size? Reviews of products on furniture websites commonly feature users who document challenges specific to building a particular piece of furniture, like needing a hammer to insert dowels or a drill when pre-drilled holes do not line up even when the instructional manuals do not call for these tools. Responses to these comments demonstrate that other users adopt these process and material alterations as part of their own prospective provenance.

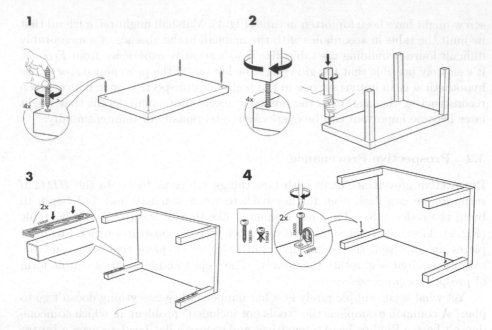

Fig. 2. Four of the eight steps for building an IKEA LACK coffee table. Source: https://www.ikea.com/us/en/p/lack-coffee-table-black-brown-40104294/

When building IKEA furniture, many users collect multiple plans before proceeding: this might include the official manual, YouTube videos, a toolbox, recommendations from reviews, and their own building experience. Models like PROV and the PROVlets account for plans; reality is an amalgamation of plans that *could* be executed in many overlapping configurations. How are these multiple possibilities documented? How can we model more comprehensive prospective provenance that better resembles real-world scenarios?

3.3 Subjunctive Provenance

Had Marshall and Ted followed the steps for building the table correctly, as depicted in Fig. 2, Lily might not have been stabbed. However, most of the time, discerning the exact time-slice that led to an error is difficult. While the flashback details what went wrong with the table's construction, in reality finding the precise step that lead to its collapse would be challenging.

Retrospectively identifying "what could have been" from a step performed in a *prospective* plan is what we call *subjunctive provenance*. We use the term subjunctive in reference to a verb tense that describes non-actual scenarios: subjunctive provenance is the documentation of the plans that *could have been* taken. It enables stories about what we *were* going to do. Separating the possible from the prospective provides a means to examine the temporal complexity of provenance. For example, subjunctive provenance can be useful for identifying errors by investigating possible paths a step could have led to. Stabbing Lily makes Marshall and Ted remember what they did wrong (*retrospective*), which calls into being the imaginings of what could have been (*subjunctive*): perhaps they made an error as early as step 1 in the manual, or they used shorter screws when they should have used longer ones. When prospective provenance is not followed properly, it is possible to look back when something goes wrong, which in turn brings up arguments about what would have happened if the plans were followed correctly.

It is also possible that a well-built table is still breakable. Had Marshall found that final screw, the table still might not have been able to hold Marshall without breaking – he's nearly two meters tall and 95 kilos. The subjunctive is helpful in discerning what provenance needs to be documented. The lives of objects can be long. At some juncture, custodians must be judicious about what to include in metadata. Changes to process and materials that do not materially alter the outcome may be rightly deemed unimportant in telling the story; even without the wood glue, Lily was going to be stabbed once Marshall hopped on the table with a sword.

The *HIMYM* example illustrates how subjunctive provenance is a useful concept dealing with situations that have already come to be, like error detection; selecting pertinent information to include in provenance documentation; and documenting the real and perceived affordances of digital technologies. Subjunctive provenance can also be forward-looking. It provides a framework to think about the complexity of the possible paths that could be taken, which can be helpful in scenarios like calculating risk and version control. Like a Bayesian inference where hypotheses based on past events are updated as new information becomes available, subjunctive provenance covers the temporal space between the past and the future. It bridges decision-making based on what has already happened with expectations about what will happen in future.

4   Discussion and Conclusion

Documenting provenance is a form of storytelling: the future is talking to the past when prospective plans become retrospective history. Simultaneously, retrospective provenance must persuade into the future: the current misinformation crisis demonstrates that provenance that seems convincing to one person may not be to another. The challenge for the person telling stories to the future is that they are speaking to a group of unknowns: it is not real-time communication. Subjunctive provenance enables a broader picture of the audiences who might be listening to the provenance story in the future. Taking these audiences into consideration when making documentation opens the possibility of better communication across time. If provenance is a story of how something comes to be, subjunctive provenance is a method of future-proofing: it can help reconcile the future and past object.

We began with provocations about the breakdown of links between prospective and retrospective provenance. We've shown that the challenges of persuading future listeners and documenting plans in the inherent complexity of the real world reveal that the temporal spectrum of provenance is rich and insufficiently defined by retrospective and prospective concepts. We identified subjunctive provenance as a potential bridge between these existing conceptions. We also applied this concept to the IKEA scenario to distinguish what subjunctive provenance can accomplish. The separate articulation of this concept suggests that future avenues of research are needed to explore how to document subjunctive provenance in ways that aid broader provenance practice.

References

1. Bettivia, R., Cheng, Y.Y., Gryk, M.: Documenting the future: navigating provenance metadata standards. Spring Nature (2022). https://doi.org/10.1007/978-3-031-18700-1
2. Conway, P.: Digital transformations and the archival nature of surrogates. Arch. Sci. **15**(1), 51–69 (2015)
3. Cook, T.: What is past is prologue: a history of archival ideas since 1898, and the future paradigm shift. Archivaria, pp. 17–63 (1997)
4. Cuevas-Vincenttin, V., et al.: ProvONE: a prov extension data model for scientific workflow provenance (2016). https://purl.dataone.org/provone-v1-dev
5. Dappert, A., Squire Guenther, R., Peyrard, S.: Digital preservation metadata for practitioners. Springer, Cham (2016). https://doi.org/10.1007/978-3-319-43763-7
6. Davidson, S.B., Freire, J.: Provenance and scientific workflows: challenges and opportunities. In: Proceedings of the 2008 ACM SIGMOD International Conference on Management of Data, pp. 1345–1350 (2008)
7. Douglas, J.: Origins and beyond: the ongoing evolution of archival ideas about provenance. Currents Arch. Think. **2**, 25–52 (2017)
8. Drucker, J.: Performative materiality and theoretical approaches to interface. DHQ: Digit. Human. Quart. **7**(1), 000143 (2013)
9. Feigenbaum, G., Reist, I., Reist, I.J.: Provenance: an alternate history of art. Getty Publications (2012)
10. Garijo, D., Gil, Y.: A new approach for publishing workflows: abstractions, standards, and linked data. In: Proceedings of the 6th Workshop on Workflows in Support of Large-scale Science, pp. 47–56 (2011)
11. Groth, P., Moreau, L.: Prov-overview: an overview of the prov family of documents (2013). https://www.w3.org/TR/prov-overview/
12. Kirschenbaum, M.G.: Mechanisms: new media and the forensic imagination. MIT Press (2012)
13. Mayernik, M.S., DiLauro, T., Duerr, R., Metsger, E., Thessen, A.E., Choudhury, G.S.: Data conservancy provenance, context, and lineage services: key components for data preservation and curation. Data Sci. J. **12**, 158–171 (2013)
14. McPhillips, T., Bowers, S., Belhajjame, K., Ludäscher, B.: Retrospective provenance without a runtime provenance recorder. In: 7th USENIX Workshop on the Theory and Practice of Provenance (TaPP 15) (2015)
15. Niu, J.: Provenance: crossing boundaries. Archiv. Manuscripts **41**(2), 105–115 (2013)
16. Nordland, L.P.: The concept of "secondary provenance": Re-interpreting ac ko mok ki's map as evolving text. Archivaria, pp. 147–159 (2004)
17. Robertson, C.: The Filing Cabinet: a vertical history of information. University of Minnesota Press (2021)
18. Sterne, J.: MP3: the meaning of a format. Duke University Press (2012)

Exploration of Accuracy, Completeness and Consistency in Metadata for Physical Objects in Museum Collections

Vyacheslav Zavalin[1]([✉]) [iD] and Oksana L. Zavalina[2] [iD]

[1] College of Professional Education, Texas Woman's University, Texas, USA
vzavalin@twu.edu
[2] College of Information, University of North Texas, Texas, USA
oksana.zavalina@unt.edu

Abstract. This exploratory study is the first one that examined student-created metadata for physical non-text resources. We applied in-depth qualitative and quantitative content analysis to the Dublin Core (DCTERMS) metadata created by the graduate students in two sections of an introductory digital library metadata course. The analysis of bibliographic records that represent paintings identified record fields in which novice metadata creators tend to make mistakes. Examples of the most common kinds of metadata errors for each quality criterion (accuracy, completeness, and consistency) are discussed and compared with results of previous relevant research. Finding of comparative analysis for the asynchronous course section and the section with synchronous class meetings are also presented. Implications are discussed, along with future directions for research.

Keywords: Metadata quality · Dublin core · Museum resources

1 Introduction

Robust metadata is key to providing equal and efficient access to information for diverse populations across the world. This applies not only to born-digital or digitized resources but also to discovery of unique valuable physical resources in cultural heritage collections such as artworks held by museums and galleries. In addition to specialized standards (Cataloging Cultural Objects, Categories for Description of the Works of Art, and Visual Resources Association Core), Dublin Core, developed with flexibility to represent a variety of resources, is often used for providing access to artworks. Once users, through online search powered by metadata, discover artworks of interest, they might use this information to plan the visit to their repository to enjoy the artworks in person. In most cases though, people who are located far away from the institution that displays the artwork in its collection or experience other barriers for in-person access (socioeconomic, health-related, etc.), can enjoy it – and other related or similar works of art – virtually. Inclusivity of access is enabled by high-quality metadata that leads potential users to the landing page for the artwork, which in addition to the work's digital image, includes valuable contextual information and provides links to related artworks and publications.

I. Sserwanga et al. (Eds.): iConference 2023, LNCS 13972, pp. 83–90, 2023.
https://doi.org/10.1007/978-3-031-28032-0_7

To ensure functionality of metadata in facilitating resource discovery, metadata quality needs to be evaluated, for evaluation results to inform improvements. Assessments of metadata in digital repositories are guided by metadata quality frameworks (e.g., [3, 18]). Multiple quality criteria proposed by these frameworks are adopted or adapted for use in evaluations. Of these, accuracy, consistency, and completeness are the most widely applied: a survey demonstrated that these 3 criteria were used by 65% or more of metadata managers [16].

Developing knowledge and skills that allow creating high-quality metadata is a priority in the metadata specialists' preparation, as shown by survey findings (e.g., [7, 8, 16]). Several studies (e.g., [1, 4, 9, 11]) examined course syllabi and found that students learn Dublin Core – the most ubiquitous metadata scheme worldwide – often with practical assignments. Case studies (e.g., [5, 8, 14, 20]) reported how the specific metadata skills are developed through readings, assignments, and other course activities. Skill building in graduate coursework was recently examined with the focus on quality of student-created Dublin Core records that represent digital text works [21].

Multiple studies analyzed the quality of metadata in repositories of digitized and born-digital content. This occasionally included metadata that represents digital images (e.g., [13]). Some of the digital repository metadata studies focused on Dublin Core or Metadata Object Description Schema (MODS) standards (e.g., [10, 12, 15, 19]). Others examined metadata created according to locally developed schema (e.g., [2, 17, 20]). However, no reports so far focused on quality in metadata representing physical works of art, and specifically on the Dublin Core metadata created by novices such as students of metadata courses. In this study, we address this gap with analysis of the student-created metadata from the introductory graduate metadata course taught at University of North Texas. In this course, students create Dublin Core Metadata Initiative Terms (DCTERMS) metadata encoded in the Extensible Markup Language (XML) syntax to represent portraits, animal paintings, still lives, seascapes and cityscapes authored by North American and European artists in 18th–20th centuries and held by the two United States' art galleries.

2   Method

The data were collected from two sections of the online metadata course that used the same learning materials and assignments and were taught simultaneously – one with weekly synchronous meetings, another asynchronously – in summer of 2022. Thirty-two DCTERMS records (23 from the synchronous section and 9 from asynchronous) were analyzed to address these research questions:

1. What are the metadata quality issues observed? How are these issues distributed in the dataset?
2. What are the differences and similarities in observed metadata quality in synchronous and asynchronous classes, for paintings and other types of resources?

The quantitative and qualitative comparative content analysis was used with the focus on the accuracy, completeness, and consistency. In this study, metadata quality issues (detailed in the Findings section) were operationally defined this way:

- *Accuracy* problems: use of metadata element not applicable to the resource, use of the metadata element intended for other data type than the one entered by student, use of the overly broad Dublin Core Metadata Element Set (DCMES 1.1) element when a specific DCTERMS element should be used, misrepresentation of resource by data values that do not apply, and typographical errors.
- *Completeness* problems: omission of applicable metadata elements (including the use of a single instance of a metadata element when multiple instances apply), and incomplete data values: unfinished sentences and/or missing important pieces of information in the overly brief data value.
- *Consistency* problems: failure to draw data values from controlled vocabularies (name authority files, subject headings, etc.) where applicable.

The analysis focused on 19 DCTERMS metadata fields which were applicable to one or more of the paintings assigned to students in this course. Descriptive statistics indicators were measured for the overall level of metadata quality problems in student-created records, and separately for accuracy, completeness, and consistency problems, as well as individually for each metadata element.

3 Findings and Discussion

Across the two sections of the course, 1 or more metadata quality errors were found in each of the 19 applicable DCTERMS fields. The number of errors per record ranged widely from 1 to 22. The average total number of quality problems per metadata record was 7.43, with the median of 6 and the standard deviation of 5.56. The total number of quality problems per metadata field in the dataset ranged even more substantially: between 2 – for the Provenance field that applies to every painting and the Alternative [title] field that only applied to under a third in this dataset – and 31 for the Subject that applies to any resource. The average total number of quality problems per metadata field in the dataset was 12.53, with the median of 10 and the standard deviation of 8.97. Table 1 shows how the quality issues distributed across DCTERMS metadata fields, including for synchronous and asynchronous sections, with significant (twofold or more) differences highlighted/. The data is presented and discussed with examples below.

Accuracy problems were observed in all, but two (Provenance and Alternative) fields analyzed, most often in the Subject (56.25% of student-created records in 2 sections of the course) and Title (28.13%). Synchronous section students made *accuracy* errors significantly more often that asynchronous section students in these 5 fields: Title, Type, Medium, Description, HasFormat, and AccessRights (Table 1). The most common Title field *accuracy* problem was appending the date of creation to the actual title, (e.g., "Still Life with a White Mug, 1764"). The most common Subject field *accuracy* problem was including terms that represent the genre of described resource which belong to the Type DCTERMS field (e.g., "Paintings, French") instead of or alongside the term(s) correctly representing its topical aboutness (e.g., "Hunting dogs"). Similarly, in the Subject field, students sometimes included geographic terms (e.g., "Toruń (Poland)") which belong to the Spatial field. In Dublin Core, Subject field is reserved only for aboutness terms other than those representing places and times.

Completeness problems were observed in 1 or more student-created records for all but 3 fields: Title, Medium, and Description. The fields with the highest levels of *completeness* errors were those that apply to every painting in this course: AccessRights (65.63% of student-created records in 2 sections) and Identifier (59.38%). AccessRights *completeness* errors distributed the following way: the field was either entirely skipped by a student or included only partial information (e.g., the student stated that the painting is currently not on view but forgot to include the names of the gallery and its specific exhibit at which this artwork is normally accessible to the viewers). Almost all students who made a *completeness* mistake in the Identifier field, included only one of the two identifiers that each painting has and omitted another. In 4 metadata fields – Temporal, Spatial, Created, and Provenance – synchronous section students made *completeness* errors significantly more often that asynchronous section students.

As the *consistency* metadata quality criterion relies heavily on the use of controlled vocabularies where they are applicable, this criterion does not apply to the free-text metadata fields: Title, Alternative, Extent, Identifier, Description, IsReferencedBy, Has-Format, Rights, AccessRights, and Provenance. Out of the 9 remaining DCTERMS fields that are applicable to all or some of the paintings that students created metadata for, 6 (66.67%) exhibited *consistency* errors in 1 or more of records across the 2 sections of the course. However, for 5 of these fields – Temporal, Spatial, Creator, Contributor, and Type – the proportion of records with *consistency* errors was very low: 3.13%. Subject field included a substantial number (15.63%) of *consistency* mistakes which fell into two categories: not using a controlled vocabulary term at all or using the non-authorized (variant) term from the authority record. In Type and Spatial fields, synchronous section students made *consistency* mistakes significantly more often than asynchronous section students. At the same time, asynchronous section students tended to make significantly more *consistency* errors than their counterparts in the Creator field.

Over a third (37%) of student-created metadata records overall included mistakes outside of the 19 applicable DCTERMS fields. Several records included the DCMES 1.1 field Coverage instead of the more specific DCTERMS field Spatial and/or Temporal (or in addition to it, with the same data value). Others included DCMES 1.1 Date (instead of the specific DCTERMS field Created or in addition to it, with the same data value), Relation (instead of or in addition to specific DCTERMS fields IsReferencedBy and HasFormat). In 18.75% of records, violations of Dublin Core one-to-one principle were observed: in addition to representing the physical painting using the information on the gallery's website, students also represented in the same record its digital image and/or the gallery website's landing page with information about it. Typical examples of these violations included use of a URL in the Identifier field, entering terms such as "JPEG" or "TIFF" in the Medium field, inclusion of the file size measured in KB in the Extent field (as opposed to dimensions of the physical painting), inclusion of the Language and/or Publisher fields. Such a practice poses a serious impediment to functionality of the metadata record as the resulting high level of ambiguity confuses the information searcher and creates roadblocks for access by not supporting the important user tasks of Identify and Select.

Table 1. Comparative frequency of accuracy, completeness, and consistency problems in DCTERMS metadata fields: synchronous and asynchronous sections

Metadata field	Accuracy problems (% of records in 2 course sections)	Accuracy problems (% of records, synchr. section)	Accuracy problems (% of records, synchr. section)	Completeness problems (% of records in 2 course sections)	Completeness problems (% of records, synchr.)	Completeness problems (% of records, asynchr.)	Consistency problems (% of records in 2 course sections)	Consistency problems (% of records, synchr.)	Consistency problems (% of records, asynchr.)
Title	**28.1**	34.8	11.1	**0**	0	0	**0**	0	0
Alternative	**0**	0	0	**6.3**	8.7	0	**3.1**	0	0
Creator	**12.5**	13	11.1	**12.5**	13	11.1	**3.1**	0	11.1
Contributor	**9.4**	8.7	11.1	**3.1**	4.3	0	**0**	0	0
Type	**12.5**	17.4	0	**28.1**	26.1	22.2	**3.1**	8.7	0
Extent	**9.4**	8.7	11.1	**43.8**	52.2	33.3	**0**	0	0
Medium	**6.3**	8.7	0	**0**	0	0	**0**	0	0
Identifier	**18.8**	17.4	22.2	**59.4**	56.5	66.7	**0**	0	0
Description	**6.3**	8.7	0	**0**	0	0	**0**	0	0
Subject	**56.3**	60.9	55.6	**18.8**	17.4	11.1	**15.6**	13.0	22.2
Temporal	**15.6**	21.7	0	**18.8**	26.1	0	**0**	0	0
Spatial	**15.6**	13.0	22.2	**21.9**	26.1	11.1	**3.1**	8.7	0
Created	**15.6**	17.4	11.1	**18.8**	21.7	11.1	**0**	0	0
IsReferncedBy	**15.6**	17.4	11.1	**12.5**	13	22.2	**0**	0	0
HasForat	**6.3**	13.0	0	**46.9**	43.5	55.6	**0**	0	0
Rights	**12.5**	13.0	0	**6.3**	8.7	11.1	**0**	0	0
AccessRights	**18.8**	26.1	11.1	**65.6**	52.2	88.9	**0**	0	0
Audience	**3.1**	4.3	0	**15.6**	17.4	11.1	**0**	0	0
Provenance	**0**	0	0	**6.3**	4.3	11.1	**0**	0	0

Finally, three students – 2 in the larger synchronous section and 1 in the smaller asynchronous section – kept in their records a few empty unused DCTERMS fields with placeholder data values (ellipses enclosed in square brackets). These placeholders were part of the XML template that students were provided with to create records to represent paintings and text resources. Students had been instructed to remove fields that are not applicable.

4 Conclusions and Future Research

As no other studies of DCTERMS metadata representing paintings or other physical museum objects exist, results of this exploratory study can be compared to findings of DCTERMS student-created metadata evaluation for digital text resources [21]. This comparison must consider that some of the DCTERMS metadata fields relevant to physical paintings (Medium and Provenance) are not applicable in representing digital text resources. Likewise, digital text resources are represented with fields non-applicable to physical paintings: Publisher, Language, TableOfContents, DateSubmitted, DateAccepted, etc. Also, unlike our study, the previous study [21] did not include IsReferencedBy and HasFormat fields. This leaves a total of 15 DCTERMS metadata fields the findings for which can be compared across the two studies.

Comparison of these two studies' findings reveals that:

- *Accuracy* issues were prevalent in both studies compared not only to *consistency* (not applicable to many free-text data fields) but also to *completeness. Accuracy* errors occurred in all analyzed metadata fields for digital text resources and most (89%) for paintings.
- Subject was the field with the highest occurrence of *accuracy* errors in both studies. However, higher proportion (56.25%) records for the paintings had them compared to records for digital text resources (29.5%). Subject analysis has traditionally been found challenging for novices. Moreover, it is easier to misapply this controlled-vocabulary field when creating a DCTERMS record for a painting as the lack of scope notes in most of the Library of Congress Subject Headings (LCSH) authority records for genre terms (intended for presenting works about these resources) prompts novices to inappropriately use them.
- Subject field also exhibited the highest proportion of *consistency* errors in both studies, which is explained by the inherent complexity of subject representation with controlled vocabularies. Somewhat lower level of Subject field *consistency* errors was observed for paintings (15.63%) than for digital text resources (24.3%), possibly due to our ongoing work on refining instruction on finding, interpreting, and applying LCSH authority records correctly.
- AccessRights was the top field with *completeness* errors in paintings metadata and one of the top 5 fields with *completeness* errors in the metadata for digital text works. Yet the level of errors in this field was significantly higher in the paintings metadata (65.63% compared to 27.00% records). This could be explained by the more multi-faceted nature of access to artworks, which are often temporarily removed from display in museums and galleries.

This study is the first one to compare the student-created metadata quality for synchronous and asynchronous metadata instruction. We found that the synchronous section students tended to make metadata quality errors substantially more often than asynchronous section students for 10 DCTERMS fields, including two (Type and Spatial) where this trend was observed for 2 out of 3 major metadata quality criteria. One possible explanation is that synchronous students are often distracted by other tasks during the class meeting they join and might not realize they miss a piece of instruction and need to review the recording later, while asynchronous students review the recordings at their own pace and are able to better focus on the material.

The small scale of this comparative exploratory study however bears limitations that need to be addressed in future research as more data becomes available. The asynchronous offering of this course at our institution is a recent development, and the number of students enrolled in it so far is small as it currently serves as overflow sections for the main synchronous section. As the course continues to be offered both synchronously and asynchronously, we will collect and comparatively analyze more data that would allow to make more definite conclusions and possibly a decision to move instruction of this course entirely into asynchronous mode.

With the shift towards online teaching in Libraries, Archives, and Museums professional degree programs since 2020, we expect that more such data would become available from other programs and could be comparatively analyzed. Future studies are also needed that evaluate metadata records for paintings created by students and other metadata creators in multiple metadata standards: DCTERMS, DCMES 1.1, MODS, and VRA Core. These studies would provide a more complete understanding of the museum metadata quality issues. They would also allow to evaluate the extent the briefness and broad definitions of Dublin Core metadata guidelines (as opposed to the much higher level of detail and specificity in the other metadata standards and/or accompanying metadata creation guidelines) have on the resulting quality of metadata that serves to provide equitable access to valuable objects in museum collections for everyone.

References

1. Alajmi, B., Rehman, S.: Knowledge organization trends in library and information education: assessment and analysis. Educ. Inf. **32**(4), 411–420 (2016)
2. Aljalahmah, S., Zavalina, O.L.: A case study of information representation in a Kuwaiti archive. In: Toeppe, K., Yan, H., Kai Wah Chu, S. (eds.) Diversity, Divergence, Dialog: 16th International Conference, iConference 2021, Beijing, China, 17–31 March 2021, Poster Descriptions, pp.1–6. IDEALS, Urbana, Illinois (2021). http://hdl.handle.net/2142/109683
3. Bruce, T.R., Hillman, D.I.: The continuum of metadata quality: defining, expressing, exploiting. In: Hillman, D., Westbrook, L. (eds.) Metadata in Practice, pp. 238–256. American Library Association, Chicago (2004)
4. Davis, J.M.: A survey of cataloging education: are library schools listening? Cataloging Classif. Q. **46**(2), 182–200 (2008)
5. Glaviano, C.: Teaching an information organization course with Nordic DC metadata creator. OCLC Syst. Serv. Int. Digit. Libr. Perspect. **16**(1), 33–40 (2000)
6. Hady, M.F.A., Shaker, A.K.: Cataloging and classification education in Egypt: stressing the fundamentals while moving toward automated applications. Cataloging Classif. Q. **43**(3/4), 407–429 (2006)

7. Hider, P.: A survey of continuing professional development activities and attitudes amongst catalogers. Cataloging Classif. Q. **42**(2), 35–58 (2008)
8. Hsieh-Yee, I.: Organizing internet resources: teaching cataloging standards and beyond. OCLC Syst. Serv. Int. Digit. Libr. Perspect. **16**(3), 130–143 (2000)
9. Hudon, M.: The status of knowledge organization in library and information science master's programs. Cataloging Classif. Q. **52**(5), 506–550 (2021)
10. Jackson, A.S., Han, M., Groetsch, K., Mustafoff, M., Cole, T.W.: Dublin core metadata harvested through OAI-PMH. J. Libr. Metadata **8**(1), 5–21 (2008)
11. Joudrey, D., McGinnis, R.: Graduate education for information organization, cataloging, and metadata. Cataloging Classif. Q. **59**(6), 576–596 (2014)
12. Kurtz, M.: Dublin Core, DSpace, and a brief analysis of three university repositories. Inf. Technol. Libr. **29**(1), 40–46 (2010)
13. Lim, S., Li Liew, C.: Metadata quality and interoperability of GLAM digital images. ASLIB Proc. **63**(5), 484–498 (2011)
14. Or-Bach, R.: Educational benefits of metadata creation by students. ACM SIGCSE Bull. **37**(4), 93–97 (2005)
15. Park, J.R., Maszaros, S.: Metadata object description schema (MODS) in digital repositories: an exploratory study of metadata use and quality. Knowl. Organ. **36**(1), 46–59 (2009)
16. Park, J.R., Tosaka, Y.: Metadata quality control in digital repositories and collections: criteria, semantics, and mechanisms. Cataloging Classif. Q. **48**(8), 696–715 (2010)
17. Phillips, M., Zavalina, O.L., Tarver, H.: Exploring the utility of metadata record graphs and network analysis for metadata quality evaluation and augmentation. Int. J. Metadata Semant. Ontol. **14**(2), 112–124 (2020)
18. Stvilia, B., Gasser, L., Twidale, M.B., Smith, L.C.: A framework for information quality assessment. J. Am. Soc. Inf. Sci. **58**, 1720–1733 (2007)
19. Weagley, J., Gelches, E., Park, J.: Interoperability and metadata quality in digital video repositories: a study of Dublin Core. J. Libr. Metadata **10**(1), 37–57 (2010)
20. Zavalina, O.L.: Integrated learning of metadata quality evaluation and metadata application profile development in a graduate metadata course. In: Sutton, S., Walk, P. (eds.) DCMI 2017: Proceedings of the 2017 International Conference on Dublin Core and Metadata Applications, pp. 93–96. Dublin Core Metadata Initiative, Washington, DC (2017). https://dcpapers.dublin core.org/pubs/article/view/3856
21. Zavalina, O.L., Burke, M.: Assessing skill building in metadata instruction: quality evaluation of Dublin core metadata records created by graduate students. J. Educ. Libr. Inf. Sci. **62**(4), 423–442 (2021)

Social Media and Digital Networks

How We Express Ourselves Freely: Censorship, Self-censorship, and Anti-censorship on a Chinese Social Media

Xiang Chen[1] , Jiamu Xie[2] , Zixin Wang[3] , Bohui Shen[4] ,
and Zhixuan Zhou[5]([✉])

[1] King Abdullah University of Science and Technology, Thuwal, Saudi Arabia
xiang.chen@kaust.edu.sa
[2] Wuhan University, Wuhan, China
2019300001053@whu.edu.cn
[3] Zhejiang University, Hangzhou, China
zixin_wang@zju.edu.cn
[4] BNU-HKBU United International College, Zhuhai, China
[5] University of Illinois at Urbana-Champaign, Champaign, USA
zz78@illinois.edu

Abstract. Censorship, anti-censorship, and self-censorship in an authoritarian regime have been extensively studies, yet the relationship between these intertwined factors is not well understood. In this paper, we report results of a large-scale survey study ($N = 526$) with Sina Weibo users toward bridging this research gap. Through descriptive statistics, correlation analysis, and regression analysis, we uncover how users are being censored, how and why they conduct self-censorship on different topics and in different scenarios (i.e., post, repost, and comment), and their various anti-censorship strategies. We further identify the metrics of censorship and self-censorship, find the influence factors, and construct a mediation model to measure their relationship. Based on these findings, we discuss implications for democratic social media design and future censorship research.

Keywords: Social media · Censorship · Self-censorship · Anti-censorship · Mediation model

1 Introduction

Sina Weibo is a Chinese social media platform providing micro-blogging services, which can be thought of as a Twitter equivalent [12]. It provides a medium for people to participate in civic life [30] and express themselves [32]. Weibo has a huge user base: according to a financial report published by Sina in 2021, the average daily active users of Weibo in December 2021 reached 249 million [19]. The implication of the large user base is that the dark side of social media,

I. Sserwanga et al. (Eds.): iConference 2023, LNCS 13972, pp. 93–108, 2023.
https://doi.org/10.1007/978-3-031-28032-0_8

e.g., fake news [31] and discrimination speech [24], can potentially affect a large population.

Nationalism and censorship of political discussion on Weibo has long been reported [5], which negatively affects people's freedom of speech. Research has been conducted to understand users' attitudes toward censorship [23], anti-censorship strategies emerging from the user community [15], and self-censorship of media [21]. However, there is a lack of understanding on how these intertwined factors interact with each other.

In this paper, we report the results of a survey study ($N = 526$) conducted with Sina Weibo users, toward understanding censorship, self-censorship, and anti-censorship practices in the current Chinese social media landscape from a user perspective, as well as their relationships.

Through the descriptive statistics, we construct the profile of Weibo users based on their demographic information, including age range, occupation, and the time and frequency of Weibo usage. We also discover the ways and topics that Weibo users are usually censored on, their self-censorship practices, and anti-censorship strategies commonly used by the respondents. Based on principal component analysis (PCA), we construct three metrics to measure the attitudes of Weibo users towards censorship and anti-censorship, namely, perceived necessity of self-censorship, impact of self-censorship on users' expression desire and mood, and support for censorship. Through correlation analysis, we find the influence factors significantly correlated to these three metrics. On top of this, we build an intermediate model for these three metrics and show the mediation effect of censorship and self-censorship: the perceived necessity of self-censorship will increase the impact of self-censorship on users' expression desire and mood, which in turn will increase support for censorship.

Thus our contributions are two-fold. First, we update previous understanding of the status quo of the censorship infrastructure and situation on Chinese social media. Second, we approach the relationship between censorship, self-censorship, and anti-censorship from a user perspective.

In the sections below, we will first discuss literature on censorship, anti-censorship, and self-censorship. Then we describe our method and results, followed by a discussion of main takeaways from this study and design implications for more democratic social media in an authoritarian regime.

2   Related Work

2.1   Censorship

Internet censorship has been extensively studied, especially in the context of authoritarian regimes [29]. Twitter has a standard interface for government agencies to request that individual tweets or accounts be censored. Tanash et al. discovered over a quarter million censored tweets out of 20 million from late 2014 to early 2015 in Turkey [20]. Most of the censored tweets were found to contain political content, often criticisms of the Turkish government. Twitter under-reported the number of censored tweets in Turkey, which might hold for other countries as well. The situation of social media censorship in China can be more unknown. The platforms are known to be closely regulated by the Chinese government and asked to censor political content, yet they never disclose how many posts or accounts they censor each year—it is a black-box. However, by applying a statistical analysis on massive social media data of Sina Weibo and Twitter, Bamman et al. uncovered a set a politically sensitive terms whose presence in a message could lead to anomalously higher rates of deletion [4].

It is argued that censorship, when detected by citizens, will have an adverse impact on their assessment of the government, because censorship signals the government's inability to address the issue being censored [27]. However, perceived government intrusion is strongly correlated with privacy concern and self-protective behavior, and trust towards other Weibo participants has a significant negative relationship with self-protective behavior [3]. Generally, Internet users have varied attitudes and perceptions of censorship. Users' demographic backgrounds, Internet usage experience, and personality are known to influence their attitudes toward censorship. Those with an authoritarian personality tend to support censorship [23]. One relevant paper uncovered common topics when Chinese users discussed censorship on Twitter, which has long been blocked by the Chinese government, namely, sharing technical knowledge, expressing political opinions, and disseminating alternative news items [28]. While these Chinese users either reside overseas or are able to use VPN to access Twitter, we sought out to understand how people blocked by the Great Firewall [11] perceived censorship.

2.2 Anti-censorship

It is possible to predict if a social media post will be censored. For example, Ng et al. used linguistic properties of social media posts to automatically predict if they were going to be censored [17]. Algorithmically bypassing the censorship of social media is also possible. Hiruncharoenvate et al. presented a non-deterministic algorithm for generating homophones that created large numbers of false positives for censors, making it difficult to locate banned conversations [13].

From a user perspective, though they have limited knowledge of natural language processing, Weibo users are found to intuitively express in machine unreadable ways, e.g., image-based content, to resist the censorship infrastructure [15]. Chinese users have also adopted variants of words, i.e., morphs, to avoid keyword-based censorship [7]. Here we use a larger-scale survey study to uncover more strategies used to resist the censorship infrastructure imposed by Weibo.

2.3 Self-censorship

It is common for social media users to exhibit some level of last-minute self-censorship of their posts, mostly for the sake of the "perceived audience", and people with more boundaries tend to self-censor more [10]. At a larger scale, media self-censorship in China has been found to increase the possibility of the publication of reports on highly politically sensitive topics [21]. In this paper, we focus on the latter purpose of self-censorship, i.e., avoid being censored. Specifically, we look into how users experience self-censorship, and how self-censorship practices are associated with censorship.

The most self-censored regimes in China include discussions of LGBTQ [14] and political issues [6], and release of music [2]. In such cases, self-censorship is not only about how to circumvent censorship, but also about people's efforts to negotiate with the authorities [2].

While censorship can potentially inspire self-censorship or anti-censorship practices, the relationship between these factors have hardly been discussed in previous literature. We bridge this research gap with this current survey study.

3   Method

3.1   Survey Flow

Through this study, we aimed to understand user attitudes toward censorship, self-censorship, and anti-censorship, as well as relationships between these factors. To this end, we designed a survey comprised of 38 questions. Below, we elaborate on each section of the survey.

Introduction and Screening. We started by introducing the concept of self-censorship. In our definition, self-censorship is "Internet users' inspection and examination of their own speech. Choices after self-censorship can be whether or not to say something, what to say, and how to say."

We filtered participants with two screening questions: (1) whether one has used Weibo, and (2) whether one has practiced self-censorship.

Demographics and Weibo Usage. To know more demographic information of the survey respondents, we asked questions regarding gender, age, occupation, location (province), yearly income, party membership, educational background, and relevant study/work experience in computer/software. We gave participants the option not to disclose party membership, given the potentially sensitive nature of this question. Though understanding the effect of demographic information on people's self-censorship choices was only a secondary goal of our investigation, it could nevertheless situate our analysis in a specific cultural context.

Since we aimed to investigate Weibo users' self-censorship choices, we also needed to ask about their usage of Weibo, including the amount of time spent on Weibo via computers (desktop and laptop) and mobile devices (mobile phone, iPad, etc.), years of experience with Weibo, usage frequency, activities on Weibo (posting, commenting, news feed, etc.), and number of followers and following.

Self-censorship. We explicitly asked participants' experience, purpose, and perspective of self-censorship, and used a five-point Likert scale ("Strongly Disagree" to "Strongly Agree") to probe their attitude toward self-censorship.

We further used three five-point Likert scales to identify participants' choices of self-censorship when posting, commenting and reposting, respectively, on Weibo. We differentiated between self-censorship choices of different topics, namely, entertainment, sports, current events, daily life, covid, humor, video games, and finance. Some of the listed topics are potentially more susceptible to self-censorship as well as censorship, such as current events and covid.

Censorship and Anti-censorship. To identify the effect of users' experiences/attitudes of censorship on self-censorship choices, we asked participants' experiences, topics and ways of being censored by Weibo, as well as common anti-censorship strategies used by Chinese people. The research team, which consisted of five researchers from China, identified a wide range of anti-censorship strategies based on their years of experience of Weibo usage. We also used a five-point Likert scale to probe participants' attitude toward censorship.

IP Address. Recently, Weibo, as well as some other social media in China, started to reveal users' IP address on their homepage and comments, possibly to crack down on discussion surrounding pandemic policy and other sensitive political topics. To identify the effect of the disclosure of IP address on users' self-censorship choices, we asked participants whether they would more strictly self-censor their speech after the change. We also asked perceived pros and cons of, and attitudes toward the revealing of IP address. Further, a user's willingness to pay for a feature can be used as a proxy for how much the user values that feature. With this in mind, we asked how much the participants were willing to pay in order to hide their IP address.

3.2 Data Collection

We recruited participants on different social media platforms in China, including WeChat and Weibo itself. Personal contacts of the authors were also requested to distribute the survey link.

Initially, we used Wenjuanxing[1], a Chinese survey design and distribution platform, to facilitate the data collection process. However, after two days, our survey was stopped and recycled by the platform, stating that our survey contained politically sensitive questions and information. Notably, all survey platforms based in China were overseen by the Chinese government, as stated in their terms of use, and one needed to use her real identity (i.e., ID card) to distribute surveys via these platforms. Thus, we alternatively used Qualtrics[2] to make the survey distribution possible.

---

[1] https://www.wjx.cn/.
[2] https://www.qualtrics.com/.

When one researcher, who had about 3,000 followers on Weibo at the time of this study, distributed the survey, heated discussion took place in the comments. Participants were enthusiastic about our topics of investigation, and over 300 surveys were filled in the first few hours. They complained that they had long suffered from censorship of Weibo, and were even unaware of their own anti-censorship or self-censorship practices. Due to the wide spread of this survey, unfortunately, the Weibo account of this researcher was suspended. After a week, the account of another researcher who had around 2,000 followers was also suspended for distributing the survey.

We gained confidence in the ethical aspect of our research and our personal safety by finding a large body of literature on quantitatively or qualitatively researching censorship practices in China.

4 Results

In the end, a total of 1,346 responses were received, but many of them were missing data or unfinished. After filtering them out, we had 526 (39%) valid questionnaires. Among them, 523 (99.4%) respondents answered they have used Weibo, while 3 (0.6%) answered they have not used Weibo, and the subsequent analysis only considered those who had used Weibo.

4.1 Descriptive Statistics

Demographic Information. Among the survey respondents, 18% of them were male, and 80% were female. Although the non-binary option was given in our questionnaire, only 2% selected it. The large majority of survey respondents were young people: people aged 18–24 accounted for 70%, and people aged 25–34 accounted for 25% of the whole population. Students accounted for 68% of the survey respondents. Since our participants were mostly students, 59% of them reported to have no income. 10% of the survey respondents had party membership, and 51% of them were members of the Communist Youth League. Some noted that they "automatically became Communist Youth League members in junior high school", and were "annoyed with the identity". Interestingly, when asked where they lived, some participants chose not to disclose, because "the revealing of IP address on Weibo has made them lose a sense of safety." People with and without computer related study/work experience were evenly distributed.

Weibo Usage. Participants preferred using mobile devices (3.0 h on average per day) to use Weibo rather than computers (1.7 h on average per day). They have used Weibo for 3.57 years on average, and 66% of them had more than five years of experience using Weibo, identifying as experienced users. The majority of our participants were also frequent Weibo users, with 89% of them using Weibo multiple times a day. Weibo was mainly used to post (80%), comment (68%), watch news (74%), make friends (30%), and following idols (31%).

Many of our participants had a relatively large fan base. 47% of them had more than 100 followers. Thus they might see a need to be mindful of what they post.

Self-censorship. Among those who ever used Weibo, 90.4% acknowledged that they had practiced self-censorship. Averaged over 3 Likert-scale questions regarding user attitudes toward self-censorship, it turned out that the participants diverged in their perception of the necessity of self-censorship. However, they largely agreed that self-censorship decreased their willingness to express (84%), and that self-censorship negatively affected their mood (80%).

Participants practiced self-censorship to bypass the censorship (57%), avoid being deleted (53%), avoid being suspended (61%), either temporarily or permanently, avoid being reported or cyberbullied (43%), and avoid being summoned by the police (48%). Other self-reported motivations for self-censorship included fear of conflicts, avoiding being noticed by acquaintances in real life, self-presentation, avoiding privacy leakage, habit, etc.

Figures 1, 2, and 3 show the user's self-censorship practices in different usage scenarios and different topics. Users tend to practice more self-censorship when it comes to current events and pandemic, and less self-censorship on such topics as humor and video games. Figures 2 and 3 reveal that users' self-censorship on reposting is more common than on commenting. One possible reason is that reposting will be displayed on their homepage, which is essentially similar to posting, while commenting is made under other users' Weibo posts, which will not cause much damage to their own Weibo accounts.

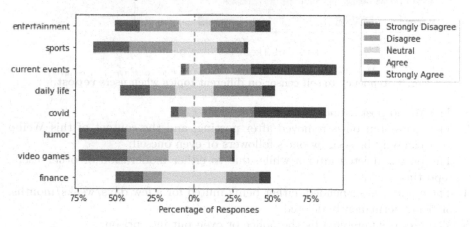

Fig. 1. Tendency to self-censor on different topics when users **post**.

Censorship. 79% of Weibo users indicated that they had been censored, and the censored topics are mostly current events (79.0%) and covid (69.0%).

Censorship can imply different processes and consequences for users and we list some commonly mentioned ones below.

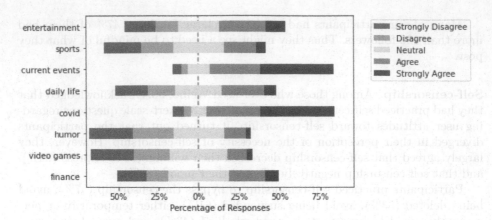

Fig. 2. Tendency to self-censor on different topics when users **comment**.

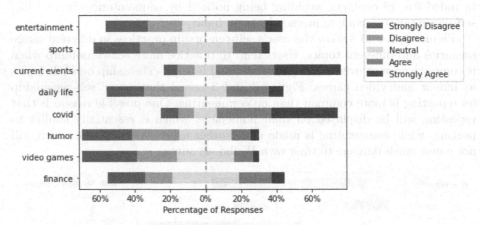

Fig. 3. Tendency to self-censor on different topics when users **repost**.

1. The Weibo post cannot be sent;
2. The repost button is removed after posting, and the content of this Weibo post can only be seen by one's followers or even oneself;
3. The post is deleted after a while, due to either moderation or other users' reporting;
4. The account is suspended, either being muted for a few days/weeks/months, or being permanently deleted;
5. The user is summoned by the police or even put into prison.

IP Address. In March, Weibo has begun to reveal users' IP locations when they post and comment, and on their account homepages, to "discourage bad behavior" [26]. This feature cannot be proactively turned off by the users.

After the IP address was displayed on their Weibo homepage and comments, nearly half of the respondents indicated that their self-censorship efforts had not changed significantly, and they would pay as much attention to self-censorship as they do now; while less than half of the respondents indicated that they would increase the extent of self-censorship.

The vast majority (81.8%) have a negative opinion regarding the act of revealing the IP address, but most (57.2%) respondents said they would continue to use Weibo despite this. Another 31.7% said that they did not know whether they would continue to use Weibo in the future.

Anti-censorship Strategies. Due to the increasing censorship, Weibo users have adopted or created the following strategies to avoid censorship of their published posts.

1. Pinyin: phonetic transcription of mandarin Chinese;
2. Acronym: initials of Pinyin;
3. Homophone: substituting Chinese characters with the same or similar pronunciation;
4. English translation;
5. Martian language: characters that look similar, composed of non-normalized character symbols such as uncommon characters, split parts of Chinese characters, or many other unicode symbols;
6. Emoji;
7. Code name, e.g., addressing pandemic personel as "Big White" who are often in white coveralls;
8. Mixing symbols among Chinese characters;
9. Reversing or shuffling the order of Chinese characters;
10. Satire;
11. Converting text to images;
12. Adding graffiti or occlusion on converted images;
13. Rotating or flipping the converted images;
14. Posting an irrelevant yet safe Weibo, and put what they really want to say in the comment or in the edit log.

The three anti-censorship strategies perceived as most effective by the respondents are satire, acronym, and homophones, which are most likely to bypass NLP-based or human moderation.

4.2   A Medication Model Connecting Censorship and Self-censorship

Identifying the Metric of Censorship and Self-Censorship. Two groups of questions in our survey asked respondents about their attitudes toward censorship and self-censorship, respectively, and were quantified using the Likert scale.

The three questions regarding users' perception of self-censorship are listed below.

1. Self-censorship is necessary for social media use;
2. Self-censorship reduces my willingness to express myself;
3. Self-censorship negatively affects my mood.

We use the Cronbach's α coefficient [9] to measure the strength of consistency of these 3 questions. Practically, a Cronbach's α of 0.7 or higher is considered acceptable. The standardized Cronbach's α coefficient of these 3 questions is 0.699, and when Question 1 is not taken into account, the coefficient of the remaining two questions rises to 0.749. Therefore, we suppose Questions 2 and 3 jointly reflect the impact of self-censorship on users' expression desire and mood, while Question 1 alone reflects the perceived necessity of self-censorship. Thus the two metrics of self-censorship are (perceived) **necessity of self-censorship** and **impact of self-censorship** on expression desire and mood. There will be scenarios like this: although self-censorship greatly affects users' mood, in order to be able to post, the users still think it necessary to practice self-censorship.

Similarly, several questions are used to probe users' attitudes toward censorship:

1. Weibo censorship is good for improving the Internet environment;
2. I would report Weibo posts holding a different opinion from mine;
3. I hope Weibo would remove the censorship mechanism;
4. Censorship shows no respect for freedom of speech;
5. I support suspending accounts disseminating extreme speech;
6. Censorship negatively affects my user experience with Weibo.

Likewise, we use the Cronbach's α coefficient to measure the strength of consistency of these 6 questions. The coefficient is 0.824, which shows a strong consistency. We further calculate the Corrected Item-Total Correlation (CITC) [33]. The CITC of Question 2 and 4 is 0.348 and 0.497, respectively, which indicates that the relationship between these two questions and the rest of the items is weak [8]. Thus we did not take these two questions into account. This is also confirmed in the principal component analysis (PCA). The result of PCA shows that if all the 6 questions are combined into one principal component, the contributions of Questions 2 and 4 are very small. After removing them, the four questions 1, 3, 5, and 6 can be combined into one principal component, which can be regarded as the metric of **support for censorship** for further exploration.

Correlation Test. After identifying the metrics to measure self-censorship and censorship, we conduct the correlation analysis and hypothesis testing.

We performed t-test and analysed the variance of the correlations between the three metrics (N: the necessity of self-censorship, I: the impact of self-censorship on users' expression desire and mood, S: support for censorship) elaborated on above, as well as other variables and influencing factors in the questionnaire.

At the significance level of $p = 0.01$, multiple variables show a significant correlation with these metrics, as seen in Table 1. Motivations of self-censorship, e.g., avoiding account suspension, and avoiding being summoned by the police, are correlated to all three metrics. Censorship/self-censorship/anti-censorship experiences, i.e., having conducted self-censorship on Weibo, having been censored on Weibo, and having used anti-censorship strategies, are also correlated to all three metrics.

The correlation of these three metrics themselves is shown in Table 2. As we can see, all three metrics are significantly correlated at the p = 0.01 level.

Table 1. Influence factors significantly correlated with the metrics of censorship and self-censorship ($p = 0.01$).

Metrics of Censorship/Self-Censorship	Influence Factors
I: Impact of Self-censorship	Avoid account suspension Avoid being summoned by the police Gender Age How long they have used Weibo Have conducted self-censorship on Weibo Have been censored on Weibo Have used anti-censorship strategies
N: Necessity of Self-censorship	Make sure Weibo posts can bypass the censorship Keep Weibo posts from being deleted Avoid account suspension Avoid being summoned by the police Use Weibo to post Have conducted self-censorship on Weibo Have been censored on Weibo Have used anti-censorship strategies
S: Support of Censorship	Make sure Weibo posts can bypass the censorship Keep Weibo posts from being deleted Avoid account suspension Avoid being summoned by the police Computer or software related experience Frequency of Weibo usage Use Weibo to post Have conducted self-censorship on Weibo Have been censored on Weibo Have used anti-censorship strategies

Mediation Model. To test the relationships among perceived necessity of self-censorship, impact of self-censorship, and support for censorship, we follow MacKinnon's four-step procedure to establish the mediation effect [16], which requires (a) a significant association between necessity and support, (b) a significant association between necessity and impact, (c) a significant association between impact and support while controlling for necessity, and (d) a significant coefficient for the indirect path between necessity and support through impact. The bias-corrected percentile bootstrap method determines whether the last condition is satisfied.

Multiple regression analysis shows that, in the first step, necessity is significantly associated with support, $b = 0.452, p < 0.001$ (see Model 1 of Table 3). In the second step, necessity is significantly associated with impact, $b = 0.396, p < 0.001$ (see Model 2 of Table 3). In the third step, when this study controls for necessity,

Table 2. The correlation of three metrics of censorship and self-censorship (**means correlation is significant at the $p = 0.01$ level).

	I	N	S
I	1	0.511**	0.396**
N	0.511**	1	0.452**
S	0.396**	0.452**	1

impact is significantly associated with support, $b = 0.296, p < 0.001$ (see Model 3 of Table 3). Finally, the bias-corrected percentile bootstrap method indicates that the indirect effect of necessity on support through impact is significant, $ab = 0.156$, $SE = 0.023, 95\%CI = [0.113, 0.202]$. The mediation effect accounted for 22.9% of the total effect. Overall, necessity will increase impact, which in turn will increase support. In other words, impact will mediate the link between necessity and support (Fig. 4 shows the mediation effect).

Table 3. The mediation effect of necessity on support.

	Model 1 (S)		Model 2 (I)		Model 3 (S)	
Predictors	b	t	b	t	b	t
N	0.452	11.564**	0.396	9.849**	0.296	7.596**
I					0.394	10.118**
R^2	0.204		0.157		0.335	
F	133.726**		97.001**		131.063**	

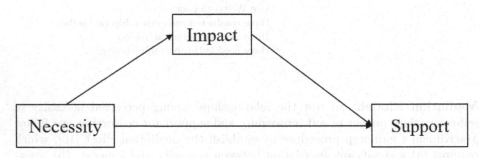

Fig. 4. Mediation model constructed by three metrics of censorship and self-censorship: the perceived necessity of self-censorship, the impact of self-censorship on users' expression desire and mood, and the support for censorship.

5 Discussion

Social media censorship, including those facilitated by AI, is found prevalent in social media, especially in authoritarian regimes [29]. It greatly negates the freedom of speech. In this paper, we reveal the difficulties of expressing in social media in China from a user's perspective, updating existing findings (e.g., [28]). We further explore the relationship between three intertwined concepts, i.e., censorship, self-censorship, and anti-censorship. Below, we reflect on main results and practical implications for more democratic social media in authoritarian regimes, and address limitations and future work in the end.

5.1 Recap of Findings

Self-censorship is common on Chinese social media. Out of 523 valid samples, 90.4% of the respondents acknowledged more or less practicing self-censorship. There was a consensus regarding the effect of self-censorship on people's willingness to express themselves and mood, which was not reported in previous literature [10,21]. Common motivations for self-censorship included bypassing the censorship, avoiding being deleted, avoiding account suspension, avoiding being summoned by the police, etc. More politically sensitive topics, which are reported to be more susceptible to censorship [4], were more often self-censored by our respondents, echoing with prior research [21]. Some examples included discussions of current events and the covid. Users also paid more attention to self-censorship when reposting than commenting.

79% of our respondents had been censored at least once. While there is not an estimation of the ratio of censored Weibo posts, like that in the Turkish context [20], we provided a number in our limited sample. The consequences of censorship ranged from being deleted to being summoned by the police and even being put into prison [22]. Three anti-censorship strategies perceived as most effective to bypass the censorship infrastructure were satire, acronym, and homophones.

To examine the relationship between censorship and self-censorship, we defined three metrics, namely, perceived necessity of self-censorship, impact of self-censorship on users' expression desire and mood, and support for censorship. We then conducted correlation analysis, hypothesis testing, and regression analysis to reveal the influence factors that had a significant correlation with these three metrics. Finally, we conducted a regression analysis on these three metrics and established a mediation model to measure their relationship. Perceived necessity of self-censorship turns out to increase the impact of self-censorship on users' expression desire and mood, which in turn will increase support for censorship. A possible explanation is that those who deem self-censorship as necessary are more likely to practice self-censorship, and are thus more likely to be affected by it in terms of expression desire and mood. Those who deem self-censorship as necessary also tend to solve the issues brought by censorship from the end of themselves, instead of questioning the censorship infrastructure. Thus they are more likely to support censorship.

5.2 Implications for Research and Design

Several design and research implications can be drawn from our survey results.

Firstly, censorship [23], self-censorship [21] and anti-censorship [15] are not independent of each other. Due to the existence of the censorship infrastructure, Weibo users have adopted a number of anti-censorship strategies to defend their expression rights. It is also because of the censorship infrastructure that Weibo users have to practice self-censorship in order to freely express themselves and to avoid unnecessary trouble. These intertwined factors should be addressed together instead of separately in censorship research. Hereby we present an example by building a mediation model of censorship and self-censorship.

Secondly, it is increasingly hard to maintain a democratic and free social media environment in China. People are censored for various topics, especially politically sensitive ones such as current events and pandemic, and in different scenarios, i.e., posting, reposting, and commenting. In a blunting manner [1], users may choose to not talk about these topics to avoid trouble. In a monitoring manner, users may proactively think of ways to resist the censorship infrastructure, e.g., English, metaphors, sarcasm, etc., as shown in our responses. On July 13, 2022, Weibo issued an announcement stating that it would carry out centralized rectification of illegal behaviors that used homophonic words, variant words and other typos to publish and disseminate "bad information" [25]. As a result, the anti-censorship strategies used by our respondents will soon or later be deemed illegal. To bypass the censorship infrastructure which is intrinsically imposed by the government, a decentralized platform which is free of centralized regulation might be a rescue [18].

5.3   Limitations and Future Work

The main limitation of our survey study is the skewed sampling, as 80% of the respondents are female. The results may not generalize to a larger population with a different demographic. Nevertheless, our results reveal novel insights into this specific subset of Weibo users. Future work could consider conducting a larger-scale survey study to obtain more generalizable results, or conducting qualitative interviews to gain more in-depth insights of people's attitudes toward censorship.

6   Conclusion

In this paper, we conducted a survey study to understand the current landscape of Chinese social media in terms of censorship, self-censorship, and anti-censorship. People's attitudes toward censorship, self-censorship practices, and anti-censorship strategies are revealed through descriptive statistics, updating findings in previous research. A mediation model is further established to understand the relationship between censorship and self-censorship. Based on the results, we suggest a shift in censorship research, focusing on the relationship between censorship, self-censorship, and anti-censorship, and potential ways of democratizing social media in an authoritarian regime.

Acknowledgements. We would like to thank the respondents who contributed to the survey data, and those who helped us distribute the survey. We also thank the anonymous reviewers for their good words and insightful feedback. We further thank Yifei Wang, Chuanli Xia, Zijie Shao, among many others, who provided useful feedback in the early stage of the study.

References

1. Aguirre, K.M.: Monitoring and blunting coping style effects on college student processing of health information via social media. The University of Texas at El Paso (2017)
2. Amar, N.: Navigating and circumventing (self) censorship in the Chinese music scene. China Perspectives, pp. 25–33 (2020)
3. Amos, C., Zhang, L., Pentina, I.: Investigating privacy perception and behavior on weibo. J. Organiz. End User Comput. **26**, 43–56 (2014)
4. Bamman, D., O'Connor, B., Smith, N.: Censorship and deletion practices in Chinese social media. First Monday (2012)
5. Cairns, C., Carlson, A.: Real-world islands in a social media sea: Nationalism and censorship on weibo during the 2012 diaoyu/senkaku crisis. Chin. Quart. **225**, 23–49 (2016)
6. Chang, C., Manion, M.: Political self-censorship in authoritarian states: The spatial-temporal dimension of trouble. Comp. Pol. Stud. **54**(8), 1362–1392 (2021)
7. Chen, L., Zhang, C., Wilson, C.: Tweeting under pressure: analyzing trending topics and evolving word choice on sina weibo. In: Proceedings of the first ACM Conference on Online Social Networks, pp. 89–100 (2013)
8. Clark, L.A., Watson, D.: Constructing validity: new developments in creating objective measuring instruments. Psychol. Assess. **31**(12), 1412 (2019)
9. Cronbach, L.J.: Coefficient alpha and the internal structure of tests. Psychometrika, **16**(3), 297–334 (1951)
10. Das, S., Kramer, A.: Self-censorship on facebook. Proceed. Int. AAAI Conf. Web Soc. Media **7**, 120–127 (2013)
11. Ensafi, R., Winter, P., Mueen, A., Crandall, J.R.: Analyzing the great firewall of china over space and time. Proc. Priv. Enhancing Technol. **1**, 61–76 (2015)
12. Gao, Q., Abel, F., Houben, G.J., Yu, Y.: A comparative study of users' microblogging behavior on sina weibo and twitter. In: International Conference on User Modeling, Adaptation, and Personalization, pp. 88–101 (2012)
13. Hiruncharoenvate, C., Lin, Z., Gilbert, E.: Algorithmically bypassing censorship on sina weibo with nondeterministic homophone substitutions. Proceed. Int. AAAI Conf. Web Social Media **9**, 150–158 (2015)
14. Ho, L.W.W.: The gay space in Chinese cyberspace: Self-censorship, commercialisation and misrepresentation. J. Current Chin. Affairs-Chin. aktuell **36**(4), 45–73 (2007)
15. Kou, Y., Kow, Y.M., Gui, X.: Resisting the censorship infrastructure in China. Hawaii International Conference on System Sciences, pp. 446–453 (2017)
16. MacKinnon, D.P.: Introduction to statistical mediation analysis. Routledge (2012)
17. Ng, K.Y., Feldman, A., Peng, J.: Linguistic fingerprints of internet censorship: the case of sina weibo. In: Proceedings of the AAAI Conference on Artificial Intelligence, pp. 446–453 (2020)

18. Sharma, T., Zhou, Z., Huang, Y., Wang, Y.: "it's a blessing and a curse": unpacking creators' practices with non-fungible tokens (NFTs) and their communities. arXiv preprint arXiv:2201.13233 (2022)
19. Sina: weibo reports fourth quarter and fiscal year 2021 unaudited financial results (2021)
20. Tanash, R.S., Chen, Z., Thakur, T., Wallach, D.S., Subramanian, D.: Known unknowns: an analysis of twitter censorship in turkey. In: Proceedings of the 14th ACM Workshop on Privacy in the Electronic Society, pp. 11–20 (2015)
21. Tong, J.: Press self-censorship in China: a case study in the transformation of discourse. Discourse Soc. **20**, 593–612 (2009)
22. Wang, A.: Two women arrested in China's Jiangsu province for helping woman locked in hut after video goes viral on social media. Vision Times (2022)
23. Wang, D., Mark, G.: Internet censorship in china: examining user awareness and attitudes. ACM Trans. Comput.-Human Inter. **22**, 1–22 (2015)
24. Wei, M., Zhou, Z.: AI ethics issues in real world: Evidence from AI incident database. arXiv preprint arXiv:2206.07635 (2022)
25. WeiboAdministrator: announcement on correcting "typos" on weibo. https://weibo.com/1934183965/LC43v6SBi
26. WeiboAdministrator: weibo will launch the function of user profile page showing the location of recent posts in the next week. https://weibo.com/1934183965/Lk9Uv04Ty
27. Wong, S.H.W., Liang, J.: Dubious until officially censored: effects of online censorship exposure on viewers' attitudes in authoritarian regimes. J. Inf. Technol. Politics, **18**, 310–323 (2021)
28. Wu, S., Mai, B.: Talking about and beyond censorship: Mapping topic clusters in the Chinese twitter sphere. Int. J. Commun. **13**, 23 (2019)
29. Xu, X., Mao, Z.M., Halderman, J.A.: Internet censorship in china: where does the filtering occur? In: International Conference on Passive and Active Network Measurement, pp. 133–142 (2011)
30. Zhang, F.: Who you@ today?: The mediating impact of social capital on sina weibo use and political expression in China. National Communication Association (NCA) 100th Annual Convention (2014)
31. Zhou, Z., Guan, H., Bhat, M.M., Hsu, J.: Fake news detection via NLP is vulnerable to adversarial attacks. arXiv preprint arXiv:1901.09657 (2019)
32. Zhou, Z., Wang, Z., Zimmer, F.: Anonymous expression in an online community for women in China. arXiv preprint arXiv:2206.07923 (2022)
33. Zijlmans, E.A., Tijmstra, J., Van der Ark, L.A., Sijtsma, K.: Item-score reliability as a selection tool in test construction. Front. Psychol. **9**, 2298 (2019)

Impact of Social Media on Self-esteem and Emotions: An Instagram-Based Case Study

Sara Martínez-Cardama[1]([✉]) [iD] and Elena Gómez-López[2]

[1] Department of Library and Information Sciences, University Carlos III of Madrid, Madrid, Spain
smarti1@bib.uc3m.es
[2] University Carlos III of Madrid, Madrid, Spain

Abstract. Social networks currently serve not only as platforms for publishing content but also as fundamental tools for accessing information. This role in providing access is mediated by a series of opaque, algorithm-based mechanisms for personalising the content. This article draws on existing literature on the relationship between possible mental health disorders and the functioning of these platforms to try to understand their effects on elements such as self-esteem and emotions. To this end, it focuses on the Instagram social network, which is prominent in the user groups corresponding to the Millennial and Z generations due to its high visual and multimedia content, its capacity for uncovering trends, and its integration with social commerce. It presents the results of a study (n = 100) of Instagram users between the ages of 18 and 39. These results provide relevant data on patterns associated with the following: time spent on the platform and excessive use, the risk of emotional loneliness or isolation, displacement of daily activities, and feelings of inferiority. They also reveal a real lack of awareness of how the algorithms on these types of platforms work and an interest in the mechanisms of disconnection and digital well being. Lastly, the results open up new possibilities for inclusion of these risks in digital literacy programmes.

Keywords: Instagram · Mental health · Self-esteem · FOMO · Digital literacy

1 Introduction

New milestones in Internet consumption were reached worldwide in 2021, especially in terms of social media. Data from the *Digital Report* published in 2022 show that 58.4% of the world's population are social media users, with this increasing annually by 10% [1] In Spain, the figure for users immersed in social networks rises to 80% of the total population [2]. The pandemic and the associated health measures, which brought generalised shutdowns and confinement orders worldwide, led to an expansion of their role, not only in terms of usage to connect people or as entertainment but also as information sources in and of themselves in which interesting content is to be found.

Of all the social networks, one of the most prominent in recent years has been Instagram. Created in 2010 for the mobile ecosystem, its growth has been exponential.

I. Sserwanga et al. (Eds.): iConference 2023, LNCS 13972, pp. 109–122, 2023.
https://doi.org/10.1007/978-3-031-28032-0_9

While its initial purpose was for users to share photos and videos with their followers and apply filters and aesthetic modifications with great visual power, since then there have been numerous updates, which created a private messaging system and made it a pioneer in the introduction of ephemeral content through its Stories (temporary content that vanishes after 24 h). Its acquisition by Facebook (now Meta) in 2012 amplified its reach, by making it possible to share content on both platforms simultaneously, and boosted its receptiveness to brand advertising and, in particular, social commerce. This resulted in a content ecosystem combining personal content, advertising by companies, and brand prescriptors (also known as influencers) [3]. The latter act not only as trendsetters but often also as authentic opinion leaders among certain sectors of the population.

The boom in these social platforms, their very configuration in terms of content presentation (based on personalisation rather than relevance), on top of the time users spend on them, have contributed to a boom in studies associated with overconsumption of them and their influence on aspects of mental health such as self-esteem, loss of emotional stability, the appearance of self-image distortions, as well as other disorders associated with sleep disturbances or depression [4–6]. Recent studies have detected this relationship in the public's self-perceived symptoms when evaluating their informational use on social media [7]. Nonetheless, limitations still exist in relation to the lack of research on specific social media platforms, socio-demographic conditioning factors, and other types of elements that can influence or aggravate the link between deteriorating mental health and excessive use of social networks.

This study limits its scope to Instagram, placing special emphasis not only on the mental health consequences of overexposure to it but also on how the content positioning and personalisation algorithms influence feelings about this network, evaluating whether this could aggravate problems associated with self-esteem or other types of syndromes, such as FoMO (fear of missing out). To this end, we present the results of a survey of Instagram users between 18 and 29 years of age in which we evaluate these risks, as well as the degree of awareness of the information filtering taking place within the platform itself.

2   Literature Review

To gain a proper understanding of the subject matter, the literature review focused primarily on access to information and its current context and on the emotional risks triggered by use of the networks.

2.1   The Context: Access to Information on Instagram and its Conditioning Factors

Originally, the platform displayed content chronologically; however, due to the nature of the platform, the average user was missing a good part of the content being posted. As the application was updated, it altered the order of appearance of the posts so as to improve the user experience on this social network [8]. This new way of presenting content was enabled by a series of algorithms, classifiers and processes for specific purposes which were used to personalise and improve the user experience and make time spent on the platform more effective [9]. The algorithms have evolved to try to ascertain the content that will be most interesting to the user based on engagement (followers' loyalty and commitment) and to establish the order for posts on this basis. This affects the Instagram Feed and Stories (content that users must first follow) and the 'Explore' session, the latter based on recommendations similar to the content the user has 'liked', spent longer viewing or saved, or on its popularity within the application. It constitutes related content for which the platform infers a probability of being of interest. The same is true of Reels, for which specific polls are taken regarding their value.

The pursuit of a better user experience is a constant across all social media platforms, and, to the extent that their algorithms have become more sophisticated and omnipresent, concern over their power has grown [10]. The so-called 'filter bubbles' [11] based on personalisation of individual results also represent a real limitation of an informational offer that relies on a pre-classification of users according to their prior online activities. It represents a 'hidden curator' which, in a sense, configures and imposes the ratings, meanings and relationships on the objects and actors we interact with [12]. In a sense, the algorithms take decisions in our name regarding the information to display, or not, for the sake of improving our user experience or presupposing what most interests us. This leads several authors to reflect on the threat of invisibility, of both the content generated itself and of the decisions taken by the algorithms. Algorithmic opacity means that many content creators on Instagram are affected by the need to play the so-called 'visibility game' [10], which involves learning to optimise their results through refinement in an ocean of algorithmic decisions. Nonetheless, the fact of being able to optimise our activity on a platform by investigating how the algorithms work obscures the necessary debate on the real and conscious capacity we have as users to understand their limits. This is especially salient in the use of platforms like Instagram for advertising purposes. Companies take advantage of personalisation algorithms that, in a general way, favour acceptance of the advertising shown on the networks, as this is normally for products or services aligned with the preferences of the user.

Thus, the companies on Instagram have not only gravitated to the platform for direct sales but also as a showcase for promotion, increasingly using strategies for reaching larger numbers of users. Growth in the use of this social network has led to a rise in the influencer profile by continually improving the ways of communicating and presenting oneself through this medium [13]. This strategy is based on the close relationship with the user through the concept of brand ambassadors. Brands intervene in their daily routines seeking to give the promotion credibility [14]. Therefore, an essential point that brands assess to optimise the work of influencers is whether their behaviour in the content they upload to Instagram appears natural, as if it were a true reflection of their daily life and their product recommendations were completely sincere. Another tool brands use is advocacy marketing, a 'word-of-mouth' recommendation technique that turns customers into participants by sparking engagement and participation. Customers express their positive opinion of the product or service, helping the company to capture new customers [15]. Sometimes the advertising message creates a fictitious reality in order to persuade and stimulate desire for the product-service [16]. Constancy plays an essential role on social networks, which seek to stimulate desire and capture consumers emotionally. The problem arises when these reference groups are idealised by users, which involves a desire not only for the products they showcase but also the lifestyle they simulate having. The desire to resemble them and imitate their lifestyle can breed frustration due to idealisation of influencers, as trying to be the same as another person produces dissatisfaction with oneself. These characteristics, in addition to the lifestyles they display, can give rise to false expectations in groups of young people, who are more vulnerable to feelings of envy or a desire to be like the influencers, triggering the risky behaviours typical of adolescents and which they do not know how to cope with [17].

2.2 Emotional Risks Triggered by Social Networks

Moderate use of social networks increases interactions and connectedness, providing benefits associated with the ability to maintain social contact despite time constraints or distance. The problem arises when constant connection to the networks gives rise to isolation, loss of control over their use, anxiety, or fear of missing out on what others are doing by not being connected [18]. The latter is known as FoMO. Different studies assert that people with low mood and less satisfaction of basic psychological needs, that is, competence, autonomy and affinity [19], displayed higher levels of FoMO. In turn, a link has been observed between high levels of FoMO and increased activity on social media [18].

According to [20] it has been insinuated that people with a higher level of FoMO display a greater tendency to have self-esteem issues. They therefore sometimes seek to idealise their identity by displaying successful experiences on their profiles in order to garner positive reactions that enable them to bolster their self-esteem through 'likes' and positive comments from followers. In general, the more severe the addiction to the networks, the greater the degree of alteration of the associated states. The frequency of use and type of content consumed by users can give rise to higher levels of anxiety, in addition to generating other types of mental health problems [21]. Furthermore, hyper-connectivity triggers isolation and a feeling of loneliness [22].

Cramer and Inkster, for RSPH, [23] try to understand the impact on the mental health of young people based on 14 questions about health and well-being. Among the results they obtained, it should be noted that the social network with the greatest negative impact on mental health was Instagram, followed by Snapchat, Facebook, Twitter and YouTube, with the latter being the social network with the least negative effects. On the other hand, social networks can also offer a window towards self-expression of the identity and the creation of social ties. Nonetheless, as [22] indicates, the problem arises when a false identity is projected through the networks, hiding fears and complexes, especially among young people, or when maximum attention is devoted to editing posts or to the best time of day to upload content to ensure that it is seen by the largest number of followers and garner the most likes and positive comments in response to it.

This is where, in contrast to the benefits, the problem of addiction arises, which can lead to other risks, such as abandonment of daily activities [24], narcissistic behaviours, erroneous assimilation of reality, social isolation, feelings of loneliness, or loss of self-esteem [25].

Following a literature review, the emotional risks related to excessive use of social networks were established in:

- Addiction [26, 27]
- Isolation [28]
- Anxiety about staying connected or irrational fear of disconnection, also known as 'Nomophobia' [26, 29]
- Loss of awareness about real time and distrust or fear regarding face-to-face interpersonal interactions [26]
- FoMO [18]
- Low levels of self-esteem [30] and high levels of narcissism [31]
- Mood swings [21, 32]
- Reduction of the time spent on other, face-to-face activities such as sports or socialising in person [33].

Nonetheless, authors like Bekalu, McCloud, & Viswanath [34] point to the need to delve more deeply into the qualitative dimensions in the research on social media and mental and emotional health, having identified improvement variables in the relationship to well-being and self-perception of health improvement. Additionally, these results differ according to the social and economic conditions within the same subtype of post or even at an individual level [35].

3 Methodology

This study was conducted through a survey in which 100 people between the ages of 18 and 39 were recruited on the Instagram platform itself by means of simple random sampling in September-October 2021. The reason for selecting this age range was the information obtained in the latest report released by The Social Media Family [2], which states that over half of the platform's users (65%) are in this age range. Supporting these figures drawn from the report, the Statista portal maintains that 62.6% of Instagram users worldwide in 2021 are between the ages of 18 and 34, with the following range, 35 to 44, accounting for 16% of the total.

For definition of the evaluation items, the study relied on identification of the leading issues addressed in the academic literature and on two preliminary interviews of professionals in the area of psychology and psychiatry. The interviews were structured around the following eight content blocks:

- The effects of social network use on the self-esteem and emotions of young people.
- Time spent using the networks and mental health.
- Comparisons between users of social networks, especially Instagram.
- Idealisation of the lifestyle depicted in the posts.
- The most negative aspects of the use of these platforms.
- Gender differences.
- The age associated with the greatest risk of experiencing low self-esteem.
- Impact of the pandemic and use of social networks.

The responses helped to define a methodological tool created on an ad hoc basis, i.e., the survey. It was designed around four evaluation items with 14 questions (Table 1).

Table 1. Description of the evaluation items and questions in the survey

Evaluation item	Questions
1. Demographic information	Gender Age
2. Frequency and use of social networks	Use of social networks Daily frequency Type of use
3. Instagram	Type of people followed Use of idealised image Reduction of time spent on other activities due to Instagram use Interest in how Instagram presents its results Level of awareness regarding how Instagram presents its results
4. Feelings and emotions on Instagram	Level of feelings of inferiority on Instagram Level of influence on content of others Concern about own reputation in relation to the content uploaded Possibility of improving mental health and leisure conditions by reducing the amount of time invested in social platforms (Instagram in particular)

4 Results

For better understanding, the results are separated according to the survey evaluation items.

4.1 Regarding the Demographic Data of the Sample

The questionnaire was posted on the Instagram social network in order to elicit responses from users between the ages of 18 and 29, the age range corresponding to its target population. It included two filter questions: age, to focus the study on the abovementioned age range; and usage of social networks, as the responses would not be valid if the participants were not users.

The majority of the responses came from users active on some social network and between the ages of 18 and 24 (68.6%), with the least information collected from people between the ages of 32 and 39 (2.9%).

The number of people for analysing the results was 100, with any responses from persons over the age of 39 being eliminated. Once the invalid responses were eliminated, the breakdown by gender was as follows: 42% men and 58% women, all of whom used some social network in their daily lives.

4.2 Regarding the Use of Social Networks

The majority of those surveyed use social networks between one and three hours per day (59%), with the next most frequent amount of time being 'between four and six hours' (30%). Just 1% of the respondents acknowledge spending more than six hours per day on social networks.

As for the type of use and purpose, three categories and one open question were defined. The three categories were the following: as an information source, as an entertainment medium, and for online shopping. The majority of the respondents (96) marked the entertainment option, followed by informational use of the networks (58) and online shopping (25). In the responses given in the open option, three categories were added: two that recognised their use as a work tool (2), their potential in activism (1), and as a source of inspiration (1) (Fig. 1).

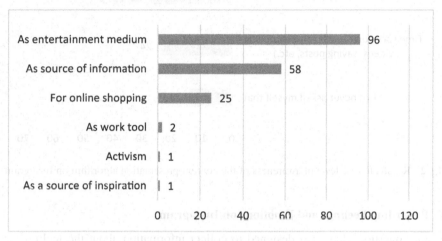

Fig. 1. Types of social network use

4.3 Regarding the Instagram Platform

The second evaluation item was designed to collect information about the type of use made of the Instagram platform, the type of followers or posts, the level of awareness of how it works, etc.

As for the type of followers, just 7% of the respondents follow only people in their immediate circle, with the rest also following accounts that post content they find interesting. The idealisation of the posts made by brands on the social network generated a massive number of responses (94%) of users who are aware of this.

One noteworthy result in this block is that 57% of the respondents acknowledge that being connected to Instagram has influenced their day-to-day activities by leading them to stop doing certain activities in order to stay connected. Within this percentage, 10% acknowledge excessive use on numerous occasions.

In relation to the algorithms used for presentation of the content, the majority of the users are interested in the methods used (84%). As for having an awareness of the actions that influence how these results are presented and how the algorithm works, the responses were varied; the most frequently marked option was the one that links the results presented only to the user's prior activity in relation to 'likes'. Nonetheless, other options such as interactions with users or the time spent on the platform were considered less. Some 14% of those surveyed acknowledge that they have never asked themselves how they work (Fig. 2).

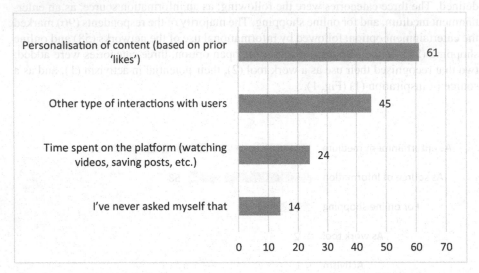

Fig. 2. Results for the level of awareness of the content presentation algorithm on Instagram

4.4 Regarding Feelings and Emotions on Instagram

The third question block was designed to collect information about the feelings and emotions triggered by use of the Instagram application.

Regarding the self-perception of a feeling of inferiority when comparing oneself with other users in the Instagram community, 8% of the responses favoured the feeling of inferiority with respect to other users, with some of them (16%) considering that they have felt inferior on numerous occasions.

If we analyse the responses to this question by gender, it becomes clear, first, that there is a percentage difference between the responses from men and women (16 more responses from women) and, second, that the latter have a greater tendency to feel inferior when comparing themselves to other users. A total of 50 women answered that they have felt influenced on some occasion or many occasions, while the total number of men who gave the same answer was 18.

In addition, to learn how the sample was influenced by content posted by other users, we used a Likert scale, where the minimum value of '1' meant seeing themselves as barely influenced and '5' meant influenced a great deal. The majority of the results correspond to low and intermediate values, with just one of the responses indicating that third-party content affected their possible decisions a great deal. In this case, 99 responses were obtained, as one of the study subjects did not answer (Fig. 3).

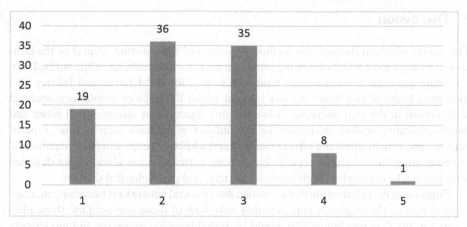

Fig. 3. Level of influence of other users in the Instagram community

The next question was to verify the level of importance and concern regarding their own reputation in relation to their posts and outside opinions of them. Just 15% of those surveyed denied the influence capacity of outside opinion in response to their posts. The gender-disaggregated data show a greater influence of outside opinion on women than on men with regard to posting content on their Instagram accounts (Fig. 4).

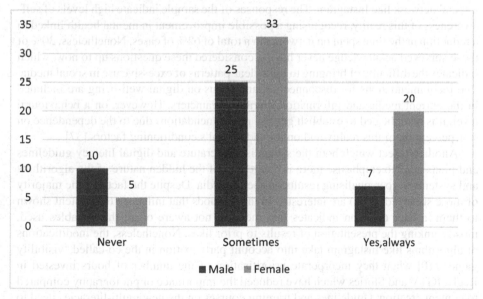

Fig. 4. Gender-disaggregated influence of outside opinion on posts.

Lastly, 62% of the respondents consider that a reduction in the time spent on social networks, specifically Instagram, would improve their quality of life and mental health. Just 8% deny that spending less time on the application would result in an improvement.

5 Discussion

The results obtained through the methodological tool demonstrate several of the concerns or issues most addressed in the literature review on the subject of the study. First, regarding time spent. Authors like Krasnova et al. [36] and Cramer and Inkster [23] indicate a range of two hours per day beyond which the risks of problems associated with mental health may increase. However, this figure is an estimate, and more and better qualitative studies are needed on the subject in domains such as time, type of activity, investment (time and effort invested) and addictive behaviour [6]. Nonetheless, in researching these domains separately, a strong correlation has always been detected with issues like depression, high levels of anxiety, and psychological distress.

Supporting the information that excessive use of social networks is becoming increasingly common, the responses indicated that only 10% of those surveyed use these platforms for less than one hour; 59% would be found between excessive and moderately responsible use, dedicating between one and three hours daily; and, finally, 30% consider that they should reduce the time they spend to avoid the risk of mental health problems, as they are on the platforms between four and six hours per day.

One important factor detected in the preliminary interviews with professionals and which emerges in the responses is the loss of control of the time spent on social networks to the detriment of activities generally of a face-to-face and everyday nature [24]. The results of the survey reflect that 57% of the sample has on some occasion (47%) or many occasions (10%) stopped doing something they were doing because they were on a social network like Instagram. The responses of the sample indicate high levels of self-awareness of this reality, recognising a possible improvement in mental health linked to a reduction in the time spent on networks in a total of 62% of cases. Nonetheless, 30% of those surveyed acknowledge never having considered these questions up to now, which indicates the difficulty of bringing to light clear patterns of excessive use in social media. The recommendations for disconnection and focus on digital well-being are included in the current media and information literacy parameters. However, on a behavioural level, it is complicated to establish general recommendations due to the dependence on self-perception of this reality and on the individual's conditioning factors [37].

Another aspect which both the specialised literature and digital literacy guidelines and plans need to emphasise more is awareness of the hidden nature of the algorithms and systems for personalising results on social media. Despite the fact that the majority of those surveyed (84%) are interested in the methods that influence the content shown to them, a later question indicates that they are not aware of all the variables used, mostly linking the presentation of results to prior likes. Nonetheless, the modifications of algorithms like Instagram take into account participation in the co-called 'visibility game' [10] when they incorporate prioritisation of the number of hours invested in Reels, IGTV and Stories which have reduced the importance of photography compared to content creation. Guidelines and training courses on the new multi-literacies need to take into account the different dimensions in content presentation and how they affect us as users or content creators. Third-party actors (companies) which, through prior negotiation, help to position themselves or adapt to the new algorithmic requirements generally intervene in these dimensions [38].

Regarding the question block associated with emotional involvement in use of the platform, 68% of the responses tended towards the feeling of inferiority with respect to other users, with a greater tendency for this observed in women than in men. These types of gender biases had already been detected in frequent studies on Instagram focused on aspects such as idealisation of the body and beauty, as well as other aspects such as maternity [39–40]. Despite the fact that 94% of those surveyed acknowledged being aware of the use of idealised images to promote products and brands, continual feelings of inferiority are produced in response to them. The same is true when analysing the endogenous factors of this idealisation, as 85% of the respondents see themselves as conditioned by outside opinions when it comes to posting content, which keeps them from showing themselves on the networks in a natural way.

6 Conclusions

Access to information marked by the parameters for personalising results affects any informational interaction in the digital world on a daily basis. While it is true that the academic literature has focused on the large-scale social and political effects that these mechanisms may have in reinforcing biases (polarisation, hoaxes, weakening of political and democratic systems), this personalisation has also had endogenous repercussions on the configuration of personality and opinions, or risks associated with mental and emotional health. Instagram is a paradigmatic case for this study, as its emphasis on visual content and loyalty-building mechanisms, together with the product prescription components that use everyday images like those of influencers, evokes real situations that may seem rosier than the users' own lives. This needs to meet certain standards contributes to problems of self-esteem or the need for outside approval of behaviours, as well as to a continual feeling of FoMO by making it necessary to post more and better content to maintain this 'idealisation bubble'.

The results of the survey offer good perspectives on the interest of the target audience in learning about the functional mechanisms of these platforms, as well as a self-awareness of the improvement in their daily lives if they were to establish disconnection mechanisms.

The study suggests paths for future research. First and foremost, to expand the survey sample to include a more distributed age percentage. Similarly, it opens up lines of action for inclusion of this content and these risks in the study plans for digital and media literacy programmes, getting away from the limitation of learning abstract categorisations of metaphors like the 'bubble filter' or 'echo chamber' concepts, which, while useful, at times are not approached from a more practical perspective. It supports, therefore, the creation of a more specific literacy based on the everyday effects in which these platforms, already constituted as authentic sociotechnical systems, configure our interests and possibly our decisions, and can even aggravate problems related to mental or emotional health.

Acknowledgements. This work has been supported by the Madrid Government (Comunidad de Madrid-Spain) under the Multiannual Agreement with UC3M in the line of Excellence of University Professors (EPUC3M02), and in the context of the V PRICIT (Regional Programme of Research and Technological Innovation).

References

1. Digital 2021: Global Overview Report — DataReportal – Global Digital Insights. https://dat areportal.com/reports/digital-2021-global-overview-report. Accessed 29 Aug 2022
2. Informe de los perfiles en redes sociales de España. https://thesocialmediafamily.com/inf orme-redes-sociales/. Accessed 29 Aug 2022
3. Araujo Pinto, P., Antunes, M.J., Pisco Almeida, A.M.: Instagram como herramienta de salud pública: un estudio sobre América del Sur. Instagram Tool Public Health Study South Am. (53), 63–81 (2021). https://doi.org/10.12795/Ambitos.2021.i53.04
4. Hinojo-Lucena, F.J., Aznar-Díaz, I., Trujillo-Torres, J.M., Romero-Rodríguez, J.M.: Uso problemático de Internet y variables psicológicas o físicas en estudiantes universitarios. Revista electrónica de investigación educativa. 23 (2021)
5. Jan, M., Soomro, S., Ahmad, N.: Impact of social media on self-esteem. Eur. Sci. J. **13**, 329–341 (2017)
6. Keles, B., McCrae, N., Grealish, A.: A systematic review: the influence of social media on depression, anxiety and psychological distress in adolescents. Int. J. Adolesc. Youth **25**, 79–93 (2020)
7. Perlis, R.H., et al.: Association between social media use and self-reported symptoms of depression in US adults. JAMA Netw. Open **4**, e2136113–e2136113 (2021)
8. Quero, J.: ¿Cómo funciona el algoritmo de Instagram?. https://jessicaquero.com/algoritmo-de-instagram/
9. Mosseri, A.: Instagram.Más detalles de cómo funciona Instagram. https://about.instagram.com/es-la/blog/announcements/shedding-more-light-on-how-instagram-works. Accessed 21 Aug 2022
10. Cotter, K.: Playing the visibility game: how digital influencers and algorithms negotiate influence on Instagram. New Media Soc. **21**, 895–913 (2019)
11. Pariser, E.: The Filter Bubble: How the New Personalized Web is Changing What We Read and How we Think. Penguin (2011)
12. Willson, M.: Algorithms (and the) everyday. Inf. Commun. Soc. **20**, 137–150 (2017)
13. Cuenca-Piqueras, C., Moreno, M.J.G., Olmos, J.C.C.: ¿ Empoderadas u objetivadas? Análisis de las ciberfeminidades en las influencers de moda1. Investigaciones Feministas. **12**, 19–31 (2021)
14. Tocci Ghitis, D.: Valores y creencias que adoptan los jóvenes de los contenidos audiovisuales de los Influencers Lifestyle. Universidad Peruana de Ciencias Aplicadas (UPC) (2020)
15. Sashi, C.M., Brynildsen, G., Bilgihan, A.: Social media, customer engagement and advocacy: an empirical investigation using Twitter data for quick service restaurants. Int. J. Contemp. Hosp. Manag. **31**(3), 1247–1272 (2019)
16. García, S.E.R.: Connotación y persuasión en la imagen publicitaria. Gazeta de Antropología. **24** (2) (2008)
17. Peralbo-Fernández, A.: El poder de los influencers en el adolescente que tienes en casa. https://www.larazon.es/familia/el-poder-de-los-influencers-en-el-adolescente-que-tienes-en-casa-HB24078483/. Accessed 29 Aug 2022
18. Serrano, M.T.: Fear of missing out (FoMO) and Instagram use: analysis of the relationships between narcisim and self-esteem. Aloma: Rev. de Psicologia, Ciències de l'Educació i de l'Esport. **38**, 31–38 (2020)
19. Przybylski, A.K., Murayama, K., DeHaan, C.R., Gladwell, V.: Motivational, emotional, and behavioral correlates of fear of missing out. Comput. Hum. Behav. **29**, 1841–1848 (2013)
20. Varchetta, M., Fraschetti, A., Mari, E., Giannini, A.M.: Adicción a redes sociales, Miedo a perderse experiencias (FOMO) y Vulnerabilidad en línea en estudiantes universitarios. Revista Digit. de Investigación en Docencia Universitaria. **14**(1) (2020)

21. Reyes, V.P., Amaya, J.A.Á., Capps, J.W.: Relación del Uso de Redes Sociales con la Autoestima y la Ansiedad en Estudiantes Universitarios. Enseñanza e Investigación en Psicología. **3**, 139–149 (2021)

22. Oliveros, G.D.: Instagram sin filtros, su impacto real en la salud mental del usuario. https://www.grupodoctoroliveros.com/instagram-sin-filtros-su-impacto-real-en-la-salud-mental-del-usuario/. Accessed 29 Aug 2022

23. RSPH: #StatusofMind. https://www.rsph.org.uk/our-work/campaigns/status-of-mind.html. Accessed 29 Aug 2022

24. Jiménez, M. de la V.M., Domínguez, S.F.: Uso problemático de internet en adolescentes españoles y su relación con autoestima e impulsividad. Avances en psicología latinoamericana. **37**, 103–119 (2019)

25. Huaytalla, K.P.C., Vega, S.R., Soncco, J.J.: Riesgo de adicción a redes sociales, autoestima y autocontrol en estudiantes de secundaria. Revista Científica de Ciencias de la Salud. **9**, 9–15 (2016)

26. Dhand, A., Luke, D.A., Lang, C.E., Lee, J.-M.: Social networks and neurological illness. Nat. Rev. Neurol. **12**, 605–612 (2016)

27. Primack, B.A., Karim, S.A., Shensa, A., Bowman, N., Knight, J., Sidani, J.E.: Positive and negative experiences on social media and perceived social isolation. Am. J. Health Promot. **33**, 859–868 (2019)

28. Anshari, M., Alas, Y., Sulaiman, E.: Smartphone addictions and nomophobia among youth. Vulnerable Child. Youth Stud. **14**, 242–247 (2019)

29. Valkenburg, P.M., Koutamanis, M., Vossen, H.G.: The concurrent and longitudinal relationships between adolescents' use of social network sites and their social self-esteem. Comput. Hum. Behav. **76**, 35–41 (2017)

30. Andreassen, C.S., Pallesen, S., Griffiths, M.D.: The relationship between addictive use of social media, narcissism, and self-esteem: findings from a large national survey. Addict. Behav. **64**, 287–293 (2017)

31. Van Rooij, A.J., Ferguson, C.J., Van de Mheen, D., Schoenmakers, T.M.: Time to abandon internet addiction? predicting problematic internet, game, and social media use from psychosocial well-being and application use. Clin. Neuropsychiatry **14**, 113–121 (2017)

32. Salcedo Culqui, I.S.: Relación entre adicción a redes sociales y autoestima en jóvenes universitarios de una universidad particular de Lima. Universidad de San Martín de Porres (2016)

33. Bekalu, M.A., McCloud, R.F., Viswanath, K.: Association of social media use with social well-being, positive mental health, and self-rated health: disentangling routine use from emotional connection to use. Health Educ. Behav. **46**, 69S-80S (2019)

34. Beyens, I., Pouwels, J.L., van Driel, I.I., Keijsers, L., Valkenburg, P.M.: The effect of social media on well-being differs from adolescent to adolescent. Sci Rep. **10**, 10763 (2020). https://doi.org/10.1038/s41598-020-67727-7

35. Krasnova, H., Widjaja, T., Buxmann, P., Wenninger, H., Benbasat, I.: Research note—why following friends can hurt you: an exploratory investigation of the effects of envy on social networking sites among college-age users. Inf. Syst. Res. **26**, 585–605 (2015). https://doi.org/10.1287/isre.2015.0588

36. Vanden Abeele, M.M.P., Halfmann, A., Lee, E.W.J.: Drug, demon, or donut? theorizing the relationship between social media use, digital well-being and digital disconnection. Curr. Opin. Psychol. **45**, 101295 (2022). https://doi.org/10.1016/j.copsyc.2021.12.007

37. Arriagada, A., Ibáñez, F.: You need at least one picture daily, if not, you're dead: content creators and platform evolution in the social media ecology. Soc. Media + Soc. **6**(3) (2020) https://doi.org/10.1177/2056305120944624

38. Sherlock, M., Wagstaff, D.L.: Exploring the relationship between frequency of Instagram use, exposure to idealized images, and psychological well-being in women. Psychol. Pop. Media Cult. **8**, 482–490 (2019). https://doi.org/10.1037/ppm0000182

39. Garcia, R.L., Bingham, S., Liu, S.: The effects of daily Instagram use on state self-objectification, well-being, and mood for young women. Psychology of Popular Media. No Pagination Specified-No Pagination Specified (2021). https://doi.org/10.1037/ppm0000350

40. Chansiri, K., Wongphothiphan, T.: The indirect effects of Instagram images on women's self-esteem: the moderating roles of BMI and perceived weight. New Media Soc. 14614448211029976 (2021). https://doi.org/10.1177/14614448211029975

Motivations, Purposes, and Means of Creating Information Cocoons Intentionally for Oneself: Looking on the Bright Side

Shiting Fu[1] [iD] and Tingting Jiang[2(✉)] [iD]

[1] School of Information Management, Wuhan University, Wuhan, Hubei, China
[2] Center for Studies of Information Resources, Wuhan University, Wuhan, Hubei, China
tij@whu.edu.cn

Abstract. Information cocoons have been criticized for their negative impact on individuals and the society. However, a newly observed phenomenon on Chinese social media is that some users are creating information cocoons intentionally for themselves. This study conducted a thematic analysis on 58 posts explicitly discussing such phenomenon collected from three popular Chinese social media platforms. The results indicate that the intentional creation of information cocoons for oneself can be driven by the self-defense or self-enhancement motivation and serve the purpose of self-control, safety, comfort, or utility. Managing information sources and affecting recommendation algorithms are the two major approaches to creating the information cocoons. This study sheds new light on the understanding of information cocoons and provides useful implications for improving recommender systems.

Keywords: Information cocoons · Filter bubble · Recommendation algorithms

1 Introduction

Information cocoons is a concept coined by Sunstein [1], which is caused by people increasingly engaging only with satisfying and pleasurable information and avoiding information and opinion they find offensive or disagreeable. The discussion of information cocoons focused on their negative effects on individuals and society, and many studies explored how to break them [2, 3]. Recently, we observed a new phenomenon in Chinese social media, in which people created information cocoons intentionally for themselves. It means that these people may think creating information cocoons is beneficial or necessary, which is contrary to the negative stereotypes of information cocoons in the previous research.

Therefore, in order to explore why and how people create information cocoons intentionally, we conducted a thematic analysis on 58 posts related to this phenomenon collected from three popular Chinese social media platforms. The results revealed people's motivations, purposes, and means of creating information cocoons intentionally. This study provides a new perspective on information cocoon research.

I. Sserwanga et al. (Eds.): iConference 2023, LNCS 13972, pp. 123–130, 2023.
https://doi.org/10.1007/978-3-031-28032-0_10

2 Literature Review

2.1 Information Cocoons and the Negative Consequences

There are many concepts related to information cocoons, such as selective exposure, filter bubble, and echo chamber. Selective exposure is a way to form information cocoons, a tendency for people to defend their attitudes, beliefs, and behaviors by seeking information likely to support them and avoiding information likely to challenge them [4]. Filter bubble is thought to enhance the information cocoons by personalization algorithms, in which a person only encounters familiar information or opinions [5]. Besides, echo chamber describes that people tend to surround themselves with only those who are socially and ideologically similar to them, thus avoiding alternative view-points, and it can also enhance their information cocoons [6]. In these research fields, researchers highlight the negative consequences of people's tendency to approach what they like and/or avoid what they dislike, e.g., stopping people from developing new perspectives, reducing creativity and innovation [7], causing more and faster negative emotional shift [8], threatening democracy, and enhancing the social polarization [9].

2.2 Alternative Perspectives on Information Cocoons

Although information cocoons have been regarded as matters of course without any extra effort, such viewpoint was questioned as researchers found it is difficult to only access to homogeneous information in daily life [10]. Instead, people faced other threats caused by online information, i.e., information explosion, information overload, information anxiety, social media fatigue, and so on. Numerous evidence shows that exposure to contradictory information may evoke confusion and frustration, and lead people to doubt and reject related information [11, 12]. And exposure to a large amount of information may lead to information overload, as the excessive quantity of information exceeds their ability to digest it [13, 14]. It will not only cause negative feelings like exhaustion and anxiety [15], but also allow people to have difficulty in locating, processing, and managing the information they really need [16]. Besides, information overload is related to various attention deficit problems and can impact people's cognitive ability [17]. Researchers advocated some approaches to deal with this problem, such as building effective information architectures, promoting information literacy, applying personal information management, etc. [18]. Overall, all these approaches focus on information filtering to narrow the gap between available information and required information [18, 19] and they work at the cost of information richness and diversity to some extent. In other words, creating an information cocoon can allow people to focus more on the satisfying, wanted and pleasurable information, which may mitigate information overload.

3 Methods

Due to the extensive discussion on information cocoon in Chinese social media, a large group of users know this terminology and would like to share their own opinions and experiences about this phenomenon. Searches were conducted on three popular Chinese social media platforms, including Weibo (https://weibo.com/login.php),

Douban (https://www.douban.com/), and Xiaohongshu (https://www.xiaohongshu.com/explore), using the query "information cocoons". The time span of the searches was "2022.05.01~2022.08.31". A total of 7281 posts were found, and 58 of them were included in the dataset for explicitly describing individuals' experiences of intentional building of and enclosing themselves in information cocoons. An inductive thematic analysis approach was applied to emerge the themes. The idea was to extract important themes from qualitative data in a bottom-up fashion. Specifically, the data analysis followed a process composed of 5 steps, i.e., generating initial codes that identify a feature of the data, combining coded data to form themes, reviewing the themes to refine them, defining and naming themes, and producing the report.

4 Results

4.1 Motivations of Creating Information Cocoons Intentionally

According to the thematic analysis results, we found motivations for crating information cocoons intentionally can be divided into the following two dimensions (see Table 1).

Self-defense motivation can drive people to wrap themselves in a comfortable and pleasant information environment to avoid negative emotions induced by overload information, counter-attitudinal information, and online disputes, as well as to avoid fears of missing out and feeling of being monitored. For example, people thought that "the internet is a swamp, I choose to close my eyes to be happy rather than open my eyes to

Table 1. Motivations of creating information cocoons intentionally

Themes	Sub-themes	Posts
Self-defense motivation	Preventing information overload	P14, P37, P53, P58
	Avoiding exposure to counter-attitudinal information	P15, P18, P21, P24, P26, P27, P39, P42
	Easing fears of missing out	P19, P25
	Keeping away from online disputes	P31, P33, P34, P41, P49, P54, P57
	Eliminating the feeling of being monitored	P4, P5
	Avoiding exposure to negative information	P28, P30, P35, P43, P44, P50, P51, P52, P55, P57
Self-enhancement motivation	Improving the efficiency of information obtained	P20, P22, P47, P57
	Improving the accuracy of information obtained	P9, P12, P13, P16, P26
	Improving the quality of information obtained	P1, P17, P23, P32

be painful (P28)", and "I was overwhelmed by the flood of negative news and decided to keep these out of the door (P13)".

Self-enhancement motivation can drive people to create information filters to obtain desired information with more accuracy and high-quality, and minimize the cost of time and energy in the meanwhile. For example, people thought that "the clutter information made me unable to think, and I'm tired to choose what to read and what to believe (P14)", and "I would like to train the algorithm work for me (P1)".

4.2 Purposes of Creating Information Cocoons Intentionally

The results indicate that people's purposes of creating information cocoons intentionally can be divided into the following four dimensions (see Table 2).

Self-control. People regarded the construction of an information cocoon as a procedure of "training and taming the algorithms/computers" to control their online information exposures. They wanted to create "a faucet to regulating the information flow (P1)" and named it "an accurate information feeder (P48)" or "a customized information cocoon (P30–31)".

Safety. People wanted to protect themselves from threatening and overwhelming information by creating an information cocoon. They call it "green dam (P40)", "shelter bay (P45)", "safety zoon (P52–55)", and "line of defense (P57)".

Comfort. People thought it's comfortable to stay in information cocoons, just like an "informational villa (P23)" or a "comfort zoon (P27, P56)" that is filled with their preferred information.

Table 2. Purposes of creating information cocoons intentionally

Themes	Sub-themes	Posts
Self-control	A faucet to regulating the information flow	P1
	An accurate information feeder	P48
	A customized information cocoon	P30, P31
	Consequences of training/taming algorithms	P2, P4, P5, P8, P27
Safety	Green dam	P23, P27, P40
	Shelter bay	P45
	Safety zoon	P52, P53, P54, P55, P56, P57
	Line of defense	P58
Comfort	Informational villa	P26, P23
	Comfort zoon	P32, P56
Utility	High-quality information cocoon	P17, P27, P56
	Valuable information cocoon	P12, P32,

Utility. People wanted to create an information cocoon filled with "high-quality (P26)" and "valuable (P32)" information.

4.3 Means of Creating Information Cocoons Intentionally

We divided all the means of creating information cocoons into two categories (see Table 3), i.e., managing information sources and affecting recommendation algorithms. The following actions were found to be taken to manage information sources.

Disabling Recommendations. People would turn off the recommendation algorithms for apps like TikTok, Taobao, and WeChat and then sort the information feeds by the most recent messages. They also used simplified editions of apps (e.g., Weibo intl.) to avoid the algorithmic feeds.

Managing ONE's Follower List. People would set the upper limit of the follower list, and update their follower list regularly through deleting accounts that no longer needed or interested in. Besides, they would take deliberate thinking on deciding to whether follow an account or not and shield the uninterested accounts to avoid the related information feeds.

Using RSS Readers. Some people would apply RSS reader apps to manage their information feeds in various platforms.

Two contrasting actions were taken by individuals to affect recommendation algorithms.

Approaching Wanted Information Deliberately. People would click and search similar information deliberately and interact with similar accounts to educate the algorithms, e.g., they "searched the keywords on the same topic repeatedly so that the algorithms would push more useful information related to this topic", and they also "included some keywords in the comments and posts to make the algorithm push more relevant information".

Avoiding Unwanted Information Deliberately. People would no longer interact with some information to avoid its possible reappearance. For example, they "intended to avoid arguing with people in the comment area because they didn't want to give the algorithm a wrong indicator".

Table 3. Means of creating information cocoons intentionally

Themes	Sub-themes	Codes	Posts
Managing information sources	Disabling recommendations	Turning off the recommendation algorithms	P1, P11, P22
		Using simplified editions of apps	P1, P6, P37
	Managing one's follower list	Setting the upper limit of the follower list	P1
		Updating their follower list regularly	P1, P23
		Shielding the uninterested accounts	P15, P25, P29
	Using RSS readers	Applying RSS to receive information	P1, P11
Affecting recommendation algorithms	Approaching wanted information deliberately	Clicking expected information content deliberately	P36, P38
		Interacting with expected information sources deliberately	P1
		Searching keywords about expected information deliberately	P3, P4, P9, P32
		Including keywords about expected information in comments and posts deliberately	P5
	Avoiding unwanted information deliberately	Avoiding unexpected information content deliberately	P43
		Avoiding interaction with unexpected information sources deliberately	P20

5   Discussion and Conclusions

This study conducted a thematic analysis on 58 social media posts and explored the motivations, purposes, and means of creating information cocoons intentionally.

First, the results reflect the two-sided nature of information cocoons. In contrast to previous research, this study reflected that some information cocoons may protect people from the threats of overload information and negative information, and improve the quality and effectiveness of information requirements. Thus, it's necessary to redefine the information cocoons with a dialectical view. In the online environment inundated with false and misleading information, people would like to filter the information rather than just accept it all. In this case, the information cocoons are not dilemmas that people unconsciously fall into, but a self-constructed information villa or information security room to reduce cognitive load and emotional stress.

Second, this study observes that people would exhibit some deliberate information behaviors to affect recommendation algorithms. Such phenomenon can also be described as creating filter bubbles. People who performed in this way may have a high algorithmic literacy so that they know how to make recommendation algorithms work for themselves. It suggests that filter bubbles are not inherently good or bad, but rather depend on how people use them. Besides, such phenomenon shows that users need but can't directly control the recommendation algorithms. Thus, there should be a human-algorithm interface for users, providing explanations of the recommendation algorithms mechanism, as well as explicit feedback paths for users to adjust algorithms in real time. In addition, this phenomenon has dashed the stereotype that the clicking stream data and log data reflected real behaviors in the information behavior research field, as the behaviors may be performed for training algorithms rather than satisfy specific information needs.

There are still some limitations in this study. First, further empirical evidence rather than self-reported data should be collected to verify the real benefits people obtained from such information cocoons. Second, the small sample size limited the reliability of the results. More samples should be collected to draw a solid conclusion in the future.

Acknowledgement. This research has been made possible through the financial support of the National Social Science Foundation of China under Grant No. 22&ZD325 and the National Natural Science Foundation of China under Grant No. 72074173.

References

1. Sunstein, C.R.: Infotopia: How Many Minds Produce Knowledge. Oxford University Press, New York (2006)
2. Peng, H., Liu, C.: Breaking the information cocoon: when do people actively seek conflicting information?. Proc. Assoc. Inf. Sci. Technol. **58**(1), 801–803 (2021)
3. McKay, D., Owyong, K., Makri, S., Lopez, M.G.: Turn and face the strange: investigating filter bubble bursting information interactions. In: ACM SIGIR Conference on Human Information Interaction and Retrieval, pp. 233–242 (2022)
4. Hart, W., Albarracín, D., Eagly, A.H., Brechan, I., Lindberg, M.J., Merrill, L.A.: Feeling validated versus being correct: a meta-analysis of selective exposure to information. Psychol. Bull. **135**(4), 555–588 (2009)
5. Pariser, E.: The Filter Bubble: What the Internet Is Hiding from You (2011)
6. Sunstein, C.R.: Republic.com. (2001)
7. McKay, D., Makri, S., Chang, S., Buchanan, G.R.: On birthing dancing stars: the need for bounded chaos in information interaction. In: Proceedings of the 2020 Conference on Human Information Interaction and Retrieval, pp. 292–302 (2020)

8. Vicario, M.D., Vivaldo, G., Bessi, A., et al.: Echo chambers: emotional contagion and group polarization on facebook. Sci. Rep. **6**, 37825 (2016)

9. Gossart, C.: Can digital technologies threaten democracy by creating information cocoons. In: Transforming Politics and Policy in the Digital Age, pp. 145–154 (2014)

10. Dahlgren, P.M.: A critical review of filter bubbles and a comparison with selective exposure. Nordicom Review **42**(1), 15–33 (2021)

11. Chang, C.: Men's and women's responses to two-sided health news coverage: a moderated mediation model. J. Health Commun. **18**(11), 1326–1344 (2013)

12. Nagler, R.H.: Adverse outcomes associated with media exposure to contradictory nutrition messages. J. Health Commun. **19**(1), 24–40 (2014)

13. Maier, C., Laumer, S., Eckhardt, A., Weitzel, T.: Giving too much social support: social overload on social networking sites. Eur. J. Inf. Syst. **24**(5), 447–464 (2015)

14. Bright, L.F., Kleiser, S.B., Grau, S.L.: Too much facebook? an exploratory examination of social media fatigue. Comput. Hum. Behav. **44**, 148–155 (2015)

15. Bawden, D., Robinson, L.: The dark side of information: overload, anxiety and other paradoxes and pathologies. J. Inf. Sci. **35**(2), 180–191 (2009)

16. Zhang, S., Zhao, L., Lu, Y., Yang, J.: Do you get tired of socializing? an empirical explanation of discontinuous usage behaviour in social network services. Inf. Manage. **53**(7), 904–914 (2016)

17. Jones, S.L., Kelly, R.: Dealing with information overload in multifaceted personal informatics systems. Hum.-Comput. Interact. **33**(1), 1–48 (2018)

18. Koltay, T.: The bright side of information: ways of mitigating information overload. J. Documentation **73**(4), 767–775 (2017)

19. Davis, N.: Information overload, reloaded. Bull. Am. Soc. Inf. Sci. Technol. **37**(5), 45–49 (2011)

Left and Right Retweets! Curation Logics During Black History Month

Yiran Duan(✉), Jeff Hemsley, Alexander Owen Smith, and LaVerne Gray

Syracuse University, Syracuse, NY 13244, USA
yduan12@syr.edu

Abstract. This study investigates what information that was spread the most on Twitter regarding #BlackLivesMatter during the Black History Month of February 2022. We distinguished political affiliation through a series of interpretations of network structure and content. In doing so, we observed different political groups offering unique curated information flows on Twitter. Using qualitative coding, our findings confirmed that opinion leaders affiliated with different political groups or movements tend to curate different kinds of messages. Our findings also show that opinion leaders on the political left discuss #BlackLivesMatter in a clear supportive way towards the movement, while the ones on the political right describe the movement in a more provocative way. Further, we observed that opinion leaders in the political right group have more dense connections than the political left group. This work contributes to the bodies of literature using the theory of curated logics, the influence of opinion leaders, viral information, and the empirical work around #BlackLivesMatter on Twitter.

Keywords: BlackLivesMatter · Black History Month · Curation logics · Virality · Twitter

1 Introduction

The killing of the unarmed African American, George Floyd by former police officer Derek Chauvin in Minneapolis, Minnesota on May 25th, 2020, started nation-wide protests police brutality. On Twitter, the hashtag #BlackLivesMatter (#BLM) trended and, more than two years later, still remains as a well-used hashtag. Indeed, we wonder if Black Lives Matter is still a social movement or if it has become a semi-main-stream, ongoing discussion within Twitter, part of the fabric of today's society. However, not all of the messages tagged with #BlackLivesMatter are supportive of the movement, and in fact, Pew polling data shows that roughly 42% of adults in the U.S. held a negative view of the movement [12]. Both supportive and non-supportive messages can go viral with the hashtag, and as [17] argue, what goes viral is generally a reflection of what society views as important at that moment.

To get a better understanding of what people are seeing as important reflections of #BLM, we collected tweets and retweets with #BLM related hashtags during Black History Month (February) 2022. In this work we leverage the concept of opinion leaders

I. Sserwanga et al. (Eds.): iConference 2023, LNCS 13972, pp. 131–142, 2023.
https://doi.org/10.1007/978-3-031-28032-0_11

[15], people who are followed by, and have some influence over, other social media users. We also use the theory of *curation logics* [20], which posits that actors' decision to share, or curate content is driven by the incentives they face and the social norms within which they are embedded. The opinion leaders in our study are the users who posted the most retweeted tweets during the month of February 2022. Given the limited space of this paper, we only selected the top 10 most retweeted tweets from our dataset.

Using social network analysis, our findings show that information that is positively related to #BlackLivesMatter got the most attention (most retweeted) compared to non-supportive messages. However, some of the most retweeted posts that on the top 10 list viewed the #BLM organization negatively. For these users, we manually categorized them into roles, and qualitatively analyzed the top 10 most shared retweets into explicit groups. We find that there is roughly the same amount of supportive and unsupportive retweeted tweets about #BLM on the top 10 list, and these supportive and unsupportive tweets formed two opposing clusters. Also, the links among the unsupportive cluster are denser than the ones of the supportive cluster.

This work contributes to the bodies of literature using the theory of curated logics [20], the influence of opinion leaders [15], viral information [17], and the empirical work around #BlackLivesMatter on Twitter [2, 4, 6, 7, 14, 16, 21].

2 Background Studies and Related Work

#BlackLivesMatter (BLM) began in 2013 as a collective of Black organizers and self-identified Black/Queer feminists, Patrisse Cullors, Alicia Garza, and Opal Tometi [6–8, 19]. They organized in response to the death of Trayvon Martin and George Zimmerman's acquittal. Their organizational interests are in ending police brutality and racist bias in law enforcement [21, 23]. While initial uptake of the hashtag #BlackLivesMatter was small [9], since the killing of George Floyd on May 25th, 2020, the use of the hashtag has trended several times and become a common tag [2]. Within the networks of people tweeting and retweeting about BLM, most tweets hardly get noticed since a very tiny percentage of what gets shared ever goes viral, or even reaches more than a single user's followers [17].

In order for content to spread, or go viral, it typically needs a few key ingredients [17]. Here we focus on *context* and *message sender*. *Context* operates here as content which surrounds the tweet during the time it was posted. If context and content are well connected, the tweet is more likely to go viral. In this study, our temporal context is Black History Month. While BlackLivesMatter is relatively new, Black History month has history going back 1926 when Dr. Carter G. Woodson proposed memorizing Black History [3]. However, Congress didn't enact a supporting law until 1986 [22]. Dr. Woodson also started a series of events titled "Negro History Week' during the 2nd week of February in the United States in 1926 [3]. To be more specific, in 1969, Black educators at Kent State University proposed every February to be Black History Month. In 1975, President Gerald Ford sent out the Message on the Observance of Black History Week, stating that "to recognize the important contribution made to our nation's life and culture by our Black citizens" (*Message on the Observance of Black History Week.|The American Presidency Project*, n.d.). By 1986, Congress designated February "National Black (Afro-American) History Month by passing Public Law 99–244 in 1986 [22].

Another key ingredient for virality has to do with who is sending the message [17]. Messages sent by influential actors, like opinion leaders, are more likely to go viral. Opinion leaders are actors in networks that follow events or news carefully, and then offer their own view or interpretation of it for others [15]. To understand the logic by which these opinion leaders share viral content about #BlackLivesMatter during Black History Month we turn to [20]'s theory of *curated logics*, which are presented through the term of *curated flows*: how people select information to share into their own networks. In this view, to *curate* is to "select, organize, and filter information to fulfill a need" [20:313]. Curation decisions are based on the incentives and social norms that actors face within their own networks. As such, we might expect that actors in different networks that share information regarding #BlackLivesMatter might face different incentives and norms. Thus, the kinds of content actively shared on each network are different. Therefore, it is reasonable to think that people's unique political networks face different incentives and norms in discussing #BlackLivesMatter during Black History Month.

Given the above, we propose the following research questions:

RQ1: What are the most shared tweets about #BlackLivesMatter on Twitter during Black History Month 2022?

RQ2: Who are the users that generated most shared tweets about #BlackLivesMatter on Twitter during Black History Month 2022 and how are they connected?

3 Methods

We designed this project by looking into the data we collected from Twitter. We collected tweets from February 1st to March 15th, 2022, to make sure that viral events that happened at the end of February are included. During this time, Twitter users posted 939,257 tweets matching the term BlackLivesMatter or BLM. Of these, 705,953 of the tweets were retweets.

To provide a descriptive overview of our data, we utilized social network analysis. Previous studies have shown that Twitter data is particularly suitable for visualizing social network analysis [5]. We used Rstudio to sort the top 10 most retweeted tweets during the timeframe, and then created a retweet network that shows the retweeting relations among all the retweets. We then used Gephi, an open-source network visualization software to generate the retweet network of our data (Fig. 1).

Each node in Fig. 1 represents a user in our data collection, and each edge/link represents one user retweeting another. The node size shows the in-degree of a user, which means that the more someone gets retweeted, the bigger the node is. The text labels are proportional with the node size to indicate who generated the most retweeted tweet during our data collection period. The ForceAtlas 2 algorithm was applied to generate the layout [13]. The algorithm aims to show communities by grouping nodes together who are more closely linked. The layout was optimized to support graphical interpretation. We colored Fig. 1 based on modularity– the strength of division of a network into groups. Since modularity is exclusive, the links between two hubs only show the same color of one hub.

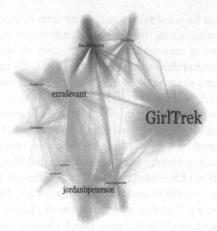

ezralevant

GeoffBennett

GirlTrek

jordanbpeterson

Fig. 1. The top 10 users who generated the most retweeted tweets during February 2022

4 Results

As Fig. 1 shows, the network has 10 hubs, each of those represents one of our opinion leaders. The nodes connected to them are Twitter users who retweeted them. This shape of network serves as an example of a "broadcast network" [18], which refers to the idea that news related tweets often have a one-to-many structured network, in which many Twitter users repeat what the news creator tweets. While several of these are notably not news personalities, bios from each twitter handle confirm that the four of our opinion leaders are news reporters or pundits.

It is interesting that six of these handles are not explicitly news related but appear to be influential in the network. For each of our opinion leaders, the following table lists their username (Twitter handle), profile description, the tweet in the top 10 retweets and their number of retweets. Based on the profile information listed in each of the accounts, we assigned a category to describe their roles. This step involved the 3 researchers in our team to come to a mutual agreement of defining the categories.

As Table 1 shows, the most retweeted in our dataset asserts the view that a 12-year-old Black girl suffered unfair treatment for wearing a swimsuit that says BlackLivesMatter during a swim meet. This tweet further advocates for speaking up about the incident, especially given that it was Black History month. Users retweeted this post 28,755 times, which is almost double of the 2nd most retweeted tweet (retweeted 14,688 times) on our list.

The 2nd most retweeted post claims that GoFundMe, a crowd-funding platform, is confiscating funds donated to a Canadian trucking protest and giving the money to the Black Lives Matter organization. The trucker protest was popular in both the U.S. and Canada among conservative groups. The 3rd most retweeted post on our list actually quoted the 2nd most popular tweet; this tweet expressed a critical view of the trucker protest fund confiscation. Table 1 shows that the 2nd and 3rd most retweeted tweets almost have the same number of retweets, and both tweets are critical of the same event.

Table 1. Summary of the top 10 tweets

Ranking	Username	Profile description	Role	Retweeted times	Tweet	Annotation
1	GirlTrek	Started as 10-week walking challenge, 10 years ago, by 2 friends (@vanessatreks + @morgantreks), is now a global movement of 1M + Black women	Activist	28755	Leidy, a 12-year-old Black girl was nearly disqualified for wearing her Black Lives Matter swimsuit. What we're not gonna do is be silent about this. Especially during Black History month	News-support
2	ezralevant	Journalist, publisher of Rebel News—telling the other side of the story. Awarded the Queen's Diamond Jubilee Medal for advancing freedom of expression	Writer	14688	At the request of Trudeau, @GoFundMe has just stolen $9,000,000 from the truckers. Rather than automatically refunding it to the donors, they say they're going to give it to groups of their own choosing. What a windfall for Black Lives Matter, Greenpeace, and Planned Parenthood!	Critique
3	jordanbpeterson	Best-Selling Author l Clinical Psychologist l #1 Education Podcast l Listen to the podcast here	Writer	13545	This is far worse than mere theft. Government-sanctioned appropriation from citizens funding lawful opposition. This sets a very very dark precedent @JustinTrudeau @gofundme	Critique
4	GeoffRBennett	PBS News Weekend' Anchor l @NewsHour Chief Washington Correspondent l@NBCNews & @MSNBC Political Analyst l Always @Morehouse	News anchor	7413	The Missouri Supreme Court on Tuesday indefinitely suspended the law licenses of two St. Louis attorneys who waved guns at Black Lives Matter protesters in 2020	News

(continued)

Table 1. (*continued*)

Ranking	Username	Profile description	Role	Retweeted times	Tweet	Annotation
5	joncoopertweets	Former National Finance Chair of Draft Biden, LI Campaign Chair for Barack Obama. Hit "Super Follow" for tips to boost your messaging and grow your followers!	Politician	5834	I kneel with Eminem and Colin Kaepernick in support of Black Lives Matter. Who joins us?	Support
6	jsparkblog	Hospital chaplain. Korean American. 6th degree black belt. Ex-atheist. Loves Jesus. Writing a second book, on grief	Health care worker	5549	In Korean, the phrase Black Lives Matter translates to Black Lives Are Precious. You more than matter. You are more than worthy of protection. Black lives are beloved, cherished, dignified, and made in the Image Divine. #BlackHistoryMonth	Support
7	Firstdoctorr	Health Coach, Medical Doctor, Author, Traveler, CEO @Telemed_Clinic Email - peteratangwho@yahoo.com	Health care worker	5145	Salary cut - Fined £250.000 - Lost Adidas sponsorship - May spend 4 years in prison An entire career gone for kicking his cat? Black athletes worldwide, this is the time to speak up against systemic racism. It is Zouma today, it may be you tomorrow. #BlackLivesMatter	Support

(continued)

Table 1. (*continued*)

Ranking	Username	Profile description	Role	Retweeted times	Tweet	Annotation
8	libsoftiktok	All videos belong to their respective owners. Libsoftiktok@gmail.com. DM submissions	Influencer	4903	A school in DC forced kindergarteners to march around with BLM signs and chant "Black Lives Matter"	News-support
9	mehdirhasan	Host, @mehdihasanshow on @MSNBC and NBC's @peacockTV	News anchor	3326	Compare Fox's coverage of the Canadian truckers protests versus Fox's coverage of Black Lives Matter protests and tell me that white privilege doesn't exist	News-opposition
10	AndrewKerrNC	Investigative Reporter Soon: @FreeBeacon// DM for Signal	Reporter	3267	BREAKING: Black Lives Matter's national arm just went and shut down ALL its online fundraising streams following a @dcexaminer investigation that exposed the charity's shocking lack of financial transparency	News-opposition

This raises the question of how many of the people who retweeted one, also retweeted the other. We will unpack this question using Figs. 2 and 3 below.

Going down the top 10 retweet list, we can see that the 4th, 7th, 8th, and 10th most retweeted posts are also news related. However, based on the words used in the posts, only one post, from @Firstdoctorr, shows clear support of the #BlackLivesMatter movement. The 4th most retweeted post on our list holds a neutral stance towards #BlackLivesMatter, while 8th and 10th most retweeted posts show unsupportive attitudes.

Figure 1 also shows that some opinion leaders are linked together by users who retweeted both. This implies that some of them may share the same audience. For example, the 2nd (from @ezralevant) and 3rd (from @jordanbpeterson) most retweeted posts appear to share more links than any other pair of nodes. To further explore the audience's overlap, we used Rstudio's iGraph package to create Fig. 2 to show our ten opinion leaders with weighted links based on how many twitter users retweeted both. Figure 2 represents an example of social network analysis. The color shows the different groupings. There are two main clusters, which we believe reflects political group affiliations. The user with a neutral standpoint (colored in purple) is connected to both left (blue) and right (red) groups. Using Rstudio, we created Fig. 3 to show the clusters and the distance between users clearly in a dendrogram form.

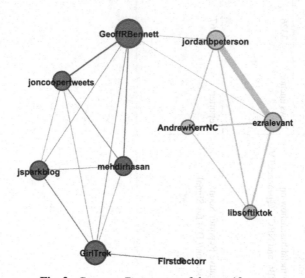

Fig. 2. Common Retweeters of the top 10 users

5   Discussion

This study investigates viral #BlackLivesMatter informational patterns. Specifically, we focus on the curation logics of opinion leaders in the context of Black History Month in 2022. We distinguished political affiliation through a series of interpretations of network structure and content. In doing so, we successfully observed different political groups offering unique curated information flows on Twitter. Using qualitative coding, we first

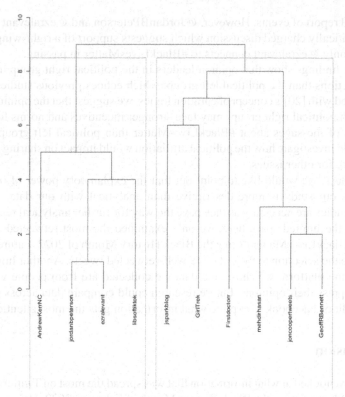

Fig. 3. A dendrogram of the top 10 users.

confirmed that opinion leaders affiliated with different political groups or movements tend to curate different kinds of messages. Then we composed a social network graph (Fig. 2) and a dendrogram (Fig. 3) which further illustrate the structure of opinion leaders from different clusters.

Based on distinctions in information behavior among opinion leaders affiliated with different political groups, we suggest that these opinion leaders face different curation logics [20], which reflects what information they choose to spread. For example, opinion leaders who are pundits and journalists with a specific political standpoint may have an incentive to appeal to their audience that have a similar view with them. Therefore, we expect them to post things that target their audience, which is what we have found. Indeed, among our top 10 users who tweeted about #BlackLivesMatter during February 2022, those organizing into different network clusters, i.e. their political affiliation, characterize the movement differently. The ones that are on the political left discuss #BlackLivesMatter in a clear supportive way towards the movement, while the ones on the political right describe the movement in a more provocative way. By only communicating within their networks, the opinion leaders of each political group curate consistent political contexts for their audience. Furthermore, an interesting, weakly connected relationship between @GeoffRBennett, @JordanBPeterson, and @ezralevant suggests an informational report of events. However, @JordanBPeterson and @ezralevant are offering more politically charged discussion which suggests support of a right-wing event in Canada that only @ezralevant connects to #BlackLivesMatter in passing.

Also, our findings show that opinion leaders in the political right group have more dense connections than the political left group, which echoes previous studies [10, 11, 24]. Combined with [20]'s concept of curation logics, we suggest that the opinion leaders affiliated with political right groups may face stronger incentives and norms for posting certain types of messages about #BlackLivesMatter than political left groups. Future research could investigate how the political affiliation would impact on sharing messages to the network for other issues.

Nevertheless, we would like to point out that the explanatory power of our results is limited, as our study is more descriptive than analytical with our data. However, descriptive studies are necessary as they pave the way for further analytical research [1]. Also, due to the limited space here, we only examined the most retweeted 10 tweets containing #BlackLivesMatter during the Black History Month of 2022. Future research could enlarge the selection to look at more well-retweeted tweets. Another limitation of our study is the platform we chose: the data we collected are from people who chose Twitter to express their opinions. Future research could compare data across platforms such as Reddit or Facebook to explore what information gets the most attention.

6   Conclusion

In this work we looked at what information that was spread the most on Twitter regarding #BlackLivesMatter during the Black History Month of February 2022. Using social network analysis and qualitative coding, we find differences in different groups of opinion leaders curation behavior within #BlackLivesMatter. We offer some observations about the differences in logics (incentives and norms) that they might face.

This work contributes to the bodies of literature using the theory of curated logics [20], the influence of opinion leaders [15], viral information [17], and the empirical work around #BlackLivesMatter on Twitter [2, 4, 6, 7, 14, 16, 21]. Our work also shows the analytical usefulness of the framework of curated flows [20]. And while space requirements limited our ability to delve more deeply into how the concept of opinion leaders and curation logics can update the concept of virality, we intend to follow up this theoretical work.

References

1. Brünker, F., Wischnewski, M., Mirbabaie, M., Meinert, J.: The Role of Social Media during Social Movements – Observations from the #metoo Debate on Twitter (2020). http://hdl.handle.net/10125/64030. Accessed 15 May 2022
2. Carney, N.: All lives matter, but so does race: black lives matter and the evolving role of social media. Hum. Soc. 40(2), 180–199 (2016). https://doi.org/10/gf3gsp

3. Doharty, N.: I felt dead: applying a racial microaggressions framework to Black students' experiences of black history month and black history. Race Ethn. Educ. **22**(1), 110–129 (2019). https://doi.org/10.1080/13613324.2017.1417253

4. Edrington, C.L.S., Lee, N.: Tweeting a social movement: black lives matter and its use of twitter to share information, build community, and promote action. J. Public Interest Commun. **2**(2), 289–289 (2018). https://doi.org/10/gkmr32

5. Freelon, D., Karpf, D.: Of big birds and bayonets: hybrid Twitter interactivity in the 2012 presidential debates. Inf. Commun. Soc. **18**(4), 390–406 (2015). https://doi.org/10/gctm2g

6. Freelon, D., McIlwain, C., Clark, M.: Quantifying the power and consequences of social media protest. New Media Soc. **20**(3), 990–1011 (2018). https://doi.org/10/gdfpb5

7. Freelon, D., McIlwain, C.D., Clark, M.: Beyond the hashtags:# Ferguson,# Blacklivesmatter, and the online struggle for offline justice. Center Media Soc. Impact Am. Univ. Forthcoming (2016)

8. Gallagher, R.J., Reagan, A.J., Danforth, C.M., Dodds, P.S.: Divergent discourse between protests and counter-protests:# BlackLivesMatter and# AllLivesMatter. PloS One **13**(4), e0195644 (2018). https://doi.org/10/gdchmm

9. Ge, J., Gretzel, U.: Emoji rhetoric: a social media influencer perspective. J. Mark. Manag. **34**(15–16), 1272–1295 (2018). https://doi.org/10/gg2wn5

10. Himelboim, I., Smith, M., Shneiderman, B.: Tweeting apart: applying network analysis to detect selective exposure clusters in twitter. Commun. Methods Meas. **7**(3–4), 195–223 (2013). https://doi.org/10.1080/19312458.2013.813922

11. Hogan, B.: Analysing Social Networks Via the Internet. 13 (2007)

12. Hurst, K.: U.S. teens are more likely than adults to support the Black Lives Matter movement. Pew Research Center. https://www.pewresearch.org/fact-tank/2022/06/15/u-s-teens-are-more-likely-than-adults-to-support-the-black-lives-matter-movement/. Accessed 19 Sept 2022

13. Jacomy, M., Venturini, T., Heymann, S., Bastian, M.: ForceAtlas2, a continuous graph layout algorithm for handy network visualization designed for the gephi software. PLoS ONE **9**(6), e98679 (2014). https://doi.org/10.1371/journal.pone.0098679

14. Jones, K., Nurse, J.R.C., Li, S.: Out of the Shadows: Analyzing Anonymous' Twitter Resurgence during the 2020 Black Lives Matter Protests. arXiv preprint http://arxiv.org/abs/2107.10554 (2021)

15. Katz, E., Lazarsfeld, P.: Personal Influence: The Part Played by People in the Flow of Mass Communications. Transaction Publishers (1955)

16. Mundt, M., Ross, K., Burnett, C.M.: Scaling social movements through social media: the case of black lives matter. Social Media+ Soc. **4**(4), 2056305118807911 (2018)

17. Nahon, K., Hemsley, J.: Going Viral. Polity Press Cambridge, Cambridge, UK (2013)

18. Smith, M., Rainie, L., Shneiderman, B., Himelboim, I.: Mapping Twitter Topic Networks: From Polarized Crowds to Community Clusters. Pew Research Center: Internet, Science & Tech (2014). https://www.pewresearch.org/internet/2014/02/20/mapping-twitter-topic-networks-from-polarized-crowds-to-community-clusters/. Accessed 19 Sept 2022

19. Stewart, L.G., Arif, A., Nied, A.C., Spiro, E.S., Starbird, K.: Drawing the lines of contention: networked frame contests within #BlackLivesMatter discourse. In: Proceedings of the ACM on Human-Computer Interaction 1, CSCW, pp. 1–23 (2017). https://doi.org/10/gf3gsk

20. Thorson, K., Wells, C.: Curated flows: a framework for mapping media exposure in the digital age: curated flows. Commun. Theory **26**(3), 309–328 (2016). https://doi.org/10/f878cg

21. Tillery, A.B.: What kind of movement is black lives matter? the view from twitter. J. Race, Ethn. Polit. **4**(2), 297–323 (2019). 10/gh7smx

22. Wood, M.: Research Guides: Black History Month: A Commemorative Observances Legal Research Guide: History and Overview. https://guides.loc.gov/black-history-month-legal-resources/history-and-overview. Accessed 10 Aug 2022

23. Black Lives Matter (BLM). Library of Congress, Washington, D.C. 20540 USA. https://www.loc.gov/item/lcwaN0016241/. Accessed 19 Sept 2022

24. Conservatives Moral Foundations Are More Densely Connected Than Liberals' Moral Foundations. https://doi.org/10.1177/0146167220916070

Libraries

Another Named Storm! Building Resiliency Through Florida's Essential Public Libraries

Denise M. Gomez⬤, Faye R. Jones⬤, and Marcia A. Mardis^(✉)⬤

Florida State University, Tallahassee, FL 32306, USA
mmardis@fsu.edu

Abstract. Florida public librarians are impacted by at least one named storm a year and are statutorily designated as essential providers of emergency services. To understand how resiliency can be improved through the services of public libraries, we surveyed Florida's public library directors about their public library systems' preparedness for natural disasters to identify policies and procedures libraries may have to enhance community resilience. Through our survey, we documented that few public librarians severely affected by 2018's Hurricane Michael had formal disaster plans in place and expressed desires to respond to adverse events as part of an integrated community-wide response. Although library staff members were considered essential workers, few library leaders regularly attended local emergency management meetings. While librarians worked more often with county and local government partners during disaster preparation, response, and recovery, library directors reported that local governments lacked an awareness of the services libraries provided during crises. This study's results have implications for improving community resilience in and through libraries by generating new knowledge for practitioners and researchers about proactive policy creation and implementation.

Keywords: Libraries · Disaster management · Community resilience

1 Introduction

Climate disasters are on the rise [1] and increasingly impacting people, infrastructure, and communities. For example, Florida receives at least one named storm, along with other natural disasters, each year. Though public librarians are statutorily considered first responders [2], many Florida public library systems are not integrated into their community's disaster response and lack consistently documented procedures. The 2019 IMLS Heritage Health survey [3] reflected that only 25% of small and rural libraries in the U.S. have a disaster plan, while our interviews with public librarians severely affected by Hurricane Michael in the Florida Panhandle corroborated that in this region, librarians had few formal disaster plans in place [4].

Disaster plans are "actively maintained document[s] containing procedures and information needed to prevent, mitigate, prepare for, respond to, and recover from emergencies" [5]. They are used at all levels of government, public agencies, and private

I. Sserwanga et al. (Eds.): iConference 2023, LNCS 13972, pp. 145–156, 2023.
https://doi.org/10.1007/978-3-031-28032-0_12

organizations. Existing disaster plans fail when they are not consistently assessed and improved; staff lacks experience with disaster response; and planning does not address necessary elements or is implemented incorrectly [6]. Library systems often have out-dated plans or plans focused solely on collections and library infrastructure, without accounting for staff and community needs. Though most public libraries are extensions of local government, how emergency management personnel collaborate with library leaders to effectively allocate library staff and resources is underexplored, despite the obvious potential harm to the community.

To explore the topic of disaster preparedness in Florida's public libraries in natural disasters, we surveyed Florida public library directors about their experiences with disaster planning, relationships with emergency management organizations, expected roles of staff, and the types and applications of disaster plans they used. We were guided by two research questions:

RQ1: What elements of disaster preparedness, response, and recovery are public library leaders using in preparing for disasters?
RQ2: What issues do public library leaders in Florida face when planning for and responding to natural disasters?

2   Literature Review

2.1   Library and Disaster Management

Public libraries strengthen their communities by providing lifelong learning and innovation [7–9] and people turn to libraries in moments of need [10]. Public libraries are among the first anchor institutions to reopen following disasters, providing climate-controlled safe spaces, critical information, communications technologies, and workspaces for first responders [4]. Community members turn to the library for aid, technology access, and social connection [11]. States along the Gulf of Mexico fell victim to several devastating storms during 2004 and 2005 and public librarians helped communities prepare for those storms by distributing emergency information and physical aid; caring for vulnerable community members in need; working with relief organizations; assisting with cleaning up storm damage; and providing shelter [11].

Librarians also rise to community needs even when their own facilities are affected. Although the Federal Emergency Management Agency (FEMA) did not recognize libraries as essential community organizations in 2008, librarians from Cedar Rapids Public Library worked feverishly to set up an alternate location to provide services to their community when their own library was devastated by flood waters [12]. Despite their efforts and those of librarians who routinely answered the call following disasters, libraries were considered nonessential services, prompting FEMA to deny their request for temporary facilities. Others lobbied for FEMA to change their policy on libraries and in 2011, the Stafford Act was amended, designating libraries "as essential community organizations, adding public libraries to the category of essential community services, including police, fire protection/emergency services, medical care, education, and utilities" [10].

Despite this recognition, libraries and local emergency management organizations are often disconnected, with leaders who are often not aware of library staff's disaster support activities or many patrons' dependency on the library during disaster response and recovery [13, 14]. Libraries and library staff are "often engaged in...relief efforts by accident or through ad hoc efforts, not by design" [11, p. 210], and are not immediately considered as a resource by emergency managers, with a former FEMA director commenting, "I think you're really on to something there, I mean, where else are they going to go? Libraries have back-up generators for power, they have the Internet, they have people who will help you. I guess we never really thought of the role libraries could play" [15, p. 722]. Disaster responders often only recall libraries as disaster resource providers resources after prompting, even if librarians provided resources and worked collaboratively with local agencies [10].

2.2 Disaster Plans in Libraries

Many libraries lack formalized plans for use during disasters [10, 14, 16] leading librarians to a "delayed and hindered...coordinated response" [10]. This disconnect is long-standing: researchers studying library disaster planning two decades ago focused on circulating collections and building maintenance, but also suggested improving communications with emergency management personnel, but only as they related to building and safety issues [17–19]. Many plans that were in place followed this format, protecting library collections and equipment which often presented the bulk of the library's capital, and included procedures for staff and patron safety during a disaster [14]. However, plans have lacked detail on how librarians could prepare for a disaster, leaving them "reactionary to events as they unfolded" [14, p.37].

Following disasters, when power and telecommunication grids are down, libraries are inundated by community members hoping for continued Internet access to reconnect with the outside world. Continuity planning, or the continuous function of operations throughout the disaster, is often overlooked in disaster planning [20]. Following Hurricanes Katrina and Rita, library leaders in Louisiana concluded existing disaster plans were insufficient to protect community members, insisting the "focus had to be on business continuity, suggesting "the value of libraries lies in their ability to connect patrons to loved ones, help them find information, and establish some normalcy" following a disaster" [21, p.37]. Some librarians have created a continuity of operation plan (COOP) as an addendum to the disaster plan, which "provides the organization with the means to address the numerous issues involved in performing essential functions and services during an emergency" [6, p.44]. Throughout disasters like hurricanes and floods, librarians prioritize reopening and assisting patrons in disaster recovery even without plans in place; however, librarians benefit from regularly thinking critically about community needs and planning out necessary resources to provide a continuity of service to expedite the library's disaster response.

For many library disaster plans, a COOP will be an important guide to continuing operations. Though community needs planning should happen in conjunction with emergency management personnel, libraries are often not included in county emergency management plans [3, 22] and are rarely considered during emergency planning sessions [22].

2.3 Barriers to Disaster Management

Coordinated disaster management is an emerging field shaped by disaster response. FEMA was created following natural disasters in the 1960s and 1970s to create a federal coordinated response during large scale disasters [6], though local disaster preparation is left to the states and local governments to organize without a federally mandated protocol. As a result, disaster response varies greatly among states and between rural and urban areas, as does the relationship between emergency management and their community. A lack of relationship between libraries and emergency management agencies has been seen as a barrier to disaster management [16]. Though some library staff work with emergency management officials to provide workshops to the public, others have been met with resistance by emergency management personnel unaware of the resources that libraries could provide in disasters [10].

Even librarians have varied perceptions of expected response to disasters. In a national survey of over 1500 librarians [22], respondents stated that they believed their primary role in disasters was "protecting library collections and maintaining normal services" [22, p.407] and far surpassed their participation in emergency planning and response teams. Although library collections affected by disasters are at risk for mold and bacteria damage [23], responding to community needs in times of crisis requires certain skills that may require additional training and practice. Few librarians participate in emergency preparedness training and many library staff have been unable to participate in disaster management training or planning events due to conflicting staff priorities [16], resulting in few librarians with the skills to respond to any disaster phase [24]. Training in disaster preparedness, response, and recovery improves librarians' response and benefits the community [10].

2.4 Library Needs in Disaster Management

Although library collections are extremely valuable and collections are important to include within disaster management plans, patrons' continued access to the library for information, connectivity, and assistance during disaster response and recovery is critical and could be incorporated into local emergency management response. A lack of collaboration between librarians and emergency management personnel could lead to duplicating efforts and wasting resources. For example, 2005's Hurricane Katrina prompted the Louisiana State Museum director to suggest cultural institutions needed to be "integrated into local emergency management plans" [25, p.39], while Louisiana State Library leaders suggested that public librarians need to coordinate their disaster response efforts with local emergency management and maintain positive relationships that would encourage librarians to be included in local disaster plan discussions [21]. Working with emergency management personnel better positions library leaders to anticipate community needs, resources they could provide, and roles and responsibilities of their staff, thus enabling a better disaster response through more efficient planning.

Staff with sufficient training to implement emergency plans provide a more expeditious response in times of crisis [10] and prepare staff for dealing with the personal and professional effects of disasters [26]. Library staff often contend with also being victims of home destruction, displacement, and familial obligations.

Disaster plans are an element of community resiliency because they provide a blueprint to follow in chaotic circumstances. Florida libraries are at greater risk to natural disasters and implementing an appropriate plan would help them better serve the community, but we need to explore the current state of library disaster plans and preparedness,

3 Method

We used a survey with nominal and ordinal measurement scales and short answer responses to identify issues faced by public library directors in Florida when planning for, responding to, and recovering from disasters. The survey can be seen at https://bit.ly/Lib DisasterSurvey. Our aim was to understand, from a public library director perspective, public libraries' practices and needs for disaster planning, response, and recovery. We reviewed and validated the survey with our advisory board, which includes Chief Officers of State Library Agencies (COSLA) and Public Library Association (PLA) members, state climatologists, emergency operations officers, information science faculty, and public librarians.

3.1 Data Collection and Analysis

Our study is based in Florida, with 146 public library directors each leading a library system in one of 67 state counties. To identify the state's public library directors, we used county library websites. We worked directly with leaders of the Florida Department of State and the Division of Library and Information Services (DLIS) to confirm names and contact information. The survey instrument (available at https://bit.ly/LibDisasterS urvey) consisted of 31 questions and concluded with submission upload requests for existing disaster plan documents. Questions centered on librarians' roles and relationships in disaster management; plans and policies for disaster management; and librarians' unmet disaster management needs.

We opened the survey from September 2021 to February 2022 and received 50 total responses (N = 50), for a return of 34%, though only 38 were completed in its entirety. Twenty percent of respondents were from state-designated rural counties. We received plans from 13 library systems. We analyzed the data using descriptive statistics and open coding with thematic analysis for short answer question responses.

4 Results

4.1 Library Directors and Natural Disasters

Relationship with Emergency Management. Our preliminary survey findings survey revealed that of the 44 that responded to this question, 82% (n = 36) held a leadership role during a disaster and most of their libraries were affected primarily by pandemic and hurricane-related disasters in the last decade. As Fig. 1 depicts, although 27 of 44 (61%) library directors have library staff who are considered essential workers, only 10 library leaders regularly attended Emergency Operations Center (EOC) meetings. Only one library director sat on the EOC board and assisted in decision-making. Almost half of the respondents were not directly involved with the local government's emergency operations center and remained on standby for the next steps during disasters.

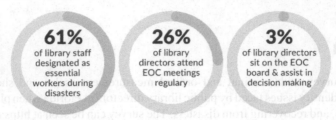

61%
of library staff designated as essential workers during disasters

26%
of library directors attend EOC meetings regulary

3%
of library directors sit on the EOC board & assist in decision making

Fig. 1. Florida libraries and their roles in emergency operations centers (EOC)

4.2 Libraries and Natural Disasters

Library Readiness. Library directors felt confident in their readiness for previously experienced natural disasters in Florida, with 69% (n = 29) of 42 respondents indicating their libraries were very prepared for hurricanes and 59% (n = 24) of 41 respondents were very prepared for pandemics. They were less confident about disasters with minimal warning time, as out of 39 of this question's respondents, 23 (59%) reported feeling only somewhat prepared for tornadoes, and 20 (51%) felt somewhat prepared for floods. Understandably, many respondents reported that their libraries were not prepared for tsunamis and earthquakes as both are not impossible, but rarely experienced, in Florida. The infrastructure of buildings, however, was a concern, with 22 (60%) of 37 participants claiming old and deteriorating buildings were sometimes or always a barrier to disaster management activities. Poor infrastructure could allow for storms to penetrate through the building and damage collections and equipment.

4.3 Disaster Preparedness

Preparing for Disasters. Many library directors prepared for catastrophic events by discussing potential disasters and responses in organizational meetings; attending disaster meetings or trainings outside of the organization; and providing information to community members on disaster-related issues. Only 48% (n = 20) of 42 respondents to this question held disaster-related training within the library and library directors expressed concern for staff ill-prepared for emergency-related roles or duties that lack clear explanation or training.

Risk assessment and mitigation is the first phase in disaster preparation because it is "the process of identifying risks to which an institution is vulnerable and determining how the impacts…may be diminished or eliminated" [27, p.1]. Library organizations would assess their risks of hazards to staff and patrons, physical buildings, materials, and technology infrastructure during this phase, however, less than half of those in our study engaged in structural mitigation measures, conducted vulnerability assessments, or considered long-term recovery strategies. Funding is an issue, as nearly 73% (n = 27) of 37 participants indicated that having an adequate budget to design, conduct, or evaluate disaster response was sometimes or always a barrier.

Although libraries worked more often with county and local government partners than other outside organizations during disaster preparedness, response, and recovery, approximately 24 of 37 library directors felt local governments lacked an awareness of the services their libraries provided to the community during a disaster. One participant expressed the need to "convince local government (that) library is integral to disaster recovery" and another felt libraries should be incorporated into local government emergency plans. Identifying and building relationships with community agencies can strengthen the ability and effectiveness of disaster management [16]. Only 18 of 44 question respondents had existing relationships with community partners that could aid in disaster response.

Status of Disaster Plans. Regarding the status of existing disaster plans and policies, we found of 40 respondents, only 10 reported that local government entities included public libraries in their COOPs, and even with libraries generating their plans, less than 10 libraries surveyed had written disaster plans to accommodate their needs in disaster management as shown in Fig. 2.

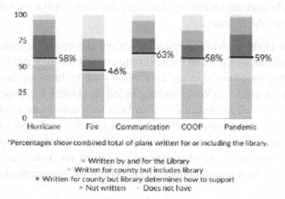

*Percentages show combined total of plans written for or including the library.

■ Written by and for the Library
▪ Written for county but includes library
■ Written for county but library determines how to support
▪ Not written   Does not have

Fig. 2. Disaster plans currently in place for hurricanes, fires, communications, continuity of operations (COOP), and pandemics.

Many library directors did not report having plans, services, or equipment in place for vulnerable populations. Of the 36 respondents, only four library directors indicated they have plans that address assisting seniors, children, persons with disabilities, persons from low socioeconomic circumstances, and persons experiencing homelessness.

4.4 Disaster Response

During disaster response, library directors indicated library infrastructure is used primarily for library functions by 28 of 39 (72%) library systems, although in later questions,

17 of 36 respondents provided space for external agencies. Twelve of 33 library directors responded that their libraries were used for aid distribution and only five had libraries that are always or sometimes used for shelters.

Assets and Barriers to Disaster Management. We asked library directors what they saw were their strongest assets and they expressed strengths in terms of highly competent and caring staff, customer service, communications, skill in information retrieval, as well as commitment to their community. Many of Florida's library leaders and staff have prior experience with disaster response and recovery and the library's value to the community extends to its role as a technology resource, information hub, and partner to local government and community agencies.

We also inquired about the challenges they face in disaster management. When their community is victim to a disaster, their staff is also impacted, and the desire to help the community must be balanced with the safety of their staff. There are issues with convincing local government that the library is integral to disaster management. Many library staff do not have training in emergency-related roles and are unclear of their responsibilities during disasters and the library's technology infrastructure is often inadequate. Some libraries lack generators to maintain power and communications and either do not have disaster plans or the plans they do have are insufficient for the needed response. Participants were also uncertain about the future, as one participant wrote, "The biggest challenge is the unknown – if an event happens, how bad is it?" Staff may not be able to get through and access the building for days, weeks, or not at all depending on the magnitude of the disaster.

Library Needs in Disaster Management. Library directors indicated a tremendous need for generators that could assist with climate control for their collections and supply relief to community members seeking assistance with technology and disaster-related forms. Technology upgrades in Wi-Fi and upgraded bandwidth facilitate government and volunteer agencies as well as community members with communication and technology needs. Staff needs training opportunities that are specific to disaster-related roles and responsibilities, preferably through on-demand online delivery so scheduling is flexible to staff needs. Library directors also expressed a need for a defined disaster plan for libraries, formally written and in collaboration with local government plans.

4.5 Disaster Recovery

During the disaster recovery phase, nearly 32 of 36 library directors who responded to this question reported working often or sometimes with county and local government. In comparison, 15 of 34 library directors worked with non-profit and volunteer organizations. Only 14 of 35 library directors worked with FEMA and 10 worked with Red Cross, although one participant noted these agencies are coordinated directly through local government officials. Library directors noted issues with staffing during recovery due to displacement of staff, lack of updated contact lists, or issues with communication lines. Some staff were reallocated to emergency management roles outside of their daily work, leaving a minimal number of staff for libraries to reopen and provide needed assistance to their community. Libraries lacked sufficient generators to maintain collections and communication technology resources.

5 Discussion

In this section, we discuss the survey results in the context of our research questions.

5.1 What Elements of Disaster Preparedness, Response, and Recovery Are Public Library Leaders Using to Prepare for Disasters?

Library leaders are talking about disasters with their staff. Still, less than half held training or prepared staff for emergency management roles, leaving some staff uninformed about emergency-related duties. Librarian turnover, such as retirements at the director level, can also have grave consequences for community resiliency. Though more than half have disaster plans and are working with emergency management officials, there are still 40% that lack written or properly maintained disaster plans or report poor collaboration with local government officials, leaving some libraries in reactionary positions during disaster response and recovery and possibly leading to less efficient assistance for their communities in need [16].

Less than half of the library systems in the study are engaged in mitigation strategies where vulnerabilities are assessed in building infrastructure, technology concerns, and social capital, which could result in increased damage and related costs in disasters. Following and maintaining a well-implemented disaster plan could address these elements and better prepare Florida libraries to deal with disasters in their communities. Disaster plans should serve the needs of the library, staff, and surrounding community, so assessing those needs when writing disaster plans are essential. Library leaders, however, may not be formally trained in disaster management. This has implications on several levels and could lead to a domino effect of sorts. Without proper understanding of disaster management, library leaders may overlook the need to assess vulnerabilities, which would weaken disaster preparation and lead to inefficient disaster response and recovery. It may be solutions can be found through education and collaboration. Within academia, those preparing future library leaders for success could include emergency management certification focused on libraries, encompassing not only facilities and collections, but also delineating continuity of operations and providing community aid in the aftermath of disasters. Unfortunately, implementing education certifications could take time. Current library leaders could collaborate with their local government's emergency management team, perhaps calling on their emergency management expertise to assist in mitigation strategies and disaster preparation for both the library system and the general public and fostering a closer relationship between the two entities.

5.2 What Issues Do Public Library Leaders in Florida Face when Planning for and Responding to Natural Disasters?

Library leaders have issues with building and technology infrastructure, staffing, inadequate or no disaster plan, and an absent relationship with local government emergency management. Library directors would benefit from working with local government officials to integrate libraries into their emergency management disaster plans in a way that accommodates both parties and utilizes library staff and resources to their best advantage. For example, the role of librarians as "information specialists' to maximize information access, retrieval, and dissemination to communities may be highly overlooked by county government and EOC leaders.

Libraries could also better prepare for disasters by creating and maintaining their own disaster and continuity of operation plans, addressing possible events and protocol for disaster preparation, response, and recovery. Local library disaster plans need to address building infrastructure, assessing building construction and window replacement needs so storms are less likely to wreak havoc inside libraries. Updating old HVAC units could address climate control needs for collections and equipment, as well as pandemic issues. Another aspect raised by library directors was technology infrastructure, and they would need to consider Wi-Fi and bandwidth needs that would suit their community's population. Additionally, library directors should anticipate their community's likely needs during disasters and possible ways staff and library resources can meet those needs, so a conscientious plan of action can be formulated for staff roles and responsibilities. Library leaders who want a voice in how libraries and staff will be utilized during disasters must build relationships with local emergency management leaders. Establishing relationships before emergencies strike, perhaps through joint preparedness workshops to the public, could expose those in emergency management to the information resources available at the library, both in information access and staff that are trained information specialists, and allow for opportunities to share how libraries can contribute towards community needs during disasters.

Library leaders would also benefit from using their voices through targeted public relations campaigns, sharing how they help the community in the aftermath of disasters. Many library programs encourage patrons to share experiences through their own stories or by documenting with photos, creating displays of community resilience [4]. This could be an opportunity to include the library's own stories and invite local government and community organizations to share their stories as well. An opening reception for this type of exhibit could bring more exposure, showing how those in the community rely on libraries following disaster events.

6 Conclusion

Our study explored how libraries are using the elements of disaster preparation, response, and recovery and the issues library leaders face when planning for and responding to natural disasters. Regardless of the status of their disaster plans, librarians heeded the call when needed in their communities. As disasters are more frequent in our changing climate, library leaders expressed the need to prepare their staff and create a more efficient plan that works in tandem with the local government response.

Our next steps include analyzing the submitted disaster plans to understand commonalities and differences, especially the main themes or elements of the plans. Focus groups of library directors will be conducted to conduct in-depth analyses of the elements of a plan and determine the extent to which modifications are needed based on library locale (e.g., rural versus urban libraries). We are also in the process of surveying Florida county Emergency Operations Center directors to identify perspective gaps in community disaster response.

Even without those additional insights, the research featured in this paper will inform disaster planning, facilitate the design of disaster plan workbooks, models, and COOPs, and generate new knowledge about key aspects of policy creation and implementation in disaster management that can strengthen community resiliency through Florida's essential libraries. This study is important because it emphasizes that many emergency management officials do not recognize the value libraries bring to disaster management. By formally partnering with emergency managers, library directors can clearly communicate that library staff are trained information specialists, poised to "understand the diverse community information needs of the local population and…how to best meet those needs" [28, p.2].

Acknowledgment. This research was supported, in part, by Institute for Museum and Library Services (IMLS) award LG-246371-OLS-20.

References

1. World Meteorological Organization, World Meteorological Organization (WMO). https://public.wmo.int/en/media/press-release/weather-related-disasters-increase-over-past-50-years-causing-more-damage-fewer
2. State of Florida Legislature. http://www.leg.state.fl.us/statutes/index.cfm?App_mode=Display_Statute&URL=0200-0299/0252/0252.html
3. Hahn, T.B., Weeks, A.C., Aversa, E., Barlow, D., Jaeger, P.: Strengthening the public library's role in times of crisis: a preliminary investigation. University of Maryland (2006)
4. Mardis, M.A., Jones, F.R., Tenney, C.S., Leonarczyk, Z.: Constructing knowledge about public librarians' roles in natural disasters: a heuristic inquiry into community resiliency in Florida's Hurricane Michael. Libr. Trends **69**, 768–789 (2021)
5. Society of American Archivists, SAA Dictionary: disaster plan. https://dictionary.archivists.org/entry/disaster-plan.html
6. Fagel, M.J.: Principles of Emergency Management: Hazard Specific Issues and Mitigation Strategies. CRC Press/Taylor & Francis Group (2012)
7. Leon County Public Library, Leon County. https://cms.leoncountyfl.gov/Library/LibraryInformation/Mission
8. Library, M.-D.P., Miami-Dade County. https://mdpls.org/about-us#:~:text=Our%20Mission,personal%20growth%20and%20limitless%20opportunities
9. New York Public Library, The New York Public Library. https://www.nypl.org/help/about-nypl/mission
10. Patin, B.: What is essential?: Understanding community resilience and public libraries in the United States during disasters. In: 83rd Annual Meeting of the Association for Information Science & Technology, vol. 57, no. 1, p. e269 (2020)
11. Jaeger, P.T., Bertot, J.C., McClure, C.R., Rodriguez, M.: Public libraries and internet access across the United States: a comparison by state 2004–2006. Inf. Technol. Libr. **26**, 4–14 (2007)
12. Library, C.R.P.: FEMA Recognizes Libraries as Essential Community Organizations. Cedar Rapids Public Library (2011)
13. Young, E.: The role of public libraries in disasters. New Vis. Public Aff. **10**, 31–38 (2018)
14. Bishop, B.W., Veil, S.R.: Public libraries as post-crisis information hubs. Public Libr. Q. **32**, 33–45 (2013)
15. Veil, S.R., Bishop, B.W.: Opportunities and challenges for public libraries to enhance community resilience. Risk Anal. **34**, 721–734 (2014)

16. Carnes, S.: Investigating options for increased awareness and use of disaster preparedness, response, and recovery resources among libraries and librarians (part one of a two-part series). J. Hosp. Librariansh. **18**, 115–126 (2018)
17. Smith, R.D.: Disaster recovery: problems and procedures. IFLA J. **19**, 12 (1992)
18. Morgan, G., Smith, J.G.: Disaster management in libraries: the role of a disaster plan. South Afr. J. Libr. Inf. Sci. **65**, 62–72 (1997)
19. Watkins, C.: Chapter report: disaster planning makes (dollars and) sense. Am. Libr. **27**, 9–10 (1996)
20. Kuzyk, R.: Serving through disaster: continuity planning is the new mantra in disaster planning, helping to keep key services alive. Libr. J. **132**, 26–29 (2007)
21. Hamilton, R.: The state library of Louisiana and public libraries' response to hurricanes: issues, strategies, and lessons. Public Libr. Q. **30**, 40–53 (2011)
22. Zach, L.: What do I do in an emergency? the role of public libraries in providing information during times of crisis. Sci. Technol. Libr. **30**, 404–413 (2011)
23. Silverman, R.: Toward a national disaster response protocol. Libr. Cult. Rec. **41**, 497–511 (2006)
24. Rattan, P.: Role of library and information centres in disaster management. Libr. Philos. Pract. **886**, 1–11 (2013)
25. Clareson, T., Long, J.S.: Libraries in the eye of the storm. Am. Libr. **37**, 38–41 (2006)
26. Jorgensen, C., Marty, P.F., Braun, K.: Connecting to collections in Florida: current conditions and critical needs in libraries, archives, and museums. Libr. Q. **82**, 453–476 (2012)
27. Northeast Document Conservation Center, Northeast Document Conservation Center. https://www.nedcc.org/free-resources/preservation-leaflets/3.-emergency-management/3.3-emergency-planning
28. Hagar, C.: Public library partnerships with local agencies to meet community disaster preparedness and response needs. In: ISCRAM 2015 Conference, p. 8. (2015)

Digital Experiences in Physical Spaces: Virtual Reality and Public Libraries in Aotearoa New Zealand

Katia Grodecki[1] and Anne Goulding[2]

[1] Tauranga City Libraries, Tauranga, New Zealand
[2] Victoria University of Wellington, Wellington, New Zealand
anne.goulding@vuw.ac.nz

Abstract. Presents selected results from research exploring the use and role of virtual reality (VR) in public libraries in Aotearoa New Zealand. Interviews with public library staff responsible for VR services in 9 public libraries found that digital inclusion and supporting communities' digital literacy skills and experiences were the key motivations behind the introduction of VR. The aim of attracting a more diverse user base was also presented as an important reason for adopting the technology. VR can be used for education or entertainment purposes and the libraries recognised the validity of programming covering both, although the earlier adopters were moving towards more educative and creative activities incorporating VR. Discussion of the role of the public library space for VR services highlighted its importance as a safe space for experimentation for groups with less access to technology, reinforcing its positioning as a site for digital equity within communities. It is concluded that VR can contribute to the continuing development of the public library as a participatory physical space, with co-creation and dialogic activities supported by digital technologies.

Keywords: Public libraries · Virtual reality · Immersive technology · Digital inclusion · Library space

1 Introduction

Immersive technology is changing how people consume information and media by bringing together the physical and digital worlds. Virtual reality (VR) specifically has experienced rapid growth over the last decade as head-mounted consoles and controls have become more widely available and more affordable [1]. With the use of a stand-alone headset or a headset connected to a computer or game console, we are invited into a virtual world that immerses us in experiences such as games, roller coaster rides, museum visits, or explorations of travel destinations. Although the gaming and entertainment purposes of VR have dominated discussions of the technology, VR also offers opportunities for formal and informal learning and, in this capacity, has been introduced into educational institutions and their libraries [2].

I. Sserwanga et al. (Eds.): iConference 2023, LNCS 13972, pp. 157–170, 2023.
https://doi.org/10.1007/978-3-031-28032-0_13

Previous research into the use of VR in libraries has focused primarily on its application in academic libraries and has explored the challenges and opportunities of the technology and perceptions of library staff and users [3–5]. Discussion of the use of VR in public libraries is less common but public libraries internationally and in Aotearoa New Zealand have introduced VR programming in recent years [6, 7], indicating a growing recognition of its potential for drawing in new audiences and enhancing educational programs. The grounds for the inclusion of VR programs in public libraries lie in their learning remit, open safe spaces, and their role in supporting community-based digital inclusion. Libraries today are focused on making connections [8] - connecting people with each other as well as with ideas, knowledge, and creativity, increasingly through technology. Digital technologies now play a vital role in people's learning experiences, and, for many, the public library is the only free, open, public space where they can encounter and experiment with new technology to support their learning.

The introduction of VR into public libraries fits with the public library mission of supporting community access to technology and widening learning experiences but successful implementation of the technology requires more in-depth knowledge of why and how public libraries are using VR than that currently available in the research literature. The use of VR has been little researched in the public library context and we lack a clear understanding of its role in supporting the public library's purpose within communities and its impact on the library or community. Clarity on the motivations behind public libraries' introduction of VR, the aims of their programming around VR, and indications of future plans for the technology will provide insights for other public library services considering adopting VR, including effective practice in its implementation and any potential challenges to consider. Drawing on research undertaken for a master's research project [9], this paper explores the intersection of digital technology and physical space within public libraries in Aotearoa New Zealand and addresses the following research questions:

– RQ 1: What are the motives behind the introduction and implementation of VR in Aotearoa New Zealand's public libraries?
– RQ 2: How is VR used in Aotearoa New Zealand's public libraries?

2 Literature Review

The literature on VR in libraries focuses primarily on academic libraries, with some mention of public libraries. Before reviewing some of the studies, though, it is important to have some background on the educational uses of VR as this is often the motivation for introducing the technology into libraries.

2.1 VR and Learning

VR is continuing to undergo testing in the study of such subjects as biology, anatomy, and archaeology, allowing learners to study 3D models in VR instead of using more traditional online platforms [10–12]. In addition to formal learning opportunities, there are also examples of community-based learning using VR, such as learning to understand dementia through first-person interactive virtual experiences [13], immersive learning and therapy for neurodiversity [14, 15], or with visual art sessions for stroke rehabilitation [16]. Many participants in studies of both formal and informal learning using VR found their experiences entertaining and engaging because of their perception of the experiences as realistic [10, 17] and this can be motivating for participants. Game-based learning programs can inspire students by setting new challenges for their progress through interactive incentives [12] and while the entertainment and educational values of VR might appear to be competing against each other, gamification generally is considered to have positive engagement capabilities for learners [18, 19]. Gamification through VR can be employed to engage those in formal learning situations in schools and universities and also those participating in more informal learning experiences in spaces such as museums [20] and libraries [21].

2.2 VR in Libraries

Although the learning potential of VR is clear, the motivation behind the implementation of VR in libraries, and specifically public libraries, is primarily to offer users access to popular technology. Massis [22] suggests that VR is a tool for teaching library users about information literacy while encouraging and supporting engagement with new technology. With this approach, Massis [22] argues that VR in libraries uses a hybrid of entertaining content, the goal of which is primarily educational. However, subsequent studies by other authors conclude that educational opportunities with VR are often not the main target for library users; instead, users engage with VR in an exploratory manner [3, 4]. Since VR can be used for both educational and entertainment purposes, the two applications can be seen as drastically different or complementary, depending on the strategy of the implementing library. In their study of VR use by university students, Frost et al. [23] found that the majority were interested in extracurricular uses of VR but suggested that library staff should collaborate with faculty to help students engage with the technology to enhance their academic experiences too. Sample [24] and Valenti et al. [25] found that new students' anxiety declined following a virtual tour and orientation program respectively, indicating that VR can engage students and provide valuable learning experiences.

Conventional learning-focused uses of VR may not be directly applicable to public libraries, and there may be implications for the types of learning-focused content that can be developed and offered as part of public libraries' educational programs and services to their user communities [26, 27]. While an education focus would fit the mandate of an academic or school library, public libraries might take a more relaxed approach toward VR that, nonetheless, supports their overall digital strategy. The aim of the libraries in implementing VR may be to merely allow users to engage with the technology without a specific agenda. There could be obstacles to that engagement in the community, however. Dahya et al. [28] found that users within that community felt that VR platforms do not feature enough visible diversity to reflect the user community and suggested that this could be off-putting for some. A more targeted approach may be more successful such as that described by Hall [29] who discusses a VR program used as a learning tool for veterans and seniors in California. The program encouraged participants to share personal memories from their past travels after immersing themselves in a virtual travel experience. This storytelling-based approach, delivering a specialized program to a distinct group of users, offers a different framework for delivering learning-based VR that appeals to users' interests. It is important to consider, however, the challenge of meeting the needs of the numerous demographic groups who use the public library. While Hall [29] presents a case where a specifically designed outreach program brought VR into the community and presented carefully selected content for a niche group, public libraries may find it a challenge to engage a diverse user base while also striving to address the unique needs of different groups through access to digital technologies [27]. This issue was explored in the research reported here as part of a study exploring Aotearoa New Zealand public library experiences of introducing VR and lessons learnt in its implementation.

3 Method

An environmental scan was undertaken to identify public libraries in Aotearoa New Zealand providing VR services. The websites and social media pages of all public library services in Aotearoa New Zealand were searched and the results showed that, in late February 2022, 15 public library services offered VR. A qualitative approach was taken, and semi-structured interviews were the main data-gathering technique with the aim of allowing participants to share the unique stories behind the development of VR programs and their experiences of implementing VR in their libraries. A combination of purposive and convenience sampling resulted in interviews with nine participants. Having identified libraries with VR services, those managing the VR programs in all 15 libraries were invited to participate in an interview and nine responded positively. All interviews were via Zoom and were recorded. All data relating to the individual and participating libraries were de-identified to protect the confidentiality of participants and their organizations. The participants were asked questions about the introduction of VR, any user groups prioritized, programs offered, challenges faced, the role of VR within the library's digital strategy and their experiences of implementing VR. The interviews were transcribed and NVivo 12 was used to assign inductive codes aligning with the research questions. The codes were then organized into themes relevant to the research objectives and questions as well as reflecting additional topics arising during the interviews [30, 31].

4 Findings

Table 1 presents an overview of the provision of VR in the participating libraries at the time the research was undertaken (early 2022). All the libraries adopted VR technology between 2016 and 2020 with two introducing it very soon before the start of the COVID-19 pandemic in early 2020.

Table 1. VR provision in participating libraries

	Date of Interview	Date Introduced	Number of Headsets	Type(s) of Headset(s)	Methods of VR programme delivery						Age limit
					Lending	In-library daytime programmes	After-school and school holidays	Special events	Community outreach in schools and rest homes	Room booking	
Library 1	15/03/2022	about 2019	5	3 Oculus Quest 2 used within the library; 2 Oculus Quest for lending	Yes	No	Yes	Yes	Yes	No	8+
Library 2	21/03/2022	2020	1	Oculus Quest 2	No	Yes	Yes	Planned	Planned	Planned	13+
Library 3	21/03/2022	2020	1	Oculus Quest	No	Yes	Yes	Yes	Yes	No	None
Library 4	21/03/2022	about 2019	2	HTC VIVE; Oculus Quest	No	No	Yes	Yes	No	No	None
Library 5	21/03/2022	about 2017	1	PlayStation 4 VR	No	No	Yes	Yes	Yes	Yes	12+
Library 6	22/03/2022	2016-2017	2	Playstation VR; HTC VIVE	No	No	Yes	Yes	No	Trialled briefly	None
Library 7	24/03/2022	2019-2020	6	4 Oculus Quest; 1 Quest 2; 1 Quest Go	No	No	Yes	Yes	Yes	No	13+
Library 8	4/4/2022	2018-2019	2 + classroom set	Oculus Quest; HTC Vive; cardboard VR classroom set	No	Yes	Yes	Yes	Yes	No	12+
Library 9	19/04/2022	2017-2018	4 + classroom set	3 HTC VIVE; 1 PlayStation VR; Blake NZ-VR classroom set	No	Yes	Yes	Yes	Yes	No	12+

4.1 Aims and Uses of VR in Libraries

In response to RQ1, the analysis found that all the participants highlighted digital inclusion as the motivation behind the adoption of VR with the aim of making more technology available and promoting digital literacy within the community. Librarian 7 linked this with the Māori concept of kaupapa – "principles and ideas which act as a base or foundation for action" [32], in this case, the strategy or policy of providing collective community resources:

> It was introduced with the intent of offering an upper form of digital experience. We're incredibly focused on accessibility and removing as many barriers to using and participating in digital stuff as possible. Many people can't afford VR sets or might be intrigued by the technology but have no other way to interact with it. So, we invest in that on behalf of our community so they will have those opportunities. It links to a wider kaupapa around extending the thinking around why libraries have collections in the first place. If you think about a community as able to afford a much larger, richer collection by pulling all their money together through their rates, they can then collectively afford the resources, like books. If you extend your thinking, it can apply to all manner of things, like VR, 3D printers for their community, PlayStation 5. All those kinds of things that individual families might not be able to afford on their own.

The positioning of the library as a collective, community good is evident in the participant's words as is the promotion of the role of the library in extending digital opportunities to those who may not otherwise be able to access them.

Another aim of VR evident in the participants' responses was to attract more and a wider cross-section of local people to the library. The argument that VR can be a good strategy to draw teens, particularly, into the library space and introduce them to the other services and programs offered was often made by participants. Librarian 2 said:

That was a big point for me because … teens' usage is a big struggle for us. Something like [VR] was a great way to draw them into the library and then once they're kind of familiar with using the library then next you start going, "Hey, you know we've got these other programs that are going on. Do you want to take part in it next?"

Conversely, Librarian 5, who worked primarily with teens in her role, spoke about VR as a valuable program in its own right, rather than a gateway to other library services, saying that it is important to learn about the teens' patterns with the access and use of the library and to work to meet their needs. While some of the libraries expressed an agenda to use VR as an introduction to other programs and services, therefore, others promoted VR because of its merits as an interesting technology offered by the library. Librarian 8 commented that VR for teens in Library 8's youth space offered teens variety within the library and helped to promote it as a safe space for them. Three participants also emphasized the benefits of VR for users who are neurodiverse or have physical disabilities. They had worked with users with autism or dementia, as well as those who use wheelchairs, to assist them with accessing travel experiences through VR.

Although VR was considered by all participants as a way of attracting new users to the library, its success in this regard was also questioned. None of the participating libraries kept statistics on how frequently users returned to the library specifically for VR programs, but the participants commented that most of their users did not tend to return to the library for that purpose. According to Librarian 4:

We do have a few frequent [users] who like to enjoy it. There is a guy who is doing one of the design programs. He's getting quite good with the software and is starting to be able to design stuff, but the vast majority are a one-hit-wonder. They come in; they try it. Sometimes the kids tend to come back, but not over and over and over again.

Despite this, all the participants said that VR continued to attract new users to the library and had become an effective promotional tool. Three of the participating libraries that were early adopters of VR suggested that there is a wide potential to explore the educational aspect of VR and had plans to teach users how to design games and experiences using the technology, enabling users to generate content that reflected their interests and experiences.

VR offers an immersive digital experience but still requires sufficient physical space to enable users to move safely, a point emphasized by all participants. Furniture was also required for older users or those who chose to sit while using the technology. In libraries without a dedicated VR room, participants said that the staff isolated the playing area, using bollards or ropes, to prevent others from walking through the space while the VR is in use. This raises the issue of how digital technologies impact the physical space of the library, fellow library users and the other services and activities within the library building.

Aside from programming in the library, a range of outreach programs was also offered by the participating libraries. Taking the VR equipment out to schools was common, particularly in remote areas, to introduce the technology to students who may rarely come to the library and are therefore unaware of the range of facilities and programs offered. 5 participants had also used VR at local events to promote the library more generally, indicating that VR can work as a stand-alone attraction to bring people into the library. Before COVID-19, several of the participating libraries offered VR via community outreach as well as in the library by visiting schools or rest homes and they would also take their VR to special events, such as festivals, to showcase the technology. In addition, community groups sometimes collaborated with the library using VR. According to Librarian 4: "I've done some work with a local lady who was doing a study on people with dementia and using VR with them and they actually created a VR simulator for them to use." Librarian 4 described a project with migrants in the community: "We also had a group of migrant women come in. We've done things with them with Google Earth, so they can go back and check out their hometowns and they show it on the big screen to show people where they came from". These examples show that while VR can be a novelty and entertainment for some users, there is also educational value in the technology.

4.2 Entertainment Versus Education

Returning to the discussion of gaming versus education uses of VR outlined in the literature review, participants explained that they worked to provide a balanced blend of entertainment-focused and educational VR experiences. An age-related distinction was evident; while older adults largely tended to use VR for informal learning armchair-style expeditions, younger users often received their first introduction to VR via games. Seven of the participants said that they sought to promote the educational aspects of the technology, particularly when visiting schools as noted by Librarian 1:

We have conversations with the teachers and ask about what they cover over the term. We had one school that was learning about the pyramids, so we used a VR headset and the app Wander to go over the pyramids and actually see them. We had one where they were doing underwater and the ocean [using] an app called Ocean Rift that allows you to experience different sea creatures.

Library 1's after-school and school holiday VR programs were more relaxed, however, aiming to introduce users to the technology without a strict curriculum-based agenda. Following such introductions, Librarian 1 was planning for the next steps with VR, which would allow the users to learn about design: "I think now that they've done quite a bit of the programmes, our next step will be to change it up a little bit, maybe do some virtual reality design".

There was some discussion about the educational value of gaming. For example, Librarian 3 suggested that, to a certain extent, many experiences on VR constitute education through gamification; whether playing a game or exploring an app that teaches the user about human anatomy, the user receives an introduction to a new technology:

Although it is gamification, it is learning how to use the navigation. A new thing that came out a year or two ago was hand tracking. Before it was all [about using] controls and now you can navigate by pinching. There are a couple of games that are games but they're for learning how to navigate the system, so that was the great thing for (users), that they pick up the ball and put it on fire but they're learning navigation to get around.

Librarian 8 also said that she worked with the local schools to explain to the teachers the merits of VR. "Many of them thought, at first, that it's just for gaming," she said, explaining that she is not opposed to gaming because it, too, offers education opportunities: "I strongly advocate for gaming because I know there is a lot of negativity. I have talked to the media class at the local college and we talk about the story aspect of gaming and the narrative aspect. It can be quite a valuable experience as well if you highlight it". Library 9, which was one of the first to introduce VR in 2017, was trialling a partnership with BLAKE NZ-VR, an organization that works with schools to offer VR-based programs that educate students about nature conservation and sustainability. Like the other libraries, Library 9 was planning to move beyond the initial introduction of VR as entertainment toward specific educational programs. According to Librarian 9:

Now we're getting more experience in terms of what software and platforms we can use. I think we're moving toward more structured educational VR, but we're still at the entertainment side and even our programs are just dipping their toes in. It's just having the time to design that kind of programming.

Librarian 9 was also working with local Pasifika (Pacific Islands peoples) communities to address the existing disparities between the Pākehā (New Zealanders of European ancestry) and the Māori and Pasifika communities in STEM careers. With a friend, Librarian 9 had established a privately funded trust for STEM-focused education for isolated Pasifika communities in the region. The aim is to create a more inclusive environment by working intensively with the communities of users for whom access to the library and its resources presents a challenge due to prohibitive geographical distances and socioeconomic and cultural factors. Librarian 9 explained that it is important for libraries to learn about the needs of the Māori and Pasifika communities and to teach the children in those communities about the prospects of STEM careers:

Just having access and creating a space where it's safe for whole families to play with technology, normalize the use of it, and make it not scary has a massive benefit. I always see a huge sense of pride in the kids when they teach their parents how to use technology. That confidence with tech and knowing that it's not a space that they can't be a part of is always a massive driver for me personally. That extends out to the whole community, but definitely those communities that don't see technology as a career path. It's really massive to make sure that they have access to [STEM education] and that they feel confident and have a good learning space for that.

Librarian 9's emphasis on the need for safe, welcoming spaces for disadvantaged groups to experience technology is an important one, discussed further below.

5 Discussion

All the participating libraries offered a variety of games and exploratory experiences to their users through their VR programs, and although the majority do not prioritize specific user groups, making the technology available to everyone, they have programs designed specifically for teens, seniors and other groups within their communities. One of the commonly mentioned motives for the introduction of VR in libraries was to attract non-users (primarily teens) into the library space. The libraries would typically reach teens and seniors through in-house programs and digitally inclusive outreach by travelling to schools and rest homes, especially in remote areas where people might not otherwise have access to library services and programs [27]. The focus on programs for teens and seniors allows the participating libraries to choose a variety of VR experiences for those groups. The libraries offer those users an opportunity to learn about the technology, as well as its capabilities but some of the participating libraries are starting to consider the next steps to direct their work with the technology toward programs focused more closely on the educational applications of VR, specifically in working with schools. Without data from the participating libraries regarding returning users and their perceptions of the technology and related experiences, it is challenging to understand the next steps that the libraries could take to harness VR beyond the purposes of mere introduction to the technology, however. The importance of evaluating library programs and services to improve and develop them has been emphasized in the literature [33].

Initiatives that identify a specific challenge and highlight a discrepancy between the needs of a community group and the programs offered by the library are particularly important to consider in any evaluation activities. Hartnett et al. [27] discuss the perception of public libraries as inclusive communities that are working actively to address the challenges of the digital divide. In this research, Librarian 9 spoke about bringing STEM-focused educational programming to Pasifika groups, while other libraries reached schools and remote communities via mobile vehicles. The important role that public libraries play in extending opportunities for digital engagement to specific groups who may not have had extensive experience with technology [34, 35] is evidenced again in this research. For those with limited income, libraries can open up access to new technologies by making them available for collective use as noted by Librarian 9, with one study finding that the greatest demand for gaming programs in public libraries came from low-income communities [36].

Another important point here is that those in low-income households may not only lack the funds to purchase new technologies but also the space in which to experiment. The participants in this study often highlighted the need for adequate space for VR, unlikely to be available in all homes. The provision of VR services in libraries gives users the space to play and be creative that they may lack elsewhere and use technology that has physical as well as digital attributes. The impact of digital technologies on library spaces has been considered previously, often focused on the development of the information or learning commons in academic institutions [37]. In public libraries, Crawford Barniskis [38] explored the spatial arrangements of makerspaces, noting that the arrangements made for the provision of library services and programs indicate the prioritization of certain groups or activities and Black and Pepper [39] have discussed how technology has changed library architecture but there has been little consideration of how internal spaces in the public library, and people's use of these, is impacted by the integration of digital technologies like VR and associated programming and this would be an interesting avenue for future studies on the topic.

One promising avenue for the development of programs may draw on the ideas presented by Dahya et al. [28] and Ellern and Cruz [40] who discuss VR content creation, either by the libraries themselves or by their users. As public libraries are increasingly positioned as participatory community organizations [41], they are seeking new ways to engage local people as active participants and facilitate connections around ideas and content. By supporting users' content creation, libraries will be helping local communities share their stories and providing them with digital skills at the same time. The physical public library space can play an important role as a site for digital participatory practice, supporting users' technology learning and also opening up dialogue with those the library may otherwise find hard to reach. This would also support users' creativity. The role of public libraries as creative spaces has been a developing trend in the last decade or so [42] representing a shift in emphasis from content provision to content production, and inspiring users' creativity [43]. In this respect, VR content creation can be considered part of the developments that brought makerspaces and fab labs into public libraries.

Much is made of the tension between the educational and entertainment purposes of VR but the findings of this study suggest that they are not dichotomous but complementary. The participants recognized the value of learning through play in line with research showing that gaming can develop multiple literacies [36], and support creativity and experimentation [44]. Video games have been shown to have a host of educational benefits. They can increase general knowledge and promote skills like teamwork, leadership, problem-solving [36, 45], pattern recognition, spatial reasoning [46], critical thinking [36], and perseverance [47]. Gaming has been found to be a good way into technology for those with limited skills because it is less daunting to play technology-based games than to learn to use a computer [36] and VR has the potential to develop similar skills and competencies as users work alone or with others to progress through apps and games. Participants in this study confirmed that their VR services and programs developed important ICT skills as well as collaborative and problem-solving skills. Ultimately, the participants' comments emphasized that public libraries provide resources for learning *and* leisure and VR programs support both.

Librarian 9 talked of the importance of a safe, welcoming space for disadvantaged groups to experiment with technology, suggesting that the public library can be successful in this regard. Libraries are recognized as key spaces for digital inclusion where librarians regularly support users with their digital needs and activities [27]. A motivation to develop further technology-based programs was evident in participants' responses, both to excite people about digital technologies and to encourage a more diverse user group into the library space. While there is some evidence that users who attend technology-based programs will interact with other library services [36, 49, 50], further research is required to evidence a clear link. In any case, VR provision should arguably be supported as a valuable service in its own right rather than as a way of increasing the use of others, as emphasized by some participants in this study. Perhaps more important is the impact on the image of the library that the introduction of technologies like VR can have. The positioning of the library as a vibrant community space that welcomes groups of people to meet and interact around technology may encourage greater use alongside enhanced community connections and dialogue.

To summarize the response to the research question, for RQ 1, the motives behind the introduction and implementation of VR in public libraries in Aotearoa New Zealand focused on offering library users a variety of equitable digital opportunities and attracting a wider audience into the libraries, including teens. RQ 2 focuses on how VR has been implemented in the responding public libraries. The analysis shows that VR services are offered both in the library space and via community outreach to schools and seniors in care homes. The subject of VR for entertainment and/or educational purposes is relevant to both research questions. Although younger audiences have been primarily interested in using VR for entertainment, opportunities exist for education through gamification, and some libraries have begun exploring the prospect of teaching their users how to design experiences for VR.

6 Limitations and Future Research

Although the nine participating libraries formed an effective sample for a project of this scope and nature, a larger sample would have provided additional and more diverse data and it would have been interesting to explore the experiences and plans of more libraries offering VR services. The research data would have been further enriched by capturing users' experiences too, focusing on their perceptions of the technology, the available content, and the role of VR within the library. Furthermore, by observing the libraries' VR users, we would gain a better understanding of behaviors with the technology in the library. Such insights would help to inform the libraries' evaluation of their VR programs and plans for future implementation. While outside the scope of this project, there is potential for user studies in the future including community perspectives on the integration of technology like VR into the library space. Research focusing on how digital technologies shape library spaces and patrons' behavior and how digital and physical spaces interact with one another in the public library would provide a greater depth of understanding of digital-physical dynamics in public libraries.

7 Conclusion

This research contributes to the body of knowledge on how public libraries and their spaces support digital inclusion in communities which continues to be a key agenda for libraries. The evidence presented in this paper indicates that it was driving much of the implementation of VR services in the participating public libraries as well as participants' ideas for future developments using the technology. VR content creation programs run by the libraries would position the libraries as active players in community-based digital skills initiatives, and the dialogic potential of VR would also strengthen their co-creation and community participation activities. Although VR presents users with virtual representations of worlds and places, their interactions with these digital spaces take place within a physical location, usually the library itself, connecting them with the library, its services and other users within the space. This blending of physical and digital environments, sometimes termed "phygital" [51], has been discussed previously in light of public library developments during COVID-19 [52] and has generally referred to people accessing digital public library services from their homes. With VR services, however, public libraries are supporting people's experiences of virtual places within a familiar physical space. The physical and digital convergence provided by VR offers libraries opportunities to become more participatory and engaged with communities and groups beyond their usual clientele and offers library users the chance to have new digital experiences within a trusted, safe physical environment.

References

1. Grand View Research: Virtual reality market size, share & trends analysis. https://www.gra ndviewresearch.com/industry-analysis/virtual-reality-vr-market

2. Grant, C.R., Rhind-Tutt, S.: Is your library ready for the reality of virtual reality? What you need to know and why it belongs in your library. In: Proceedings of the Charleston Library Conference (2018). https://doi.org/10.5703/1288284317070

3. Cook, M., et al.: Challenges and strategies for educational virtual reality. Inf. Technol. Libr. **38**(4), 25–48 (2019). https://doi.org/10.6017/ital.v38i4.11075

4. Greene, D., Groenendyk, M.: An environmental scan of virtual and augmented reality services in academic libraries. Libr. Hi Tech **39**(1), 37–47 (2021). https://doi.org/10.1108/LHT-08-2019-0166

5. Suen, R.L.T., Chiu, D.K.W., Tang, J.K.T.: Virtual reality services in academic libraries: deployment experience in Hong Kong. Electron. Libr. **38**(4), 843–858 (2020). https://doi.org/10.1108/EL-05-2020-0116

6. Ranford, C.: Virtual reality to become reality at Marlborough libraries. Stuff (2021). https://www.stuff.co.nz/national/politics/local-democracy-reporting/300311176/vir tual-reality-to-become-reality-at-marlborough-libraries. Accessed 2 Sept 2022

7. Selwyn Libraries - Virtual Reality. Selwyn Libraries. https://www.selwynlibraries.co.nz/ whats-on/virtual-reality. Accessed 2 Sept 2022

8. Lankes, R.D., Silverstein, J., Nicholson, S.: Participatory networks: the library as conversation. Inf. Technol. Libr. **26**(4), 17–33 (2007)

9. Author (2020)

10. Erolin, C., Reid, L., McDougall, S.: Using virtual reality to complement and enhance anatomy education. J. Vis. Commun. Med. **42**(3), 93–101 (2019). https://doi.org/10.1080/17453054.2019.1597626

11. Education Gazette editors: Real-world opportunities with virtual reality. Aotearoa New Zealand Educ. Gazette **100**(7), 32–36 (2021). https://gazette.education.govt.nz/articles/real-world-opportunities-with-virtual-reality/. Accessed 2 Sept 2022

12. Shackelford, L., Huang, W.D., Craig, A., Merrill, C., Chen, D.: Relationships between motivational support and game features in a game-based virtual reality learning environment for teaching introductory archaeology. EMI Educ. Media Int. **56**(3), 183–200 (2019). https://doi.org/10.1080/09523987.2019.1669946

13. Sari, D.W., et al.: Virtual reality program to develop dementia-friendly communities in Japan. Australas. J. Ageing **39**(3), e352–e359 (2020). https://doi.org/10.1111/ajag.12797

14. Boyd, L.E., Day, K., Stewart, N., Abdo, K., Lamkin, K., Linstead, E.J.: Leveling the playing field: supporting neurodiversity via virtual realities. Technol. Innov. **20**(1), 105–116 (2018). https://doi.org/10.21300/20.1-2.2018.105

15. Soccini, A.M., Cuccurullo, S.A.G., Cena, F.: Virtual reality experiential training for individuals with autism: the airport scenario. In: Bourdot, P., Interrante, V., Kopper, R., Olivier, A.-H., Saito, H., Zachmann, G. (eds.) EuroVR 2020. LNCS, vol. 12499, pp. 234–239. Springer, Cham (2020). https://doi.org/10.1007/978-3-030-62655-6_16

16. Marylyn, A., Wünsche, B.C., Lottridge, D.: Virtual reality art-making for stroke rehabilitation: field study and technology probe. Int. J. Hum. Comput. Stud. **145**, 102481 (2021). https://doi.org/10.1016/j.ijhcs.2020.102481

17. Gorman, D., Hoermann, S., Lindeman, R.W., Shahri, B.: Using virtual reality to enhance food technology education. Int. J. Technol. Des. Educ. 1–19 (2021). https://doi.org/10.1007/s10798-021-09669-3

18. Lo, C.K., Hew, K.F.: A comparison of flipped learning with gamification, traditional learning, and online independent study: the effects on students' mathematics achievement and cognitive engagement. Interact. Learn. Environ. **28**(4), 464–481 (2018). https://doi.org/10.1080/10494820.2018.1541910

19. Park, S., Kim, S.: Is sustainable online learning possible with gamification?—the effect of gamified online learning on student learning. Sustainability **13**(8), 4267 (2021). https://doi.org/10.3390/su13084267

20. Nofal, E., Panagiotidou, G., Reffat, R.M., Hameeuw, H., Boschloos, V., Moere, A.V.: Situated tangible gamification of heritage for supporting collaborative learning of young museum visitors. J. Comput. Cultural Heritage **13**(1), 1 (2020). https://doi.org/10.1145/3350427

21. Degiorgis, D., et al.: The impact of Virtual Reality (VR), social media and gamification on learner engagement: re-imagining an online study space for university students. In: EDULEARN22 Proceedings, pp. 9198–9204 (2020). IATED. https://doi.org/10.21125/edulearn.2022.2206

22. Massis, B.: Using virtual and augmented reality in the library. New Libr. World **116**(11/12), 796–799 (2015). https://doi.org/10.1108/NLW-08-2015-0054

23. Frost, M., Goates, M., Cheng, S., Johnston, J.: Virtual reality: a survey of use at an academic library. Inf. Technol. Libr. **39**(1), 1–12 (2020). https://doi.org/10.6017/ital.v39i1.11369

24. Sample, A.: Using augmented and virtual reality in information literacy instruction to reduce library anxiety in nontraditional and international students. Inf. Technol. Libr. **39**(1), 1–29 (2020). https://doi.org/10.6017/ital.v39i1.11723

25. Valenti, S., Lund, B., Wang, T.: Virtual reality as a tool for student orientation in distance education programs: a study of new library and information science students. Inf. Technol. Libr. **39**(2), 1–12 (2020). https://doi.org/10.6017/ital.v39i2.11937

26. Bertot, J.C., Real, B., Jaeger, P.T.: Public libraries building digital inclusive communities: data and findings from the 2013 Digital Inclusion Survey. Libr. Q. **86**(3), 270–289 (2016). https://doi.org/10.1086/686674

27. Hartnett, M., Butler, P., Mentis, M., Carvalho, L., Kearney, A.: Public libraries as spaces for digital inclusion: connecting communities through technology. Institute of Education, Massey University (2020). https://www.librariesaotearoa.org.nz/public-libraries-as-spaces-for-digital-inclusion.html. Accessed 3 Sept 2022

28. Dahya, N., King, W.E., Lee, K.J., Lee, J.H.: Perceptions and experiences of virtual reality in public libraries. J. Doc. **77**(3), 617–637 (2021). https://doi.org/10.1108/JD-04-2020-0051

29. Hall, J.: Journey with veterans: virtual reality program using google expeditions. Inf. Technol. Libr. **39**(4), 1–3 (2020). https://doi.org/10.6017/ital.v39i4.12857

30. Nowell, L.S., Norris, J.M., White, D.E., Moules, N.J.: Thematic analysis: striving to meet the trustworthiness criteria. Int. J. Qual. Methods **16**(1), 1–13 (2017). https://doi.org/10.1177/1609406917733847

31. Ormrod, J. E., Leedy, P. D.: Practical Research: Planning and Design, 12th edn. Pearson Education (2020)

32. Te Ahukaramū Charles Royal: 'Papatūānuku – the land - Whakapapa and kaupapa', Te Ara - the Encyclopedia of New Zealand. http://www.TeAra.govt.nz/en/papatuanuku-the-land/page-8

33. Goulding, A: Storytelling for the evaluation of GLAM programmes and services. In: Haddow. G., White, H. (eds.) Assessment as Information Practice, pp. 29–52. Routledge (2021)

34. Casselden, B.: Not like riding a bike: How public libraries facilitate older people's digital inclusion during the Covid-19 pandemic. J. Librariansh. Inf. Sci. (2022)

35. Gustafsson, M., Wihlborg, E.: 'It is unbelievable how many come to us': a study on community librarians' perspectives on digital inclusion in Sweden. J. Commun. Inform. **17**, 26–45 (2021)

36. Levine, J.: Gaming and libraries update: broadening the intersections. Library Technol. Report. **44**(3) (2008)

37. Oliveira, S.M.: Trends in academic library space: from book boxes to learning commons. Open Inform. Sci. **2**(1), 59–74 (2018)

38. Crawford Barniskis, S.: Creating space: the impacts of spatial arrangements in public library makerspaces (2016). http://library.ifla.org/1384/

39. Black, A., Pepper, S.: From civic place to digital space: the design of public libraries in Britain from past to present. Libr. Trends **61**(2), 440–470 (2012)

40. Ellern, G.D., Cruz, L.: Black, white, and grey: the wicked problem of virtual reality in libraries. Inf. Technol. Libr. **40**(4) (2021). https://doi.org/10.6017/ital.v40i4.12915

41. Rasmussen, C.H.: The participatory public library: the Nordic experience. New Libr. World **117**(9/10), 546–556 (2016). https://doi.org/10.1108/NLW-04-2016-0031

42. Boyle, E., Collins, M., Kinsey, R., Noonan, C., Pocock, A.: Making the case for creative spaces in Australian libraries. Aust. Libr. J. **65**(1), 30–40 (2016). https://doi.org/10.1080/00049670.2016.1125756

43. Nicholson, K.: Collaborative, creative, participative: trends in public library innovation. Public Libr. Q. **38**(3), 331–347 (2019). https://doi.org/10.1080/01616846.2019.1571399

44. Adams, S.: The case for video games in libraries. Libr. Rev. **58**(3), 196–202 (2009)

45. Gumulak, S., Webber, S.: Playing video games: learning and information literacy. Aslib Proc. New Inform. Perspect. **63**(2/3), 241–255 (2011)

46. Neiburger, E., Gullett, M.: Out of the basement: the social side of gaming. Young Adult Library Serv. **5**(2), 34–36, 38 (2007)

47. Winner, M.: Why video games matter. Libr. Media Connect. **33**(5), 36–37 (2015)

48. Hunter, C.: The Minecraft craze at the public library. Public Libraries Online (2014). http://publiclibrariesonline.org/2014/05/the-minecraft-craze-at-the-public-library/

49. McNicol, S.: The shape and state of gaming in UK libraries. Libr. Inf. Res. **35**(110), 50–64 (2011)

50. Nicholson, S.: Library gaming census report (2009). https://scottnicholson.com/pubs/CensusReport2007ALA.pdf

51. Ballina, F.J., Valdes, L., Del Valle, E.: The physical experience in the smart tourism destination. Int. J. Tour. Cities **5**(4), 656–671 (2019)

52. Reid, P.H., Mesjar, L.: "Bloody amazing really": voices from Scotland's public libraries in lockdown. J. Doc. (2022). https://doi.org/10.1108/JD-03-2022-0067

What Do We Do with the Fruits of Open Educational Practices? A Case for Open Educational Collections

Diana Daly(✉) (iD)

University of Arizona, Tucson, AZ 85721, USA
didaly@arizona.edu

Abstract. In this article perspectives are offered by an instructor, author, and researcher involved in the open textbook *Humans R Social Media* and resulting OEC (Open Educational Collection) developed at a large southwestern university. The iVoices OEC is described as the unplanned fruit of teaching in connection with Open Educational Practices (OEP). OECs in general are discussed as logical outcomes of pedagogical theories including open pedagogy in general, and the theories of Funds of Knowledge and Universal Design for Learning as well as user privacy protection strategies. Lessons learned are offered as recommendations for planning future OEPs and OECs including changes in memoranda language, budgeting for collection management assistance, and clearer partnerships with institutional repositories. This case study of an open textbook and accompanying OEC is offered to deepen understanding of open pedagogy in praxis.

Keywords: Open educational collections · Open pedagogy · Open educational practices · Open textbooks · Funds of knowledge · Universal design for learning

1 Introduction

A growing body of work supports the value of open pedagogy and Open Educational Practices (OEP), but less work has focused on the collections of student content that can result from such practices. This article lays out implementation of an instructor-designed, multimodal open textbook project, and then management of the unplanned Open Educational Collection (OEC) of personal student stories about technologies it produced. Lessons learned are offered as a model for planning future OECs including changes in memoranda language, budgeting for collection management assistance, and partnerships with institutional repositories. This case study of the open textbook *Humans R Social Media* [6] and multimedia OEC iVoices [15] respectively first published in May and October 2021 respectively, and in continuous production through spring 2023 is offered to deepen understanding of open pedagogy in praxis.

2 Conceptual Framework

Humans R Social Media or *HRSM* is a textbook originally produced for a large general education course on social media, then developed into a multiyear project designed

I. Sserwanga et al. (Eds.): iConference 2023, LNCS 13972, pp. 171–179, 2023.
https://doi.org/10.1007/978-3-031-28032-0_14

following the principles of open pedagogy [9, 16]. Beginning in Fall 2020, students in the course for which *HRSM* was created by this author were trained in storytelling and media production. They were first invited to present their identities and experiences with social technologies, then to openly license the content they created for integration in the textbook. Such practices of creation and use of Open Educational Resources (OER) have been framed as Open Educational Practices or OEP [2, 7]. The groundwork for these open culture frameworks in education has been built in part through the growth of participatory cultures online [11], seeded by active user approaches to Web 2.0 sites inviting user participation in creation of video, audio, and graphical content. OEP like those in *HRSM* cultivate student agency through enabling student participation not only as learners, but as creators of course content in the media modalities that increasingly characterize the social networking landscape.

iVoices was designed with pedagogical theories at its foundation, as well as user privacy protection measures documented by new media scholars. First, the project was intended to activate critical "Funds of Knowledge" [8, 13] students have around personal and group uses of technologies at home and among peers, knowledge they can share through stories they tell and creative work they produce around new technologies in their lives. Channeling of such content in this project is a manifestation of the collective value of experiences with technologies formed within the contexts of families, communities, and cultures. Additionally, this project was designed toward Universal Design for Learning [14], offering flexibility in instructional content modality and practices with the understanding that accessibility for specific populations would benefit learners more broadly. Finally, user privacy protection strategies were observed by researchers [10] including "white-walling" [1], migrating student content out of the environments where it was created to remove digital traces of identity not intended for sharing.

3 Initiation of the iVoices Project

In Fall of 2020, iVoices Student Media Lab was launched at a large, southwestern university in the United States. The project was initiated by the author with support from an institutional fellowship funding education-based scholarship. The author had previously taught a large general education course on social media for eight semesters, during which she had piloted the production of course audio content in the form of a podcast featuring student stories. iVoices was funded beginning in her ninth semester teaching the course, with the goal of integrating student stories into curricula and scholarship around technologies. Project funds were used to hire student media lab instructors, fund media production equipment and subscriptions, and buy out instructor time from other courses. As originally envisioned, the project was to include three phases: *Teaching*, *Publishing*, and *Research*. The crucial and rewarding *Collection* phase only emerged through praxis.

4 The (Planned) Teaching Phase

As planned in the Teaching Phase of iVoices, the team trained students to produce media and digital stories about their experiences with technologies, and then offered students the option to openly license their work for reuse including in the textbook. This phase began with the original source for the open textbook: a simple 10-chapter textbook the author had written and continuously updated beginning in 2017, *Humans are Social Media* [5]. As a member of the Open Educational Network, the institution's libraries offered the open source Pressbooks for institutional use when this project began, opening the possibility of having students as eBook contributors. Before the semester began, a graduate assistant and the author migrated *Humans are Social Media* from its previous host to Pressbooks and modified the title to *Humans R Social Media* [6]. The team then created a new draft version of the textbook in Pressbooks for work by the students, giving them the sense of contributing to the textbook while offering a key layer of privacy and security.

Once the semester began, the iVoices team of undergraduate media lab workers with skills in video, audio, and graphic media production helped design assignments that would immerse students in the world of online, social media as creators. Assigned projects (Table 1) included composing text-based stories, audio stories, videos, and graphics. Projects were low stakes in grade value and scaffolded to build confidence with writing multimodally for the web; each was worth no more than 10% of the student's grade, and several were due per semester. For accessibility for all students, following the principles of Universal Design for Learning, instructions were in multiple

Table 1. Assignment components

	Text	Audio	Video	Graphics
Fall 2020	4 × 500 word posts* 1 short bio* 1 new glossary term*	1 narrative audio story*** 1 interview-based audio story** 1 optional narrative audio story**	1 optional video story***	1 graphic profile picture (1 version without and 1 version with background)
Spring 2021	3 × 600 word posts* 1 short bio*	1 narrative audio story 1 audio story featuring reused sound bites**	1 interview-based video story** 1 animated video story**	1 graphic profile picture (1 version without and 1 version with background) 1 meme
Fall 2021	2 × 600 word posts* 5 tweet-style posts* 1 × 300 word post*	1 narrative audio story**	1 video story*** 1 rigged animation video (Option 1 of 2)	1 graphic profile picture* 1 infographic (Option 2 of 2)

* Design preferred and workshops offered in Open Source Software.
** Creative Commons music required.
***Could optionally include Creative Commons music (or no music).

formats such as videos, writing, and live workshops, with ample repetition. Teaching was informed by formative assessments to gauge students' levels of comfort and experience with technologies, levels of satisfaction with the course as it progressed, and ideas for improvements.

Included in workshops and extra credit assignments offered to students were walk-throughs of Creative Commons, and open licensing resource use and sharing opportunities. Students were also offered shortcuts for integrating Creative Commons content in their work, such as the iVoices Innovation Park, a playlist of short, Creative Commons-licensed tracks composed by our media lab for class reuse. To help the class find other reusable music for audio stories, students were given extra credit for sharing music they found in a class forum, provided they included the Title, Artist, Source and License or TASL [3], and provided the license was reusable for the book. All written posts were designed, and all media presented in each student's Pressbooks chapter.

At the end of the semester, students were invited to openly license their content Attribution 2.0 Generic (CC BY) through a Memorandum of Understanding (MOU) (Table 2). The MOU was based on an agreement shared through the Rebus community [12] and workshopped with the Institution's Scholarly Communications and Open Education librarians. The MOU has been adapted across semesters to better suit project workflow and perceived understandings and preferences of students in the course (Table 3).

Table 2. License elections in the memorandum of understanding

	Class size at MOU election	Elected CC BY on all work	Elected CC BY on some work	Elected All Rights Reserved	Did not fill out the MOU	Contributed openly licensed work
Fall 2020 original MOU	113	82	n/a*	20	7	73%
Fall 2020 revised MOU*	113	22	0	1	90	19%
Spring 2021	130	45	26	41	18	55%
Fall 2021	144	47	30	54	13	54%

* In Fall 2020 students were not offered some of the options offered in subsequent semesters, including selection of projects and name redaction options. Out of ethical concern and desire for consistency it was decided to offer those students a revised MOU with the expanded options, emailed to students the following Fall. Only a fraction of students responded, perhaps due to the time that had passed since they had been in the course (11 months).

In all, the Teaching phase of iVoices ran successfully and as planned. The students of the course who participated in a survey conducted by the institution's Open Education

Table 3. Identity modification elections in the memorandum of understanding

	Chose open licensing	Chose full name	Chose first name only	Chose different name**	Chose to be fully deidentified
Fall 2020 revised MOU*	22	11	9	n/a	2
Spring 2021	71	36	18	n/a	17
Fall 2021	77	30	22	3	22

*In the original Fall 2020 MOU, students were not offered name options.

Librarian at the end of the first semester, 62% said the *HRSM* project had greater educational value than traditional learning activities (n = 85), and this percentage rose to 75.5% when students participating in the second semester of the project were surveyed (n = 94) [4]. In this measure and all others including mastery of core academic content and collaborative learning, majorities of students rated the outcomes of this open pedagogy project better than or the same as traditional class activities, while percentages of students who rated the outcomes of this open pedagogy project as worse than traditional class activities were all in the single digits. Themes found in students' open-ended responses included terms like *hands-on, interactive, relevance, engaging, creativity,* and *connecting*. At the time of this writing, results were not available for the third semester survey.

5   The (Unplanned) Collection Phase

The author has an accredited master's degree in library and Information Science MLIS), yet when designing iVoices had not considered the issues that would arise in curating products of the *Teaching* phase. Collection principles including storage, selection, and privacy protection were not central foci in the literature consulted on open pedagogy. Still, a need for collection strategies emerged as content produced in the first two semesters' *Teaching* phases began to amass. The author decided to build a public collection because students' stories, graphics, and other content were licensed CC BY, making it legal for anyone to reuse straight from the textbook even if there were no additional OEC published. Fortunately, this project was housed within School of Information with a MLIS program which allowed the author to recruited graduate interns to organize the growing collection of student work. Regretfully, the original budget did not include or plan for this assistance in the project, so these internships were unpaid.

Refining of the *Collection* phase has ultimately led to the following sequence of processes.

1. Organization
2. Migration
3. Transcription and identity modification (distinct processes performed in tandem)
4. Collection and Dataset creation

5.1 Organization

Following the issuing of course grades, the MOU response report generated by the survey platform Qualtrics was used to organize submitted student work URLs by license elections. Content with All Rights Reserved was set aside or removed in accordance with the Family Educational Rights and Privacy Act (FERPA).

5.2 Migration

After training in ethics including human subjects research training modules by an Institutional Review Board, the teams of interns or student workers were given editorial access to the Pressbooks draft book containing submitted student work. The team migrated openly licensed content reports to Google Sheets & Google Drive, which afforded version histories and ease of collaboration, and deleted All Rights Reserved content before adding columns for transcription, description, and metadata. At various stages throughout the collection phase, the team copied the spreadsheet and resumed work from the copy to ensure references to any unshared content in the version history are deleted.

Metadata fields for the openly licensed project components became column headers designed to capture what essential data. Content headings or titles and written passages were pasted directly into fields, including longer written assignments with 600-word minimums. Fields were created for attribution of reused media using the TASL model. Visual content is linked to the downloaded.jpg or.png files. Audio and video story sections contained links to the audio or video file, ideally, .mp3 or .wav and .mp4 or .mov, respectively.

5.3 Transcription

UDL was a crucial principle behind the *Collection* phase as it was in the *Teaching* phase, with content organized for broad human accessibility and engagement. All audio and video were transcribed—pasting transcriptions in the spreadsheet in addition to linking them—to afford searchability of key topics. Transcription was begun in Descript, a program which performed machine-transcription, and then human-corrected by the team. Select audio and video projects also contained descriptions by interns of the content meanings not captured in existing text or transcription; for example, in the Soundbyte-based Audio Story assignment, which led to many stories with sound featuring more prominently than language. Machine learning image classification (with a CIFAR-10 library based on the Convolution Neural Network by Tensorflow) were explored to aid in describing images.

5.4 Identity Modification

Review of student stories openly licensed in the first semester revealed very personal content, including discussion of online harassment and eating disorders. Recognizing that such content was both valuable and sensitive, in the second semester the MOU was altered to begin offering removal of authoring students' last names or full names in the MOU, as well as use of a different name in the third semester. Eventually a revised

MOU was offered to students from the first semester with these name options offered as well. Across all three semester MOUs, 55% of students elected some form of identity modification or name change for their work. The time-consuming process of identity modification resulting from these decisions included removal of first names, full names, and other identifiers of students and people mentioned in their stories; and editing of images of students and other identifying visual information such as Instagram handles. Identity modification of openly licensed content turned out to be skilled work, practiced as a careful negotiation between rights of authorship and protections of privacy requested by contributing students and those mentioned in their stories.

5.5 Collection and Dataset Creation

The final process within the *Collection* phase was to finalize one human-readable collection and one machine-readable (cleaned) dataset. Each human-readable collection hosted in Google Drive was a color-coded spreadsheet with images and text files appearing when hovered over and direct links to all content. A version of the collection cleaned for machine readability including filenames and key words was created. Three collections with each of these components has been made available through the iVoices website [15].

6 Reflection

While collection has not previously been a primary focus of the nascent literature on open pedagogy and OEP, theoretical underpinnings of iVoices and *HRSM* remind us that collection was always a fundamental outcome of this work. First, considering iVoices was designed to activate students' critical Funds of Knowledge (FoK), the author could have predicted that the collective value of these cultural resources would manifest in an actual collection. Following user privacy protection strategies such as white-walling, the team repeatedly replicated this student content outside the site of creation to remove digital traces of identity that may have remained in platform memory, leading to a corpus of work outside of the environment where it had been created. Additionally, Universal Design for Learning led to the further replication of content in different formats toward accessibility, such as video and audio story derivations including transcriptions and migration to more easily rendered and downloadable formats. Considering the privacy protection strategies and the theoretical framework including FoK and Universal Design for Learning, it follows that iVoices and *HRSM* would coalesce in collections reflecting how students were taught and what students came to know. In the end, the best reasons this work can offer for not planning the OEC resulting from this project include absence from the literature, lack of confidence that students would share as generously as they did, and privacy protection processes added iteratively to the project as the personal nature of the stories became clear.

7 Conclusion

Planning for OECs will add significant work but also clear value to open pedagogy projects. Lessons learned in this project are offered here as recommendations for future planning of OECs and OEPs. First, the author recommends the language and options offered by the MOU focus not on *contribution* (to an open textbook, for example) but instead on *open licensing and the broad reuse it affords*. Second, considering most students who openly licensed work chose some form of identity modification in this project, the author recommends identity modification options be added to future MOUs, particularly when solicited student content includes personal experiences. Third, the author recommends budgeting for collection and dataset organization assistance by interns pursuing MLIS or related degrees. Fourth and finally, the author advises forming early partnerships with institutional repositories as part of the OEC planning process, and designing MOU language, collections, and datasets with these partners. As for the iVoices collection and datasets, these unplanned fruits of this open pedagogy project have been developed and publicly released thanks to factors including a successful *Teaching* phase with institutional support, knowledgeable creative labor by students, robust open culture and pedagogy infrastructures, and the singular serendipity of being surrounded by librarians.

Acknowledgements. The iVoices project was funded in part by the Center for University Education and Scholarship at University of Arizona and has benefited significantly from the work of interns in the iSchool's MLIS program.

References

1. Asiri, F., Millard, D.: Unpacking privacy practices in SNSs: users' protection strategies to enforce privacy boundaries. In: 2018 21st Saudi Computer Society National Computer Conference (NCC), pp. 1–6 (2018). https://doi.org/10.1109/NCG.2018.8593046
2. Bali, M., Cronin, C., Jhangiani, R.S.: Framing open educational practices from a social justice perspective. J. Interact. Media Educ. **2020**(1) (2020)
3. Creative Commons: Best practices for attribution—creative Commons (n.d.). https://wiki.cre ativecommons.org/wiki/best_practices_for_attribution Accessed 12 Nov 2021
4. Cuillier, C., Daly, D.: Open pedagogy: independence and interdependence in teaching about new media. AoIR Selected Papers of Internet Research (2021). https://doi.org/10.5210/spir. v2021i0.12157
5. Daly, D.: Humans are Social Media. The University of Arizona (2017)
6. Daly, D and students: Humans R Social Media, Winter 2022 Open Textbook Edition. The iVoices Media Lab. The University of Arizona (2021). https://ivoices.ischool.arizona.edu/ humans-r-social-media
7. Ehlers, U.-D.: Extending the territory: From open educational resources to open educational practices. J. Open Flexible Distance Learn. **15**(2), 1–10 (2011)
8. Gonzalez, N., Moll, L.C., Amanti, C.: Funds of Knowledge: Theorizing Practices in Households, Communities and Classrooms. Erlbaum, Mahwah, NJ (2005). https://doi.org/10.4324/ 9781410613462
9. Hegarty, B.: Attributes of open pedagogy: a model for using open educational resources. Educ. Technol. 3–13 (2015)
10. Marwick, A.E., boyd, d.: Networked privacy: how teenagers negotiate context in social media. New Media Soc. **16**(7), 1051–1067 (2014). https://doi.org/10.1177/1461444814543995
11. Jenkins, H.: Fans, Bloggers, and Gamers: Exploring Participatory Culture. NYU Press, New York, NY, and London, England (2006)

12. Mays, E., et al.: A Guide to Making Open Textbooks with Students. Pressbooks, Montreal, Canada (2017)
13. Moll, L.C., Amanti, C., Neff, D., Gonzalez, N.: Funds of knowledge for teaching: using a qualitative approach to connect homes and classrooms. Theory Practice **31**(2), 132–141 (1992)
14. Rose, D.H., Meyer, A.: Teaching every student in the digital age: universal design for learning. ERIC (2002)
15. iVoices Media Lab: The iVoices Media Lab 2021 CC BY Dataset (2021). Retrieved from https://ivoices.ischool.arizona.edu/research
16. Tietjen, P., Asino, T.I.: What is open pedagogy? Identifying commonalities. Int. Rev. Res. Open Distrib. Learn. **22**(2), 185–204 (2021)

Terminology Preferences of the LGBTQ+ Community: A User Study

Heather Moulaison-Sandy[1]([✉]) [iD], Ngoc-Minh Pham[1] [iD], Karen Snow[2] [iD],
and Brian Dobreski[3] [iD]

[1] University of Missouri, Columbia, MO, USA
moulaisonhe@missouri.edu
[2] Dominican University, River Forest, IL, USA
[3] University of Tennessee, Knoxville, TN, USA

Abstract. The LGBTQ+ community is a group with a specific identity where the literature has identified the potential for such mismatches. To investigate the problem of LGBTQ+ terminology from a user's perspective, 10 LGBTQ+ users of library catalogs were interviewed. Participants were asked to describe an LGBTQ+ title, *The Queer Advantage*, to identify subject terminology that could be used to query a library catalog, and to react to the title's assigned Library of Congress Subject Headings (LCSH). Results indicate that participants had a very different focus when describing the title and formulated largely non-expert queries that did not align with the LCSH terminology. They found the LCSH terms to be accurate but academic, and not aligned with their approach. Findings from this study shed light on the ways in which LGBTQ+ users alter their language in interacting with library systems, but at the same time, indicate that the subject terminology used in libraries may not meet the needs of the LGBTQ+ community. Limitations to this study are presented, and further research is explored.

Keywords: User studies · LGBTQ+ community · Controlled vocabularies

1 Introduction

Not enough is known about the way that members of underrepresented groups interact with information systems. Expectations surrounding subject terminology and access represent one such problem. Although a number of studies have examined the inadequacies of current vocabularies in supporting access to topics related to LGBTQ+ individuals (e.g., [1]) and projects to address LGBTQ+ information access (e.g., [2]), a gap nonetheless exists in the understanding of how LGBTQ+ individuals expect to be able to query information systems such as library catalogs.

User studies are one way to begin to explore subject access for members of the LGBTQ+ community. The current study's investigation is threefold, seeking to understand the spontaneous usage of terminology surrounding an LGBTQ+ title, *The Queer Advantage*, query formulation by LGBTQ+ users of library systems, and the suitability of formally assigned subject terminology as perceived by the users.

I. Sserwanga et al. (Eds.): iConference 2023, LNCS 13972, pp. 180–188, 2023.
https://doi.org/10.1007/978-3-031-28032-0_15

1.1 Research Questions

RQ1: What terminology do LGBTQ+ library users use to describe *The Queer Advantage*?

RQ2: How does user terminology change when suggesting subject queries for the library catalog?

RQ3: How well do the Library of Congress Subject Headings (LCSH) used at the Library of Congress describe the title from the perspective of members of the LGBTQ+ community?

2 Review of the Literature: The Challenge of Subject Access for LGBTQ+ Information

Information access is difficult for LBGTQ+ users when searching LGBTQ+ topics in library systems. In a 2013 study of catalog usage by homeless LGBTQ+ youth, the authors noted such a difference between user and system terminologies that they proposed developing a crosswalk ontology [3]. LIS researchers have long acknowledged the problem of non-expert query formulation when using information systems like library catalogs (e.g., [4]), resulting in less-than-optimal results; these seem to be compounded by the potential for a mismatch between the terminology preferred by members of the LGBTQ+ community and the metadata included in library catalogs [2]. This mismatch in terminology manifests as a misalignment between terms used to describe a resource and terms used in retrieval. Though recent years have seen increased attention to LGBTQ+ concerns and libraries, much of the research has focused on collections and services [5, 6]. Examinations of information seeking tend to focus on health information [7], leaving general library catalog behavior of LGBTQ+ users understudied.

Though not the only source of terminology for subject metadata in the library catalog, LCSH is the predominant subject heading list used in libraries in the United States and is widely used in other countries as well [8]. Curry's 2005 [9] study found that reference librarians were often unsuccessful in assisting with queries concerning LGBTQ+ topics due to not knowing the appropriate search terms. Traditionally, LCSH has relied on literary warrant as the guiding principle behind adding or changing terminology, meaning that terms well established in the published literature have received priority [10]. As a result, LCSH has received much criticism (e.g., [11, 12]) for its inadequacy in representing information from marginalized perspectives. More recently, work by Adler and Tennis [1] highlighted issues surrounding LCSH's treatment of gender and sexuality. In advocating for the use of an alternative vocabulary, Fischer [13] noted that even after extensive criticism and improvements, LCSH terminology remains inadequate in representing LGBTQ+ topics. Such findings echo longstanding observations on how libraries may struggle to provide adequate subject access to members of LGBTQ+ community.

Recent trends have seen libraries exploring beyond LCSH to alternative means of subject representation in order to better serve LGBTQ+ users and other marginalized groups. For example, the Homosaurus is a vocabulary designed to represent identities and concepts from the perspective of the LGBTQ+ community, which some libraries have begun adopting [13, 14]. Bullard et al. [2] have reported on the Out on the Shelves initiatives, including the design of alternative classification and subject heading systems intended to center the perspectives of the Canadian LGBTQ+ community. While these developments offer the potential for better representation and access, most libraries in the United States are still reliant on LCSH for subject metadata. Better understanding of how LGBTQ+ users react to current library metadata can provide insights to both the improvement of current systems and the development of new, alternative ones.

3 Methodology

Participants identifying as part of the LGBTQ+ community were recruited from Reddit and Facebook online forums for readers in July 2022; participants had a degree of domain expertise as well as prior experience using library catalogs, the two broad factors that would potentially support *search expertise* [4]. Interviews took place over the summer 2022 via Zoom.

One of the titles discussed during the interviews was *The Queer Advantage: Conversations with LBGTQ+ Leaders on the Power of Identity* by Andrew Gelwicks [15]. Published in 2020, this title presents interviews with leading members of the LGBTQ+ community. Participants were given information about the title ahead of time that included cover art, the table of contents, and publisher descriptions. They were specifically instructed not to look up any further information, neither in library catalogs nor on bookseller websites.

Table 1. Age range and LGBTQ+ identity of study participants.

Participant #	Age	Participant's self-described identity
P1	18–24	Butch Lesbian
P2	45–54	Gay man (he/him)
P3	18–24	Genderfluid lesbian
P4	25–34	Lesbian
P5	25–34	Bisexual, cisgender
P6	35–44	Queer, homoromantic
P7	25–34	Cis female, Pansexual
P8	45–54	Lesbian woman
P9	18–24	Queer and trans (he/they)
P10	18–24	Nonbinary female

Among our 10 participants, four participants were from the 18–24 age group, three participants were from the 25–34 age group, one participant was from the 35–44 age group, and two participants were from the 45–54 age group. A range of identities was used by participants to describe themselves. Table 1 represents age and identity information, as captured through their survey responses.

To explore participants' perceptions of the LCSH, we conducted open ended structured interviews. Interviews were chosen since it enables the exploration of what is "in and on someone's mind" [16]. Interview participants were asked three open ended questions, which are: (1) Imagine you are talking to a friend who is also a member of the LGBTQ+ community, what would you say this book is about? (2) If you wanted to locate this book in a library catalog, searching by subject, what terms would you type into the search box? (3) In your opinion, how well do these terms describe the book? If you could alter these subject headings, would you change them? If so, how would you change them? (asked after interviewer presented the participant with the LCSH assigned to *The Queer Advantage*). The interviews were recorded with the consent of the participants and transcribed through the Zoom e-conferencing software. The transcripts were later cleaned by research team members.

Transcripts were analyzed using MAXQDA software [17] in two rounds. Data from six participants was analyzed in round one. Prominent bits of data that appeared potentially relevant to the research question were notated and open coded [18]. Open codes were grouped into different themes relevant to each research question using the axial coding [18]. The results for the first round of the analysis were then discussed by three members in the research team for triangulation purposes. The second round involved data from another four interviews. Categories from the first round of analysis were constantly compared, using the constant comparative method of qualitative data analysis [18], with those obtained from the rest of the interviews. The final analysis results were then examined by all the research team members.

4   Results and Discussion

4.1   Describing the Title for the LGBTQ+ Community

The first question about *The Queer Advantage* asked participants to consider how they would describe the title for other members of the LBGTQ+ community. Participants tended to focus on the people featured, their accomplishments, and their fields of endeavor. The human element was key, rather than the specific way in which the individuals were LGBTQ+ or other aspects of identity that would be considered minority, such as race or gender. This does not reflect the "othering" that can take place in information systems, but rather is indicative of inclusivity [1].

Celebrity Interviewees as Success Stories. All the participants in this study mentioned roles, such as 'leaders,' 'celebrities,' 'famous people,' 'movers and shakers,' 'public figure,' 'icon queers,' etc. in their description of the title, such as

P7: *'It has a lot of people across different aspects of the world. You do have some actors. You have some people who are in politics.'*

Some of the language the participants used included '*queerness as a source of power*' (P9), '*how their identity has had an impact on their leadership*' (P8), '*...overcome the stigma or the barriers that their identities or society's opinions about their identities have put in their path*' (P2), and '*leadership and how being queer can be an advantage*' (P1).

Umbrella Identity Terms. All the participants in this study tended to use neutral and umbrella identity terms to portray individuals represented. All the participants (10/10) employed a variation of LGBT including 'LGBTQ,' 'LGBT+,' and 'LGBTQ+' in their description of the title. The second most common term used in the participants' responses was the term 'queer' (9/10 participants). However, one participant expressed concern about the neutrality of the term 'queer.'

> P9: '*...I know a lot of older LGBTQ people aren't comfortable with that since it's a reclaimed slur so I, like, I would personally want to lean towards something more neutral.*'

Format. Format was also discussed by the participants. Some of the terms used by the participants included '*biography*' (P3), '*memoir*' (P3), '*anthology*' (P9), '*interview*' (P7), '*nonfiction*' (P2, P3, P4, P5, P6, P7), '*real life story*' (P4), and '*conversations*' (P2).

4.2 Proposed Subject Query Terms

Next, participants were asked to brainstorm subject terms they would use to query the library catalog for *The Queer Advantage* if they did not have author or title information available. Because queries were provided verbally to interviewers, no system support or search feedback was offered. Overall, participants provided two-term queries that did not map to LCSH terms for the title. Drawing from Smith's [4] analysis of expert searcher practices, the queries provided were largely non-expert, despite participant status as domain experts and their prior experience with library catalogs. We believe this suggests that LCSH terminology as applied to this title is not optimal for members of the LGBTQ+ community [e.g., 2, 3]. See Table 2.

Proposed search terms were generally shortened versions of the longer explanations they provided previously. In other words, participants had two separate subject vocabularies for describing the title – one they would use when engaging in normal conversation, and an abbreviated version of the vocabulary for use when querying the library catalog. Terms that were not part of their daily language were not generally presented as options when building queries; however, participants did seem to acknowledge that the language used in library catalogs would be more academic (P3). Two participants suggested searching for proper names, suggesting misunderstanding of the way subject terms are supplied in library catalogs [e.g., 9]. This might be indicative of a deeper problem with catalog searching that relates to when and how headings are provided.

Table 2. Search terms proposed by respondents for the title.

Participant #	Original search terms
P1	*Queer leadership*
P2	*Queer identity, queer conversations, queer people interviews, gay interview, queer nonfiction, gay nonfiction, proper names (e.g., Adam Rippon)*
P3	*LGBTQ+ nonfiction, biography, memoir, LGBTQ+ history*
P4	*Interview about LGBTQ, a real-life story of LGBTQ,*
P5	*Queer nonfiction, LGBTQ nonfiction, LGBTQ interviews, queer interviews*
P6	*LGBTQ nonfiction, queer, interview*
P7	*LGBT interviews*
P8	*Queer leadership, queer biography, proper names (e.g., Billie Jean King, Margaret Cho, George Takei)*
P9	*LGBTQ heroes, LGBTQ history, queer history*
P10	*LGBTQ identity*

4.3 Perceived Fitness of the Library of Congress Subject Headings

The third and final question revolved around participant impressions of the Library of Congress Subject Headings used in the Library of Congress catalog.

The two subject heading strings assigned by the Library of Congress were the following:

- Sexual minorities–Interviews.
- Sexual minorities–Identity.

Participants did not raise any concern with the use of the terms 'Interviews' and 'Identity' as part of the subject heading strings.

Overwhelmingly, however, 'Sexual minorities' was perceived to be problematic, reflecting the potential for harm that terms can represent [1].

Describing Identity. The term 'Sexual minorities' fails to make the marginalized identities pertaining to groups under the LGBTQ+ umbrella visible, as evidenced by the response of P4 and P6.

P4. '*The term should be a bit related to LGBTQ because when I see sexual minority, I just feel OK this book is not meant for me, so I don't go for it.*'

P6. '*....by using sexual minorities, you're taking away the way LGBT people, their experiences intersect with other marginalized groups so there's you know women being interviewed.*'

Sex and *gender* seem to be viewed as synonymous terms in the LCSH term 'Sexual minorities'. That the two terms are not viewed as the same among the LGBTQ+ community members can be seen in the response by P10. Titles about LGBTQ+ community members are not exclusively about their sexuality, as mentioned by P6.

P6. *'They're not just talking about their sexual identity.'*

P10: *'Sexual minorities? I feel like they should be gender.'*

Perceptions of Utility. Overall, there was a lack of perceived usefulness of the term 'Sexual minorities' assigned to the title due to the discrepancy between the language participants said they would use when searching for the title [e.g., 2].

P1. *'I would never search for those terms.'*

P8. *'I would never say sexual minorities. I'm confident my students would never use a term like that.'*

The term seems not to be in the daily vocabulary habits of participants, as indicated by P1, P2, and P4, thereby limiting its utility in query formulation.

P1. *'I think this is terrible. 'Sexual minorities.'*

P2. *'It's not a term that we're going to associate with this book.'*

P4. *'I wouldn't have been typing sexual minorities because that would not even pop into my head.'*

Participants (P8) also noted that the use of 'Sexual minorities" makes the work less accessible to the very community who would be most interested in reading it.

Recommendations for Improvement. Participants recommended using subject terms related to individuals featured and themes which they had earlier used to describe the title as search terms/subject headings. Many went back to the terms they had wanted to use to query the catalog in response to question 2. For example, P1 had used words such as *'leadership,'* *'notable queer,'* to describe the title and recommended that keywords such as *'queer leadership,'* *'icon queer,'* should be in the subject headings instead of 'sexual minorities.' Likewise, P2 used words such as *'modern leaders,'* *'visible people in the queer community,'* *'openly queer,'* *'openly gay,'* *'succeed,'* *'famous ones,'* *'stigma,'* *'barriers,'* *'identities'* to describe the title. After, viewing the Library of Congress subject headings, P2 recommended that the subject headings should be terms like *'queer interviews,'* *'queer identity,'* *'queer leaders,'* *'LGBTQ leader interviews,'* *'LGBTQ public figures,'* *'queer public figures,'* and *'gay public figures.'*

P5. *'I think there's an aspect of it that to me feels like the book is very specifically geared towards how people in these communities have created, have gone on to obtain celebrity status and to me that feels like that's a factor that's missing from this.'*

Participants expressed their need for the subject headings to emphasize the visibility of marginalized group identities, in this case, LGBTQ+ groups, rather than to focus on the aspect relating to a perceived minority status (P8 and P9). Since 'Sexual minorities' failed to reflect who the title is about, some participants suggested using culturally sensitive and relevant terminology such as 'LGBT', 'LGBTQ', 'LGBTQ+' and 'queer' as an alternative, as mentioned by P1, P3, and P4.

P1. *'I would get rid of them and search for queer leadership, um, perhaps.'*

P3. *'...I would change the wording. I would say LGBT+ or potentially queer.'*

P4. *'I would still go for LGBT. I would know it covers everything. It's not about lesbian alone or gay so I would know it cover everything.'*

At the same time, participants did not view the term 'Sexual minorities' as 'inaccurate' or 'offensive' descriptor (P3) even if they would not use the term. As such, it is likely not useful for retrieval, as indicated by P1 and P2.

P1: *'Yeah, I would never search for those terms (sexual minorities).'*

P2. *'So, it's technically correct but I don't think it'd be very useful for actually trying to find the book.'*

5 Future Study and Conclusion

This study takes the novel approach of interviewing members of a marginalized group (the LGBTQ+ community) to probe their preferred terminology for describing resources relating to their LGBTQ+ identity. Limitations include the interview methodology, which was deemed appropriate for a small-scale study while Covid-19 was still active. Findings show that LGBTQ+ users struggled with interpreting LCSH terms for this resource. While "LGBTQ" and "queer" were the most commonly identified search terms that users would try in a catalog search, they used a range of deeper terminology when spontaneously describing the title. Findings from this study shed light on the ways in which LGBTQ+ users alter their language in interacting with the library, but at the same time, indicate that the subject terminology used in libraries may not meet the needs of the LGBTQ+ community.

Future work in this project will investigate other LGBTQ+ titles on different topics and will compare the preferred terminology of LGBTQ+ users to other controlled vocabularies. The LIS literature has consistently recommended that specialized vocabularies be used to support access to resources for members of marginalized communities, but if the true barrier to access is the catalog and not the vocabulary, or if other vocabularies are not sufficient for supporting enhanced access anyway, then a completely new approach to considering access will be in order. This paper represents one step in understanding the needs of marginalized users.

Acknowledgements. We would like to thank the iSchools, Inc. for funding to support this work. In addition, we gratefully acknowledge the contributions of Kathryn Scott Arbuckle and Amy Snyder.

References

1. Adler, M., Tennis, J.T.: Toward a taxonomy of harm in knowledge organization systems. Knowl. Organ. **40**(4), 266–272 (2013). https://doi.org/10.5771/0943-7444-2013-4-266
2. Bullard, J., Dierking, A., Grundner, A.: Centering LGBT2QIA+ subjects in knowledge organization systems. Knowl. Organ. **47**(5), 393–403 (2020). https://doi.org/10.5771/0943-7444-2020-5
3. Nichols, F., Cortez, E.: Breaking down the barriers: creating empathetic ontologies for LAMBDA Initiative. In: The 21st International BOBCATSSS Conference, p. 49 (2013)
4. Smith, C.L.: Domain-independent search expertise: a description of procedural knowledge gained during guided instruction. J. Am. Soc. Inf. Sci. **66**(7), 1388–1405 (2015)
5. Adler, M.: Meeting the needs of LGBTIQ library users and their librarians: a study of user satisfaction and LGBTIQ collection development in academic libraries. In: Greenblatt, E. (ed.) Serving LGBTIQ Library and Archives Users: Essays on Outreach, Service, Collections and Access, pp. 184–192 (2010)
6. Montague, R.-A.: Leading and transforming LGBTQ library services. Paper presented at: IFLA WLIC 2015 - Cape Town, South Africa in Session 128 - LGBTQ Users SIG (2015)
7. Morris, M., Roberto, K.: Information-seeking behaviour and information needs of LGBTQ health professionals: a follow-up study. Health Inform. Library J. **33**(3), 204–221 (2016). https://doi.org/10.1111/hir.12139
8. Library of Congress: Process for adding and revising Library of Congress subject headings (n.d.). https://www.loc.gov/aba/cataloging/subject/lcsh-process.html
9. Curry, A.: If I ask, will they answer? Evaluating public library reference service to gay and lesbian youth. Ref. User Serv. Quar. **45**(1), 65–75 (2005)
10. Barité, M.: Literary warrant. Knowl. Organ. **45**(6), 517–536 (2018). https://doi.org/10.5771/0943-7444-2018-6
11. Berman, S.: Prejudice and Antipathies: A Tract on the LC Subject Heads Concerning People. Scarecrow Press, Metuchen, N.J. (1971)
12. Olson, H.: The Power to Name: Locating The Limits of Subject Representation in Libraries. Kluwer (2002)
13. Fischer, R.K.: Using Homosaurus in a public library consortium. Presented at the Core Cataloging & Classification Research Interest Group Meeting Virtual Interest Group Week (2021). https://ala-events.zoom.us/rec/play/XSFemqLHbaOxNFAAkavyfXeg_zgpl5P epbIm_ixeFQJvvjyx7JwqnsUB6omwW0g9TsPF7nmtgulxrO79.b2x2VWR_u-tR1sCC?con tinueMode=true&_x_zm_rtaid=P4vpKQ8hTf2lDUvf7qNATQ.1643582921802.3f0dfe9b1 eb7e21231798dd8b9be08ce&_x_zm_rhtaid=803. Accessed 30 Jan 2022
14. Hardesty, J.L., Nolan, A.: Mitigating bias in metadata. Inf. Technol. Libr. **40**(3), 1–14 (2021). https://doi.org/10.6017/ital.v40i3.13053
15. Gelwicks, A.: The Queer Advantage: Conversations with LBGTQ+ Leaders on the Power of Identity. Hachette Go (2020)
16. Patton, M.Q.: Qualitative Research & Evaluation Methods: Integrating Theory and Practice. Sage Publications (2014)
17. VERBI Software: MAXQDA 2022 [computer software]. Berlin, Germany: VERBI Software (2021). Available from maxqda.com
18. Merriam, S.B., Tisdell, E.J.: Qualitative Research: A Guide to Design and Implementation. Wiley (2016)

Exploring the Concept of *Library Use:*
A Research Review

Rachel Fleming-May(✉) (iD)

University of Tennessee, Knoxville, TN 37996, USA
rfm@utk.edu

Abstract. This paper revisits an analysis and typology of the concept of "library use," published in 2011 [1] with the objectives of using the Evolutionary Concept Analysis (ECA) method to review subsequent discussion of the concept in the Library and Information Science (LIS) scholarly and professional literature for significant developments and, if needed, facilitating revision of the typology. Findings highlight emerging themes in discussions of library use and an addition to the library use typology.

Keywords: Concepts in LIS · Library use · Assessment

1 Introduction

As can likely be said of most scholarly disciplines, concepts are "all-present and pervasive" in Library and Information Science [2, p. 1527]. Despite this ubiquity, LIS scholars have frequently drawn notice to the discipline's failure to define "basic concepts", particularly in the context of establishing their individual roles in theory [3, p. 459]. This shortcoming also creates challenges that are especially apparent when they must be operationalized as variables for research design.

The concept of *information use* is an example of a concept central to LIS that "many have struggled with how to conceptualize and study" [4, p. 282]. This difficulty certainly extends to at least one area of Information Behavior in context: *library use*. Despite high-profile scholars' having pointed out the need to clarify "library use" for more than a half century, studies claiming to focus on use of library resources, spaces, and services continue to suffer from a lack of conceptual clarity. Often, library use is treated as a primitive concept: an idea so fundamental to a discipline's epistemological structure as to be undefinable.

In 2011 the author used the Evolutionary Concept Analysis (ECA) method to investigate if this was, in fact, the case. On the contrary, review of a large sample of the Library and Information Science (LIS) scholarly and professional literature published between 1876 and 2008 revealed that library use is a concept with several distinct facets, described in a typology of library use [1].

The intervening years have seen an increased focus on establishing measures of value and return on investment in library resources, services, and facilities, and highlighted the importance of clarifying what, exactly, "using the library" and its resources means,

I. Sserwanga et al. (Eds.): iConference 2023, LNCS 13972, pp. 189–196, 2023.
https://doi.org/10.1007/978-3-031-28032-0_16

and how that use can be tied to measures of impact. This paper revisits the typology through the LIS literature published in the intervening years to ascertain if explanations of library use have become more explicit, and if revisions to the typology are required.

1.1 Understanding Library Use

The question of how best to understand and measure library use is not a new one; Brenda Dervin and Douglas Zweizig began raising it in earnest in the late 1970's. To that point, library use had typically been expressed in terms of output measures such as book circulation and door counts, a practice Dervin questioned, pointing out the premise that "that there is something of value to be obtained as a result of measuring library activities" might be flawed [5, p. 16]. Reflecting the social sciences' larger "cognitive turn" of the time, Dervin and Zweizig called for those studying "library use" to move from centering library-centric measures to exploring the role of the library and its resources in addressing the needs of the individuals who make use of it [6]. A few years later Abraham Bookstein demonstrated that failing to define "library use" in survey design may lead to very different answers from two respondents whose actual behavior is identical. Bookstein surveyed students in the University of Chicago Graduate Library School to ascertain which activities they considered "uses" of the library. Among several activities, only 53% considered making an unsuccessful attempt to check out a book to be a "use" of the library, while even fewer (32%) believed visiting the library to return a book to be library use [7, p. 89]. Without clear operationalization of the concept, Bookstein argued, "a considerable portion of the variability reported in library use may in fact be variability in how one interprets what constitutes a use of the library" [7, p. 86].

A Typology of Library Use. During research on the topic conducted several years after these publications, the author discovered that most empirical research continued referring to "library use" as a monolith rather than a collection of actions, processes, and measures. That project employed the Evolutionary Concept Analysis method to identify several sub-types (or "dimensions") of "library use", including.

Library use as:

- an *abstraction*, or general topic without further explanation or attachment to specific examples of the type of library use being discussed (undergraduate students' library use)
- an *instance* or transaction, a discrete event that can be measured and/or tracked quantitatively. Output measures (item circulation or log-on to a library-subscribed online resource). The most common
- a *process* on the part of the user to achieve a purpose unique to the user ("going to the library" to research how to create a business plan) [1, p. 308–9]. What Kyrillidou terms "use in the life of the user" [8, p. 42].

At that time, most operationalizations of library use in the LIS literature could be described as output measures, or examples of the "instance" dimension of library use rather than having shifted focus toward the user as Dervin, Zweizig, and others recommended thirty years earlier.

2 "LIbrary Use" in the LIS Literature, 2009–2022

The typology of library use developed by the author in 2011 demonstrated that "library use" has many meanings that are not always articulated, even in the context of empirical study. The purpose of this short paper is two-fold: revisiting the original typology of library use to determine if it requires revision and ascertaining if "library use" is being defined more frequently and clearly in the LIS literature in the years since the initial study, particularly in the context of measurement. Clear understanding of "library use" remains important because data concerning "use" of library services, facilities, and/or resources are frequently the basis for significant decisions regarding staffing, collection management, service provision, and other types of resource allocation. Prominent initiatives including the Association of College and Research Libraries (ACRL) *Value of Academic Libraries* Report emphasize the importance of demonstrating the value and impact of library resources, facilities, and services, typically understood as dependent on "use" [9]. Clear operationalization of "library use" remains essential.

2.1 Theoretical Framework and Method

The theoretical framework for the 2011 typology of library use was based on Beth Rodgers' Evolutionary Concept Analysis (ECA) [10]. ECA is one of several formal methods of Concept Analysis used in nursing scholarship to explore the significance of concepts within one or more specific contexts. While some concept analyses in are specific to health ("Psychological Distress") [11], other projects explore the significance of more general concepts in a health- or nursing-related context ("Routine") [12]. Concept Analysis is a long-standing and rich tradition of scholarship in nursing; searching the CINAHL database of nursing and allied health literature for items with "concept analysis" or "analysis of a concept" in the title retrieves nearly 2000 items published since 2000. Rodgers' ECA model calls for reviewing the nature of a concept within a specific context, often a sub-set of a discipline's scholarly or professional literature. The published record of a discipline provides a useful record of its discourse at the time of publication, and editorial and peer review processes serve to establish a paper's "trustworthiness" [13, p. 905] within the discipline.

ECA requires close review of the concept as it appears in the data set, noting the following characteristics of each instance:

- Those events, activities, etc., to which the concept refers (referents)
- The concept's defining characteristics (attributes)
- Events taking place or conditions existing prior to the concept's appearance (antecedents)
- Outcomes of the phenomenon or concept (consequences)
- Other ideas appearing in close proximity to the concept or are used as its synonyms *(closely related concepts)* [10, p. 91–92].

Following review, these characteristics are aggregated and analyzed for themes.

While data collection and analysis for this paper is also based on ECA, the 2011 typology provided an additional frame for analysis. Individual discussions of library use were categorized as abstraction, instance, or process to identify possible gaps or other necessary revisions.

The data set was gathered through searches of Library and Information Science Source (LISS), Library, Information Science, and Technology Abstracts (LISTA), and Library and Information Sciences Abstracts (LISA) for articles published since 2010 in a short list of English-language journal titles established as relevant by being designated a "core title" by both LISS and LISA, and influential, as assessed by considering Clarivate's Journal Impact Factor (JIF) and Scimago Journal Reports' SJR scores.

The purpose of Concept Analysis is not to establish "the" definition of a concept, but to explore its use within the specified context. Because ECA is exploratory, data set assembly errs on the side of inclusivity. That goal is reflected in the strategy for searching the three databases:

- Articles with "use" or "usage" in the title *and* abstract of the article
- A variation of "library" in the article title or abstract (to distinguish articles about "library use" from those about information or other resource use).

Because "use" is a common word in general vernacular, it was necessary to review the retrieved items closely for relevance. Items not directly related to "library use" were discarded. Further review for the characteristics specified for ECA revealed several items of limited significance, which were discarded from the data set. It should also be noted that articles discussing use of a single library resource or service (e.g., e-books) were not included in the final data set as the objective was exploring library use as a collection of activities rather than a single type. The final data set was comprised of 68 articles published between 2009 and 2022.

3   Findings: Library Use in the LIS Literature, 2009–22

The volume of literature related to the topic of library use remains considerable, and the nature of this short paper precludes extensive discussion of individual works, but it is possible to identify several themes, illustrated by specific works from the data set.

Most works can be organized into a few general categories:

- Explanatory or descriptive accounts of the behaviors of individuals who share one or more characteristics, such as occupation [14], age range [15], nationality [16], or geographic area of residence [17]
- Descriptions of use behaviors associated with a specific library [18] or type of library [19]
- Descriptions of a specific type of use behavior, such as "in-house" [20, 21]
- "Before-and-after" analyses of changes to library use in after a change or event. These may be internal, such as addition of a service or refurbishment of a space [22], or external, such as the COVID-19 pandemic [23].

3.1 Use-as-Instance

Many of these accounts include data, frequently examples of the library use typology's "use-as-instance": numeric, transactional accountings of activities like book circulations and door counts collected automatically by library systems. A significant number of these attempt to "link ostensibly objective indicators of [user] success" to library usage [24, p. 459], typically as a means of demonstrating the value of said library. This approach is especially common in research about students' use of college and university libraries, perhaps in response to the Association of College and Research Libraries' Value of Academic Libraries Report [9] which emphasized the importance of finding ways to demonstrate connections between library use and student success, typically measured in metrics such as grade point average or retention [25]. The "library cube" is one such model. Developed at the University of Wollongong Library, it connects individual students' library use (operationalized as checking out books and searching for and downloading articles from electronic resources), their demographic profile, and measures of academic performance. Although the authors acknowledge that "borrowing a book does not automatically translate into learning" [26, 27, p. 31] and emphasize the library cube can only describe correlation between the three variables, it has undoubtedly become an influential approach [28].

Studies of this type that do not rely on automated output measures typically describe findings from surveys that ask respondents to self-report library use behavior. Anderson and Garcia's survey captures a wide range of behaviors, including seeking assistance at various service points, accessing facilities such as electrical outlets, searching for and locating information resources both in the facility and remotely, participating in instruction in library resources, and visiting physical spaces in multiple buildings. Respondents were also asked to self-report their grade point average and identify the extent to which they connect library resources and services with their academic success [24].

Whether based on data collected automatically or self-reported activity, these studies only demonstrate a correlative relationship between library use measures and student success. As Anderson and García mention, "it is noteworthy that these library-use indicators are all student self-directed library research activities that require engagement, activity, and often some sort of procedural follow-through from the student" [24, p. 460]. In other words, isn't it possible that a high-achieving student might simply be more likely to check out and download materials to support their research or avail themselves of the library as a place for quiet study?

3.2 Use as Process

"Use as Process" is the library use typology dimension that comes closest to the goal of prioritizing "library use in the life of the user." Rather than focusing on discrete events or activities, a process-oriented approach to understanding library use can include multiple individual and groups of actions carried out over a short or long period of time. As was the case when conducting the original library use concept analysis, very few papers in the current data set take this approach, perhaps because this type of study requires extensive engagement with individuals to ascertain the role of the library in their lives (generally) or in accomplishing a specific goal (specifically).

While most items continue to reflect the "instance" dimension of library use, some authors recognize that understanding library use is "not as straightforward as producing quantitative data" [29, p. 140] and employ user-centered research methods including surveys, focus groups, observations, and interviews. Chen and Huang [30] and Chen et al. [31] explored medical students' needs and behaviors in the context of their institution's change to a problem-based learning (PBL) curricular approach. Interested in exploring how the PBL approach might affect students' information needs and attendant uses of the library's facilities, resources, and services, the researchers conducted semi-structured interviews with a group of students. The interviews covered a wide range of subjects, focusing not only on students' information needs and behaviors vis-à-vis the library, but those addressed by resources and entities unrelated to the library. This expansion allowed researchers to grasp the entirety of the students' information needs, seeking, and use, and the role of the library's resources, services, and facilities in addressing them. Aabø and Audunson [29] used a mixed-method approach to study users' motivation for and behavior while visiting a collection of public libraries in Norway. In addition to observation, the researchers involved short interviews in which "users were asked what activities they were performing in the library that day, the context and life sphere to which these activities were linked, and their general library use, for example, frequency of visiting the library" [29, p. 142] In other words, the role of the library in their lives. Further analysis addresses the public library's place in society more generally, emphasizing the importance of the library as a kind of crossroads of the community.

3.3 Use as Abstraction or Something Else?

The "abstraction" dimension of library use represents instances of the concept that are removed from specific examples or operationalization, as in the interview protocol included as an appendix to a recent study of undergraduates' behavior: "Do you use the library? How? a. If yes, which ones? How often? Why do you use those resources or spaces? b. If no, why not?" [32, p. 396]. The "abstraction" dimension of use can be understood as an amorphous collection of behaviors; the authors in the preceding example could be asking respondents about any number of activities related to library facilities, collections, or resources…and the respondents could have any number of activities in mind. While the "abstraction" dimension of library use remains common in the LIS literature, review of the data set for this project revealed an additional dimension of the library use concept that the 2011 typology did not identify as distinct: use as behavior. This dimension could be understood as library use activities or instances of use observed without context. In other words, the activities an individual is perceived as engaging in (studying, attending a meeting, using the computer, browsing the new fiction) without a deeper understanding of the reasons for or benefits of said activities, and without the capacity for measurement instances of use typically provide. Describing findings from a survey of public library users, Richter, et al., provide an example, reporting "69% of respondents reported 'looking for library materials'" as their most common activity while visiting the library. [33, p. 436] While this is gratifying, without knowing why a person was looking for library materials, if they were successful, or the outcome of this activity, what remains is a behavior rather than a fuller understanding of the role of library materials in the lives of respondents. Because these descriptions lack context, they are too obscure to be understood as examples of use as a process. As these descriptions typically refer to observed or reported behaviors, they are more specific than "use as abstraction."

4 Conclusion

This short paper provides an overview of recent representations of "library use" in the professional and scholarly literature of LIS. An additional objective was reviewing the 2011 Library Use Typology for possible revision; indeed, a new dimension has emerged through this updated analysis: Use-as-behavior.

Evolutionary Concept Analysis finds that statistical measures, or "instances" of library use remain prominent, although some authors recognize a need for more nuanced understanding users' experience of library use [32]. Valorization of statistical methods and the large samples made possible by automated collection of usage data are a possible impediment to reaching this goal. The (aforementioned) semi-structured interviews conducted by Chen and their co-authors involved only 20 students [30, 31], a reasonable number of participants for an interpretive project, but a number many researchers more inclined toward quantitative approaches might consider shockingly small. The fact remains, however, that it is impossible to understand the role of library or information use in the life of the individual when the individual is one of 2000 survey respondents or represented by a collection of data points.

References

1. Fleming-May, R.A.: What is library use? Facets of concept and a typology of its application in the literature of library and information science. Libr. Q. **81**, 297–320 (2011)
2. Hjørland, B.: Concept theory. J. Am. Soc. Inform. Sci. Technol. **60**, 1519–1536 (2009)
3. Vakkari, P.: Information Seeking in Context. A Challenging Metatheory. Presented at the Information Seeking in Context, Tampere, Finland (1996)
4. Kari, J.: Diversity in the conceptions of information use. Inform. Res. Int. Electron. J. **15** (2010)
5. Dervin, B.: Useful theory for librarianship – communication, not information. Drexel Library Quar. **13**, 16–32 (1977)
6. Zweizig, D.L., Dervin, B.: Public library use, users, uses. In: Voigt, M., Harris, M.H. (eds.) Advances in librarianship, pp. 231–55. Acad press (1977)
7. Bookstein, A.: Sources of error in library questionnaires. Library Res. **4**, 85–94 (1982)
8. Kyrillidou, M.: From input and output measures to quality and outcome measures, or, from the user in the life of the library to the library in the life of the user. J. Acad. Librariansh. **28**, 42–46 (2002). https://doi.org/10.1016/S0099-1333(01)00299-3
9. Oakleaf, M.: The Value of Academic Libraries: A Comprehensive Research Review and Report. Association of College and Research Libraries, Chicago (2010)
10. Rodgers, B.L.: Concept analysis: an evolutionary view. In: Concept Development in Nursing: Foundations, Techniques, and Applications, pp. 77–102. Saunders (2000)
11. Ridner, S.H.: Psychological distress: concept analysis. J. Adv. Nurs. **45**, 536–545 (2004)
12. Zisberg, A., Young, H.M., Schepp, K., Zysberg, L.: A concept analysis of routine: relevance to nursing. J. Adv. Nurs. **57**, 442–453 (2007)

13. Kling, R., McKim, G.: Scholarly communication and the continuum of electronic publishing. J. Am. Soc. Inform. Sci. **50**, 890–906 (1999)
14. Hartman, K.A.: Retaining intellectual capital: retired faculty and academic libraries. Ref. User Serv. Quar. **48**, 384–390 (2009)
15. Merga, M.K., Roni, S.M.: Choosing strategies of children and the impact of age and gender on library use: insights for librarians. J. Libr. Adm. **57**, 607–630 (2017)
16. Arshad, A.: Effects of students' demographic and academic characteristics on library use: a perspective from Pakistan. Portal Librar. Acad. **21**, 1–21 (2021)
17. Johnson, C.A., Griffis, M.R.: The effect of public library use on the social capital of rural communities. J. Librariansh. Inf. Sci. **46**, 179–190 (2014)
18. Jara, M., et al.: Patterns of library use by undergraduate students in a Chilean University. Portal Librar. Acad. **17**, 595–615 (2017)
19. Parker, J.B.: Who uses the public library, and who cares? J. Libr. Adm. **54**, 318–326 (2014)
20. Han, X., Song, M., Li, C., Zhu, Q.: Can in-house use data of print collections shed new light on library practices? Statistical evidence from a five-year longitudinal study in China. J. Librariansh. Inf. Sci. **51**, 938–949 (2019)
21. Godfrey, B., Stoddart, R.: Managing In-library use data: putting a web geographic information systems platform through its paces. Inf. Technol. Libr. **37**, 34–49 (2018)
22. Ramsden, B.: Evaluating the impact of learning space. Ref. Serv. Rev. **39**, 451–464 (2011)
23. De Groote, S., Scoulas, J.M.: Impact of COVID-19 on the use of the academic library. Ref. Serv. Rev. **49**, 281–301 (2021)
24. Anderson, L., Vega García, S.: Library usage, instruction, and student success across disciplines: a multilevel model approach. C&RL. **81**, 459–492 (2020)
25. Haddow, G.: Academic library use and student retention: a quantitative analysis. Libr. Inf. Sci. Res. **07408188**(35), 127–136 (2013)
26. Cox, B., Jantti, M.: Discovering the impact of library use and student performance. EDUCAUSE Review (2012)
27. Cox, B.L., Jantti, M.: Capturing business intelligence required for targeted marketing, demonstrating value, and driving process improvement. Library Inform. Sci. Res. **34**, 308–316 (2012). https://doi.org/10.1016/j.lisr.2012.06.002
28. Robertshaw, M.B., Asher, A.: For a meta-analysis of findings from studies utilizing this approach, see Unethical Numbers? A Meta-analysis of Library Learning Analytics Studies. Library Trends. **68**, 76–101 (2019). https://doi.org/10.1353/lib.2019.0031
29. Aabø, S., Audunson, R.: Use of library space and the library as place. Libr. Inf. Sci. Res. **07408188**(34), 138–149 (2012)
30. Chen, K.-N., Huang, I.-T.: Library use by medical students engaging in problem-based learning: a taiwanese case study. Libri Int. J. Librar. Inform. Serv. **62**, 248–258 (2012)
31. Chen, K., Lin, P., Chang, S.-S., Sun, H.: Library use by medical students: a comparison of two curricula. J. Librariansh. Inf. Sci. **43**, 176–184 (2011)
32. Mayer, J., Dineen, R., Rockwell, A., Blodgett, J.: Undergraduate student success and library use: a multimethod approach. Coll. Res. Libr. **81**, 378–398 (2020)
33. Richter, S., Bell, J., Jackson, M.K., Lee, L.D., Dashora, P., Surette, S.: Public library users: perspectives of socially vulnerable populations. J. Libr. Adm. **59**, 431–441 (2019). https://doi.org/10.1080/01930826.2019.1593711

Shared LGBTQ+ Identity
in Librarian-Community Partnerships

Jesselyn Dreeszen Bowman(✉) ⓘ and Vanessa Kitzie ⓘ

University of South Carolina, Columbia, USA
Dreeszej@email.sc.edu, Kitzie@mailbox.sc.edu

Abstract. This project addresses whether library staff can build relevancy and trust with the populations they serve through shared identities. Specifically, it examines the results of a project partnering academic librarians with LGBTQ+ community leaders to co-create an information resource for the leader's community. Twenty-one leader-librarian pairs were recruited. Data was collected through monthly diaries and focus groups at the project's conclusion. Data was qualitatively analyzed to determine if and how the presence or absence of shared identities affected the partnerships. Findings indicate that when librarians are working with marginalized communities, sharing that marginalized identity could help reduce relational barriers. When librarians share LGBTQ+ identities with community members, the community members feel more comfortable with the librarians and feel a more significant investment in supporting the information needs of LGBTQ+ communities. Library directors and university administrators need to consider strategies such as LGBTQ+ affinity groups and professional development to foster safe library spaces where LGBTQ+ librarians can feel safe disclosing their identities to their communities.

Keywords: Academic libraries · LGBTQ+ populations · Community partnerships

1 Introduction

A challenge characterizing librarian outreach to underserved populations is that these populations might not view libraries or librarians as relevant or may mistrust them [14]. Hiring and promoting library staff with shared identities may address this challenge as they initiate outreach and engagement efforts with populations whose identities they share. Advantages of shared identities include a better sense of what is relevant to the population and heightened trust [9]. This project investigates this observation by examining the results of a project partnering North American librarians with LGBTQ+ community leaders from a southeast state to co-create a health information resource for the leader's community. Findings demonstrate how librarians can leverage shared identities with community leaders to facilitate outreach and collaboration with an underserved population. This study addresses the following research questions:

I. Sserwanga et al. (Eds.): iConference 2023, LNCS 13972, pp. 197–206, 2023.
https://doi.org/10.1007/978-3-031-28032-0_17

RQ 1) How, if at all, does the presence of shared identities between LGBTQ+ community leaders and librarians foster relationship building?
RQ 2) How, if at all, does the absence of shared identities between LGBTQ+ community leaders and librarians affect the relationship?

2 Literature Review

Library sciences once overlooked the LGBTQ+ community or felt that serving its needs would be too niche or a political act when a cornerstone of librarian ethics is neutrality [3]. Recently, librarians have acknowledged that neutrality is impossible and that librarians must concentrate efforts on supporting the marginalized communities most in need of service [8]. MLIS programs are now considering the needs of LBGTQ+ communities. Some programs even have classes dedicated entirely to LGBTQ+ communities (The University of South Carolina, n.d.). There has been a proliferation of sessions at professional conferences that address serving LGBTQ+ communities (e.g., American Association on School Librarians, 2021). It remains unclear if the LGBTQ+ communities feel this shift in intention.

Despite the potential role of libraries as "safe spaces" for LGBTQ+ communities, it remains unclear if the LGBTQ+ communities feel this shift in attention [14]. A factor that has been found to motivate LGBTQ+ to use the library is if library staff share their LGBTQ+ identities, especially within healthcare contexts [4, 11] Less evident in the literature is a discussion of how LGBTQ+ library workers manage their visibility in the workplace or when collaborating with LGBTQ+ users and communities (Fisher et al. 2019). This paper addresses the research gap by examining the relationship between LGTBQ+ community leaders, who perform their work within healthcare contexts and LGBTQ+ library workers, focusing on how these workers identities might facilitate community engagement.

In this paper, we define identity as produced between people and within social relations [10]. Identities are intersectional and interdependent rather than diverse and separate, and certain identity intersections take salience in various contexts [7]. Therefore, while LGBTQ+ identities are the focal point of the research, we also consider how these identities interact with other social locations, such as race and class, to characterize relationships between librarians and community leaders.

3 Methods

This research is part of a larger project that identified a cohort of LGBTQ+ community leaders from a Southeast state to receive community health worker training. As part of the project, leaders worked with health sciences librarians from across North America to create a health information resource for the leaders' communities. Examples of final resources created include an inclusive intake form, a social networking application for pansexual adults who come out later in life, and a webseries about how to navigate the health insurance marketplace geared towards transgender and nonbinary young adults. See https://bit.ly/lgbtqia_chws for more information.

3.1 Recruitment

We recruited 21 leader-librarian pairs from May–August 2021. We recruited LGBTQ+ leaders from the PI's research network and a contact list of visible LGBTQ+ communities and affinity3 groups in [redacted]. We contacted health sciences librarians from North America through the Medical Library Association listserv. Health sciences librarians

Table 1. LGBTQ+ leader demographics

Category	Label	N
Sexuality	Pansexual	5
	Queer	4
	Bisexual	3
	Gay	2
	Demisexual	2
	Polyamorous	1
	Lesbian	1
	Homosexual	1
Gender identity	Female	5
	Cisgender	3
	Queer	3
	Transgender	3
	Male	2
	Non-binary	3
	Demigirl	1
	Masculine	1
Race/ethnicity	Black	5
	White	3
	LatinX/Latine	2
	Multiracial	1
Age	25–44	9
	18–24	2
Education	Bachelor's	5
	Some college credit	4
	Associate's	1
	Master's	1

Note: Participants used multiple labels to describe their identities were not limited to [redacted] due to their small number. Those interested in participating attended a meeting and completed questionnaires collecting basic demographic information and their motivation for participating. We selected leaders and librarians based on their questionnaire responses and objectives for maximal variety regarding intersectional identities. We prioritized librarians with LGBTQIA+ identities or experiences working with LGBTQ+ communities. We paired librarians with leaders based on mutual interests and areas of expertise. Tables 1 and 2 show LGBTQ+ leader and librarian demographics.

Table 2. Librarian demographics

Category	Label	N
Sexuality	Straight	5
	Queer	4
	Gay	2
	Bisexual	2
	Asexual	1
	Questioning	1
Gender identity	Female	8
	Ciswoman	2
	Male	2
	Transgender	1
	Non-binary	1
	Genderqueer	1
Race/ethnicity	White	9
	Black	2
	Caribbean non-Latino	1
	Southeast Asian	1
Age	45–64	7
	25–44	6
Education	Master's	12
	Doctorate	1

Note: Participants used multiple labels to describe their identities

3.2 Data Collection

Data collection ranged from September 2021 - April 2022 and consisted of monthly diaries and focus groups. Each participant kept diaries they submitted to the research team at the end of each month. Diaries could be written responses or audio recordings. Participants responded to the same questions each month, which elicited the following themes: 1. What occurred with the partnership within the last month. 2. Forms of support and challenges experienced in this period. 3. Any additional information to share or questions to ask.

This paper focuses on the last two data sources: monthly diaries and focus groups. Each participant kept diaries they submitted to the research team at the end of each month. Diaries could be written responses or audio recordings. Participants responded to the same questions each month, which elicited the following themes:

1. What occurred with the partnership within the last month.
2. Forms of support and challenges experienced in this period.
3. Any additional information to share or questions to ask.

We held four 120-min focus groups of 5–6 people each asking participants to reflect on the project, including their partnerships. We divided groups by participant time-leaders and librarians. The protocol included several questions asking about the partnership (e.g., What identities do you have that you think influenced your relationship with your partner?) and used techniques and tools to encourage collective participation (e.g., list-making using virtual whiteboards). We audio-recorded focus groups and, along with any audio diaries, used Otter.ai to generate and refine verbatim transcripts for analysis.

3.3 Data Analysis

We employed open, in vivo, descriptive, and process-based coding (Saldaña 2013) to develop inductive codes that addressed the research questions. The authors coded 20% of the diaries and focus group transcripts using the research questions as parent coding categories. We then met twice to discuss emergent codes. During these discussions and subsequent coding, we employed the constant comparative method (Charmaz 2014), to identify and compare emergent codes to existing ones. The first author created a codebook based on this discussion and used it to code the rest of the data.

4 Findings

We organize findings by research question, illustrating each with lightly edited participant quotes. We use pseudonyms for all participants.

RQ1. How, if at all, does the presence of shared identities between LGBTQ+ community leaders and librarians foster relationship building? Leaders and health science librarians felt that shared identities developed a shared understanding of the leader's community needs. These included identifying as Black, transgender, gay, or a mother. Tony, a leader, expressed, "[my librarian] identifies as trans male So, I mean, that in itself was pretty easy to understand, like, why we feel like we need to do this." Avery, the librarian paired with Tony, wrote in his diary, "I feel that the partnership is going well. I'm in an interesting situation in that my leader partner and I share quite a few things in common: we are both transmen, live in southern states that both present issues for LGBT+ citizens, and have experience working with our local communities."

Avery felt that sharing this transgender identity led to more "organic" conversations and removed "potential early barriers" in their relationship. Drew, a librarian, noted that sharing a gay male identity helped his leader, Hileah Rainey, feel more comfortable with him. "Well, I think being gay I think helped him feel a little more comfortable opening up to me, also, knowing that I had volunteered at an [organization] in my earlier days. So he was comfortable talking about HIV AIDS and education, and things like that." Drew's leader agreed that because Drew was also a "member of the gay community, there was no learning curve." Had Drew not shared that gay identity with his leader, there may have been a barrier with Hileah Rainey being less willing to open up to Drew.

In four cases, the librarian shared identities with the leader because they both are LGBTQ+. When the librarians identified as LGBTQ+, they noted a personal and professional commitment to the project. Molly, who identifies as queer, indicated that she "was inspired to work with LGBTQIA+ communities because of my own identity as a person". Celina, who also identifies as queer, referenced a "personal investment" in and "personal connection" to the project. Sharing an LGBTQ+ identity helped librarians feel invested in the project because of their experiences. The leaders also noted the importance of the LGBTQ+ identities of the librarians. Celina's partner Emma expressed being "pleased" with her partner due to her genuine interest in Emma's idea. The librarian's LGBTQ+ identities led to excitement and passion for the project.

It was not only shared LGBTQ+ identities that brought partners together. Tyrech, a leader, noted that they and their librarian are Black, which facilitated their relationship. One pair was both mothers, and the leader and librarian identified the importance of sharing that experience. Elizabeth the librarian, wrote in her diary,

> We had a great meeting, and as with the meeting before, we enjoy exchanging stories and getting to know each other. While my children are older and both girls, rather than her one boy, there are many child-rearing issues we discuss, as well as many working mother issues we can commiserate with.

Partners also noted the commonality between librarians and leaders in that they are helping professionals who share commitments to their patrons or communities. Librarian Elizabeth wrote in her diary, "leaders and librarians are both helping professions, so our dedication to our jobs is similar." Lacking LGBTQ+ identities, partners found connections through professional identities or other social identities.

RQ2. How, If At All, Does the Absence of Shared Identities Between LGBTQ+ Community Leaders and Librarians Affect The Relationship? When there are not shared identities, there may be additional barriers to relationship building caused by mistrust. Leader Zayne was immediately mistrustful of zir librarian Alice who ze identified as "older and cisgender." Zayne felt "standoffish" towards zir librarian because she is an older cisgender woman while Zayne is young and trans. This lack of shared identity created a gulf between the two and impeded their relationship in the early stages of the project. In the initial brainstorming, Zayne felt like Alice wasn't listening to zim and expressed frustration that Alice wasn't hearing zim. Alice's patience, persistence, and showing a steady commitment to the project and Zayne's ideas improved the relationship throughout the project. Alice proved herself to Zayne through professional competence and compassion. As the relationship evolved, Zayne reflected:

> She's like super knowledgeable … And she was like, 'Oh, you should actually get a common licensure [creative commons license]. And I was like, what is that? It's something you'll see [on my resource]. And so that was really cool. And then she actually was able to talk to me. Code switched into LGBTQ language, which I thought was very impressive. I actually like her a lot. She was very considerate of me as a trans person.

Alice was compassionate to Zayne. When ze felt stressed about moving apartments, Alice asked for a video tour of the new apartment. Alice proved herself trustworthy and dependable, and slowly, Zayne opened up to her: "she always got back to me - check this out for me or can you look this up, and she always know how to handle it no matter what it was, which was awesome." When the pair lacked shared identities, the librarian's empathy skills could improve the relationship and build trust.

Sharing an LGBTQ+ identity was not always sufficient for fostering a strong partnership when librarians and leaders did not share other social identities. Leader Emma, who is pansexual and Black, struggled with her partner, who was bisexual and white. Even though the women shared sexuality, Emma doubted that Celina, a white woman, would be able to understand her perspective as a Black woman: "I went in, like looking at her sideways. I was just like, 'Oh God, here's another white woman.'" These racial differences also led to conflict in their partnership related to the resource Emma envisioned:

> And because I'm so much into intersectionality, there were like conversations we would have and it was just it go in one ear …My project is about pansexuality. So, she's like … why not just focus on like bisexuality or like lesbians? The first meeting was a lot of me saying no, that's not what I want.

In instances where the leader and librarian did not share any significant identities, they still attempted to find commonality through shared interests. This attempt could indicate that partners felt finding common ground was vital to relationship building and positively impacted the project. Robert, a transgender leader, was initially reticent of his older cisgender, heterosexual female librarian. During their initial brainstorm, Robert said his librarian was not hearing him. After months of meetings and relationship building, Robert felt close to his librarian. He said, "we had so many things in common," and referenced movies, politics, and Harry Potter. While Robert and his librarian did not share any identities, Robert could feel close to his librarian through shared interests. Leader Gloria noted the things she had in common with her librarian and mentioned not shared identities but shared interests and experiences: "We love animals. We love birds… She has visited [country] which is my home country."

Avery, who did share a transgender identity with his leader, still mentioned that he didn't want his partner to feel like Avery was taking control of the direction of the project:

There was some trust already, just because we have similar backgrounds, but I think there was trust building needed to, I think, assure them that I wasn't going to come in [and] dictate everything. And I think that that helped somewhat to make it so they felt that they could be more open about what they wanted to do.

Several other librarians noted in the focus group that they were hesitant to lead the project and wanted to give their leaders agency to identify the needs of their communities and guide the resource creation process. Even when librarians did share identities with leaders, the librarians were clear that more work was needed to strengthen the relationship. As Avery noted above, there was still trust-building required to build the information resources successfully. While shared identities were essential, librarians still needed to demonstrate a willingness to give leaders agency and to value their lived experience and knowledge of what resources would most benefit their communities.

5   Discussion

Findings indicate that when librarians are working with marginalized communities, sharing that marginalized identity or identities could help reduce relational barriers. When librarians share LGBTQ+ identities and other salient intersectional identities with community members, the community members feel more comfortable with the librarians and feel a more significant investment in supporting the information needs of LGBTQ+ communities. Therefore, a possible solution for academic libraries that seek to partner with LGBTQ+ communities is to hire more LGBTQ+ librarians, specifically those with salient identity intersections across social locations such as race and class.

Librarians may have ethical concerns about disclosing their LGBTQ+ identities to community members; their role as information experts means they must maintain firm boundaries and not share their personal experiences or identities. But findings denote such disclosure benefits the relationship between experts and community members. Sharing that these librarians have a personal and professional commitment to serving LGBTQ+ communities could make community members more willing to trust the librarians and accept their help, thereby strengthening the relationship and the project. However, librarians must feel safe enough to disclose their LGBTQ+ identities to community members. Library directors and university administrators need to consider strategies to foster safe library spaces where LGBTQ+ librarians can be their whole selves. These strategies include affinity groups for LGBTQ+ employees and professional development with a focus on gender and sexuality.

Even without shared identities, leader-librarian relationships could thrive when librarians exhibited empathy and compassion and made efforts to bond with leaders. Such soft skills are important for providing high quality service to all user groups.

MLIS programs should continue to implement ways to teach librarians these skills and helping them build meaningful personal connections with the communities they serve. There is also a need for cultural humility training. Sharing one or more identities with a community does not alleviate all barriers, and librarians must be mindful and respectful of the intersecting identities in their communities.

6 Conclusion

Presence and absence of shared LGBTQ+ identities among academic librarians and LGBTQ+ leaders have consequences for collaborations. Shared identities led to an early reduction of barriers and a meaningful personal connection to the project on the part of librarians. Lacking shared identities could lead to mistrust on the part of the community member. And sharing an LGBTQ+ identity was not always enough when partners lacked other social identities such as race.

A significant limitation of this project relates to the overall lack of health science librarians in [redacted]; as a result, we had to pair leaders with librarians who did not reside in their state. Several leaders expressed that they wished they could work with health sciences librarians from [redacted] who would better understand their background and experience. Another challenge with the limited number of health science librarians was that it was not always possible to pair librarians and leaders based on shared identities. Finally, this project specifically explored the relationships between health sciences librarians and LGBTQ+ community leaders. The applications of this project to other settings, for example, public librarians partnered with LGBTQ+ communities, still need to be explored.

Findings have several implications concerning fostering relationships between academic librarians and marginalized communities. Communities may feel wary of the experts based on previous negative experiences with experts claiming to have their best interests. Relationship building is needed to build a bond between experts and community members before the two can successfully work together. Sharing identities with community members reduces barriers. It is essential to consider that experts who share the marginalized identities of their community partners may be more able to build relationships that shift unavoidable power imbalances. Experts must also possess soft skills such as empathy and a willingness to invest time and effort in relationship building.

References

1. American Association of School Librarians: AASL National Conference (2021). https://national.aasl.org/. Accessed 9 Dec 2022
2. American Public Health Association (APHA): Community health workers (2021). https://www.apha.org/apha-communities/member-sections/community-health-workers. Accessed 9 June 2022
3. Attwell, V.: "In all areas, I cater to the majority": An Investigation of LGBT+ Provision in School Libraries from the Librarian's Perspective. School Libraries Worldwide (2020)
4. Fikar, C.R., Keith, L.: Information needs of gay, lesbian, bisexual, and transgendered health care professionals: results of an internet survey. JMLA **92**(1), 56–65 (2004)
5. Charmaz, K.: Constructing Grounded Theory, 2nd edn. Sage, Thousand Oaks, CA (2014)
6. Conron, K., Mimiaga, M., Landers, S.: A population-based study of sexual orientation identity and gender differences in adult health. Am. J. Public Health **100**(10), 1953–1960 (2010)
7. Crenshaw, K.: Mapping the Margins: Intersectionality, identity Politics, and violence against women of color. Stanford Law Rev. **43**(6), 1241–1299 (1991)
8. Drabinski, E.: Are libraries neutral? [Conference Session]. American Library Association Midwinter Conference, Denver, CO, United States (2018). http://www.emilydrabinski.com/are-libraries-neutral/

9. Fisher, Z., Krueger, S.G., Malamud, R.G., Patillo, E.: What It means to be out: queer, trans, and gender nonconforming identities in library work. In: Baer, A., Cahoy, E., Schroeder, R. (eds.) Libraries Promoting Reflective Dialogue in a Time of Political Polarization, pp. 71, 90. ACRL Publications, Chicago (2019)
10. Lawler, S.: Identity: Sociological Perspectives. Wiley (2015)
11. Morris, M., Roberto, K.R.: Information seeking behavior and information needs of LGBTQ health professionals: a follow-up study. Health Inform. Librar. J. **33**(3), 204–221 (2016). https://doi.org/10.1111/hir.12139
12. Saldaña, J.: The Coding Manual for Qualitative Researchers, 2nd edn. Sage, Thousand Oaks, CA (2013)
13. University of South Carolina: Master of library and information science. College of Information and Communication (n.d.). https://sc.edu/study/colleges_schools/cic/academic_programs/masters/master_of_library_and_information_science/index.php. Accessed 9 Sept 2022
14. Wexelbaum, R.S.: Do libraries save LGBT students?. Library Management (2018)

Bridging the Research-Practice Gap in China's Librarianship through Library Societies: A Pilot Study

Wei Feng(✉) and Lihong Zhou

School of Information Management, Wuhan University, Wuhan 430072, China
fengwei211@whu.edu.cn

Abstract. The integration of research and practice is the basic guarantee for librarianship, but there is still a research-practice gap in China's librarianship. Library Society of China (LSC) is an important force to promote the integration of research and practice in China. This pilot study employed an inductive case study approach. Five core members of LSC were interviewed using a semi-structured question script designed based on the theoretical framework of Community of Practice (CoP). According to the theory of CoP, this paper carried out the analysis procedure and summarized the development experience of LSC in bridging the research-practice gap from three perspectives: micro-level identity, meso-level practice, and macro-level cooperation. The research findings can provide indications and strategies for bridging the research-practice gap in other countries and other related disciplines.

Keywords: China · Community of practice · Librarianship · Library society · Research-practice gap

1 Introduction

An overall and harmonious development of librarianship depends on the interaction between theoretical research and practical work [1]. In any case, librarianship should be rooted in theory and practice integration, and research should be integrated and intertwined with practice [2, 3]. However, librarianship has a research-practice gap [4–8] often resulting from both researchers and practitioners [9, 10]. Thus, how to close this gap is an ongoing issue in library and information research [7, 11, 12].

In China, it is not new to suggest that there is a research-practice gap in librarianship. Although the practice of libraries has advanced significantly in China since the beginning of Reform and Opening-Up in 1978, some Chinese scholars remained focused on fundamental issues in the 1950s. This has led to the reality that research and practice are unrelated [13–15]. Since entering the 21st century, with the profound impact of technology on librarianship, researchers have heavily focused on technology but lack concern about practical problems, making it difficult for library practitioners to keep up with the pace of scientific research [16, 17].

I. Sserwanga et al. (Eds.): iConference 2023, LNCS 13972, pp. 207–216, 2023.
https://doi.org/10.1007/978-3-031-28032-0_18

To bridge the research-practice gap, both Chinese researchers and practitioners transferred the focus to the library development strategy [18–22]. Although the study of development strategy yielded excellent insights, this effort did not significantly bridge the research-practice gap. Librarians are driven to participate in the work of professional library associations in today's society, which is undergoing significant changes brought on primarily by new technologies and globalization[23]. Bridging the research-practice gap through library associations has gradually become a new solution [9, 24, 25].

The Library Society of China (LSC) has successfully established itself as a vital hub connecting research and practice. But the efforts of LSC to close the gap have not been the subject of studies. Therefore, LSC will be employed as a case study to explore how library societies bridge the research-practice gap. The following research questions are formulated to further this study:

RQ1. How does LSC bridge the research-practice gap in China's librarianship?

RQ2. How the research findings can be used for establishing strategies?

2   Theoretical Basis

Community of Practice (CoP) referred to "groups of people who share a concern, a set of problems, or a passion about a topic, and who deepen their knowledge and expertise in this area by interacting on an ongoing basis" [26]. The theory of CoP was founded to bridge the knowledge gap between apprentices and experts [27, 28]. The domain, the practice, and the community are the three constructs that distinguish a CoP from other types of communities [26].

Practitioners and researchers join LSC for the shared vision of librarianship, and that is the "domain". Then they share a repertoire of resources, address recurring problems, and keep sustained interaction with other members [26, 28], that is the "practice". All members in LSC, who have bonded due to their shared interest (domain), form a "community". Therefore, LSC is a typical CoP, which contains many subordinate CoPs, like provincial library societies; and is also part of the larger CoPs, like IFLA.

The problem of the research-practice gap has been studied through the lens of CoP theory [29, 30]. Developed from Wenger's core constructs of CoP, this research adopts the following three themes to form the preliminary framework:

(1) *Micro-level identity*: This perspective pays more attention to individuals who are very small units of CoP. Instead of personal identity, identity in CoP is professional, working, and social. Its revolution is molded by others' reactions [31] or complicated interactions between individuals [32] in their social environment [33].

(2) *Meso-level practice*: The meso-level practice has served as the micro-macro connection [34] between identity and cooperation. A CoP is not merely a community of interest but practice. Through practice, participants build a common repertory of resources, including experiences, stories, tools, and approaches to reoccurring problems [26, 28].

(3) *Macro-level cooperation*: Macro-level is the larger abstract level that sort of stands above the other two levels. Lave and Wenger (1991) [35] introduced the concept

of legitimate peripheral learning, which evolved into cooperative learning. Cooperative learning is also a way to link learning with participation and build shared knowledge in CoP [36].

3 Research Method and Processes

3.1 Literature Review

The theoretical framework was constructed through a systematic literature review, which was carried out from January to March 2022. Academic articles about CoP were retrieved from two research databases: Web of Science and Scopus. The database search returned a total of 245 articles, 124 from Web of Science and 121 from Scopus. After careful screening, 48 articles were included for literature analysis. The screening and selection processes are demonstrated in the Preferred Reporting Items for Systematic Reviews and Meta-Analysis (PRISMA) flow diagram (see Fig. 1).

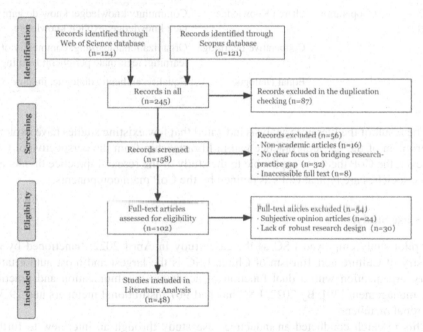

Fig. 1. PRISMA diagram on article screening processes.

The approach of thematic analysis was used in literature analysis, which is defined as a systematic approach using coding to represent qualitative data [37]. In the specific coding process, the research team combined open, axial, and selective coding, as suggested by Corbin and Strauss (1998) [38]. The three themes, outlined in Sect. 2, served as a beginning point for the data analysis, supplying an initial and speculative collection of thematic codes, theoretical themes, and linkages. The literature analysis was conducted using MAXQDA software and pointed to the themes and codes shown in Table 1.

Table 1. Themes, sub-themes, and codes derived from the literature review.

Perspective	Theme	Sub-theme	Codes
Micro-Level	Identity	Common Vision	Values, enterprise, visions, missions
		Participants	Members, researchers and practitioners, organizational structure
		Identity Acceptance	Professional identity, status, standing, sharpen expertise, shape identity
Meso-Level	Practice	Mutual Engagement	Relationship building, participating in activities, further interaction, continuing motivation to participate
		Reflection on Practice	Reflective practice, reflective narratives, reflective research work
		Situated Learning	Learning culture, learning environment, learning situation
Macro-Level	Cooperation	Shared Knowledge	Community knowledge; know-do gap; tacit knowledge; explicit knowledge
		Cooperative Learning	Organizational learning, community of learning, legitimate peripheral learning
		Equal Dialogue	Equality, authentic dialogue, inquiry

The result of the literature analysis indicated that few existing studies have explored the problem of the research-practice gap in librarianship from the perspective of CoP. However, the CoP theory is applicable to the study of the research-practice divide, and library societies are typical CoPs as defined by the CoP main components.

3.2 Case Study

This pilot study employed LSC as the case study in April 2022. Sanctioned by the Ministry of Culture and Tourism of China, LSC is the largest and most authoritative library organization with a dual function of academic communication and practical work management [39]. By 2022, LSC has had 967 institutional members and 29,396 individual members.

This research conducted an inductive case study through an interview to further explore the research questions. A semi-structured question script was designed to obtain interview data. The interview questions were based on the CoP framework. In the actual interview process, the order and content of the interview questions were flexibly adjusted according to the respondents' answers, allowing the interviewees to carry out appropriate expansion and discussion without leaving the subject. A total of 5 researchers and practitioners were interviewed and each review lasted from forty minutes to one hour. Information of the interviewees is shown in Table 2.

Table 2. Personal information of interviewees.

Interviewees	Personal information
A	Director of a provincial library society in China, Deputy director of a provincial public library in China
B	Librarian of a university library which is an institutional member of LSC
C	Director of the professional group under one committee of LSC, Professor of one of the top LIS schools in China
D	Member of one committee of LSC, Professor of one of the top LIS schools in China
E	Professor of one of the top LIS schools in China, Once won the *Talent Young Award of LSC*

With consent from interviewees, the interviews were recorded and transcribed into word files, averaging about 10,000 Chinese characters each. Although there were only 5 interviewees in this research, each of them was the focus of LSC and was interviewed very deeply. The analysis of the interview data inherited the thematic analysis strategy used in Sect. 3.1. And themes and codes that emerged from the literature analysis were adopted as the starting point for the analysis of the interview transcripts.

4 Research Findings

4.1 Identity

The data analysis showed that LSC has formed different identity acceptance systems for young scholars and practitioners. Although this system "has not been formally written into regulations" (Interview E), it has imperceptibly affected the mutual acceptance of researchers and practitioners in LSC and laid the foundation for mutual engagement at theoretical and practical levels.

Researchers in Library Science. LSC primarily plays the role of promoting academic communication in the transition of young scholars from green to practiced hands. Firstly, the academic conferences held by LSC are open to all researchers and practitioners. "The academic papers [of young scholars] will not be refused directly instead with more encouragement and attention during reviewing" (Interview B). LSC provides young scholars more opportunities to be recognized and known by "giving conference paper rating awards and inviting young scholars to deliver oral reports" (Interview A). Particularly, LSC has held *Youth Academic Forum* as a platform for young scholars to communicate and learn since 2002, so that they can "emerge in the academic community" (Interview D). In addition, LSC has set up *Young Talent Award* and other evaluation mechanisms. Each provincial library society can recommend outstanding young scholars to participate in the evaluation to "obtain the chance to be recognized by other scholars" (Interview E).

Practitioners in Library Work. Since 2001, LSC has actively assisted some national ministries to "carry out the work of professional qualification for librarians, such as drafting professional qualification reports, formulating national professional standards, and compiling vocational teaching syllabi" (Interview C). Although a professional qualification system for librarians has not been formally established, "the membership registration process [of LSC] has the same effect as professional qualification" (Interview A). Because LSC membership candidates must submit corresponding materials with previous acknowledgment of their affiliations and the provincial library societies. Under the provisions of the membership system of LSC, the professional qualification for librarians is equivalent to the procedure of "first determining the job and then certifying through registered members" (Interview A).

4.2 Practice

LSC has led a series of practical work, in which reading promotion, assessment and rating, and continuing education are the most frequently mentioned cases. LSC fully mobilizes the academic and practical forces to participate in practice together, so that "the scholars can find problems in practice, actively reflect these practical problems to academia, and provide solutions [from the theoretical level]" (Interview B). These practices "reflect the stronger ability of LSC to narrow the research-practice gap in China's librarianship" (Interview A).

Reading Promotion. LSC has formed a mature working mode in reading promotion to narrow the research-practice gap. For instance, to summarize the practical experience and reflect on the practice process, LSC has "organized a series of seminars and funded several research projects to explore the theory and practice of reading promotion" (Interview D). And LSC often holds some evaluation activities (e.g., Excellent Reading Promotion Case Selection, Excellent Reading Promoter Selection, etc.) and "distributes them to the provincial library societies to implement, while LSC also actively participates in the international excellent work case evaluation" (Interview C).

Assessment and Rating. Since 1994, the Chinese government has begun to carry out the work of National Public Library Assessment and Rating (NPLAR) every four years, which is a process of "refining problems from the practical level to the theoretical level" (Interview A and B). As the executive organization, LSC has gradually undertaken more responsibility, like formulating assessment standards in the third NPLAR in 2006, conducting training for relevant staff before assessment in 2008 and 2012, etc. Generally, "NPLAR is divided into two parts: standard setting and specific implementation, respectively responsible by researchers and practitioners" (Interview A). Library practitioners would summarize the practical problems during the implementation of NPLAR, so that researchers can "explore solutions, basically forming a 'theory-practice-theory' closed loop" (Interview C).

Continuing Education. Continuing education for librarians can "ensure their professionalism and advancement" (Interview A). So LSC "delegated theoretical experts to train librarians and preach at libraries to help them understand the latest developments in the discipline, realizing the dissemination of theoretical research results to the practice" (Interview E). Practitioners can selectively receive guidance and suggestions from the theorists according to the needs of practical work. At the same time, continuing education is also a good opportunity for researchers to learn about the practice. With knowledge from practice, researchers will "carry out relevant research that is more instructive to practice" (Interview B).

4.3 Cooperation

Sharing Knowledge. The external cause of equality and cooperation between researchers and practitioners is the establishment of their relationship through mutual engagement, while the internal cause is the sharing and flowing of knowledge between the two communities. "The knowledge of researchers comes from their learning and thinking, while that of practitioners comes from practice" (Interview A). Due to the applicability and practicality of library science [40], the knowledge source of researchers is essentially the same as that of practitioners. The meso-level practice provided by LSC enables their knowledge to flow and share. In this process, the two sides "share their tacit knowledge to become the common community knowledge of LSC, creating a mutually compatible knowledge system in the community of LSC" (Interview D and E).

Cooperative Learning. The macro-level cooperation involves two aspects, one is that LSC as a CoP cooperates with the sub-CoPs at the internal level, and the other is LSC as a CoP cooperates with other external CoPs. As for the inner collaboration within LSC, the subordinate library societies basically "keep the same pace with LSC to arrange work, [which is passive cooperation;] while pursuing certain innovations, [which is active learning]" (Interview A and B). As far as external cooperation, LSC, as one of the initiators and members of IFLA, actively participates in the relevant activities of IFLA and serves the development of global librarianship by sending talents to IFLA. On the other hand, LSC actively communicates with other national library associations by "co-hosting library forums, sending library researchers and practitioners to study abroad and absorb experience, providing training and assistance for libraries in developing countries" (Interview A). The cooperative learning of LSC has contributed to "bridging the research-practice gap of not only China's librarianship but also international librarianship" (Interview B).

Equal Dialogue. Researchers of LSC have the responsibility to assist relevant national ministries in formulating library-related laws, standards, norms, etc. Although theoretical researchers cannot focus on practice, "long-term theoretical thinking allows them to have a deeper insight into the problem, so they can play a major role in the formulation of relevant standards" (Interview A). Researchers in library science need to "carry out some theoretical explorations higher than practice to build a complete discipline system and enhance the influence of library science" (Interview A). Therefore, only the equal dialogue between researchers and practitioners can "achieve interactive integration of discipline construction and practice" (Interview C).

5 Discussion and Conclusion

5.1 Discussion

The research findings reveal that LSC has been a major force in bridging the research-practice gap in librarianship but also, that the CoP theory is especially useful for explaining LSC's operating mechanism from identity, practice, and cooperation, which are potentially interrelated and influential.

After participating in LSC, researchers and practitioners gain identity acceptance from other participants and society. Then, they mutually engage in activities organized by LSC and establish relationships with each other. The two communities grow together through situated learning. Researchers reflect and study practical problems, while practitioners improve practice with theories. Next, based on the shared knowledge system established in practice, researchers and practitioners carry out cooperative learning inside and outside LSC, achieving equal dialogue and integration of both communities.

Through understanding the connection and priorities of different constructs, three main strategies to bridge the research-practice gap through library societies are formulated specifically: (1) Establishing the identity acceptance mechanism for researchers and practitioners; (2) Providing researchers and practitioners with mutual engagement chances in each other's situation; (3) Promoting the continuous dialogue through designed and performed practice.

5.2 Conclusion

This pilot study explores how to bridge the research-practice gap in librarianship with library society as a solution through the lens of the CoP theory. Using an inductive case study approach, the authors analyzed the operating mechanism of LSC from identity, practice, and cooperation. The research findings provide some implications and strategies for spanning the research-practice gap in librarianship, and the CoP theory can be employed as a new theoretical lens for library science.

Several limitations can be addressed in future work. A sample size of only 5 interviewees is not enough. The research findings will be more reliable and abundant with more informants. The applicability of CoP theory in library science remains further explored. And due to the length limitation of the short paper, not all codes are shown in the research findings. In the future, this study plans to conduct in-depth research on the work of LSC with the theory of CoP and investigate more national library societies to explore how to bridge the research-practice gap in librarianship.

References

1. Ardanuy, J., Urbano, C.: The academic-practitioner gap in Spanish library and information science: an analysis of authorship and collaboration in two leading national publications. J. Librariansh. Inf. Sci. **51**, 317–330 (2019). https://doi.org/10.1177/0961000617726125
2. Harris, L.: Spanning the theory-practice divide in library and information science. JASIST. **58**, 606–607 (2007). https://doi.org/10.1002/asi.20440

3. Case, D.: Looking for Information: A Survey of Research on Information Seeking, Needs, and Behavior, Part 1. Emerald Publishing Group, Bingley, UK (2012)
4. Bawden, D.: Smoother pebbles and the shoulders of giants: the developing foundations of information science. J. Inf. Sci. **34**, 415–426 (2008). https://doi.org/10.1177/0165551508089717
5. Feather, J.: LIS research in the United Kingdom: reflections and prospects. J. Librariansh. Inf. Sci. **41**, 173–181 (2009). https://doi.org/10.1177/0961000609337096
6. Klobas, J.E., Clyde, L.A.: Beliefs, attitudes and perceptions about research and practice in a professional field. Libr. Inf. Sci. Res. **32**, 237–245 (2010). https://doi.org/10.1016/j.lisr.2010.07.004
7. Ponti, M.: A LIS collaboratory to bridge the research-practice gap. Libr. Manag. **29**, 265–277 (2008). https://doi.org/10.1108/01435120810869066
8. Liu, Y., Xie, H., Gu, Y.: The academic-practitioner gap in LIS: an explanation based on practical relevance and scientific rigor. Library and Information Service. **60**, 32–41 (2016) (in Chinese). https://doi.org/10.13266/j.issn.0252-3116.2016.24.005
9. Matteson, M.: The YBP student writing award winner - integrating theory and practice: the role of the professional library association. Libr. Leadersh. Manag. **22**, 10–14 (2008). https://doi.org/10.5860/llm.v22i1.1710
10. Hall, H., Cruickshank, P., Ryan, B.: Closing the researcher-practitioner gap: an exploration of the impact of an AHRC networking grant. Journal of Documentation **75**(5), 10561081 (2019). https://doi.org/10.1108/JD-12-2018-0212
11. Ipadeola, O., Ogungbade, A.: From classroom to the field of library practice: the gaps and its cost in the librarianship profession. Library Philosophy and Practice (e-journal) (2021)
12. Booth, A.: Bridging the research-practice gap? the role of evidence based librarianship. New Review of Inf. Library Res. **9**, 3–23 (2003). https://doi.org/10.1080/13614550410001687909
13. Qiu, C., Huang, X.: Research on the library science research in the new period of China. Journal of Library Science in China, 31–39 (1982) (in Chinese)
14. Chai, C.: Library science in the ten years reform: comments on the study of measure taken to solve problem of "theory divorced from practice". Journal of Library Science in China, 39–41+92 (1991) (in Chinese)
15. Chai, C.: A review of the discussion on the disconnection between theory and practice of library science in the ten years of reform. Library and Information Service, 13–17 (1991) (in Chinese)
16. Cong, J.: The divorce between theory and practice in library science research and the strategies concerned. Library and Information Service 89–91 (2001) (in Chinese)
17. Xiong, W.: A study on the discipline progress and existing problems of China's library science after 1949. Library and Information Service, 37–41 (2003) (in Chinese)
18. Huang, C.: Some thoughts on the development strategy of librarianship in China. Journal of Library Science in China 15–22+32 (1986) (in Chinese)
19. Xiang, Y.: Suggestions on the development strategy of China's librarianship. Journal of Library Science in China 36–39 (1998) (in Chinese)
20. Wu, W., Luo, Z.: Research on the development strategy of China's librarianship. Journal of Library Science in China 7–13+79 (1997) (in Chinese)
21. Yan, D., Lin, S.: Thinking on the development strategy of university librarianship. Journal of Library Science in China 67–69+94–95 (1989) (in Chinese)
22. Han, J.: The research of the development strategy - the enlightening idea of the Chinese library's modernization. Library 4–7 (1996) (in Chinese)
23. Horvat, A., Mišetić, M.: The Role of a Professional Library Association Today **56**, 1–12 (2013)
24. Haddow, G.: Communicating research to practice: the role of professional association publications. Library and Information Res. **34**, (2011). https://doi.org/10.29173/lirg332

25. Eldredge, J.: Integrating research into practice. J. Medical Library Association: JMLA. **104**, 333–337 (2016). https://doi.org/10.3163/1536-5050.104.4.017

26. Wenger, E., McDermott, R., Snyder, W.: Cultivating Communities of Practice: A Guide to Managing Knowledge. Harvard Business School Press, Boston, MA (2002)

27. Galvani, R.: The Apprentice's Tale: Entry to Multiple Communities of Practice for Working Class Boys. UCL (University College London), London, UK (2017)

28. Li, L.C., Grimshaw, J.M., Nielsen, C., Judd, M., Coyte, P.C., Graham, I.D.: Evolution of wenger's concept of community of practice. Implement. Sci. **4**, 11 (2009). https://doi.org/10.1186/1748-5908-4-11

29. Bone, T.J.: Bridging the Theory-to-Practice Gap: A Multivariate Correlational Study Exploring the Effects of a Graduate Online Learning Environment as a Community of Practice Framework (2013)

30. Tavakoli, P.: Connecting research and practice in TESOL: a community of practice perspective. RELC J. **46**, 37–52 (2015). https://doi.org/10.1177/0033688215572005

31. Ibarra, H.: Provisional selves: experimenting with image and identity in professional adaptation. Administrative Science Quarterly - ADMIN SCI QUART. **44**, 764–791 (1999). https://doi.org/10.2307/2667055

32. Williams, J.: Identity and learning within communities of practice. In: Williams, J. (ed.): Constructing New Professional Identities: Career Changers in Teacher Education. pp. 25–40. SensePublishers, Rotterdam (2013). https://doi.org/10.1007/978-94-6209-260-0_4

33. Gomes, W.B., Teixeira, M.A.P.: Autonomous career change among professionals: an empirical phenomenological study. J. Phenomenol. Psychol. **31**, 78–96 (2000)

34. Serpa, S., Ferreira, C.: Micro, meso and macro levels of social analysis. Int. J. Social Science Studies **7**, 120 (2019). https://doi.org/10.11114/ijsss.v7i3.4223

35. Lave, J., Wenger, E.: Situated Learning: Legitimate Peripheral Participation. Cambridge University Press (1991). https://doi.org/10.1017/CBO9780511815355.

36. Lastrucci, E., Pascale, A.: Cooperative learning through communities of practice. International Journal of Digital Literacy and Digital Competence. **1**, 11–21 (2010). https://doi.org/10.4018/jdldc.2010040102.

37. King, N., Horrocks, C., Brooks, J.: Interviews in Qualitative Research. SAGE, London (2018)

38. Strauss, A.L., Corbin, J.M.: Basics of Qualitative Research (3rd ed.): Techniques and Procedures for Developing Grounded Theory. Sage Publications, Thousand Oaks (1998)

39. Library Society of China: Introduction to Library Society of China. https://www.lsc.org.cn/cns/channels/1297.html. Accessed 12 Dec 2022

40. Shearer, K.: The impact of research on librarianship. J. Educ. Librariansh. **20**, 114–128 (1979). https://doi.org/10.2307/40322626

Automation of University Library Operations: An Analysis of the COVID-19 Pandemic Experience in the United Kingdom and Nigeria

Gbenga Adetunla[1,2]( ) , Diane Rasmussen Pennington[1,3], and Gobinda Chowdhury[1]

[1] University of Strathclyde, 26 Richmond Street, Glasgow G1 1XH, UK
{gbenga.adetunla,gobinda.chowdhury}@strath.ac.uk
[2] Ekiti State University, Ado Ekiti 362103, Nigeria
[3] Edinburgh Napier University, Edinburgh EH10 5DT, UK
d.pennington@napier.ac.uk

Abstract. This study examined how automation systems enhanced the operations of university libraries in Nigeria and the United Kingdom (UK) during the COVID-19 pandemic. It reviewed literature on the extent of automation, effectiveness of the use of automation technology and ascertained the challenges of automation in the operations of university libraries during COVID-19 lockdown in Nigeria and the United Kingdom. Findings revealed that most university libraries in the UK are fully automated while university libraries in Nigeria are either partially automated or not automated. During the COVID-19 lockdown, university libraries in the UK were able to provide services, while Nigerian libraries were unable to render services. UK and Nigeria were both faced with challenges during the lockdown. Some UK libraries could not optimally provide services due to insufficient licenses for digital content. In Nigeria, there were several socio-technical issues such as inadequate staff access to computers and the internet, poor power supply, and a lack of ICT skills. The study concluded that university libraries in Nigeria should embrace more technology if they want to be effective in their operations and be able to compete favourably in the global space.

Keywords: Library automation · Integrated library system · University library operation · COVID-19 pandemic

1 Introduction

A library is an integral organ of a university which functions in line with the university's vision and mission to achieve its goals. A university library is charged with the responsibility of collection, processing, storage, and dissemination of recorded information for the purpose of reading, teaching, life-long learning, and research. The operations of the university library follow through an entire chain from collection development to information dissemination, such as acquisition, cataloguing, and circulation [2].

© The Author(s), under exclusive license to Springer Nature Switzerland AG 2023
I. Sserwanga et al. (Eds.): iConference 2023, LNCS 13972, pp. 217–225, 2023.
https://doi.org/10.1007/978-3-031-28032-0_19

Acquisition operations involve the selection and purchase of materials or resources, selection of vendors, negotiating consortium pricing, arranging standing orders, and selecting individual titles or resources [10]. Cataloging and classification are core functions of the library, dealing with the organization and arrangement of library holdings for easy location, creating multiple access points for easy retrieval, and creating advanced search terms i.e., title, author's name, publisher, date, and place of publication etc. [16]. Circulation and reference services are the main service points. They provide lending services, facilitate return of loaned items, renew materials, and collect fines [22].

The advent of Information and Communication Technologies (ICT) has influenced the use of technology in the day-to-day operations of university libraries, and this has brought about the concept of library automation. It has transformed library operations from manual processes to the use of computer technologies [29]. University libraries now use Library Management Systems (LMS) to automate their core operations for more efficient service delivery.

COVID-19 halted almost every aspect of human endeavor, shutting down economic, social, and industrial activities across the globe. The education sector was not spared, including universities. University libraries shut down their physical operations.

University libraries in the United Kingdom (UK) and Nigeria have invested heavily in automation systems [10, 35]. Their adoption presumably is to significantly improve the quality of services rendered; services that are limitless in time and space. It therefore became useful to explore how automation enhanced the operations of university libraries in Nigeria and the UK during the pandemic. Resulting from this, our research questions were as follows:

1. What is the extent of automation within university libraries in Nigeria and the United Kingdom?
2. How did automation enhance the operations of university libraries during COVID-19 lockdown in Nigeria and the UK?
3. What were the challenges of automation in the operations of university libraries during COVID-19 lockdown in Nigeria and the UK?

2   Methodology

This study used a literature review to appraise published literature in line with the research questions. The University of Strathclyde Library's discovery layer, SUPrimo, was used to find sources published between 2019–2022. Google Scholar was also used to find other relevant sources. The Boolean keyword approach was used to search, and a set of inclusion criteria was applied on titles and abstracts of located resources. 36 relevant sources were reviewed for this study (Table 1).

Table 1. Breakdown of searches and selection of resources.

Boolean keywords	Search engines and number of resources	Inclusion criteria	Number of resources by inclusion criteria
("higher education library*" OR "university library*" AND "online services" OR "library automation" OR "digital library operation*") ("covid 19 pandemic" OR "covid-19") AND ("United Kingdom" AND "Nigeria")	Library and Information Science Abstracts (LISA): 453 Library, Information Science, and Technology Abstracts (LISTA): 506 Sage: 7 Google Scholar: 64	**Themes:** • Library automation • COVID-19/pandemic • Digital library environment • University library operations/services • Nigeria • United Kingdom **Language:** English **Full text**	10 5 2 19 36
Totals	1031		36

3 Literature Review

The review resulted in a general background on library automation, the extent of automation in university library operation, the operations of university libraries during COVID-19 lockdown, and the challenges of automation in the operations of university libraries during lockdown in the UK and Nigeria.

3.1 Library Automation

The advent of ICT has shaped our day-to-day activities. ICT could be described as a diverse set of technological tools and resources used for creating, storing, managing, and communicating information in the digital space [11]. Organizations now use ICT to carry out their operations. Libraries are now automating their operations for more efficient service delivery. Library automation is the application of technologies in the day-to-day operations of the library [7]. This term is often interchangeable with library computerization, mechanization, and the use of LMS.

Library automation dates to the 1950's and 1960's in the United States of America and the UK respectively [23, 32]. In 1968, the three major libraries in Birmingham, UK (Birmingham Public Libraries, University of Aston, and University of Birmingham) came together under a project known as the Birmingham Libraries Co-operative Mechanization Project (BLCMP) to develop an automation system. This laudable project initially gained the attention and funding of the Scientific and Technical Information Office and later the British Library Research and Development Department. Over the years, the BLCMP cooperative cataloguing scheme gained the interest of other libraries, and its membership began to expand. BLCMP was later commercialized, and this gave birth to the first indigenous library management system in the UK. The BLCMP Library System (BLS) incorporated all modules and a database of 7.5 million bibliographic records. By the end of the 1980s, over 50 libraries in the UK had incorporated BLS [31].

Developing countries such as Nigeria began automation in the 1980s. The first known university library automation efforts involved Ahmadu Bello University, Nnamdi Azikiwe University, University of Nigeria Nsukka and University of Lagos [3]. In 1992, the National University Commission attracted World Bank funding to install The Information Navigator Library software in 20 participating federal universities' libraries [6].

Over the years, there has been an expansion of automation systems in the UK and Nigerian university libraries, and it has proven successful operationally. Despite the successes, there was a rise and fall in the use of these automation systems, and this became a concern for the libraries. Studies have examined the issues around automated operations and systems in the UK and Nigeria. In the UK, staff training and inadequate finance were major pitfalls. In Nigeria, lack of technical knowledge, incompetence in software development, and poor hardware maintenance were the issues [3, 14]. In a bid to overcome these challenges, libraries started looking for a better alternative. In the late 1990s, open-source ILS started surfacing, with features that seemed to provide solutions to their problems.

Open-source ILS are non-proprietary software or software made available for free to users [29]. Examples include Avanti, MicroLCS, PhpMyLibrary, Emilda, and Koha. Many libraries in the UK and Nigeria have embraced their use. There have been several efforts to identify which open-source software is most appropriate for library operations. Koha is the most used open-source ILS in university libraries, and the significant justifications for the adoption are user-friendliness, richer features, low cost of purchase, low cost of maintenance, and a support community [21, 26, 33].

3.2 Extent of Automation in University Libraries' Operation

The automation process of the European Community (EC) libraries in the 1970s involved 12 countries including the UK. They automated their circulation operations first and later their cataloging, while acquisition work was carried out using teleordering systems offered by Whitaker and Blackwell in the UK, and Springer in Germany and Scandinavia. The serial operations were recorded using traditional Kardex. Interlibrary operations were not automated at the local libraries level, but within regional or national networks [36].

By the end of the 1980s, ILS were available for a variety of housekeeping operations, especially with the use of microcomputers. The modules available were Cataloguing, OPAC, Circulation, Acquisitions, Serials, and Interlibrary Loans [31]. By the 1990s, over 50 university libraries in the UK were fully automated. Libraries at Staffordshire

University, University of Hertfordshire, University of the Arts London, and Loughborough University eventually operated services in virtual environments: the use of Web 2.0 platforms, provision of downloadable content such as e-books, e-audiobooks, vodcasts, and podcasts, and 24/7 online services such as renewals and reservations [21].

E-learning has become an integral part of higher education in the UK. University teaching operations are heavily reliant on Learning Management Systems which is alternatively known as Virtual Learning Environment (VLE) software. It provides the digital backbone to many university courses and enables institutions to manage administration and deliver courses and exams online. For libraries in the UK to maintain their relevance, library software vendors have developed solutions to support teaching and learning such as reading list software [34]. These include Talis' Aspire, Ex Libris' Leganto, and SirsiDynix's BLUEcloud. They integrate library resources, student registrations, and university bookstores [35].

In Nigeria, university libraries have resorted to various ILS, but Koha has gained much popularity, with over 100 universities using it [33]. Even though Koha captures most operations, usage is low. In one study, only cataloging in the Nimbe Adedipe Library at the Federal University of Agriculture Abeokuta was automated, while the Olabisi Onabanjo University Library had automated only cataloguing and circulation [1]. In an investigation of public university libraries in north central Nigeria, only the cataloging routine was automated [16]. Comparing the extent of automation in a private and a public university library; most operations of the private university library were automated, while the public university only had automated cataloguing and circulation [26]. One assessment found that only 5% of university libraries in Nigeria are fully automated, while the remaining 95% are either not automated or partially automated [19].

3.3 University Libraries Operations During COVID-19 Lockdown

COVID-19 created a worldwide health crisis. The World Health Organization pronounced the emergency as a pandemic on March 11, 2020, which propelled the United Nations Education and Scientific Council to advise that academic activities across the globe should be closed, and most governments yielded to this. Libraries were closed to avoid physical contact but attempted to provide services through online and virtual/remote approaches [17]. According to a 2020 report by the National Authorities of Public Libraries in Europe (NAPLE), which consists of twenty European nations including the UK, most of the libraries in these nations were shut down and focused on online services. Most staff worked from home while some were made to report to work under strict social distance monitoring. Libraries in the NAPLE countries provided services such as click and collect and home delivery. Librarians focused on e-services with the use of the library's software and social media platforms by providing all essential information through these [24]. In one UK example, the University of Edinburgh made operations on Microsoft Teams compulsory. Necessary training and support were given to staff. All library staff were subjected to at least one new digital skill course which formed a key indicator in their annual performance reviews [20].

However, the International Federation of Library Associations (IFLA) advised that even though the decision to close a library must be adhered to following assessment of the relative risks, the closure of libraries in almost all countries of the world implied redundancy. IFLA further advised that libraries should go virtual [9]. This was timely advice as it was the best alternative to get the libraries running so they could meet their expected purpose. Unfortunately, Nigerian libraries were yet to fully go digital, making it difficult to function during the lockdown. They had no time to plan for a transition of operation. Their traditional methods of rendering information services became redundant during the pandemic. Most libraries in Nigeria were shut down due to the fast spread of the virus, especially in public universities, with very few providing information on their websites or via social media while they complied with the "work from home" order by the federal government [4, 8, 15, 18].

3.4 Automation Challenges in the Operations of University Libraries During COVID-19 Lockdown

Libraries around the world made significant effort to stay relevant and keep operating during lockdown. UK libraries were mostly able to respond to the call of this crucial time, but despite their efforts, their operations faced challenges. Some libraries expressed frustration as most part of their traditional operations which were supplementary to their digital services needed to be reinvented. These include reference services, e-book acquisitions models, vendor relationships, liaison services, etc. [5].

Also, the situation at the time required that all services be rendered online. The demand for e-resources increased and libraries struggled to meet the demand. Libraries suddenly found their existing licensing arrangements insufficient. As such, more funding was required to purchase licenses for more online content and increase access to titles for popular materials. This adaptability created serious pressure on budgets [28].

In Nigeria, libraries were not able to go virtual during the lockdown due to the issues surrounding technology emergence. Even though most university libraries had automation installations, managerial and technological problems existed. Before the pandemic, studies exposed some of the factors impeding the functionalities of their automation systems. Amongst many were poor internet access, poor funding, inadequate ICT skills, unreliable power supply, lack of trained personnel and inadequate training facilities [12, 13, 25]. The inability of library management and staff to explore and use the right technology to provide virtual services efficiently was caused by poor technology infrastructure, lack of retooling opportunity, and poor expertise in handling technology during the lockdown [22].

Other challenges identified were issues associated with the process of learning to work remotely and the inadequacies of working from home. Most homes in Nigeria do not have internet access unlike in the UK. This meant there was no internet service provision for library staff to work from home and in most cases, they were subjected to pay for data/broadband access themselves. Also, a lack of technological infrastructure such as computer systems and other hardware were impeding factors; most library staff did not have personal computers at home [10].

4 Findings

Automation systems are holistic and run on a complete operation circle. As far back as the 1990s, most university libraries in the UK have been fully automated while even now, most university libraries in Nigeria are either partially automated or not automated. By implication this means the status of university library automation in Nigeria is more than three decades behind the UK. This assertion was corroborated in [27] by concluding that most libraries in developing nations are under-automated.

During lockdown, university libraries in the UK were able to appreciably leverage automation to provide services. Also, management encouraged and provided training to staff where required. Unfortunately, Nigerian libraries were unable to go digital, making it difficult to render services. The best decision by their management was to shut down operations.

University library operations in the UK and Nigeria were both faced with challenges during the lockdown. Some UK libraries could not optimally provide services due to insufficient licenses for digital content. In Nigeria, there were several socio-technical issues such as inadequate staff access to computers and the internet, poor power supply, and a lack of ICT skills. For university libraries to stay relevant and overcome the challenges of operations in a digital environment, they must embrace and be more conscious of technology [22].

5 Conclusions and Recommendations

The COVID-19 lockdown was a challenging time for university libraries across the globe. The pandemic exposed the wide dearth of socio-technical infrastructure and library automation worldwide. It is obvious that the way forward is to be up to date with technology, increase digital service provision, and embrace remote operations. The transition from traditional library services to operating in the digital environment is indispensable. The digital environment in UK university libraries is commendable as they were able to leverage technology to keep their operations running during the lockdown. On the other hand, university library operations in Nigeria halted because they lacked adequate technological infrastructure and expertise that could function in that epoch.

The world has started a new work-life pattern: a hybrid operation which is a blend of physical and virtual/remote operation. It has therefore become necessary for university libraries in the UK to put substantial effort in purchasing more digital content licenses and embrace the SCONUL initiatives of promoting content creation through open access and open education research in their universities. On the other hand, university library management in Nigeria should fully embrace the use of technology and provide basic infrastructure that will allow operation in a digital environment. Primary attention should be placed on fast internet bandwidth, computer systems/hardware and digital training of staff on emerging automation technology.

References

1. Adegbore, A.M.: Automation in two Nigerian university libraries. Library Philosophy and Practice 2(3), 1217 (2010)

2. Aina, L.O.: Library and Information Science Text for Africa. Third World Services, Ibadan, Nigeria (2004)
3. Alabi, G.A.: Computer usage in Africa: trends, problems and prospects. Niger. Libr. Inf. Sci. Rev. **5**(1&2), 1–6 (1987)
4. Ameh, G.J., Ukwuoma, H.C., Oye, P.O.: COVID-19 pandemic and evolving library and information services: lessons for Nigeria. Int. J. Dev. Management Rev. (INJODEMAR) **16**(1), 75–87 (2021)
5. Appleton, L.: Accelerating the digital shift: how a global pandemic has created an environment for rapid change in academic libraries. New Rev. Acad. Librariansh. **27**(3), 257–258 (2021). https://doi.org/10.1080/13614533.2021.1994184
6. Atanda, L.A.: Impact of library automation in Nigerian universities. Research J. Library and Information Sci. **2**(4), 21–25 (2018)
7. Boateng, H., Agyemang, F., Dzandu, M.: The pros and cons of library automation in a resource challenged environment: a case study of KNUST Library. Library Philosophy and Practice 1061 (2014)
8. Chibuzor, L.D., Mole, A J.: Academic staff use of Electronic Resources (ER) in Nigerian university libraries during the COVID-19 lockdown period. Library Philosophy and Practice 5341 (2021)
9. COVID-19 and the global library field. https://www.ifla.org/covid-19-and-the-global-library-field/. Accessed 15 Dec 2022
10. Dauda. I.A.: Implications of Integrated Library Systems (ILS) switching costs in Nigerian university libraries, MSc Information Science thesis (2017)
11. Dzandu, L., Dadzie, P.: Facilitating ICT adoption among research scientists in Ghana. Library Philosophy and Practice 1 (2012)
12. Emasealu, H.U.: Automation of academic libraries and web development: a reverie or reality. Int. J. Knowledge Content Dev. Technol. **9**(1), 43–56 (2019)
13. Fadehan, O.A., Hussaini, A.: Educational needs of librarians in the digital environment: case studies of selected academic libraries in Lagos State, Nigeria. Library Philosophy and Practice 476 (2010)
14. Herring, J.E., Mackenzie, J.A.: Planning for Library Automation: Aberdeen City Libraries: 7 (Library Automation Case Study). Library Association Publishing, London (1986)
15. Ifijeh, G., Yusuf, F: Covid-19 pandemic and the future of Nigeria's university system: the quest for libraries' relevance. The Journal of Academic Librarianship **46**(6), 102226 (2020)
16. Igbudu, M.T., Asen, A.T., Tyopev, C.M.: Influence of Koha software on technical operations of the public university libraries in north central Nigeria. Int. J. Library Science **9**(1), 1–6 (2020)
17. Jegede, D.: Perception of undergraduate students on the impact of COVID-19 pandemic on higher institutions development in federal capital territory Abuja, Nigeria. Electronic Res. J. Social Sciences and Humanities **2**(2), 211–222 (2020)
18. Kasa, M.G., Yusuf, A.: Experience of an academic library during the COVID-19 pandemic. Library Philosophy and Practice (e-journal), 4456 (2020)
19. Lawal-Solarin, E.O., Allison, G.O., Justice, J.I.: Contemporary library automation issues in Nigeria. In: Library Automation: The Nigerian Experience, pp. 162–172. University of Ibadan, Nigeria (2018)
20. Lingstadt, K., Tate, D.: Collaboration and change within library & university collections: perspectives from the University of Edinburgh. ABI Technik **40**(4), 346–356 (2020)
21. McGarvey, V.: Staffordshire University's Koha journey: taking an integrated approach to supporting an open source library management system. Insights **31**, 21 (2018)
22. Momah, P.O.: Post COVID-19 reference services: NIIA Library, the way forward. J. Humanities Social Sci. **25**(9), 36–41 (2020)

23. Mutula, S.: IT diffusion in Sub-Saharan Africa: implications for developing and managing digital libraries. New Libr. World **105**(7/8), 281–289 (2004)
24. NAPLE Sister Libraries Annual Report 2020. https://www.naplesisterlibraries.org/naple-sis ter-libraries-annual-report-2020/. Accessed 15 Dec 2022
25. Oghenetega, L., Umeji, E., Obue, C.: Challenges associated with the use of ICT facilities in public library of Nigeria. Dev. Country Stud. **4**(22), 1–5 (2014)
26. Omopupa, K.T., Adedeji, A.A., Kehinde, A.A., Abdulsalam, A.U., Abubakar, H.: Comparative study of Koha usage in Bowen University and University of Ilorin libraries. J. University Res. **3**(3), 98–106 (2020)
27. Padmavathi, N., Ramani, M.: Koha acquisition module: a study of Bangalore university library. Int. J. Res. Analytical Rev. **9**(1), 10–16 (2019)
28. Poole, N.: British librarianship in the time of Covid-19. Alexandria: The Journal of International and National Library and Information Issues **30**(2–3), 264–270 (2021)
29. Poulter, A.: Open source in libraries: an introduction and overview. Libr. Rev. **59**(9), 655–661 (2010)
30. Sharma, A.: The impact of ICT in library automation in the selected libraries of Dehradun: a case study. Library Philosophy and Practice 1180 (2014)
31. Stubley, P.: Automation with BLCMP in academic libraries in the United Kingdom. High. Educ. Eur. **14**, 33–42 (1989)
32. Tedd, L.A.: Library management systems in the UK: 1960s–1980s. Libr. Hist. **23**, 301–317 (2007)
33. Tella, A., Dina, N., Olaniyi, O.T., Memudu, S.A., Oguntayo, S.A.: Assessment of the use of Koha library software in four selected university libraries in Nigeria. J. Applied Inf. Science Technol. **10**(2), 1–15 (2017)
34. The automatic university – a review of datafication and automation in higher education. https://www.ucu.org.uk/article/10826/The-automatic-university---a-review-of-dataficat ion-and-automation-in-higher-education. Accessed 15 Dec 2022
35. Trends in the library technology market – a UK perspective. https://www.cilip.org.uk/news/ 552340/Trends-in-the-library-technology-market--a-UK-perspective.htm. Accessed 15 Dec 2022
36. Walckiers, M.: Library automation in Europe. In: Proceedings of the 1991 IATUL Conferences, Paper 5 (1991)

Human-Computer Interaction
and Technology

What Makes a Technology Privacy Enhancing? Laypersons' and Experts' Descriptions, Uses, and Perceptions of Privacy Enhancing Technologies

Houda Elmimouni[1](✉) (iD), Erica Shusas[2] (iD), Patrick Skeba[3] (iD),
Eric P. S. Baumer[3] (iD), and Andrea Forte[2] (iD)

[1] Luddy School of Informatics, Computing, and Engineering, Bloomington, IN, USA
helmimo@iu.edu
[2] College of Computing and Informatics, Drexel University, Philadelphia, PA, USA
[3] Computer Science and Engineering, Lehigh University, Bethlehem, PA, USA

Abstract. What makes a technology privacy-enhancing? In this study, we construct an explanation grounded in the technologies and practices that people report using to enhance their privacy. We conducted an online survey of privacy experts (i.e., privacy researchers and professionals who attend to privacy conferences and communication channels) and laypersons that catalogs the technologies they identify as privacy enhancing and the various privacy strategies they employ. The analysis of 123 survey responses compares not only self-reported tool use but also differences in how privacy experts and laypersons explain their privacy practices and tools use. Differences between the two samples show that privacy experts and laypersons have different styles of reasoning when considering PETs: Experts think of PETs as technologies whose primary function is enhancing privacy, whereas laypersons conceptualize privacy enhancement as a supplemental function incorporated into other technologies. The paper concludes with a discussion about potential explanations for these differences, as well as questions they raise about how technologies can best facilitate communication and collaboration while enhancing privacy.

Keywords: Privacy · Privacy enhancing technologies · Privacy behaviors · Privacy experts · Privacy laypersons

1 Introduction

In order to design privacy tools that people can use and benefit from, technologists need to understand what lay people *think* privacy-enhancing technologies (PETs) are, how they *think* they work, and how effective they *think* these technologies are [14,24,44]. Characterizations of what constitutes a privacy-enhancing technology (e.g., [27]) are well established in the expert communities that research and develop privacy tools, but past work has shown that experts and laypersons have different conceptions of privacy [41] and of specific tools [23]. Researchers and designers lack an understanding of what people

I. Sserwanga et al. (Eds.): iConference 2023, LNCS 13972, pp. 229–250, 2023.
https://doi.org/10.1007/978-3-031-28032-0_20

believe makes a technology good or bad for privacy. How do people, especially laypersons, determine what counts as a privacy–enhancing technology? How do privacy experts and laypersons describe the technologies and strategies they use to protect their privacy? Prior work has established the value of investigating differences between lay and expert approaches to privacy. User experience studies of specific PETs have provided insight about usability barriers to adoption [17,22], and researchers have used creative methods to understand how laypersons and experts conceptualize privacy [32,41]. Models have been developed to explain rationales that may guide adoption of PETs [15], and economists have long theorized about the tradeoffs involved in making privacy decisions [1,43]. Unfurling the privacy paradox—when people's stated privacy concerns and real-world behaviors contradict each other—has occupied scholars in many fields who have applied a variety of theoretical framings [33], including institutional vs. social privacy concerns [55], apathy or lack of control [30], and dual-process theory [42]. To provide further context for understanding people's sometimes puzzling practices and decisions about privacy, it is important to know what they believe a privacy-enhancing technology *is*. In this study we use a sociotechnical perspective to lay the basis for a grounded explanation of privacy-enhancing technology use by cataloging the technologies and related strategies identified as privacy-enhancing by privacy experts and by laypersons.

To construct an inventory of privacy-enhancing technologies used by privacy experts and laypersons and to collect short explanations of their use, we developed and deployed a survey. Adapting methods used by Oates et al. [41] to collect data from experts and laypersons, we recruited privacy experts by soliciting participants from the PETs and HCI privacy research communities, and we recruited laypersons using a demographically-matched panel procured by Qualtrics.

Our contributions include three key findings and a discussion of their implications.

1. One impetus for examining privacy laypersons' practices was to discover whether they reference technologies and strategies for everyday privacy practices that resemble those of experts. In their descriptions of everyday technology use, we found that the *laypersons applied heuristic reasoning* in determining which tools and practices enhanced (or reduced) their privacy while, as expected, the *experts often demonstrated a more technical style of reasoning* when thinking about PETs.
2. Experts and laypersons reported some common technology use and privacy behaviors. However, from the list of technologies reported by each sample, we understand that *ease of use impacts laypersons' use of PETs but does not impact the experts' use as much*. Some laypersons use technologies because they are user friendly or avoid using other technologies because they have usability issues. On the other hand, the *experts reported technologies and behaviors that require dedicated attention* and are often less widely known (e.g., using PETs with difficult user experience, varying their online behaviors, or opening social media in a browser with no other websites concurrently open).

3. Among the technologies popularly mentioned in each sample, *laypersons reported technologies with a primary function other than privacy protection.* In contrast, *technologies cited by experts tend to foreground privacy protection* as a primary function.

We conclude with a discussion that addresses some of the social features of privacy tools use and proposes human-centered design recommendations for privacy-enhancing technologies grounded in the above findings. Specifically, our findings point to the importance of using privacy-enhancing technologies as a substrate for Internet tools with other primary functions.

2 Related Work

Privacy-enhancing technologies (PETs) are tools designed to help people achieve desired experiences of privacy. Privacy-enhancing technology as an area of scholarship has traditionally had a strong emphasis in contributions around the design and effectiveness of technologies themselves. For example, Goldberg et al.'s foundational work on PETs [27] concluded that well-designed technologies—not social interventions and policies subject to "the whims of bureaucrats" (p. 108)—would be the best solutions for individuals to protect their privacy as they ventured online. In later updates to this work, Goldberg rereviewed the state of the art and concluded with a set of general design requirements that reflected a growing interest in human-centered concerns: PETs must be usable, deployable, effective, and robust in order to have broad impact [26]. In the intervening years, interest in social, political, and cultural features of PETs adoption has become a routine feature of PETs scholarship; to understand why people use PETs, researchers need to understand how people make sense of them.

2.1 Conceptualization of Privacy and Comparison of Experts and Laypersons

Research has offered frameworks for users' conceptualization of privacy as well as potential factors that might influence online privacy behavior. Baumer and Forte [5] suggest that rather than conceptualizing privacy in terms of literacy, it might be beneficial to analyze people's everyday approaches to protecting their data, which include a person's perceived risks when interacting with technologies, the strategies employed to manage the perceived risks, and the results of those strategies. Kang et al. [32] similarly suggest the experience of privacy violation, rather than an individual's level of literacy or know-how, shapes online privacy practice. In addition, socioeconomic factors may contribute to how people engage with technologies [3,37,54]. Being a member of groups that suffer inequality and discrimination puts individuals at higher risk of privacy violations and makes them susceptible to disproportionate harms as a result of such violations [38].

Some research has been done to investigate the differences between experts and laypersons in their conceptualizations of privacy as a concept.

Research by Oates et al. [41] used a qualitative analysis of 366 illustrations created by laypersons, privacy experts, children, and adults to reveal that many drawings from laypersons displayed a strong distinction between private and public spaces, while drawings from experts were more likely to illustrate more nuanced privacy spaces and control over information. In an interview study investigating expert and layperson understandings of the anonymity system, Tor, experts showed a deeper understanding of Tor's underlying operation and focused more on the technical details of Tor's operations, while laypersons were more likely to situate Tor within a broader sociotechnical landscape [23]. Chua et al. [16] looked at novice and expert users of "Social-Local-Mobile services" (SoLoMo) and found that in both groups, "covert" channels (that run in the background) triggered higher privacy concerns than "overt" channels (that respond to explicit requests). However, novice users with different life goals and less experience with mobile applications demonstrated lower privacy concerns than expert users.

2.2 Methods of Seeking Privacy

Many privacy researchers have used Altman's canonical description of privacy as an ongoing process of boundary regulation to examine privacy strategies online [2,4,20,50]. Lampinen et al. [34] have categorized strategies for boundary regulation as behavioral, such as self-censorship or creating fake accounts, and mental strategies, such as trusting others. Stutzman and Hartzog [50] grouped these strategies into pseudonymity, practical obscurity (obscuring one's profile through modification of privacy settings, pseudonymity, technical separation), and transparent separation, such as maintaining multiple profiles without obscuring identity.

In general, the literature suggests two broad categories into which strategies for maintaining privacy online fall:

1. *Technical Approaches* focus on specific technologies. Anonymous browsers (e.g. Tor browser), Virtual Private Networks (VPNs), non-tracking search engines (e.g. DuckDuckGo), or browsers and plugins/extensions [18]. Anonymous email clients enable individuals to send emails without revealing their origin. Forte et al. [20] refer to the use of Tor and IP-blocking strategies as technical approaches and suggest them among one of two ways that people can counter privacy threats. Proxy servers, Secure Sockets Layer (SSL) technology, and cookie managers [51] are also technical approaches to seeking some degree of privacy and/or anonymity.
2. *Operational Approaches* involve more behavioral strategies. Previous work has described creating multiple accounts [20], or throwaway accounts [4,35] to dissociate one's self from certain online actions and information sharing. Other examples of operational approaches to seeking privacy include modifying one's behavior or using language meant to obstruct authorship attribution [11].

2.3 PETs Adoption Motivations and Barriers

Motivations to adopt PETs, as well as potential barriers to use [7,49] are also important factors for understanding expert and layperson PET adoption. In proposing a model to explore how consumers choose between competing PETs, Caulfield et al. [15] consider the context in which a technology is used; the requirement for the level of privacy that a technology must provide in order for an individual to be willing to use it; the belief, or perception, of the level of privacy a technology provides; and the relative value of privacy in relation to how much the individual is willing to trade it for other attributes. Vemou and Karyda [52] suggest lack of awareness of privacy risks and PETs, lack of technical skill, the complexity and diversity of the risks involved in privacy management, direct and indirect costs, and privacy being a cultural value as potential factors for the limited adoption of PETs on social networking sites. Research has found varying amounts of usability issues with the Tor browser and Tor deployment tools that hinder the adoption of Tor as a widespread anonymity system and suggests that usability issues hinder the widespread adoption of Tor [17,21,22]. The reputation of Tor as being used for illegal activities and its consequences such as being a target of investigations also hinders Tor use and adoption [29,56].

Although models that explore usability issues and motivations can help scholars understand what factors influence decisions, questions remain. What PETs are most salient to people and which do they use in their daily lives? Do experts and laypersons differ? What technologies do people seek out and what technologies do people *avoid* in order to enhance their privacy? We set out to understand what makes a technology a PET—not based on scholarly definitions but grounded in a sociotechnical understanding of the technologies and practices that people (both privacy experts and laypersons) report using to enhance their privacy.

3 Study Design

To generate an inventory of privacy-enhancing technology examples as understood by both privacy experts and laypersons, we developed and administered a survey via Qualtrics to two separate samples. This study was approved by the IRBs at Drexel and Lehigh University where all authors were affiliated at the time of data collection.

3.1 Recruitment

We targeted two groups: privacy experts and privacy laypersons. We defined experts as privacy researchers and privacy professionals who contribute to privacy literature as one of their research areas and/or attend to communication channels and conferences centered around privacy. Given the inherent complexities in defining both "expertise" [25] and "privacy" [40], we did not determine an *a priori* skill set to identify privacy experts. Instead we used a similar approach to Oates et al. [41], who assembled data from experts by collecting data (illustrations in their case) in venues where experts can be found. Similarly Ion et al. [31] and Busse et al. [13] defined their expert samples as people attending privacy conferences.

Thus, to recruit privacy experts, we advertised the study in expert venues. First, we searched for recent privacy-related publications of members of the CHI 2020 subcommittee on privacy and security, and emailed subcommittee members and their co-authors a link to the study. Second, we asked the Privacy-Enhancing Technologies Symposium Twitter account to retweet our recruitment message on Twitter, which they did. This recruitment approach yielded 49 responses in fall (September-October) 2019. No incentives were offered to complete the survey.

To recruit privacy laypersons, we used the demographic profile of our expert sample to acquire a sample from the general population of survey takers on Qualtrics that reflected our expert sample in terms of age, gender, and education level. This departs from Oates et al. [41]'s method of recruiting laypersons by ensuring demographic alignment between our two samples. In this way, we decrease the chance that any differences are due to differences in, say, education but are instead due to differences in privacy expertise. Similary to Oates et al. [41], we also assume that recruiting participants without specifically targeting channels where privacy experts are likely to be found will result in a sample that can be treated as "laypersons." Like Oates et al. [41], we acknowledge it is possible that privacy experts could have responded to the Qualtrics panel, just as laypersons could have been included in the expert sample. During the analysis, we identified one respondent in the laypersons' sample who shared many characteristics with the expert sample. Otherwise, the groups exhibited largely divergent behaviors around and conceptualizations of PETs, which lends confidence to our recruitment-based approach to identifying experts and laypersons.

We recruited 99 participants from Qualtrics in spring (early March) 2020[1]. The minimal eligibility criteria to participate in the survey included being 18 or older and being able to read English.

3.2 Participants

A total of 148 survey responses were collected during the period the surveys were active, of which 123 were included in the final dataset—46 from the privacy expert sample and 77 from the laypersons' sample (See Table 1 for details about participants). The participants who were excluded did not answer the questions about technologies or practices and/or provided nonsensical text like entering random words. Whereas the majority of our participants reported residing in the USA, 16 of our privacy experts sample reported other countries (Canada, France, India, Italy, Switzerland, UK, Germany). Table 1 shows demographics for both samples. Because of the relative uncertainty involved in recruiting experts via

---

[1] A total of 106 Qualtrics participants were solicited: 6 as a preliminary test and 100 additional participants. However, only 99 entered any data in the survey. Qualtrics data collection was limited to U.S. respondents and ended before widespread emergence of the COVID-19 pandemic in the United States.

social networks and work-of-mouth vs laypersons via a survey panel commissioned from Qualtrics, the number of participants in each sample is uneven.

Table 1. Cross tabulation of participant demographics from the two samples.

Demographics		Privacy experts ($n = 46$)	Privacy laypersons ($n = 77$)
Gender	Man	22(48%)	39(51%)
	Woman	20(43%)	38(49%)
	Not specified	2 (4%)	0 (0%)
Age	Min	22	22
	Max	69	67
	Avg	35	36
Education	Doctorate	25(54%)	38(49%)
	Master	13(28%)	25(32%)
	Bachelor	4 (9%)	13(17%)
	Some college/university	1 (2%)	0 (0%)
	Some secondary/high school	0 (0%)	1 (1%)
	Blank	3 (7%)	0 (0%)

3.3 Survey Protocol

An identical survey was deployed to the privacy expert sample and to the laypersons' sample. The survey included both closed- and open-ended questions to allow both for systematic numeric reports of things like technology use frequency and for respondents to express details about their privacy technology use, privacy behaviors, and motivations.

The survey began with an explanation that we were interested in technology use related to privacy: *the purpose of this survey is to understand what technologies you and other people use to protect your privacy while using computers, phones, and other electronic devices.* We intentionally did not define privacy for participants or introduce the term "privacy enhancing technology" in order to allow participants to articulate their understandings through their responses and examples of technologies. The survey included an initial semi-open portion that asked participants to freely list technologies they are familiar with in multiple categories: browsers with special features like ad-blockers, pop-up blockers, or private browsing mode, anonymous browsers, privacy-enhancing search engines, encrypted communications, and other privacy technologies. These categories were derived from both scholarly and popular articles that listed types of privacy-enhancing technologies to establish a baseline with which to compare expert and layperson responses. In the first question we asked "Which of the following types of technologies are you familiar with? please provide as many examples that you can think of (leave blank if don't know of any)." For each category mentioned above, we asked them to provide up to three examples of technologies they are familiar with. The participants' answers were then piped and used in follow-up questions about the frequency of and motivations for using the technologies they cited. Respondents were also asked about the technologies they avoid to protect their privacy and any other ways they protect their privacy online. The survey concluded with a short demographic section about gender, age, and education level. With the exception of the two questions verifying eligibility, answering any question was not obligatory.

3.4   Data Analysis

The expert and layperson data were first analyzed separately in the same manner. We designed the study not to enable making statistical inferences about differences between the practices of the two participant groups, but rather to offer descriptions of the practices employed by each sample. Thus, data from close-ended questions were analyzed using descriptive statistics as a way of providing insights about the practices described. The answers to open-ended questions, on the other hand, were analyzed using thematic analysis [10] to examine differences in the ways participants wrote about privacy and their practices. We identified themes by coding the data line-by-line [9]. Thematic analysis goes beyond identifying and counting occurrences of words or phrases to identifying implicit ideas [28]. The first and second authors used Dedoose to collaboratively code the data. Each of the coders independently coded the data and then discussed discrepancies to converge on a shared understanding and codebook. Multiple coders were used, not to verify their correctness, but to facilitate a critical process and strengthen the conceptual integrity of the codes [39]. All the authors repeatedly discussed themes identified in the data and connections among them. The first and second authors then worked together on collapsing themes into affinity groups [6]. For instance, privacy-related motivations for using privacy technologies were grouped together separately from non-privacy-related motivations. After coding and affinity grouping data from the expert and layperson data sets separately, the findings from each were compared and further analyzed to identify differences and commonalities. We report our findings about both samples' privacy-enhancing technologies use and privacy behaviors in the next section.

4   Findings

The themes that emerged from analysis of survey data describe reported use of privacy-enhancing technologies and behaviors among privacy experts and laypersons in our sample. First, to aid comparisons, we identify a list of PETs mentioned by both samples.

The lists of technologies identified by privacy experts and laypersons included 29 common technologies. The expert sample further identified 40 technologies that were not mentioned by the laypersons, and the laypersons cited 51 technologies that were not mentioned by the experts. Most of these technologies were only cited once or twice.

To make a comparative analysis more tractable and to address unevenness of sample size, we focus only on the technologies that are mentioned by at least 10% of either sample. The list includes 16 technologies, 15 of which were mentioned at least once by both groups of respondents (See Fig. 1). In the sections below we examine qualitative differences between the technologies reported by each group.

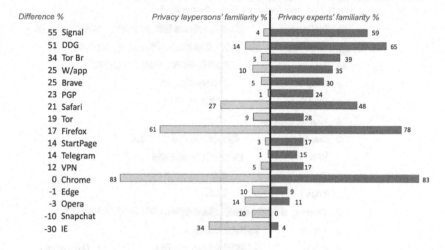

Fig. 1. Percent of privacy experts and laypersons who mentioned each PET, ordered by difference in percent between the two samples.

The remainder of this section uses these lists of technologies to analyze: PETs named by each sample; frequency of use; various classes of PETs; classifications of PETs; technologies respondents seek out, as well as technologies they avoid; respondents' motivations for using PETs; and other reported privacy strategies.

4.1 Reported PETs and Frequency of Use

As a first point of comparison, the technologies that laypersons reported using tend to advertise main functions other than privacy protection—for example, Snapchat. Snapchat's website emphasizes creativity, social connection, and self-expression, proclaiming that "Snapchat is a camera... that is connected to your friends."[2] On the other hand, experts' reported technology use emphasized technologies that promote privacy protection as a primary function such as Tor or Signal. In comparison to Snapchat, Signal is a chat app that promotes itself first as a privacy tool; the website proclaims that "Signal is the most scalable encryption tool we have" and includes an endorsement from Edward Snowden[3].

---

[2] https://whatis.snapchat.com accessed 9/15/2022.
[3] https://www.signal.org/ accessed 9/15/2022.

Use frequency data reinforces this finding about privacy as a primary or secondary feature of the technologies cited by both samples (see Fig. 2). For example, the biggest discrepancies in daily/weekly reported use by experts vs laypersons were Tor Browser, Whatsapp, and Telegram, all of which advertise privacy as a central feature. Snapchat was not cited by any expert.

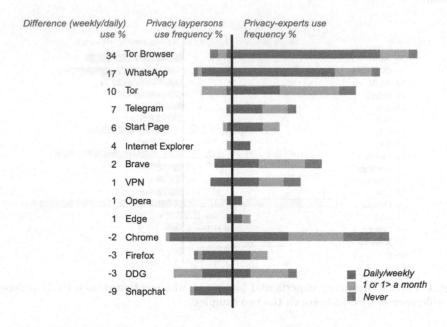

Fig. 2. Frequency of PET use reported by experts and laypersons.

Survey respondents were prompted to list examples of PETS in different categories, such as web browsers, encrypted communications tools, or anonymous browsers. Categories are powerful indicators of meaning [8] and the ways respondents categorized PETs reflect the ways they conceptualize the tools. We noted that the way experts categorized technologies reflected their expert understanding of the common traits of different technologies.

Recall that 29 technologies were listed by both the expert and laypersons' sample; however, the two samples frequently diverged in their categorization of technologies on this shared list. In some cases there was agreement, for instance, most experts and laypersons agreed that WhatsApp is an encrypted communication technology and DuckDuckGo is a privacy-enhancing search engine. On the other hand, some technologies were categorized differently. For example, Chrome is categorized by experts as a web browser while the laypersons' categorization of Chrome included anonymous browser, encrypted communication, and privacy-enhancing search engine in addition to web browser. Brave was categorized by experts as either an anonymous browser or web browser, but laypersons additionally categorized it as a privacy-enhancing search engine.

4.2   Technologies Sought Out and Technologies Avoided

The divergence of expert and layperson perceptions of PETs also manifests in the technologies they reported avoiding or seeking to protect their privacy. We extracted lists of technologies sought out and avoided from open-ended responses (see Table 2 and Table 3).

Table 2. Technologies avoided.

Expert		Common	Layperson
Google Chrome	Cloud storage	Amazon Echo	Bitly
Tinder	Credit cards	Facebook	Capital One
Twitter	Epic Games Launcher	Siri	Instagram
Venmo	File sharing websites	Social networks	Internet Explorer
Voice Assistant	Fitness trackers		URL shortener
Wifi; public/shared	Game/casino websites		Link manager
Windows OS	Google Home		Public computers
Smart devices/IoT	Google search		Ring doorbell
Laptop/cell phone cameras	Amazon.com		USAA
Apps which collect data	LinkedIn		
Centralized messaging apps	Personal assistants		
Closed-source software/hardware			

Table 3. Technologies sought out.

Expert	Common	Layperson
DuckDuckGo	Ad blockers	Laptop encryption
Instagram stories	Two-factor authentication	Security apps for mobile
Open source software	Virtual private networks	Norton
Password generator		PayPal
Protonmail		
Telegram		
Tor browser		
Tor		
Ublock		

We also coded answers related to what technologies people reported avoiding and/or seeking out. For instance, in the case where a participant mentions that they use technology 'x' or they try to avoid technology 'y'.

Affinity diagramming for the technologies avoided show that both groups avoid some IoT technologies such as Echo and Alexa, social media platforms such as Facebook, banking technologies such as credit cards and "capitalone", shared public platforms such as WiFi or computers, certain browsers and certain websites. However, experts report a greater number of technologies they avoid.

The smaller sample of 46 privacy experts group generated 33 responses describing 51 unique technologies avoided. The larger sample of 77 laypersons yielded only 30 responses and 19 unique technologies avoided. Note that when multiple services were listed (Google home, Google search) or both concrete examples (Amazon Echo) and the concomitant abstract categories (Voice assistant), these were counted separately.

Abstract categories were unique to the expert list. A number of privacy experts listed Internet of Things (IoT), voice assistants, and personal assistants as entire categories of things to be avoided. In contrast, the layperson list included concrete examples of IoT technologies like "Ring Doorbell" or "Amazon Echo" but did not identify classes of things to be avoided, with the exception of "social media". Similarly, avoiding credit cards appears on the expert list, whereas laypersons listed specific banks but not credit cards in general. The presence of abstractions suggests that experts understand of privacy threats underlying their avoidance of specific technologies, whereas laypersons did not signal this same understanding.

Participants were asked to describe strategies they use to protect their privacy in an open-ended question. Responses to all open-ended questions were coded to identify technologies participants reported seeking out to protect their privacy. The list of technologies above is not expected to be exhaustive but informative and can prompt insights about some of the technologies both groups want to use, try to use, or actually use.

4.3   PETs Use Motivation

For each technology they reported using, survey respondents were asked why they used it. The reported motivations for PETs use show that experts' main reasons for using PETs are privacy centered whereas laypersons' motivations are often not privacy related.

Affinity diagramming for the coded motivation responses revealed four main themes of motivations. Some categories overlap. For instance "privately doing things" overlaps with "avoiding tracking" since one might avoid tracking in order to do something privately, however, we used participants' explanations to differentiate A. purposeful efforts to maintain privacy during specific activities in order to conceal those activities from B. avoiding tracking as a general practice for all activities as a defensive measure against surveillance. Below we explain them with more details and quotes from the data. Here we refer to an expert participant as 'E' and a layperson participant as 'L'.

- **Avoiding things: such as not be tracked, malware, cookies, surveillance, history data.** For example, E46 reported using private browsing mode to avoid creating a digital profile based on previous searches. She wrote: *"searching for things i would not like to have in my digital profile (for example buying pregnancy clothes for my sister in law. i don't want my entire amazon recommendations to be around pregnancy)."* Similarly, L66 reported using private browsing mode to avoid leaving a history that could be tracked.

He reported: *"Private browsing protects you from people with access to your computer snooping at your browsing history - your browser won't leave any tracks on your computer. It also prevents websites from using cookies stored on your computer to track your visits."*

– **Protecting things: such as password, email, financial information, anonymity.** In some cases, although privacy experts and laypersons may share the same motivation, the technology they use to achieve privacy differs. E6 reported using StartPage to protect personal information. He stated: *"Routine protection from sharing too many personally-attributed interests with major search engine companies."* Similarly, E39 uses OpenPGP to protect his email: *"to keep my mails confidential. mostly through autocrypt. I try to encrypt everything from trivial mails to confidential ones."* On the other hand, L29 mentions using Chrome to protect their information: *"It is very secure for me to search the internet without worrying leak of information."*

– **Privately doing things: such as private communication, illegally downloading movies, accessing suspicious websites, and searching about people.** As noted, while "privately doing things" seems to be similar to "avoiding being tracked," the coding of these instances reflects the expressions of the participants, which emphasize keeping specific actions out of sight rather than potential aggregate tracking threats. For example, E23 mentions using Tor to download illegal movies so that his identity cannot be connected with that specific action but does not describe using it as a general practice to avoid tracking.

– **Other non-privacy motivations: better experience, required, fun, curiosity and default.** Both groups mentioned a better browsing experience, fun, convenience, popularity, curiosity and the fact that the technology is either default or required to interact with some of their social connections. The latter motivation appears frequently in the data and reflects the impact of the social aspects of PETs adoption and use. For example E46 uses Signal because it was required by a friend. She reported: *"some of my friends are quite serious about their privacy so they only use signal for chatting and i downloaded it particularly for them. i also once had a friend who shared very serious and private info about themselves and used a fake account on signal in case i decided to somehow take screenshots or show anyone this content then they could claim it is not theirs."* L46 used DuckDuckGo just to try it out. She mentions: *"I tried it out when I first heard about it a couple of years ago but prefer Google Chrome."*. L60 uses Brave and says: *"It pays you."*

As demonstrated in the excerpts above, privacy experts and laypersons reported some common motivations for using PETs. Some of these motivations are privacy related and some others are not. Both groups reported using PETs to **avoid** malware, being tracked, accepting cookies, and personal data collection, to **protect** passwords, email, and other personal information and to privately **do things** such as communicating with others.

While experts mentioned some non-privacy-related motivations such as fun and curiosity, their list of privacy-related motivations was more detailed and extensive and included technical features of online interaction, such as hiding their network address, accessing multiple accounts, avoiding having metadata known about them, blocking scripts, accessing prohibited content, and searching sensitive topics. Laypersons often used generic terms to describe motivations such as keeping activities private, communicating, protecting privacy and personal reasons like "it is good," "it pays you," or "I like it."

4.4   Other Privacy Strategies

Affinity diagramming of the data showed privacy behavior similarities at the level of general overarching themes but we noted differences between the two samples in some specific behaviors. The overarching themes include:

- Being aware and checking behaviors: such as being aware of data shared with others and checking links before clicking.
- Limiting/avoiding certain behaviors: limiting personal data shared, social media logins/use. data retention.
- Deleting/disabling behaviors:turning off/not using location-based services, deleting/managing cookies
- Using fake/disposable/different identifiers: such as emails, personal information, user names
- Managing passwords: not reusing important passwords, using password managers or generators
- Using physical privacy devices: device camera covers and privacy screens

Privacy behaviors reported by laypersons are practices that we interpret to be general practices that are well-known and widely advocated such as limiting social media use, device use, and data sharing. The experts' behaviors on the other hand included more idiosyncratic and resource-intensive practices that required more time and attention. Some experts reported going beyond limiting social media use, device use, and data sharing to limiting internet and technology use in general. In addition, some privacy experts mentioned more complicated and detailed strategies such as: opening Facebook and Linkedin incognito with no other websites open at the same time, intentionally engaging in inconsistent use behavior, and using their own server for services.

Although the sample of experts is smaller than the layperson sample (46 privacy experts vs 77 laypersons), the data generated by privacy experts sample includes more privacy behaviors (34) compared to the number of privacy behaviors generated by the layperson sample (24).

5   Discussion and Implications

The above analysis suggests that privacy experts and laypersons have different styles of reasoning and approach privacy issues differently; experts conceive of PETs as technologies whose primary function is protecting or enhancing privacy or that are promoted as such. Laypersons, in contrast, think of privacy enhancement as an add-on functionality to tools like browsers, chat applications, and websites. This discussion compares our main finding with results from the related literature and then considers the finding's implication for future work.

5.1 Comparison with Prior Work

Technical vs. Heuristic Understanding of PETs. In many of the differences described above, the expert sample often demonstrated a more technical understanding of PETs and attended to specific implementation details thereof. In contrast, the laypersons tended to apply heuristic reasoning in determining which tools and practices enhanced (or reduced) their privacy. For example, as described above (Sect. 4.2), laypersons described avoiding individual products or companies (e.g., Capital One, Internet Explorer), while experts described avoiding more broad categories of technologies defined by some common technical detail (e.g., public or shared Wifi, "smart" IoT devices, fitness trackers). Similarly, in the motivations described above (Sect. 4.3), respondents from the expert sample described strategies that reveal an understanding of how data are aggregated and analyzed, e.g., not "sharing too many personally attributed interests with major search engine companies." In contrast, respondents from the layperson sample made higher level statements, such as describing Chrome as being "very secure [...] without worrying leak of information."

Such differences align somewhat with work by Gallagher et al. [23] on the Tor anonymity system. They found that experts have a deeper understanding of Tor's underlying architecture and focused on the technical details of Tor's operations–similar to our findings about experts' engagement with more technical details–, while laypersons were more likely to situate Tor within a broader sociotechnical landscape. Also the work by [41] on laypersons and privacy experts suggests that experts were more likely to illustrate more nuanced data privacy spaces and control over information than laypersons. While the work by [23] focused only on comparing the use of Tor by laypersons and experts, our study considers all the salient technologies to the experts and laypersons as well as reported privacy behaviors. In addition, contrary to the [41] study that focused on how privacy is defined, our focus is to learn about what PETs are for each sample.

This finding raises questions about the role of expertise in informing everyday privacy practices. We have discussed literature that frames privacy practices as outcomes of experiences of violation [32] or need [3,37,54] as opposed to reflecting a particular level of "literacy" [23]; yet, our findings in this survey suggest that privacy experts' practices differ from those of laypersons. Specifically, experts more often attended to the technical details of such systems, while laypersons applied higher level heuristic reasoning. While perhaps unsurprising, given the respective backgrounds of these two samples, this difference also highlights a key point. Experts do not simply have *more knowledge* or a *better understanding* of PETs than laypersons; rather, the two samples in this study demonstrated fundamentally *different styles* of reasoning about their privacy. This is not to say that expertise is irrelevant. Expertise matters, but perhaps not in the ways that we might expect. For instance, experts and laypersons may differ in the ways that their PETs use is influenced by the PETs used in their social network. Indeed, such differences represent an important area for future work.

Difficult User Experience vs. Good User Experience. Based on the findings about use motivations that show some laypersons use technologies because they are user friendly or avoid using other technologies because they have usability issues, we understand that the UX of PETs impact their use. The PETs that our expert respondents reported more use of appear to require more dedicated attention and technology skills. Concerns about the relationship between privacy and usability are a perennial topic; indeed an entire conference, the *Symposium on Usable Privacy and Security*, is dedicated to addressing the problem of unusable privacy and security tools. In our sample, experts were far more likely to use Tor browser, an open source project that has long-documented usability weaknesses [17,21,36] than, for example, Internet Explorer, which (despite ubiquitous grumblings about all browsers' failings) is designed to be a general-use consumer product. In the same vein, privacy behaviors reported by laypersons seem to be popular and widely-advocated (e.g., strong password, consideration of audience). On the other hand, the privacy behaviors that are reported by the experts are complex in that they require multiple steps and prerequisite knowledge.

What might entice people to overcome the barriers associated with a more difficult user experience? We found that experts and laypersons alike reported social interaction as a motivation for adopting privacy enhancing technologies. Some participants adopted PETS because a heightened level of privacy protection was required by a more concerned or more vulnerable social contact. This suggests that privacy may have a transitive property and that communication and collaboration technologies in particular occupy an important design space for privacy-enhancing technologies.

Privacy: Primary Concern vs. Afterthought. The survey data show that experts are more likely to approach privacy as a primary concern, while laypersons tend to think about other aspects first and then later consider privacy. This is evidenced by the salient technologies for each sample, their reported frequency of using them, as well as each sample's reported motivations for that usage. The experts reported they are mostly familiar with Signal, Tor browser, Brave, Tor, VPN, and StartPage, all of which include privacy enhancement as a primary function. In contrast, the laypersons reported that they are mostly familiar with Internet Explorer, Snapchat, and Edge, which do not place as much emphasis on privacy. The use frequency reveals similar findings as the laypersons use Chrome, Snapchat, and Firefox more frequently while the experts report use of Tor browser/Tor more often.

This distinction is only partly a question of the technology itself and how it is presented to users. For instance, a technology such as PGP is first and foremost a privacy technology, whereas a technology such as Chrome is first and foremost a web browser. However, examples such as the Tor browser, which foregrounds privacy while having the primary function of browsing the web, end up in a blurry middle. Similar points could be raised about Signal (a messaging app that foregrounds privacy) or DuckDuckGo (a search engine that foregrounds privacy).

Instead, the distinction to be made here revolves around how users *conceive of* these technologies. The qualitative analysis of open-ended responses makes it clear that the privacy experts in our sample conceive of certain technologies being first and foremost about protecting their privacy. In contrast, the laypersons in our sample are more likely to conceive of privacy as an added feature included in another technology they are already using.

These findings highlight how the definition of PETs in the literature does not align with privacy laypersons' use and perceptions of PETs, but with the experts'. PETs are for "protecting personal identity" [12], "protecting or enhancing an individual's privacy," and "minimizing the collection and use of personal data" [47]. Privacy experts perceive PETs as technologies where privacy protection/enhancement is the primary function. The laypersons' sample, in contrast, often describes other kinds of technologies as PETs, particularly those where privacy protection/enhancement is a secondary or tertiary function.

5.2 Implication: Privacy Protection as an Embedded Feature in Everyday Life Technologies

Our grounded data examines which technologies are salient to privacy experts and laypersons and shows which technologies and practices for enhancing privacy are used. It reveals that privacy experts and laypersons conceive of PETs somewhat differently. In the expert sample, PETs are reported to be technologies that are designed for privacy purposes primarily, whereas laypersons define PETs as technologies that help them achieve their tasks but have privacy as a secondary or tertiary function. Furthermore, our findings about use motivations show that some laypersons use technologies because they are user friendly while avoiding other technologies because they have usability issues.

At least two possible interpretations could account for this finding, each with slightly different implications. First, this finding aligns with other studies showing that a difficult UX is one justification for why laypersons do not use PETs [17,22,45,48,53]. This finding also builds on that prior work by suggesting that usability issues are more of a deterrent for laypersons than they are for experts. This interpretation suggests that designers prioritize the usability and UX of technologies whose primary function is privacy protection. Second, another possible interpretation is that laypersons simply do not know about the privacy dedicated technologies, either because they do not know other people using them or because such technologies were never advertised to them. This interpretation suggests that energy be put into information dissemination efforts.

An alternative strategy could address either of these interpretations. Whether laypersons do not know about privacy dedicated technologies or have difficulty using them, laypersons could be served by designing privacy in the technologies they use in their everyday life. Goldberg posits that:

> In order for a technology to be useful, it must be possible for everyday users doing everyday things to obtain it and benefit from it. This means it needs to be compatible with their preferred operating system, their preferred web browser, their preferred instant messaging client, and so on. Ideally, the technology would be built right in so that the user doesn't even need to find and install separate software packages. [26, p. 15]

Our findings add emphasis to Goldberg's assertion. Not only would such an arrangement be *ideal* for the uptake of technologies with strong privacy protections. Rather, these findings suggest having PETs "built right in" may be *necessary* for them to be adopted by a diverse user base whose expertise lies outside the field of privacy.

Thus, we suggest that designers of Internet tools should be aware of the privacy needs and desires of users and embed privacy features that would help them protect their privacy. By using that approach, users do not need to take extra steps to explore, to understand, and to learn about privacy and privacy tools.

6   Limitations and Conclusion

This study's findings are grounded in the data collected via two identical surveys, one addressed to privacy experts and one to laypersons.

Most of this study's limitations revolve around data collection. For example, our data rely on participants self-reporting their behaviors. Some participants might experience "social desirability bias and thus may over report their behavior," [19] while other participants may forget or misrepresent their behavior. Other limitations pertain to our sampling procedures. For example, we do not know if our laypersons' sample includes some privacy experts. Additionally, demographically matching the laypersons' sample and the expert sample resulted in participants with PhDs being dramatically over-represented among laypersons. Although higher education levels have been correlated with higher levels of privacy concern [46], the effect of oversampling high academic achievement among the laypersons' sample on practices and strategies is not known. Furthermore, our expert sample includes a few international respondents, but the laypersons all reside in the U.S. We do not know what cultural differences might be at play; for example, some experts from Europe may have reported using technologies that are popular in Europe but relatively unknown in the U.S and vice versa. We believe the international character of the privacy research community mitigates some of this concern since the privacy experts were recruited based on their participation in conferences that annually publish and meet together. Importantly, in the survey instruments, we provided an example of categories of technology we wanted to prompt people to name and describe, including Tor for "anonymous browser," Snapchat for "encrypted communication," and Duck-DuckGo for "privacy-enhancing search engine." It is notable that, although the presence of these illustrative examples could have triggered additional mentions of them in the data, there is no obvious indication that the example technologies are over represented. For instance, despite being used as an example, Snapchat was mentioned by no experts as an example of encrypted communication. While this might suggest a limitation in the sense that the examples primed the participants, the variety of responses that we got back suggests that respondents were not constrained by the examples that we provided. The same survey questions were administered to both samples and each sample came up with different technologies.

Our findings revealed that both experts and laypersons share some technical approaches (technology use) and operational approaches (privacy behaviors) to protect their privacy. However, they have different reasoning styles. The way each sample conceives of privacy-enhancing technologies differs according to which technologies they use and for what motivations. Our data reveal that privacy experts leverage their technical understanding of technologies to inform use of technologies and strategies that are complex, have a difficult UX, and have a primary function of privacy protection. For the laypersons, privacy is sought through technologies that have privacy as a secondary or tertiary function. Finally, experts were more likely to report technologies they avoid and avoidance strategies and to link them to abstract categories which suggests they understand threats underlying their avoidance of specific technologies. We conclude by underscoring opportunities for technology designers to embed privacy features in the design of everyday life technologies to serve a wider cross-section of people.

Acknowledgements. This material is based on work supported in part by the NSF under Grants No. CNS-1814533 and CNS-1816264.

References

1. Acquisti, A., Taylor, C., Wagman, L.: The economics of privacy. J. Econ. Liter. **54**(2), 442–92 (2016)
2. Ahern, S., Eckles, D., Good, N.S., King, S., Naaman, M., Nair, R.: Over-exposed? privacy patterns and considerations in online and mobile photo sharing. In: Proceedings of the SIGCHI conference on Human factors in computing systems. pp. 357–366 (2007)
3. Ames, M.G., Go, J., Kaye, J., Spasojevic, M.: Understanding technology choices and values through social class. In: Proceedings of the ACM 2011 Conference on Computer Supported Cooperative Work, pp. 55–64 (2011)
4. Andalibi, N., Haimson, O.L., De Choudhury, M., Forte, A.: Understanding social media disclosures of sexual abuse through the lenses of support seeking and anonymity. In: Proceedings of the 2016 CHI Conference on Human Factors in Computing Systems, pp. 3906–3918 (2016)
5. Baumer, E.P., Forte, A.: Undoing the privacy paradox with data styles (2017)
6. Beyer, H., Holtzblatt, K.: Contextual design. Interactions **6**(1), 32–42 (1999)

7. Borking, J.J.: Why adopting privacy enhancing technologies (pets) takes so much time. In: Gutwirth, S., Poullet, Y., De Hert, P., Leenes, R. (eds.) Computers, Privacy and Data Protection: an Element of Choice, pp. 309–341. Springer, Dordrecht (2011). https://doi.org/10.1007/978-94-007-0641-5_15
8. Bowker, G.C., Star, S.L.: Sorting things out: classification and its consequences. MIT press (2000)
9. Boyatzis, R.E.: Transforming qualitative information: thematic analysis and code development. Sage (1998)
10. Braun, V., Clarke, V.: Using thematic analysis in psychology. Qual. Res. Psychol. **3**(2), 77–101 (2006)
11. Brennan, M., Afroz, S., Greenstadt, R.: Adversarial stylometry: circumventing authorship recognition to preserve privacy and anonymity. ACM Trans. Inf. Syst. Secur. (TISSEC) **15**(3), 1–22 (2012)
12. Burkert, H., et al.: Privacy-enhancing technologies: typology, critique, vision. Technology and privacy: The new landscape, pp. 125–142 (1997)
13. Busse, K., Schäfer, J., Smith, M.: Replication: no one can hack my mind revisiting a study on expert and non-expert security practices and advice. In: Fifteenth Symposium on Usable Privacy and Security ({SOUPS} 2019), pp. 117–136 (2019)
14. Caulfield, T., Ioannidis, C., Pym, D.: On the adoption of privacy-enhancing technologies. In: Zhu, Q., Alpcan, T., Panaousis, E., Tambe, M., Casey, W. (eds.) GameSec 2016. LNCS, vol. 9996, pp. 175–194. Springer, Cham (2016). https://doi.org/10.1007/978-3-319-47413-7_11
15. Caulfield, T., Ioannidis, C., Pym, D.: On the adoption of privacy-enhancing technologies. In: Zhu, Q., Alpcan, T., Panaousis, E., Tambe, M., Casey, W. (eds.) GameSec 2016. LNCS, vol. 9996, pp. 175–194. Springer, Cham (2016). https://doi.org/10.1007/978-3-319-47413-7_11
16. Chua, W.Y., Chang, K.T.T., Wan, M.P.H.: Information privacy concerns among novice and expert users of solomo. In: PACIS (2014)
17. Clark, J., Van Oorschot, P.C., Adams, C.: Usability of anonymous web browsing: an examination of tor interfaces and deployability. In: Proceedings of the 3rd symposium on Usable privacy and security, pp. 41–51 (2007)
18. Evangelho, J.: Why you should ditch google search and use duckduckgo. Forbes (2018)
19. Fisher, R.J.: Social desirability bias and the validity of indirect questioning. J. Consumer Res. **20**(2), 303–315 (1993)
20. Forte, A., Andalibi, N., Greenstadt, R.: Privacy, anonymity, and perceived risk in open collaboration: A study of tor users and wikipedians. In: Proceedings of the 2017 ACM Conference on Computer Supported Cooperative Work and Social Computing, pp. 1800–1811 (2017)
21. Gallagher, K.: Measurement and improvement of the tor user experience, Ph. D. thesis, New York University Tandon School of Engineering (2020)
22. Gallagher, K., Patil, S., Dolan-Gavitt, B., McCoy, D., Memon, N.: Peeling the onion's user experience layer: examining naturalistic use of the tor browser. In: Proceedings of the 2018 ACM SIGSAC Conference on Computer and Communications Security, pp. 1290–1305 (2018)
23. Gallagher, K., Patil, S., Memon, N.: New me: understanding expert and non-expert perceptions and usage of the tor anonymity network. In: Thirteenth Symposium on Usable Privacy and Security ({SOUPS} 2017), pp. 385–398 (2017)
24. Garg, V., Camp, J.: Heuristics and biases: implications for security design. IEEE Technol. Soc. Mag. **32**(1), 73–79 (2013)

25. Gobet, F., Ereku, M.H.: What Is Expertise? Psychology Today (2016)
26. Goldberg, I.: Privacy-enhancing technologies for the internet, ii: five years later. In: Dingledine, R., Syverson, P. (eds.) PET 2002. LNCS, vol. 2482, pp. 1–12. Springer, Heidelberg (2003). https://doi.org/10.1007/3-540-36467-6_1
27. Goldberg, I., Wagner, D., Brewer, E.: Privacy-enhancing technologies for the internet. In: Proceedings IEEE COMPCON 97. Digest of Papers, pp. 103–109. IEEE (1997)
28. Guest, G., MacQueen, K.M., Namey, E.E.: Applied thematic analysis. Sage Publications (2011)
29. Harborth, D., Pape, S., Rannenberg, K.: Explaining the technology use behavior of privacy-enhancing technologies: the case of Tor and Jondonym. Proceed. Privacy Enhancing Technol. 2020(2), 111–128 (2020)
30. Hargittai, E., Marwick, A.: "what can i really do?" explaining the privacy paradox with online apathy. Int. J. Commun. 10, 21 (2016)
31. Ion, I., Reeder, R., Consolvo, S.: "... no one can hack my mind": comparing expert and non-expert security practices. In: Eleventh Symposium On Usable Privacy and Security ({SOUPS} 2015), pp. 327–346 (2015)
32. Kang, R., Dabbish, L., Fruchter, N., Kiesler, S.: "My data just goes everywhere:" user mental models of the internet and implications for privacy and security. In: Eleventh Symposium On Usable Privacy and Security ({SOUPS} 2015), pp. 39–52 (2015)
33. Kokolakis, S.: Privacy attitudes and privacy behaviour: a review of current research on the privacy paradox phenomenon. Comput. Secur. 64, 122–134 (2017). https://doi.org/10.1016/j.cose.2015.07.002. https://linkinghub.elsevier.com/retrieve/pii/S0167404815001017
34. Lampinen, A., Tamminen, S., Oulasvirta, A.: All my people right here, right now: Management of group co-presence on a social networking site. In: Proceedings of the ACM 2009 International Conference on Supporting Group Work, pp. 281–290 (2009)
35. Leavitt, A.: " this is a throwaway account" temporary technical identities and perceptions of anonymity in a massive online community. In: Proceedings of the 18th ACM Conference on Computer Supported Cooperative Work & Social Computing, pp. 317–327 (2015)
36. Lee, L., Fifield, D., Malkin, N., Iyer, G., Egelman, S., Wagner, D.: A usability evaluation of Tor launcher. Proceed. Priv. Enhan. Technol. 2017(3), 90–109 (2017)
37. Marwick, A., Fontaine, C., Boyd, D.: "nobody sees it, nobody gets mad": social media, privacy, and personal responsibility among low-ses youth. Soc. Media+ Soc. 3(2), 2056305117710455 (2017)
38. McDonald, N., Forte, A.: The politics of privacy theories: moving from norms to vulnerabilities. In: Proceedings of the 2020 CHI Conference on Human Factors in Computing Systems, pp. 1–14 (2020)
39. McDonald, N., Schoenebeck, S., Forte, A.: Reliability and inter-rater reliability in qualitative research: norms and guidelines for CSCW and HCI practice. Proc. ACM Hum.-Comput. Interact. 3(CSCW), 1–23 (2019). https://doi.org/10.1145/3359174
40. Mulligan, D.K., Koopman, C., Doty, N.: Privacy is an essentially contested concept: a multi-dimensional analytic for mapping privacy. Philos. Trans. Royal Soc. A: Math. Phys. Eng. Sci. 374(2083), 20160118 (2016). https://doi.org/10.1098/rsta.2016.0118

41. Oates, M., et al.: Turtles, locks, and bathrooms: understanding mental models of privacy through illustration. Proceed. Privacy Enhan. Technol. **2018**(4), 5–32 (2018). https://content.sciendo.com/view/journals/popets/2018/4/article-p5.xml
42. Phelan, C., Lampe, C., Resnick, P.: It's creepy, but it doesn't bother me. In: Proceedings of the 2016 CHI Conference on Human Factors in Computing Systems, pp. 5240–5251 (2016)
43. Posner, R.A.: The economics of privacy. Am. Econ. Rev. **71**(2), 405–409 (1981)
44. Renaud, K., Volkamer, M., Renkema-Padmos, A.: Why doesn't jane protect her privacy? In: De Cristofaro, E., Murdoch, S.J. (eds.) PETS 2014. LNCS, vol. 8555, pp. 244–262. Springer, Cham (2014). https://doi.org/10.1007/978-3-319-08506-7_13
45. Ruoti, S., Andersen, J., Zappala, D., Seamons, K.: Why Johnny still, still can't encrypt: evaluating the usability of a modern PGP client. arXiv preprint arXiv:1510.08555 (2015)
46. Sheehan, K.B.: Toward a typology of internet users and online privacy concerns. Inf. Soc. **18**(1), 21–32 (2002)
47. Shen, Y., Pearson, S.: Privacy enhancing technologies: A review. HP Laboratories **2739**, 1–30 (2011)
48. Sheng, S., Broderick, L., Koranda, C.A., Hyland, J.J.: Why Johnny still can't encrypt: evaluating the usability of email encryption software. In: Symposium On Usable Privacy and Security, pp. 3–4. ACM (2006)
49. Spiekermann, S.: The challenges of privacy by design. Commun. ACM **55**(7), 38–40 (2012)
50. Stutzman, F., Hartzog, W.: Boundary regulation in social media. In: Proceedings of the ACM 2012 Conference on Computer Supported Cooperative Work, pp. 769–778 (2012)
51. Turner, E.C., Dasgupta, S.: Privacy on the web: an examination of user concerns, technology, and implications for business organizations and individuals. Inf.Syst. Manage. **20**, 8–18 (2006)
52. Vemou, K., Karyda, M.: A classification of factors influencing low adoption of pets among sns users. In: International Conference on Trust, Privacy and Security in Digital Business, pp. 74–84. Springer (2013)
53. Whitten, A., Tygar, J.D.: Why Johnny can't encrypt: a usability evaluation of PGP5.0. In: USENIX Security Symposium, vol. 348, pp. 169–184 (1999)
54. Yardi, S., Bruckman, A.: Income, race, and class: exploring socioeconomic differences in family technology use. In: Proceedings of the SIGCHI Conference on Human Factors in Computing Systems, pp. 3041–3050 (2012)
55. Young, A.L., Quan-Haase, A.: Privacy protection strategies on facebook: the internet privacy paradox revisited. Inf. Commun. Soc. **16**(4), 479–500 (2013)
56. Zabihimayvan, M., Sadeghi, R., Doran, D., Allahyari, M.: A broad evaluation of the tor english content ecosystem. In: Proceedings of the 10th ACM Conference on Web Science, pp. 333–342 (2019)

A Critique of Using Contextual Integrity to (Re)consider Privacy in HCI

Huichuan Xia[✉] [iD]

Department of Information Management, Peking University, Beijing, China
huichuanxia@pku.edu.cn

Abstract. Privacy is a complicated and extensively discussed topic in human-computer interaction (HCI) research and practice. Helen Nissenbaum's contextual integrity (CI) theory, which examines privacy by the integrity of entrenched information collection and flow norms in a particular context, has been a popular theoretical lens to consider privacy in HCI. Many HCI scholars have also advocated and applied the CI theory to investigate privacy issues in various contexts. However, this article critiques using the CI theory when its original positions and limitations about context, norms, and physical privacy are somewhat dismissed in HCI research. Finally, this article proposes that privacy contains specific universal and fundamental values that are not necessarily context-dependent.

Keywords: Contextual integrity · Privacy · HCI

1 Introduction

Privacy is a widely studied but complicated concept. In human-computer interaction (HCI), privacy has been considered important for research but difficult to define or measure [3]. Such a difficulty is due to several possible reasons. First, since Warren and Brandeis's (1890) first definition of privacy as a right to be let alone, privacy has become a notoriously conflated and complex concept. For example, Alan Westin defined it as a person's psychological state and value associated with the fundamental human right of freedom [22]; Altman and Petronio, on the other hand, defined privacy as a process of an individual or collective boundary control to allow or deny information accessibility [1, 15]. However, privacy scholars may have preferred perspectives but are hardly ready to reach a consensus [4]. Second, since the burgeoning development of the internet and ubiquitous computing, defining privacy as a static state or dynamic control became increasingly difficult to describe, prescribe, or address privacy issues in the evolving HCI field, which itself is a moving target [8]. Hence, some scholars tried to define privacy more generically or contextually. Most notably, Daniel Solove developed a taxonomy of privacy to describe different categories of information and physical privacy risks referencing Wittgenstein's terminology of "game" or "family" (e.g., the term family is defined by its constituting members and structure, not the semantic meaning of this word) [18]. Helen Nissenbaum proposed the contextual integrity (CI) theory of privacy, which sets the integrity of the canonical or entrenched information collection and distribution

I. Sserwanga et al. (Eds.): iConference 2023, LNCS 13972, pp. 251–256, 2023.
https://doi.org/10.1007/978-3-031-28032-0_21

norms in a given context as the benchmark of privacy protection or violation [12–14]. Accordingly, if a certain activity violates any canonical information collection or flow norm, such activity is privacy-intrusive; otherwise, it is non-intrusive.

Between Solove's taxonomy of privacy and Nissenbaum's CI theory, the latter seems to be more popularized in HCI, and only a few HCI studies have leveraged the taxonomy of privacy as their theoretical lens (e.g., [23]). We posit that it is because the CI theory has several conspicuous merits for HCI research. First, the CI theory emphasizes the "contextual" nature of privacy, which pertains to the diverse and comprehensive research domains in HCI. For example, the CI theory has been applied to study users' interactions with the Internet of Things (IoT) [16], personal blogs [7], smartphones [9], password management [10], and even COVID-19 surveillance technologies [20]. Arguably, these studies suggest that every HCI domain may be regarded as a research context in which there exist "appropriate norms" that can be perceived or at least expected by users. Second, as Louise Barkhuus pointed out almost one decade ago, it was problematic for HCI scholars to aim to obtain "universal answers" to users' "general privacy practices" because HCI could involve so many different and state-of-the-art technologies [3]. In this sense, the CI theory provided a "more specific vocabulary" to investigate users' views, behaviors, and expectations of information sharing regarding a particular phenomenon [3]. Despite these merits, we posit that the CI theory also has a few limitations that some scholars may have neglected, which could impact the validity of privacy research in HCI. Below, we list three of them in the CI theory for discussion.

2   The Limitations of the CI Theory for Privacy Research in HCI

2.1   A Static View of "Context" Falls Short of Describing Dynamic Contexts

Nissenbaum did not give a concrete definition of "context" in the CI theory but referred to this term generally as

> "structured social settings characterized by canonical activities, roles, relation-ships, power structures, norms (or rules), and internal values (goals, ends, purposes)" [14] (p. 132).

However, she seemed to hold a static view of the context, meaning that a context has clear boundaries and structures, and people know or are informed what information may be collected and flowing to what parties and whether such acts are appropriate to the norms in that context. For example, in her recounts and analyses of surveillance in public spaces and RFID technology, she argued that people in these contexts were conscious of the appropriate boundaries and rules of information collection and distribution. However, not every circumstance in HCI has a clear boundary or a prescription for a subject to know whether an action is appropriate. As Paul Dourish pointed out, a context may not be stable or defined in advance but dynamically arises from subjects' activities in ubiquitous computing or HCI more broadly [5]. Hence, we posit that the CI theory may fall short of describing or prescribing actions in some emerging or dynamic contexts in HCI.

For example, scholars have been leveraging crowd work platforms such as Amazon Mechanical Turk (MTurk) to conduct surveys and experiments, which can be grossly termed crowd work-based research. However, crowd work-based research is a relatively new and dynamic context compared to conventional sociological surveys or lab research. It is still under discussion whether it is appropriate for scholars to collect MTurk workers' demographic information for research purposes since MTurk workers have numerous privacy concerns [6, 17, 23]. We argue that crowd work-based research is still an evolving HCI research context far from stable or delineated. Hence, the appropriate information collection and distribution "norms" are still arising and mutating from the collective and interactive activities between crowd workers and scholars. Furthermore, as Tobias Matzner noted, when considering information flow, sometimes people cannot tell where exactly a context ends and another begins to render the flow across the boundary becomes inappropriate or not [11]. Therefore, to conclude this point, the CI theory's relatively static stance on context may fall short of describing various dynamic and emerging contexts in HCI.

2.2 The Canonical Norms in a Context Do Not Always Equate to Perceived Norms

Nissenbaum contended that there were "canonical" or "entrenched" norms of information collection and flow in a given context that people could use as the benchmark to evaluate whether certain information collection and distribution activities violate them [14]. In her original purpose, Nissenbaum advocated for the existence of such canonical norms to critique the private/public dichotomy and the opinion that there was no privacy in a public space. For example, she argued that even in public spaces, people still held the norm that private information should not be collected or flowing to government agencies without due notice, warrant, or procedures, and therefore, there was still privacy in public places [14]. However, applying this original stance in the CI theory to HCI may be problematic. On the one hand, related to our arguments in the previous subsection, a context in HCI may be dynamically emerging or created in which no canonical or entrenched norms are settled or identifiable. On the other hand, when using the CI theory to measure users' privacy concerns or expectations in HCI, some scholars might have equated the CI theory's *canonical* norms to participants' *perceived* norms in a context, which are not necessarily identical.

For example, Apthorpe et al. surveyed 1,731 American adults on MTurk to discover privacy norms in smart home IoT [2]. Even though they had a fairly large sample size and measured 3,840 "acceptable" information flow suggestions from the participants [2], we still regard the final results as not being tantamount to "canonical" privacy norms in smart home IoT. First, their sample may be biased toward the U.S. population and people that are tech-savvy enough to understand IoT. However, these participants' perceptions of privacy norms may not accurately reflect the under-represented users in other countries, cultures, or groups. Hence, it could be a problem if we universalize or extrapolate such "perceived" privacy norms to be "entrenched" when we design smart home IoT not only for the U.S. but for the populations in other parts of the world. Second, as discussed above, smart home IoT may still be an evolving and dynamic context without unaminously acknowledged or entrenched privacy norms. As state-of-the-art technologies become more connected and integrated into smart home IoT, the authors' identified privacy norms perceived by MTurk workers in 2018 might change or evolve nowadays or in the future. Thus, it is unlike the social contexts, such as surveillance in the public sphere in Nissenbaum's original critique, that have become well-recognized. However, it should be noted here that we aim not to critique a specific HCI study per se but rather to raise awareness of the potential pitfall of operationalizing the canonical norms in the CI theory to be respondents' perceived norms in a survey.

2.3 Privacy Risks Are Not Only Informational But Can also Be Physical

Nissenbaum's CI theory is primarily about information privacy risks and protection, but as Solove commented, privacy risks can also be physical [18]. For example, when stalking occurs physically or online, or when a stranger invades a private space, it is more concerning about physical privacy violations than information privacy breaches. In HCI, we argue that although most privacy divulgence and protection are about information, there are still some circumstances when physical privacy risks are also involved. In this sense, the CI theory may be insufficient to depict a whole picture of privacy issues in these contexts. We use human-drone interaction (HDI) research as a case to illustrate this point. For example, Wang et al. conducted a qualitative study of people's privacy perceptions of drones in the U.S. [21]. They found that the participants were not only worried about what information might be collected and how it might be distributed but also expressed their concerns about drones' physical size, speed, flying height, noise, and even color because they would be uncomfortable if a drone were too small that could be spying or too noisy that could be disturbing when they were alone [21]. We argue that these privacy concerns in HDI were not about any information collection or flow norms being breached per se but rather about their physical space being intruded upon. In this sense, the CI theory may not be easily or readily applicable in describing or prescribing privacy issues in HDI.

Despite it, we may not blame the CI theory for encompassing all aspects of privacy because every theory has its focus, boundary, and limitations. Instead, we reflect that, as HCI scholars, we may need to be more prudent in "contextualizing" every privacy problem. In 2012, when the CI theory was still relatively new to HCI scholars, Louise Barkhuus advocated for using it in HCI so that the research lens, solutions, and recommendations would be more specific to measure and address privacy in a certain context. We agreed with this suggestion but also proposed that one decade since, we should be cautious of reaching the other extreme, namely, perceiving every privacy issue or value as contextual. Perhaps, Solove's [19] reminder should echo in HCI more than before:

> "[m]erely calling for more context in conceptualizing privacy throws the issue back into the hands of those who are struggling over a particular problem without telling them how to make sense of it." [19], (p. 173).

3 Conclusion

In this short paper, we made a few primitive reflections on using the CI theory in HCI. However, as aforementioned, our primary goal is not to falsify or negate the value of the CI theory but instead to raise some awareness for further discussion in the HCI scholarship. Also, in our view, privacy may have certain fundamental and universal values that should not be easily regarded as context-specific. For example, Alan Westin depicted people's universal privacy feelings across different cultures and the fundamental relation between privacy protection and human freedom [22]. We propose that such values of privacy could be studied deeper and more extensively across different research contexts in HCI.

References

1. Altman, I.: The environment and social behavior: privacy, personal space, territory, crowding. Brooks/Cole Pub. Co. (1975)
2. Apthorpe, N., et al.: Discovering smart home internet of things privacy norms using contextual integrity. Proc. ACM Interact. Mob. Wearable Ubiquitous Technol. 2(2), 1–23 (2018). https://doi.org/10.1145/3214262
3. Barkhuus, L.: The mismeasurement of privacy: using contextual integrity to reconsider privacy in HCI. In: Proceedings of the 2012 ACM annual conference on Human Factors in Computing Systems - CHI '12, p. 367. ACM Press, Austin, Texas, USA (2012). https://doi.org/10.1145/2207676.2207727
4. Bélanger, F., Crossler, R.E.: Privacy in the digital age: a review of information privacy research in information systems. MIS Quarterly 35(4), 1017 (2011). https://doi.org/10.2307/41409971
5. Dourish, P.: What we talk about when we talk about context. Pers. Ubiquit. Comput. 8(1), 19–30 (2004). https://doi.org/10.1007/s00779-003-0253-8
6. Fowler, C., et al.: Frustration and ennui among Amazon MTurk workers. Behav Res., 117 (2022). https://doi.org/10.3758/s13428-022-01955-9.
7. Grodzinsky, F.S., Tavani, H.T.: Applying the "Contextual Integrity" Model of Privacy to Personal Blogs in the Blogosphere 3, 11
8. Grudin, J.: A moving target—the evolution of human-computer interaction. In: Human-Computer Interaction Handbook. pp. 1–40. Taylor & Francis (2012)
9. King, J.: How come i'm allowing strangers to go through my phone? smartphones and privacy expectations. SSRN Journal (2012). https://doi.org/10.2139/ssrn.2493412.
10. Kumar, P.C., et al.: Strengthening children's privacy literacy through contextual integrity. MaC. 8(4), 175–184 (2020). https://doi.org/10.17645/mac.v8i4.3236
11. Matzner, T.: Why privacy is not enough privacy in the context of "ubiquitous computing" and "big data." J. Inf. Commun. Ethics Soc. 12(2), 93–106 (2014). https://doi.org/10.1108/JICES-08-2013-0030
12. Nissenbaum, H.: A contextual approach to privacy online. Daedalus 140(4), 32–48 (2011). https://doi.org/10.1162/DAED_a_00113
13. Nissenbaum, H.: Privacy as contextual integrity. Washington Law Rev. 79, 119 (2004)
14. Nissenbaum, H.: Privacy in Context - Technology, Policy, and the Integrity of Social Life. Stanford Law Books (2010)
15. Petronio, S.: Boundaries of Privacy: Dialectics of Disclosure. Suny Press (2002)
16. Shaffer, G.: Applying a contextual integrity framework to privacy policies for smart technologies. J. Inf. Policy 11(1), 222–265 (2021). https://doi.org/10.5325/jinfopoli.11.2021.0222

17. Shmueli, B., et al.: Beyond Fair Pay: Ethical Implications of NLP Crowdsourcing. arXiv: 2104.10097 [cs]. (2021)
18. Solove, D.: A Taxonomy of Privacy. University of Pennsylvania Law Rev. **154**(3), 477 (2006)
19. Solove, D.: Understanding Privacy. Harvard University Press (2008)
20. Vitak, J., Zimmer, M.: More than just privacy: using contextual integrity to evaluate the long-term risks from COVID-19 surveillance technologies. Social Media + Society **6**(3), 205630512094825 (2020). https://doi.org/10.1177/2056305120948250
21. Wang, Y., et al.: Flying eyes and hidden controllers: a qualitative study of people's privacy perceptions of civilian drones in the US. Proceedings on Privacy Enhancing Technol. **2016**(3), 172–190 (2016). https://doi.org/10.1515/popets-2016-0022
22. Westin, A.F.: Privacy and Freedom. Ig Publishing (2015)
23. Xia, H., et al.: "Our privacy needs to be protected at all costs": crowd workers' privacy experiences on amazon mechanical turk. Proc. ACM Hum.-Comput. Interact. 1, CSCW, pp. 1–22 (2017). https://doi.org/10.1145/3134748

Audience Video Game Engagement in a Live Streaming Context: Examining the Role of Perceived Influence of Game Streamers from the Self-determination Perspective

Xiaoyu Chen[1]([⊠]) [ID], Yan He[1], Han Zheng[2] [ID], and Jiahui Lu[3]

[1] School of Cultural Heritage and Information Management, Shanghai University, Shanghai, China
{xiaoyu-chen,heyan}@shu.edu.cn
[2] School of Information Management, Wuhan University, Wuhan, China
hanzheng@whu.edu.cn
[3] Department of Sociological Studies, University of Sheffield, Sheffield, UK
jlu55@sheffield.ac.uk

Abstract. Despite the increasing popularity of game streamers on live streaming platforms, the understanding of how perceived influence of game streamers affects audience video game engagement is limited. To address the research gap, this paper develops a research model by combining the self-determination theory with extant live-streaming literature. Results from an online field survey suggest that perceived influence of game streamers is positively associated with satisfying audiences' needs for autonomy, competence, and relatedness, further promoting their video game engagement. Theoretical and practical implications are also discussed.

Keywords: Audience · Game streamers · Live streaming · Self-determination theory · Video game engagement

1 Introduction

The rise of live streaming profoundly shapes the video game industry. Video game live streaming (hereafter referred to as game streaming) enables streamers to play video games while chatting with viewers in real time, becoming increasingly popular among video game lovers [1]. For example, Twitch—a globally popular live streaming platform where streamers broadcast their play live—has attracted over 3 million concurrent viewers [2]. Professional and amateur game players can broadcast themselves playing games through a live stream or a prerecorded video to target audiences. Meanwhile, audiences freely choose streamers they like to follow and watch their plays. The audiences gradually learn about play styles and skills favored by the streamers and are even influenced to engage in the game.

I. Sserwanga et al. (Eds.): iConference 2023, LNCS 13972, pp. 257–267, 2023.
https://doi.org/10.1007/978-3-031-28032-0_22

In practice, several large video game publishers have paid millions of dollars to famous game streamers to attract more audiences [3]. Extant literature has suggested that game streamers may benefit the game industry by motivating audience video game engagement [4]. Generally, game streamers are usually viewed as trustworthy and valuable influencers that draw audiences to play the games and even persuade them to purchase virtual products for level up in the games. In such context, the role of perceived influence of game streamers seems significant to audience video game engagement [5].

Although perceived influence of game streamers receives growing scholarly attention, two research gaps still exist in the literature. First, the underlying mechanism of how perceived influence of game streamers motivates audience video game engagement remains unknown. Audience video game engagement can be primarily attributed to their self-determination to acquire gameplay skills and techniques by watching streamers' live shows with commentary [6]. However, there is limited knowledge of the relationships between perceived influence of streamers, audiences' self-determination and video game engagement. For this reason, the current study draws upon the self-determination theory and live-streaming literature to propose a theoretical model for explaining how perceived influence of game streamers affects audience video game engagement.

Second, the extent to which perceived influence of game streamers can determine audience video game engagement has not been empirically validated. There are some doubts in the literature about perceived influence of game streamers in light of some evidence that greater popularity does not necessarily indicate a greater influence on audience attitudes and behaviors [6–8]. It is still questionable about the actual importance of perceived influence of game streamers, as typical digital influencers, on audience video game engagement [4]. To this end, our proposed model was empirically tested using a field survey of 300 participants with rich experience of watching game streaming.

The study holds both theoretical and practical significance. Theoretically, it contributes to related literature by shedding light on how perceived influence of game streamers motivates audiences' self-determination process as well as their video game engagement. In practice, our research may inform related practitioners who want to harness game streamers on live streaming platforms to promote audience consumption of video games.

2   Literature Review

2.1   Linking Perceived Influence of Game Streamers to Audiences' Psychological Needs

Extant live-streaming literature suggests that popular game streamers can develop a unique display of attitudes that makes them attractive to target audiences while seeming natural on camera [5]. A streamer's personality and performance quality can be more important to audiences than actual playing skills, indicating that the relationship between streamers and audiences is similar to that between influencers and fans [7]. By sharing live shows with commentary, game streamers may evoke audiences' positive feedback on playing the game [6]. This study thus conceptualizes perceived influence of game streamers as the extent to which streamers can shape their audiences' attitudes toward streamed video games. According to the literature [9, 10], their psychological needs are satisfied when audiences perceive that the streamers are influential and impactful.

Self-determination theory (SDT) proposes three primary types of psychological needs, namely, autonomy, competence and relatedness. Autonomy refers to the extent to which a person can self-control one's actions in a game [11]. Competence refers to one's need for challenges and feelings of effectiveness at meeting those challenges set by the game [11]. Relatedness reflects a person's tendency to "connect with and be integral to and accepted by others" [12]. Prior studies have suggested that audiences' self-determination is significantly related to perceived influence of social commerce sellers who broadcast themselves in a live streaming context [10]. Nonetheless, previous research has not examined whether perceived influence of game streamers satisfies audiences' three basic psychological needs. Hence, we propose three hypotheses.

H1: Perceived influence of game streamers is positively related to satisfying the audience's need for autonomy.

H2: Perceived influence of game streamers is positively related to satisfying the audience's need for competence.

H3: Perceived influence of game streamers is positively related to satisfying the audience's need for relatedness.

2.2 Psychological Needs and Video Game Engagement

Video game engagement refers to the extent to which an audience intends to play a video game [13]. The existing literature has linked SDT to individuals' video game engagement [14, 15]. SDT is frequently used to explain the relationship between human behavior and basic psychological needs [16]. It posits that a user's behavioral intention is driven by one's satisfaction with three primary needs: autonomy, competence, and relatedness [17, 18]. With regard to autonomy, audiences who love to watch streamers playing video games are usually those who can voluntarily determine when and how to play the games. In terms of competence, after watching their favorite streamers' performances, they may be confident to master and play the game well. For relatedness, audiences may communicate both with game streamers and each other, thereby making the platform "the home of gaming community" [1].

Furthermore, we argue that the need for relatedness can be afforded by audiences' gained value from their experience on a live streaming platform. This is because such value acquisition may strengthen one's connection to the game community [1]. The existing literature draws on three distinctive values that audiences may derive from stream-watching experiences: utilitarian value, hedonic value, and symbolic value [8, 10]. Utilitarian value represents an audience's expected utility from a live streaming platform. Hedonic value is an audience subject experience of fun and playfulness by watching video games. Symbolic value refers to symbolic meanings and social codes that an audience receives from the live streaming platform. Therefore, relatedness is conceptualized as a second-order construct consisting of three first-order constructs—utilitarian value, hedonic value, and symbolic value. Hence, we propose three hypotheses.

H4: Autonomy is positively related to audience video game engagement.

H5: Competence is positively related to audience video game engagement.

H6: Relatedness, consisting of utilitarian value, hedonic value and symbolic value, is positively related to audience video game engagement.

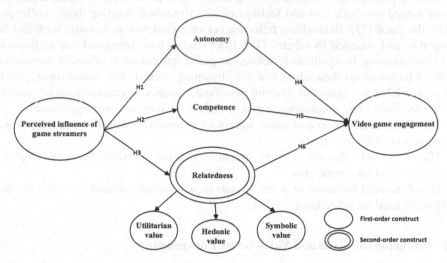

Fig. 1. Research model

3 Methods

All constructs in this study were measured using items adapted from the existing literature. Specifically, perceived influence of game streamers [9], autonomy [11], competence [11], relatedness (i.e., utilitarian value hedonic value and symbolic value) [10], and audience video engagement [19] were assessed using multiple Likert-type items ranging from 1 ("strongly disagree") to 7 ("strongly agree"). Table 1 presents the operationalization of the constructs and related references. After being approved by the institutional review board of the first author's affiliated institution, we collected the data through a field survey, and the questionnaires were hosted on Qualtrics. We recruited eligible participants with rich experience of watching game streaming from crowdworkers on Amazon Mechanical Turk (AMT).

The proposed model was assessed using a structural equation modeling (SEM) approach, and the analytical tool—SmartPLS 3—was adopted for data analysis [20]. The partial least squares (PLS) algorithm is "preferable to other techniques by allowing each indicator to vary in how much it contributes to the composite score of the latent variable" [21]. Moreover, PLS uses the ordinary least squares regression and bootstrapping techniques, which are suitable for exploring a theoretical model with a relatively small sample [21].

Table 1. Measures of related constructs

Construct	Items	Reference
Video game engagement	**E1**: "Generally, I like to get involved in discussions about the video game I watch on a livestreaming platform." **E2**: "I enjoy playing video games while watching them played by others on a livestreaming platform." **E3**: "I like to play the video game I watched on a live streaming platform." **E4**: "I often participate in activities related to the video game I watched on a livestreaming platform."	Abbasi et al. (2016)
Perceived influence of game streamers	When watching video games on a livestreaming platform: **P1**: "The game streamer I follow suggests helpful gameplay skills to me." **P2**: "I enjoy watching video games broadcasted by the game streamer I follow." **P3**: "My video game watch experience is often shaped by the game streamer I follow."	Jiménez-Castillo & Sánchez-Fernández, (2019)
Autonomy	**A1**: "I feel a sense of autonomy when watching gameplay videos on a livestreaming platform." **A2**: "I can determine how to do freely when watching gameplay videos on a livestreaming platform."	Ryan & Deci, 2000
Competence	**C1**: "I can search for new gameplay skills and relevant techniques when watching video games on livestreaming platforms." **C2**: "I can satisfy my needs when I watch video games on a livestreaming platform." **C3**: "I believe I can learn how to play a game when watching related streaming videos on a livestreaming platform."	Ryan & Deci, 2000

(continued)

Table 1. (*continued*)

Construct	Items	Reference
Utilitarian value	**UV1**: "Watching gameplay videos on a live streaming platform is beneficial to me." **UV2**: "A livestreaming platform allows me to stay in touch with the latest information on gaming videos." **UV3**: "I learn something by watching gaming videos on a live streaming platform." **UV4**: "The gameplay videos on a live streaming platform meet my expectations."	Wongkitrungrueng & Assarut, 2020
Hedonic value	**HV1:** "Watching gameplay videos on a livestreaming platform is entertaining." **HV2:** "Watching gameplay videos on a livestreaming platform makes me happy." **HV3:** "Watching gameplay videos on a livestreaming platform gets me excited."	Wongkitrungrueng & Assarut, 2020
Symbolic value	When watching video games on a live streaming platform: **SV1:** "I feel that I can identify with the game streamer I follow." **SV2:** "I feel that the game streamer I follow has the same taste as me." **SV3:** "I am eager to tell my game friends/acquaintances about the game streamer I follow."	Wongkitrungrueng & Assarut, 2020

4   Preliminary Results

4.1   Descriptive Statistical Analysis

Table 2 presents the demographic characteristics of the survey sample (N = 300). Of them, 62% were male viewers, while females accounted for 38%. Most of them were aged from 21 to 30 (59.33%) and received education from universities (70.33%). In terms of watching game streaming experience, over 50% of participants had 4 or 5 years

of experience. In terms of the frequency of playing video games, over 70% of participants reported that they played 4–6 times per week or above. Notably, the most popular
livestreaming platforms included Twitch, YouTube and TikTok.

Table 2. Sample demography

Variable	Category	Frequency (%)
Gender	Male	186 (62.00%)
	Female	114 (38.00%)
Age	21–30	178 (59.33%)
	31–40	96 (32.00%)
	41–50	15 (5.00%)
	51–60	9 (3.00%)
	> 60	2 (0.67%)
Education level	Below Bachelor	24 (8.00%)
	Bachelor	211 (70.33%)
	Master or above	65 (21.67%)
Experience of watching game streaming	01 year	12 (4.00%)
	23 years	67 (22.33%)
	45 years	154 (51.33%)
	6 years or above	67 (22.33%)
Frequency of playing video games	Never	5 (1.67%)
	13 times a week	82 (27.33%)
	46 times a week	102 (34.00%)
	Every day or above	111 (37.00%)
Most popular livestreaming platform	Twitch	195 (65.00%)
	YouTube	45 (15.00%)
	TikTok	32 (10.67%)
	Others	28 (9.33%)

Note: Sample size = 300

The measurement model was assessed in terms of convergent validity and discriminant validity. As shown in Table 3, for all the constructs, values of Cronbach's alpha,
composite reliability (CR) and rho_A were above 0.70, and values of average variance
extraction (AVE) were above 0.50, demonstrating satisfactory reliability and convergent validity [20, 22]. To assess discriminant validity, we used the criterion that the
AVE square root of each construct exceeded its correlations with other constructs. As
shown in Table 4, the AVE square roots were greater than the correlations, indicating
satisfactory discriminant validity of the constructs [23].

Table 3. Reliability and validity assessment

Construct	Cronbach's Alpha	CR	AVE	rho_A
PI	0.78	0.87	0.69	0.78
A	0.76	0.89	0.80	0.77
C	0.80	0.88	0.71	0.80
UV	0.85	0.90	0.68	0.85
HV	0.81	0.89	0.72	0.82
SV	0.85	0.91	0.77	0.85
VE	0.77	0.85	0.59	0.77

Note: PI = perceived influence of game streamers; A = autonomy; C = competence; UV = utility value; HV = hedonic value; SV = symbolic value; VE = audience video engagement

Table 4. Discriminant validity assessment

	PI	A	C	UV	HV	SV	VE
PI	**0.83**						
A	0.49	**0.90**					
C	0.71	0.56	**0.84**				
UV	0.68	0.63	0.78	**0.83**			
HV	0.66	0.57	0.72	0.71	**0.85**		
SV	0.62	0.54	0.52	0.59	0.56	**0.88**	
VE	0.59	0.63	0.72	0.68	0.66	0.62	**0.77**

Note: PI = perceived influence of game streamers; A = autonomy; C = competence; UV = utility value; HV = hedonic value; SV = symbolic value; VE = audience video engagement

4.2 Inferential Statistical Analysis

Our data analysis supported all the hypotheses, as shown in Fig. 2. Specifically, perceived influence of game streamers was positively related to autonomy ($\beta = 0.49$, $p < 0.001$), competence ($\beta = 0.71$, $p < 0.001$), and relatedness ($\beta = 0.76$, $p < 0.001$). Moreover, autonomy ($\beta = 0.20$, $p < 0.01$), competence ($\beta = 0.31$, $p < 0.001$) and relatedness ($\beta = 0.37$, $p < 0.001$) were positively associated with audience video game engagement (See Fig. 2).

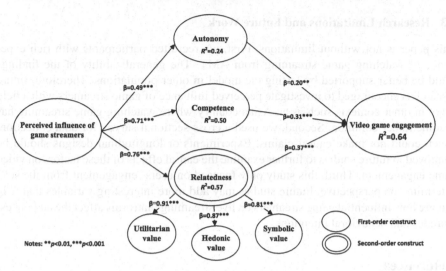

Fig. 2. Research model with PLS results

5 Discussions and Conclusion

5.1 Theoretical Implications

Based on the results above, the current study seeks to move the extant literature forward in three ways. First, it advances our understanding of the role of perceived influence of game streamers in audience game engagement by developing and validating a theoretical model. Specifically, this study suggests that perceived influence of game streamers can promote audiences' needs for autonomy, competence, and relatedness, which further motivate their video game engagement. Second, it enriches the self-determination theory by contextualizing the concepts of autonomy, competence, and relatedness within a game streaming setting. In particular, relatedness is conceptualized into three dimensions: utilitarian value, hedonic value, and symbolic value that audiences derive from watching game streaming. Last, it extends the literature by bridging the perceived influence of game streamers with audiences' psychological needs and video game engagement. This deepens our understanding of the role of influential game streamers in audience video engagement in the context of watching others' game streaming.

5.2 Practical Implications

On the practical front, the study may inform both game streamers and operators of livestreaming platforms. Game streamers can leverage their influence on target audiences to strengthen game engagement by promoting audiences' sense of autonomy, competence and relatedness when watching their gameplay. In addition, live streaming platform operators are encouraged to improve the platform affordances and functionalities to promote the audiences' perception of game streamers' practices and video game consumption.

5.3 Research Limitations and Future Work

This paper is not without limitations. First, we recruited participants with rich experience of watching game streaming from AMT. The generalizability of the findings could be better supported by testing the model in other populations. Therefore, future research is encouraged to investigate perceived influence of game streamers with a field study in other contexts such as an Asian country where watching game streaming has become rather common. Second, we used a cross-sectional survey for data collection, which could not make causal claims. Experiments or longitudinal designs should be employed in future studies to further examine the causal effects of these factors on video game engagement. Third, this study only focused on users' engagement from the self-determination perspective. Future studies may add more interesting variables that help capture how influential game streamers on live streaming platforms affect the audiences' attitudes and behavioral intentions.

References

1. Johnson, M.R., Woodcock, J.: The impacts of live streaming and Twitch.tv on the video game industry. Media, Culture & Society **41**(5), 670–688 (2019). https://doi.org/10.1177/016344 3718818363
2. Statistics: Average number of concurrent viewers on Twitch from 2nd quarter 2018 to 3rd 2021. https://www.statista.com/statistics/761122/average-number-viewers-on-youtube-gaming-live-and-twitch/. Accessed 25 May 2022
3. Needleman, S.E.: Top 'live-streamers' get $50,000 an hour to play new videogames online. The Wall Street Journal (2019). https://www.wsj.com/articles/top-live-streamers-get-50-000-an-hour-to-play-new-videogames-online-11558184421
4. Lim, J.S., Choe, M.J., Zhang, J., Noh, G.Y.: The role of wishful identification, emotional engagement, and parasocial relationships in repeated viewing of live-streaming games: a social cognitive theory perspective. Comput. Hum. Behav. **108**, 106327 (2020). https://doi.org/10.1016/j.chb.2020.106327
5. Alvarez, K.P.B., Chen, V.H.H.: Community and capital: experiences of women game streamers in Southeast Asia. ACM Trans. Social Comput. **4**(3), 1–22 (2021). https://doi.org/10.1145/3481888
6. Xu, X.Y., Luo, X.R., Wu, K., Zhao, W.: Exploring viewer participation in online video game streaming: a mixed-methods approach. Int. J. Inf. Manage. **58**, 102297 (2021). https://doi.org/10.1016/j.ijinfomgt.2020.102297
7. King, R., De La Hera, T.: Fortnite streamers as influencers: a study on gamers' perceptions. The Computer Games J. **9**(4), 349–368 (2020)
8. Zhao, Q., Chen, C.D., Cheng, H.W., Wang, J.L.: Determinants of live streamers' continuance broadcasting intentions on Twitch: a self-determination theory perspective. Telematics Inform. **35**(2), 406–420 (2018). https://doi.org/10.1016/j.tele.2017.12.018
9. Jiménez-Castillo, D., Sánchez-Fernández, R.: The role of digital influencers in brand recommendation: examining their impact on engagement, expected value and purchase intention. Int. J. Inf. Manage. **49**, 366–376 (2019). https://doi.org/10.1016/j.ijinfomgt.2019.07.009
10. Wongkitrungrueng, A., Assarut, N.: The role of live streaming in building consumer trust and engagement with social commerce sellers. J. Bus. Res. **117**, 543–556 (2020). https://doi.org/10.1016/j.jbusres.2018.08.032

11. Ryan, R.M., Rigby, C.S., Przybylski, A.: The motivational pull of video games: a self-determination theory approach. Motiv. Emot. **30**(4), 344–360 (2006). https://doi.org/10.1007/s11031-006-9051-8

12. Deci, E.L., Ryan, R.M.: Handbook of Self-Determination Research, 1st edn. University of Rochester Press, Rochester, NY (2013)

13. Przybylski, A.K., Rigby, C.S., Ryan, R.M.: A motivational model of video game engagement. Rev. Gen. Psychol. **14**(2), 154–166 (2010). https://doi.org/10.1037/a0019440

14. Lin, H.H., Wang, Y.S., Chou, C.H.: Hedonic and utilitarian motivations for physical game systems use behavior. Int. J. Human-Computer Interaction **28**(7), 445–455 (2012). https://doi.org/10.1080/10447318.2011.618097

15. Peng, W., Lin, J.H., Pfeiffer, K.A., Winn, B.: Need satisfaction supportive game features as motivational determinants: an experimental study of a self-determination theory guided exergame. Media Psychol. **15**(2), 175–196 (2012). https://doi.org/10.1080/15213269.2012.673850

16. Deci, E.L., Eghrari, H., Patrick, B.C., Leone, D.R.: Facilitating internalization: the self-determination theory perspective. J. Pers. **62**(1), 119–142 (1994). https://doi.org/10.1111/j.1467-6494.1994.tb00797.x

17. Deci, E., Ryan, R.: Self-determination theory. In: Van Lange P.A., Kruglanski, A.W., Higgins, E.T. (eds): Handbook of theories of social psychology: volume 1, pp. 416–437. SAGE Publications Ltd, London (2012). https://doi.org/10.4135/9781446249215.n21

18. Zhang, Y.: Understanding the sustained use of online health communities from a self-determination perspective. J. Am. Soc. Inf. Sci. **67**(12), 2842–2857 (2016). https://doi.org/10.1002/asi.23560

19. Abbasi, A.Z., Ting, D.H., Hlavacs, H.: A revisit of the measurements on engagement in videogames: a new scale development. In: Wallner, G., Kriglstein, S., Hlavacs, H., Malaka, R., Lugmayr, A., Yang, H.-S. (eds.) ICEC 2016. LNCS, vol. 9926, pp. 247–252. Springer, Cham (2016). https://doi.org/10.1007/978-3-319-46100-7_25

20. Ringle, C.M., Wende, S., Becker, J.M.: SmartPLS 3. Boenningstedt: SmartPLS GmbH (2015). http://www.smartpls.com

21. Zha, X., Huang, C., Yan, Y., Yan, G., Wang, X., Zhang, K.: Understanding extended information seeking: the perspectives of psychological empowerment and digital libraries attachment. Aslib J. Inf. Manag. **72**(5), 705–724 (2020)

22. Fornell, C., Larcker, D.F.: Structural equation models with unobservable variables and measurement error: algebra and statistics. J. Mark. Res. **18**(3), 382–388 (1981)

23. Gefen, D., Straub, D.: A practical guide to factorial validity using PLS-graph: tutorial and annotated example. Commun. Assoc. Inf. Syst. **16**(1), 91–109 (2005)

A Surprise Birthday Party in VR: Leveraging Social Virtual Reality to Maintain Existing Close Ties over Distance

Samaneh Zamanifard(✉) and Guo Freeman

Clemson University, Clemson, SC 29634, USA
{szamani,guof}@clemson.edu

Abstract. This paper explores how social virtual reality, a novel 3D virtual social interaction space that provides embodied and immersive experiences, can be leveraged to maintain existing close interpersonal relationships over distance. Based on 672 Reddit posts and comments, our findings show that in addition to initiating and building new relationships with online strangers, social VR platforms' unique features, including physicality, the enhanced sense of presence, and the broad range of shared embodied activities, can also help maintain various types of established close ties (e.g., parent-child, friends, siblings, and romantic partners) over distance in a nuanced way. This work contributes to understanding the increasingly important role of social VR in innovating modern computer-mediated relationships and can inform the future design of social VR to better support people's social needs and interpersonal connections.

Keywords: Social VR · Interpersonal relationships ·
Computer-mediated relationships · Close ties

1 Introduction

Actively maintaining various forms of existing close interpersonal relationships is not only the most important psychological and behavioral dynamics of loving and caring for others [27] but also significantly affects people's social lives and daily performance [1,12,42]. In modern social lives, varied communication technologies have been widely used to sustain such relationships, especially over distance, including emails [28,55], text messages [15,25], video chats [38,40], social networking sites [4,7,13,14,26,48], and online gaming [31,43]. However, prior research also reveals two shortcomings in maintaining existing close ties over distance through these technologies: (1) they often mainly focus on facilitating text, video, or voice communication but lack considerations of crucial experiential qualities; and (2) they often fall short of providing embodiment and immersive experiences that simulate everyday face-to-face activities, which are crucial to maintain existing close ties [6,21,37,46,47,52].

© The Author(s), under exclusive license to Springer Nature Switzerland AG 2023
I. Sserwanga et al. (Eds.): iConference 2023, LNCS 13972, pp. 268–285, 2023.
https://doi.org/10.1007/978-3-031-28032-0_23

In this paper we focus on how social virtual reality (VR), a 3D virtual ecosystem where multiple users can socialize and interact with each other through head-mounted displays [32,35] (Figs. 1 and 2), can be leveraged to address these limitations by maintaining and sustaining existing close interpersonal relationships over distance in a nuanced way. While investigating social dynamics and relationship building in social VR is becoming a growing research agenda in computing and Human-Computer Interaction studies, existing work tends to focus on building and fostering relationships among online strangers through social VR [2,16,33,54]. Yet, little is known about how social VR may also be used to support existing interpersonal relationships over distance, which may demonstrate different nature, dynamics, and impacts on one's social life and psychological well-being compared to interacting with strangers.

Fig. 1. AltspaceVR (https://www.altvr. com/)

Fig. 2. VRChat (https://www.vrchat. com/)

Therefore, based on 672 Reddit posts and comments about social VR users' experiences of using social VR to maintain their existing close social relationships, we explore three research questions:

RQ1: What types of existing relationships do people use social VR to maintain?

RQ2: In which ways do they use social VR to maintain such relationships?

RQ3: What are some potential risks when using social VR to maintain such relationships?

This work thus contributes to understanding the increasingly important role of social VR in modern social lives. We extend existing social VR literature by (1) focusing on existing social connections rather than new relationships between strangers, and (2) by providing new empirical evidence of how social VR can be leveraged to benefit various close ties over distance, such as parent-child, friendships, and romance, as well as potential risks. Our work contributes towards a better understanding of modern computer-mediated relationships and informs the future design of social VR to better support people's everyday social lives and interpersonal connections.

2   Computer-Mediated Relationships and Social VR

Belongingness is essential for maintaining people's psychological well-being [5,22]. Keeping connections with those one cares for and loves can also significantly affect one's mental health [5,12,29,42]. Most traditional social science studies appear to agree that an interpersonal relationship refers to a strong, deep, or close association/acquaintance between two or more people, involving experiences that range from the mundane to the aesthetic [49], and as a specific sort of knowing, loving, and caring for a person [27]. Such relationships are demonstrated as various forms such as friendship (a freely chosen association), family (which establishes roles and identities), and romance (based on passion, intimacy, and commitment).

However, in today's modern society, many people are forced to live separately from their close ties for various reasons, such as education, career, military, or simply moving away from family. It has been reported that millions of Americans are involved in Long Distance Relationships (LDRs) with their lovers, parents, friends, children, siblings, or other relatives [53]. Therefore, people often rely on various computer-mediated methods to stay connected with their geographically separated close ties. First, people tend to use technologies to compensate for face-to-face communication with their remote existing close ties, such as via emails, instant messages, phone calls, and social networking sites [10,14,45,56]. These technologies have been used to maintain various types of close bonds, including parent-child [13], couples [7], friends [26], and grandparent-grandchild [4]. However, in contrast with face-to-face communication, these technologies lack critical mechanisms for intimacy building that often happen in offline interaction [30,50,51].

Second, in addition to fulfilling communication needs, maintaining existing close ties also requires a sense of closeness and being a part of each other's daily activities despite from a distance. As a result, technologies for simulating physical connections [6,21,37,46,47,52] and shared activities [9,20,24,39,41,43, 44,58,59] have been used for sustaining existing close ties over distance, such as touching during a phone conversation [46], haptic device to simulate a kiss [50], cooking together through wearable devices [9], and playing puzzle games together [43]. Yet, many existing technologies seem to provide limited support for certain essential experiential qualities that are crucial for maintaining existing close ties, including physical touch, body language, shared memories, and collaborative activities as daily routine [17,19,37,38]. There also seem to be limited solutions for providing embodied and immersive experiences to resemble daily offline world activities (e.g., dancing, dating, and playing sports together), which significantly influence existing close relationships.

In this paper, we focus on the potential of social VR to address the above-mentioned issues in maintaining existing close ties over distance. In social VR, users can create and customize partially or fully body tracked avatars (i.e., their avatar body corresponds to their body movement in the offline world in real-time) and interact and socialize with each other through such avatars. In doing so, social VR users are able to conduct and enjoy social activities in a highly realistic 3D virtual environment similar to a face-to-face manner, such as walking in a public place, watching a movie, playing games, participating in a concert, and having a party. Social VR also provides other nuanced technological features such as sense of presence, body tracking, synchronous voice conversation, and the simulated touching features, making it unique compared to traditional communication technologies [35,36]. Popular social VR platforms include VRchat, Rec Room, Bigscreen, AltspaceVR, Meta Horizon, and so forth. They tend to afford diverse activities and social atmospheres. For example, Rec Room focuses on VR gaming; VR Chat supports a wide range of creative activities and avatar customization; AltspaceVR is well known for its diverse event and professional development, and High Fidelity VR highlights large-scale public events and performance [35].

Acknowledging the nuances of social VR spaces, there has been a growing research agenda in HCI to investigate interaction dynamics and relationship building in social VR [2,8,16,54]. Most existing social VR research on relationship building tends to focus on how this technology is leveraged to initiate and build relationships between online strangers. Nevertheless, little is known about how it can also be used to maintain existing close relationships over distance, which may significantly differ from meeting and fostering new interpersonal bonds. This paper thus aims to expand prior research regarding relationship building in social VR by focusing on how social VR can be used to maintain various types of existing close interpersonal relationships and potential risks in this process.

3 Methods

Data Collection. We focus on first-person and narrative accounts of people's experiences of using various social VR applications to maintain and support their existing close ties over distance. Many social VR users highly engage in popular online forums to share their experiences of VR with others who have similar experiences. Therefore, to collect data, we used keyword search (e.g., family, friend, sibling, etc.)[1] on 18 social VR related subreddits on Reddit (e.g., r/VRchat, r/bigscreen, etc.)[2], a popular international online forum to share opinions and personal stories, to collect posts and comments regarding how people experience social VR in their existing close ties over distance. Once the initial dataset was collected, we read through each collected post and comment to filter out irrelevant posts (e.g., a post about buying a VR headset for parents but not about

---

[1] List of keywords contains: Long distance relationship, LDR, parent, family, father, dad, bf, mother, mom, daughter, son, grandma, grandpa, grandparent, brother, sister, sibling, cousin, friends, friendship, boyfriend, gf, girlfriend, husband, fiance, wife, keep in touch, maintain a relationship, stay connected.

[2] Subreddits used in this research include: r/AltspaceVR, r/VRchat, r/Anyland, r/bigscreen, r/ChilloutVR, r/FacebookHorizons, r/HighFidelity, r/LDR, r/LongDistance, r/OculusQuest, r/oculus, r/RecRoom, r/RecRoomVR, r/sansar, r/SocialVR, r/TheWaveVr, r/vTime, and r/Coronavirus.

engaging in social VR together with parents) and redundant data (e.g., posts including more than one keywords, for instance, "I watched a movie with my daughter and son"). As a result, 672 posts and comments were used for further analysis. Despite using public Reddit data, we removed any possibly identifiable information from the dataset (e.g., usernames) to protect Reddit users' privacy.

Data Analysis. We then conducted an in-depth qualitative analysis of the collected data [11]. First, the first author closely read through the collected data line by line to have a whole picture of how people use social VR to maintain existing close relationships with others. Second, the first author identified a set of initial themes emerging in the data that can be used to answer our RQs through open coding [11], including types of close relationships that people use social VR to maintain (RQ1), how exactly they use social VR to stay connected with their geographically separated close ties (RQ2), and potential risks in this process (RQ3). Finally, both authors iteratively and collaboratively synthesized and revised these themes through axial coding and focused coding [11] to provide a rich description about the role of social VR in maintaining existing close ties over distance.

4 Findings

In this section, we first describe the types of existing close relationships that people often use social VR to maintain and support (RQ1). We then identify three ways through which social VR can be leveraged to maintain such relationships (RQ2). We also highlight potential privacy risks emerging in this process (RQ3).

4.1 Social VR-Supported Existing Close Ties

Our findings show that social VR, beyond just building relationships among strangers, indeed can be leveraged to maintain almost all types of existing close relationships over distance, including family relationships (e.g., with parents, children, and siblings), friendships, and romantic relationships.

Sustain Family Relationships over Distance. Many posts highlight that social VR helps people stay connected with family members such as parents, children, and siblings even when they are not in the same location. For example, a user commented that they used social VR to communicate and have fun with their sibling who was not co-located with them: *"I use Altspace to hang out with my sister who lives across the country."* Another user appreciated how AltspaceVR helped them connect with their son: *"I use Altspace to meet and chat with my son in Germany. There are some great worlds for us to wander around in together. I'm also looking into building a world for some events In October. I think it has great potential."* For this user, social VR gave them the opportunity to stay connected with their son, who lived in a different country, by embarking family journeys together remotely. This user also mentioned their plan to have a family party in AltspaceVR in the future.

In particular, some posts highlight the importance of leveraging social VR to stay connected with family members during the global COVID-19 pandemic: *"I just want to say how thankful I am right now to have recroom to meet up with my millennial kids each day to play paintball together in this time of social isolation. We are in 3 different states, and one is in another country. We are having the best time; 2 or 3 of us partied up in regular games, 4 or 5 of us in private team battles, nearly every day this week. It means a lot to me."* According to the user, though the pandemic posed significant challenges on travels and face-to-face meetings, their family across several US states were still able to engage in various family activities (e.g., playing games together) regularly through social VR platforms such as Rec Room, which helped them maintain connections while people could not travel to visit each other.

Keep Friendship Alive Remotely. Social VR is also beneficial for maintaining existing friendships despite people not being geographically co-located. A user explained how they still could connect with their friends in Rec Room after they moved away: *"This platform actually helped me stay in touch with my best friend after they moved to another state."* Similar to how social VR helps family members stay connected during the global COVID-19 pandemic, it also helps people maintain their existing friendships during lock-down: *"As someone who has been VERY isolated the past year due to the pandemic, vr has made it a breeze. My friends all bought headsets and I even bought 2 for some other friends. We have weekly hangouts in VR and sometimes even more. I recommend it."* For these users, in a unique situation like COVID when people are asked to keep social distance and reduce face-to-face meetings, social VR provides valuable opportunities for safe social gatherings with friends in a highly immersive virtual world.

In particular, compared to traditional social media, social VR does not limit users to just texting, video calls, or playing a specific game. Rather, in social VR, users are able to engage in various types of social experiences that resemble real-life activities with their friends, as this post shared: *"Me and a friend have just spent the best part of 2 h or so switching rooms, trying out 3D movies, playing games, and browsing youtube. All the things that make Bigscreen great (and it really is)."* According to this post, the variety of activities that social VR provides and their similarity to offline social activities significantly benefit maintaining friendships even over distance, which we will also discuss in Sect. 4.2.

Stay Connected with Long Distance Romantic Partners. Our data also show that social VR is commonly used to maintain long-distance romantic relationships. For example, a user shared their experiences in VRChat: *"I got my long-distance boyfriend a Quest 2 just to play VRChat together, and we've been having an absolute blast together."* VRChat helped this couple have an amusing or thrilling experience while they could not be together physically. For them, social VR seems to mitigate the geographical barrier and help them build a sense of physical togetherness. Another user shared a similar sentiment about how social VR helped them maintain their long-distance romantic relationship: *"We actually didn't meet in VRC. We met in the Rec Room. But still, VRChat has definitely made our relationship stronger. VR is an amazing thing for long-distance relationships!"* This user appreciated how social VR, such as VRChat and Rec Room, not only allowed them to start a long distance romantic relationship but also helped them maintain the romance over distance. They even commented that engaging in social VR could make their relationships "stronger" while they were not physically co-located.

4.2 Using Social VR to Maintain Existing Close Ties

As Reddit users acknowledge that social VR can be leveraged to maintain various types of existing close relationships, they also highlight several ways through which social VR makes this happen.

Building a Sense of Physically Being Together. In VR, presence is a subjective feeling that a user has a sense of being in the mediated virtual environment [57]. In our data, users commented that they were able to build a sense of physically being together because of the use of a motion-controlled avatar with a complete representation of the avatar body [23]. Building this sense of physical togetherness thus becomes a significant way to maintain their existing close ties over distance. One post described: *"It's a long-distance relationship at this point. VRChat helps because we can do more things together than if there wasn't VRChat. It's as close as we can be together without actually being together."* According to this poster, VRChat helped their long distance romantic relationship in a way similar to face-to-face communication, which led to a strong sense of physical togetherness without being physically co-located (*"as we can be together without actually being together"*). Another post shared a similar story about how VRChat helped their family mitigate distance by creating a sense of physical closeness: *"VRChat lets me stay in touch with my parents. My mom got me and my dad a headset each as a Christmas present. And with me studying abroad, VRChat helps make the distance between us feel not so big."*

Especially, a poster well summarized how the sense of physically being together in social VR differs from that in other social platforms: *"It gives a focused presence. While you might not be able to see your friends'faces, you can hear their voices and see their avatars. You're 'present'with them in a space, as opposed to a Discord or Teams or Zoom or whatever call. There you are, 'present,'but you're looking at a screen, and you have all the distractions of the real space you're in. Like the Facebook chat with other people, that recipe you wanted to look up or something on your floor...In the VR space, you're focused on the interaction with your friends more - being social around the things you normally would when watching a movie, or a show, or showing vacation photos, but are probably prevented from doing now because of covid or because your friend lives far away."* According to this user, in contrast to traditional social networking platforms such as Facebook and Whatsapp, where users interact through text, audio, and videos, social VR introduces a new form of communication by combining one's physical body with an avatar body in an immersive way. As a result, instead of simply "viewing" their communication on a computer screen, social VR users seem to have a stronger sense of presence and co-presence with others due to full body tracked avatars and the resembled face-to-face communication. Both features contribute to maintaining a solid close tie even over distance.

Facilitating Physical Contacts to Recall Familiar Moments. Social VR offers a combination of technological uniqueness such as embodied avatar, full-body tracking, and a broader spectrum of communication modes, including verbal and non-verbal interactions such as voice, gestures, proxemics, gaze, and facial expression. These unique features thus help people to recall familiar moments they cherish in their existing close ties through simulated physical contacts. A user shared their experience in VRChat: *"VRChat allows for a sense of intimacy that is hard to describe. Obviously, you're not actually sitting right beside your important person, nuzzling and cuddling with them, but VRChat can do a particularly amazing job at tricking the brain into thinking you are. Laying out in the full body in front of a mirror in a quiet room with my important person, hugging a pillow and pretending it's them, it all combines to make you feel like you are really together, as much as you can be while being apart."* This poster were able to leverage multiple social VR features to recall and re-create valuable personal moments with their loved ones: they were able to stay in a quiet and private virtual room together, simulate the action of hugging by full body tracking (e.g., hugging in VR requires moving one's physical body in the offline world to hug, such as hug a pillow), and see their actions through a virtual mirror. All of these add important physicality to the VR-mediated virtual experiences, making such experiences more vivid, realistic, and similar to those moments that happened in the offline world before.

Another user shared a similar story: *"Usually, it's a few hours of playing VRChat with other friends first, and then another 1 to 2 h of just us two looking for cozy/beautiful/interesting worlds and chatting. Last night we found a very scenic Japanese shrine or something and chatted for about an hour while she kinda sat in front of me, and I had my arms around her waist."* This poster pointed out how VRChat helped him and his long distance romantic partner physically and experientially recreate physical intimacy and reminded them of similar moments they spent together in the offline world before (e.g., *"I had my arms around her waist"*).

Simulating Offline Activities to Create New Shared Memories. Reddit users also highlight how social VR helps them create new shared memories with their close ties as they can engage in various simulated social activities that resemble offline social gatherings, such as traveling, playing games, hosting parties, sharing meals, and watching movies. They especially mention two types of activities that significantly help them stay connected with their family members, friends, and romantic partners over distance: watching movies together and engaging in immersive bonding social events.

1. Watching movies together. In social VR, users can watch a movie together either in a public place that resembles a movie theatre, or in a private room that simulate watching a movie with friends at home (Fig. 3). For example, a father shared how he could watch movies in Big Screen with their children, who were geographically separated: *"My children live on the west coast, and my other children and I live on the east coast. The big screen provides the opportunity for all of us to 'go to the movies' together and talk. It had been the best movie experience I've had with my family... ever!!!."* For this users, social VR is not merely a virtual place to meet up and hang out. Rather, the value of social VR lies in how it can seamlessly resemble family bonding activities, such as watching movies with his children. While this family could not get together in the offline world due to distance issues, watching a movie together in social VR is a comparable, or even better, family gathering experience.

Watching movies together is also important to people who want to use social VR to maintain existing friendships or romantic relationships. One post mentioned, *"Him and I ended up building a world together for ourselves with a video player and furniture so we have our movie nights in VR. It's cool too being able to invite friends over and just hang out in what is essentially our house."* This couple not only designed and created their own personal space in VRChat as their "house" but also were able to watch movies together in their house either with each other or with their friends. For them, this is similar to hosting a movie watch party or enjoying personal time together in their house in the offline world.

Fig. 3. Watching a movie together in Big Screen (Source: https://www.bigscreenvr. com/)

2. Engaging in immersive bonding social events. Many social VR platforms allow users to design and create their own private spaces, invite guests, and host immersive social events. Many users thus leverage such features to engage in various types of bonding events with their existing close ties. One user posted, *"Serenity Cove is a great place for hanging out with friends. I have parties there with my friends every single night, and before we end off our nights, we always go to the secret cave up top inside the skull and just stare at the beautiful sunset background and talk."* This user used one pre-designed virtual place in social VR to spend time with their friends (e.g., enjoying the sunset), relax, and reinforce their bonding.

Others also hold special events such as birthday parties in social VR to hang out with friends and loved ones. One user posted, *"He threw me a virtual reality surprise birthday party in VRChat with all my friends; we shot fireworks, played laser tag, and did an escape room. When we got off of VR, we called each other and just had fun talking to each other until we fell asleep. His present to me was a video that he made with a slide show of our memories together and coordinating the party and everything. It was a good day."* In this example, when people are geographically separated and cannot spend special days such as birthdays together, social VR becomes a satisfactory alternative. This poster was able to have a birthday party with friends in a way similar to how their birthday party could have been held offline – fireworks and games. These virtual activities also seem to become new shared memories that they cherish, as shown in how such events are recorded and documented (e.g., as video recordings and slideshows).

4.3 Privacy Concerns Regarding Maintain Existing Relationships Through Social VR

As our findings have shown, Reddit users in general consider using social VR to maintain various types of existing close relationships a positive and beneficial experience. However, they also express several issues, especially regarding emergent privacy concerns, in this process.

Above all, in order to use social VR services and enjoy its full technical features, certain self disclosure is almost mandatory. For example, users have to give up part of their personal information such as voice, gestures, facial expressions, and body movements to engage in immersive and embodied interactions in social VR [34]. In this sense, maintaining existing relationships in social VR may inevitably leak personal information regarding one's offline identity, especially when people interact with their existing close ties in public social VR places. One poster complained, *"[In social VR], my friend would NONSTOP use my real name, our location, etc. as a way to kind of 'brag' about how close we are. This has become an issue to me."* In this example, this poster's offline friend revealed important personal information about them without consent, including real life names and locations. For this poster, this may become a serious privacy issue as online strangers may overhear their conversations and get to know their offline identities.

Another poster shared a similar experience, *"I met these two very nice people who I became quite close with. Then suddenly my friend from real life joins and fucking starts ruining it for me. He starts off by calling me by my real name, talking about how we go to the same school and stuff like that, and that bothers me a lot. Me and the people I just met decide to join a new world, suddenly he appears outta nowhere ruining the mood once again."* This example shows how privacy issues in social VR may lead to certain conflicts between the VR world and the offline world. On the one hand, this poster's friend revealed personal information about the user's offline identity, which violated their privacy. On the other hand, the friend followed the poster around and kept interrupting this poster's online interaction with others. As a result, tensions may emerge between this poster's offline life (e.g., existing social connections) and VR life (e.g., making new friends in social VR).

This type of privacy concern when using social VR for existing close ties is not only limited to people who are offline friends. A user shared how their sibling revealed personal information about them: *"I had a real big problem playing games with my big sister because she kept calling me by my real name in front of everybody. Not to mention she kind of cramped my style."* According to this poster, using social VR to maintain existing close ties seems to lead to a double privacy challenge: while they already have difficulties in protecting their personal information (e.g., have to use voice in social VR), they also need to ensure that people whom they know in the offline world (e.g., friends and family members) do not accidental or intentionally reveal their offline identities.

5   Discussion

Grounded in our findings, in this section we first discuss how our research sheds light on unique ways through which social VR may address the limitations of conventional communication technologies to innovate modern computer-mediated relationships and better support and maintain existing close ties over distance. We then identify potential design directions to further support existing relationships through social VR.

5.1   Innovating Modern Computer-Mediated Relationships Through Social VR

As prior literature has shown, on the one hand, traditional computer-mediated relationships often lack tangible aspects of offline interaction [30,50,51]. On the other hand, even some technologies exist for simulating physical offline experiences (e.g., touching) [6,21,37,46,47,52], they are still limited in terms of their support for body language, shared memories, and collaborative activities as a daily routine, which play crucial roles in sustaining close interpersonal bonds. Therefore, one important insight from our findings lies in the unique ways through which social VR may address the two main limitations of conventional communication technologies for mediating existing offline relationships. This is especially valuable during the COVID-19 pandemic, where social distancing and lockdowns placed additional challenges for close ties over distance.

First, when using traditional on-screen social media to maintain existing close ties, people often lack a sense of physical closeness [6,21,37,46,47,52]. In contrast, social VR users leverage a combination of motion-controlled avatars with partial or full body tracking features and synchronous voice communication to build a sense of being physically together. This unique combination thus adds crucial experiential qualities (e.g., "being together") to their effort to maintain existing close ties.

Second, while conventional on-screen communication technologies often lacks the capability to simulate face-to-face collaborative activities [9,20,24,39,41, 43,44,58,59] social VR addresses these issues by offering unique physicalized experiences through embodied immersive events and non-verbal interactions such as gestures, proxemics, gaze, and facial expression. These features thus help users engage in shared activities and create new memories similar to face to face interaction while they are not co-located. For example, our findings show that social VR users feel that hugging, nuzzling, kissing, and cuddling with their loved ones in social VR (e.g., in a private room) can be felt as natural and realistic as in the offline world.

Third, while social VR has been perceived as generally beneficial for initiating and building new relationships among online strangers [2,16,18,33,54], our findings reveal that it helps people to sustain existing relationships in nuanced ways. In our study, people reported successful examples of leveraging social VR to maintain almost all types of existing interpersonal relationships over distance, such as family relationships (e.g., with parents, children, and siblings), friendships, and romantic relationships. Our findings also highlight people's different approaches when using social VR for maintaining existing close ties versus building new connections with online strangers. For example, people who aim at using social VR to maintain their existing close ties often have a clearly defined plan on what they would do together in social VR for that purpose (e.g., scheduling a movie watch activity or planning a birthday party in social VR). In contrast, people who aim at using social VR to build new connections often tend to explore the VR space spontaneously (e.g., randomly visiting certain virtual places to meet new people).

Similarly, to maintain existing relationships, people often focus on recalling/recreating familiar moments in VR that resemble what they already did in the offline world before, rather than exploring new experiences with strangers to build relationships from zero. In addition, rather than going to public places alone to meet people, people who endeavor to maintain existing close ties emphasize the importance of engaging in immersive bonding special events and spending time together with their existing close ties in carefully designed private virtual places (e.g., celebrating special occasions such as birthdays at private parties) in order to create new shared memories beyond geographical distance.

In summary, these findings (1) highlight the unique advantages of leveraging social VR to maintain existing close ties over distance compared to traditional computer-mediated long distance relationships; and (2) shed light on the different user preferences and behavioral patterns when using social VR for existing close ties versus for building new relationships among online strangers. Yet, our research also points out the emergent privacy dilemmas when using social VR for maintaining existing close ties. On the one hand, social VR can be leveraged to both building new connections and supporting existing offline relationships.

On the other hand, how to maintain a fine line between people's VR world and offline world becomes an emergent challenge. For example, some users prefer to keep their personal information and offline identity private when interacting with online strangers in social VR. However, their existing close ties, who are also present in social VR, may intentionally or unintentionally disclose such information and violate their privacy. Therefore, how to better protecting people's personal information and privacy when the boundary between the two worlds blur will require future research.

5.2 Designing Future Social VR Spaces to Support Existing Ties

Grounded in our findings, we identify two potential design directions to further support and innovate how interpersonal relationships can be supported and mediated through social VR. These design directions are neither complete nor exhaustive as they are the main directions emerging based on users' comments, posts, and our findings. Yet, we consider that they may benefit developers/designers who strive to design more socially supportive and family-friendly VR technology in the future.

Designing Family-Friendly Social VR Activities and Events. Our findings highlight the importance of engaging in mundane everyday activities for sustaining existing close ties. Replicating offline-world activities such as watching movies and having birthday parties in social VR allows users to experience their familiar offline-world activities and recreate shared memories virtually but in a way similar to face to face interaction. This thus significantly contributes to a sense of physical closeness and intimacy. Therefore, it would be valuable for future social VR spaces to provide more family-friendly places and offer more social activities that people can engage with their existing connections, such as private customized virtual places for dating, weddings, or celebrating birthdays and anniversaries.

The Ability to Categorize Friends for Privacy Purpose. Grounded in the privacy dilemma shown in our data, we also believe that providing users with the ability to further categorize their social VR friends will be beneficial. In doing so, social VR users can have more control over their availability status - e.g., shown as family time, friend time, fun time, and so forth. For example, if a user set their status as family time, only their friends in the family category can approach and interact with them. This may help people set up a fine line between their VR world/connections and existing close ties/offline world, while both can co-exist and be supported in social VR spaces.

5.3 Limitations

Our study mainly draws on Reddit posts, leading to a potential bias toward social VR users who are also active Reddit users. Therefore, our future work will focus on collecting a larger sample of social media data from diverse platforms to further confirm our findings. Since Reddit is an anonymous forum, it is also challenging to verify users' demographic information. We thus plan to conduct semi-structured in-depth interviews and a large-scale survey with a broader participant pool with diverse demographics to investigate people's unique strategies, challenges, and expectations for using social VR to sustain their existing relationships. In addition, while prior work has shown that older adults also engaged with online technologies [4] and social VR [2,3], in our research, we did not find any data regarding how older adults may leverage social VR to support their existing close ties (e.g., grandparent-grandchild relationships). Therefore, our future work also aims to further explore how older adults can use social VR to maintain close relationships with their friends, family, and grandchild.

6 Conclusion

Maintaining belongingness and close connections with people we care for and love is crucial for our psychological and behavioral well-beings [5,29,42]. How would emerging computing technologies affect this dynamic, especially over distance? In this paper, we have explored how social VR is innovating modern computer-mediated relationships by supporting almost all types of existing close relationships in nuanced ways, such as through building a sense of physically being together, facilitating physical contacts to recall familiar moments, and simulating offline activities to create new shared memories. Despite these novelties and benefits, our findings also point to the potential privacy risks and tensions when using social VR to support existing offline relationships - e.g., concerns regarding protecting people's personal information when the boundary between the two worlds blur. As the emerging metaverse paradigm continues to grow and innovate future social interactions, we hope that these insights will inform future research and design directions to create safer and more supportive social VR spaces for people's social needs and interpersonal connections.

Acknowledgement. This work was partially supported by the National Science Foundation award 2112878.

References

1. Ackerman, M.S.: The intellectual challenge of CSCW: the gap between social requirements and technical feasibility. Human-Comput. Inter. **15**(2–3), 179–203 (2000). https://doi.org/10.1207/S15327051HCI1523_5
2. Baker, S., et al.: Interrogating social virtual reality as a communication medium for older adults. Proceed. ACM Human-Comput. Inter. **3**(CSCW), 1–24 (2019). https://doi.org/10.1145/3359251
3. Baker, S., Waycott, J., Carrasco, R., Hoang, T., Vetere, F.: Exploring the design of social vr experiences with older adults. In: Proceedings of the 2019 on Designing Interactive Systems Conference, pp. 303–315 (2019). https://doi.org/10.1145/3322276.3322361

4. Bangerter, L.R., Waldron, V.R.: Turning points in long distance grandparent-grandchild relationships. J. Aging stud. **29**, 88–97 (2014). https://doi.org/10.1016/j.jaging.2014.01.004
5. Baumeister, R.F., Leary, M.R.: The need to belong: desire for interpersonal attachments as a fundamental human motivation. Psychol. Bull. **117**(3), 497 (1995). https://doi.org/10.4324/9781351153683-3
6. Beuthel, J.M., Bentegeac, P., Fuchsberger, V., Maurer, B., Tscheligi, M.: Experiencing distance: wearable engagements with remote relationships. In: Proceedings of the Fifteenth International Conference on Tangible, Embedded, and Embodied Interaction, pp. 1–13 (2021). https://doi.org/10.1145/3430524.3446071
7. Billedo, C.J., Kerkhof, P., Finkenauer, C.: The use of social networking sites for relationship maintenance in long-distance and geographically close romantic relationships. Cyberpsychol. Behav. Soc. Netw. **18**(3), 152–157 (2015). https://doi.org/10.1089/cyber.2014.0469
8. Blackwell, L., Ellison, N., Elliott-Deflo, N., Schwartz, R.: Harassment in social virtual reality: Challenges for platform governance. Proceed. ACM Human-Comput. Inter. **3**(CSCW), 1–25 (2019). https://doi.org/10.1145/3359202
9. Chai, M.Z., Soro, A., Roe, P., Brereton, M.: Cooking together at a distance: sustain connectedness for long distance families. In: Proceedings of the 2017 CHI Conference Extended Abstracts on Human Factors in Computing Systems, pp. 2437–2444 (2017). https://doi.org/10.1145/3027063.3053183
10. Chan, M.: Multimodal connectedness and quality of life: examining the influences of technology adoption and interpersonal communication on well-being across the life span. J. Comput.-Mediat. Commun. **20**(1), 3–18 (2015). https://doi.org/10.1111/jcc4.12089
11. Charmaz, K.: Constructing grounded theory: a practical guide through qualitative analysis. Sage (2006)
12. Cohen, S., Wills, T.A.: Stress, social support, and the buffering hypothesis. Psychol. Bull. **98**(2), 310 (1985). https://doi.org/10.1037/0033-2909.98.2.310
13. Duque, G., San Antonio, D., Brazil, L.: A correlational study on social media involvement and parental relationship among students of Asia pacific college. In: DLSU Research Congress 2017 De La Salle University, Manila, Philippines (2017)
14. Ellison, N.B., Steinfield, C., Lampe, C.: The benefits of facebook "friends:" social capital and college students' use of online social network sites. J. Comput.-Mediated Commun. **12**(4), 1143–1168 (2007). https://doi.org/10.1111/j.1083-6101.2007.00367.x
15. Findlay, B.: Preference for SMS versus telephone calls in initiating romantic relationships. Austr. J. Emerg. Technol. Soc. **2**(1), 48–61 (2004)
16. Freeman, G., Acena, D.: Hugging from a distance: building interpersonal relationships in social virtual reality. In: ACM International Conference on Interactive Media Experiences, pp. 84–95 (2021). https://doi.org/10.1145/3452918.3458805
17. Freeman, G., Bardzell, J., Bardzell, S.: Revisiting computer-mediated intimacy: In-game marriage and dyadic gameplay in audition. In: Proceedings of the 2016 CHI Conference on Human Factors in Computing Systems, pp. 4325–4336 (2016). https://doi.org/10.1145/2858036.2858484
18. Freeman, G., Maloney, D.: Body, avatar, and me: the presentation and perception of self in social virtual reality. Proceed. ACM Human-Comput. Inter. **4**(CSCW3), 1–27 (2021). https://doi.org/10.1145/3432938

19. Gooch, D., Watts, L.: sleepyWhispers: sharing goodnights within distant relationships. In: Adjunct proceedings of the 25th Annual ACM Symposium on User Interface Software and Technology, pp. 61–62 (2012). https://doi.org/10.1145/2380296.2380322
20. Günther, S., et al.: Checkmate: Exploring a tangible augmented reality interface for remote interaction. In: Extended Abstracts of the 2018 CHI Conference on Human Factors in Computing Systems, pp. 1–6 (2018). https://doi.org/10.1145/3170427.3188647
21. Gutzmann, L.: Utilization of social media in strengthening communication in long distance relationships (2018)
22. Hassenzahl, M., Heidecker, S., Eckoldt, K., Diefenbach, S., Hillmann, U.: All you need is love: current strategies of mediating intimate relationships through technology. ACM Trans. Comput.-Human Inter. (TOCHI) 19(4), 1–19 (2012). https://doi.org/10.1145/2395131.2395137
23. Heidicker, P., Langbehn, E., Steinicke, F.: Influence of avatar appearance on presence in social VR. In: 2017 IEEE Symposium on 3D User Interfaces (3DUI), pp. 233–234. IEEE (2017). https://doi.org/10.1109/3DUI.2017.7893357
24. Heshmat, Y., et al.: Geocaching with a beam: Shared outdoor activities through a telepresence robot with 360 degree viewing. In: Proceedings of the 2018 CHI Conference on Human Factors in Computing Systems, pp. 1–13 (2018). https://doi.org/10.1145/3173574.3173933
25. Holtzman, S., Kushlev, K., Wozny, A., Godard, R.: Long-distance texting: text messaging is linked with higher relationship satisfaction in long-distance relationships. Journal of Social and Personal Relationships, p. 02654075211043296 (2021). https://doi.org/10.1177/02654075211043296
26. Huq, M., et al.: Maintaining long-distance childhood friendships using digital technology (2021)
27. Jamieson, L., Ekerwald, H.: Intimacy. personal relationships in modern societies. Cambridge/Oxford: Polity Press/Blackwell Publishers Ltd. (1998). Acta Sociol. 43(2), 183–185 (2000). https://doi.org/10.1177/000169930004300210
28. Johnson, A.J., Haigh, M.M., Becker, J.A., Craig, E.A., Wigley, S.: College students' use of relational management strategies in email in long-distance and geographically close relationships. J. Comput.-Mediat. Commun. 13(2), 381–404 (2008). https://doi.org/10.1111/j.1083-6101.2008.00401.x
29. Kawachi, I., Berkman, L.F.: Social ties and mental health. J. Urban Health 78(3), 458–467 (2001). https://doi.org/10.1093/jurban/78.3.458
30. Kontaris, D., Harrison, D., Patsoule, E.E., Zhuang, S., Slade, A.: Feelybean: communicating touch over distance. In: CHI2012 Extended Abstracts on Human Factors in Computing Systems, pp. 1273–1278 (2012). https://doi.org/10.1145/2212776.2212439
31. Lu, X.: The distance: a cooperative communication game to long-distance players, Ph. D. thesis, University of Southern California (2018)
32. Maloney, D., Freeman, G., Robb, A.: Social virtual reality: ethical considerations and future directions for an emerging research space. In: 2021 IEEE Conference on Virtual Reality and 3D User Interfaces Abstracts and Workshops (VRW), pp. 271–277. IEEE (2021). https://doi.org/10.1109/VRW52623.2021.00056
33. Maloney, D., Freeman, G., Wohn, D.Y.: "Talking without a voice" understanding non-verbal communication in social virtual reality. Proceed. ACM Human-Comput. Inter. 4(CSCW2), 1–25 (2020). https://doi.org/10.1145/3415246

34. Maloney, D., Zamanifard, S., Freeman, G.: Anonymity vs. familiarity: self-disclosure and privacy in social virtual reality. In: 26th ACM Symposium on Virtual Reality Software and Technology, pp. 1–9 (2020). https://doi.org/10.1145/3385956.3418967

35. McVeigh-Schultz, J., Kolesnichenko, A., Isbister, K.: Shaping pro-social interaction in VR: an emerging design framework. In: Proceedings of the 2019 CHI Conference on Human Factors in Computing Systems, pp. 1–12 (2019). https://doi.org/10.1145/3290605.3300794

36. McVeigh-Schultz, J., Márquez Segura, E., Merrill, N., Isbister, K.: What's it mean to" be social" in VR? mapping the social VR design ecology. In: Proceedings of the 2018 ACM Conference Companion Publication on Designing Interactive Systems, pp. 289–294 (2018). https://doi.org/10.1145/3197391.3205451

37. Mueller, F., Vetere, F., Gibbs, M.R., Kjeldskov, J., Pedell, S., Howard, S.: Hug over a distance. In: CHI'05 extended abstracts on Human factors in computing systems, pp. 1673–1676 (2005). https://doi.org/10.1145/1056808.1056994

38. Neustaedter, C., Greenberg, S.: Intimacy in long-distance relationships over video chat. In: Proceedings of the SIGCHI Conference on Human Factors in Computing Systems, pp. 753–762 (2012). https://doi.org/10.1145/2207676.2207785

39. Neustaedter, C., Heshmat, Y., Jones, B., Forghani, A., Xiong, X.: Shared family experiences over distance in the outdoors. In: McCrickard, D.S., Jones, M., Stelter, T.L. (eds.) HCI Outdoors: Theory, Design, Methods and Applications. HIS, pp. 155–174. Springer, Cham (2020). https://doi.org/10.1007/978-3-030-45289-6_8

40. Neustaedter, C., et al.: Sharing domestic life through long-term video connections. ACM Trans. Comput.-Human Inter. (TOCHI) 22(1), 1–29 (2015). https://doi.org/10.1145/2696869

41. Oduor, E., Neustaedter, C.: The family room: a multi-camera, multi-display family media space. In: Proceedings of the Companion Publication of the 17th ACM Conference on Computer Supported Cooperative Work & Social Computing, pp. 289–292 (2014). https://doi.org/10.1145/2556420.2557640

42. Oxman, T.E., Berkman, L.F., Kasl, S., Freeman, D.H., Jr., Barrett, J.: Social support and depressive symptoms in the elderly. Am. J. Epidemiol. 135(4), 356–368 (1992). https://doi.org/10.1093/oxfordjournals.aje.a116297

43. Pan, R., Neustaedter, C., Antle, A.N., Matkin, B.: Puzzle space: a distributed tangible puzzle for long distance couples. In: Companion of the 2017 ACM Conference on Computer Supported Cooperative Work and Social Computing, pp. 271–274 (2017). https://doi.org/10.1145/3022198.3026320

44. Pan, R., Singhal, S., Riecke, B.E., Cramer, E., Neustaedter, C.: "MyEyes" the design and evaluation of first person view video streaming for long-distance couples. In: Proceedings of the 2017 Conference on Designing Interactive Systems, pp. 135–146 (2017). https://doi.org/10.1145/3064663.3064671

45. Park, N., Lee, H.: Social implications of smartphone use: Korean college students' smartphone use and psychological well-being. Cyberpsychol. Behav. Soc. Netw. 15(9), 491–497 (2012). https://doi.org/10.1089/cyber.2011.0580

46. Park, Y.W., Baek, K.M., Nam, T.J.: The roles of touch during phone conversations: long-distance couples' use of poke in their homes. In: Proceedings of the SIGCHI Conference on Human Factors in Computing Systems, pp. 1679–1688 (2013). https://doi.org/10.1145/2470654.2466222

47. Park, Y.W., Lim, C.Y., Nam, T.J.: CheekTouch: an affective interaction technique while speaking on the mobile phone. In: CHI2010 Extended Abstracts on Human Factors in Computing Systems, pp. 3241–3246 (2010). https://doi.org/10.1145/1753846.1753965

48. Pouwels, J.L., Valkenburg, P.M., Beyens, I., van Driel, I.I., Keijsers, L.: Social media use and friendship closeness in adolescents' daily lives: an experience sampling study. Dev. Psychol. **57**(2), 309 (2021). https://doi.org/10.1037/dev0001148

49. Rooney, V.: Maintaining intimacy at a distance: an exploration of human-computer interaction's approach to mediating intimacy. Behav. Inf. Technol. **33**(9), 882–891 (2014). https://doi.org/10.1080/0144929X.2013.791722

50. Saadatian, E., et al.: Mediating intimacy in long-distance relationships using kiss messaging. Int. J. Hum Comput Stud. **72**(10–11), 736–746 (2014). https://doi.org/10.1016/j.ijhcs.2014.05.004

51. Singhal, S., Neustaedter, C., Antle, A.N., Matkin, B.: Flex-N-Feel: emotive gloves for physical touch over distance. In: Companion of the 2017 ACM Conference on Computer Supported Cooperative Work and Social Computing, pp. 37–40 (2017). https://doi.org/10.1145/3022198.3023273

52. Slater, M., Wilbur, S.: A framework for immersive virtual environments (five): speculations on the role of presence in virtual environments. Presence: Teleoper. Virt. Environ. **6**(6), 603–616 (1997). https://doi.org/10.1162/pres.1997.6.6.603

53. Stafford, L.: Maintaining long-distance and cross-residential relationships. Routledge (2004). https://doi.org/10.4324/9781410611512

54. Sykownik, P., Graf, L., Zils, C., Masuch, M.: The most social platform ever? a survey about activities amp; motives of social VR users. In: 2021 IEEE Virtual Reality and 3D User Interfaces (VR), pp. 546–554 (2021). https://doi.org/10.1109/VR50410.2021.00079

55. Utz, S.: Media use in long-distance friendships. Inf. Commun. Soc. **10**(5), 694–713 (2007). https://doi.org/10.1080/13691180701658046

56. Valkenburg, P.M., Peter, J., Schouten, A.P.: Friend networking sites and their relationship to adolescents' well-being and social self-esteem. Cyberpsychol. Behav. **9**(5), 584–590 (2006). https://doi.org/10.1089/cpb.2006.9.584

57. Walther, J.B., Parks, M.R.: Cues filtered out, cues filtered. In: Computer-mediated Communication and Relationships. Handbook Interpers. Commun. **3**, 529–563 (2002)

58. Yang, L., Jones, B., Neustaedter, C., Singhal, S.: Shopping over distance through a telepresence robot. Proceed. ACM Human-Comput. Inter. **2**(CSCW), 1–18 (2018). https://doi.org/10.1145/3274460

59. Yarosh, S., Cuzzort, S., Müller, H., Abowd, G.D.: Developing a media space for remote synchronous parent-child interaction. In: Proceedings of the 8th International Conference on Interaction Design and Children, pp. 97–105 (2009). https://doi.org/10.1145/1551788.1551806

"Monday Feels Like Friday!" - Towards Overcoming Anxiety and Stress of Autistic Young Adults During Times of Isolation

Roberto Palma[✉], Ho Ching Lam, Ashima Shrivastava, Ethan Karlinsey,
Kohl Nguyen, Prab Deol, Moushumi Sharmin, and Shameem Ahmed

Western Washington University, Bellingham, WA 98225, USA
{palmar,hochinl,shrivaa,karline,nguye269,singhp4,sharmim,
ahmeds}@wwu.edu

Abstract. Autistic young adults are at a higher risk of experiencing elevated mental and psychological distress during times of isolation, such as the COVID-19 pandemic, due to the challenges related to uncertainty and abrupt changes in every aspect of daily life. In this research, we aim to develop participant-centric interventions for assisting autistic young adults in addressing their anxiety and stress during times of isolation. We first conducted an exploratory literature review to gather the design requirements for an effective stress management technology. Based on our findings, we designed our initial high-fidelity prototype, Mind-Bot, a mindfulness and AI-based chatbot application. We conducted an in-depth qualitative study (semi-structured interviews with 15 autistic young adults and a cognitive walkthrough with 20 participants who have training in HCI and usability evaluation techniques) to identify the design and usability issues to improve the effectiveness of MindBot.

Keywords: COVID-19 pandemic · Autism Spectrum Disorder · Mental health · Stress & anxiety · Young adults

1 Introduction

1 in 44 children in the USA has been diagnosed with Autism Spectrum Disorder (ASD) [1]. Moreover, almost half a million autistic children in the USA will be adults by 2025 [2]. This transformation to adulthood can be challenging for them due to their inherent social communication impairments, dependence on family, and susceptibility to experiencing mental health conditions, along with a general struggle to address unexpected changes in activities, situations, or expectations [3].

The COVID-19 pandemic pushed global healthcare structures to their limits, and it is especially difficult for people suffering from stress, anxiety, and mental health conditions [21]. Twenge and Joiner conducted a study in 2020 and compared mental distress experienced by participants pre- and post-COVID [6]. They found that only

---

R. Palma and H. C. Lam contributed equally to this work.

I. Sserwanga et al. (Eds.): iConference 2023, LNCS 13972, pp. 286–305, 2023.
https://doi.org/10.1007/978-3-031-28032-0_24

22% of participants reported experiencing moderate to severe mental distress in 2018 compared to 70% during the COVID-19 pandemic [6]. For autistic young adults, COVID-19 caused more challenges due to the abrupt changes in their daily routine and structure, the transition to remote learning, lack of access to needed resources (e.g., face-to-face therapy sessions), social isolation, and stressors affecting their caregivers due to job loss or change in career [8]. Researchers reported a significant increase in stress, anxiety, and other mental health problems for autistic individuals due to the COVID-19 pandemic [14].

Even in regular times, compared to neurotypicals, autistic individuals are more likely to experience higher anxiety and other mental health conditions [31]. The uncertain and unpredictable living environment persisting during times of isolation, such as the COVID-19 pandemic, along with pre-existing impairments in social communication and social behavior in autistic young adults, resulted in peer interactions that were difficult and limited and caused concern in parents [20].

Due to the prevalence and impact of anxiety in autistic young adults, techniques for addressing anxiety have received increased research attention [5]. Two major approaches that are extensively used to overcome anxiety and stress are Mindfulness-Based Cognitive Therapy (MBCT), a subpart of Cognitive-Behavioral Therapy (CBT) [7], and the usage of AI chatbots [19, 23].

Our current research aims to develop participant-centric interventions for assisting autistic young adults in addressing anxiety and stress issues during prolonged times of isolation, such as the COVID-19 pandemic. To fulfill our goal, we conducted research in multiple phases. First, we conducted a literature review to understand the existing approaches, elicit the needs of autistic young adults, and gather the design requirements to design an effective anxiety management technology. As our findings indicated the potential of a mobile-based solution, in the second phase, we developed a high-fidelity prototype of a mindfulness and AI-based chatbot app called MindBot. In the third phase, we conducted an in-depth qualitative study with autistic young adults (N = 15) to understand their challenges, needs, and experiences surrounding anxiety and stress management technology during times of isolation. Our other goal for this phase was to receive qualitative feedback on the feasibility and potential usefulness of Mind-Bot. Finally, we conducted a cognitive walkthrough (N = 20) to evaluate the usability and learnability issues of MindBot to enhance its effectiveness.

2 Related Work

According to the World Health Organization (WHO), "Mental health is a state of mental well-being that enables people to cope with the stresses of life, realize their abilities, learn well and work well, and contribute to their community" [43]. Resilience is connected to well-being, which focuses on developing an ability to intervene and cope with stress and adapting to new and/or challenging situations [22]. Autistic individuals are generally not well-accustomed to unexpected changes and struggle to deal with uncertainty, and depend on various outside resources (e.g., health, social care, therapies) that were difficult to maintain during the pandemic [38]. The COVID-19 pandemic highlighted the importance of developing digital adaptations of traditional interventions as effective alternatives to face-to-face therapeutic sessions, which cannot be carried out during isolation [39]. In addition, Alonso-Esteban et al. emphasized the importance of including online counseling, mindfulness measurement, and monitoring programs for periods of isolation in educational and treatment centers [40].

As mentioned above, autistic individuals often face challenges in managing such situations, which escalate their stress levels. Getting inspiration from prior research, we are showcasing the effectiveness of AI chatbots, CBT, MBCT, and Guided Imagery in providing better interventions. This section will briefly summarize these methods offered as intervention and support.

2.1 Cognitive Behavior Therapy (CBT), Mindfulness-Based Cognitive Therapy (MBCT), and Guided Imagery

Cognitive Behavioral Therapy (CBT), a psychological treatment where an individual works with a psychotherapist in multiple sessions, has been considered an effective technique for young adults to treat their anxiety disorders [24, 25]. Ellis et al. showed the efficacy of an online-based CBT program in addressing anxiety symptoms [4].

Mindfulness has been described as "the awareness that emerges through paying attention on purpose, in the present moment, and non-judgmentally to the unfolding of experience moment by moment" [15]. Within the array of MBCT online programs, autistic individuals have demonstrated tremendous improvement [10]. MBCT may positively impact internalizing and externalizing problems, autism symptoms such as social communication impairment, and psychological well-being [16]. For immediate impact, short-term structured mindfulness meditation is also practiced among young adults [17]. Researchers reported that short-term mindfulness could increase coping flexibility and help improve stress management in durations as short as two weeks [18].

The Guided Imagery technique, an alternative anxiety-controlling therapy, purposefully and consciously induces mental images to obtain the desired outcome [12]. Besides healthcare settings, the Guided Imagery technique can address other challenges available in various settings [11]. Bigham et al. showed that Guided Imagery exercise could lessen the perceptions of cognitive and emotional stress [13]. As cultivating mindfulness and guided imagery is devoid of side effects, it is safe for autistic individuals to practice this irrespective of their health conditions.

2.2 AI Chatbot

A chatbot is "a computer program designed to simulate conversation with human users, especially over the internet" [23]. Prior studies reported the promise of chatbots to assist in addressing mental health problems [30]. A chatbot provides conversational flexibility and may facilitate interactions with individuals who hesitate to seek mental health advice due to stigmatization [33]. To address the mental health issues of young adults, it is important to respond with appropriate interventions based on their mental and emotional states. A well-designed chatbot can provide a practical, evidence-based, and attractive solution by understanding the needs of young adults. This is especially applicable to young adults who may find it difficult to share stressful feelings even with their loved ones. A chatbot can provide an alternative avenue free from this feeling of judgment and reprimand when sharing the stressful situations they are experiencing [37].

3 Research Methodology

We conducted our research in multiple phases. Below, we discuss the phases of our research methodology.

3.1 Phase 1: Exploratory Literature Review

In the first phase, we conducted an exploratory literature review to identify papers focused on designing and/or delivering software-based interventions to autistic young adults to overcome anxiety and stress. We primarily used Google Scholar, ACM Digital Library, and IEEE Xplore to find relevant papers. Our search resulted in over 35 articles related to CBT and MBCT, chatbots in mental health, and the effect of COVID-19. However, not all articles were specific to autistic individuals.

3.2 Phase 2: MindBot Development

Our literature review led us to include MBCT and chatbot features in our initial prototype design, dubbed as MindBot, which consists of three primary stress management features (MBCT, AI chatbot, and Instant) and other secondary features.

3.3 Phase 3: Qualitative Study

In phase 3, we conducted an in-depth qualitative study. It had two subparts: a semi-structured interview and a cognitive walkthrough.

Semi-structured Interview
We conducted a semi-structured interview (N = 15) via zoom to understand the challenges faced by autistic young adults related to mental health conditions, current coping strategies, and their needs and expectations from any stress management technology. We started recruitment after receiving approval from the Institutional Review Board (IRB) of Western Washington University. We contacted autistic young adults via email, and various social media platforms, including Discord, Reddit, and Facebook, and recruited 15 autistic (self-reported) participants. Our participants were in the age group 20–34 (avg = 26.3 years). Only one participant was female. According to the CDC, autism is much more common among males (around four times) than females [1]. Such disparity may have contributed to the gender imbalance among our participants. Our participants had different professions, while some had two professions (student and driver). Nine participants lived with their parents, three had their own families (spouse and/or children), and two lived alone. See Table 1 for participants' demographic information.

Each interview session lasted up to 90 min. We asked 12 questions and allowed tangents to learn about the holistic experience of our participants. See Table 2 for sample questions asked during the interview session.

Table 1. Demographic information of participants

Gender	Age (Years)	Profession	Family status
Male = 14 Female = 1	20–34 Information not available = 2	College student = 9 Commercial driver = 3 Software Engineer = 1 Barber = 1 Barista = 1 Unemployed = 1	Living with parents = 9 Has own family = 3 Living alone = 2 Information not available = 1

Table 2. Sample interview questions

How was your last year? How did the pandemic affect your life, if at all?
Many people suffered from anxiety and elevated levels of stress during this pandemic. Did you go through anxiety or any mental health issues because of the pandemic?
What was your coping mechanism to address stress and anxiety issues, and how did you manage your stress and anxiety?
Do you believe any technology could help you intervene through your stress and anxiety? Why or why not?

In the last part of each interview, we showed our participants a high-fidelity prototype of MindBot. The goal of this demonstration was to identify useful features, features that are considered limiting and receive feedback regarding MindBot.

We transcribed the audio recordings of the interviews and imported those transcriptions into ATLAS.ti cloud [32]. For some participants, there was a slight language barrier since English was not their first language. We tried our best to clarify and correctly transcribe their words. We applied thematic analysis to perform qualitative coding. In the first coding phase, we applied initial coding (open coding in grounded theory [34]) and identified 48 codes. Some codes are as follows: Pandemic: Daily Schedule, Pandemic: Changes due to Pandemic, Coping: Distraction, Technology: Expectation from Technology. In the second coding phase (axial coding), we utilized the initial codes to link interview data from each participant. We performed a systematic comparison of their answers to understand their situations and emotions better. We identified seven high-level themes: User Profile, Technology Feedback, Suggestions from Users, Stress, Pandemic, Coping During Pandemic, and Design Implications. We finalized our major themes in the theoretical coding (selective coding in the grounded theory) phase.

Cognitive Walkthrough

In the last phase of our research, we conducted a cognitive walkthrough [9, 41] of MindBot, a standard technique utilized to evaluate the usability and learnability issues present in computing systems. We recruited 20 participants who have training in HCI and usability evaluation techniques, enabling them to identify design problems that could hinder the effective use of MindBot. To provide access to MindBot, we shared a web link with our participants. Through this link, each participant completed four major tasks and answered questions that enabled them to identify design issues and suggest possible improvements to address such issues. We will report the cognitive walkthrough process in Sect. 4.

4 Findings

4.1 Finding from Exploratory Literature Review

While there have been many approaches for designing interventions to address the anxiety and stress of autistic individuals, only a few are effective and are accessible to the growing autistic population. For instance, various music interventions demonstrate that participating in such interventions effectively addresses some core challenges, including social and peer interaction observed in autistic adolescents and young adults [35, 36]. However, it was not proven if the software or online-based systems can be effective in this regard, which is one of our primary goals. Research articles revealed that CBT-based interventions, both offline and online, can be effective in helping autistic individuals [5, 8].

Our findings suggest that a web or mobile-based application will effectively deliver interventions since autistic young adults feel more comfortable with technologies than with face-to-face solutions [8]. Such systems may reduce several potential burdens (e.g., economic, and social burdens, sensory issues, and demands of travel to a place outside of home) of face-to-face therapy sessions. Though the range varies from 22–84%, researchers agree that autistic young adults in the USA go through psychosocial issues and anxiety disorders [26], making it harder for them to seek traditional face-to-face interventions. Although such systems will not replace face-to-face interventions, technological platforms could be a promising complement or accessible alternative.

Our findings also suggest that the best option to gain immediate results in managing anxiety and stress is to integrate mindfulness-based therapy and a base of CBT [5], as CBT and MBCT interventions can make autistic young adults feel comfortable. In addition, we found that interventions should be based on individual participants' needs and lifestyles. Interventions that provide motivational messages to the participants and focus on the roots of their stress would help reduce anxiety and better prepare them to receive MBCT treatments.

4.2 MindBot Development

Our exploratory research guided the design and development of a prototype system, MindBot. See Fig. 1 for the home screen and main menu. First, the welcome page greets the user, and following login/sign-up, MindBot displays the main menu.

The first major feature included in MindBot is MBCT (see Fig. 2). This page directs users to choose the type of mindfulness therapy they would like to perform. The page also provides access to audio sessions, where a therapist guides the users in a mindfulness session.

The second important feature is an AI chatbot (see Fig. 3) that leads the users to a page that gives the option to either begin chatting or receive kind messages. Both options lead to a text conversation window where the user can commence a conversation with an AI chatbot. If the user chooses to receive a kind message, the AI chatbot will send a kind message. If the user chooses to chat, the AI chatbot will begin the conversation by asking the user about their day. To improve the quality of the AI chatbot, this page enables sending a message to the application developers if a particular chat response is deemed inappropriate by the user. In addition, during a conversation, the avatar of the AI chatbot will change to reflect the emotion associated with the user's input. Finally, the user can access the 'Let's Chat' and the 'Kind Message' options during a conversation. Users can also receive a kind message while conversing with the AI chatbot.

Additional features include the ability to edit user profiles and provide a way to change the chatbot's avatar to match the users' preferences (see Fig. 4). MindBot prototype also includes the following options: 1) change the app's appearance, and 2) save message history. Changing the appearance will change the app's look for the users, while the save message history is intended to archive the user's conversation history. Users have the ability to turn off this feature.

To implement MindBot, which is compatible with both Android and iOS devices, we used React-Native, Python (as a backend framework), and firebase (as data hosting storage). The current version of MindBot has a functional login system and main screen (see Fig. 1). It also has a mindfulness page (see Fig. 2) which includes categories of mindfulness code (randomly display selected mindfulness messages), yoga videos (a list of selected mindfulness yoga videos from YouTube), relaxation music (a list of free mindfulness music from the internet), and activity list (a list of mindfulness activity). The mindfulness page is currently in the testing phase, which we developed based on the feedback we received from the semi-structured interviews (will be discussed in

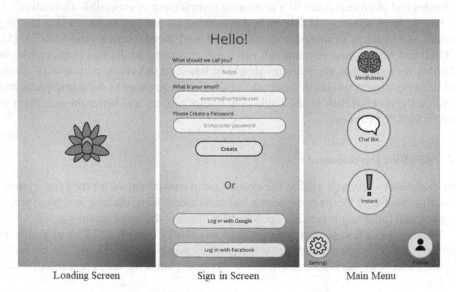

Loading Screen   Sign in Screen   Main Menu

Fig. 1. Home and main menu of MindBot

Fig. 2. Mindfulness and chatbot (before screen)

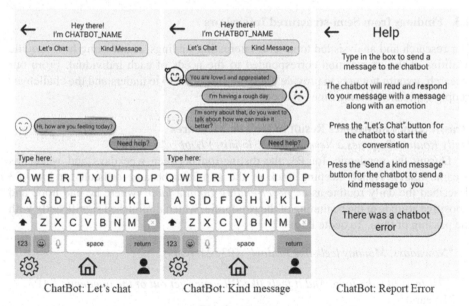

Fig. 3. Chatbot

Sect. 4.3.3). For testing kind messages, messaging emojis, and messages between server and client, we used the DialoGPT model from hugging face, which has simple conversation functionality [42]. We completed the profile section (see Fig. 4), where users can set up their preferences such as theme color, font size, removing chat history, and deleting accounts. We are currently implementing the AI chatbot.

Fig. 4. Profile & settings

4.3   Findings from Semi-structured Interviews

Our research and analysis led to several interesting findings, manifesting how specific qualities of the intervention corresponded to the needs of each individual. From our research, we aim not only to provide interventions but also to understand the challenges people experience during times of social isolation.

Drastic Times Sometimes Result in Drastic Measures
Daily Routine Becomes a Never-Ending (Infinite) Loop
During the pandemic, for P3, the distinction between weekdays and weekends became blurry. Hence, keeping track of the activities became difficult for him. P3 described the daily routine as a *"never-ending infinite loop"* where he had hope and a positive attitude at the beginning of the pandemic, which diminished significantly with the passing of time. To quote P3:

"Nowadays, Monday feels like Friday!" (P3, 21 years).

"[It] feels like the loop. And it feels like I'll never get out of the pandemic." (P3, 21 years).

P5 talked about his struggle with his routine, which stressed him out.

"I went through a lot during the pandemic because it really affected my daily life... I was thinking about... how it could stop so I could get back to my daily routine. So that really made me stressed and anxious to see the end of it." (P5, 32 years).

Strange Social Life
According to WHO, almost 18% of the United States population suffers from mental health issues, and it increased to 40% due to COVID-19 [44]. The COVID-19 pandemic also increased the risk of psychological distress among autistic adults [45]. This changing landscape has resulted in severe stress and made it exhausting to feel motivated and incorporate positive thoughts and emotions. Also, being unable to meet with friends added to our participants' loneliness. Although being in touch with friends was still possible online, P1 experienced a difference between in-person and online meetings. P1 stated.

"I actually lost one of my best friends from I guess lack of engagement. We used to drive to college every day. Once it became clear that we can't hang out everyday, it just kinda fizzled out I would say." (P1, 24 years).

P14 voiced his inability to see his friends due to the pandemic. To quote P14,

"I wasn't able to see my friends... I wasn't able to cope, and I couldn't see my friends" (P14, 29 years).

On the contrary, P2 and P13 looked at the pandemic positively. The pandemic allowed P13 to communicate with others better, while P2 had more time due to fewer physical interactions with friends and used these times for productive activities (e.g., study). To quote P2,

"I can really focus on my studies very well since there are minimal interactions with friends. (P2, 21 years).

Taking (Illegal) Drugs
Our participants had experienced uncertainties, social and physical isolation, and substantial changes to their daily lives, including losing income sources, job and career changes, and family time. These changes contributed to engaging in activities that they would otherwise refrain from. For instance, P8 is a commercial driver who drove on high-paying routes. Due to the pandemic, high-paying routes became non-functional, and he had to do low-paying jobs instead. His inability to support his family even brought suicidal thoughts. The following quote from P8 highlights his mental anguish,

"I almost feel like I should die... I should commit suicide. But I feel that my kids will need me, and what am I going to tell my kids?" (P8, 32 years)

When asked if he used a digital resource to reduce his ill feelings, he mentioned a website called digital pills. He further explained:

"It's a website where you get some prescriptions on mental health issues... [it guides] you through different mental health prescriptions, even when you think of committing suicide." (P8, 32 years)

P4, a student and barista by profession, started taking drugs to resolve his stress during the pandemic. To quote P4,

"I actually got on some drugs ...[I]t actually helped calm me down." (P4, age unknown)

P4 did not elaborate further on the types of drugs he was taking, but the conversation hinted that the drugs were not prescribed by his medical team. P4 was trying to focus on school and work simultaneously and, as someone short on time, found a quick solution to calm himself down. P11 also reported starting drugs during the pandemic. To quote P11,

"I took some drugs. At some point, I had issues with sleeping at night. I could not really sleep at night. So, I had to take drugs... to sleep." (P11, 25 years)

P11 confirmed that no doctor prescribed these drugs, and she thought taking them would be a good idea.

Mental Health Support
Current Coping Mechanism

Research shows that autistic individuals demonstrate resilience through coping despite being exposed to heightened stress and anxiety resulting from uncertainty and limited opportunities for in-person social interaction [29]. Despite all the psychosocial challenges that they were going through, our participants made efforts to move past this difficult situation.

P2 and P3 used online streaming and watching movies as coping mechanisms. P1 and P2 watched horror movies as they built up the tension and made them forgetful about their stressful situations. P2 mentioned,

"The reason I like horror movies is the kind of tension that you have when watching the movie, so that's the most enjoyable part of watching horror movies for me!" (P2, 21 years).

Therapies played a vital role in our participants' survival during the pandemic by helping them organize their thoughts. The feeling of not being alone helped them address their mental health issues. Our participants also felt that having pets could be helpful during such times. They considered taking care of pets as their "personal therapy." P3 practiced meditation and watched YouTube videos of guided meditation, which helped to reduce anxiety and stress. To quote P3,

"I like [to] meditate often, that helps me relax. That's very good for stress, just like 20-minute meditation." (P3, 21 years)

Role of Technology

Our participants showed enthusiasm for technological solutions to reduce stress and anxiety. P1 talked about having a VR headset and how being immersed in a different world distracted their minds and shifted focus away from unwanted feelings. P1 stated,

"I'm looking into getting an Oculus Rift VR headset for my birthday, like a week. I was really interested in trying that to see if ... the immersion of those type of games would be alleviating." (P1, 24 years)

P10 believed that even using a phone for everyday things (e.g., listening to music or having a workout device) could reduce some mental anxiety. To quote P10,

"It gives the clear evidence that.... I can recoup my mental situation with mobile apps." (P10, 26 years)

P8, a commercial driver, shared his opinions in the following way.

"If I could have an application or technology that can detect my stress, and tell me, I'm driving too much, I should .. Relax myself. That will be very, very lucrative for me." (P8, 32 years)

P15 used the Calm [27], an application that provides resources to people who suffer from stress and anxiety. P15 explained what features of the app he liked:

"I actually like ... the availability of... different musics and the reminder... It relax[es] my nerves." (P15, 25 years)

P9 wished to have a technology that could give him something to do based on ongoing context (what was happening at that moment). P11 talked about how she could give details about her situation and the technology (e.g., app) could tell her how to reduce her stress. P12 discussed a technology that would be able to provide a user with solutions based on what the user describes to the technology (e.g., chatbot). P3 considered technology could be useful. However, he was skeptical that excessive use of technology could become a source of stress. To quote P3,

"If you're just like watching like Twitch streams all day... If you have work to do and the technology is distracting then that definitely contributes to stress." (P3, 21 years)

Feedback on MindBot
MindBot Prototype Impressed Our Participants
    In the last part of each interview, we demonstrated MindBot to our participants over zoom. We wanted to gather feedback about MindBot and its features from autistic young adults, as the feedback would help us better understand which features were considered useful and which features needed to be redesigned or removed. Overall, our participants considered MindBot's idea innovative and mentioned that they would be interested in using it. The following quotes highlight this.

"This whole idea and project are so good. I almost feel jealous not to be a part of research like this myself. This seems really well thought [out] the way it is designed." (P1, 24 years)

"For this one, I will give it 100% and say, Bravo! Because for me, as I said earlier, I don't share most of my problems with people. So, considering my knowledge on chatbots, this is a perfect idea." (P2, 21 years)

"One of the features that I do enjoy about this app is a chatbot... Instead of go seeing a therapist, now just communicating with the bot. It's, to an extent, nice." (P6, 31 years)

"I love everything about the app. It's fun. I actually love the instant feedback. The instant is good. I can use it to get instant mental help services, prescriptions, and services." (P7, 34 years)

"According to what I'm seeing it, it's very, very perfect. I like it." (P14, 29 years)

Improving Chatbot
We also received insightful suggestions to improve MindBot. One clear design implication is that participants recommended ways to make the AI chatbot more friendly. Instead of a separate app, they wanted to communicate with the bot via the phone's messaging application like they would with their friends with actual phone numbers. They also mentioned that having a delayed response from the bot would be considered genuine and thought-out. P1 mentioned,

"I feel like if it replies right away, right when I say something, it would almost be a little less genuine." (P1, 24 years).

P1 and P2 suggested including users' hobbies and interests so that the chatbot could follow up by asking about these interests. P3 emphasized improving the bot's avatar since he would not like the bot to appear *"like a cold robot."* To make the bot more human-like, P1 offered that the bot could follow up with users after a conversation and send reminders to come back and talk (like a human friend).

Participants wanted to add more empathetic responses and to have a continuous conversation over multiple days. They envisioned the bot sending a follow-up message the next day asking how users were holding up after a stressful night.

Participants liked the idea of saving the chat history option. Having control over what specific chat messages would be saved would empower users to protect their sensitive messages. To quote P3:

"It will be cool to have the option of saving specific messages. Personally, I like saving messages but not all so that I would remember the conversation afterward." (P3, 21 years).

P9 wanted a notification feature to remind him to speak with the chatbot, while P13 wanted a feature where the chatbot could "speak" rather than "chat" with the user.

Other Suggestions
Our participants provided additional suggestions. P1 noted that the big red help button on the chat page was out of place and distracting. P2 wanted MindBot available on web browsers. P2 often put their phones aside to take a break and thought that having MindBot on mobile and the web would be helpful. P5 wanted an option to play music, see funny images or emojis, and send positive messages from the chatbot to other users. P6 and P9 suggested having a forum for people using the app. In addition, P9 was interested in

talking with other app users. P7 wanted a timer feature in MindBot. P10 suggested that the app should provide a sense of it being real, not too technical. P12 mentioned that the instant feature could ask users a question and tell users what they can do. P15 wanted to see a sleep feature, instrumental music, and an image of hope for the instant.

4.4 Findings from the Cognitive Walkthrough

In this section, we focus on findings from the cognitive walkthrough. To enhance the effectiveness of MindBot, we conducted a cognitive walkthrough of the system (N = 20). As cognitive walkthrough requires expert users with experience in evaluation techniques and Human-Computer Interaction, we recruited participants from a graduate level Human-Computer Interaction course who were trained on applying cognitive walkthrough on computing applications. As this type of evaluation requires specific skills and knowledge in user interface design and computing systems, we did not recruit participants who lacked such skillset.

Each cognitive walkthrough participant completed the following four tasks that enabled them to identify usability and learnability issues associated with them:

- Task 1: Log in to the app by creating an account
- Task 2: Prompt the Chatbot to start a conversation
- Task 3: Respond to Chatbot messages with emotion
- Task 4: Log out of the app.

After performing each task, each participant answered the following four questions.

- Q1: Did you achieve the right outcome?
- Q2: Did you notice that the correct action is available?
- Q3: Did you associate the correct action with the outcome you expected to achieve?
- Q4: If the correct action was performed, did you see that progress was being made towards the intended outcome?

Table 3 shows the responses of our participants, which shows that our participants successfully performed Tasks 1, 2, and 4 (90% to 100% success rate). For Task 3, we see that 18 participants (90%) achieved the right outcome for Q1. However, only 11 (55%), 12 (60%), and 12 (60%) participants were successful for Q2, Q3, and Q4, respectively. We analyzed participants' comments to understand the underlying reason for the lower success rate for Task 3. MindBot was initially designed where users needed to compose a chat message first. Users could choose emojis to represent their emotions when they pressed the send button. Users found this sequence of operations confusing. This finding inspired us to implement an emoji keyboard in our updated version, discussed in Sect. 5 (see Fig. 6).

Table 3. Cognitive walkthrough responses

Task #	Question #	# Of Successful Participants
Task 1	Q1	20 (100%)
	Q2	20 (100%)
	Q3	19 (95%)
	Q4	19 (95%)
Task 2	Q1	19 (95%)
	Q2	19 (95%)
	Q3	20 (100%)
	Q4	20 (100%)
Task 3	Q1	18 (90%)
	Q2	11 (55%)
	Q3	12 (60%)
	Q4	12 (60%)
Task 4	Q1	19 (95%)
	Q2	19 (95%)
	Q3	19 (95%)
	Q4	18 (90%)

5   Discussion

Our findings suggest that mobile-based applications can potentially deliver interventions effectively. As mentioned earlier, such solutions are not a replacement for face-to-face intervention, but they show promise.

5.1   Design Implications

Our findings also led us to three design implications, which are discussed below.

A Need for Mental Health Resources and Education

As mentioned earlier, some of our interview participants took extreme measures (e.g., suicidal thoughts, and taking illegal drugs) during the pandemic. This finding inferred the following expectations of the participants.

- A service to alleviate their stress.
- An emergency support system to get help in extreme situations (e.g., suicidal thoughts and ideation).
- A support system for diagnostic services and alternatives to extreme measures.

To meet these expectations, a mobile-based technology can be designed to provide mental health resources and educate users on appropriate drug use, especially for those with suicidal thoughts.

Social Aspect
Connecting with others during the pandemic was crucial for P9, P10, and P14. Similarly, P6 and P9 wanted a forum in the MindBot app to share their experiences and frustrations with other autistic young adults. A question may arise if a traditional social media platform (e.g., Facebook) is better in this regard. Facebook already has a remarkable existing user base, and it is straightforward to set up a Forum on Facebook. However, we believe that the MindBot forum could offer benefits beyond an existing social network. For example, it will bring a small number of people actively looking to reduce their stress together in one place. It may include an unconventional way of providing a social aspect. One idea is to design a night sky-like digital board, where each star represents an autistic user. Such visualization can offer a sense of solidarity to autistic individuals.

Stress Management Guide
Technology can play an important role by automatically detecting stress and informing users how to deal with it. Islam et al. provided an affordable mobile and wearable technology-based solution to predict the stress of autistic college students [28]. Integrating such a solution with MindBot could be beneficial. After detecting the stress, MindBot may provide a stress management guide to aid users through particular scenarios.

5.2 Future Goals and Current Status of MindBot

Our future goal is to develop MindBot 2.0 by addressing suggestions provided by our participants and by evaluating MindBot with other autistic individuals. We have improved a few features by addressing recommendations by our participants. Figures 5 and 6 show some screenshots of this refined MindBot. Figure 5 shows that MindBot has separated registration and sign-in pages. We have also combined the settings and account pages as setting pages, implemented theme color and font size options for user preferences, and added a "delete account" option (Fig. 6). For the chatbot page, we implemented a feature that allows users to select emotion emojis for each message.

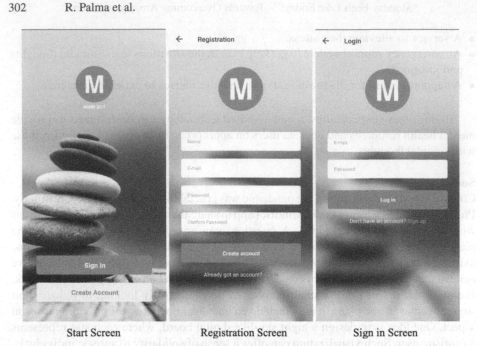

Start Screen   Registration Screen   Sign in Screen

Fig. 5. Start, registration, and sign-in screen

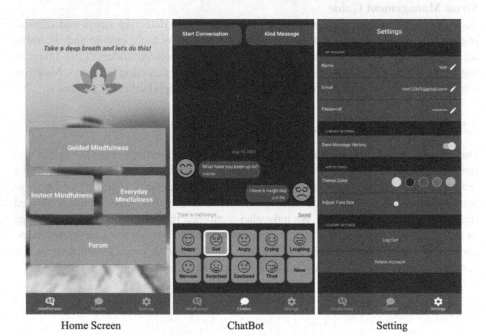

Home Screen   ChatBot   Setting

Fig. 6. Home, chatbot, and setting screen.

6 Conclusion

Our research highlighted the need for effective intervention techniques to reduce the stress and anxiety of autistic young adults during prolonged isolation. In MindBot, we incorporated MBCT and an AI Chatbot to help autistic individuals to manage their stress and anxiety. We identified various problems that autistic individuals experienced during the pandemic due to increased mental health issues. We also shed light on specific reasons that caused stress in autistic individuals because of the need to adapt to the pandemic lifestyle. We believe that by focusing on constructive and optimistic coping mechanisms and building positive energy, technology like MindBot can lead to an effective approach to addressing autistic young adults' mental health conditions during and after the pandemic.

References

1. Data & Statistics on Autism Spectrum Disorder. https://www.cdc.gov/ncbddd/autism/data.html. Accessed 15 Dec 2022
2. Roux, A.M., Shattuck, P.T., Rast, J.E., Rava, J.A., Anderson, K.: A. National Autism Indicators Report: Transition into Young Adulthood. Philadelphia. A.J. Drexel Autism Institute, Drexel University (2015)
3. White, S.W., et al.: Psychosocial treatments targeting anxiety and depression in adolescents and adults on the autism spectrum: review of the latest research and recommended future directions. Curr. Psychiatry Rep. **20**(10), 82 (2018)
4. Ellis, L.A., Campbell, A.J., Sethi, S., O'Dea, B.M.: Comparative randomized trial of an online cognitive-behavioral therapy program and an online support group for depression and anxiety. J. Cyberther. Rehabil. **4**(4), 461–467 (2011)
5. Luxford, S., Hadwin, J.A., Kovshoff, H.: Evaluating the effectiveness of a school-based cognitive behavioural therapy intervention for anxiety in adolescents diagnosed with autism spectrum disorder. J. Autism Dev. Disord. **47**(12), 3896–3908 (2017)
6. Twenge, J.M., Joiner, T.E.: Mental distress among US adults during the COVID-19 pandemic. J. Clin. Psychol. **76**(12), 2170–2182 (2020)
7. Krusche, A., Cyhlarova, E., Williams, J.M.G.: Mindfulness online: an evaluation of the feasibility of a web-based mindfulness course for stress, anxiety and depression. BMJ Open **3**(11), e003498 (2013)
8. Stadheim, J., Johns, A., Mitchell, M., Smith, C.J., Braden, B.B., Matthews, N.L.: A qualitative examination of the impact of the COVID-19 pandemic on children and adolescents with autism and their parents. Res. Dev. Disabil. **125**, 104232 (2022)
9. Rieman, J., Franzke, M., Redmiles, D.: Usability evaluation with the cognitive walkthrough. In: Conference Companion on Human Factors in Computing Systems, pp. 387–388 (1995)
10. Salem-Guirgis, S., et al.: MYmind: a concurrent group-based mindfulness intervention for youth with autism and their parents. Mindfulness **10**(9), 1730–1743 (2019)
11. Skeens, L.M.: Guided imagery: a technique to benefit youth at risk. National Youth-at-Risk Journal **2**(2), 92 (2017)
12. Veena, D., Alvi, S.: Guided imagery intervention for anxiety reduction. Indian J. Health Well Being **7**(2), 198 (2016)
13. Bigham, E., McDannel, L., Luciano, I., Salgado-Lopez, G.: Effect of a brief guided imagery on stress. Biofeedback **42**(1), 28–35 (2014)

14. Oomen, D., Nijhof, A.D., Wiersema, J.R.: The psychological impact of the COVID-19 pandemic on adults with autism: a survey study across three countries. Molecular Autism **12**(1), 1–21 (2021)
15. Kabat-Zinn, J.: Mindfulness-based interventions in context: past, present, and future. Clin. Psychol. Sci. Pract. **10**(2), 144–156 (2003)
16. Ridderinkhof, A., de Bruin, E.I., Blom, R., Bögels, S.M.: Mindfulness-based program for children with autism spectrum disorder and their parents: Direct and long-term improvements. Mindfulness **9**(3), 773–791 (2018)
17. Myint, K., Choy, K.L., Tin, T.S., Lam, S.K.: The effect of short-term practice of mindfulness meditation in alleviating stress in university students. Biomedical Research-India **22**(2) (2011)
18. Jones, D.R., Lehman, B.J., Noriega, A., Dinnel, D.L.: The effects of a short-term mindfulness meditation intervention on coping flexibility. Anxiety Stress Coping **32**(4), 347–361 (2019)
19. Grové, C.: Co-developing a mental health and wellbeing Chatbot with and for young people. Front. Psych. **11**, 1664 (2020)
20. Furar, E., et al.: The impact of COVID-19 on individuals with ASD in the US: parent perspectives on social and support concerns. PLoS ONE **17**(8), e0270845 (2022)
21. Bäuerle, A., et al.: An e-mental health intervention to support burdened people in times of the COVID-19 pandemic: CoPE It. J. Public Health **42**(3), 647–648 (2020)
22. Wu, G., et al.: Understanding resilience. Frontiers in Behavioral Neuroscience **7**, 10 (2013)
23. Bond, R.R., et al.: Chatbots to support mental health & wellbeing: early findings from chatpal use during COVID-19 lockdown. In: 9th European Conference on Mental Health (2020)
24. Higa-McMillan, C.K., Francis, S.E., Rith-Najarian, L., Chorpita, B.F.: Evidence base update: 50 years of research on treatment for child and adolescent anxiety. J. Clin. Child Adolesc. Psychol. **45**(2), 91–113 (2016)
25. Cognitive Behavioral Therapy (CBT). https://www.mayoclinic.org/tests-procedures/cognitive-behavioral-therapy/about/pac-20384610. Accessed 15 Dec 2022
26. Vasa, R.A., Mazurek, M.O.: An update on anxiety in youth with autism spectrum disorders. Curr. Opin. Psychiatry **28**(2), 83 (2015)
27. Calm app. https://www.calm.com/. Accessed 15 Dec 2022
28. Islam, T.Z., et al.: College life is hard! - shedding light on stress prediction for autistic college students using data-driven analysis. In: IEEE 45th Annual Computers, Software, and Applications Conference (COMPSAC), pp. 428–437 (2021)
29. den Houting, J.: Stepping out of isolation: autistic people and COVID-19. Autism in Adulthood **2**(2), 103–105 (2020)
30. Gaffney, H., Mansell, W., Tai, S.: Conversational agents in the treatment of mental health problems: mixed-method systematic review. JMIR Mental Health **6**(10), e14166 (2019)
31. Autism Spectrum Disorder and Anxiety/Depression. https://adaa.org/understanding-anxiety/autism-anxiety-depression. Accessed 15 Dec 2022
32. Atlas.ti cloud. https://cloud.atlasti.com/. Accessed 15 Dec 2022
33. Radziwill, N.M., Benton, M.C.: Evaluating Quality of Chatbots and Intelligent Conversational Agents. arXiv preprint arXiv:1704.04579 (2017)
34. Strauss, A., Corbin, J.M.: Grounded Theory in Practice. Sage (1997)
35. Hillier, A., Greher, G., Poto, N., Dougherty, M.: Positive outcomes following participation in a music intervention for adolescents and young adults on the autism spectrum. Psychol. Music **40**(2), 201–215 (2012)
36. Eren, B.: The use of music interventions to improve social skills in adolescents with autism spectrum disorders in integrated group music therapy sessions. Procedia Soc. Behav. Sci. **197**, 207–213 (2015)
37. Santos, K.A., Ong, E., Resurreccion, R.: Therapist vibe: children's expressions of their emotions through storytelling with a chatbot. In: Proceedings of the Interaction Design and Children Conference, pp. 483–494 (2020)

38. Pellicano, E., et al.: COVID-19, social isolation and the mental health of autistic people and their families: a qualitative study. Autism **26**(4), 914–927 (2022)
39. MacEvilly, D., Brosnan, G.: Adapting an emotional regulation and social communication skills group programme to teletherapy, in response to the COVID-19 pandemic. Irish Journal of Psychological Med. 1–6 (2020)
40. Alonso-Esteban, Y., López-Ramón, M.F., Moreno-Campos, V., Navarro-Pardo, E., Alcantud-Marín, F.: A systematic review on the impact of the social confinement on people with autism spectrum disorder and their caregivers during the COVID-19 pandemic. Brain Sci. **11**(11), 1389 (2021)
41. Wharton, C., Rieman, J., Lewis, C., Polson, P.: The cognitive walkthrough method: a practitioner's guide. In: Usability Inspection Methods, pp. 105–140 (1994)
42. Zhang, Y., et al.: Dialogpt: Large-Scale Generative Pre-Training for Conversational Response Generation. arXiv preprint arXiv:1911.00536 (2019)
43. Mental health: strengthening our response. https://www.who.int/news-room/fact-sheets/detail/mental-health-strengthening-our-response. Accessed 15 Dec 2022
44. Mental Health. https://www.who.int/health-topics/mental-health#tab=tab_1. Accessed 15 Dec 2022
45. Bal, V.H., et al.: Early pandemic experiences of autistic adults: predictors of psychological distress. Autism Res. **14**(6), 1209–1219 (2021)

Self-tracking to Manage Chronic Illness: Exploring User Agency in Apps for Diabetes Self-management

Rachel Tunis(✉) ⓘ

University of Texas, Austin, USA
rtunis@utexas.edu

Abstract. Self-tracking through wearable devices and mobile applications is becoming increasingly common, especially for health measures. In particular, self-tracking tools hold great potential to help patients with chronic illnesses with self-management, as they can allow for continuous data collection and provide trends and insights that can help patients navigate their daily lives. This study examines 18 mobile apps for diabetes self-management and uses thematic analysis and computer-mediated discourse analysis to understand the key messages being communicated to users through App Store descriptions. The specific focal concept is *agency*; the study explores the extent to which app descriptions discuss affordances which allow users to manage their health in their own life contexts, according to their own preferences and goals, or whether apps, based on their descriptions, undermine users' agency. The study finds that app descriptions imply different possible modes of agency: apps may be used to afford users maximum ease and convenience (alleviating burden and delegating more agency to the apps) and/or to equip users with an improved capacity to manage their own health (strengthening their own capacity for agency). Beyond these different possible modes of agency, however, this study finds that overall, based on these apps' self-descriptions, user agency is limited. Despite plentiful mentions of flexibility, personalization, customization, and context, there are few indications that apps' interfaces and functionalities can meaningfully incorporate and adapt to users' context, preferences, and goals.

Keywords: Health technology · Health information · Self-tracking · Self-management · Diabetes · Chronic illness · Agency

1 Introduction

As technology becomes increasingly embedded in our lives, digital self-tracking tools (i.e., wearables or smartphone apps) have been rapidly gaining uptake, particularly in the health space [13]. In addition to the unprecedented ability to collect and display health information in real-time, self-tracking tools have a didactic element that can help patients see trends and patterns in their data and link cause and effect. While most self-tracking

I. Sserwanga et al. (Eds.): iConference 2023, LNCS 13972, pp. 306–314, 2023.
https://doi.org/10.1007/978-3-031-28032-0_25

research focuses on healthy consumers, self-tracking tools can be of immense value to patients with chronic health conditions, providing novel access to data and insights and enabling more independent, self-driven health management [2]. Recent studies have begun to explore self-tracking tools for patients with chronic conditions such as diabetes [21], HIV [30], Parkinson's Disease [23], Multiple Sclerosis [3], mental illness [32], and more. Ensuring thoughtful design of these tools is extremely important because data that is inaccurate, misleading, or presented in an undesirable way may result in anxieties, disruptions, and direct adverse health impacts that may be a matter of life or death.

Caution around the way that self-tracking tools are designed is certainly warranted. Previous research has demonstrated that they are often not designed in ways that support people's changing health status, goals, or practices, and that they often make assumptions about what and how people want to track [14, 24]. This paper focuses on mobile apps for diabetes self-management and uses the concept of agency to consider whether users are afforded opportunities to track according to their own goals and preferences. By analyzing apps' public-facing descriptions, this study explores how apps position themselves to users and considers the role of agency in the features and affordances they describe.

2 Background

Diabetes is one of the most prevalent chronic conditions in the world and requires consistent and attentive self-management. Diabetics must ensure that their blood glucose is always within a stable range, taking care to avoid extremes in either direction. This is a complex process that involves anticipating one's activities and their impacts on blood glucose. Indeed, Jull et al. estimate that many diabetics must make as many as 600 different decisions daily [16]. To assist with self-management, devices that continuously measure patients' blood glucose can feed data to apps which can help patients keep track of their blood sugar levels, identify trends, and understand contributors to high or low readings.

In practice, self-management looks different for everyone, as patients have very different goals and life contexts. Raj et al. [27] have demonstrated that apps for diabetes self-management lack a "contextualized understanding" of patients' circumstances and practices and thus are not sufficiently able to give people the most appropriate support or guidance. Research has also shown that patients have different preferences for how to go about tracking and managing their health data. Costello and Veinot [8], for example, describe five approaches that people take when interacting with their health information: avoiding, receiving, asking, verifying, and seeking. Adams et al. also demonstrate a distinction between those who prefer numeric tools for self-tracking and those who prefer more qualitative tools [1]. Such evidence suggests that self-management tools should allow patients to track flexibly, according to their own preferences and needs. We thus turn to the concept of agency.

Agency has long been debated in many fields, but its usage in science and technology studies (STS) and, more specifically, actor-network theory (ANT), is adopted here. ANT considers social actors to be an amalgamation of associations—constantly shifting assemblages of the people, places, discourses, ideas, objects, technologies, and so on [18]. Importantly, ANT ascribes agency to any "actor" that "modif[ies] a state of affairs by making a difference." Thus, technologies like self-tracking tools have agency in that their affordances can "authorize, afford, encourage, permit, suggest, influence, block, render possible, forbid, and so on" [18]. Put more directly, when it comes to technology, "human agents conspicuously do not call all the shots"; rather, "material and human agencies are mutually and emergently productive of one another" [25]. Duus et al., writing on self-tracking tools, for example, propose the concept of the "agency pendulum", wherein the human and the tracker can influence behaviors and decisions at different times, depending on how the human configures the tool and their attitudes toward it [12].

Prior research on diabetes self-management technologies supports these ideas, finding that assemblages of personal preferences, relationships, informational resources, tools, and particular contexts constantly affect one another, influencing patients' actions and the meanings they attribute to self-management tools [9, 16]. Careful consideration of these assemblages allows us to identify different elements and actors within them and their impacts on patients. Thinking about the agency of self-tracking tools themselves can help contextualize situations in which patients cannot foresee or control tools' actions, which might undermine their agency to track as they wish and, further, might have consequential mental and physical health impacts [20].

3 Methods

To extract and analyze themes from app descriptions, the first step was selecting a sample of diabetes self-management apps. This was done by searching the App Store using the term "diabetes" *and* either "manage*" "track*", "log*", "journal*", "record*," *or* "diary." This search was conducted in June 2022. The following inclusion criteria were used to select the sample[1]: (1) the app focused on holistic diabetes management (i.e., not just tracking one aspect such as meals), (2) allowed for data integration from an external sensor device (i.e., glucose monitor or smartwatch), (3) not linked to a single brand-name product or device, (4) in English, (5) at least 25 App Store ratings, (6) publicly available and free to download (not including the option for separate, in-app purchases), and (7) updated since 2020. The search yielded 168 results, of which 150 were excluded due to failing to meet the inclusion criteria. The final sample consisted of 18 apps. To ensure other apps that fit the criteria had not been overlooked, the author cross-checked the App Store on multiple devices (iPhone, iPad, and MacBook) and referenced online articles listing top apps for diabetes management.

---

[1] Search terms and inclusion criteria are adapted from Caldeira et al.'s [6] study of mobile apps for mood tracking.

After the final sample was identified, App Store descriptions for each app were manually retrieved in July 2022. Thematic analysis [5] and computer-mediated discourse analysis [15] were used to capture key themes. Following Braun & Clarke's approach, the entire dataset was coded, and themes were generated, consolidated, and distilled until they were distinct and clear. Herring's computer-mediated discourse analysis was used to understand how agency was operationalized through word choice and other semantic decisions. Language invoking agency was specifically extracted during coding of the dataset. Following Tanninen et al. [31], the expectation was not to see the word "agency" used explicitly, as it is not common in everyday speech. Rather, the approach was to assess what common discourse features and terms invoked the idea of users' freedom to track as they wished, in accordance with their own goals and preferences.

4 Findings

Three broad themes emerged from the thematic analysis. First, *ease and convenience* (Fig. 1) relates to the features and mechanisms allowing users to log their data, interpret it (e.g., visualizations or descriptions of trends), and access it, with minimal stress, burden, or confusion. This theme is invoked by nearly every app; descriptions include phrases such as "quick and easy input," "least possible effort," or "in just a few clicks." One description states that the app is "designed to get your entries in as quickly as possible, with controls close to your thumbs" [11].

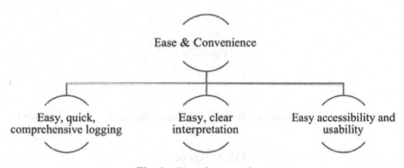

Fig. 1. Ease & convenience

The second theme, *improved health management capacity* (Fig. 2) relates to the bigger picture of health and disease management. Language that appeals to this theme often references daily routines of disease management and how the app helps users plan around elements of their daily lives, so they feel more in control. One app description claims: "With more information, you are able to plan into the future. Spend less time carb counting and tracking insulin, and more time on the things you love" [26]. App descriptions also frequently invoke language referencing progress or improvement, using phrases like "level up" or "manage your diabetes better." Some apps do this by implying obligation or duties (i.e., "ensure you are diligent…" or "make sure you check…"), while others appeal to their ability to help users develop a better understanding of factors that affect their disease, leading to more confidence and control.

Fig. 2. Improved health management capacity

Finally, Fig. 3. Demonstrates how *agency*, the third theme, is operationalized in app descriptions. Agency is discussed indirectly, through references to flexibility, customization, personalization, and context. These terms are primarily used to describe app features; for example, users can add "notes" providing context to data or customize their target blood sugar ranges. Beyond basic customizable features and results that are "personalized" (i.e., based on users' unique data and measurements), opportunities for delineating preferences, setting goals, and meaningfully incorporating context are limited. For example, few app descriptions mention that users can set goals in the app, and no app description indicates that the app's interface or functionality adapts to the context the user provides or goals they input.

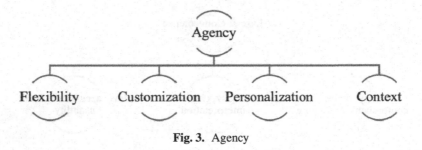

Fig. 3. Agency

5 Discussion

The themes resulting from this analysis are, in a way, paradoxical. The first theme, ease and convenience, illustrates apps' tendency to emphasize their potential to alleviate burden by making self-management as easy as possible. This aligns with much previous research that has found burden to be a significant barrier to consistent self-tracking [13]. On the other hand, the second theme, improved health management capacity, implies that by regularly using the app and its functionalities, users will build their skills and abilities such that they feel more in control self-managing their condition and overall health. These two themes indicate different ways that users might enact agency. Using Bandura's description of different modes of agency [4], the ease and convenience theme can be said to imply *proxy agency*, or a reliance on other entities to act on one's behalf to secure desired outcomes, thus alleviating burden. The improved health management capacity theme implies more direct control, or *personal agency*. The balance in how much an app appeals to ease and convenience vs. improved health management capacity can be seen as an example of an "agency pendulum" [12], providing hints towards apps' expectations of how users might enact agency.

Despite the implication of multiple possible modes of agency, the findings here indicate that apps *limit* agency in that their interfaces and functionalities do not allow for meaningful adjustments based on users' goals, preferences, and life contexts. This is consistent with prior research—Costa-Figuereido et al. [7] found, for example, that users of fertility self-management apps can "choose what to track, but only within the possibilities offered... [users] usually cannot manipulate data the way they want or choose how to analyze, compare, and visualize data at different levels of detail... the feedback they receive is pre-defined and often generic." Munson et al. [24] caution that *flexibility* is not the same as *supporting individualized goals*, which requires that a system support re-configuration aligning with user goals. This and other research [10] emphasize that health apps can do a better job providing actionable guidance that is tailored to users' context and goals, especially when they face an undesirable situation or forecast.

5.1 Limitations and Future Research Directions

App descriptions provide only a single lens into understanding how agency is distributed in the sociomaterial assemblages that make up self-tracking apps. As such, this study is limited in that it provides a limited lens which does not reflect an examination of the functionalities of apps themselves, nor the experience of users. Future research could consist of walkthroughs of apps [19] to examine the alignment between apps' descriptions and available features, as well as interviews with users to understand their experiences and how they use various "creative tactics" [29] to make space for agency within apps' imposed structures. Some research has begun to explore novel designs allowing users to set their own parameters for self-management tools and has found that this can be an empowering practice that supports agency [3, 22]. Such work that explicitly considers the optimal distribution of agency for users to have their needs met is important, as prior research has also warned about delegating too much agency to technological tools, given that the rationales behind their design are typically far from transparent [17, 28]. If the distribution of agency is too skewed towards tools rather than users, there is a risk that users might be steered towards certain choices without the awareness of the underlying platform's structure and motives and, as a result, their own preferences might be deprioritized and undermined.

6 Conclusion

This study analyzes the key themes communicated through app descriptions of diabetes self-management apps and their connections to how users might enact agency. Findings reveal that apps appeal to both how they can help alleviate burden *and* how users might build their own skills and abilities to exercise more control and agency. Still, this study finds that agency in apps for diabetes self-management is limited, because features offering flexibility and customization provide limited opportunities for the configuration of app interface and functionality to truly adapt to users' needs, preferences, goals, and larger life contexts.

Bandura, in discussing agency, has written that "agency involves not just deliberative ability to make choices and action plans but the ability to give shape to appropriate courses of action and to motivate and regulate their execution" [24]. True agency thus requires a larger view of users' life contexts, preferences, and the options available to them (or resources needed by them) to achieve their goals. Self-management tools that incorporate more context, as well as guidance and informational resources that *adapt* to that guidance, will be better positioned to allow users a more meaningful version of agency.

References

1. Adams, P., Murnane, E.L., Elfenbein, M., Wethington, E., Gay, G.: Supporting the self-management of chronic pain conditions with tailored momentary self-assessments. In: Proceedings of the 2017 CHI Conference on Human Factors in Computing Systems, pp. 1065–1077 (2017). https://doi.org/10.1145/3025453.3025832
2. Appelboom, G., LoPresti, M., Reginster, J.-Y., Connolly, E.S., Dumont, E.P.L.: The quantified patient: a patient participatory culture. Curr. Med. Res. Opin. **30**(12), 2585–2587 (2014). https://doi.org/10.1185/03007995.2014.954032
3. Ayobi, A., Marshall, P., Cox, A., Chen, Y.: Quantifying the body and caring for the mind: self-tracking in multiple sclerosis. In: Proceedings of the 2017 CHI Conference on Human Factors in Computing Systems, pp. 6889–6901 (2017). https://doi.org/10.1145/3025453.3025869
4. Bandura, A.: Social cognitive theory: an agentic perspective. Annu. Rev. Psychol. **52**, 1–26 (2001). https://doi.org/10.1146/annurev.psych.52.1.1
5. Braun, V., Clarke, V.: Using thematic analysis in psychology. Qual. Res. Psychol. **3**(2), 77–101 (2006). https://doi.org/10.1191/1478088706qp063oa
6. Caldeira, C., Chen, Y., Chan, L., Pham, V., Chen, Y., et al.: Mobile apps for mood tracking: an analysis of features and user reviews. In: AMIA Annual Symposium Proceedings Archive, pp. 495–504 (2017)
7. Costa Figuereido, M., Huynh, T., Takei, A., Epstein, D., Chen, Y.: Goals, life events, and transitions: examining fertility apps for holistic health tracking. JAMIA Open **4**(1) (2021). https://doi.org/10.1093/jamiaopen/ooab013
8. Costello, K., Veinot, T.: A spectrum of approaches to health information interaction: from avoidance to verification. J. Assoc. Inf. Sci. Technol. **71**(8), 871–886 (2019). https://doi.org/10.1002/asi.24310
9. Danesi, G., Pralong, M., Pidoux, V.: Embodiment and agency through self-tracking practices of people living with diabetes. In: Ajana, B. (Ed.), Metric Culture, pp. 117–135. Emerald Publishing Limited, Bingley (2018). https://doi.org/10.1108/978-1-78743-289-520181007
10. Desai, P., Mitchell, E., Hwang, M., Levine, M., Albers, J., et al: Personal health oracle: explorations of personalized predictions in diabetes self-management. In: Proceedings of the 2019 CHI Conference on Human Factors in Computing Systems, pp. 1–13 (2019). https://doi.org/10.1145/3290605.3300600

11. DiabetesPro. https://apps.apple.com/us/app/diabetes-pro/id1137466950. Accessed 15 Sept 2022

12. Duus, R., Cooray, M.: Page, N: Exploring human-tech hybridity at the intersection of extended cognition and distributed agency: a focus on self-tracking devices. Front. Psychol. (2018). https://doi.org/10.3389/fpsycg.2018.01432

13. Epstein, D., Caldeira, C., Costa Figueiredo, M., Lu, X., Silva, L.M., et al.: Mapping and taking stock of the personal informatics literature. Proc. ACM Interact. Mob. Wearable Ubiquitous Technol. 4(4), 1–38 (2020). https://doi.org/10.1145/3432231

14. Epstein, D., Ping, A., Fogarty, J., Munson, S.: A lived informatics model of personal informatics. In: Proceedings of the 2015 ACM International Joint Conference on Pervasive and Ubiquitous Computing, pp. 731–742 (2015). https://doi.org/10.1145/2750858.2804250

15. Herring, S.C.: Computer-mediated discourse analysis: an approach to researching online behavior. In: Barab, S.A., Kling, R., Gray, J.H. (Eds.) Designing for Virtual Communities in the Service of Learning, pp. 338–376. Cambridge University Press (2004). https://doi.org/10.1017/CBO9780511805080.016

16. Jull, J., Witteman, H.O., Ferne, J., Yoganathan, M., Stacey, D.: Adult-onset type 1 diabetes: a qualitative study of decision-making needs. Can. J. Diabetes 40(2), 164–169 (2016). https://doi.org/10.1016/j.jcjd.2015.09.080

17. Lanzing, M.: "Strongly Recommended" revisiting decisional privacy to judge hypernudging in self-tracking technologies. Philos. Technol. 32(3), 549–568 (2018). https://doi.org/10.1007/s13347-018-0316-4

18. Latour, B.: Reassembling the Social: An Introduction to Actor-Network Theory. Oxford University Press Inc, New York (2005)

19. Light, B., Burgess, J., Duguay, S.: The walkthrough method: an approach to the study of apps. New Media Soc. 20(3) (2016). https://doi.org/10.1177/1461444816675438

20. Lomborg, S., Langstrup, H., Andersen, T.O.: Interpretation as luxury: heart patients living with data doubt, hope, and anxiety. Big Data Soc. (2020). https://doi.org/10.1177/2053951720924436

21. Mamykina, L., Heitkemper, E.M., Smaldone, A.M., Kukafka, R., Cole-Lewis, H.J., et al.: Personal discovery in diabetes self-management: discovering cause and effect using self-monitoring data. J. Biomed. Inform. 76, 1–8 (2017). https://doi.org/10.1016/j.jbi.2017.09.013

22. Maxwell, H., O'Shea, M., Stronach, M., Pearce, S.: Empowerment through digital health trackers: an exploration of Indigenous Australian women and physical activity in leisure settings. Ann. Leisure Res. 24(1), 150–167 (2019). https://doi.org/10.1080/11745398.2019.1674677

23. Mishra, S., Klasnja, P., Woodburn, J.M., Hekler, E., Omberg, L., et al.: Supporting coping with Parkinson's Disease through self tracking. In: Proceedings of the 2019 CHI Conference on Human Factors in Computing Systems, pp. 1–16 (2019). https://doi.org/10.1145/3290605.3300337

24. Munson, S.A., Schroeder, J., Karkar, R., Kientz, J.A., Chung, C.F., et al.: The importance of starting with goals in N-of-1 studies. Front. Dig. Health (2020). https://doi.org/10.3389/fdgth.2020.00003

25. Pickering, A.: The mangle of practice: agency and emergence in the sociology of science. Am. J. Sociol. 99(3), 559–589 (1993)

26. Quin: Diabetes Management. https://apps.apple.com/us/app/quin-diabetes-management/id1159135459. Accessed 15 Sept 2022

27. Raj, S., Toporski, K., Garrity, A., Lee, J.: "My blood sugar is higher on the weekends": finding a role for context and context-awareness in the design of health self-management technology. In: Proceedings of the 2019 CHI Conference on Human Factors in Computing Systems, pp. 1–13 (2019). https://doi.org/10.1145/3290605.3300349

28. Sax, M.: Optimization of what? for-profit health apps as manipulative digital environments. Ethics Inf. Technol. **23**(3), 345–361 (2021). https://doi.org/10.1007/s10676-020-09576-6

29. Sharon, T.: Healthy citizenship beyond autonomy and discipline: tactical engagement with genetic testing. BioSocieties **10**, 295–316 (2015). https://doi.org/10.1057/biosoc.2014.29

30. Swendeman, D., Ramanathan, N., Baetscher, L., Medich, M., Scheffler, A., et al.: Smartphone self-monitoring to support self-management among people living with HIV: perceived benefits and theory of change from a mixed-methods randomized pilot study. JAIDS J. Acquir. Immune Defic. Syndr. **69**(Suppl 1), S80–S91 (2015). https://doi.org/10.1097/QAI.0000000000000570

31. Tanninen, M., Lehtonen, T.-K., Ruckenstein, M.: Trouble with autonomy in behavioral insurance. Br. J. Sociol. **73**(4), 786–798 (2022). https://doi.org/10.1111/1468-4446.12960

32. Young, A.S., Choi, A., Cannedy, S., Hoffman, L., Levine, L.: passive mobile self-tracking of mental health by veterans with serious mental illness: protocol for a user-centered design and prospective cohort study. JMIR Res. Protoc. **11**(8), e39010 (2022). https://doi.org/10.2196/39010

Virtual Reality Interventions for Autistic Individuals: Research Trends and Practices

Ngoc-Minh Pham[(✉)] [iD], Shangman Li[iD], and Heather Moulaison-Sandy[iD]

University of Missouri, Columbia, USA
phamngocminhclc@gmail.com

Abstract. Autism is a lifelong neurodevelopmental disorder that impacts individuals across different genders, ages, races, ethnicities, and socioeconomic groups. One promising, multidisciplinary area of research interest in this space is Virtual Reality (VR). This project reviews domestic and international collaboration patterns and scholarly interest relating to VR applications for autistic individuals. The analysis uses 215 empirical papers screened and selected from 1,050 papers retrieved from the Web of Science database. Findings show that (a) papers on this topic are largely the product of collaborations, with the number of domestically collaborated papers (183 papers (86%)) over six times higher than that of internationally collaborated papers (30 papers (14%)) and with the top 3 countries with collaboratively authored papers being US (n = 100), UK (n = 32), and India (n = 20); (b) collaboration has increased over time; and (c) domestically collaborated papers tend to be on the rise, most notably since 2018. In terms of research trends relating to VR for autistic individuals, topics of study are comparable between domestically collaborated papers and internationally collaborated papers, with a few notable exceptions relating to the focus of study.

Keywords: Autistic individuals · Virtual reality · Collaboration patterns · Research trends

1 Introduction

Autism is a lifelong neurodevelopmental disorder characterized by deficits in two core domains: (1) social communications and social interactions and (2) restricted repetitive patterns of behaviors, interests, and activities [1]. Autism (also termed autism spectrum disorder (ASD) and closely associated with the neurodevelopmental disorder Asperger syndrome (Asperger's)) is increasingly prevalent since it was first observed and recorded in the 1940s. As many as 1 in 44 children have been identified with autism in the US [2]. Autistic individuals come from all racial, ethnic, and socioeconomic groups.

Virtual Reality (VR) technology is successfully paired with interventions for autistic individuals. VR offers the opportunity to simulate the real world as it is or create completely new worlds based on computer graphics [3]. Autistic individuals tend to have a natural affinity for screen-based technology, and the controlled environment provided by the computer is beneficial [4]. VR-based worlds can be designed to facilitate

© The Author(s), under exclusive license to Springer Nature Switzerland AG 2023
I. Sserwanga et al. (Eds.): iConference 2023, LNCS 13972, pp. 315–325, 2023.
https://doi.org/10.1007/978-3-031-28032-0_26

the understanding of skills and concepts, and the learning to perform certain tasks [5]. Autistic individuals need effective and appropriate interventions to address their skill delays and impairments to thrive in social contexts and independent living settings, and VR offers opportunities to stimulate safe, repeatable, and diversifiable social environments for training and learning [3]. However, little is known about the way research in this emerging area of study has been carried out.

2 Research Questions

This exploratory research project seeks to analyze the scholarly body of literature in VR for autistic individuals published from 1996 to 2021. Understanding the nature of trends in this line of research in terms of national and international collaborations can contribute to future directions of research collaboration and interventions, which in return may lead to more efficient support services for autistic individuals using cutting-edge technologies like VR. To achieve our goal of understanding research trends in research on VR interventions for autistic individuals, we seek to answer the two following research questions.

RQ1: What are scientific collaboration trends in VR applications for autistic individuals and in what way have patterns of collaboration evolved over time, both domestically and internationally?
RQ2: What are the research approaches and topical trends evident in this literature in terms of VR interventions for autistic individuals?

3 Review of the Literature

3.1 Collaboration in Research

Collaboration enables scientists to make use of others' complementary expertise, resources, and ideas. Therefore, collaboration enhances the efficiency of scientific production, improves research quality (e.g., [6, 7]), and fosters advances of science in a shorter time [8]. Collaboration in the research community ensures the high quality of study through examinations of research topics of interest and discussion from different scholarly perspectives [9]. Further, international research collaborations appear to show greater research contributions to scientific fields in terms of sharing ideas, resources, and research impacts [10, 11].

The increasingly interdisciplinary and complex nature of modern science together with the benefits of collaboration has encouraged scientists to get involved in collaborative research. Multiple-authored papers tend to increasingly dominate single-authored papers [6]. Though international collaborations (ICs) are on the rise [8, 12], they are lower in proportion to domestic collaborations (DCs) [8, 13] and have a slower momentum than DCs [8, 14]. Internationally collaborated papers (ICPs) of the two most dominant countries in research publication outputs, the USA and China, account for 34.7% and 25.9% respectively of their total publications [13]. ICPs in the top five countries regarding research publications range from 25.9% to 54.7% [13]. Though lower in proportion to domestically collaborated papers (DCPs), ICPs still account for a significant proportion of a country's publication outputs, accounting for at least 20% of a country's scientific publications in general [13].

3.2 Trends in Virtual Reality Interventions for Autistic Individuals

Collaborative research on VR interventions for autistic individuals is not uncommon in this field of science. This is because the design and development of the interventions and research require expertise from different domains, for instance, evidence-based interventions for autistic behaviors, computer programming for VR environments, instructional design with multimedia components. At the same time, the significance of interdisciplinary collaboration in VR-related interventions is continuously realized by the research community. Collaborations among engineering, computer science, new media, arts, education, healthcare, and so forth can be witnessed, both domestically and internationally [15, 16].

Topically, studies on VR interventions for autistic individuals tend to focus on social skills [3, 17, 18]. Besides social skills, VR interventions for autistic individuals have been reported to target independent living skills such as driving skills, job interview skills, safety skills such as pedestrian skills and skills with following road signs [19]. The use of VR games as interventions is also reported as a line of research in the field [19]. Although reviews on VR applications in skill training support for autistic individuals published in empirical studies have been conducted and have made some contributions to the exploration of topical trends, to date, no rich understanding of research trend similarities and differences between DCPs and ICPs have been carried out. Hence, we identify the need for conducting this research to assess this gap.

4   Methodology

The data for this research was drawn from the Web of Science-All Databases (WoS). Cursory searches were conducted on Google Scholar and the WoS, starting with "autism" and "virtual reality". Google Scholar was not used to pull data since Google Scholar does not support data retrieval from their system. The titles, abstracts, and keywords of the returned literature were examined for the nature and variations of the two original keywords. To make sure the research results included all the variations of the two original keywords, we also examined and included keywords used in prior systematic reviews on VR interventions for autistic individuals [20–22]. Table 1 shows the keywords used in the search query.

Our initial search, conducted on July 7th, 2022, by two researchers in the team, identified 1,050 papers published between 1994 and 2021. The dataset included authors, abstract, title, language, and publication type; the dataset was then imported to R Studio [23], where duplicates, blank abstracts, non-English sources, and documents which were not journal publications or conference proceedings were excluded. This reduced the manuscripts to $n = 842$. Titles and abstracts were combined as a new variable and then used for further data selection and for the text mining analysis.

Table 1. Keywords in the search query.

Term one	Term two
Virtual Reality, VR, virtual learning environment, virtual environment, virtual world, 3D virtual world, MUVE, CAVE, head-mounted display	Autism, Asperger, ASD, pervasive developmental disorder, PDD-NOS

To determine which manuscripts were eligible to be used, we developed inclusion and exclusion criteria based on the PICo framework for qualitative studies [24]. For Population (P), manuscripts had to have autistic individuals as the focus of the research and as research participants. Regarding Interest (I), papers had to describe the use of a VR system. For Context (Co), the VR system had to have been used to deliver an intervention for autistic individuals. Two researchers in the team first met and worked together to apply the criteria with the first 10 manuscripts in the dataset. Any discrepancies in the understanding in the criteria were discussed until consensus was reached. After that, the two researchers worked independently to select the papers, and then met to compare and discuss the results. A total of 215 papers published from 1996 to 2021 remained after applying these criteria.

We used R Studio [23] to establish collaboration patterns, and the text mining feature 'word frequencies' for unigram and bigram frequencies in MAXQDA Pro [25] to understand the topical research trends. When using the 'word frequencies' function in MAXQDA, we applied the stop word removal using the built-in standard list of stop words and lemmatization. Words like 'virtual', 'reality', 'autism' were excluded as stop words. We also used the heatmaps by VOSviewer [26] for further understandings of the results from the n-gram analysis.

5 Findings

5.1 Authorship Trends

Papers on VR for autistic individuals are largely the product of collaborations, which is in alignment with the literature [8, 12–14]. Out of 215 papers, 213 (99%) are multiple authored papers and only two papers (1%) are single authored. Of the collaboratively authored papers (n = 213), the number of DCPs is over six times higher than that of ICPs, 183 papers (86%) and 30 papers (14%) respectively. The top 3 countries with collaboratively authored papers are US (n = 100), UK (n = 32), and India (n = 20) (Table 2). For these, ICPs are outnumbered by DCPs. ICPs are 11 papers (11%), 12 papers (37%), and 7 papers (35%) for US, UK, and India respectively.

Collaboration, in general, has increased over time. The first paper in this line of research was a single authored paper, published in 1996. Since then, on average, papers in this line of research have been authored by at least three authors. From 2004 to 2007, the average number of authors per paper ranged from 3 to 3.5. From 2008 to 2021 saw the increase in the average number of authors per article, as compared to 2004 to 2007, with most of the years averaging 5 or more authors per paper (see Fig. 1).

Table 2. Collaborations in the top five countries.

#	Country	Collaboratively authored papers (% of N = 213)	DCPs (% of n)	ICPs (% of n)
1	USA	100 (47%)	89 (89%)	11 (11%)
2	UK	32 (15%)	20 (63%)	12 (37%)
3	India	20 (9%)	13 (65%)	7 (35%)
4	Spain	12 (6%)	10 (83%)	2 (17%)
5	Italy	10 (5%)	8 (80%)	2 (20%)

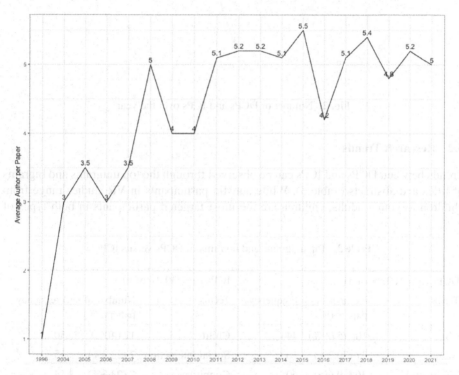

Fig. 1. Average number of authors per paper, by year

Likewise, the trends in publications between domestic and international author teams can be assessed. DCPs take place at a higher rate than ICPs (Fig. 2). Despite the fluctuations in the number of publications over the year, DCPs tend to be on the rise, most notably since 2018. Despite the rise in the number of publications from ICPs since 2015, the number of international publications in this line of research is consistently low over the year.

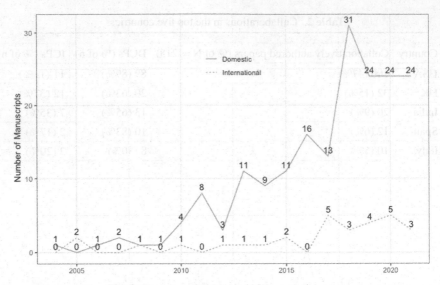

Fig. 2. Number of DCPs and ICPs over the year

5.2 Research Trends

Trends between DCPs and ICPs can be observed through the top unigrams and bigrams of titles and abstracts (Table 3). While autistic participants in VR studies range from children to young adults, children are the most targeted participants in both types of

Table 3. Top unigrams and bigrams in DCPs versus ICPs.

DCPs (n = 183, % of n)			ICPs (n = 30, % of n)		
Terms	Number of papers (%)	Frequency	Terms	Number of papers (%)	Frequency
Child	106 (57.9%)	444	Child	12 (40%)	50
Adult	37 (20.2%)	102	Social interaction	7 (23.3%)	15
Social skill	36 (19.6%)	60	Cognitive	7 (23.3%)	14
Game	33 (18.0%)	107	Adolescent	7 (23.3%)	11
Adolescent	33 (18.0%)	67	Game	6 (20.0%)	20
Social communication	23 (12.6%)	44	Social communication	6 (20.0%)	9
Joint attention	12 (6.6%)	38	Gaze	5 (17.0%)	9
Emotion recognition	10 (5.5%)	15	Attention	4 (13.3%)	14
Drive skill	8 (4.3%)	12	Adult	4 (13.3%)	7
Job interview	7 (3.8%)	33	Emotion	3 (10.0%)	10

collaborations (term: *child*, 58% in DCPs and 40% in ICPs). The clinical focus of the papers in both types of collaboration is on addressing core deficit areas of autistic individuals, which are deficits in communication and problems with social interaction. Social skills received the most attention (e.g., term: *social skill*, 19.6% in DCPs and term: *social interaction*, 23.3% in ICPs). The use of VR-based games to support skill training are also made up of a significant portion of the selected papers in both DCPs and ICPs (i.e., term: *game*, 18.0% in DCPs and 20.0% in ICPs). The differences in research trends between DCPs and ICPs are noticeable in the focus of training skills which can lead to economic autonomy such as job interview skills and adult independent living skills such as driving, which is a trend in DCPs (e.g., term: *drive skill*, 4.3% and term: *job interview*, 3.8%), but not in ICPs.

To have a richer understanding of the research trends between DCPs and ICPs, we also use heatmaps (Figs. 3 and 4) generated by VOSviewer [26]. Clusters of terms in Fig. 3 show that topical trends in DCPs include the use of VR games for improving emotions and interactions for children (terms: *game, child, emotion, interaction*), usability evaluations to gauge cognitive load and eye gaze in VR environments for autistic children (terms: *usability study, cognitive load, eye gaze, child*), VR for learning enhancement in the classroom for autistic children (terms: *child, learning, classroom, attention*), VR to reduce anxiety/phobia for autistic children (terms: *child, anxiety, phobia*), and VR for training independent living skills for autistic young adults (terms: *virtual interview training and transition age groups*). Two observable trends in ICPs include VR for improving social communication skills (term: *social communication skill*) and for enhancing emotion and attention skills for children (term: *emotion, attention, emotion, child*).

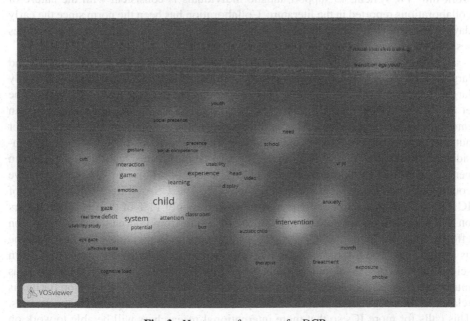

Fig. 3. Heatmap of n-grams for DCPs

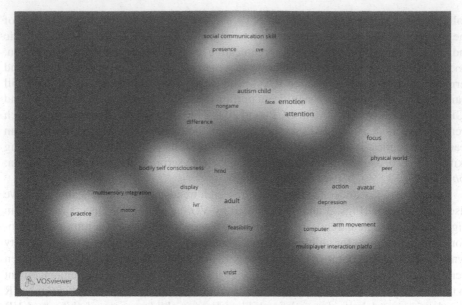

Fig. 4. Heatmap of n-grams for ICPs

6   Discussion, Limitations, and Future Work

The results of our study indicate that in general, domestic and international collaborative work into VR systems to support autistic individuals is consistent with the nature of collaborations reported in the literature. Collaboration has been the norm since the early days of this line of research. The finding in the trend in multiple authored papers echoes results reported in the scientific literature (e.g., [6, 7]).

Specifically, work in VR interventions for autistic individuals is collaborative and largely domestic. Despite the increase in the number of ICPs, DCPs have a considerably larger share and greater momentum. This finding corroborates the finding by Maisonobe et al. [8] that despite globalization, domestic research teams are more common than international research teams. What is interesting is the proportion of ICPs on VR for autistic individuals observed in the top five countries in terms of publications is considerably lower than that of ICPs in the top five countries in scientific publications in general identified in the literature (e.g., [13]). The proportion of ICPs in the top five countries in our study ranges from 11% to 37%. The USA, which has over 34% of IC publications in scientific research in general, has only 11% of their research papers on VR interventions for autistic individuals, resulting from international collaboration efforts. Also, we found the ICPs among the top players in this line of research can be as low as 11%. The disproportion in ICPs of this line of research compared to ICPs in scientific fields in general indicates that ICs in this line of research have not received as much attention as other lines of scientific research. One plausible explanation for this is related to the affordability and availability of VR-based technology in most countries. This calls for more ICs so that more international researchers will be able to work on this topic thanks to the benefits of ICs such as knowledge and resource sharing.

The comparison of DCPs and ICPs shows that scholarly interests in this line of research are comparable, but DCPs have more topical research trends. The target skills in both DCPs and ICPs found in this study are quite like the findings in the literature which show that social and communication skills [3, 17] and games [19] tend to be the focus of research on VR intervention for autistic individuals. Our current study also found that this line of research has focused more on autistic children than on autistic teenagers and autistic young adults as research participants in both DCPs and ICPs. This calls for more collaborative research work in this line of research, domestically and internationally, for a better understanding of how to design VR interventions to support autistic teenagers and young adults, especially when these demographic groups tend to be faced with greater barriers to support services to undertake usually daily activities than autistic children [27]. Also, among the prominent research trends in DCPs is the focus on economic autonomy and independent living skills for young adults, but this trend is not observed in ICPs.

Limitations to the current study include the approach to assembling the corpus. Anecdotally, the way that autistic individuals have been described in the literature has changed rapidly over the years. Even if the terminology surrounding VR has remained relatively constant, being certain of recall as it pertains to papers about work with autistic individuals is less certain. Also, the findings of this study relating to the topical research trends were derived from the title and abstract analysis rather than the full-text analysis. Future research could carry out a full-text analysis for deeper insights of research trends on this topic. This paper also did not explore topical trends in this line of research over time. This is an area future research could investigate as well.

Although it does not pertain to the research questions this paper asks, future research should consider the nature and impact of collaborations in this area in relation to national variations in recognizing needs for support services for autistic individuals [28, 29], misinformation about the disorder [30], and the perspectives of families and autistic individuals themselves towards autism in general and an autism diagnosis [31]. In the corpus under study, out of almost 200 countries in the world, only 31 countries were represented. How can research teams in the countries not represented be enticed to participate in study in this important area of research?

7   Conclusion

Our current study's findings about DC and IC patterns in research on VR interventions to improve the quality of life of autistic individuals are in alignment with findings in other areas of scientific work, implying that this work continues in a standard fashion. We consider such findings are promising. This project likewise considers the topical nature of work to support autistic individuals over the past 20 years and finds that interest on the part of DCs is very similar topically to work done through ICs but more diverse and targeting participants of wider age ranges.

Acknowledgements. We would like to thank Dr. Janine Stichter, a professor in the Department of Special Education and Thompson Center for Autism & Neurodevelopmental Disorders, for her insights of the terminology surrounding autism used in this paper and for proofreading the paper for us.

References

1. American Psychiatric Association: Diagnostic and Statistical Manual of Mental Disorders. 5th ed. American Psychiatric Publishing (2013)
2. Maenner, M.J., et al.: Prevalence and characteristics of autism spectrum disorder among children aged 8 years - autism and developmental disabilities monitoring network, 11 sites, United States 2018. MMWR Surveill. Summ. **70**(11), 1–16 (2021). https://doi.org/10.15585/mmwr.ss7011a1
3. Bellani, M., Fornasari, L., Chittaro, L., Brambilla, P.: Virtual reality in autism: State of the art. Epidemiol. Psychiatr. Sci. **20**(3), 235–238 (2011). https://doi.org/10.1017/S2045796011000448
4. Hardy, C., Ogden, J., Newman, J., Cooper, S.: Autism and ICT: a Guide for Teachers and Parents. Routledge (2016)
5. Chittaro, L., Ranon, R.: Web3D technologies in learning, education and training: Motivations, issues, opportunities. Comput. Educ. **49**(1), 3–18 (2007). https://doi.org/10.1016/j.compedu.2005.06.002
6. Ahn, J., Oh, D.-H., Lee, J.-D.: The scientific impact and partner selection in collaborative research at Korean universities. Scientometrics **100**(1), 173–188 (2013). https://doi.org/10.1007/s11192-013-1201-7
7. Gazni, A., Didegah, F.: Investigating different types of research collaboration and citation impact: a case study of Harvard University's publications. Scientometrics **87**(2), 251–265 (2011). https://doi.org/10.1007/s11192-011-0343-8
8. Maisonobe, M., Eckert, D., Grossetti, M., Jégou, L., Milard, B.: The world network of scientific collaborations between cities: domestic or international dynamics? J. Informet. **10**(4), 1025–1036 (2016). https://doi.org/10.1016/j.joi.2016.06.002
9. Rigby, J., Edler, J.: Peering inside research networks: Some observations on the effect of the intensity of collaboration on the variability of research quality. Res. Policy **34**(6), 784–794 (2005). https://doi.org/10.1016/j.respol.2005.02.004
10. Levitt, J.M., Thewall, M.: Does the higher citation of collaborative research differ from region to region? a case study of economics. Scientometrics **85**(1), 171–183 (2010). https://doi.org/10.1007/s11192-010-0197-5
11. Adams, J.: The fourth age of research. Nature **497**(4751), 557–560 (2013). https://doi.org/10.1038/497557a
12. Coccia, M., Wang, L.: Evolution and convergence of the patterns of international scientific collaboration. Proc. Natl. Acad. Sci. **113**(8), 2057–2061 (2016). https://doi.org/10.1073/pnas.1510820113
13. Zanotto, S.R., Haeffner, C., Guimarães, J.A.: Unbalanced international collaboration affects adversely the usefulness of countries' scientific output as well as their technological and social impact. Scientometrics **109**(3), 1789–1814 (2016). https://doi.org/10.1007/s11192-016-2126-8
14. Nguyen, T.V., Ho-Le, T.P., Le, U.V.: International collaboration in scientific research in Vietnam: an analysis of patterns and impact. Scientometrics **110**(2), 1035–1051 (2016). https://doi.org/10.1007/s11192-016-2201-1
15. Cai, S., Zhang, L., Zuo, W., Feng, X.: A probabilistic collaborative representation-based approach for pattern classification. In: Proceedings of the IEEE Conference on Computer Vision and Pattern Recognition, pp. 2950–2959 (2016)
16. Lorenzo, G., Newbutt, N., Lorenzo-Lledó, A.: Global trends in the application of virtual reality for people with autism spectrum disorders: conceptual, intellectual and the social structure of scientific production. J. Comput. Educ. **9**(2), 225–260 (2022). https://doi.org/10.1007/s40692-021-00202-y

17. Lorenzo, G., Lledó, A., Arráez-Vera, G., Lorenzo-Lledó, A.: The application of immersive virtual reality for students with ASD: a review between 1990–2017. Educ. Inf. Technol. **24**(1), 127–151 (2018). https://doi.org/10.1007/s10639-018-9766-7

18. Parsons, S., Mitchell, P.: The potential of virtual reality in social skills training for people with autistic spectrum disorders: Autism, social skills, and virtual reality. J. Intellect. Disabil. Res. **46**(5), 430–443 (2002). https://doi.org/10.1046/j.1365-2788.2002.00425.x

19. Mak, G., Zhao, L.: A systematic review: the application of virtual reality on the skill-specific performance in people with ASD. Interact. Learn. Environ. 1–14 (2020). https://doi.org/10. 1080/10494820.2020.1811733

20. Glaser, N., Schmidt, M.: Systematic literature review of virtual reality intervention design patterns for individuals with autism spectrum disorders. Int. J. Hum.–Comput. Interact.1–36 (2021). https://doi.org/10.1080/10447318.2021.1970433

21. Karami, B., Koushki, R., Arabgol, F., Rahmani, M., Vahabie, A.: Effectiveness of virtual reality-based therapeutic interventions on individuals with autism spectrum disorder: a comprehensive meta-analysis. Front. Psychiatry (12), 665326. https://doi.org/10.31234/osf.io/ s2jvy

22. Mesa-Gresa, P., Gil-Gómez, H., Lozano-Quilis, J.-A., Gil-Gómez, J.-A.: Effectiveness of virtual reality for children and adolescents with autism spectrum disorder: An evidence-based systematic review. Sensors **18**(8), 2486 (2018). https://doi.org/10.3390/s18082486

23. RStudio Team, RStudio: Integrated development environment for R [Manual] (2020). http:// www.rstudio.com/

24. Butler, A., Hall, H., Copnell, B.: A guide to writing a qualitative systematic review protocol to enhance evidence-based practice in nursing and health care: the qualitative systematic review protocol. Worldviews Evid.-Based Nurs. **13**(3), 241–249 (2016). https://doi.org/10. 1111/wvn.12134

25. VERBI Software: MAXQDA 2022 [computer software]. VERBI Software (2021). maxqda.com

26. van Eck, N.J., Waltman, L.: VOSviewer, a computer program for bibliometric mapping. Leiden University (2018)

27. Miller, I.T., Miller, C.S., Wiederhold, M.D., Wiederhold, B.K.: Virtual Reality air travel training using Apple iPhone X and Google cardboard: a feasibility report with autistic adolescents and adults. Autism adulthood **2**(4), 325–333 (2018)

28. Thoresen, S.H., Fielding, A., Gillieatt, S., Blundell, B., Nguyen, L.: A snapshot of intellectual disabilities in Lao PDR: challenges for the development of services. J. Intellect. Disabil. **21**(3), 203–219 (2017). https://doi.org/10.1177/1744629517704535

29. Kim, S.Y., Cheon, J.E., Gillespie-Lynch, K., Kim, Y.-H.: Is autism stigma higher in South Korea than the United States? examining cultural tightness, intergroup bias, and concerns about heredity as contributors to heightened autism stigma. Autism **26**(2), 460–472 (2022). https://doi.org/10.1177/13623613211029520

30. Yu, L., Stronach, S., Harrison, A.J.: Public knowledge and stigma of autism spectrum disorder: comparing China with the United States. Autism **24**(6), 1531–1545 (2020). https://doi.org/ 10.1177/1362361319900839

31. Smith, I.M., MacDonald, N.E.: Countering evidence denial and the promotion of pseudoscience in autism spectrum disorder: countering evidence denial in ASD. Autism Res. **10**(8), 1334–1337 (2017). https://doi.org/10.1002/aur.1810

Towards a Useful Chinese Annotation Tool: An Examination of Annotators' Practice and Needs

Wenqi Li[1,2] , Tzu-Yi Ho[2] , and Jun Wang[1,2(✉)]

[1] Department of Information Management, Peking University, Beijing 100871, China
junwang@pku.edu.cn
[2] Research Center for Digital Humanities, Peking University, Beijing 100871, China

Abstract. With the rapid development of digital humanities research and the digitization of ancient Chinese books, annotation has become a critical pre-processing activity to extract information for quantitative analysis and to prepare training corpus for natural language processing models. Since manual annotation is a repetitive and time-consuming task that occupies the majority of humanities scholars' time, humanities scholars are looking for tools to facilitate annotation. However, existing tools cannot fulfill the annotation needs of humanities scholars. Few studies have investigated current annotation practices and requirements of humanities scholars, not to mention Chinese annotators. This paper explores Chinese humanities scholars' annotation practice, needs, and expectations of annotation tools based on interviews with 12 participants from different humanities disciplines. The interview transcripts are coded in three steps: open coding, axial coding, and selective coding. Six main categories are identified. We described the analysis results of three categories: annotation practice, feature requirements, and user experience. We further discussed the design implications and requirements of the research environment and the limitations of the work and future work.

Keywords: Digital humanities · User behavior · Text annotation

1 Introduction

Annotation is commonly used in traditional humanities studies to facilitate close reading and text interpretation [1]. It is one of the "scholarly primitives" of humanities research [2]. For Chinese humanities scholars, especially those dealing with ancient Chinese texts, annotation has always been an essential yet time-consuming part of their research. Annotations used to be conducted on printed books or text editors. Most often, the annotations serve as notes for subsequent interpretation and writing. Still, they can expand to more formulaic tasks, including punctuation, named entity annotation, part-of-speech, syntactic structure, and so on.

I. Sserwanga et al. (Eds.): iConference 2023, LNCS 13972, pp. 326–340, 2023.
https://doi.org/10.1007/978-3-031-28032-0_27

Annotation tasks vary by discipline. For example, history studies rely on named entity annotation to extract persons, relations, time, and location of events. Meanwhile, linguistic studies focus more on lexical and grammar-level annotation, such as part-of-speech tagging. Annotation needs are also determined by language. Chinese annotation differs from English in that there are more complex semantics and a lack of linguistic norms. These annotations are fundamental to ancient book collation and quantitative linguistic or history studies.

With the thriving of digital humanities and the growing digitization of ancient Chinese books, it is now possible to leverage computational methods for book collation and large-scale text analysis. In this case, annotation has also become a foundational pre-processing activity to extract information for quantitative analysis and to prepare training corpora for natural language processing models. Annotation tools are needed to increase their productivity and transform the annotated texts into machine-operable data that can be retrieved, calculated, and used for algorithms.

Many annotation tools with different functions and user interfaces are developed to support annotation [3–5], but most are too complicated for users of humanities background. While most annotation tools are built for corpora of English, only a few tools are designed for Chinese annotators, especially ancient Chinese, such as Markus [6] and LoGaRT [7]. Yet these tools are specific to entity annotation tasks and need improvement in user experience. It is imperative to design and develop an annotation tool that takes into consideration both Chinese annotation tasks and annotators' habits and needs. Yet few studies have focused on how humanities scholars annotate and what kind of tools they need, not to mention Chinese annotators' practice and needs.

Therefore, this study is aimed at exploring the following research questions:

1. What are the annotation tasks and needs of Chinese humanities scholars?
2. What are the desired features of an annotation tool for Chinese humanities scholars?

2 Related Works

There is an abundance of annotation tools. Neves and Sava [8] built a directory of 93 annotation tools and set 31 criteria to help annotators choose the most suitable tool. We surveyed the annotation tools in this directory and selected eight tools to test out in depth. The selection criteria include continuous updates, the activity of online communities, detailed documentation, and functionalities. The selected tools are YEDDA, WebAnno, Brat, FoLia, Catma, Tagtog, LoGaRT, and Markus. Their annotation features, supporting features, and configuration requirements were examined and compared. One of the issues with these tools is that the installation is too complicated. Some of the powerful tools need users to download the installation package first and then setup with a specific programming language [4, 9], which could be intimidating for humanities scholars with limited technical skills. Various annotation tasks are supported by different tools, such as generating dependency syntax trees [9] and metadata annotation [10]. Other desired supporting features include but are not limited to collaborative proofreading [3, 4], shortcuts customization [3], and visual display of multi-level annotation [5].

Although some of the tools support Chinese annotation [3–5, 9], they are not intended and designed towards it. Chinese annotation differs from English annotation in that there are no explicit word boundaries, and most of the ancient texts are not punctuated [11]. The biggest drawback of these tools is the auto-annotation accuracy in Chinese, while auto-annotation is one of the most important features that appeal to humanities scholars. There are two annotation tools designed specifically for Chinese annotators – Markus [6] and LoGaRt [7]. Their annotation features are not as powerful, but they are both interfaced with critical Chinese resources, such as the China Biographical Database (CBDB) [12] and Chinese local gazetteer collections, either to work with or refer to. The design of these annotation tools can give us a preliminary understanding of the common annotation tasks and features. Yet none of the tools mentioned thorough user studies, not to mention the practice and needs of Chinese annotators.

As technologies have profoundly impacted humanities research, scholars expressed their need for better tools for text analysis as well as annotation standards [13]. Despite the many tools and digital humanities platforms available, the adoption and satisfaction rate is not ideal due to the high learning curve and complex user interfaces, which roots in a lack of understanding of user behaviors and requirements [14]. Studies have emerged to design digital humanities platforms and tools for Chinese documents and users [15–17]. But few studies have dug into users' needs. Given and Wilson recently documented the behaviors and needs of humanities scholars in performing digital humanities research in general and pointed out the importance of flexibility of digital tools, including choosing data to input and manipulating outputs [18]. Annotation is an important work in digital humanities and can be very complicated depending on scholars' research objectives. A more focused examination of scholars' annotation practice and needs is necessary.

3   Methods

3.1   Data Collection

The study adopted a qualitative methodology to explore the annotation behaviors and needs of humanities scholars working with Chinese texts ("annotators" hereafter). Data were collected mainly through semi-structured interviews. We first got a preliminary understanding of humanities annotation by investigating existing annotation tools and relevant literature to develop the interview script. We employed purposive sampling to cover typical areas of study so that all types of annotation tasks can be considered. A total of 12 participants were recruited for interviews through referrals and snowball sampling, including four faculty members, one postdoc, five Ph.D. students, and two Master's students. Their areas of study covered ancient Chinese philosophy, history, literature, historical geography, and linguistics (see Table 1). The first four interviews were conducted by the first two authors together to ask questions from different perspectives. Most interviews (11) were conducted face-to-face and one interview was conducted online due to geographic limitations. The average length of the interviews is one hour. The interviews were recorded and transcribed for data analysis. We also collected their annotation work artifacts, such as Word documents, Excel spreadsheets, and screenshots of annotation tools, to triangulate and get a better picture of their actual annotation work [19]. The data collection stopped as no more new categories on annotation practice, feature requirements, and user experience, which are the core concerns of the current study, emerged in the coding process.

Table 1. Participants in the semi-structured interviews

Participant no.	Title	Area of study
1	Ph.D. student	History
2	Professor	Linguistics
3	Professor	Historical geography
4	Assistant professor	Philosophy
5	Professor	Linguistics
6	Post-doc	Linguistics
7	Ph.D. student	Historical geography
8	Ph.D. student	Literature
9	Ph.D. student	History
10	Ph.D. student	Literature
11	Master's student	History
12	Master's student	Literature

3.2 Data Analysis

The data was coded and analyzed inductively guided by existing literature and platform features. We adopted the three-step coding procedure that includes open coding, axial coding, and selective coding [20, 21]. The first two authors, both experienced in product design and participated in digital humanities projects, employed in-vivo coding to code three of the interview transcripts separately and discussed the coding process together to rule out bias in promoting validity. The second author then finished the rest of the open coding process. The codes were then formed into 14 sub-categories and 6 categories in the axial coding process. The categories include discipline characteristics, perceptions of technologies, annotation practices, feature requirements, user experience, and research environment (see Table 2).

In the selective coding stage, we established theoretical connections between the six categories. Discipline characteristics and annotators' perceptions of technologies are related to their disciplinary background and determine their annotation practice, including annotation tasks and needs, which further inform the design of annotation tools. To better support their annotation practice, the annotation tool needs to provide desirable features to guarantee utility as well as user experience. Meanwhile, research environment is the cornerstone of all these aspects. It shapes the discipline characteristics, technology perceptions, and annotation practice subliminally, and the annotation tool design should also consider the research environment. On the other hand, understanding annotation practice can also provide insights into constructing the research environment (see Fig. 1).

Table 2. Axial coding results

Category	Sub-categories	Example codes
Discipline characteristics	Disciplinary research culture	Primary sources, domain literacy, independent research, slow adaptation to technologies
	Linguistic features of Chinese	Semantic complexity, diverse writing style, temporal contexts, character evolvement
	Paradigm debates	Value of digital humanities, cautious about statistics
Perception on technologies	Perceived value	Reduce workload, convenience, scalability
	Perceived risks & doubt	Low accuracy, black box, poor usability, limited intelligence
Annotation practice	Annotation tasks	POS tagging, syntax analysis, semantics annotation, annotation hierarchy, pre-processing, machine annotation
	Current workarounds	Text editor, structured spreadsheet, existing annotation tools, collaboration mechanism
Feature requirements	Annotation features	Auto-annotation, disambiguation, draw relations, customize tag-sets
	Supporting features	Text import, embedded thesaurus, data export, search, basic statistics
	Collaboration & crowdsourcing	Proofreading mechanism, user management, crowdsourcing quality control, modification tracing
User experience	Flexibility	Compatible formats, reusable tags, interface with other platforms
	Usability	Efficiency, interaction complexity, ease of use, learning curve

(*continued*)

Table 2. (*continued*)

Category	Sub-categories	Example codes
Research environment	Databases & platforms	CBDB, digital humanities platforms, high-quality database
	Standard & regulations	Annotation standard, copyright protection

In this paper, we focus on the descriptive analysis of annotation practices, feature requirements, and user experience so as to fill in the gap and inform the design of annotation tools. The connections and causal relationships with other categories will also be mentioned as needed.

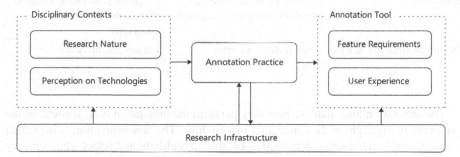

Fig. 1. Selective coding - Theoretical connections of the code categories

4 Findings

4.1 Annotation Practice

Participants have their own expressions on what they annotate. Linguistic annotators use more concrete concepts to describe their tasks, such as part-of-speech tagging and constituent parsing for syntax analysis. Meanwhile, annotators in history may just view their task as "event annotation" instead of articulating them as semantics annotation or decompose it as named entity and relation annotation. For annotators dealing with multiple types of tasks, the tasks are inherently hierarchical, from the phonetic of a character, the lexical category of a word, the grammar of a sentence, and the content of a paragraph to the structure and style of the whole document. We refer to an existing annotation type system in the natural language processing realm [22] to summarize and make uniform the annotation task types participants mentioned (see Table 3). In addition to these tasks, punctuation annotation is unique to ancient Chinese texts which are usually not punctuated, and it's also a foundational task that help scholars to understand the texts. Among all the task types, semantic annotation is the most common task. It includes named entities, domain entities, entity relationships and attributes. Linguistic annotators deal with the most complex annotation tasks, while history and philosophy annotators mainly focus on semantic annotation.

Table 3. The hierarchical annotation tasks

Annotation tasks	Annotation unit	Areas of study
Punctuation	Position	Linguistics, literature, history, philosophy
Phonetics	Character	Linguistics
Part-of-speech	Character, word	Linguistics
Syntax	Character, word, phrase, position, relation	Linguistics, literature
Semantics	Character, word, phrase, relation, sentence, paragraph	Linguistics, literature, history, philosophy, historical geography
Document structure & style	Paragraph, document metadata	Linguistics, literature

The annotation units indicate how they perform the annotation task. It could be the text chunk to highlight or the connection line to draw. The annotation unit is important to tool design because annotators need to be able to highlight and select whatever they want to put tags on. For linguistic annotators, the annotation unit is usually a word, a phrase, or a character, especially in Chinese. And in semantic annotation, named entities like time, location, person, and official positions are the most frequently used annotation units, while phrases sentences, or paragraphs can also be the target units. For example, historical geography annotators mentioned, "We sometimes need to read through the whole paragraph to determine the disaster's severity to tag." The position is used in cases where the target is omitted, especially in the case of zero anaphora. The relation is annotated for dependency syntax parsing, such as subject-predicate relation, verb-object relation, and prepositional object, or semantic relations like governance relations and temporal roles. As for the document level, the text genre, version, and paragraph structures are usually annotated, and the annotation unit is a paragraph or can directly be reflected as document metadata.

Despite their willingness of adopting annotation tools, none of them have found the perfect tool to use and some of them stopped considering tools after a bad experience on the first attempt. The main reason is that the tools can't support their annotation tasks, such as selecting a position to annotate. Other drawbacks include the difficulty of installation, poor learnability, and inefficiency. Currently, Word documents and Excel spreadsheets are the most used workarounds, as the former gives them the flexibility to select any annotation unit, and the latter enables them to establish relationships and yields structured data for further analysis. Some of the annotators mentioned if there were tools to be used in the future, they would like their existing annotations in Word documents or text editors to be ingested as well.

4.2 Feature Requirements

Annotation Features. According to our participants, the annotation features most in need are tag set customization, auto-annotation, and entity disambiguation and resolution.

Tag Set Customization. Tag sets are closely related to annotation tasks and should be defined by annotators according to their research objectives. for POS tagging and syntax tagging, the tags may be virtually the same, but annotators still want to be able to adjust the tags freely, especially for semantic annotation where domain entities and attributes are very specific. For example, one participant commented on an annotated Chinese corpus, "the tag set they designed is too ambitious. You could tell they put lots of thoughts into trying to incorporate all the possible elements into the system. But it really depends on the contexts, whether you want to dig deep into the linguistic inquiry. for me, entities like person, location, and book titles are enough. it could be painful if you have to choose among a bunch of tags you don't need in the first place." Another participant also described the complexity of the semantic annotation, "events are complicated. The attributes of a disaster event are not limited to time and location, there are type, severity, damage, and scope of influence. And there are logistical relations to deal with. I'M not sure any tools can support such a complex tag set." Another reason that annotators are used to customizing tag sets is the lack of standards, which is also very important for building machine learning corpus and collaboration. Tags of basic linguistic elements and named entities should be uniform across tools so that annotators can migrate and integrate annotated data easily. Such a set of Chinese annotation standards is a vital part of the research environment and would require the collective wisdom of scholars across disciplines.

Auto-annotation. Participants have a love-hate feeling for auto-annotation. on the one hand, they would like to leave the preliminary annotations for machines to handle – "I just want the simple things automatically marked out for me, like all the places and persons. And then I only need to do the brain work instead of wasting time on the repetitive labor." On the other hand, they cannot fully trust the machine – "I know it is easy for the machine to extract the information, but the extraction process needs judgment sometimes. And I Don't know if the people who wrote the algorithm have enough domain knowledge and humanities background. If I have to go over all the annotations for accuracy check, then it is still time-consuming. "They expect the auto-annotation can be an iterative human-machine collaborative process. The machine can pre-annotate first, then while annotators modify the pre-annotation results, the machine can actively absorb and learn from the modifications to optimize its algorithm. "When I made some adjustments, theoretically this machine can also know what adjustments i have made...the machine will learn instantly and can give me some suggestions, and then i can edit on top of it. it is a constant learning process." They also prefer that the machine can provide a confidence level on the annotation so that annotators can set a threshold and identify the annotations that need to be checked manually.

Entity Disambiguation and Resolution. In the most common named entity annotation tasks, different words can refer to the same entity (entity resolution), or identical words can refer to different entities according to the contexts (entity disambiguation). To address these issues, the annotation tool should provide a unique id to each entity, so that an index of entities can be generated for future information retrieval and statistics. "For example, Mengde is the Alias of Cao Cao. If we only annotate both of them as a person without assigning them the same id, how can we include mengde when counting the number of times the person cao cao is mentioned in the texts?" also, participants mentioned that the id should be uniform across documents and even across platforms. Yet There's a lack of a universal entity library or thesaurus to refer to. "Markus is embedded with some reference books and databases that provide ids for entities, such as CBDB for person IDs. It is a good start but far from enough, because CBDB is not a database dedicated to recording persons, instead it's for relationships." Standardized entity libraries, dictionaries, or thesauri are also much-needed parts of the research environment development.

Supporting Features. The supporting features include pre-annotation features and post-annotation features.

Pre-annotation Features. Pre-processing is needed before annotation including text conversion and auto-punctuation. Most annotation tools require users to upload text documents to annotate or paste texts directly. But text formats are not always available. "The majority of our research materials are not even in text formats. There are lots of scanned pdf documents and images. None of the tools can handle these annotations. "OCR is the most preliminary function for these documents to be converted into operable texts. Annotators sometimes use open-source OCR tools for pre-processing, yet the accuracy of the recognition result is not ideal. "If the image is blurry, slanted, or crooked, the recognition result is not something you can count on. But the fundamental issue is that the OCR technology is not there yet. "Auto-punctuation is important for ancient Chinese texts where no punctuation is used for sentence breaks. Despite the pretty high accuracy of auto-identified sentence breaks, some annotators majoring in ancient text collation and linguistics still want to be able to modify or directly upload their own punctuated version. "The Texts I use to annotate are all punctuated according to my own interpretation. I Don't want to use just someone else's version, but a mixture of a well-collated version and my own. it is the best version in my view. "Nevertheless, some annotators think punctuation doesn't need to be one hundred percent accurate, as long as it can help understand the text. Another pre-annotation feature is to provide an overview of the texts, such as a comparison of different versions and distant reading [23]. "Maybe the tool can provide a rough preview of the texts like the keyword distribution so that I would know which chapters I should focus on first. I think LoGaRt has such features".

Post-annotation Features. The final goal of annotation is to prepare inter-operable data for digital humanities analysis and machine learning. analysis, search, and statistics are the basic need. In terms of search, what they need is not only keyword search, but instead, they want entity search which relies on entity resolution. Linguistics would also want to search by syntax rules. "I want to figure out how many times the character "Zhi" is preceded by a noun or adjective, so i need to search for these two conditions first." It would be useful if the tool can offer a customized and easy-to-understand query builder. statistics can be as simple as tag frequencies. Annotators view these as "Nice to Have" Features for an annotation platform. "at the end of the day, you'll take the data to whichever analysis tool that you normally use. For me, I just need an excel spreadsheet that i can upload to ArcGIS. This depends on scholars' discipline…but i think it is still very convenient if some preliminary analysis can be provided, like a one-stop service" Therefore, exporting the data in formats compatible with various analysis tools is very important.

Collaboration and Crowdsourcing. Many humanities scholars tend to do research alone [24]. Yet in digital humanities projects, it is necessary to collaborate with others to deal with large-scale texts. "Mostly I work alone, and so are my students. but in this zero-anaphora annotation project, I needed to collaborate with two of my colleagues. We spent over two years and annotated more than 10,000 cases. You Can't imagine how long it would take if i were to do this alone. "However, participants may still prefer to annotate independently due to concerns of collaboration, even if it took them much more time. "I did this by myself because I was afraid that multiple people working together may mess up. of course, It would be much better if multiple people can annotate simultaneously because the annotation workload in such a text analysis project is huge. It took me three months to get it done by myself. "The concerns do exist as confirmed by the seven participants who had collaboration experience. major issues include modification tracking, user management, and quality control, and most people are still using traditional workarounds since there are no suitable collaboration platforms.

First of all, being able to track contributions and editions made by each collaborator is important, especially when proofreaders find disagreements and make modifications. "We used to use the online collaboration platform Shimo. But we found that it doesn't support tracing back, so we switched back to Excel. For example, if a student overwrites another's annotations during proofreading on Shimo, it doesn't leave modification traces. Yet the disagreements may reflect very interesting research questions. And the process of resolving disagreements is actually a manifestation of academic discussion." Second, user management is critical for large-scale collaborative projects, especially for those building corpora and databases or crowdsourced projects. Participants mentioned that "a rigorous user management system is the basic guarantee of high-quality annotation." The tool should support the project owner to create multiple roles with different levels of permissions, such as contributor and proofreader. Then these roles and tasks can be assigned to fellow annotators. Being able to track user contributions is also important for principal investigators to evaluate the collaborators' work. Third, features to assist quality control are needed. Participants suggested that the best way to ensure quality is for multiple people to work on the same tasks and then compare the results to resolve disagreements. In this case, automatic result comparison is useful in efficiently revealing the issues. Yet for projects with limited annotators, a proofreading mechanism is often used instead. Designated proofreaders review contributors' annotations and make modifications, and the principal investigator may conduct a final spot check. In this case, features to facilitate the exchange of information among annotators are needed, such as easy commenting and modification tracing. This is especially important if collaboration occurs online. "We used to sit together to do this so that we can discuss whenever needed. Due to the Covid pandemic, the exchange of ideas doesn't come naturally anymore. Remote collaboration is difficult."

None of the participants have participated in or initiated crowdsourcing projects for annotation. Most of them are worried about crowd annotators' expertise. For easier tasks like named entity annotation or POS tagging, it is easier to recruit crowd annotators. But other tasks demand higher levels of domain knowledge. "The work we do requires domain knowledge. At least you need to have a history background, and geographic knowledge is also required sometimes. I don't think we can recruit the right annotators by crowdsourcing." This also makes them doubt whether crowdsourced projects can be trusted. "If some database is annotated by crowdsourcing, I would definitely question its reliability. If it's a renowned project, maybe I can trust its operating mechanism knowing that it has been verified by peers." Therefore, if the annotation tool were to be designed for crowdsourcing, the examination of annotators' qualifications and the quality check mechanism need to be considered.

4.3 User Experience

Usability. Usability requirements mentioned by participants include ease of use and efficiency. Ease of use is a decisive factor in whether annotators will adopt the tool. For annotators working with traditional workarounds like word and excel, lack of error prevention is the main issue. THEre's a greater chance of typos as everything is entered manually. As much as they would like to try new tools, they find existing tools hard to learn and too complicated to use. Several participants have tried existing annotation tools and gave up eventually either due to the long learning curve or the complex interfaces. "I'M Not good with technical stuff. It takes time to learn. once you learned, there may be a great chance that IT's not useful at all. So why bother?" "the whole process from importing texts to annotating is very complicated. I'D rather do it manually." detailed user manuals should be provided to ease the learning phase. intuitive user interfaces should be designed to simplify the annotation process instead of burdening annotators.

On the other hand, efficiency is the factor that affects annotators' retention. To improve efficiency, shortcuts are must-haves according to almost all the participants. The shortcuts should be intuitive, universal, and customizable. The tools should also allow annotators to save shortcuts, tag sets, and other configurations to apply to future projects to minimize repetitive work. "Once I have the project all set up, I'd like to reuse it in other projects, like the color of tags because the text to be annotated may be different, yet the projects may probably head in a similar direction. Or you can offer a file management system to have different files managed in the same configuration, that way I can also merge the results easily as everything is consistent." Another way to improve efficiency is batch annotation or modification, which is especially useful when they want to make changes to auto-annotation results, conduct entity disambiguation or resolution or make modifications during proofreading. But batch modification needs to be done cautiously. Contexts need to be provided for every item to be annotated or modified for double check. "For example, Cao Cao is a person, but Cao Cao Zhuan (Cao Cao's Biography) is a book. It's all about the contexts."

Flexibility. The participants hope that the tool can interface with some common databases and tools, including but not limited to CBDB, CBeta, ArcGis, and CHGIS. They also acknowledged that copyright needs to be resolved first. While such bilateral cooperation with other platforms is difficult to achieve, being able to import and export data in a variety of common formats is crucial. particularly, they would like to directly export data in formats compatible with their analysis tools. Not only the formats should be compatible, but also the tags should be able to be used by other annotators working on other tools so that the annotated data can be well integrated for the greater good. This again relies on annotation standards to be established as part of the research environment. The standard should cover as many annotation tasks as possible. Meanwhile, it should be extensible so that different disciplines can build their domain standards upon it. The ability to customize the tag sets, shortcuts and other configurations contribute to the flexibility. Annotators also want to have control over the dictionary or thesaurus used for the auto-annotation. overall, annotators' needs, and expectations of the annotation tool are determined by their discipline characteristics and specific annotation tasks. providing extensibility and customization can give annotators the flexibility they need.

5 Discussion

The study contributes theoretically by summarizing different types of annotation tasks and their current workarounds. This adds to existing literature, where only specific tasks concerning the authors' areas of study are examined [11, 25], by providing a holistic understanding of the annotation practice of Chinese humanities scholars across disciplines. The annotation tasks are hierarchical and include annotation of punctuation, phonetics, part-of-speech, syntax, semantics, and document structure and style. The hierarchy also manifests in the annotation units, ranging from characters, words, positions, phrases, sentences, and paragraphs, to documents. Annotation tools should support cross-hierarchy annotations and a flexible selection of annotation units. The tasks also vary by discipline, where linguistic scholars are faced with the most diverse and especially granular tasks, while scholars in history and philosophy are more concerned with entity annotation. Although we didn't discuss it in-depth in this paper, the theoretical coding result suggests that discipline characteristics, scholars' perceptions of technologies, and the research environment all have potential impacts on the annotation practice and the design of annotation tools. These theoretical relations are interesting topics to be explored in the future.

The study also provides practical design implications for annotation tools. The desired features can be wrapped up in an annotation workflow. First of all, the tool should allow users to import various file formats other than a text file, meanwhile, provide pre-processing features such as OCR and auto-punctuation so that documents of various formats can be converted to readable texts. Then the tool should enable users to define their own tag set while providing universal annotation standards to be based on so that the annotated data is interoperable. Next, the tool should be able to automatically annotate for the user based on an embedded dictionary or trained algorithms. As users modify the auto-annotated results, the tool should learn and adjust the algorithm accordingly. When users annotate manually, the tool should enable them to annotate with customized shortcuts and perform batch modifications. Particularly, the tool should support assigning IDs for entities for disambiguation and resolution. The IDs can be assigned by users or integrated from existing databases. After the annotation, the tool should allow users to search either by keywords or entity. Basic statistics can be provided for preliminary distant reading. For users who prefer to perform further analysis or use the annotated data for machine learning. The tool should allow them to export the data in compatible formats. This concludes the whole annotation work cycle. Moreover, to support the annotators who need to collaborate with others or crowdsource their tasks, it is necessary to further implement a robust user management system, modification tracking, and quality control assistance such as result comparison. Many features stated above contribute to the usability and flexibility of the tool, which are the two most valued aspects of user experience.

Nevertheless, these tool features need to be built upon some critical research environment, which has a long way to go and demands far more dedication. First, a set of Chinese annotation standards need to be established based on the linguistics characteristics as well as scholars' needs. There are already some specific annotation schemes designed for modern Chinese linguistics, such as [25, 26]. The new standard should consider ancient Chinese and try to incorporate existing ones so that existing data can be integrated or migrated easily. Second, databases, dictionaries, or thesaurus are needed for training auto-annotation algorithms and entity disambiguation and resolution. Copyright and technical issues should be resolved for direct use. Furthermore, to acknowledge the efforts of annotating the data and building databases, a sound data property protection system should be established to regulate data citation and attribution.

The goal of the paper is to provide a preliminary understanding of Chinese scholars' annotation practice and needs and provide insights into the design of Chinese annotation tools. We interviewed scholars with diverse academic backgrounds. As shown in the study, different research disciplines are faced with different annotation tasks, and their expectation of the annotation tool could also vary by their disciplinary research culture and their perceptions of technologies. As the study findings are based on a limited number of participants, we may not be able to cover all kinds of annotation practices and requirements. In this paper, we mainly focused on the common aspects of the practice and needs, while the differences and comparisons across disciplines were not covered in the current scope. Thus, the design implications are more focused on generally applicable features. More in-depth investigations of these differences are needed to make the tool more flexible and usable – to provide features supporting specific disciplinary annotation tasks and be able to customize according to personal habits. Future research can perform usability studies or experiments on existing tools or newly designed tools to collect observational or quantitative data on the topic. Moreover, the design implications are derived from interviews with Chinese annotators and thus are intended to inform the design of Chinese annotation tools for humanities scholars. Whether the implications can be extended to the annotation tool of other languages and other research disciplines are to be further validated.

Acknowledgment. The authors thank the reviewers for their valuable feedback. This work is supported by the National Natural Science Foundation of China (Grant No. 72010107003).

References

1. Porter-O'Donnell, C.: Beyond the yellow highlighter: teaching annotation skills to improve reading comprehension. English J. **93**, 82–89 (2004). https://doi.org/10.2307/4128941
2. Unsworth, J.: Scholarly primitives: what methods do humanities researchers have in common, and how might our tools reflect this. In: Symposium on Humanities Computing: Formal Methods, Experimental Practice. King's College, London (2000)
3. Yang, J., Zhang, Y., Li, L., Li, X.: YEDDA: a lightweight collaborative text span annotation tool. arXiv:1711.03759 [cs] (2018)
4. Yimam, S.M., Gurevych, I., Eckart de Castilho, R., Biemann, C.: WebAnno: a flexible, web-based and visually supported system for distributed annotations. In: Proceedings of the 51st Annual Meeting of the Association for Computational Linguistics: System Demonstrations. pp. 1–6. Association for Computational Linguistics, Sofia, Bulgaria (2013)
5. Stenetorp, P., Pyysalo, S., Topić, G., Ohta, T., Ananiadou, S., Tsujii, J.: BRAT: a web-based tool for NLP-assisted text annotation. In: Proceedings of the Demonstrations at the 13th Conference of the European Chapter of the Association for Computational Linguistics, pp. 102–107. Association for Computational Linguistics, Avignon, France (2012)
6. Ho, Brent, H.I., De Weerdt, H.: MARKUS - text analysis and reading platform. http://dh.chinese-empires.eu/beta/. Accessed 15 Aug 2022
7. Chen, S.-P., Yeh, C., Che, Q., Wang, S.: LoGaRT: local gazetteers research tools (software). https://www.mpiwg-berlin.mpg.de/research/projects/logart-local-gazetteers-research-tools. Accessed 15 Aug 2022
8. Neves, M., Seva, J.: Annotationsaurus: a searchable directory of annotation tools. arXiv:2010.06251 [cs] (2020)
9. Van Gompel, M., Başar, E., Neumann, A., Van Der Klis, M.: Proycon/flat: v0.11. https://zenodo.org/record/6567192 (2022). https://doi.org/10.5281/ZENODO.6567192
10. Gius, E.,et al.: CATMA. https://zenodo.org/record/1470118 (2022). https://doi.org/10.5281/ZENODO.1470118
11. Bin, L., Lu, W., Xiaohe, C., Dongbo, W.: Digital humanity based ancient text annotation and visualization – a case study on Zuozhuan knowledgebase. J. Acad. Lib. **38**, 70–80 (2020)
12. Harvard University, Academia Sinica, Peking University: China Biographical Database Project (CBDB). https://projects.iq.harvard.edu/cbdb/home. Accessed 25 Aug 2022
13. Toms, E.G., O'Brien, H.L.: Understanding the information and communication technology needs of the e-humanist. J. Documentation. **64**, 102–130 (2008). https://doi.org/10.1108/00220410810844178
14. Gibbs, F., Owens, T.: Building Better Digital Humanities Tools: Toward broader audiences and user-centered designs. DHQ. 006 (2012)
15. Gao, D., He, L., Liu, J., Li, Z.: Construction over operation? a study of the usage of digital humanities databases in China. Aslib J. Inf. Manag. **74**, 1–18 (2021). https://doi.org/10.1108/AJIM-03-2021-0087
16. Chen, C.-M., Chang, C., Chen, Y.-T.: A character social network relationship map tool to facilitate digital humanities research. Library Hi Tech. ahead-of-print (2021). https://doi.org/10.1108/LHT-08-2020-0194
17. Cuijuan, X., Lihua, W., Wei, L.: Shanghai memory as a digital humanities platform to rebuild the history of the city. Dig. Sch. Humanit.. **36**, 841–857 (2021). https://doi.org/10.1093/llc/fqab023
18. Given, L.M., Willson, R.: Information technology and the humanities scholar: documenting digital research practices. J. Am. Soc. Inf. Sci. **69**, 807–819 (2018)
19. Pickard, A.J.: Research Methods in Information. Facet Publishing, London (2013)

20. Corbin, J., Strauss, A.: Basics of Qualitative Research: Techniques and Procedures for Developing Grounded Theory. SAGE Publications (2014)

21. Matthew, B., Miles, A., Huberman, M., Saldana, J.: Qualitative Data Analysis: A Methods Sourcebook. SAGE Publications, Inc. (2014)

22. Hahn, U., et al.: An annotation type system for a data-driven NLP pipeline. In: Proceedings of the Linguistic Annotation Workshop. pp. 33–40. Association for Computational Linguistics, Prague, Czech Republic (2007)

23. Moretti, F.: Graphs, Maps, Trees: Abstract Models for a Literary History. Verso (2005)

24. Stone, S.: Humanities scholars: information needs and uses. J. Documentation **38**, 292–313 (1982)

25. Zhou, Q.: Annotation scheme for Chinese treebank (in Chinese). J. Chin. Inf. Process., 1–8 (2004)

26. Academia Sinica: Academia Sincia Balanced Corpus of Modern Chinese. http://asbc.iis.sinica.edu.tw/. Accessed 29 Aug 2022

Information Retrieval

Similarity Visualizer Using Natural Language Processing in Academic Documents of the DSpace in Ecuador

Diego Vallejo-Huanga[1]([✉]) [iD], Janneth Jaime[2], and Carlos Andrade[2]

[1] Universidad Politécnica Salesiana, IDEIAGEOCA Research Group, Quito, Ecuador
dvallejoh@ups.edu.ec
[2] Universidad Politécnica Salesiana, Department of Computer Science,
Quito, Ecuador
{ljaimep,candradev5}@est.ups.edu.ec

Abstract. Due to the widespread use of the Internet, users have the ease of accessing collections of university academic documents stored in virtual libraries whose information is of an unstructured type. In recent years, the production and publication of scientific documents in Ecuador have increased considerably, so the search and classification of documents is a fundamental task within information retrieval computer systems. Intelligent search systems allow found information with a high degree of accuracy and similarity. For the development of this project, academic documents from the Ecuador Network of Open Access Repositories (RRAAE) were retrieved using a glossary of terms in the area of science and technology. For the recovery of documents, the web scraping technique was used and its results were stored in a cloud database in JSON format. In the recovered documents, NLP techniques were applied to clean and homogenize the unstructured information. Two similarity metrics were used to measure the divergence between the retrieved documents, and similarity matrices were generated based on the title, keywords, and abstract, which were then unified into a weighted matrix. The results of the system are displayed in a web interface that, through the use of graphs, shows the relationship between the linked documents. The operation of the similarity system was validated through functional tests through experimentation with a collection of 30 queries with indexed and non-indexed terms in the input of the information retrieval system. The experiments showed that for indexed terms, the system performs better.

Keywords: Vector cosine similarity · Web scraping · Connected papers · Jaccard · Artificial intelligence · University repositories · DSpace · Graphs

1 Introduction

During the last years, the volumes of information have grown due to the appearance of new technologies [25], which allow the user to access a large collection of documents through simplified search strings. The largest amount of information

© The Author(s), under exclusive license to Springer Nature Switzerland AG 2023
I. Sserwanga et al. (Eds.): iConference 2023, LNCS 13972, pp. 343–359, 2023.
https://doi.org/10.1007/978-3-031-28032-0_28

disseminated in the network is of unstructured type [32], therefore, it is necessary to have intelligent search systems that allow finding correlated information, with a high degree of accuracy and similarity.

In generic form, similarity can be defined as the correlation between two or more objects in which common features can be found [18]. In computer science, a similarity metric is used as a measure of divergence between various instances [27]. Thus, several concepts in the field of Artificial Intelligence (AI) and Machine Learning (ML) incorporate this notion to be able to find patterns in various datasets that allow the prediction to be executed between two or more objects [15]. Natural Language Processing (NLP) is a subdiscipline of ML that combines computational linguistics using rule-based models, statistical models, and deep learning. [24]. NLP has made it possible to improve search systems, due to their inherent ability to assimilate the human colloquial language, allowing Information Retrieval (IR) systems to have more accurate results [5,16,22,35].

The massive use of the Internet meant that many collections of documents were published in digital format to facilitate their search. A survey conducted by Deloitte in 2019, evaluated 12 institutions in the United States and Canada on issues related to the adoption of AI as a service tool in social welfare. [6]. The results show that it exists an 80% of unstructured texts, which are the most significant standardized, generating a greater disorganization of information and difficulties in the search, collection, and analysis of textual data [1,10]. In this context, the International Federation of Library Associations (IFLA) [12] proposes to implement ML algorithms to improve document retrieval, with the aim of automating content classification using NLP.

Within the report carried out by Deloitte for Latin America, a comprehensive panorama was presented in the implementation of computational linguistics. This has allowed one to advance and automate the development of institutional university repositories, Registry of Open Access Repositories (ROAR), and Directory of Open Access Repositories (OpenDOAR) in the Ranking Web of Repositories. The report showed that several countries in the region have digital repositories to implement an open-access digital strategy that contributes to a network of virtual libraries for the storage of complete text files, scientific articles, books, and theses. Thus, Brazil has 45 repositories, Colombia with 26, Ecuador with 24, and Argentina with 19.

Ecuador is one of the 12 countries surveyed in Latin America that have digital repositories, with an approximate collection of 300000 documents [21]. Due to the high demand for digital documents from institutional repositories, Ecuador had to implement transversal policies to manage, organize, and store these documents. Academic and scientific information in Ecuador is not centralized and presents difficulties in access and search, as each institutional repository has its own policies, styles, and organization of information [20].

DSpace is a software that provides open-access administrative tools and facilitates the management of digital collections of documents. Generally, university communities use it for the management of their institutional academic repository [2]. In Ecuador, DSpace is used mainly as a de facto standard in university repositories, but most universities have worked independently on the construction of their institutional repositories, that is, through academic policies that establish each of the versions of DSpace. To try to group the information, the Ecuadorian government implemented the Ecuador Open Access Repositories Network (RRAAE) [26], used at the educational level to have access to academic work, where some of the documents hosted in the DSpace tool are retrieved at the national level. RRAAE is managed and administered by the Ecuadorian Corporation for the Development of Research and Academia (CEDIA).

The use of AI and NLP techniques in the field of scientific documents and institutional repositories is poor [7,28]. These techniques allow us to develop much more efficient and accurate search tools, which allow users to navigate comfortably and perform better searches for obtaining consistent results. The RRAAE does not have ML algorithms that automate search processes and ensure the quality of information retrieved.

Some of the university institutional repositories in Ecuador have missing files and the information retrieval processes, when entering a query, are not very relevant and with few similarities between the retrieved documents. This article presents a tool that allows the visualization of similarities between academic documents, that are recovered from topics related to the computational area, from several university repositories hosted within the RRAAE in Ecuador. After the information retrieval stage, the related documents are represented by a graph that allows one to visualize the relationship between them, making the information more intelligible to the user.

1.1 Previous Work

Several investigations focused on the classification and grouping of documents based on similarity metrics [19]. The similarity of documents is one of the factors intrinsically related to the field of AI and is often an expensive task due to the vast number of Internet documents. There are several algorithms and methodologies for searching and indexing similar documents, such as ML-based methods with classification tasks, clustering, and content-based systems [13,23].

Thus, the research of Yeh et al. [34] provides a review of machine learning approaches and document rendering techniques, using a training dataset of 862 articles drawn from FlyBase and 213 new articles were used for the test phase. The data were cleaned, except for the change in a format considered important for the definition of the characteristic of each token. A binomial classification task was executed, where the system returns a Boolean depending on the new article's membership in the already trained group of specific topics. The results of the classification evaluation had a recall of 85%.

Han et. al. [11] present a simple document classification clustering algorithm based on the centroid. The analysis shows that the measure of similarity allows for dynamically adjusting the documents belonging to different classes and densities, with the aim of grouping the documents according to the dependencies between the terms of the different classes. Then, allows the classification of a new document belonging to different areas based on the highest percentage of similarity, for which the clustering algorithm uses the cosine distance. The results show that better performance is obtained compared to the kNN and C4.5 algorithms.

Vijayarani et al. [31], evaluate the performance of the classification algorithms, Naïve Bayes and Lazy, with a dataset of 80,000 instances and four attributes, with the Weka software platform. The algorithms analyzed a collection of clean and standardized text documents. The classifiers had a performance of 85.7% accuracy for the Naïve Bayes algorithm and 89.9% for Lazy.

In [14], an empirical evaluation of similarity models is carried out in text documents, taking as ground truth peer review by 83 university students. The evaluation was carried out by 29 men and 54 women with a mean age of 19.6 years, who evaluated the documents with a range of similarity between 0 and 1. Around 350 documents were used, with a length of corpus variable between 51 to 126 words. The average recall between the predicted correlations of the similarity measures and the evaluation results for each university student was 0.605. Measures of similarity used for experimentation were: Jaccard, cosine distance, and the overlap coefficient.

Currently, there is a web tool developed by Alex Tarnavsky Eitan, Eddie Smolyansky, Itay Knaan Harpaz, and Sahar Perets, called *Connected Papers* [3], which analyzes approximately 50,000 scientific articles from different databases such as arXiv [17], Semantic Scholar [4,8], PubMed [33], etc. and look for similarities between them. In this tool, the user searches for a topic of scientific interest, and the application calculates the similarity with other documents. For the representation of relationships in graphical form, use the force-directed graph [9], which starts from the similarity metric of the documents, taking as a parameter the citation and bibliography of the articles to obtain a relationship between them. The recovered articles are mostly related to the area of medical sciences, and the tool can only retrieve documents that have a DOI as a unique identifier. On the other hand, our research proposes to develop a similar visualizer paper documents from the university repository DSpace of Ecuador, analogous to *Connected Papers*, taking into account the particularity of Ecuadorian articles, repositories, and research.

2   Methodology and Materials

2.1   Information Retrieval and Dataset Generation

To establish measures of similarity between different documents, it was necessary to generate a dataset of academic articles from the DSpace of Ecuadorian Universities. No academic institution nationwide has an API that allows direct communication and extraction of information from its repository. The CEDIA network, in collaboration with the Secretary of Higher Education, Science, Technology, and Innovation (Senescyt), through the RRAAE project, grouped several repositories of academic and scientific institutions in the same space. The RRAAE collects the documents from the university repositories periodically, which makes use of the DSpace software, and allows the administration of a large number of documents for better organization and grouping.

The collection of documents was carried out with web scraping. This technique initially extracts information from the HTML code of the RRAAE according to a set of terms that were pre-established with lexemes related to the area of science and technology. The set of lexemes was obtained from information sources from organizations that standardize the international nomenclature for the fields of science and technology, such as UNESCO, Incibe, NextU, and Oracle. Given that these organizations present a wide set of terminology, a sampling of specific terms was carried out, avoiding general lexemes that are usually used in other areas. Therefore, the glossary was limited to a total of 332 items, which can be consulted in the open source repository GitHub https://github.com/JanneJaime/visualizador_similitud/blob/main/palabras_permitidas.xlsx.

The dataset collected from the RRAAE is a collection of academic documents $D_i (i = 1, ..., n)$, where $n = 8378$ is the total number of retrieved documents. For each D_i, seven attributes were recovered, allowing for a broad and unambiguous description of each document. The three attributes used to describe the content of the academic document and on which similarity metrics will be applied are the *Title* T_i, the *Keywords* PC_i, and the *Abstract* R_i. For the variables T_i and PC_i similarity measure will be used Jaccard, while for R_i, which contains a greater amount of tokens repeated, the cosine similarity [29]. The remaining four attributes *ID*, *ISBN*, *Repository name*, *Publication date*, and *Author*. These attributes serve as informative fields in the document and are displayed in the results of our web tool.

2.2 Development Methodology

The development of the project was divided into three phases with the aim of optimizing resources, segmenting specific processes, and reducing response times for the Web tool in the extraction, cleaning, processing, storage, and presentation of D_i. Development used Python 3.9.7 [30] as a programming language executed through an interpreter, i.e., there is no need for compilation. The experiments were carried out on a Microsoft Azure Server with 4 GB of RAM and 500 GB of storage.

For the first phase, the data set with D_i documents retrieved based on terms related to science and technology. Web scraping used the Python library *Beatiful-Soup* to extract the information in HTML format from the RRAAE repository. The multiprocessing technique through threads was also applied. When querying the RRAEE, 20 results are obtained per page, and the implementation of threads allows one to retrieve all the results in a single execution time. In addition, it was synchronized with a method called *barrier*, which blocks the threads until they have completed each task. When these techniques were applied for the extraction of D_i, a shorter processing time was obtained that lasted approximately nine hours.

The collection of documents recovered from the RRAAE was stored in JSON format. This information, of unstructured type, is stored in the cloud database

Firebase, which has two NoSQL services. One of these services, called *Realtime Database*, allows reading and writing data in real-time, and in its free version, it has a storage limit of 1 GB with a data transfer of 360MB per day. The second service is *Firestore*, which is a flexible and scalable database service that offers several quotas of operations in its free version. Offer 50,000 operations for reading, 20,000 for writing, and 20,000 operations for data deletion, per day. This free service was used for this project, which allows the handling of information on a large scale and with cloud deployment.

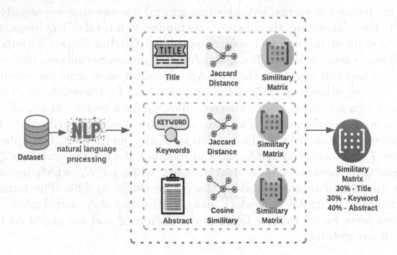

Fig. 1. Implementation of the NLP processes on the retrieved documents and calculation of the weighted similarity matrix.

Figure 1 shows the architecture of the second phase, which takes as input the query of D_i documents housed in *Firestore* and applies various NLP techniques. NLP processes allow normalization, cleaning of special characters, conversion to lowercase letters, tokenization, and elimination of stop words in the corpus texts of articles recovered in Spanish.

For each D_i were extracted T_i, PC_i, and R_i attributes. In the first two attributes, the level of similarity of the entire collection of documents is calculated using the coefficient Jaccard. This coefficient measures the similarity between two datasets and the operating range is $J \to \mathbb{R} \in [0, 1]$, where a value close to 0 implies low similarity between documents, while a value close to 1 indicates a high degree of similarity, with $j \neq i, (j = 1, ..., n)$. Eq. 1 shows the index particularization J for T_i y PC_i.

$$J(T_i, T_j) = \frac{|T_i \cap T_j|}{|T_i \cup T_j|}$$

$$J(PC_i, PC_j) = \frac{|PC_i \cap PC_j|}{|PC_i|}$$

(1)

To measure the divergence of the *Abstract* attribute, R_i, a bag of words is used that applies *Term Frequency Inverse Document Frequency* (TF-IDF) as a weighting system and uses the vector cosine similarity metric. In this model, documents are considered vectors in a multidimensional space, in which the Salton cosine measures their separation angle $cos \to \mathbb{R} \in [0,1]$. Thus, this coefficient for a pair of documents i y j is defined by Eq. 2.

$$\cos(\vec{R}_i, \vec{R}_j) = \vec{R}_i \cdot \vec{R}_j = \sum_{i=1}^{|n|} R_i R_j \ , \tag{2}$$

For each of the three attributes T_i, PC_i y R_i, a similarity matrix was generated, using its corresponding metric. To unify the three matrices, a weighting process is carried out in each matrix, thus, in the matrix of titles and keywords, a weighting of 0.3 and for the summary matrix a value of 0.4. This implies that in this model R_i provides more information, for the calculation of the similarity, than the other two attributes. As a result, a weighted similarity matrix is obtained MT. The Algorithm 1 refers to the process of generating MT.

Algorithm 1. Weighted Similarity Matrix
***
Input: D_i
Output: MT
 1: Step 1: Initialization
 2: $T_i \leftarrow [1, ..., n]$;
 3: $R_i \leftarrow [1, ..., n]$;
 4: $PC_i \leftarrow [1, ..., n]$;
 5: **for** $i \leftarrow 1, n$ **do**
 6: Step 2: Attribute Extraction
 7:    $T_i \leftarrow D_i[Title]$;
 8:    $PC_i \leftarrow D_i[Keywords]$;
 9:    $R_i \leftarrow D_i[Abstract]$;
10: Step 3: NLP
11:    $T_i \leftarrow NLP(T_i)$;
12:    $PC_i \leftarrow NLP(PC_i)$;
13:    $R_i \leftarrow NLP(R_i)$;
14: **end for**
15: Step 4: Similarity Matrix
16: $M_{T_i} \leftarrow Jaccard(T_i)$;
17: $M_{PC_i} \leftarrow Jaccard(PC_i)$;
18: $M_{R_i} \leftarrow Cosine(R_i)$;
19: Step 5: Weighing
20: $M_{T_i} \leftarrow (M_{T_i} * 0.3)$;
21: $M_{PC_i} \leftarrow (M_{PC_i} * 0.3)$;
22: $M_{R_i} \leftarrow (M_{R_i} * 0.4)$;
23: Step 6: Total Matrix
24: $MT \leftarrow (M_{T_i} + M_{PC_i} + M_{R_i})$;

For the execution of the second phase, the *Google Collaboratory* Jupyter Notebook was used to execute Python code. This development environment provides free access to storage and processing resources in the cloud. Since the collection of documents is from $n = 8378$, the resulting weighted similarity matrix, MT, is a square matrix of $n \times n$. The generation of this matrix requires computational resources and processing time for its calculation. The virtual machine assigned by *Google Colaboratory*, is elastic in nature, that is, it assigns computational resources in a variable way depending on the process to be executed. For matrix generation MT a virtual machine was allocated up to 12.68 GB in RAM, and a 107.72 GB disk and the approximate time execution was three hours. In this sense, the RI web system will not calculate the matrix MT in real time but will use a plain text file .TXT that contains the pre-calculated matrix and is stored on the web application server. Before a new query, the system will only extract a submatrix of MT, therefore, the latency to search for similarities between documents is low.

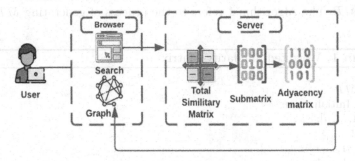

Fig. 2. Process of presentation of similarity results between documents linked by means of a graph.

The scheme of Fig. 2 shows the processes executed in the third phase to obtain the relationship between the linked documents by means of a graph. In this stage, a viewer was implemented to show the relationship between D_i. The process invokes MT and computes a submatrix SM, which satisfies a query Q made by the user. The submatrix SM calculates the graph of the relative neighborhood, with the Python function *returnRNG*, and returns an adjacent array MA which has the same dimension as SM. Algorithm 2 summarizes the process for generating the adjacency matrix. For one Q it is verified that the value of each D_i, which corresponds to the node N in the graph, is greater than 0, and thus it is guaranteed that there is a link E between the nodes. Finally, it is sent to the web front-end, in a file with extension JSON, the information of the nodes obtained from each of the links that are assigned in a dictionary with the keys origin-destiny. The front-end is responsible for displaying the similarity results between Q and D_i to the users through an interactive graph. In addition, its informative attributes can be displayed in each document.

2.3   Development of the Back-end and Front-end of the Application

For the development of the web page, the client-server model is used, made up of three blocks: API, back-end, and front-end, as shown in Fig. 3. The API performs web scraping operations on the RRAAE page to retrieve academic documents. A parameter was implemented that limits the response time to 15 s, and when this is exceeded, the next document continues. The result of the entire operation is a set of documents in JSON format.

The back-end was developed with the Python programming language using the Flask framework. For the design of the software, the Model View Controller (MVC) architecture pattern was used, which facilitates the connection with the database *Firestore*, where the collection of documents obtained by the API is housed. Finally, within the back-end the *MT* and *SM* of the documents are calculated for consultation by the user.

For the development of front-end languages, *HTML5*, *CSS3*, and *JavaScript* were used to structure, design, and give interactivity to the system. Furthermore,

---

Algorithm 2. Adjacency Matrix

Input: MT, D_i, Q
Output: N, E
 1: Step 1: Initialization
 2: $SM \leftarrow SM \subset MT$;
 3: $MT \leftarrow read(MT)$;
 4: $Q \leftarrow read(Q)$;
 5: Step 2: NLP
 6: $Q \leftarrow NLP(Q)$;
 7: Step 3: Query Database
 8: $D \leftarrow searchD_i(Q)$;
 9: Step 4: Generate Sub-array
10: **for** $i \leftarrow 1, n$ **do**
11:     **for** $j \leftarrow i + 1, n$ **do**
12:         $SM_{i,j} \leftarrow MT.item((D_i, D_j))$;
13:     **end for**
14: **end for**
15: Step 5: Adjacency Matrix
16: $MA \leftarrow returnRNG(SM)$;
17: Step 6: Node Links
18: **for** $i \leftarrow 1, n$ **do**
19:     **for** $j \leftarrow i + 1, n$ **do**
20:         **if** $MA_{i,j} > 0$ **then**
21:             $E(Origin : D_i, Destiny : D_j)$;
22:         **end if**
23:     **end for**
24: **end for**
25: Step 7: Response
26: $N \leftarrow D$;
27: $E \leftarrow E$;

---

the multi-platform library was used *Bootstrap* to generate the adaptive design of the Web and the library *D3* to visualize links and nodes in the form of a graph. The interaction of the HTML elements are executed with the library *JQuery* and *AJAX*, which make requests to the server, in the background, with the aim of obtaining documents to complement the graph.

2.4   Functional Description of the Web Tool

The web application consumes academic articles from the RRAAE, with the aim of providing the user with the possibility of searching and viewing, through a graph, all the documents related to a query regarding the technological area.

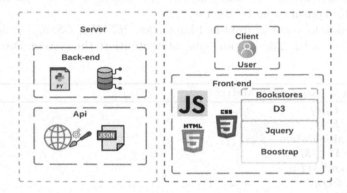

Fig. 3. Web architecture of the client-server model for viewing academic documents.

The home page, as shown in Fig. 4, allows the user to enter a specific query. To execute this process, the user must press the button *Search*, and the system will display similar documents recovered for the query. If no results are found, a message indicating this fact will be displayed on the screen. With the indexes (ID) of the retrieved documents, we proceed to generate the submatrix SM, from the global similarity matrix MT and calculate the adjacency matrix MA to identify the links that each node has in relation to each document. This information is sent to front-end for displaying the results obtained.

Search results are listed on the left side of a new window with their respective attributes. Meta-data displayed on the Web include the unique identifier of the document (ID), the full name of the document, the authors of the manuscript, the year of publication, and the university repository where it is hosted. The user can access the complete document through a hyperlink that will redirect him to the RRAAE repository. In the right section of this same page, a canvas is available, where the relationship graph between documents will be displayed. When the user interacts with the list of results and clicks on one of them, the graph with similar linked nodes is displayed. This last graph is of a dynamic type, ergo, the user can interact with the graph and when passing the cursor

Fig. 4. Search interface on the main web page for the information retrieval system

over each node, some attributes of the document are displayed. Figure 5 displays the result of a search and retrieval of academic documents related to that entry.

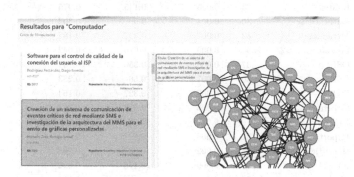

Fig. 5. Visualization page of the links between nodes of each academic document given a specific search.

3   Experiments and Results

The experiments aim to validate the operation of the Web tool. Therefore, functional tests were carried out, using a heuristic method, which does not explore all the possible outputs of the system. To begin with, certain lexemes were selected to be entered as search parameters for the retrieval of academic documents. Two criteria were used for the selection of terms; the first criterion is to select certain lexemes from the glossary of the 332 terms compiled above, to be extracted from the RRAAE. The set of elements is made up of 215 elements of a token that represent the 65% of the entire glossary and 117 for two or more tokens, which represent the 35% of the dataset. The second search criterion took into account lexemes that are not found within the established glossary but related to the technological area.

For the first experiment, 30 indexed terms were randomly selected from the set of established elements, representing 10% of the dataset. In Table 1 the number of documents retrieved is displayed for each word N_{D_i}, the range, and the mean μ_{SM_i}, of each submatrix of similarities generated by the input lexeme. The range of similarities in the documents is expressed by means of the minimum (Min) and maximum (Max) of the resulting SM. For example, for the word *Metadata*, 32 documents were recovered, where the submatrix SM of similarities has a range between the minimum of 0.007 and the maximum of 0.357, with a mean value of 0.182.

Table 1. Lexemes, number of retrieved documents, measures of dispersion, and central tendency of the similarity sub-matrices for the first experiment.

Lexeme	N_{D_i}	Min	Max	μ_{SM_i}
Modem	39	0.006	0.329	0.167
Driver	30	0.004	0.263	0.133
Router	33	0.005	0.145	0.075
Authenticity	30	0.004	0.6	0.302
Metadata	32	0.007	0.357	0.182
Pentest	9	0.009	0.076	0.042
OSI	37	0.006	0.356	0.181
USB	30	0.007	0.56	0.283
FAT	34	0.002	0.327	0.164
Switch	16	0.009	0.567	0.288
Cracker	13	0.012	0.15	0.081
Export	32	0.008	0.6	0.304
Heuristics	34	0.002	0.335	0.168
IO	32	0.009	0.176	0.092
Machine	30	0.01	0.127	0.068
Domain	39	0.008	0.6	0.304
Bit	32	0.008	0.6	0.304
Browser	34	0.003	0.55	0.276
URL	35	0.009	0.6	0.304
HTTP	30	0.001	0.488	0.244
Computer system	32	0.016	54	0.278
Deep learning	30	0.007	0.6	0.303
Bandwidth	35	0.007	0.6	0.303
Smart machine	36	0.007	0.55	0.278
Business to business	30	0.016	0.533	0.24
Information search	32	0.009	0.6	0.304
Public key	35	0.003	0.3	0.151
Reputation system	30	0.009	0.172	0.09
Linear programming	31	0.008	0.6	0.304
Computerized system	32	0.009	0.565	0.287
	31 ±7	0.007 ± 0.003	0.428 ± 0.1821	0.227 ± 0.1474

Figure 6 represents the sub-matrix of similarities of the term *Metadata*, where the intensity of the color indicates the similarity that each instance has. It is observed that all recovered documents are related to the established Q, and SM will be the input parameter that will allow the adjacency matrix MA, to be created as a graph.

On the other hand, the second experiment aims to observe the result of words that are not found in the pre-established glossary. The experiment was performed with 10 non-indexed terms, as shown in Table 2, with the same attributes as Table 1. It is important to remember that these items were not used as input parameters of the information retrieval system, ergo, it would be expected to obtain more generic documents related to other areas.

In Table 1, the functional tests for the first experiment are shown, where the mean for the 30 values of μ_{SM_i} is 0.227 with a deviation of 0.147. For the second experiment, in Table 2, the mean value of μ_{SM_i} is 0.307 with a deviation of 0.012. These results indicate that the documents retrieved in the first experiment generate matrices with higher similarities, probably because the lexemes used for this case were inputs from the IR system.

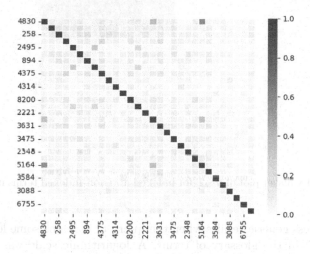

Fig. 6. Similarity sub-matrix of word *Metadata*

The results of the contrast of the means are visualized by the box-and-whisker plot in Fig. 7. The top of the diagram shows the average μ_{SM_i} of the Di indexed and their quartile dispersion. At the bottom is the group of non-indexed documents, where it is observed that the distribution is low between the papers.

In Fig. 8, the number of documents retrieved was considered, both for indexed and non-indexed terms and evaluated in a diagram that allows for observing the differences of means and interquartile dispersions. In the first experiment, an average of 31 documents were recovered; in the second experiment, the average was 476. The latter implies that the information retrieval system obtains more

Table 2. Lexemes, number of retrieved documents, measures of dispersion, and central tendency of the similarity sub-matrices for the second experiment.

Lexeme	N_{D_i}	Min	Max	μ_{SM_i}
File	249	0.001	0.602	0.301
Logic	1045	0.001	0.619	0.31
Circuits	82	0.002	0.6	0.301
Sentences	14	0.012	0.6	0.306
Information	2983	0.001	0.685	0.343
Memory	205	0.001	0.602	0.301
Buffer	24	0.009	0.6	0.304
Flowchart	10	0.012	0.6	0.306
Machine	121	0.001	0.6	0.300
Source code	31	0.007	0.6	0.303
	476 ± 933	0.0046 ± 0.0048	0.6108 ± 0.0267	0.3072 ± 0.0119

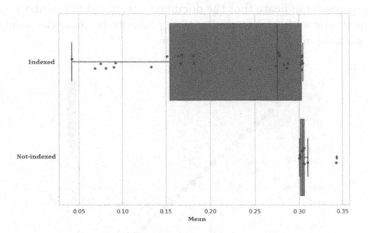

Fig. 7. Box-and-whisker plot of μ_{SM_i} for indexed and non-indexed terms in the glossary

accurate and less generic results when the query Q contains some lexeme of the pre-established in the glossary of terms. A logarithmic scale was used in the box-and-whisker diagram because of the significant difference in magnitudes to be compared.

Finally, in Fig. 9, queries are made using the terms of Tables 1 and 2 of one or more tokens. The retrieval of documents consisting of lexemes of a token with non-indexed terms presents a more significant number of papers collected than queries made with two or more tokens not indexed. Querying the terms of one or more indexed tokens results in a more uniform number of documents collected.

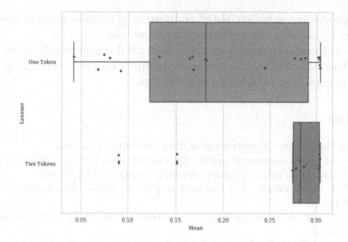

Fig. 8. Box-and-whisker plot of the number of documents retrieved by indexed and non-indexed terms.

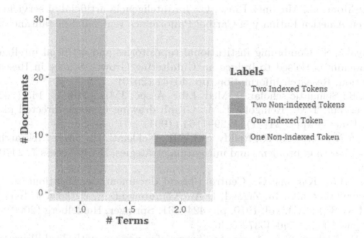

Fig. 9. Frequency diagram of one or more tokens for the experimental process

4   Conclusions and Future Work

This research project collected academic documents from repositories of universities in Ecuador stored in the RRAAE. With this information, a Web search engine was built to find the most similar documents according to the search carried out by the user. Documents were collected using Web scraping and NLP to perform data cleansing and calculate Jaccard and cosine similarity metrics. The work is limited to using a search engine based on divergence metrics. However, as prospects, the intelligent recommendation method could be used to recommend relevant documents to users while retrieving documents, to improve users' retrieval satisfaction. In addition, the system in future versions could use large-scale processing and distributed computing of massive texts in the software architecture, to improve the performance of the tool.

This project's scope is limited to the search for documents related to technical terms, and the matrix of similarities must be updated every certain period since the computational cost of its generation is high.

References

1. Assessing the quality of unstructured data: an initial overview
2. DSpace: An open source dynamic digital repository. https://doi.org/10.1045/january2003-smith. https://dspace.mit.edu/handle/1721.1/29465
3. Eitan, A.T., Smolyansky, E.: Connected papers. https://www.connectedpapers.com/ (2019)
4. Ammar, W., et al.: Construction of the literature graph in semantic scholar. In: NAACL (2018)
5. Cambria, E., White, B.: Jumping NLP Curves: a review of natural language processing research. IEEE Comput. Intell. Mag. **9**(2), 48–57 (2014). https://doi.org/10.1109/MCI.2014.2307227
6. Gómez Mont, C., Martinez Pinto, C.: La inteligencia artificial al servicio del bien social en América Latina y el Caribe: Panorámica regional e instantáneas de doce países
7. Ekanayaka, S.: Combining institutional repositories and artificial intelligence: AI in Academia is Poised to Induce an Unfaltering Growth Stance in Research and Innovation. Research Information, pp. 40–41 (2020)
8. Fricke, S.: Semantic scholar. J. Med. Libr. Assoc. JMLA **106**(1), 145 (2018)
9. Fruchterman, T.M., Reingold, E.M.: Graph drawing by force-directed placement. Softw. Pract. Exper. **21**(11), 1129–1164 (1991)
10. Ghazi, A.N., Petersen, K., Reddy, S.S.V.R., Nekkanti, H.: Survey research in software engineering: problems and mitigation strategies. IEEE Access **7**, 24703–24718 (2018)
11. Han, E.-H.S., Karypis, G.: Centroid-based document classification: analysis and experimental results. In: Zighed, D.A., Komorowski, J., Żytkow, J. (eds.) PKDD 2000. LNCS (LNAI), vol. 1910, pp. 424–431. Springer, Heidelberg (2000). https://doi.org/10.1007/3-540-45372-5_46
12. Irvall, B., Nielsen, G.S.: Access to libraries for persons with disabilities: checklist. IFLA Professional Reports, No. 89. International Federation of Library Associations and Institutions (2005). https://eric.ed.gov/?id=ED494537 iSSN: 0168-1931 Publication Title: International Federation of Library Associations and Institutions (NJ1)
13. Kurian, S.K., Mathew, S.: Survey of scientific document summarization methods. Comput. Sci. **21**, 3356 (2020)
14. Lee, M.D., Pincombe, B., Welsh, M.: An empirical evaluation of models of text document similarity. In: Proceedings of the Annual Meeting of the Cognitive Science Society, vol. 27 (2005)
15. Mair, C., et al.: An investigation of machine learning based prediction systems. J. Syst. Softw. **53**(1), 23–29 (2000). https://doi.org/10.1016/S0164-1212(00)00005-4. https://www.sciencedirect.com/science/article/pii/S0164121200000054
16. Mayr, P., et al.: Introduction to the special issue on bibliometric-enhanced information retrieval and natural language processing for digital libraries (BIRNDL). Int. J. Digit. Libr. **19**(2), 107–111 (2018)

17. McKiernan, G.: arXiv. org: The los alamos national laboratory e-print server. Int. J. Grey Literat. **1**(3), 127–138 (2000)
18. Medin, D.L., Goldstone, R.L., Gentner, D.: Respects for similarity. Psychol. Rev. **100**(2), 254–278 (1993). https://doi.org/10.1037/0033-295X.100.2.254. http://doi.apa.org/getdoi.cfm?doi=10.1037/0033-295X.100.2.254
19. Mohammed, A.J., Yusof, Y., Husni, H.: Document clustering for knowledge discovery using nature-inspired algorithm (2014)
20. Pazmiño-Maji, R., Naranjo-Ordoñez, L., Conde-González, M., García-Peñalvo, F.: Learning analytics in Ecuador: an initial analysis based in a mapping review. In: Proceedings of the Seventh International Conference on Technological Ecosystems for Enhancing Multiculturality, pp. 304–311 (2019)
21. Saltos, W.R.F., Barcenes, V.A.B., Benavides, J.P.C.: Una mirada a los repositorios digitales en ecuador. RECIAMUC **2**(1), 836–863 (2018)
22. Sánchez, D., Martínez-Sanahuja, L., Batet, M.: Survey and evaluation of web search engine hit counts as research tools in computational linguistics. Inf. Syst. **73**, 50–60 (2018)
23. Sebastiani, F.: Machine learning in automated text categorization. ACM Comput. Surv. (CSUR) **34**(1), 1–47 (2002)
24. Sintoris, K., Vergidis, K.: Extracting business process models using natural language processing (NLP) techniques. In: 2017 IEEE 19th Conference on Business Informatics (CBI), vol. 01, pp. 135–139 (2017)
25. Sosin, A., et al.: How to increase the information assurance in the information age. J. Defense Resour. Manage. (JoDRM) **9**(1), 45–57 (2018)
26. Sumba, F.: Red de repositorios de acceso abierto del ecuador-rraae. In: X Conferencia Internacional de Bibliotecas y Repositorios Digitales (BIREDIAL-ISTEC) (Modalidad virtual, 25 al 29 de octubre de 2021) (2021)
27. Suryakant, Mahara, T.: A new similarity measure based on mean measure of divergence for collaborative filtering in sparse environment. Procedia Comput. Sci. **89**, 450–456 (2016). https://doi.org/10.1016/j.procs.2016.06.099. https://www.sciencedirect.com/science/article/pii/S1877050916311644
28. Tonon, L., Fusco, E.: Data mining as a tool for information retrieval in digital institutional repositories. Proceed. CSSS **2014**, 180–183 (2014)
29. Vallejo-Huanga, D., Morillo, P., Ferri, C.: Semi-supervised clustering algorithms for grouping scientific articles. Procedia Comput. Sci. **108**, 325–334 (2017)
30. Van Rossum, G., et al.: Python programming language. In: USENIX Annual Technical Conference, vol. 41, pp. 1–36. Santa Clara, CA (2007)
31. Vijayarani, S., Muthulakshmi, M.: Comparative analysis of Bayes and lazy classification algorithms. Int. J. Adv. Res. Comput. Commun. Eng. **2**(8), 3118–3124 (2013)
32. Weiss, S.M., Indurkhya, N., Zhang, T., Damerau, F.: Text mining: predictive methods for analyzing unstructured information. Springer Science & Business Media (2010). https://doi.org/10.1007/978-0-387-34555-0
33. White, J.: Pubmed 2.0. Med. Ref. Serv. Quart. **39**(4), 382–387 (2020)
34. Yeh, A.S., Hirschman, L., Morgan, A.A.: Evaluation of text data mining for database curation: lessons learned from the KDD challenge cup. Bioinform. **19**(suppl_1), 331–339 (2003)
35. Yue, X., Di, G., Yu, Y., Wang, W., Shi, H.: Analysis of the combination of natural language processing and search engine technology. Procedia Eng. **29**, 1636–1639 (2012)

Information Retrieval Research in Academia and Industry: A Preliminary Analysis of Productivity, Authorship, Impact, and Topic Distribution

Jiaqi Lei[1]([✉]) [ID], Yi Bu[1] [ID], and Jiqun Liu[2] [ID]

[1] Department of Information Management, Peking University, Beijing 100871, China
radium@stu.pku.edu.cn, buyi@pku.edu.cn
[2] School of Library and Information Studies, The University of Oklahoma, Norman, OK 73019, USA
jiqunliu@ou.edu

Abstract. Due to the increasingly diversified research topics, approaches, and applications, there is a growing trend of scientific collaboration between academia and industry in information retrieval (IR) research. However, the characteristics in productivity, authorship, impact, and topics for publications by researchers from academia and industry and by academia-industry collaboration still remain understudied. In this paper, we examine the features and differences regarding productivity, authorship, and impact of the three types of studies and also pay special attention to the research problems and topics that attract and foster academia-industry collaborations in the recent two decades of IR studies. To this end, we analyzed 36,072 research papers published by 52,419 authors from 2000–2021 in the field of IR from ACM Digital Library. We find that the three categories have clear preferences in terms of selecting which academic conferences for publication. Regarding author teams, the industry community prefers small teams or solo-authored publications compared with the academic community. As for impact, papers by academia-industry collaboration tend to have higher citation impact compared with the research where only one community is involved. The thematic analysis of academia-industry collaborative papers and co-authorship network analysis reveal the preferred choice of research topics and the continuous "centrality" of researchers from academia. Knowledge from the study offers a new perspective for analyzing the advance and emerging trends in IR research and further clarifies the cross-community collaborations and scientific contributions of academia and industry.

Keywords: Information retrieval · Bibliometrics · Productivity · Scientific collaboration

1 Introduction

Information retrieval (IR) research seeks to characterize, support, and improve the process of retrieving relevant information and documents that satisfy users' information needs [1]. As an interdisciplinary research field that emphasizes the value of evaluation and brings together the knowledge and methods of computer science, library and information studies, human-computer interaction, and other related fields, IR usually attracts the attention and research efforts from both academia and industry. Particularly, in recent two decades, as search systems become increasingly ubiquitous in different modalities of human-information interactions (e.g., desktop search, mobile search, conversational/spoken information seeking), both researchers and system developers from academia and industry have examined and contributed to various aspects of IR algorithms, interactive search systems, user models, as well as evaluation techniques. In addition, recent advances in natural language processing, deep learning, and AI techniques also mark a series of unique contributions from industry researchers to the area and cause a resurgent interest in developing and evaluating modern intelligent search systems [3, 7, 10]. To illustrate the diverse contributions from different communities and depict the trend of recent development in IR theories, techniques, and applications, it will be useful to examine the research outputs (i.e., scientific publications) from academia and industry and also characterize the scientific collaborations between scholars from the two communities within IR.

In addition to conducting individual user studies and simulation-based experiments, previous studies have also systematically reviewed the general trends, topics of interests, and open challenges in different sub-areas of IR and synthesized the knowledge learned from the summarized publications. For instance, Huang and Keyvan (2022) surveyed the techniques, tools, and methods applied in understanding ambiguous queries in Conversational Search Systems (CSS) that are widely applied in workplace and everyday-life settings, such as chatbots, Apple's Siri, Amazon Alexa, and Google Assistant. The open questions involved in related studies, such as ambiguous query clarification and search result re-ranking, are widely examined and discussed by published research from both academia, industry, and collaborative projects involving both sides [6, 9, 11]. In addition, algorithmic fairness, accountability, transparency, and ethics (FATE) as an emerging topic also attracts attentions from both academic and industrial scholars in IR and gives rise to a series of publications, industry sessions, collaborative workshops, tutorials, and funding projects [2, 4, 5]. The FATE-IR research brings together a diverse group of researchers and practitioners who contribute to both the conceptualization and technical aspects for the research agenda on responsible IR [8].

Previous surveys and workshops on IR problems mainly focused on summarizing the problems and progresses and synthesizing the knowledge learned from individual studies. However, how researchers from different communities contribute to the advance of knowledge in IR and collaborate with each other still remain largely unclear. To address this gap, the current study aims to answer the following research questions:

RQ 1: What are the patterns of productivity and preferred venues of information retrieval studies by Academia, Industry, and Academia-Industry Collaboration?

RQ 2: What are the differences regarding the patterns of authorships for the three types of studies?

RQ 3: What are the differences regarding the impact of publications by the three types of studies? and

RQ 4: What are the research topics of academia-industry collaborative publications in information retrieval?

Knowledge learned from our study offers a new perspective for analyzing the advances and trends in IR research and further clarify the scientific contributions of academic and industrial communities.

2   Data Source and Processing

Empirical data employed in our analysis mainly comes from ACM Digital Library as it contains the majority of articles in the field of information retrieval. ACM assigns one or more CCS tags to each paper. In this paper, we select 11 CCS tags that are closely related to the field of information retrieval from all CCS tags, namely digital libraries and archives, document representation, information retrieval query processing, users and interactive retrieval, retrieval tasks and goals, retrieval models and ranking, evaluation of retrieval results, search engine architectures and scalability, specialized information retrieval, web search engines, and content ranking. In this paper, we obtain all 36,072 scientific publications in 2000–2021 from ACM digital library based on the 11 selected CCS tags in March 2022 (Later referred to as the ACM dataset).

When the raw ACM dataset are obtained, there are some papers that did not contain author institution information. To fix this issue, we manually screen 55 topics recorded in the Microsoft Academic Graph (MAG) dataset[1] that are closely related to the field of information retrieval and match MAG author institution information with the ACM dataset. The ACM dataset contains a total of 52,419 authors, and ultimately 4,533 authors are not matched to an institution (~8.65%).

The GRID[2] (Global Research Identifier Database) assigns a type to each institution, which includes both academia and industry. In this study, author institutions in the ACM dataset are normalized and then match with the institutions in GRID, this labels each author as either academia or industry. We further classify a scientific publication into four types, namely publications purely authored/co-authored by people from academia (Academia), publications purely authored/co-authored by people from industry (Industry), publications co-authored by people from both academia and industry (Academia-Industry Collaboration), and others. We find that the four types have 24,474, 1,446, 5,657, and 1,724 publications, respectively in ACM. This indicates that most papers in information retrieval are authored/co-authored within the academic community, followed by the number of papers published collaboratively between academia and industry, and the type with the fewest number of papers published entirely by researchers from the industrial community. This paper mainly focuses on the former three types, with a total of 33,178 papers. Figure 1 shows the specific process of data processing.

---

[1] https://www.microsoft.com/en-us/research/project/microsoft-academic-graph/.
[2] https://www.grid.ac.

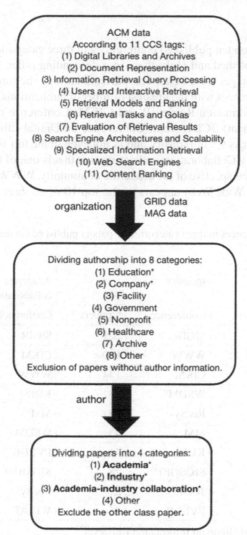

ACM data
According to 11 CCS tags:
(1) Digital Libraries and Archives
(2) Document Representation
(3) Information Retrieval Query Processing
(4) Users and Interactive Retrieval
(5) Retrieval Models and Ranking
(6) Retrieval Tasks and Golas
(7) Evaluation of Retrieval Results
(8) Search Engine Architectures and Scalability
(9) Specialized Information Retrieval
(10) Web Search Engines
(11) Content Ranking

organization   GRID data
                    MAG data

Dividing authorship into 8 categories:
(1) Education*
(2) Company*
(3) Facility
(4) Government
(5) Nonprofit
(6) Healthcare
(7) Archive
(8) Other
Exclusion of papers without author information.

author

Dividing papers into 4 categories:
(1) **Academia***
(2) **Industry***
(3) **Academia-industry collaboration***
(4) Other
Exclude the other class paper.

Fig. 1. Flow chart of data processing. "*" indicates the focus of this current paper

3   Results

This section presents the results from analyzing the pre-processed ACM publication dataset introduced above. The results are organized under accordingly to specific RQs they address. Since the analysis methods are fairly straightforward in our preliminary study, we combine the introduction of methods and corresponding results under separate sub-sections.

3.1 Productivity

Table 1 presents the top ten published conferences in three categories according to the number of papers published and ranks them in a descending order. Figure 2 shows the corresponding percentages for a better comparison. Among the three types of papers, we find that the conferences with the greatest number of publications are SIGIR (Special Interest Group on Information Retrieval) and CIKM (Conference on Information and Knowledge Management). JCDL (Joint Conference on Digital Libraries) ranks 4th in Academia, while it ranks 9th in Industry and is not even in the top 10 conference list in the Academia-Industry Collaboration, indicating that this is one of the more important conferences from the perspective of the academic community. WWW (The International Conference of World Wide Web) appears in the top 10 of all three categories, but the

Table 1. Top 10 conferences in three categories of papers published (in descending order of the number of articles).

Academia		Industry		Academia-industry collaboration	
Conference	# papers	Conference	# papers	Conference	# papers
SIGIR[a]	2,652	SIGIR	221	SIGIR	911
CIKM[b]	1,803	WWW	150	CIKM	702
WWW[c]	1,125	CIKM	134	WWW	481
JCDL[d]	1,082	WSDM[e]	53	KDD	282
MM[f]	990	RecSys	49	MM	274
WI-IAT[g]	809	MM	45	WSDM	242
SAC[h]	585	KDD[i]	41	PVLDB	164
RecSys[j]	477	SIGSOFT[k]	28	SIGMOD[l]	122
PVLDB[m]	415	JCDL	27	RecSys	102
ICMR[n]	408	PVLDB	25	WI-IAT	98

[a] SIGIR: Special Interest Group on Information Retrieval
[b] CIKM: International Conference on Information and Knowledge Management
[c] WWW: The International Conference of World Wide Web
[d] JCDL: Joint Conference on Digital Libraries
[e] WSDM: Web Search and Data Mining
[f] MM: International Conference on Multimedia
[g] WI-IAT: Web Intelligence and Intelligent Agent Technology
[h] SAC: Symposium on Applied Computing
[i] KDD: Knowledge discovery in data mining
[j] RecSys: ACM conference on Recommender systems
[k] SIGSOFT: ACM SIGSOFT Software Engineering Notes
[l] SIGMOD: International conference on Management of data
[m] PVLDB: Proceedings of the VLDB Endowment
[n] ICMR: International Conference on Multimedia Retrieval

rank position in Industry is higher than that of Academia and Academia-Industry Collaboration, which may hint that the research focuses of the industrial community on information retrieval is the field of Internet technologies.

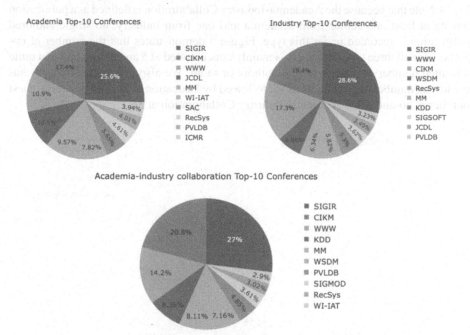

Fig. 2. The top 10 conferences where the three types of research were published

We also pay special attention to CHIIR (Conference on Human Information Interaction and Retrieval) which is a new conference venue under ACM SIGIR for facilitating the dissemination and discussion of diverse research on user-centered aspects of information interaction and information retrieval.[3] We adopt the following formula as the normalization to visually compare the differences in distribution:

$$P_i = (N_i/A_i)/\sum_{i=1}^{3}(N_i/A_i)$$

where i represents a paper's type, i.e., Academia ($i = 1$), Industry ($i = 2$) and Academia-Industry Collaboration ($i = 3$) respectively, P_i is the number of CHIIR articles in each category, N_i refers to the number of articles published in CHIIR in the three categories, and A_i indicates the total number of articles in the three categories. We find that the percentage of papers published in CHIIR conferences is 53.4% for Academia (i.e., P_1), 23.3% for Industry, and 23.3% for the Academia-Industry Collaboration. This result indicates that CHIIR as a user-oriented information seeking and retrieval research venue attracts more research attention from academic scholars.

---

[3] https://chiir.org/.

3.2 Authorship

Is there any difference regarding their authorship pattern? To explore this, we present the distribution of the number of co-authors of publications in each category, as shown in Fig. 3. Note that because the Academia-Industry Collaboration is defined as a publication having at least one author from academia and one from industry, no single-authored publication is recorded under this type. Figure 3 demonstrates that the number of co-authors for all three types of papers is mainly concentrated at 5 and below, and that quite a limited number of articles have 8 authors or more. We also notice that Industry has the lowest number of co-authors at 15, followed by Education at 24, and that the highest number of co-authors is Academia-Industry Collaboration at 36.

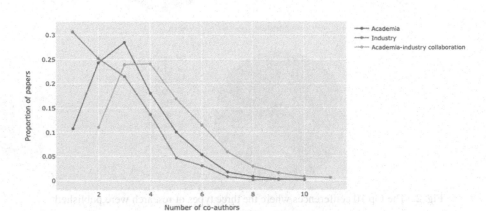

Fig. 3. Distribution of the number of co-authors for each type of publications

As seen in Fig. 3, when the number of co-authors is greater than 3, the percentage of articles written by both Academia authors and Academia-Industry Collaboration co-authors is greater than the percentage of articles written by Industry co-authors, which indicates that when studies involve researchers from the academic community, there is a tendency towards larger-group collaborations. Also, the results indicate that the number of solo-authored publications in Industry is much higher than in that of Academia. This might be interpreted by the fact that IR studies in academia are often conducted by lab-based teams under funded projects and may involve broad collaborations among faculty members, senior researchers, and graduate students. In particular, for user-centered IR evaluation research, teams may involve researchers with diverse backgrounds (e.g., system developers, user experience designers and researchers, statisticians, and machine learning scientists), resulting in higher number of co-authors on publications.

3.3 Impact

We use the number of citations received by papers to estimate the impact of scientific publications as many previous bibliometric analyses did (e.g., [12]). Figure 4 presents the distribution of the number of citations. To make the changes more intuitive and obvious, the number of papers (y-axis in the graph) is logarithmized and the curves are smoothed. We observe that the number of papers of all three types of papers decreases with the increase of citations, and the decreasing trend of Industry is the most obvious, while the decreasing trend of Academia-Industry Collaboration is more moderate. When the number of citations is fewer than 2, the number of papers of Industry is the largest; after that, the proportion of Academia-Industry Collaboration papers is always greater than that of Academia and Industry. It can be surmised that in IR, academic and industrial collaboration in publishing papers, which usually combine both the research insights and advanced techniques from both sides, tend to have a greater impact than publishing papers within the two communities alone.

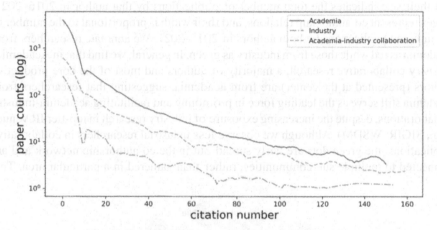

Fig. 4. Citation distribution of the three types of papers

3.4   Academia-Industry Collaborative Publications: Topic Analysis

To further explore the preference of Academia-Industry Collaboration on research topics, this paper extracts the top five most important topics of Academic-Industry collaborative papers from the textual information using the titles and abstracts of collaboration papers and the LDA topic model. Following previous studies [13], our work chooses to generate 5 topics using LDA, and 5 topic words are selected as representatives for each topic. The results are shown in Table 2. Overall, the topic words jointly present a set of system-oriented topics and application-focused sub-domains that attract a majority of Academia-Industry Collaboration, such as Web search, image and video retrieval, and recommender systems. Besides, we have also observed the emergence of user and social factors in Academia-Industry Collaboration. This finding echoes the growing trend of user-oriented interactive IR research during recent years.

Table 2. Research topics for Academia-Industry collaborative papers

Topic 1	data	system	application	information	network
Topic 2	user	recommendation	system	social	recommender
Topic 3	question	data	query	system	based
Topic 4	search	web	query	user	information
Topic 5	retrieval	image	based	video	learning

The data extracted from papers published during 2016–2021 are selected to construct a co-authorship network (see Fig. 5). In the network visualization, dots represent authors, and their size indicates the total number of publications by that author in 2016–2021. Edges represent co-authorship relations, and their width is proportional to the number of co-authored publications by both authors in 2016–2021. We annotate researchers from academia as red while those from industry as green. In general, we find that in Academia-Industry collaborative research, a majority of authors and most of the core productive authors (presented at the center) are from academia, suggesting that researchers from academia still serve as the leading force in promoting and facilitating academia-industry collaborations, despite the increasing exposure of industry research in top-tier IR venues (e.g., SIGIR, WSDM). Although we observe less industrial researchers in collaborative publications, the green dots are fairly spread out in the co-authorship network and are connected to multiple sub-communities, rather than gathered in a particular area. This

Fig. 5. Visualization of the co-authorship network. Red dots represent researchers from academia while green ones indicate those from industry. (Color figure online)

result indicates that academia-industry collaborations connect to and cover a relatively wide range of subareas. Also, the small emerging collaborations and topics (e.g., conversational IR, fairness and explainability, ML-based recommender systems[4]) on the edge of the network may lead new research trends and inspire further scientific collaborations between academia and industry.

4 Conclusions

This paper explores several characteristics (i.e., productivity, authorship, impact, and topic distribution) of information retrieval research by analyzing and comparing research publications from academia, industry, and academia-industry collaboration. In terms of preferred venues and productivity, all three types of papers were published mostly at SIGIR and CIKM. Regarding other venues, while WWW is more industry-centered, JCDL and CHIIR tends to be more academia-oriented. Publications from academia-only teams tend to involve larger co-author groups. Citation impact paints a different picture— we find that research publications from academia-industry collaboration are likely to have a greater impact than those published within the two communities separately.

When we focus on academic-industry collaborative papers, empirical results show that representative words by LDA jointly present a set of system-oriented topics and application-focused subdomains. We also observe that core and productive researchers in academia-industry collaborative research are mainly from the academic community, indicating that "academic researchers" still serve as the leading force in promoting and facilitating collaboration between academia and industry.

With respect to the limitations of our study, although the GRID data are used for matching between institutions and types of researchers, and the accuracy of some data is sampled by manual checking, there are still cases of inaccurate matching. Moreover, in this paper, we only obtained some descriptive metadata of the paper instead of the full-text data. This limitation calls for future research to implement topical analyses with more state-of-art NLP techniques.

Knowledge from our study offers a new perspective for analyzing the advance and emerging trends in IR research and helps clarify the cross-community collaborations and scientific contributions of academia and industry. Future research can further examine the divergence in impacts on different subareas of IR research and application across varying communities.

References

1. Kobayashi, M., Takeda, K.: Information retrieval on the web. ACM Comput. Surv. (CSUR) **32**(2), 144–173 (2000)
2. Castillo, C.: Fairness and transparency in ranking. ACM SIGIR Forum **52**(2), 64–71 (2019)

---

[4] The specific topics and subareas of collaboration are extracted and inferred from individual research papers and main authors' research profiles available via Google Scholar and DBLP.

3. Culpepper, J.S., Diaz, F., Smucker, M.D.: Research frontiers in information retrieval: report from the third strategic workshop on information retrieval in Lorne (SWIRL 2018). ACM SIGIR Forum **52**(1), 34–90 (2018)
4. Ekstrand, M.D., Burke, R., Diaz, F.: Fairness and discrimination in retrieval and recommendation. In: Proceedings of the 42nd International ACM SIGIR Conference on Research and Development in Information Retrieval, pp. 1403–1404, July 2019
5. Gao, R., Shah, C.: Addressing bias and fairness in search systems. In: Proceedings of the 44th International ACM SIGIR Conference on Research and Development in Information Retrieval, pp. 2643–2646, July 2021
6. Gao, J., Xiong, C., Bennett, P.: Recent advances in conversational information retrieval. In: Proceedings of the 43rd International ACM SIGIR Conference on Research and Development in Information Retrieval, pp. 2421–2424, July 2020
7. Li, H., Lu, Z.: Deep learning for information retrieval. In: Proceedings of the 39th International ACM SIGIR Conference on Research and Development in Information Retrieval, pp. 1203–1206 (2016)
8. Olteanu, A., et al.: FACTS-IR: fairness, accountability, confidentiality, transparency, and safety in information retrieval. ACM SIGIR Forum **53**(2), 20–43 (2021)
9. Thomas, P., Czerwinksi, M., McDuff, D., Craswell, N.: Theories of conversation for conversational IR. ACM Trans. Inf. Syst. (TOIS) **39**(4), 1–23 (2021)
10. Yates, A., Nogueira, R., Lin, J.: Pretrained transformers for text ranking: BERT and beyond. In: Proceedings of the 14th ACM International Conference on Web Search and Data Mining, pp. 1154–1156, March 2021
11. Zamani, H., Dumais, S., Craswell, N., Bennett, P., Lueck, G.: Generating clarifying questions for information retrieval. In: Proceedings of the Web Conference 2020, pp. 418–428, April 2020
12. Bornmann, L.: Measuring impact in research evaluations: a thorough discussion of methods for, effects of and problems with impact measurements. High Educ. **73**, 775–787 (2017)
13. Zhang, C., Bu, Y., Ding, Y., Xu, J.: Understanding scientific collaboration: homophily, transitivity, and preferential attachment. J. Assoc. Inf. Sci. Technol. **69**(1), 72–86 (2018)

Career-Based Explainable Course Recommendation

Jacob Striebel[1]($\boxtimes$), Rebecca Myers[1], and Xiaozhong Liu[2]

[1] Luddy School of Informatics, Computing, and Engineering, Indiana University,
Bloomington, IN 47408, USA
{jstrieb,rsciagli}@indiana.edu
[2] Department of Computer Science, Worcester Polytechnic Institute,
Worcester, MA 01609, USA
xliu14@wpi.edu

Abstract. The type and quality of education that a student receives can have a profound impact on their career. In contrast to education that is not intentionally organized to help students achieve specific career objectives, career-based education seeks to provide students with the skills that are required to achieve specific career goals. In this work, we propose a course recommendation framework that is designed to recommend courses based directly on their ability to teach skills relevant to a user-specified career goal. Within our framework, course recommendations are generated in a transparent manner, using skills to bridge between jobs and courses in a knowledge-based inference procedure. Due to the procedure's transparency, our system is able to provide faithful template-based explanations detailing why each recommended course was chosen for recommendation. Our framework contrasts with other course recommendation systems in the literature that lack the ability to explain their choices and therefore may lack trustworthiness from the perspective of a user. The proposed framework has several applications, including assisting students with course planning, as well as aiding with curriculum evaluation and development by providing insight into the usefulness of specific courses to specific careers. We conduct a preliminary evaluation of our system, and its performance is competitive against two baselines. We provide all the resources needed to reproduce our results. (http://github.com/striebel/cbecr)

Keywords: Career-based education · Course recommendation · Explainable recommendation · Knowledge graph · Information retrieval

1 Introduction

An important function of education is to mitigate mismatches between workers' skills and labor markets' needs [3]. However, as the pace of economic transformation around the world continues to accelerate, researchers have observed that many educational institutions are struggling to align their programs with the

I. Sserwanga et al. (Eds.): iConference 2023, LNCS 13972, pp. 371–382, 2023.
https://doi.org/10.1007/978-3-031-28032-0_30

needs of the contemporary economy [12]. Furthermore, even when programs do offer highly relevant courses, students are not always well equipped to judge the relative usefulness of offered courses to their career goals. The present work addresses these problems by proposing a framework for course recommendation (illustrated in Fig. 1), which recommends courses based directly on their ability to teach skills most important to achieving a specific career goal. The proposed framework relies on constructing a heterogeneous knowledge graph (KG) by integrating job, course, and skill data, followed by performing knowledge-based inference directly over the KG, which we hypothesize will enable improved recommendation explainability over alternative approaches. The main contribution of this work is its investigation of the following two research questions:

1. Does the integration of job, course, and skill data into a KG followed by performing knowledge-based inference directly over the KG represent a viable avenue for improving the explainability of career-based course recommendation, as opposed to alternative approaches that do not directly link jobs and courses via skills?
2. If a KG-based approach does improve explainability, does this improvement come with a cost to performance on the core course recommendation task, and, if it does, do any strategies suggest themselves for minimizing this cost?

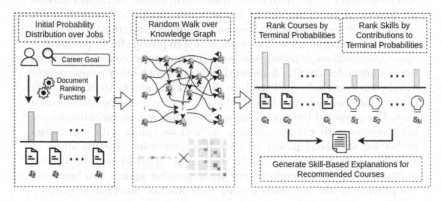

Fig. 1. Proposed framework for career-based explainable course recommendation

1.1   Knowledge Graphs and Explainable Recommendation

Currently, the most common way to approach a problem like recommendation using a knowledge graph is to follow an unsupervised node-vectorization procedure [9] and then recommend target nodes (e.g., courses) based on their proximity to source nodes of interest (e.g., jobs) in the vector space [7]. There has been much recent work on trying to learn better vector representations for nodes in a knowledge graph, such as by using meta-paths which encode graph topological

information including node and edge type [6,13,15,19]. However, while continuous feature representations of nodes in a knowledge graph can be extremely
useful in improving performance of a task like recommendation, attempts to
make them explainable have tended to be post hoc; that is, the way explanations are generated using them has usually been independent of the recommendation procedure so that generated explanations do not necessarily describe the
underlying recommendation process [1]. Therefore, one solution that has been
suggested for exploiting the benefits of a knowledge graph data representation
while also allowing for faithful explanation is to conduct inference directly over
the graph itself [20,23]. This is the direction taken in the present work.

1.2   Course Recommendation

It is currently more common for uninterpretable collaborative filtering techniques
to be used in course recommendation than graph-based approaches [8]. Graph-
based approaches have though received some recent attention [4,11]. Relatively
sophisticated course recommendation systems have been previously constructed
that take into account several types of constraints, such as pre- and corequisite
constraints and scheduling constraints [10,14]. However, existing efforts have
not yet meaningfully addressed course recommendation explainability, which is
a main focus in the present work.

2   Methods

This section describes our proposed framework for career-based explainable
course recommendation, including construction of the KG (Sect. 2.1) and our
knowledge-based inference procedure that operates over the KG (Sect. 2.2).

2.1   Knowledge Graph Schema

The basis of our KG is the job, course, and skill data sets described in Table 1.
The schema which we use to integrate these three data sets into a KG is based
on similar schemata that have recently been used successfully in the career–
education domain [11,22,23]. Specifically we define our KG as

$$G = (V, E, \tau, \sigma), \tag{1}$$

with each component defined in Table 2. Each vertex in the KG corresponds to
a job, course, or skill; that is, V is equal to the union of J, C, and S. The graph
edges are directed; e.g., $v \to u \in E$ denotes an edge from $v \in V$ to $u \in V$. In
addition to each edge having a source and target vertex, each edge also has a
type: the edge type function is defined as $\tau : E \mapsto \mathfrak{T}$, where $\mathfrak{T}$ is the set of edge
types, so that $\tau(v \to u) = t$ means that $t \in \mathfrak{T}$ is the type of edge $v \to u \in E$,
which we denote as $v \xrightarrow{t} u \in E$. Furthermore, each edge is assigned a weight
which quantifies its salience. Specifically, the edge salience function $\sigma : E \mapsto \mathbb{Q}^+$
is defined so that $\sigma(v \to u) = w$ denotes that $w \in \mathbb{Q}^+$ is the weight of edge
$v \to u \in E$ (Fig. 2).

Table 1. Summary of the basic data sets used to construct the knowledge graph

Name	Description
J	A collection of job advertisements
C	A collection of course syllabi
S	A collection of interrelated skill terms

Table 2. Summary of the knowledge graph schema components

Name	Description
V	The set of knowledge graph vertices
E	The set of knowledge graph edges
τ	The edge type function
σ	The edge salience function

Fig. 2. Visualization of the KG constructed according to the schema presented in Subsect. 2.1, using the data sets described in Subsect. 3.1.

Table 3. Summary of edge types

Edge type	Visualization	Notation	Description
req	• → •	$j \xrightarrow{\text{req}} s$	Job j requires skill s
sub	• → •	$s \xrightarrow{\text{sub}} r$	Skill s is a subclass of skill r
sup	• → •	$s \xrightarrow{\text{sup}} r$	Skill s is a superclass of skill r
tby	• → •	$s \xrightarrow{\text{tby}} c$	Skill s is taught by course c
cse	• → •	$c \xrightarrow{\text{cse}} c$	Course self-edge (bookkeeping)

Edge Types. The set of edge types is defined as

$$\mathfrak{T} = \{\text{req}, \text{sub}, \text{sup}, \text{tby}, \text{cse}\}, \tag{2}$$

with each of the five types defined in Table 3. As an example, if we have two vertices $v, u \in V$ that are connected by an edge $v \to u \in E$ and it is also the case that $\tau(v \to u) = \text{req}$, it follows that v denotes a job in J, u denotes a skill in S, and, moreover, in order to perform the job v, the skill u is required. This situation is compactly denoted $v \xrightarrow{\text{req}} u \in E$.

Edge Salience. The edge salience function σ is piecewise and is made up of five subfunctions, each of which corresponds to one of the five edge types, and the subfunctions are defined in Table 4. The edge salience function is used subsequently to define a transition probability matrix over the KG, which is a critical component of our recommendation algorithm.

2.2 Algorithm

The algorithm proceeds by calculating the probability that a random walk over the KG of T timesteps will terminate at any course in C, where the start state

Table 4. Definition of the salience subfunction for each edge type

Edge type	Salience subfunction
req	$\sigma(j \xrightarrow{\text{req}} s) = $ freq. of s in j / $\sum_{j' \in J}$ freq. of s in j'
sub	$\sigma(s \xrightarrow{\text{sub}} r) = $ mean outgoing edge weight from s
sup	$\sigma(s \xrightarrow{\text{sup}} r) = $ mean outgoing edge weight from s
tby	$\sigma(s \xrightarrow{\text{tby}} c) = $ freq. of s in c / $\sum_{c' \in C}$ freq. of s in c'
cse	$\sigma(c \xrightarrow{\text{cse}} c) = $ unit weight

in the random walk is based on an initial probability distribution over J generated from a user-provided job query string. The courses in C are then ordered for recommendation by their probabilities of being the terminal step in the random walk. Random walk over KG is an approach to recommendation that is both unsupervised and lends itself well to explanation [18,21]. Table 5 provides a summary of the objects used in the subsequent description of the algorithm.

Table 5. Summary of objects used in the algorithm

Name	Description
T	The final timestep in the random walk; $0 < T$
t	The current timestep; $0 < t \leq T$
V_i	The i-th vertex in an ordering of all vertices in the KG
E	The transition probability matrix; dimensions $|V| \times |V|$
$E_{.i}$	The probability of transitioning from any vertex in V to V_j; a column vector of length $|V|$
E_{ij}	The probability of transitioning from V_i to V_j; a scalar
p	The state probability matrix; dimensions $|V| \times (T+1)$
p_0	The initial probability distribution over all vertices in V; a row vector of length $|V|$
p_{0i}	Probability of random walker starting at V_i; a scalar
p_t	Probability of being at any vertex after timestep t; a row vector of length $|V|$
p_{ti}	Probability of being at vertex V_i after timestep t; a scalar
q	Array of probability-contributions-to-state matrices; dimensions $|V| \times |V| \times T$
q^i	Probability-contributions-to-V_i matrix; dimensions $|V| \times T$
$q^i_{.t}$	Probability-contributions-to-V_i-during-timestep-t vector; a column vector of length $|V|$
q^i_{jt}	Given that a random walker is in state i (i.e., at vertex V_i) after timestep t, this is the probability that the walker arrived in state i from state j

Transition Probability. The definition of our transition probability matrix is given in equation (3), which specifies the probability of traversing any edge

$v \to u \in E$ as the salience of the edge normalized by the sum of the saliences of all edges that have v as their source.

$$E_{ij} = \begin{cases} \sigma(V_i \to V_j)/\sum_{u' \in \{u:v \to u \in E\}} \sigma(V_i \to u') & \text{if } V_i \to V_j \in E \\ 0 & \text{else} \end{cases} \quad (3)$$

Course Recommendation. The initial probability distribution p_0 over V is defined in the following manner: if $V_i \in S$ or $V_i \in C$, then p_{0i} equals 0; otherwise $V_i \in J$ and p_{0i} equals the normalized BM25 score of the job posting V_i calculated using a user-provided job name as a query string. The probability of a random walker being at any vertex V_i after timestep t, where $0 < t \leq T$, is then given by

$$p_t = p_{t-1} E \; . \quad (4)$$

Once p_T has been calculated, the best course recommendation is given by $V_{\hat{i}}$, where

$$\hat{i} = \underset{\{i:V_i \in C\}}{\operatorname{argmax}} p_{Ti} \; . \quad (5)$$

In addition to the algorithm recommending a single most relevant course, the ordering of the probabilities in p_T also define an ordering of all courses in C according to their relevance to the specified job of interest.

Explanation Procedure. Once a recommended course $V_{\hat{i}}$ is identified, the skills that most strongly link the course to the job of interest can also be found. This is done by calculating the probability of a random walker being in state V_j after step $T - 1$ and transitioning to state $V_{\hat{i}}$ during the final step of the random walk T; that is,

$$q^{\hat{i}}_{\cdot T} = p_{T-1}{}^{\mathrm{T}} \circ E_{\cdot \hat{i}} \; . \quad (6)$$

Once $q^{\hat{i}}_{\cdot T}$ is obtained, the skill that most strongly links the originally selected job to the recommended course $V_{\hat{i}}$ is equal to $V_{\hat{j}}$, where

$$\hat{j} = \underset{\{j:V_j \in S\}}{\operatorname{argmax}} q^{\hat{i}}_{jT} \; . \quad (7)$$

In addition to $V_{\hat{j}}$ being the skill that most strongly links $V_{\hat{i}}$ to the user-provided job of interest, the probabilities given in $q^{\hat{i}}_{\cdot T}$ also allow all skills in S to be ranked by how strongly they contributed to $V_{\hat{i}}$'s recommendation.

Explanation Template. Once a course has been recommended and its most salient skill terms have been identified, we present this information to the user through an explanation template, which has been shown to be a successful technique for delivering explanations to a user [16,17,20].

The explanation template developed for this project contains four slots which are filled using the user-specified career of interest, the recommended course, and the two skills taught in the course which are most relevant to the career of interest. An example of the filled template is:

In "Introduction to Embedded Systems Design" you will learn "Microcontrollers" and "Programmable Devices" which are important for the job "Embedded Systems Engineer."

3   Evaluation

This section presents a preliminary evaluation of our framework for career-based explainable course recommendation, including a description of the three data sets that were used in our experiments (Sect. 3.1), a description of the two baseline models that we evaluated our framework against (Sect. 3.2), and a description of the evaluation procedure we followed (Sect. 3.3).

3.1   Data Sets

In this preliminary work, we concentrated on course recommendation for careers within a single industry. We chose the microelectronics industry because it is critical to the economy and to society, yet it represents an area of the labor market that continues to evolve rapidly and therefore may be difficult to align coursework with [2].

For the project, three data sets were newly collected which contain job posts, course syllabi, and skill terms. The data sets are summarized in Table 6. The jobs data set J contains 1,277 job posts obtained from the Indeed employment website (indeed.com). These advertisements are for a variety of positions within the US microelectronics industry. The courses data set C contains 1,269 syllabi obtained from three providers of massive open online courses (MOOCs): Coursera (coursera.org), edX (edx.org), and Udemy (udemy.com). 27% of the collected courses are on microelectronics topics, 21% are on science and technology topics not directly related to microelectronics, and the remaining 52% cover areas outside of science and technology. The skills data set S contains 12,133 terms which are the names of all Wikipedia articles and categories that are within four steps of the Electrical Engineering category in Wikipedia's article–category graph.

Table 6. Summary of the data sets

Data set	Contents
J	1,277 microelectronics-industry job posts
C	1,269 MOOC syllabi
S	12,133 technical-skill terms

3.2   Baseline Models

In our preliminary evaluation, two baselines are used. The first is the BM25 document ranking function, which takes a query string as input and assigns a score to each document in a corpus based on the document's relevance to the query string. The query string used is the title of the user-selected job of interest in J and the scored documents are the course syllabi in C. The second baseline algorithm is the cosine similarity between the user-selected job in J and each of the course syllabi in C. The features that are compared are the non-stopwords in the selected job post and in each course syllabus. Both baselines use the most frequently occurring non-stopwords in the syllabus of a recommended course as that recommendation's explanation terms used to fill the template.

3.3   Model Comparison

To conduct the preliminary evaluation, we asked a graduate student who has reviewed literature on microelectronics education to serve as our scorer. The scorer's first task was to choose several job posts from the data set J that represent a diverse mix of job types currently in demand in the microelectronics industry. Seven job posts were chosen, and the title of each chosen job is listed in Table 7.

Table 7. Job posts sampled for model evaluation

Job title
"Associate Field Service Representative - Portland"
"Bead Blast Technician"
"Electronic Technician"
"Summer 2021 Robotics Intern"
"Systems Engineer"
"Test Engineer"
"Tester II - Semiconductor Product Validation"

For each of the seven jobs, a ranked list of twenty course recommendations and explanations was generated using our framework and the two baselines. This produced 60 course recommendations and 60 corresponding explanations for each job, totaling 420 courses and 420 explanations. After anonymizing which system generated which recommendations and explanations, the course recommendations and explanations were delivered to the scorer. Each recommended course was scored on a four-point relevance scale with respect to the input job, and each explanation was scored on a four-point adequacy scale with respect to how well it explained why the recommended course would be useful to the input job. From these scores, precision and normalized discounted cumulative gain (NDCG) at five, ten, and twenty were calculated separately for each of the three systems' recommendations and explanations.

4   Results

The results of the preliminary evaluation are reported in Figs. 3 and 4 for the recommendation and explanation tasks, respectively. For each evaluation metric on both tasks, the proposed system outperformed the two baselines. The KG system's performance on the explanation task validates our hypothesis that integrating job, course, and skill data into a KG and performing inference directly over the KG can improve a course recommendation system's ability to explain its recommendations: this result suggests a positive answer to our first research question. The KG system's superior performance on the recommendation task is also notable and encouraging because an important goal when designing an explainable recommendation system is to achieve high explanation performance, without sacrificing the performance of the system's core recommendation functionality [20]: this second result may suggest a negative answer to our second research question; important follow-up work to our preliminary evaluation will be to compare our framework's performance against more sophisticated (unexplainable) baselines, which will allow us to better analyze the competitiveness of our system on the recommendation task considered independently of the explanation task.

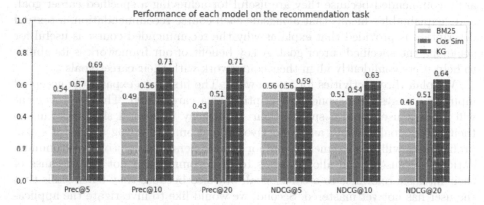

Fig. 3. Recommendation performance. BM25 is the widely used document ranking function, Cos Sim stands for cosine similarity, and KG stands for knowledge graph and refers to the propsed random-walk-over-KG system. Prec abbreviates precision and NDCG stands for normalized discounted cumulative gain. The @5, @10, and @20 suffixes indicate that a metric was calculated using the top 5, 10, or 20 course recommendations generated by each system for each input job title.

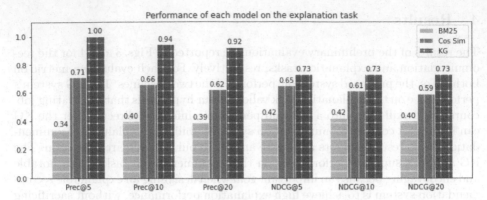

Fig. 4. Explanation performance. Abbreviations are defined in the caption of Fig. 3.

5   Discussion and Conclusion

In this work we have proposed a course recommendation framework that is both career based and explainable, where "career based" means that courses are recommended because they are useful for achieving a specified career goal, and "explainable" means that alongside each course recommendation, a textual description is provided that explains why the recommended course is useful for achieving the specified career goal. A key benefit of our framework is its ability to help users confidently align their coursework with their career goals.

We plan three activities for future work. The first is to expand the accepted input to our system beyond a description of a career goal. This improvement will allow a user to also specify their proficiency in several skills relevant to their career goal through an interactive evaluation. Collecting a student's skill proficiencies will be extremely useful for further personalizing course recommendations, because it will allow courses to be recommended not just because of their intrinsic relevance to a career goal, but also because they teach skills that the user has not yet mastered. Second, we would like to investigate the applicability of more sophisticated natural language generation techniques for creating explanations [5], in contrast to the template-based approach used in the present work. Finally, we plan to conduct a more comprehensive evaluation of the system via a user study, which will include comparison against additional baselines.

Acknowledgment. We acknowledge support from the U.S. Department of Defense [Contract No. W52P1J-22-9-3009]. The views and conclusions contained in this document are those of the authors and should not be interpreted as representing the official policies, either expressed or implied, of the U.S. Department of Defense or the U.S. Government. The U.S. Government is authorized to reproduce and distribute reprints for Government purposes, notwithstanding any copyright notation here on.

References

1. Ai, Q., Zhang, Y., Bi, K., Croft, W.B.: Explainable product search with a dynamic relation embedding model. ACM Trans. Inf. Syst. **38**(1), February 2020. https://doi.org/10.1145/3361738
2. Bonnaud, O., Fesquet, L., Bsiesy, A.: Skilled manpower shortage in microelectronics: a challenge for the French education microelectronics network. In: 2019 18th International Conference on Information Technology Based Higher Education and Training (ITHET), pp. 1–5 (2019). https://doi.org/10.1109/ITHET46829.2019.8937384
3. Börner, K., Scrivner, O., Gallant, M., Ma, S., Liu, X., Chewning, K., Wu, L., Evans, J.A.: Skill discrepancies between research, education, and jobs reveal the critical need to supply soft skills for the data economy. Proc. Natl. Acad. Sci. **115**(50), 12630–12637 (2018). https://doi.org/10.1073/pnas.1804247115
4. Bridges, C., Jared, J., Weissmann, J., Montanez-Garay, A., Spencer, J., Brinton, C.G.: Course recommendation as graphical analysis. In: 2018 52nd Annual Conference on Information Sciences and Systems (CISS) (2018). https://doi.org/10.1109/CISS.2018.8362325
5. Chowdhery, A., et al.: Palm: scaling language modeling with pathways. arXiv preprint arXiv:2204.02311 (2022)
6. Dong, Y., Chawla, N.V., Swami, A.: Metapath2vec: Scalable representation learning for heterogeneous networks. In: Proceedings of the 23rd ACM SIGKDD International Conference on Knowledge Discovery and Data Mining, pp. 135–144. Association for Computing Machinery, New York (2017). https://doi.org/10.1145/3097983.3098036
7. Gogoglou, A., Bruss, C.B., Nguyen, B., Sarshogh, R., Hines, K.E.: Quantifying challenges in the application of graph representation learning. In: 2020 19th IEEE International Conference on Machine Learning and Applications (ICMLA), pp. 1519–1526 (2020). https://doi.org/10.1109/ICMLA51294.2020.00234
8. Gong, J., et al.: Attentional graph convolutional networks for knowledge concept recommendation in moocs in a heterogeneous view. In: Proceedings of the 43rd International ACM SIGIR Conference on Research and Development in Information Retrieval, pp. 79–88. Association for Computing Machinery, New York (2020). https://doi.org/10.1145/3397271.3401057
9. Grover, A., Leskovec, J.: Node2vec: scalable feature learning for networks. In: Proceedings of the 22nd ACM SIGKDD International Conference on Knowledge Discovery and Data Mining. pp. 855–864. Association for Computing Machinery, New York (2016). https://doi.org/10.1145/2939672.2939754
10. Jing, X., Tang, J.: Guess you like: course recommendation in moocs. In: Proceedings of the International Conference on Web Intelligence, pp. 783–789. Association for Computing Machinery, New York (2017). https://doi.org/10.1145/3106426.3106478
11. Li, N., Suri, N., Gao, Z., Xia, T., Börner, K., Liu, X.: Enter a job, get course recommendations. In: iConference 2017 Proceedings. 2, pp. 118–122 (2017). http://hdl.handle.net/2142/98865
12. Martinez, W.: How science and technology developments impact employment and education. Proc. Natl. Acad. Sci. U.S.A. **115**(50), 12624–12629 (2018). https://doi.org/10.1073/pnas.1803216115
13. Nguyen, D., Malliaros, F.D.: Biasedwalk: Biased sampling for representation learning on graphs. In: 2018 IEEE International Conference on Big Data (Big Data), pp. 4045–4053 (2018). https://doi.org/10.1109/BigData.2018.8621872

14. Parameswaran, A., Venetis, P., Garcia-Molina, H.: Recommendation systems with complex constraints: a course recommendation perspective. ACM Trans. Inf. Syst. **29**(4), December 2011. https://doi.org/10.1145/2037661.2037665
15. Seo, S., Oh, B., Lee, K.H.: Reliable knowledge graph path representation learning. IEEE Access **8**, 32816–32825 (2020). https://doi.org/10.1109/ACCESS.2020.2973923
16. Tao, Y., Jia, Y., Wang, N., Wang, H.: The fact: taming latent factor models for explainability with factorization trees. In: Proceedings of the 42nd International ACM SIGIR Conference on Research and Development in Information Retrieval, SIGIR 2019, pp. 295–304. Association for Computing Machinery, New York (2019). https://doi.org/10.1145/3331184.3331244
17. Wang, N., Wang, H., Jia, Y., Yin, Y.: Explainable recommendation via multi-task learning in opinionated text data. In: The 41st International ACM SIGIR Conference on Research Development in Information Retrieval, SIGIR 2018, pp. 165–174. Association for Computing Machinery, New York (2018). https://doi.org/10.1145/3209978.3210010
18. Wang, X., Wu, H., Hsu, C.H.: Mashup-oriented api recommendation via random walk on knowledge graph. IEEE Access **7**, 7651–7662 (2018)
19. Wang, Z., Li, L., Li, Q., Zeng, D.: Multimodal data enhanced representation learning for knowledge graphs. In: 2019 International Joint Conference on Neural Networks (IJCNN) (2019). https://doi.org/10.1109/IJCNN.2019.8852079
20. Zhang, Y., Chen, X.: Explainable recommendation: a survey and new perspectives. Found. Trends Inf. Retr. **14**(1), 1–101 (2020). https://doi.org/10.1561/1500000066
21. Zheng, L., Liu, S., Song, Z., Dou, F.: Diversity-aware entity exploration on knowledge graph. IEEE Access **9**, 118782–118793 (2021). https://doi.org/10.1109/ACCESS.2021.3107732
22. Zhu, G., Chen, Y., Wang, S.: Graph-community-enabled personalized course-job recommendations with cross-domain data integration. Sustainability **14**(12) (2022). https://doi.org/10.3390/su14127439
23. Zhu, G., Kopalle, N.A., Wang, Y., Liu, X., Jona, K., Börner, K.: Community-based data integration of course and job data in support of personalized career-education recommendations. In: Proceedings of the Association of Information Science and Technology, vol. 57 (2020). https://doi.org/10.1002/pra2.324

A Benchmark of PDF Information Extraction Tools Using a Multi-task and Multi-domain Evaluation Framework for Academic Documents

Norman Meuschke[1]([✉]) [iD], Apurva Jagdale[2], Timo Spinde[1] [iD],
Jelena Mitrović[2,3] [iD], and Bela Gipp[1] [iD]

[1] University of Göttingen, 37073 Göttingen, Germany
{meuschke,spinde,gipp}@uni-goettingen.de
[2] University of Passau, 94032 Passau, Germany
{apurva.jagdale,jelena.mitrovic}@uni-passau.de
[3] The Institute for Artificial Intelligence R&D of Serbia, 21000 Novi Sad, Serbia

Abstract. Extracting information from academic PDF documents is crucial for numerous indexing, retrieval, and analysis use cases. Choosing the best tool to extract specific content elements is difficult because many, technically diverse tools are available, but recent performance benchmarks are rare. Moreover, such benchmarks typically cover only a few content elements like header metadata or bibliographic references and use smaller datasets from specific academic disciplines. We provide a large and diverse evaluation framework that supports more extraction tasks than most related datasets. Our framework builds upon DocBank, a multi-domain dataset of 1.5 M annotated content elements extracted from 500 K pages of research papers on arXiv. Using the new framework, we benchmark ten freely available tools in extracting document metadata, bibliographic references, tables, and other content elements from academic PDF documents. GROBID achieves the best metadata and reference extraction results, followed by CERMINE and Science Parse. For table extraction, Adobe Extract outperforms other tools, even though the performance is much lower than for other content elements. All tools struggle to extract lists, footers, and equations. We conclude that more research on improving and combining tools is necessary to achieve satisfactory extraction quality for most content elements. Evaluation datasets and frameworks like the one we present support this line of research. We make our data and code publicly available to contribute toward this goal.

Keywords: PDF · Information extraction · Benchmark · Evaluation

1 Introduction

The Portable Document Format (PDF) is the most prevalent encoding for academic documents. Extracting information from academic PDF documents is crucial for numerous indexing, retrieval, and analysis tasks. Document search, recommendation, summarization, classification, knowledge base construction, question answering, and bibliometric analysis are just a few examples [31].

I. Sserwanga et al. (Eds.): iConference 2023, LNCS 13972, pp. 383–405, 2023.
https://doi.org/10.1007/978-3-031-28032-0_31

However, the format's technical design makes information extraction challenging. Adobe designed PDF as a platform-independent, fixed-layout format by extending the PostScript [24] page description language. PDF focuses on encoding a document's visual layout to ensure a consistent appearance of the document across software and hardware platforms but includes little structural and semantic information on document elements.

Numerous tools for information extraction (IE) from PDF documents have been presented since the format's inception in 1993. The development of such tools has been subject to a fast-paced technological evolution of extraction approaches from rule-based algorithms, over statistical machine learning (ML) to deep learning (DL) models (cf. Sect. 2). Finding the best tool to extract specific content elements from PDF documents is currently difficult because:

1. Typically, tools only support extracting a subset of the content elements in academic documents, e.g., title, authors, paragraphs, in-text citations, captions, tables, figures, equations, or references.
2. Many information extraction tools, e.g., 12 of 35 tools we considered for our study, are no longer maintained or have become obsolete.
3. Prior evaluations of information extraction tools often consider only specific content elements or use domain-specific corpora, which makes their results difficult to compare. Moreover, the most recent comprehensive benchmarks of information extraction tools were published in 2015 for metadata[1] [54], 2017 for body text [6], and 2018 for references[2] [53], respectively. These evaluations do not reflect the latest technological advances in the field.

To alleviate this knowledge gap and facilitate finding the best tool to extract specific elements from academic PDF documents, we comprehensively evaluate ten state-of-the-art non-commercial tools that consider eleven content elements based on a dataset of 500 K pages from arXiv documents covering multiple fields.

Our code, data, and resources are publicly available at
http://pdf-benchmark.gipplab.org

2   Related Work

This section presents approaches for information extraction from PDF (Sect. 2.1), labeled datasets suitable for training and evaluating PDF information extraction approaches, and prior evaluations of IE tools (Sect. 2.2).

2.1   Information Extraction from PDF Documents

Table 1 summarizes publications on PDF information extraction since 1999. For each publication, the table shows the primary technological approach and

---

[1] For example author(s), title, affiliation(s), address(es), email(s).
[2] Refers to extracting the components of bibliographic references, e.g., author(s), title, venue, editor(s), volume, issue, page range, year of publication, etc.

Table 1. Publications on information extraction from PDF documents.

Publication[a]	Year	Task[b]	Method	Training Dataset[c]
Palermo [44]	1999	M, ToC	Rules	100 documents
Klink [27]	2000	M	Rules	979 pages
Giuffrida [18]	2000	M	Rules	1,000 documents
Aiello [2]	2002	RO, Title	Rules	1,000 pages
Mao [37]	2004	M	OCR, Rules	309 documents
Peng [45]	2004	M, R	CRF	CORA (500 refs.)
Day [14]	2007	M, R	Template	160,000 citations
Hetzner [23]	2008	R	HMM	CORA (500 refs.)
Councill [12]	2008	R	CRF	CORA (200 refs.), CiteSeer (200 refs.)
Lopez [36]	2009	B, M, R	CRF, DL	None
Cui [13]	2010	M	HMM	400 documents
Ojokoh [42]	2010	M	HMM	CORA (500 refs.), ManCreat FLUX-CiM (300 refs.),
Kern [25]	2012	M	HMM	E-prints, Mendeley, PubMed (19K entries)
Bast [5]	2013	B, M, R	Rules	DBLP (690 docs.), PubMed (500 docs.)
Souza [52]	2014	M	CRF	100 documents
Anzaroot [3]	2014	R	CRF	UMASS (1,800 refs.)
Vilnis [56]	2015	R	CRF	UMASS (1,800 refs.)
Tkaczyk [54]	2015	B, M, R	CRF, Rules, SVM	CiteSeer (4,000 refs.), CORA (500 refs.), GROTOAP, PMC (53K docs.)
Bhardwaj [7]	2017	R	FCN	5,090 references
Rodrigues [48]	2018	R	BiLSTM	40,000 references
Prasad [46]	2018	M, R	CRF, DL	FLUX-CiM (300 refs.), CiteSeer (4,000 refs.)
Jahongir [4]	2018	M	Rules	10,000 documents
Torre [15]	2018	B, M	Rules	300 documents
Rizvi [47]	2020	R	R-CNN	40,000 references
Hashmi [22]	2020	M	Rules	45 documents
Ahmed [1]	2020	M	Rules	150 documents
Nikolaos [33]	2021	B, M, R	Attention, BiLSTM	3,000 documents

[a] Publications in chronological order; the labels indicate the first author only.
[b] (B) Body text, (M) Metadata, (R) References, (RO) Reading order, (ToC) Table of contents
[c] Domain-specific datasets: Computer Science: CiteSeer [43], CORA [39], DBLP [51], FLUX-CiM [10,11], ManCreat [42]; Health Science: PubMed [40], PMC [41]

the training dataset. Eighteen of 27 approaches (67%) employ machine learning or deep learning (DL) techniques, and the remainder rule-based extraction (Rules). Early tools rely on manually coded rules [44]. Second-generation tools use statistical machine learning, e.g., based on Hidden Markov Models (HMM) [8], Conditional Random Fields (CRF) [29], and maximum entropy [26]. The most recent information extraction tools employ Transformer models [55].

A preference for—in theory—more flexible and adaptive machine learning and deep learning techniques over case-specific rule-based algorithms is observable in Table 1. However, many training datasets are domain-specific, e.g., they exclusively consist of documents from Computer Science or Health Science, and comprise fewer than 500 documents. These two factors put the generalizability of the respective IE approaches into question. Notable exceptions like Ojokoh et al. [42], Kern et al. [25], and Tkaczyk et al. [54] use multiple datasets covering different domains for training and evaluation. However, these approaches address specific tasks, i.e., header metadata extraction, reference extraction, or both.

Moreover, a literature survey by Mao et al. shows that most approaches for text extraction from PDF do not specify the ground-truth data and performance metrics they use, which impedes performance comparisons [38]. A positive exception is a publication by Bast et al. [5], which presents a comprehensive evaluation framework for text extraction from PDF that includes a fine-grained specification of the performance measures used.

2.2   Labeled Datasets and Prior Benchmarks

Table 2 summarizes datasets usable for training and evaluating PDF information extraction approaches grouped by the type of ground-truth labels they offer. Most datasets exclusively offer labels for document metadata, references, or both.

Table 2. Labeled datasets for information extraction from PDF documents.

Publication[a]	Size	Ground-truth Labels
Fan [16]	147 documents	Metadata
Färber [17]	90 K documents	References
Grennan [21]	1 B references	References
Saier [49,50]	1 M documents.	References
Ley [30,51]	6 M documents	Metadata, references
Mccallum [39]	935 documents	Metadata, references
Kyle [34]	8.1 M documents	Metadata, references
Ororbia [43]	6 M documents.	Metadata, references
Bast [6]	12,098 documents	Body text, sections, title
Li [31]	500 K pages	Captions, equations, figures, footers lists, metadata, paragraphs, references, sections, tables

[a] The labels indicate the first author only.

Only the DocBank dataset by Li et al. [31] offers annotations for 12 diverse content elements in academic documents, including, figures, equations, tables, and captions. Most of these content elements have not been used for benchmark evaluations yet. DocBank is comparably large (500 K pages from research papers published on arXiv in a four-year period). A downside of the DocBank dataset is its coarse-grained labels for references, which do not annotate the fields of bibliographic entries like the author, publisher, volume, or date, as do bibliography-specific datasets like unarXive [21] or S2ORC [34].

Table 3 shows PDF information extraction benchmarks performed since 1999. Few such works exist and were rarely repeated or updated, which is sub-optimal given that many tools receive updates frequently. Other tools become technologically obsolete or unmaintained. For instance, pdf-extract[3], lapdftext[4], PDF-SSA4MET[5], and PDFMeat[6] are no longer maintained actively, while ParsCit[7] has been replaced by NeuralParsCit[8] and SciWING[9].

Table 3. Benchmark evaluations of PDF information extraction approaches.

Publication[a]	Dataset	Metrics[b]	Tools	Labels[c]
Granitzer [19]	E-prints (2,452 docs.), Mendeley (20,672 docs.)	P, R	2	M
Lipinski [32]	arXiv (1,253 docs.)	Acc	7	M
Bast [6]	arXiv (12,098 docs.)	Custom	14	NL, Pa RO, W
Körner [28]	100 (German docs.)	P, R, F_1	4	Ref
Tkaczyk [53]	9,491 documents	P, R, F_1	10	Ref
Rizvi	8,766 references	F_1	4	Ref

[a] The labels indicate the first author only.
[b] (P) Precision, (R) Recall, (F_1) F_1-score, (Acc) Accuracy
[c] (M) Metadata, (NL) New Line, (Pa) Paragraph, (Ref) Reference, (RO) Reading order, (W) Words

As Table 3 shows, the most extensive dataset used for evaluating PDF information extraction tools so far contains approx. 24,000 documents. This number is small compared to the sizes of datasets available for this task, shown in Table 2. Most studies focused on exclusively evaluating metadata and reference extraction (see also Table 3). An exception is a benchmark by Bast and Korzen [6],

---

[3] https://github.com/CrossRef/pdfextract.
[4] https://github.com/BMKEG/lapdftext.
[5] https://github.com/eliask/pdfssa4met.
[6] https://github.com/dimatura/pdfmeat.
[7] https://github.com/knmnyn/ParsCit.
[8] https://github.com/WING-NUS/Neural-ParsCit.
[9] https://github.com/abhinavkashyap/sciwing.

which evaluated spurious and missing words, paragraphs, and new lines for 14 tools but used a comparably small dataset of approx. 10 K documents.

We conclude from our review of related work that (1) recent benchmarks of information extraction tools for PDF are rare, (2) mostly analyze metadata extraction, (3) use small, domain-specific datasets, and (4) include tools that have become obsolete or unmaintained. (5) A variety of suitably labeled datasets have not been used to evaluate information extraction tools for PDF documents yet. Therefore, we see the need for benchmarking state-of-the-art PDF information extraction tools on a large labeled dataset of academic documents covering multiple domains and containing diverse content elements.

3   Methodology

This section presents the experimental setup of our study by describing the tools we evaluate (Sect. 3.1), the dataset we use (Sect. 3.2), and the procedure we follow (Sect. 3.3).

3.1   Evaluated Tools

We chose ten actively maintained non-commercial open-source tools that we categorize by extraction tasks.

1. **Metadata Extraction** includes tools to extract titles, authors, abstracts, and similar document metadata.
2. **Reference Extraction** comprises tools to access and parse bibliographic reference strings into fields like author names, publication titles, and venue.
3. **Table Extraction** refers to tools that allow accessing both the structure and data of tables.
4. **General Extraction** subsumes tools to extract, e.g., paragraphs, sections, figures, captions, equations, lists, or footers.

For each of the tools we evaluate, Table 4 shows the version, supported extraction task(s), primary technological approach, and output format. Hereafter, we briefly describe each tool, focusing on its technological approach.

Adobe Extract[10] is a cloud-based API that allows extracting tables and numerous other content elements subsumed in the *general extraction* category. The API employs the Adobe Sensei[11] AI and machine learning platform to understand the structure of PDF documents. To evaluate the Adobe Extract API, we used the Adobe PDFServices Python SDK[12] to access the API's services.

Apache Tika[13] allows metadata and content extraction in XML format. We used the tika-python[14] client to access the Tika REST API. Unfortunately, we found that tika-python only supports content (paragraphs) extraction.

---

[10] https://www.adobe.io/apis/documentcloud/dcsdk/pdf-extract.html.
[11] https://www.adobe.com/de/sensei.html.
[12] https://github.com/adobe/pdfservices-python-sdk-samples.
[13] https://tika.apache.org/.
[14] https://github.com/chrismattmann/tika-python.

Table 4. Overview of evaluated information extraction tools.

Tool	Version	Task[a]	Technology	Output
Adobe Extract	1.0	G, T	Adobe Sensei AI Framework	JSON, XLSX
Apache Tika	2.0.0	G	Apache PDFBox	TXT
Camelot	0.10.1	T	OpenCV, PDFMiner	CSV, Dataframe
CERMINE	1.13	G, M, R	CRF, iText, Rules, SVM	JATS
GROBID	0.7.0	G, M, R, T	CRF, Deep Learning, Pdfalto	TEI XML
PdfAct	n/a	G, M, R, T	pdftotext, rules	JSON, TXT, XML
PyMuPDF	1.19.1	G	OCR, tesseract	TXT
RefExtract	0.2.5	R	pdftotext, rules	TXT
ScienceParse	1.0	G, M, R,	CRF, pdffigures2, rules	JSON
Tabula	1.2.1	T	PDFBox, rules	CSV, Dataframe

[a] (G) General, (M) Metadata, (R) References, (T) Table

Camelot[15] can extract tables using either the *Stream* or *Lattice* modes. The former uses whitespace between cells and the latter table borders for table cell identification. For our experiments, we exclusively use the Stream mode, since our test documents are academic papers, in which tables typically use whitespace in favor of cell borders to delineate cells. The Stream mode internally utilizes the PDFMiner library[16] to extract characters that are subsequently grouped into words and sentences using whitespace margins.

CERMINE [54] offers metadata, reference, and general extraction capabilities. The tool employs the iText PDF toolkit[17] for character extraction and the Docstrum[18] image segmentation algorithm for page segmentation of document images. CERMINE uses an SVM classifier implemented using the LibSVM[19] library and rule-based algorithms for metadata extraction. For reference extraction, the tool employs k-means clustering, and Conditional Random Fields implemented using the MALLET[20] toolkit for sequence labeling. CERMINE returns a single XML file containing the annotations for an entire PDF. We employ the Beautiful Soup[21] library to filter CERMINE's output files for the annotations relevant to our evaluation.

GROBID[22] [35] supports all four extraction tasks. The tool allows using either feature-engineered CRF (default) or a combination of CRF and DL models realized using the DeLFT[23] Deep Learning library, which is based on TensorFlow and Keras. GROBID uses a cascade of sequence labeling models for different components. The models in the model cascade use individual label

---

[15] https://github.com/camelot-dev/camelot.
[16] https://github.com/pdfminer/pdfminer.six.
[17] https://github.com/itext.
[18] https://github.com/chulwoopack/docstrum.
[19] https://github.com/cjlin1/libsvm.
[20] http://mallet.cs.umass.edu/sequences.php.
[21] https://www.crummy.com/software/BeautifulSoup/bs4/doc/.
[22] https://github.com/kermitt2/grobid.
[23] https://github.com/kermitt2/delft.

sequencing algorithms and features; some models employ tokenizers. This approach offers flexibility by allowing model tuning and improves the model's maintainability. We evaluate the default CRF model with production settings (a recommended setting to improve the performance and availability of the GROBID server, according to the tool's documentation[24]).

PdfAct formerly called Icecite [5] is a rule-based tool that supports all four extraction tasks, including the extraction of appendices, acknowledgments, and tables of contents. The tool uses the PDFBox[25] and pdftotext[26] PDF manipulation and content extraction libraries. We use the tool's JAR release[27].

PyMuPDF[28] extends the MuPDF[29] viewer library with font and image extraction, PDF joining, and file embedding. PyMuPDF uses tesseract[30] for OCR. PyMuPDF could not process files whose names include special characters.

RefExtract[31] is a reference extraction tool that uses pdftotext[32] and regular expressions. RefExtract returns annotations for the entire bibliography of a document. The ground-truth annotations in our dataset (cf. Sect. 3.2), however, pertain to individual pages of documents and do not always cover the entire document. If ground-truth annotations are only available for a subset of the references in a document, we use regular expressions to filter RefExtract's output to those references with ground-truth labels.

Science Parse[33] uses a CRF model trained on data from GROBID to extract the title, author, and references. It also employs a rule-based algorithm by Clark and Divvala [9] to extract sections and paragraphs in JSON format.

Tabula[34] is a table extraction tool. Analogous to Camelot, Tabula offers a *Stream* mode realized using PDFBox, and a *Lattice* mode realized using OpenCV for table cell recognition.

3.2   Dataset

We use the DocBank[35] dataset, created by Li et al. [31], for our experiments. Figure 1 visualizes the process for compiling the dataset. First, the creators gathered arXiv documents, for which both the PDF and LaTeX source code was available. Li et al. then edited the LaTeX code to enable accurate automated annotations of content elements in the PDF version of the documents. For this purpose, they inserted commands that formatted content elements in specific

---

[24] https://GROBID.readthedocs.io/en/latest/Troubleshooting/.
[25] http://pdfbox.apache.org/.
[26] https://github.com/jalan/pdftotext.
[27] https://github.com/ad-freiburg/pdfact.
[28] https://github.com/pymupdf/PyMuPDF.
[29] https://mupdf.com/.
[30] https://github.com/tesseract-ocr/tesseract.
[31] https://github.com/inspirehep/refextract.
[32] https://linux.die.net/man1/pdftotext.
[33] https://github.com/allenai/science-parse.
[34] https://github.com/chezou/tabula-py.
[35] https://github.com/doc-analysis/DocBank.

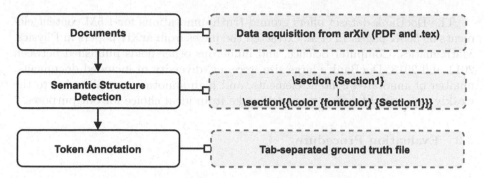

Fig. 1. Process for generating the DocBank dataset.

colors. The center part of Fig. 3 shows the mapping of content elements to colors. In the last step, the dataset creators used PDFPlumber[36] and PDFMiner to extract and annotate relevant content elements by their color. DocBank provides the annotations as separate files for each document page in the dataset.

Table 5 shows the structure of the tab-separated ground-truth files. Each line in the file refers to one component on the page and is structured as follows. Index 0 represents the token itself, e.g., a word. Indices 1-4 denote the bounding box information of the token, where (x0, y0) represents the top-left and (x1, y1) the bottom-right corner of the token in the PDF coordinate space. Indices 5-7 reflect the token's color in RGB notation, index 8 the token's font, and index 9 the label for the type of the content element. Each ground-truth file adheres to the naming scheme shown in Fig. 2.

Table 5. Structure of DocBank's plaintext ground truth files.

Index	0	1	2	3	4	5	6	7	8	9
Content	token	x0	y0	x1	y1	R	G	B	font name	label

Source: https://doc-analysis.github.io/docbank-page.

Prefix	Identifier	Postfix	Page
8.tar_	1501.04311	.gz_pippori_	27.txt

Fig. 2. Naming scheme for DocBank's ground-truth files.

---

[36] https://github.com/jsvine/pdfplumber.

The DocBank dataset offers ground-truth annotations for 1.5M content elements on 500K pages. Li et al. extracted the pages from arXiv papers in Physics, Mathematics, Computer Science, and numerous other fields published between 2014 and 2018. DocBank's large size, recency, diversity of included documents, number of annotated content elements, and high annotation quality due to the weakly supervised labeling approach make it an ideal choice for our purposes.

3.3   Evaluation Procedure

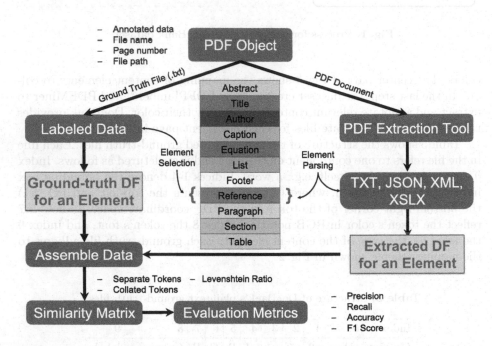

Fig. 3. Overview of the procedure for comparing content elements extracted by IE tools to the ground-truth annotations and computing evaluation metrics.

Figure 3 shows our evaluation procedure. First, we select the PDF files whose associated ground-truth files contain relevant labels. For example, we search for ground-truth files containing *reference* tokens to evaluate reference extraction tools. We include the PDF file, the ground-truth file, the document ID and page number obtainable from the file name (cf. Figure 2), and the file path in a self-defined Python object (see *PDF Object* in Fig. 3).

Then, the evaluation process splits into two branches whose goal is to create two pandas data frames—one holding the relevant ground-truth data, and the other the output of an information extraction tool. For this purpose, both the ground-truth files and the output files of IE tools are parsed and filtered for the relevant content elements. For example, to evaluate reference extraction via

CERMINE, we exclusively parse reference tags from CERMINE's XML output file into a data frame (see *Extracted DF* in Fig. 3).

Finally, we convert both the *ground-truth data frame* and the *extracted data frame* into two formats for comparison and computing performance metrics. The first is the *separate tokens* format, in which every token is represented as a row in the data frame. The second is the *collated tokens* format, in which all tokens are combined into a single space-delimited row in the data frame. Separate tokens serve to compute a strict score for token-level extraction quality, whereas collated tokens yield a more lenient score intended to reflect a tool's average extraction quality for a class of content elements. We will explain the idea of both scores and their computation hereafter.

We employ the *Levenshtein Ratio* to quantify the similarity of extracted tokens and the ground-truth data for both the separate tokens and collated tokens format. Eq. (1) defines the computation of the *Levenshtein distance* of the extracted tokens t_e and the ground-truth tokens t_g.

$$lev_{t_e,t_g}(i,j) = \begin{cases} max(i,j), & \text{if } min(i,j) = 0, \\ min \begin{cases} lev_{t_e,t_g}(i-1,j)+1 \\ lev_{t_e,t_g}(i,j-1)+1 \\ lev_{t_e,t_g}(i-1,j-1)+1_{(t_{ei} \neq t_{ej})} \end{cases} & \text{otherwise.} \end{cases}$$

(1)

Equation (2) defines the derived Levenshtein Ratio score (γ).

$$\gamma(t_e, t_g) = 1 - \frac{lev_{t_e,t_g}(i,j)}{|t_e| + |t_g|}$$

(2)

Equation (3) shows the derivation of the *similarity matrix* (Δ^d) for a document (d), which contains the Levenshtein Ratio (γ) of every token in the extracted data frame with separate tokens E^s of size m and the ground-truth data frame with separate tokens G^s of size n.

$$\Delta^d_{m \times n} = \gamma \left[E^s_i, G^s_j \right]^{m,n}_{i,j}$$

(3)

Using the $m \times n$ similarity matrix, we compute the *Precision* P^d and *Recall* R^d scores according to Eqs. (4) and (5), respectively. As the numerator, we use the number of extracted tokens whose Levenshtein Ratio is larger or equal to 0.7. We chose this threshold for consistency with the experiments by Granitzer et al. [19]. We then compute the F^d_1 score according to Eq. (6) as a token-level score for a tool's extraction quality.

$$P^d = \frac{\#\Delta^d_{i,j} \geq 0.7}{m}$$

(4)

$$R^d = \frac{\#\Delta^d_{i,j} \geq 0.7}{n}$$

(5)

$$F_1^d = \frac{2 \times P^d \times R^d}{P^d + R^d} \tag{6}$$

Moreover, we compute the *Accuracy* score A^d reflecting a tool's average extraction quality for a class of tokens. To obtain A^d, we compute the Levenshtein Ratio γ of the extracted tokens E^c and ground-truth tokens G^c in the collated tokens format, according to Eq. (7).

$$A^d = \gamma[E^c, G^c] \tag{7}$$

Figures 4 and 5 show the similarity matrices for the author names 'Yuta,' 'Hamada,' 'Gary,' and 'Shiu' using separate and collated tokens, respectively. Figure 4 additionally shows an example computation of the Levenshtein Ratio for the strings *Gary* and *Yuta*. The strings have a Levenshtein distance of six and a cumulative string length of eight, which results in a Levenshtein Ratio of 0.25 that is entered into the similarity matrix. Figure 5 analogously exemplifies computing the Accuracy score of the two strings using collated tokens.

	Yuta	Hamada	Gary	Shiu1,
Yuta	1.0	0.2	0.25	0.2
Hamada	0.2	1.0	0.2	0.0
Gary	0.25	0.2	1.0	0.0
Shiu	0.25	0.0	0.0	0.8

		Y	u	t	a
	0	1	2	3	4
G	1	2	3	4	5
a	2	3	4	5	4
r	3	4	5	6	5
y	4	3	4	5	6

Fig. 4. <u>Left</u>: Similarity matrix for author names using separate tokens. <u>Right</u>: Computation of the Levenshtein distance (6) and the optimal edit transcript (yellow highlights) for two author names using dynamic programming.

	Yuta Hamada Gary Shiu1,
Yuta Hamada Gary Shiu	0.957

Fig. 5. Similarity matrix for two sets of author names using collated tokens.

4   Results

We present the evaluation results grouped by extraction task (see Figs. 6, 7, 8 and 9) and by tools (see Table 6). This two-fold breakdown of the results facilitates identifying the best-performing tool for a specific extraction task or content element and allows for gauging the strengths and weaknesses of tools more easily. Note that the task-specific result visualizations (Figs. 6, 7, 8 and 9) only include tools that support the respective extraction task. See Table 4 for an overview of the evaluated tools and the extraction tasks they support.

Figure 6 shows the cumulative F_1 scores of CERMINE, GROBID, PdfAct, and Science Parse for the metadata extraction task, i.e., extracting title, abstract, and authors. Consequently, the best possible cumulative F_1 score equals three. Overall, GROBID performs best, achieving a cumulative F_1 score of 2.25 and individual F_1 scores of 0.91 for *title*, 0.82 for *abstract*, and 0.52 for *authors*. Science Parse (2.03) and CERMINE (1.97) obtain comparable cumulative F_1 scores, while PdfAct has the lowest cumulative F_1 score of 1.14. However, PdfAct performs second-best for title extraction with a F_1 score of 0.85. The performance of all tools is worse for extracting authors than for titles and abstracts. It appears that machine-learning-based approaches like those of CERMINE, GROBID, and Science Parse perform better for metadata extraction than rule-based algorithms like the one implemented in PdfAct[37].

Figure 7 shows the results for the reference extraction task. With a F_1 score of 0.79, GROBID also performs best for this task. CERMINE achieves the second rank with a F_1 score of 0.74, while Science Parse and RefExtract share the third rank with identical F_1 scores of 0.49. As for the metadata extraction task, PdfAct also achieves the lowest F_1 score of 0.15 for reference extraction. While both RefExtract and PdfAct employ pdftotext and regular expressions, GROBID performs efficient segregation of cascaded sequence labeling models[38] for diverse components, which can be the reason for its superior performance [36].

Figure 8 depicts the results for the table extraction task. Adobe Extract outperforms the other tools with a F_1 score of 0.47. Camelot ($F_1 = 0.30$), Tabula ($F_1 = 0.28$), and GROBID ($F_1 = 0.23$) perform notably worse than Adobe Extract. Both Camelot and Tabula incorrectly treat two-column articles as tables and table captions as a part of the table region, which negatively affects their performance scores. The use of comparable *Stream* and *Lattice* modes in Camelot and Tabula (cf. Sect. 3.1) likely cause the tools' highly similar results. PdfAct did not produce an output for any of our test documents that contain tables, although the tool supposedly supports table extraction. The performance of all tools is significantly lower for table extraction than for other content elements, which is likely caused by the need to extract additional structural information. The difficulty of table extraction is also reflected by numerous issues that users opened on the matter in the GROBID GitHub repository[39].

---

[37] See Table 4 for more information on the tools' extraction approaches.
[38] https://grobid.readthedocs.io/en/latest/Principles/.
[39] https://github.com/kermitt2/grobid/issues/340.

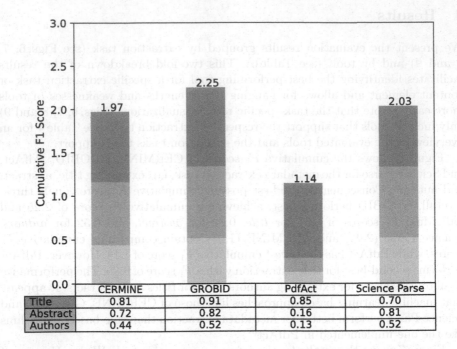

	CERMINE	GROBID	PdfAct	Science Parse
Title	0.81	0.91	0.85	0.70
Abstract	0.72	0.82	0.16	0.81
Authors	0.44	0.52	0.13	0.52

Fig. 6. Results for metadata extraction.

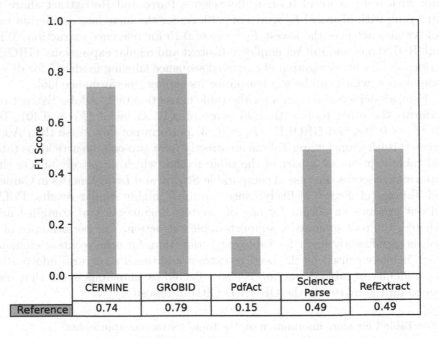

	CERMINE	GROBID	PdfAct	Science Parse	RefExtract
Reference	0.74	0.79	0.15	0.49	0.49

Fig. 7. Results for reference extraction.

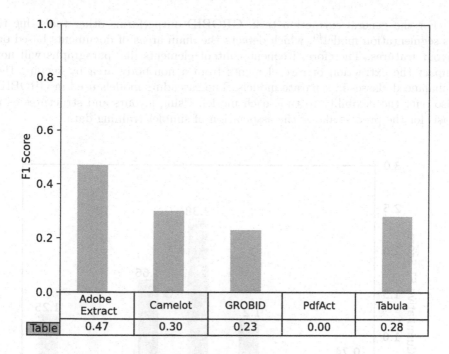

Table	Adobe Extract	Camelot	GROBID	PdfAct	Tabula
	0.47	0.30	0.23	0.00	0.28

Fig. 8. Results for table extraction.

Figure 9 visualizes the results for the general extraction task. GROBID achieves the highest cumulative F_1 score of 2.38, followed by PdfAct (cumulative $F_1 = 1.66$). The cumulative F_1 scores of Science Parse (1.25), which only support paragraph and section extraction, and CERMINE (1.20) are much lower than GROBID's score and comparable to that of PdfAct. Apache Tika, PyMuPDF, and Adobe Extract can only extract paragraphs.

For paragraph extraction, GROBID (0.9), CERMINE (0.85), and PdfAct (0.85) obtained high F_1 scores with Science Parse (0.76) and Adobe Extract (0.74) following closely. Apache Tika (0.52) and PyMuPDF (0.51) achieved notably lower scores because the tools include other elements like sections, captions, lists, footers, and equations in paragraphs.

Notably, only GROBID achieves a promising F_1 score of 0.74 for the extraction of sections. GROBID and PdfAct are the only tools that can partially extract captions. None of the tools is able to extract lists. Only PdfAct supports the extraction of footers but achieves a low F_1 score of 0.20. Only GROBID supports equation extraction but the extraction quality is comparatively low ($F_1 = 0.25$). To reduce the evaluation effort, we first tested the extraction of lists, footers, and equations on a two-months sample of the data covering January and February 2014. If a tool consistently obtained performance scores of 0, we did not continue with its evaluation. Following this procedure, we only evaluated GROBID and PdfAct on the full dataset.

For the general extraction task, GROBID outperforms other tools due to its segmentation model[40], which detects the main areas of documents based on layout features. Therefore, frequent content elements like paragraphs will not impact the extraction of rare elements from a non-body area by keeping the imbalanced classes in separate models. The cascading models used in GROBID also offer the flexibility to tune each model. Using layouts and structures as a basis for the process allows the association of simpler training data.

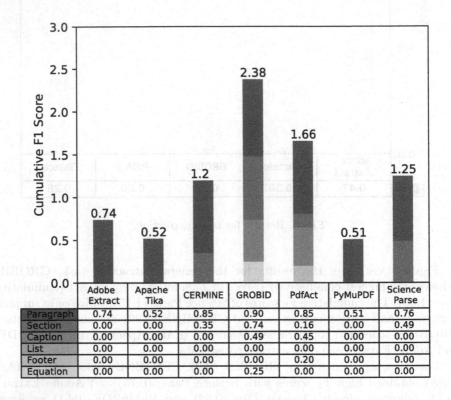

	Adobe Extract	Apache Tika	CERMINE	GROBID	PdfAct	PyMuPDF	Science Parse
Paragraph	0.74	0.52	0.85	0.90	0.85	0.51	0.76
Section	0.00	0.00	0.35	0.74	0.16	0.00	0.49
Caption	0.00	0.00	0.00	0.49	0.45	0.00	0.00
List	0.00	0.00	0.00	0.00	0.00	0.00	0.00
Footer	0.00	0.00	0.00	0.00	0.20	0.00	0.00
Equation	0.00	0.00	0.00	0.25	0.00	0.00	0.00

Fig. 9. Results for general data extraction.

The breakdown of results by tools shown in Table 6 underscores the main takeaway point of the results' presentation for the individual extraction tasks. The tools' results differ greatly for different content elements. Certainly, no tool performs best for all elements, rather, even tools that perform well overall can fail completely for certain extraction tasks. The large amount of content elements whose extraction is either unsupported or only possible in poor quality indicates a large potential for improvement in future work.

---

[40] https://grobid.readthedocs.io/en/latest/Principles/.

Table 6. Results grouped by extraction tool.

Tool[a]	Label	# Detected	# Processed[b]	Acc	F_1	P	R
Adobe Extract	Table	1,635	736	**0.52**	**0.47**	**0.45**	**0.49**
	Paragraph	3,985	3,088	0.85	0.74	0.72	0.76
Apache Tika	Paragraph	339,603	258,582	0.55	0.52	0.43	0.65
Camelot	Table	16,289	**11,628**	0.27	0.30	0.23	0.44
CERMINE	Title	16,196	14,501	0.84	0.81	0.81	0.81
	Author	**19,788**	14,797	0.43	0.44	0.44	0.46
	Abstract	19,342	16,716	0.71	0.72	0.68	0.76
	Reference	**40,333**	35,193	0.80	0.74	0.71	0.77
	Paragraph	361,273	348,160	0.89	0.85	0.83	0.87
	Section	**163,077**	139,921	0.40	0.35	0.32	0.38
GROBID	Title	16,196	16,018	**0.92**	**0.91**	**0.91**	**0.92**
	Author	**19,788**	**19,563**	**0.54**	**0.52**	**0.52**	**0.53**
	Abstract	19,342	**18,714**	0.82	**0.82**	**0.81**	0.83
	Reference	**40,333**	**36,020**	**0.82**	**0.79**	**0.79**	**0.80**
	Paragraph	361,273	**358,730**	0.90	**0.90**	**0.89**	**0.91**
	Section	**163,077**	**163,037**	**0.77**	**0.74**	**0.73**	**0.76**
	Caption	**90,606**	**62,445**	**0.57**	**0.49**	**0.47**	0.51
	Table	**16,740**	8,633	0.24	0.23	0.23	0.23
	Equation	**142,736**	**96,560**	**0.26**	**0.25**	**0.20**	**0.32**
PdfAct	Title	**17,670**	**16,834**	0.85	0.85	0.85	0.86
	Author	13,110	2,187	0.14	0.13	0.12	0.18
	Abstract	**21,470**	4,683	0.17	0.16	0.15	0.20
	Reference	30,263	12,705	0.19	0.15	0.17	0.20
	Paragraph	**361,318**	357,905	0.85	0.85	0.80	0.89
	Section	129,361	87,605	0.21	0.16	0.12	0.25
	Caption	83,435	53,314	0.45	0.45	0.40	**0.52**
	Footer	**32,457**	**26,252**	**0.23**	**0.20**	**0.25**	**0.16**
PyMuPDF	Paragraph	339,650	258,383	0.55	0.51	0.41	0.65
RefExtract	Reference	**40,333**	38,405	0.55	0.49	0.44	0.55
Science Parse	Title	11,696	11,687	0.79	0.70	0.70	0.70
	Author	471	471	**0.54**	**0.52**	**0.52**	**0.53**
	Abstract	14,150	14,149	**0.83**	0.81	0.73	**0.90**
	Reference	**40,333**	35,200	0.55	0.49	0.49	0.50
	Paragraph	**361,318**	355,529	0.79	0.76	0.76	0.76
	Section	**163,077**	158,556	0.54	0.49	0.49	0.50
Tabula	Table	10,361	9,456	0.29	0.28	0.20	0.46

[a] Boldface indicates the best value for each content element type.
[b] The differences in the number of detected and processed items are due to PDF Read Exceptions or Warnings. We label an item as processed if it has a non-zero F_1 score.

5   Conclusion and Future Work

We present an open evaluation framework for information extraction from academic PDF documents. Our framework uses the DocBank dataset [31] offering 12 types and 1.5M annotated instances of content elements contained in 500K pages of arXiv papers from multiple disciplines. The dataset is larger, more topically diverse, and supports more extraction tasks than most related datasets.

We use the newly developed framework to benchmark the performance of ten freely available tools in extracting document metadata, bibliographic references, tables, and other content elements in academic PDF documents. GROBID, followed by CERMINE and Science Parse achieves the best results for the metadata and reference extraction tasks. For table extraction, Adobe Extract outperforms other tools, even though the performance is much lower than for other content elements. All tools struggle to extract lists, footers, and equations.

While DocBank covers more disciplines than other datasets, we see further diversification of the collection in terms of disciplines, document types, and content elements as a valuable task for future research. Table 2 shows that more datasets suitable for information extraction from PDF documents are available but unused thus far. The weakly supervised annotation approach used for creating the DocBank dataset is transferable to other LaTeX document collections.

Apart from the dataset, our framework can incorporate additional tools and allows easy replacement of tools in case of updates. We intend to update and extend our performance benchmark in the future.

The extraction of tables, equations, footers, lists, and similar content elements poses the toughest challenge for tools in our benchmark. In recent work, Grennan et al. [20] showed that the usage of synthetic datasets for model training can improve citation parsing. A similar approach could also be a promising direction for improving the access to currently hard-to-extract content elements.

Combining extraction approaches could lead to a one-fits-all extraction tool, which we consider desirable. The Sciencebeam-pipelines[41] project currently undertakes initial steps toward that goal. We hope that our evaluation framework will help to support this line of research by facilitating performance benchmarks of IE tools as part of a continuous development and integration process.

References

1. Ahmed, M.W., Afzal, M.T.: FLAG-PDFe: features oriented metadata extraction framework for scientific publications. IEEE Access **8**, 99458–99469 (2020). https://doi.org/10.1109/ACCESS.2020.2997907
2. Aiello, M., Monz, C., Todoran, L., Worring, M.: Document understanding for a broad class of documents. Int. J. Doc. Anal. Recogn. **5**(1),1–16 (2002). https://doi.org/10.1007/s10032-002-0080-x

---

[41] https://github.com/elifesciences/sciencebeam-pipelines.

3. Anzaroot, S., Passos, A., Belanger, D., McCallum, A.: Learning soft linear constraints with application to citation field extraction. In: Proceedings of the 52nd Annual Meeting of the Association for Computational Linguistics (Volume 1: Long Papers), pp. 593–602. Association for Computational Linguistics, Baltimore, Maryland (2014). https://doi.org/10.3115/v1/P14-1056

4. Azimjonov, J., Alikhanov, J.: Rule based metadata extraction framework from academic articles. arXiv CoRR 1807.09009v1 [cs.IR], pp. 1–10 (2018). https://doi.org/10.48550/arXiv.1807.09009

5. Bast, H., Korzen, C.: The Icecite research paper management system. In: Lin, X., Manolopoulos, Y., Srivastava, D., Huang, G. (eds.) WISE 2013. LNCS, vol. 8181, pp. 396–409. Springer, Heidelberg (2013). https://doi.org/10.1007/978-3-642-41154-0_30

6. Bast, H., Korzen, C.: A benchmark and evaluation for text extraction from PDF. In: 2017 ACM/IEEE Joint Conference on Digital Libraries (JCDL), pp. 1–10. IEEE, Toronto, ON, Canada (2017). https://doi.org/10.1109/JCDL.2017.7991564

7. Bhardwaj, A., Mercier, D., Dengel, A., Ahmed, S.: DeepBIBX: deep learning for image based bibliographic data extraction. In: Liu, D., Xie, S., Li, Y., Zhao, D., El-Alfy, E.S. (eds.) Neural Information Processing. ICONIP 2017. LNCS, vol. 10635, pp. 286–293. Springer, Cham (2017). https://doi.org/10.1007/978-3-319-70096-0_30

8. Borkar, V., Deshmukh, K., Sarawagi, S.: Automatic segmentation of text into structured records. SIGMOD Rec. 30(2), 175–186 (2001). https://doi.org/10.1145/376284.375682

9. Clark, C., Divvala, S.: PDFFigures 2.0: mining figures from research papers. In: Proceedings of the 16th ACM/IEEE-CS on Joint Conference on Digital Libraries, pp. 143–152. JCDL 2016, Association for Computing Machinery, New York, NY, USA (2016). https://doi.org/10.1145/2910896.2910904

10. Cortez, E., da Silva, A.S., Gonçalves, M.A., Mesquita, F., de Moura, E.S.: FLUX-CIM: flexible unsupervised extraction of citation metadata. In: Proceedings of the 7th ACM/IEEE-CS Joint Conference on Digital Libraries. pp. 215–224. JCDL 2007, Association for Computing Machinery, New York, NY, USA (2007). https://doi.org/10.1145/1255175.1255219

11. Cortez, E., da Silva, A.S., Gonçalves, M.A., Mesquita, F., de Moura, E.S.: A flexible approach for extracting metadata from bibliographic citations. JASIST 60(6), 1144–1158 (2009). https://doi.org/10.1002/asi.21049

12. Councill, I., Giles, C.L., Kan, M.Y.: ParsCit: an open-source CRF reference string parsing package. In: Proceedings of the Sixth International Conference on Language Resources and Evaluation. European Language Resources Association, Marrakech, Morocco (2008). https://aclanthology.org/L08-1291/

13. Cui, B.-G., Chen, X.: An improved hidden Markov model for literature metadata extraction. In: Huang, D.-S., Zhao, Z., Bevilacqua, V., Figueroa, J.C. (eds.) ICIC 2010. LNCS, vol. 6215, pp. 205–212. Springer, Heidelberg (2010). https://doi.org/10.1007/978-3-642-14922-1_26

14. Day, M.Y., et al.: Reference metadata extraction using a hierarchical knowledge representation framework. Decis. Support Syst. 43(1), 152–167 (2007). https://doi.org/10.1016/j.dss.2006.08.006

15. De La Torre, M., Aguirre, C., Anshutz, B., Hsu, W.: MATESC: metadata-analytic text extractor and section classifier for scientific publications. In: Proceedings of the 10th International Joint Conference on Knowledge Discovery, Knowledge Engineering and Knowledge Management, vol. 1, pp. 261–267. SciTePress (2018). https://doi.org/10.5220/0006937702610267

16. Fan, T., et al.: PARDA: a dataset for scholarly pdf document metadata extraction evaluation. In: Gao, H., Wang, X., Yin, Y., Iqbal, M. (eds.) CollaborateCom 2018. LNICST, vol. 268, pp. 417–431. Springer, Cham (2019). https://doi.org/10.1007/978-3-030-12981-1_29

17. Färber, M., Thiemann, A., Jatowt, A.: A high-quality gold standard for citation-based tasks. In: Proceedings of the Eleventh International Conference on Language Resources and Evaluation. European Language Resources Association, Miyazaki, Japan (2018). https://aclanthology.org/L18-1296

18. Giuffrida, G., Shek, E.C., Yang, J.: Knowledge-based metadata extraction from postscript files. In: Proceedings of the Fifth ACM Conference on Digital Libraries, pp. 77–84. DL 2000, Association for Computing Machinery, New York, NY, USA (2000). https://doi.org/10.1145/336597.336639

19. Granitzer, M., Hristakeva, M., Jack, K., Knight, R.: A comparison of metadata extraction techniques for crowdsourced bibliographic metadata management. In: Proceedings of the 27th Annual ACM Symposium on Applied Computing, pp. 962–964. SAC 2012, Association for Computing Machinery, New York, NY, USA (2012). https://doi.org/10.1145/2245276.2245462

20. Grennan, M., Beel, J.: Synthetic vs. real reference strings for citation parsing, and the importance of re-training and out-of-sample data for meaningful evaluations: Experiments with GROBID, GIANT and CORA. In: Proceedings of the 8th International Workshop on Mining Scientific Publications, pp. 27–35. Association for Computational Linguistics, Wuhan, China (2020). https://aclanthology.org/2020.wosp-1.4

21. Grennan, M., Schibel, M., Collins, A., Beel, J.: GIANT: the 1-billion annotated synthetic bibliographic-reference-string dataset for deep citation parsing [Data] (2019). https://doi.org/10.7910/DVN/LXQXAO

22. Hashmi, A.M., Afzal, M.T., Rehman, S.U.: Rule based approach to extract metadata from scientific pdf documents. In: 2020 5th International Conference on Innovative Technologies in Intelligent Systems and Industrial Applications (CITISIA), pp. 1–4. IEEE, Sydney, Australia (2020). https://doi.org/10.1109/CITISIA50690.2020.9371784

23. Hetzner, E.: A simple method for citation metadata extraction using hidden Markov models. In: Proceedings of the 8th ACM/IEEE-CS Joint Conference on Digital Libraries, pp. 280–284. JCDL 2008, Association for Computing Machinery, New York, NY, USA (2008). https://doi.org/10.1145/1378889.1378937

24. Kasdorf, W.E.: The Columbia guide to digital publishing. Columbia University Press, USA (2003)

25. Kern, R., Jack, K., Hristakeva, M.: TeamBeam - meta-data extraction from scientific literature. D-Lib Magaz. 18(7/8), 1045 (2012). https://doi.org/10.1045/july2012-kern

26. Klein, D., Manning, C.D.: Conditional structure versus conditional estimation in NLP models. In: Proceedings of the 2002 Conference on Empirical Methods in Natural Language Processing (EMNLP), pp. 9–16. Association for Computational Linguistics, Pennsylvania, Philadelphia, PA, USA (2002). https://doi.org/10.3115/1118693.1118695

27. Klink, S., Dengel, A., Kieninger, T.: Document structure analysis based on layout and textual features. In: IAPR International Workshop on Document Analysis Systems. IAPR, Rio de Janeiro, Brazil (2000)
28. Körner, M., Ghavimi, B., Mayr, P., Hartmann, H., Staab, S.: Evaluating reference string extraction using line-based conditional random fields: a case study with german language publications. In: Nørvåg, K., et al. (eds.) ADBIS 2017. CCIS, vol. 767, pp. 137–145. Springer, Cham (2017). https://doi.org/10.1007/978-3-319-67162-8_15
29. Lafferty, J.D., McCallum, A., Pereira, F.C.N.: conditional random fields: probabilistic models for segmenting and labeling sequence data. In: Proceedings of the Eighteenth International Conference on Machine Learning, pp. 282–289. ICML '01, Morgan Kaufmann Publishers Inc., San Francisco, CA, USA (2001). https://dl.acm.org/doi/10.5555/645530.655813
30. Ley, M.: DBLP: some lessons learned. Proc. VLDB Endow. 2(2), 1493–1500 (2009). https://doi.org/10.14778/1687553.1687577
31. Li, M., et al.: DocBank: a benchmark dataset for document layout analysis. In: Proceedings of the 28th International Conference on Computational Linguistics, pp. 949–960. International Committee on Computational Linguistics, Barcelona, Spain (Online) (2020). https://doi.org/10.18653/v1/2020.coling-main.82
32. Lipinski, M., Yao, K., Breitinger, C., Beel, J., Gipp, B.: Evaluation of header metadata extraction approaches and tools for scientific PDF documents. In: Proceedings of the 13th ACM/IEEE-CS Joint Conference on Digital Libraries, pp. 385–386. JCDL 2013, Association for Computing Machinery, New York, NY, USA (2013). https://doi.org/10.1145/2467696.2467753
33. Livathinos, N., et al.: Robust pdf document conversion using recurrent neural networks. Proceed. AAAI Conf. Artif. Intell. 35(17), 15137–15145 (2021). https://doi.org/10.1609/aaai.v35i17.17777
34. Lo, K., Wang, L.L., Neumann, M., Kinney, R., Weld, D.: S2ORC: the semantic scholar open research corpus. In: Proceedings of the 58th Annual Meeting of the Association for Computational Linguistics, pp. 4969–4983. Association for Computational Linguistics, Online (2020). https://doi.org/10.18653/v1/2020.acl-main.447
35. Lopez, P.: GROBID (2008). https://github.com/kermitt2/grobid
36. Lopez, P.: GROBID: combining automatic bibliographic data recognition and term extraction for scholarship publications. In: Agosti, M., Borbinha, J., Kapidakis, S., Papatheodorou, C., Tsakonas, G. (eds.) ECDL 2009. LNCS, vol. 5714, pp. 473–474. Springer, Heidelberg (2009). https://doi.org/10.1007/978-3-642-04346-8_62
37. Mao, S., Kim, J., Thoma, G.R.: a dynamic feature generation system for automated metadata extraction in preservation of digital materials. In: 1st International Workshop on Document Image Analysis for Libraries, pp. 225–232. IEEE Computer Society, Palo Alto, CA, USA (2004). https://doi.org/10.1109/DIAL.2004.1263251
38. Mao, S., Rosenfeld, A., Kanungo, T.: Document structure analysis algorithms: a literature survey. In: Proceedings Document Recognition and Retrieval X. SPIE Proceedings, vol. 5010, pp. 197–207. SPIE, Santa Clara, California, USA (2003). https://doi.org/10.1117/12.476326
39. McCallum, A.K., Nigam, K., Rennie, J., Seymore, K.: Automating the construction of internet portals with machine learning. Inf. Retrieval 3(2), 127–163 (2000). https://doi.org/10.1023/A:1009953814988

40. National Library of Medicine: PubMed. https://pubmed.ncbi.nlm.nih.gov/
41. National Library of Medicine: PubMed Central. https://www.ncbi.nlm.nih.gov/pmc/
42. Ojokoh, B., Zhang, M., Tang, J.: A trigram hidden Markov model for metadata extraction from heterogeneous references. Inf. Sci. **181**(9), 1538–1551 (2011). https://doi.org/10.1016/j.ins.2011.01.014
43. Ororbia, A.G., Wu, J., Khabsa, M., WIlliams, K., Giles, C.L.: Big scholarly data in CiteSeerX: information extraction from the web. In: Proceedings of the 24th International Conference on World Wide Web, pp. 597–602. WWW 2015 Companion, Association for Computing Machinery, New York, NY, USA (2015). https://doi.org/10.1145/2740908.2741736
44. Palmero, G., Dimitriadis, Y.: Structured document labeling and rule extraction using a new recurrent fuzzy-neural system. In: Proceedings of the Fifth International Conference on Document Analysis and Recognition, pp. 181–184. Springer (1999). https://doi.org/10.1109/ICDAR.1999.791754
45. Peng, F., McCallum, A.: Accurate information extraction from research papers using conditional random fields. In: Proceedings of the Human Language Technology Conference of the North American Chapter of the Association for Computational Linguistics: HLT-NAACL, pp. 329–336. Association for Computational Linguistics, Boston, Massachusetts, USA (2004). https://aclanthology.org/N04-1042
46. Prasad, A., Kaur, M., Kan, M.-Y.: Neural ParsCit: a deep learning-based reference string parser. Int. J. Digit. Libr. **19**(4), 323–337 (2018). https://doi.org/10.1007/s00799-018-0242-1
47. Rizvi, S.T.R., Dengel, A., Ahmed, S.: A hybrid approach and unified framework for bibliographic reference extraction. IEEE Access **8**, 217231–217245 (2020). https://doi.org/10.1109/ACCESS.2020.3042455
48. Rodrigues Alves, D., Colavizza, G., Kaplan, F.: Deep reference mining from scholarly literature in the arts and humanities. Front. Res. Metr. Anal. **3**, 21 (2018). https://doi.org/10.3389/frma.2018.00021
49. Saier, T., Färber, M.: Bibliometric-enhanced arXiv: a data set for paper-based and citation-based tasks. In: Proceedings of the 8th International Workshop on Bibliometric-enhanced Information Retrieval (BIR). CEUR Workshop Proceedings, vol. 2345, pp. 14–26. CEUR-WS.org, Cologne, Germany (2019). http://ceur-ws.org/Vol-2345/paper2.pdf
50. Saier, T., Färber, M.: *unarXive*: a large scholarly data set with publications' fulltext, annotated in-text citations, and links to metadata. Scientometrics **125**(3), 3085–3108 (2020). https://doi.org/10.1007/s11192-020-03382-z
51. Schloss Dagstuhl - Leibniz Center for Informatics, University of Trier: dblp: Computer Science Bibliography. https://dblp.org/
52. Souza, A., Moreira, V., Heuser, C.: ARCTIC: metadata extraction from scientific papers in PDF using two-layer CRF. In: Proceedings of the 2014 ACM Symposium on Document Engineering, pp. 121–130. DocEng 2014, Association for Computing Machinery, New York, NY, USA (2014). https://doi.org/10.1145/2644866.2644872

53. Tkaczyk, D., Collins, A., Sheridan, P., Beel, J.: Machine learning vs. rules and out-of-the-box vs. retrained: an evaluation of open-source bibliographic reference and citation parsers. In: Proceedings of the 18th ACM/IEEE on Joint Conference on Digital Libraries, pp. 99–108. JCDL 2018, Association for Computing Machinery, New York, NY, USA (2018). https://doi.org/10.1145/3197026.3197048
54. Tkaczyk, D., Szostek, P., Fedoryszak, M., Dendek, P.J., Bolikowski, Ł.: CERMINE: automatic extraction of structured metadata from scientific literature. Int. J. Doc. Anal. Recogn. (IJDAR) 18(4), 317–335 (2015). https://doi.org/10.1007/s10032-015-0249-8
55. Vaswani, A., et al.: Attention is all you need. In: Proceedings of the 31st International Conference on Neural Information Processing Systems, pp. 6000–6010. NIPS2017, Curran Associates Inc., Red Hook, NY, USA (2017). https://dl.acm.org/doi/10.5555/3295222.3295349
56. Vilnis, L., Belanger, D., Sheldon, D., McCallum, A.: Bethe projections for nonlocal inference. In: Proceedings of the Thirty-First Conference on Uncertainty in Artificial Intelligence, pp. 892–901. UAI2015, AUAI Press, Arlington, Virginia, USA (2015). https://doi.org/10.48550/arXiv.1503.01397

Contextualizing Session Resuming Reasons with Tasks Involving Expected Cross-session Searches

Yuan Li[✉] and Rob Capra

School of Information and Library Science,
University of North Carolina at Chapel Hill, Chapel Hill, NC 27599, USA
yuanli@email.unc.edu, rcapra@unc.edu

Abstract. Cross-session search (XSS) describes situations in which users search for information related to the same task across multiple sessions. While there has been research on XSS, little attention has been paid to users' motivations for searching multiple sessions in real-life contexts. We conducted a diary study to investigate the reasons that lead people to search across multiple sessions for their own tasks. We applied Lin and Belkin's [24] MISE theoretical model as a coding framework to analyze users' open-ended responses about their XSS reasons. We open-coded reasons that the MISE model did not cover. Our findings identified a subset of session-resuming reasons in the MISE model (i.e., spawning, transmuting, unanswered-incomplete, cultivated-updated, and anticipated) as the main reasons that caused people to start a search session in our participants' real-world searches. We also found six additional session resuming reasons rarely discussed in the context of XSS: exploring more topic aspects, finding inspiration and examples, reviewing the information found earlier, monitoring task progress, completing a search following a scheduled plan, and feeling in the mood/having the energy to search. Our results contextualize and enrich the MISE session resuming reasons by examining them in real-world examples. Our results also illustrate that users' XSS motivations are multifaceted. These findings have implications for developing assisting tools to support XSS and help design different types of search sessions to study XSS behavior.

Keywords: Cross-session search · Session resumption · Session resuming reason · Search motivation

1 Introduction

Cross-session search (XSS) describes situations in which users search for information related to the same task across multiple sessions [5,18,24,25]. In this context, the *task* refers to activities people perform in their work and life, and information-seeking and search tasks are sub-tasks of the overarching work task [21]. Previous research often attributed XSS to complex tasks or interruptions [14,18,25,27] and focused on users' XSS activities, search task types, and

© The Author(s), under exclusive license to Springer Nature Switzerland AG 2023
I. Sserwanga et al. (Eds.): iConference 2023, LNCS 13972, pp. 406–422, 2023.
https://doi.org/10.1007/978-3-031-28032-0_32

session features. In addition, previous work has developed models to extract XSS tasks, predict search task continuation (e.g., [1,18,38]), and device switching patterns when XSS involves the use of multiple devices (e.g., [10,15,38]).

XSS also plays a vital role in Information Science (IS) research. Some well-known information behavior models and theories were developed based on studies of users' information behavior in the XSS context. For example, Kulthau's [19] Information Search Process (IPS) model, the series of studies conducted by Byström and colleagues about relevance judgment, users' information need, and task complexity (e.g., [3,4]), and Vakkari's research on users' relevance criteria [37]. However, few of previous efforts examined the reasons that cause XSS.

Several pioneering researchers explored the reasons that could lead people to search for multiple sessions. Lin and Belkin [23,24] proposed a theoretical framework (the Multiple Information Seeking Episodes (MISE) model) which posits that successive searches could be caused by eight different reasons related to the searchers' perception of their information problem status. Spink et al. [33,34] found that the main reason that motivated library users to engage in successive searches was to refine or enhance the search results from previous searches. MacKay and Watters [28] found that the main reasons for people to stop a search session during the XSS process was mainly because they found the needed information for the session or their tasks were completed.

However, relatively little current research has investigated search session resuming reasons from users' perspectives for real-life tasks. Our research is an effort to fill this gap, update our understanding of XSS behaviors, and identify ways that search systems can aid users in XSS. Therefore, we ask:

RQ: What are the reasons that cause people to resume searching for real-life tasks over time?

We collected data from a diary study with twenty-five participants over two months. Based on a qualitative analysis of users' session resuming reasons for 101 sessions, we: 1) identified MISE resuming reasons that occur in real-world tasks, 2) found scenarios where MISE reasons needed elaboration or additional context, and 3) found additional resumption reasons not covered by the original MISE reasons. Our findings shed light on helping improve search engine results for XSS tasks, developing XSS assisting tools for task management, and providing insights about designing different search sessions in XSS future experimental studies.

2   Related Work

2.1   Characteristics of Cross-session Search

Prior work has documented that XSS often happens when users' tasks are complex. For instance, early research found that people searched multiple times over an extended period to explore a topic and for information problems that evolve over time   [30,32]. Donato [13] noted that XSS might be common in complex tasks because they are tasks that often involve multiple aspects; they include subtasks that require more time and effort to complete, and sometimes the information needs associated with a complex task cannot be fully satisfied by one single web page or a search session. Additional studies [17,28,31] found that information-gathering tasks were more complex and led people to search multiple sessions over time. XSS occurs across a variety of topics, including academic research projects, school work, shopping, traveling, and medical tasks [14,28,32].

Researchers have also explored the nature of XSS sessions. MacKay and Watters [28] found that, on average, students completed their XSS tasks in two to three sessions (no more than four). However, an earlier study by Spink [32] found that XSS could extend from two sessions up to more than a hundred for some tasks. Device-switching, or cross-device search, is common when users search across sessions. Wu [40] provided a comprehensive review on cross-device search.

2.2   Reasons that Lead to Cross-session Search

A few researchers have systematically investigated the reasons that lead to XSS. Lin and Belkin [23,24] proposed a theoretical model – the Multiple Information Seeking Episodes (MISE model) – which conceptualized eight different reasons that can cause successive searches:

"(1) transmuting – the problem gets elaborated and changes from its original form to a transmuted form; (2) spawning – the problem spawns subproblems; (3) transiting – the original problem transits to another, different problem; (4) rolling back – something that was thought to have been solved by a previous search turns out to be unresolved; (5) lost-treatment – the information... once found, is not available in the treatment application stage; (6) unanswered – the problem was unanswered by previous searches; (7) cultivated – occurs when a searcher is trying to stay abreast of an area of interest; (8) anticipated – the information problem has not occurred yet, but is anticipated based on the current information" [24, p. 396].

Spink et al. found that the main reason people resume searching is to extend or refine the results they found earlier. During experimental studies, people resumed search sessions to investigate different databases, to refind previous information, or to "secure more valuable information" [33,34]. XSS can also be a result of interruptions [27,31]. However, studies in this area often induce interruptions on purpose in experimental environments and focus on users' information activities after a task is resumed instead of investigating why they resume search sessions (e.g., [9–11]). Cross-device search often involves XSS when people use multiple devices to search for information for the same task. Wu [39] found that people switch devices often because they were unsatisfied with the results found using the previous device.

Our understanding of today's XSS, especially the underlying reasons that cause XSS, is still limited. There is little current research focusing on XSS reasons in *real-life task contexts* and the effects of the resumption reasons on users' XSS behaviors. It is unclear whether the previous research findings (from over 15 years ago) still reflect today's XSS behaviors. Our current study is thus motivated to address these questions.

3   Method

We conducted a diary study to investigate how and why people engage in XSS in the context of real-life tasks. The study was reviewed by the ethics board at our university.

3.1   Participant Recruitment

We sent a recruiting message through our university-wide mailing lists. To ensure that the recruited participants would conduct XSS during the study period, the recruiting email included a screening questionnaire that outlined two requirements for participation: 1) the participant should have a real-world task or project for which they had not done any searching yet, 2) the participant expected that they would search online multiple times to complete the task. We asked prospective participants to briefly describe their tasks in the screening questionnaire. These criteria helped us focus our data collection on *expected* XSS tasks that participants knew in advance would involve multiple search sessions. We selected twenty-nine volunteers and invited them to participate in the diary study. All 29 accepted and participated in the diary study.

3.2   Diary Study Process

We first scheduled an introductory meeting with each participant. During the introductory meeting, a participant first completed a consent form. Then they filled out a pre-task questionnaire to provide more details about the selected task they mentioned in the screening questionnaire (e.g., task motivation, people involved in the task, previous knowledge about the task, plans for task work processes, etc.) Next, we set up a customized Google account for the participant to use during the study period. Each participant had an individual account for themselves. The Google account was configured with bookmark links to three online questionnaires: (1) a pre-session questionnaire, (2) a post-session questionnaire, and (3) a structured daily review diary. It also included a bookmark folder for participants to save web pages they felt were useful for their tasks. The participant was then asked to login into this account on their own computer and conduct a practice task. Participants were told that the Google account would record all the search history associated with the account but that they could review it and delete any history that was irrelevant to their tasks. All the Google accounts were shared with the study moderator so that we could monitor participants' work process and remind them to fill out the questionnaires and diaries during the study period. We asked participants do all their searching for the task using the assigned Google account during the study period.

After the introductory meeting, participants worked on their tasks at their own pace. Participants were instructed that whenever they needed to search online for their selected task, they should log in to their assigned Google account. Before each search session, they were asked to complete the pre-session questionnaire. Then they could search however they wanted. When they decided to complete their session, they were asked to fill out the post-session questionnaire. Participants were also asked to complete the daily review diary at the end of each day when they worked on their task (e.g., searched or conducted other task-related activities).

Participants could search for as many sessions as needed until they completed the study. A requirement for full participation was to submit data for at least three search sessions and two daily review diaries by the end of the study. Participants who completed the diary study received USD $120 as compensation. Out of the 29 diary study participants, 15 were invited to participate in a 45-minute retrospective interview after completing the diary study. Each received an extra USD $20 for completing the interview.

3.3 Data Collected and Analysis

We collected data from twenty-nine participants, each working on one work task involving XSS. Our data collection covered about a two-month period from 08/2021 to 10/2021. Four participants withdrew from the study and their data were not included. The remaining twenty-five (n = 25) participants included 9 undergraduate students, 7 graduate students, and 9 non-student staff from our university. Participants ranged in age from 18 to 62 years and 60% were female. Their tasks included writing a screenplay, helping friends to find an apartment to rent, designing a baby shower, registering a small business, curating a LEGO collection, and writing an essay about an international problem. The 25 participants submitted a total of 101 completed pairs of questionnaires (i.e., pre-session questionnaire and post-session questionnaire for each session). They also submitted 91 daily review diaries.

To address our research questions, we conducted qualitative analysis on participants' responses to three questions: (1) an open-ended question in the *pre-session questionnaire* that asked about the reason why they started this search session, (2) an open-ended question in the *post-session questionnaire* about the reason that motivated them to start the session (we asked this again to provide two points of reference), and (3) a multiple-choice question in the *post-session questionnaire* which asked participants to select *one* choice from the list of MISE resuming reasons that best matched their *main reason for resuming the search in this session.*

Our goals for the qualitative analysis were twofold. First, we wanted to see if the participants' responses aligned well with the MISE resuming reasons, or if they included additional dimensions not in the MISE model. Second, we wanted to gain insights into how the resuming reasons manifested and what impacts they had on the search processes. To accomplish this, we started our qualitative analysis coding with the MISE resuming reasons. We then coded the participants' responses, checking our coding against their responses to the single-choice question with the MISE reasons. In many cases, our assessment matched the participants' choices. In other cases, we identified additions or modifications to the MISE categories.

We analyzed the resuming reasons for all reported search sessions, including the initial search session. This may seem unintuitive – how can you resume the initial session? We included the initial sessions for two main reasons. First, we wanted to gain a better understanding of the role of the first search session in XSS. Second, our participants' tasks were expected to involve XSS. Therefore, their initial session could be affected by their expectation and planning for the entire task process. By including the initial session, we gain a more holistic view of XSS reasons.

4 Results

In this section, we present the results of our qualitative analysis of participants' responses. We identified: (1) real-world examples of five resuming reasons present in the existing MISE model; (2) three types of MISE reasons that occurred in our data but were not related to a task *resumption*; and (3) six additional session resuming reasons that are not covered in the original MISE model. In the subsections below, we explain each of these in more detail.

4.1 MISE Reasons in Everyday XSS

Table 1 shows five XSS session resuming reasons we observed in our data that are covered by the existing MISE model. These include spawning ($n = 62$), transmuting ($n = 19$), unanswered-incomplete ($n = 9$), cultivated updated ($n = 9$), and anticipated ($n = 2$). Next, we discuss how these reasons were manifested in our data and how our analysis suggests extensions to the MISE model.

Table 1. A Summary of MISE Session resuming reasons and the related session stages during XSS

MISE reason	Initial session	Middle Session (s)	Last session	All sessions
Spawning	10	36	16	62
Transmuting	13	5	1	19
Unanswered-incomplete	0	6	3	9
Cultivated-updated	2	3	4	9
Anticipated	0	1	1	2
Total	**25**	**51**	**25**	**101**

Spawning. Spawning describes a search resumed because sub-topics or problems emerged from the original task and required the searcher to find more information [24]. Spawning was the most common resuming reason for the middle sessions (n = 36), the last session (n = 16), and across all the sessions (n = 62). We also observed spawning as a reason for the initial session (n = 10). This may seem odd but it was quite common. Often, participants had been thinking about their task prior to searching and knew it would involve multiple parts. In this way, spawning was part of their planning process and occurred before the initial search session.

We observed three ways that these sub-problems spawned: 1) based on previous knowledge, 2) based on earlier search sessions, and 3) from communication with others. In (1), the sub-problems were planned in advance based on participants' previous knowledge about the task topic and how they wanted to complete the task. For instance,

> *"I started this search session because I had been thinking about what I wanted to search the whole day, and I had a list of things that I really wanted to look up." (p121_s2)*

Secondly, sub-problems emerged during earlier search sessions. New topics might appear either because the searcher encountered some unknown but relevant concepts during earlier search sessions, or because they purposefully explored different aspects of the task and discovered new sub-topics for further investigation. Consequently, they resumed their search during a later session to look for information about the new concept(s). For instance,

> *"I came across a new definition of 'shared streets'...[during the first search session] [In this session, I want] to continue learning about the various definitions"(p120_s2)*

Thirdly, sub-tasks arose from communication with others (e.g., talking with task collaborators, or other people they consulted while working on the tasks). For instance,

> *"I had a very in-depth talk with two fellow theater artists... Hearing about other individuals' unique summer theatrical experiences peaked my interest to see if there may be a space for me." (p104_s2)*

Transmuting. Transmuting refers to a situation when a person needs more information in order to formulate their information need before they can conduct more focused searches [24]. Transmuting was a common reason for our participants to start the initial search session (n = 13), but it also motivated middle search sessions (n = 5), and in one case, even the last session during the XSS process.

We identified two types of transmutation. In the first type, users' understanding of their task transmutes to a more specified level as more knowledge is learned. To achieve this purpose, users often try to explore the topic areas to find general information related to their tasks, such as background information, general introductions, and potential information resources. With these, they can better understand how to work on their own tasks. For instance,

"I would like to research the necessities for a short children's book. What authors typically consider when writing and how to make sure a child will be able to take in and understand the topic of the book... To see how much it would cost for me to successfully execute writing the book." (p129_s1)

The other transmutation type is that users' tasks are transmuted to a narrower sub-scope compared to the original task. For instance, participants may decide to concentrate on one specific subtopic and that subtopic becomes the main problem for solving during the rest of the XSS process.

"I wanted to gain a better understanding of the different types of businesses in order to decide which one would be most applicable to my consulting business" (p116_s1)

Unanswered-Incomplete. In Lin and Belkin's original MISE [24], *unanswered* describes a situation when a searcher resumes a search session to continue to look for specific "information objects" [24, p. 396] that they did not find in the earlier search session(s). This definition implies that the previous search might have failed or been unfinished. While analyzing our data, we found that few participants mentioned resuming a session because the previous session *failed*. On the contrary, participants often explicitly stated that their previous sessions were *unfinished* and that they started the current session because they wanted to continue exploring where they had left off. In this paper, we update the original MISE code "unanswered" to "unanswered-incomplete" to reflect participants' perspectives.

The unanswered-incomplete reason is associated with the middle sessions ($n = 6$) and the last session ($n = 3$) but not for the initial sessions. This makes sense because an unanswered session starts because the searcher did not find all the needed information during the previous search session(s).

We observed two types of foci for these types of sessions. In the first type, the participant had a specific search goal and wanted to exhaust one specific information resource that they started in the previous search session. In the second type, the participant did not have a specific search goal and wanted to explore more new information in the current session. For instance:

"My goal is to continue reviewing the source I started reviewing during the last session and also review another source that has already been bookmarked...I wanted to continue to take notes I started last night" (p128_s3)

Cultivated-Updated. In the MISE, *cultivated* refers to the scenario when users do not have specific information problems to solve at hand but search for information over time to "stay abreast of an area of information of interest" [24, p. 395]. We adjusted this to *cultivated-updated* to reflect users' information search for updated information within the context of a defined task.

Among the nine (n = 9) sessions resumed because of the cultivated-updated reason, two were initial sessions, three were middle sessions, and four were last sessions. Participants for all these sessions had clear search goals, and their information needs were specific. For instance,

> *"I'd heard that the [booking] system had changed recently and wanted to know the latest." (p106_s3)*

In addition, these updated sessions could be categorized into two groups: (1) participants wanted to find the most recent information since they knew the topic area keeps changing based on previous knowledge, such as the quotes cited above.

Another type of updated session refers to cases when (2) participants found the information during previous search sessions for their tasks and wanted to check again to make sure they have the latest information before they could make decisions. For instance,

> *"I was also curious to see if any of the flight information that I had looked up before had changed" (p117_s2)*

Anticipated. In MISE, *anticipated* describes when a searcher encounters some interesting information and thinks they would resume the search again when they need the information for a different future task. Based on our analysis, we adjust this definition to include situations when participants start a session and expect to search for information that they may use for the *current work task* at a later time, as the task proceeds.

We identified two sessions (n=2) that were mainly resumed for the anticipated reason. For instance,

> *"I simply wanted to find inspiration and other artwork to put toward later use" (p114_s3)*

4.2 Other MISE Resuming Reasons in Everyday XSS

Besides the above five session resuming reasons, we did not find sessions that were *resumed* mainly for the other MISE reasons (e.g. transiting, rolling-back, or answer-lost). But we did find examples when participants described similar situations involving these MISE reasons at other points during their XSS process.

Transiting. Transiting describes when a participant is inspired by their searches for the current task and comes up with ideas for a new task that requires more searches in the future. In other words, transiting could be the resuming reason for a later search session of a different task if it happens. For instance, the following example described that the participant found some relevant information for the current task but may need more search and effort that should be separated from the current search. However, the person did not continue that new search.

> "After that I did a quick search to see if I could find some quick statistics on the benefits of taking space away from cars more generally, but determined that was another large task and stopped that search. " (p120_s4)

Rolling-Back. Rolling-back describes when a session is started because the information found from the previous session(s) did not solve the task problem. We found an example when the participant stopped an earlier session because what they found did not work. However, when restarting the search later, the participant did not continue to look for substitutes. Instead, he switched to looking for other task aspects. Therefore, this is not exactly a rolling-back case. As the following quotes show:

> "I found an app ...but [it] did not work on my laptop so I decided to end my session out of frustration" (p114_s5)

and in the next search session, the participant described:

> "once I cooled down from my incident with a poorly constructed and expensive application I needed to 'restart' my initial search for artistic tutorials and artistic inspiration" (p114_s6)

Lost-treatment. Lost-treatment refers to the situation when participants cannot access the information they found previously and need to search again. This might include re-finding the same information or looking for alternatives since the previous information or sources are no longer available.

Although we did not identify any sessions that were resumed mainly because of the lost-treatment reason, re-finding is a common strategy people use to find the information they already knew.

> "I was also mainly looking for inspiration from things I knew of, but wanted to look up thoroughly and explore more as to how they may or may not relate to my piece and what I want to present." (p108_s1)

4.3   Session Resuming Reasons Not in MISE

Besides the resuming reasons from the MISE model, we also identified six additional session resuming reasons that are not covered by the MISE model or prior work on XSS.

Exploring More Topic Aspects. Some participants mentioned that they started new sessions to explore more task aspects they may not be aware of. There are no criteria about when to stop exploring, which differs from the exploring activities of the unanswered-incomplete mode. Although participants were clear about their task goal, their exploration is less goal-oriented. Exploring might result in spawning if the searcher identified new aspects or subtasks and decided to follow the new directions. For instance,

> " I didn't have any specific topics that I wanted to learn about within [topic] because I am too new to the topic to have any idea what I would be searching for other than the general topic itself." (p128_s3)

Finding Inspirations/Examples. Participants also mentioned resuming search sessions to look for examples that are similar to their projects or to find inspirations and ideas about how to work on their own tasks. This is different from looking for examples in the anticipated reason when people looked for inspiration for future use. Instead, the search results would affect their decisions about how to work on their tasks. For instance,

> "[I was] mainly looking for inspiration from the information (songs, lyrics, poetry & literature)... to find a possible starting point for my piece. (p108_s1)

Reviewing the Information Found Earlier. Participants also mentioned resuming search sessions to review the information found previously. The purposes of reviewing may include reacquainting themselves, confirming what they knew is correct/up to date, or examining the information closer to extract more details as their task formulated in the latter sessions. For instance,

> "I was specifically searching for information that I had saved in order to make sure I cited it properly" (p125_s3)

Monitoring Task Progress. Different from gaining information, participants mentioned they wanted to conduct a search session to get a feeling about the workload and the task progress so that they could appropriately arrange their tasks and time. For example,

> "I was curious to see if only doing one [subtask] at a time would suit me better." (p102_s2)

Completing Search Following a Scheduled Plan. For tasks that participants already have a work plan, participants start a new session in order to follow the work plan. The plan might be applied to the entire task or just parts of the task. For example,

> "I'm now deciding to do one complex a day through the end of the list, so this was just my daily session!" (p102_s4)

Feeling in the Mood/Having the Energy to Search. Sometimes, participants wanted to conduct a search session just because they felt good and wanted to work on the task to make the most of their time and energy. For instance,

> *"I had a lot of energy compared to my usual amount of energy, and I surprisingly felt no brain fog after working today; in fact, I felt clearer and more energized...I felt in the research mood" (p101_s1)*

5   Discussion and Implication

In this section, we summarize the main trends observed in our results, relate them to prior research, and discuss the implications of our work.

Overall, we found that spawning, transmuting, unanswered-incomplete, cultivated-updated, and anticipated were the main reasons that led participants to begin new search sessions during XSS. The three ways how subtasks spawned from the overarching task we identified Further, we identified three ways that subtasks spawned (based on previous knowledge, earlier search sessions, and communication with others). These extend the original definition of spawning in [24] and provide evidence to support prior work indicating that complex tasks with multiple subtasks are often associated with XSS (e.g., [13, 17, 25]).

Transmuting was also a common reason in our data, especially for initial sessions. This might be because many (76%) of our participants' tasks were self-generate and thus may have been less structured compared to assigned tasks. This is in line with Agichtien et al.'s [1] finding (based on search log data) that undirected tasks were more likely to be continued over multiple sessions. Prior research found that users often look for problem definition and background information to help structure less-determined tasks [3, 6]. Our findings show that in the XSS context, the information sought during transmuting sessions can lead to a change in the scope of the original problem since participants might narrow down the scope of the task or redefine their problems. Consequently, their work processes and the final outcomes could be different depending on the information users found and used for structuring the tasks.

Unanswered-incomplete was another important resuming reason, especially for sessions later during the XSS process. Our results suggest it may be more common for participants to continue a search that was unfinished instead of continuing a previous search that failed. This could have been because, during XSS sessions, participants often aimed to find multiple pieces of information. Therefore, there were more times when they did not finish finding all the information they sought rather than not finding any useful information at all. Another reason might be that for complex XSS tasks, there were often alternative solutions, so participants were likely to find at least some useful information during a session. We also note that Wu [39] found that unanswered or unsatisfied search results may cause people to switch their search to a different device. Future work should explore how XSS search resuming reasons may be influenced by search devices.

Our results also show that in the sessions resumed because of cultivated-updated and anticipated, participants focused on looking for specific information.

This differs from the MISE model's [24] view that the purpose of these two reasons is to familiarize oneself with information that could be potentially useful for future tasks. Our findings suggest that it would be helpful to change this definition to include information that the user thinks might be helpful at some point in the future for the current work task.

Another contribution of our study is that we identified six additional session-resuming reasons that were not discussed by the MISE model and have been less explored in the context of XSS. Among these, exploring more topic aspects, finding inspirations/examples, and reviewing the information found earlier are related to existing MISE reasons, but reflect nuances of users' information needs. For instance, similar to spawning, *exploring* can lead to discovery of new information that may become subtopics for further investigation. However, in our classification, an exploring session is often less directed whereas spawning sessions often have specific focuses and goals. The new resuming reason *finding inspirations/examples* relates to the MISE reason of transmuting when people search for background information or similar experiences on how to complete their tasks. A difference is that when finding inspiration, users' task goals were often more structured and they focused more on the examples of the process and final outcome. In the original MISE transmuting, the focus is often to look for information to help structure or narrow down task scope. Our new resuming reason, "reviewing the previously found information" relates to multiple original MISE reasons. For instance, reviewing could happen in unanswered-incomplete sessions resumed when people want to reexamine what they had found to continue their previous search. It also might happen in cultivated-updated sessions when people revisit previous information resources to check for updated information. It might occur when people want to re-access information in the lost-treatment cases. However, a reviewing session aims to confirm what had been found previously. The information from the previous sources has been fully understood rather than looking for new information as in the cultivated, incompleted sessions.

Meanwhile, monitoring task progress, completing a search following a scheduled plan, and feeling in a mood/having the energy to search are non-information-need-related reasons. These reasons reflect users' metacognitive activities through the XSS process. Researchers have found that leveraging tools to support metacognitive activities can significantly improve users' interaction with the systems and affect their task outcomes during experimental tasks [2, 20, 35]. Our findings show that users have the need for and often perform metacognitive activities in their real-world XSS tasks.

Implications. Our results have several important implications. First, our results have implications for how search systems prioritize, rank, and present search results for XSS. Our findings suggest that the initial search sessions during the XSS process often start because users' tasks contain subtasks or subconcepts or because they need to explore different aspects of the topic areas to help clarify the scope of the task. Thus, when new information tasks are detected, search systems could provide diverse search results that include different aspects of the topic. For instance, using knowledge graphs and analysis of previous similar searches on the same topic, search engines could present a knowledge map that contains important concepts, subconcepts, and their relationships to help the current searcher identify, discover, and explore important areas.

Second, our results have implications for predicting users' information needs based on their activities during previous sessions. Our findings suggest that users' information needs at the session level could differ from their needs at the task level or at the search query level. For example, during a successive session resumed because of unfinished-incomplete, the user may use the same or similar search queries as they used in previous sessions to explore new task aspects rather than to review the same results they had seen earlier. Similarly, in sessions started for the cultivated-updated reason, users are likely to want the most recent or previously unseen information, in which case providing previously viewed information might be inappropriate. Given the differences among some of these reasons are subtle and hard to detect, future system design may consider ways for users to provide explicit information about what type of goals they have for a resumed session. For example, the search system could include controls such as "See your previous results" or "Explore new/unseen results".

Third, our results illustrate that users need support for metacognitive activities during XSS, such as planning, monitoring task progress, and keeping motivated over time. Researchers from the *Search as Learning* community have found that with the assistance of scaffolding tools, users performed more information search activities and metacognitive activities through the search process (versus users without the scaffolding tools [7,35]). Further investigation is needed to evaluate and extend these types of assistive tools for more complex search processes such as XSS.

Finally, our research has methodological implications for designing XSS tasks in experimental studies. We have shown that different task resumption reasons imply different goals and search behaviors. In studies investigating task resumption, these differences should be considered. For instance, researchers could design search sessions with specific resuming purposes, such as designing tasks with vague task requirements or the need for searchers to narrow down the task scope. Sessions could also be interrupted before users complete the findings for the session, and in another session, the searcher could be asked to continue the search. Multiple reasons can be contrasted to study their impacts.

6 Conclusion

We conducted a diary study to investigate cross-session starting and resuming reasons for users' real-world tasks. Using Lin and Belkin's [24] MISE model as the theoretical framework, we identified five main MISE session resuming reasons (i.e., spawning, transmuting, unanswered-incomplete, cultivated-updated, anticipated) that led participants to start a search session during their XSS. Our findings contextualized each MISE reason with the real-world examples we collected and extended the original MISE definitions with rich details. We distinguished three MISE reasons that were not found as the primary session resuming reasons but exist in XSS. We also found six additional reasons that can cause XSS. These reasons include information-need-related reasons such as exploring more topic aspects, finding inspirations and examples, and reviewing previously found information. The other three are non-information-need-related reasons, including monitoring task progress, completing a search following a scheduled plan, and feeling in the mood or having the energy to search. Our findings have implications for developing search assistance tools to support XSS activities, improving search engines to customize search results at different stages of XSS, and helping identify and predict XSS activities.

Acknowledgement. This material is based upon work supported by the National Science Foundation under Grant No. 1552587.

References

1. Agichtein, E., White, R. W., Dumais, S. T., Bennet, P.N.: Search, interrupted: understanding and predicting search task continuation. In: Proceedings of the 35th International ACM SIGIR Conference on Research and Development in Information Retrieval - SIGIR 2012, p. 315, Portland, Oregon. ACM (2012). https://doi.org/10.1145/2348283.2348328
2. Azevedo, R., Cromley, J.G., Seibert, D.: Does adaptive scaffolding facilitate students' ability to regulate their learning with hypermedia? Contemp. Educ. Psychol. **29**(3), 344–370 (2004)
3. Byström, K., Järvelin, K.: Task complexity affects information seeking and use. Inf. Process. Manage. **31**(2), 191–213 (1995)
4. Byström, K.: Information and information sources in tasks of varying complexity. J. Am. Soc. Inform. Sci. Technol. **53**(7), 581–591 (2002)
5. Capra, R., Marchionini, G., Velasco-Martin, J., Muller, K.: Tools-at-hand and learning in multi-session, collaborative search. In: Conference on Human Factors in Computing Systems Proceedings, vol. 2, pp. 951–960 (2010). https://doi.org/10.1145/1753326.1753468
6. Choi, B., Arguello, J.: A qualitative analysis of the effects of task complexity on the functional role of information. In: Proceedings of the 2020 Conference on Human Information Interaction and Retrieval (CHIIR 2020), pp. 328–332. Association for Computing Machinery, New York, March 2020. https://doi.org/10.1145/3343413.3377992
7. Choi, B., Arguello, J., Capra, R., Ward., A.R.: OrgBox: a knowledge representation tool to support complex search tasks. In: Proceedings of the 2021 Conference on Human Information Interaction and Retrieval (CHIIR 2021), pp. 219–228. Association for Computing Machinery, New York (2021). https://doi.org/10.1145/3406522.3446029
8. Crescenzi, A., Ward, A.R., Li, Y., Capra, R.: Supporting metacognition during exploratory search with the OrgBox. In: Proceedings of the 44th International ACM SIGIR Conference on Research and Development in Information Retrieval, pp. 1197–1207, July 2021
9. Czerwinski, M., Horvitz, E., Wilhite, S.: A diary study of task switching and interruptions. In: Proceedings of the SIGCHI Conference on Human Factors in Computing Systems (CHI 2004), pp. 175–182. Association for Computing Machinery, New York (2004). https://doi.org/10.1145/985692.985715

10. Wu, D., Dong, J., Tang, Y.: Identifying and modeling information resumption behaviors in cross-device search. In: The 41st International ACM SIGIR Conference on Research & Development in Information Retrieval (SIGIR 2018), pp. 1189–1192. Association for Computing Machinery, New York (2018). https://doi.org/10.1145/3209978.3210126

11. Dawe, E., Toms, E.G.: The effect of interruptions on knowledge work. In: 7th World Congress on the Management of eBusiness (2006). https://interruptions.net/literature/Dawe-WCMeB06.pdf

12. Dervin, B.: From the mind's eye of the user: the sense-making qualitative-quantitative methodology. In: Glazier, J., Powell, R. (eds.) Qualitative Research in Information Management, pp. 61–84. Libraries Unlimited, Englewood, CO (1992)

13. Donato, D., Bonchi, F., Chi, T., Maarek, Y.: Do you want to take notes? In: Proceedings of the 19th International Conference on World Wide Web - WWW 2010, p. 321, Raleigh, North Carolina (2010). https://doi.org/10.1145/1772690.1772724

14. Gomes, S., Hoeber, O.: Supporting cross-session cross-device search in an academic digital library. In: Proceedings of the 2021 Conference on Human Information Interaction and Retrieval, pp. 337–341, March 2021

15. Han, S., He, D., Chi, Y.: Understanding and modeling behavior patterns in cross-device web search. Proc. Assoc. Inf. Sci. Technol. **54**(1), 150–158 (2017). https://doi.org/10.1002/pra2.2017.14505401017

16. Jansen, B.J., Booth, D.L., Spink, A.: Determining the user intent of web search engine queries. In: Proceedings of the 16th International Conference on World Wide Web (WWW 2007), pp. 1149–1150. Association for Computing Machinery, New York, May 2007. https://doi.org/10.1145/1242572.1242739

17. Kellar, M., Watters, C., Shepherd, M.: A field study characterizing Web-based information-seeking tasks. JASIST **58**(7), 999–1018 (2007)

18. Kotov, A., Bennett, P.N., White, R.W., Dumais, S.T., Teevan, J.: Modeling and analysis of cross-session search tasks. In: Proceedings of the 34th International ACM SIGIR Conference on Research and Development in Information Retrieval (SIGIR 2011), pp. 5 14. Association for Computing Machinery, New York (2011). https://doi.org/10.1145/2009916.2009922

19. Kuhlthau, C.C.: Inside the search process: information seeking from the user's perspective. J. Am. Soc. Inf. Sci. **42**, 361–371 (1991)

20. Kuo, F.R., Chen, N.S., Hwang, G.J.: A creative thinking approach to enhancing the web-based problem solving performance of university students. Comput. Educ. **72**, 220–230 (2014)

21. Li, Y., Belkin, N.J.: A faceted approach to conceptualizing tasks in information seeking. Inf. Process. Manage. **44**(6), 1822–1837 (2008). https://doi.org/10.1016/j.ipm.2008.07.005

22. Li, Y., Capra, R., Zhang, Y.: Everyday cross-session search: how and why do people search across multiple sessions? In: CHIIR 2020 - Proceedings of the 2020 Conference on Human Information Interaction and Retrieval, pp. 163–172 (2020). https://doi.org/10.1145/3343413.3377970

23. Lin, S.: Modeling and supporting multiple information seeking episodes over the web (Order No. 3062480). Available from ProQuest Dissertations & Theses Global. (304717282) (2001). https://www.proquest.com/dissertations-theses/modeling-supporting-multiple-information-seeking/docview/304717282/se-2

24. Lin, S.J., Belkin, N.: Validation of a model of information seeking over multiple search sessions. J. Am. Soc. Inform. Sci. Technol. **56**(4), 393–415 (2005). https://doi.org/10.1002/asi.20127

25. Liu, J., Belkin, N.J.: Personalizing information retrieval for multi-session tasks: the roles of task stage and task type. In: SIGIR 2010, pp. 26–33 (2010)
26. Liu, J., Sarkar, S., Shah, C.: Identifying and predicting the states of complex search tasks. In: CHIIR 2020, pp. 193–202 (2020)
27. Morris, D., Morris, M.R., Venolia, G.: SearchBar: a search-centric web history for task resumption and information re-finding. In: Proceedings of the SIGCHI Conference on Human Factors in Computing Systems - CHI'08, pp. 1207–1216. ACM, Florence (2008). https://doi.org/10.1145/1357054.1357242
28. Mackay, B., Watters, C.: Exploring multi-session web tasks. In: CHI 2008, pp. 1187–1196). ACM, Florence (2008). http://www.ncsa.uiuc.edu/Projects/mosaic.html
29. Mitsui, M., Shah, C., Belkin, N.J.: Extracting information seeking intentions for web search sessions. In: Proceedings of the 39th International ACM SIGIR conference on Research and Development in Information Retrieval, pp. 841–844, July 2016
30. Robertson, S.E., Hancock-Beaulieu, M.M.: On the evaluation of IR systems. Inf. Process. Manage. **28**(4), 457–466 (1992). https://doi.org/10.1016/0306-4573(92)90004-J
31. Sellen, A.J., Murphy, R., Shaw, K.L.: How knowledge workers use the web. In: Proceedings of the SIGCHI Conference on Human Factors in Computing Systems (CHI 2002), pp. 227–234. Association for Computing Machinery, New York (2002). https://doi.org/10.1145/503376.503418
32. Spink, A.: Multiple search sessions model of end-user behavior: an exploratory study. J. Am. Soc. Inf. Sci. **47**(8), 603–609 (1996). https://doi.org/10.1002/(SICI)1097-4571(199608)47:8⟨603::AID-ASI4⟩3.0.CO;2-X
33. Spink, A., Griesdorf, H., Bateman, J.: A study of mediated successive searching during information seeking. J. Inf. Sci. **25**(6), 477–487 (1999)
34. Spink, A., Wilson, T.D., Ford, N., Foster, A., Ellis, D.: Information seeking and mediated searching study: Part 3. Successive searching. J. Am. Soc. Inf. Sci. Technol. **53**(9), 716–727. https://doi.org/10.1002/asi.10083
35. Stadtler, M., Bromme, R.: Effects of the metacognitive computer-tool met. a. ware on the web search of laypersons. Comput. Hum. Behav. **24**(3), 716–737 (2008).https://doi.org/10.1016/j.chb.2007.01.023
36. Taylor, R.S.: Question-negotiation and information seeking in libraries. Coll. Res. Libr. **29**, 178–194 (1968)
37. Vakkari, P., Hakala, N.: Changes in relevance criteria and problem stages in task performance. J. Documentation **56**(5), 540–562 (2000). https://doi.org/10.1108/EUM0000000007127
38. Wang, Y., Huang, X., White, R.W.: Characterizing and supporting cross-device search tasks. In: Proceedings of the Sixth ACM International Conference on Web Search and Data Mining, pp. 707–716 (2013). https://doi.org/10.1145/2433396.2433484
39. Wu, D., Dong, J., Liu, C.: Exploratory study of cross-device search tasks. Inf. Process. Manage. **56**(6), 102073 (2019)
40. Wu, D., Dong, J., Liang, S.: Cross-device Web Search. Taylor & Francis, United Kingdom (2022)

Community Informatics

Time Lag Analysis of Adding Scholarly References to English Wikipedia
How Rapidly Are They Added to and How Fresh Are They?

Jiro Kikkawa[✉] , Masao Takaku , and Fuyuki Yoshikane

University of Tsukuba, Tsukuba, Ibaraki, Japan
{jiro,masao,fuyuki}@slis.tsukuba.ac.jp

Abstract. Referencing scholarly documents as information sources on Wikipedia is important because they complement and improve the quality of Wikipedia content. However, little is known about them, such as how rapidly they are added and how fresh they are. To answer these questions, we conduct a time-series analysis of adding scholarly references to the English Wikipedia as of October 2021. Consequently, we detect no tendencies in Wikipedia articles created recently to refer to more fresh references because the time lag between publishing the scholarly articles and adding references of the corresponding paper to Wikipedia articles has remained generally constant over the years. In contrast, tendencies to decrease over time in the time lag between creating Wikipedia articles and adding the first scholarly references are observed. The percentage of cases where scholarly references were added simultaneously as Wikipedia articles are created is found to have increased over the years, particularly since 2007–2008. This trend can be seen as a response to the policy changes of the Wikipedia community at that time that was adopted by various editors, rather than depending on massive activities by a small number of editors.

Keywords: Scholarly communication · Wikipedia · Time-series analysis · Time lag analysis

1 Introduction

With the digitization of scholarly communication, numerous scholarly documents have been referenced and used online. A significant change arising from the development and dissemination of scholarly information infrastructure on the Web is the utilization of scholarly documents by various kinds of communities and people, including non-traditional readers, such as researchers and specialists. Wikipedia offers numerous references and access to scholarly documents. According to Crossref, which massively assigns Digital Object Identifiers (DOIs) to scholarly documents, Wikipedia is one of the largest referrers of Crossref DOIs as of 2015 [6].

I. Sserwanga et al. (Eds.): iConference 2023, LNCS 13972, pp. 425–438, 2023.
https://doi.org/10.1007/978-3-031-28032-0_33

Wikipedia is a free online encyclopedia that anyone can edit, and it is one of the most visited websites in the world. However, owing to its collaborative nature, significant criticism and discussion have emerged since its start regarding the accuracy and reliability of its contents. Three core content policies [3] exist in Wikipedia: "verifiability," "neutral point of view," and "no original research." Referencing scholarly documents as information sources on Wikipedia complements these policies and improves the content quality. Therefore, Wikipedia articles should be added as scholarly references as soon as possible. Moreover, the quantity and freshness of scholarly references are crucial to cover the latest academic knowledge. However, little is known about Wikipedia's scholarly references, that is, how rapidly they are added to Wikipedia articles and how fresh they are.

Therefore, we conduct a time lag analysis regarding the editors and edits for adding scholarly references to Wikipedia to answer the following research questions (hereinafter, referred to as RQs).

- **RQ1**: How does the number of Wikipedia articles with scholarly references grow over time?
- **RQ2**: How long is the time lag between the publishing date of each scholarly article and the addition of the corresponding scholarly reference to Wikipedia articles?
- **RQ3**: How long is the time lag between the creation date of each Wikipedia article and the date of the first scholarly reference added to that article?

In addition, if the time lag mentioned in RQ2 and RQ3 decreased over time, the factors causing this were investigated.

The contributions of this study are twofold. (1) We clarified the long-term changes in the use of scholarly articles in the online encyclopedia community. (2) We attempted to identify the factors behind these changes in the online encyclopedia community.

2   Related Work

2.1   Analysis of Scholarly References on Wikipedia

Scholarly bibliographic references on Wikipedia have been analyzed considering various perspectives: (1) whether the scholarly articles published in high-impact factor journals tend to be more referenced on Wikipedia [21,25]; (2) whether the scholarly articles published in open access journals tend to be more referenced on Wikipedia [19,23,25]; (3) whether the references on Wikipedia are usable as a data source for research evaluations [17]; (4) investigations regarding the characteristics of Wikipedia articles with scholarly references [23]; (5) investigations regarding the references focused on specific identifiers (e.g., DOI, arXiv, ISSN, and ISBN) [9,11,13] or research fields [23,26]; and (6) the editors and edits for adding scholarly references to Wikipedia [12,15]. Except for (6), these studies focused on the scholarly document itself.

The methodologies used in previous studies to identify scholarly references on Wikipedia can be classified as follows: (A) extracting them from either Wikipedia article texts (Wikitexts) or Wikipedia external links [9,11,13,21,25], (B) detecting Wikipedia articles containing them using web search engines [17,23,26], and (C) analyzing usage log data [19]. However, these methods are unable to identify the first appearance of each reference on the Wikipedia article, that is, when it was added and by whom.

Considering these limitations, Kikkawa et al. [12,16] proposed methods to identify the first appearances of scholarly references on Wikipedia using paper titles and their identifiers. Subsequently, they built a dataset of the first appearances of scholarly references on English Wikipedia articles. Next, they evaluated the precision for detecting the first appearance, which was overall 93.3% and exceeded 90% in 20 out of 22 research fields [12,16]. Thus, their proposed method identifies the first appearance of scholarly references with high precision regardless of the research field. They conducted a time-series analysis using this dataset and revealed the trends and characteristics of adding scholarly references to Wikipedia; they reported a seasonal growth trend in the number of editors adding references in April and November every year since 2011 [15]. In addition, they published an updated version of the dataset of the first appearances of scholarly references on English Wikipedia articles as of 1 October 2021 [14,16].

As described above, most previous studies have focused on the scholarly document itself, and little is known about the editors and their contributions to adding scholarly references to Wikipedia. In this study, we conduct a time lag analysis regarding added scholarly references to Wikipedia using the first appearances of scholarly references on English Wikipedia articles as of October 1, 2021, provided by Kikkawa et al. [14,16].

2.2 The Shift from Quantity to Quality in the Wikipedia Community

As Wikipedia is an encyclopedia compiled collaboratively by numerous anonymous editors, untrustworthy content is often created. In 2005, an article was written stating that a certain journalist was involved in the assassination of John F. Kennedy and Robert Kennedy, which became a social problem [2,5]. In response to the criticism of the Wikipedia monitoring system after this incident, Jimmy Wales—the co-founder of Wikipedia—declared in 2006 that the community has traded in quantity for the quality of its contents [1]. Thereafter, some bots and tools for anti-vandalism started patrolling the English Wikipedia to revert problematic edits. In addition, the creation of new Wikipedia articles by non-login editors, namely IP editors, was disabled.

Halfaker et al. [10] analyzed the damage done to Wikipedia editors when their edits were reverted by other editors. The analysis revealed that when edits are reverted by others, the motivation for editing is significantly reduced; nonetheless, the editors are encouraged to make good edits. However, they reported that having one's own edits reverted by an experienced editor is damaging to new participants, which damages the editor retention rate.

The Wikimedia Foundation conducted an editor trends study in 2010 [28] and reached the following conclusions: (1) The percentage of editors with less than one year of editing experience has declined sharply since 2006, indicating that the Wikipedia community has been aging. (2) The retention rate of new participants has been low since a significant drop from mid-2005 to early 2007. Finally, (3) the retention rate of those who have been editing for more than three years remained stable.

As stated above, the Wikipedia community shifted its focus from quantity to quality to improve the information quality of its contents. Accordingly, some bots and tools were adapted to patrol and revert problematic edits. Previous studies reported that the results derived from this shift, that is, the number of Wikipedia editors and their edits on the English Wikipedia, have been declining since 2006–2007 and the Wikipedia community is aging owing to the difficulty in retaining new participants. However, little is known about how the activities of adding scholarly references contribute to this shift in focus in the Wikipedia community. In this study, we aim to clarify how Wikipedia editors respond to this shift in Wikipedia communities by focusing on the addition of scholarly references.

2.3 Analysis of the Freshness of the References in Scholarly Articles

Several studies in bibliometrics have investigated the freshness of references in scholarly articles based on the citation age, which is calculated as the difference between the publication year of the scholarly articles and the publication year of the references listed in it [7,18,24,27,32]. In particular, Zhang and Glänzel [32] investigated the citation age of scholarly articles in 1992 and 2014 indexed by the Web of Science, and they revealed that the median citation age increased over time in most research fields except for fields related to chemistry. In contrast, Varga [27] pointed out that relatively new articles published after the 1990s s tend to cite more fresh articles published within 2 years by analyzing scholarly articles indexed by the Web of Science. They suggested that these citation trends were caused by advances in information technology, such as electronic publishing.

As described above, several studies have been conducted on the freshness of references in scholarly articles. However, little is known about the freshness of scholarly references on Wikipedia; thus, in this study, we analyze them according to the time lag between the publication year of the scholarly articles and the addition date of the corresponding references to Wikipedia articles.

3 Materials and Methods

3.1 Dataset

Herein, we define the term "scholarly reference" as the reference added to Wikipedia articles by which a certain paper and its research field are uniquely identifiable. We did not consider roles, such as references, being used as evidence for a certain part of the content of the Wikipedia article, those just mentioning a paper, or those listed in further readings. Subsequently, we define the term "first appearance of the scholarly reference" as the oldest scholarly reference added to each Wikipedia article. If multiple references corresponding to the same paper in the same article were found, the oldest one was treated as the first appearance.

Considering the above definition, we used the dataset published by Kikkawa et al. [14,16], in which the first appearances of scholarly references and their research fields were identified using Crossref DOIs and Essential Science Indicator categories. This dataset contains 1,474,347 scholarly references appearing in 313,240 English Wikipedia articles in the main namespace as of October 2021. The authors added a data field regarding the creation date of each Wikipedia article to the dataset.

Table 1. Data fields of the dataset

Field	Example	Description
page_title	Spyware	Title of the Wikipedia article
page_created_timestamp	2001-11-22 16:37:56 UTC	Timestamp of the Wikipedia article created
doi	10.1016/j.cose.2015.04.009	DOI corresponding to the paper
paper_published_year	2015	Published year of the paper
editor_name	Doctorg	Wikipedia editor who added the paper as a scholarly bibliographic reference to the article
editor_type	User	Type of the Wikipedia editor
revision_timestamp	2016-08-06 16:05:57 UTC	Revision timestamp of the edit

Table 1 lists the data fields included in this dataset. In this example, the scholarly reference whose DOI is "10.1016/j.cose.2015.04.009" was added to the English Wikipedia article "Spyware" at "2016-08-06 16:05:57 UTC" by the editor "Doctorg." The editor type of this editor was "User." Regarding "editor_type," each editor was classified as "User," "Bot," and "IP," which denote the human editors among the registered editors, non-human editors among the registered editors, and non-registered editors, respectively. As for "page_created_timestamp," the authors extracted this information from the Wikipedia dump file [29] and added it to the dataset. The key "paper_published_year" indicates the publishing date of the corresponding scholarly article derived from the value of "issued" on Crossref metadata, which corresponds to the earliest publishing date for the article [8].

Among the 1,474,347 scholarly references added, User editors, Bot editors, and IP editors added 1,242,839 (84.30%), 114,122 (7.74%), and 117,386 (7.96%) references, respectively. These references were added to 313,240 Wikipedia articles by 136,379 unique User editors, 81 unique Bot editors, and 58,283 unique

IP editors. The unique IP addresses of the editors are shown for the number of unique IP editors. The minimum, maximum, median, and standard deviation values of the number of scholarly references added to each Wikipedia article were 1, 513, 2, and 9.63, respectively.

3.2   Analysis Methods

We performed the following three analyses. Each analysis corresponds to an RQ.

(1) Basic Statistics of Wikipedia Articles With Scholarly References: We investigated the number of created Wikipedia articles containing scholarly references by editor types and their time-series transitions.

(2) Time Lag between Publishing Each Scholarly Article and Adding the Corresponding Reference to the Wikipedia Article: We calculated the time lag between publishing of each scholarly article and adding the corresponding reference to the Wikipedia articles. For instance, the time lag was one year ($= 2016 - 2015$) for the case presented in Table 1. We removed cases when the published year was empty or the time lag was less than zero as an error. We analyzed the characteristics and transitions of the time lag by comparing groups of created years of Wikipedia articles.

(3) Time Lag between the Creation Date of Each Wikipedia Article and the Date of Adding the First Scholarly Reference to the Corresponding Article: We first set the target as the first scholarly reference on each Wikipedia article. The reason for filtering only the oldest references was to clarify the time period without references for each article and its transitions over time. Next, we calculated the time lags between the creation date of each Wikipedia article and the date of adding the first reference to the article, that is, the time lag between the "page_created_timestamp" and "revision_timestamp" in Table 1. We converted the time lag in days from in seconds, e.g., 5370.98 days (464,052,481 s $\fallingdotseq$ 14.7 years) for the case reported in Table 1. Subsequently, we classified them into the following groups:

A. 0 days and at the same time: when the time lag was 0 s.
B. 0 days but not the same time: when the time lag was more than 0 s and less than 1 day.
C. Less than 1 month: when the time lag was 1–29 days.
D. Equal to or more than 1 month but less than 6 months: when the time lag was 30–179 days.
E. Equal to or more than 6 months but less than 1 year: when the time lag was 180–364 days.
F. Equal to or more than 1 year but less than 3 years: when the time lag was 365–1,094 days.

G. Equal to or more than 3 years but less than 5 years: when the time lag was 1,095–1,824 days.

H. Equal to or more than 5 years: when the time lag was 1,825 days or more.

We analyzed the characteristics and transitions of the time lag by comparing the groups for the creation years of Wikipedia articles.

4   Results and Discussion

4.1   Basic Statistics of Wikipedia Articles With Scholarly References

- **RQ1**: How does the number of Wikipedia articles with scholarly references grow over time?

Table 2. Number of created Wikipedia articles containing scholarly references by editor types for every 2 years (n = 313,240)

Years	Total	User editors		Bot editors		IP editors	
2001–2002	14,951	12,280	82.13%	0	0.00%	2,671	17.87%
2003–2004	34,633	25,913	74.82%	111	0.32%	8,609	24.86%
2005–2006	53,211	46,054	86.55%	174	0.33%	6,983	13.12%
2007–2008	52,395	39,592	75.56%	12,782	24.40%	21	0.04%
2009–2010	30,439	28,241	92.78%	2,103	6.91%	95	0.31%
2011–2012	23,954	23,635	98.67%	167	0.70%	152	0.63%
2013–2014	22,920	22,491	98.13%	261	1.14%	168	0.73%
2015–2016	21,677	21,298	98.25%	214	0.99%	165	0.76%
2017–2018	28,222	23,283	82.50%	4,810	17.04%	129	0.46%
2019–2020	22,151	21,926	98.98%	6	0.03%	219	0.99%
2021	8,687	8,632	99.37%	0	0.00%	55	0.63%
Overall	**313,240**	**273,345**	**87.26%**	**20,628**	**6.59%**	**19,267**	**6.15%**

Table 2 presents the number of Wikipedia articles created containing scholarly references by editor type. Regarding RQ1, the total number of articles created peaked at 53,211 in 2005–2006, and approximately 20,000–30,000 articles were consistently created every 2 years.

Most articles were created by User editors, accounting for 87.26% of the total. The percentage for the Bot editors was low, at 6.59%. Of the 20,628 articles created by the Bot editors, most were created by specific editors, such as ProteinBoxBot [4, 30] who creates articles related to human genes, accounting for 42.42% (8,750 articles), and Qbugbot [31] who creates articles about arthropods, accounting for 21.30% (4,394 articles). Because of a policy change that prohibits non-registered editors from creating new articles on the English Wikipedia, IP editors have rarely created new articles since 2006.

4.2 Time Lag between Publishing Each Scholarly Article and Adding the Corresponding Reference to the Wikipedia Article

– **RQ2**: How long is the time lag between the publishing date of each scholarly article and the addition of the corresponding scholarly reference to Wikipedia articles?

Table 3. Results regarding the time lag between publishing scholarly articles and adding the corresponding references to Wikipedia articles every 2 years (n = 1,458,546)

Years	# of the references added to Wikipedia Articles	The time lag in years				
		Max	Median	Mode	Mean	SD
2001–2002	607	131	18.0	0	25.97	27.09
2003–2004	3,818	164	11.0	0	21.52	26.32
2005–2006	35,416	174	6.0	0	13.79	19.06
2007–2008	211,750	206	6.0	5	10.31	14.13
2009–2010	135,900	207	7.0	1	12.14	17.25
2011–2012	147,498	209	7.0	0	12.51	17.50
2013–2014	157,427	196	7.0	0	12.72	17.38
2015–2016	185,958	207	6.0	0	11.97	16.72
2017–2018	221,565	201	7.0	0	12.33	16.90
2019–2020	258,928	205	7.0	0	13.07	17.51
2021	99,679	204	7.0	0	12.92	17.53

Table 3 presents the time lag between publishing scholarly articles and adding references to the corresponding papers on Wikipedia articles. A total of 15,801 references were removed if the publishing year was empty or if the time lag was less than zero. The "years" referred to when scholarly references were added to Wikipedia articles. For instance, 211,750 references were added to Wikipedia articles during 2007–2008. For these references, the maximum, median, mode, mean, and standard deviation values of the time lag are 206.0, 6.0, 5, 10.31, and 14.13, respectively. The maximum values were consistently near 200 since 2007–2008. The median, mean, and standard deviation values were stable near 6.0–7.0, 10–13, and 14–17, respectively, after 2005–2006. The mode values were either 0 or 1, except for 2007–2008. For RQ2, according to these values, the time lag was generally constant over the years.

The median values in the time lag in Table 3 were stable near 6.0–7.0 over the years, whereas the trend of the citation age of scholarly articles increased or decreased over the years in the previous studies described in Sect. 2.3. This result suggests that the character of the time lag between publishing scholarly articles and adding references for the corresponding papers on Wikipedia articles was different from that of the citation age of the scholarly articles. However, what caused this difference is unclear because they are different data sources and targets and are not directly comparable.

The reason why the mode value was 5 in 2007–2008 is that the references of the papers entitled "Generation and initial analysis of more than 15,000 full-length human and mouse cDNA sequences [20]" and "Complete sequencing and characterization of 21,243 full-length human cDNAs [22]" were added to 1,722 and 1,212 Wikipedia articles, respectively, during this period. These two papers were published in 2002–2003, and the corresponding references for these papers were added by the Bot editor ProteinBoxBot described in Sect. 4.1.

4.3 Time Lag between the Creation Date of Each Wikipedia Article and the Date of Adding the First Scholarly Reference to the Corresponding Article

– **RQ3**: How long is the time lag between the creation date of each Wikipedia article and the date of the first scholarly reference added to that article?

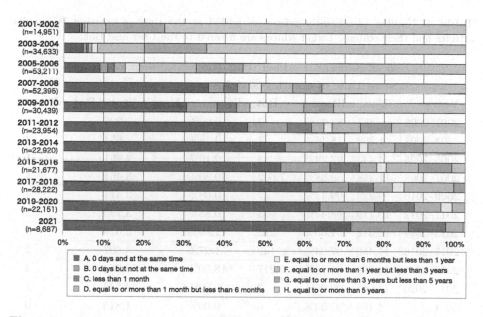

Fig. 1. Distribution of the time lag between creating the Wikipedia articles and adding the first scholarly references for every 2 years.

Figure 1 presents the distribution of the time lag between the creation Wikipedia articles and adding the first scholarly references for every 2 years. The time lag was classified into eight groups, as stated in point (3) of Sect. 3.2.

Regarding the group of "'0 days and at the same time," the percentage increased significantly from 2005–2006 to 2007–2008 (from 9.05% to 36.00%). As described in Sect. 2.2, around 2007, the co-founder of Wikipedia declared that the Wikipedia community should shift its focus from quantity to quality; thus, this increase in adding scholarly references could be seen as a response to this movement. Subsequently, it gradually increased over the years, except for 2009–2010, at 30.50%. In particular, it exceeded 50% and 60% in 2013–2014 and 2017–2018, respectively. These observations in the growth rate indicate that the cases where scholarly references were added as information sources when creating Wikipedia articles have been increasing rapidly since 2007, particularly, more than half after 2013. Furthermore, in groups A and B, the number of cases with added scholarly references within 24 h of creating Wikipedia articles has exceeded 50% since 2011–2012 and reached nearly 80% in 2019–2020. In contrast, in the early years, namely from 2001 to 2006, most of the time lag was more than or equal to 5 years. This result indicates that scholarly references were added relatively infrequently in Wikipedia articles created before 2005–2006; they were added to these articles retrospectively after five or more years. As for RQ3, according to these results, the percentage of no time lag was small in the early years, which increased significantly from 2005–2006 to 2007–2008 and has been over 50% since 2013–2014.

Table 4. Number of scholarly references added at the time of creating Wikipedia articles and their editors. Target editors are filtered to the User and Bot.

Years	# of references added to at the same time of creating articles				# of unique	
	User editors		Bot editors		User editors	Bot editors
2001–2002	483	83.71%	0	0.00%	226	0
2003–2004	1,309	78.48%	3	0.18%	654	2
2005–2006	4,443	92.29%	5	0.10%	2,291	1
2007–2008	11,258	59.68%	7,602	40.30%	3,464	4
2009–2010	9,229	99.41%	7	0.08%	3,411	4
2011–2012	10,719	98.44%	93	0.85%	3,745	2
2013–2014	12,312	97.60%	213	1.69%	3,619	3
2015–2016	11,450	97.94%	149	1.27%	3,507	2
2017–2018	14,099	81.10%	3,217	18.50%	3,754	4
2019–2020	14,003	99.06%	3	0.02%	4,543	1
2021	6,185	99.33%	0	0.00%	1,815	0
Overall	**95,490**	**88.29%**	**11,292**	**10.44%**	**25,526**	**9**

Table 4 presents the number of scholarly references added at the time of creating Wikipedia articles and their editors. IP editors were excluded here because of the small number of their contributions, as stated in Sect. 4.1. Consequently, most of the references were added by the User editors, accounting for 88.29% of the total. For every 2 years, this trend was the same, except for 2007–2008, when the Bot editor ProteinBoxBot created numerous Wikipedia articles and added references, as described previously. These references have been added by thousands of User editors. Of the unique 25,526 User editors, 19,900 (77.96%) editors added scholarly references at the time of creating articles only once. This result indicates that adding scholarly articles at the time of creating articles was adopted by various editors, rather than depending on massive activities adopted by a small number of editors.

Table 5. Top 2 editors who added the most scholarly references at the time of creating Wikipedia articles every 2 years

Years	1st editor			2nd editor		
2001–2002	Conversion script	35	6.07%	AxelBoldt	22	3.81%
2003–2004	Jfdwolff	59	3.54%	Curps	36	2.16%
2005–2006	V8rik	192	3.99%	Arcadian	148	3.07%
2007–2008	ProteinBoxBot	7,585	40.21%	WillowW	2,286	12.12%
2009–2010	Arcadian	441	4.75%	Meodipt	274	2.95%
2011–2012	Ruigeroeland	690	6.34%	Wilhelmina Will	406	3.73%
2013–2014	Dcirovic	1,291	10.23%	Ruigeroeland	1,259	9.98%
2015–2016	Daniel-Brown	1,551	13.27%	FoCuSandLeArN	503	4.30%
2017–2018	Qbugbot	2,826	16.26%	Daniel-Brown	2,283	13.13%
2019–2020	Daniel-Brown	637	4.51%	Jesswade88	576	4.07%
2021	Daniel-Brown	464	7.45%	Esculenta	225	3.61%
Overall	**ProteinBoxBot**	**8,421**	**7.79%**	**Daniel-Brown**	**5,473**	**5.06%**

Table 5 presents the top two editors who added the most scholarly references at the time of creating Wikipedia articles every 2 years. Of the 17 editors, ProteinBoxBot and Qbugbot were Bot editors, and the other 15 editors were User editors. Regarding the Bot editors, ProteinBoxBot added the most references. In particular, 40.21% of the references in 2007–2008 were added by this bot, which is the reason for the rapid increase in the group "0 days and at the same time" observed over 2007–2008, as shown in Fig. 1. Except for 2007–2008 and 2017–2018, the bot editors did not account for a high percentage. This result complements that adding scholarly articles at the time of creating articles was adopted by various editors.

5   Conclusion

We conducted a time lag analysis of adding scholarly references to the English Wikipedia as of October 2021. Consequently, we detected no tendencies for

Wikipedia articles created recently referring to more fresh references because the time lag between publishing scholarly articles and adding references for the corresponding paper to Wikipedia articles was generally constant over the years. Next, tendencies to decrease over time in the time lag between creating Wikipedia articles and adding the first scholarly references were observed. The percentage of cases where scholarly references were added at the same time as Wikipedia articles were created increased over the years, particularly since the period 2007–2008. This trend was regarded as a response to the policy changes in the Wikipedia community and adopted by various editors, rather than depending on massive activities conducted by a small number of editors. These results indicate that adding scholarly references to English Wikipedia can be conducted more rapidly, while maintaining the diversity of editors.

The limitations of this study are outlined below. First, we presented the overall picture of the decreasing time lag between creating Wikipedia articles and adding the first scholarly references; however, we were unable to identify the comprehensive factors behind this trend. For instance, not only the factors related to the policies of the Wikipedia community, but also the changes/advances, such as electronic journals and open access journals, in the scholarly publishing environment would influence the freshness of scholarly references on Wikipedia. Moreover, we were unable to cover all scholarly references added to English Wikipedia articles because the dataset used in this study depends on Crossref DOIs and Essential Science Indicators. However, the findings of this study are valuable for illustrating/understanding long-term changes in the usage of scholarly articles in the online encyclopedia community as information sources to improve content quality.

The directions for future research are as follows. First, we will conduct a time lag analysis focusing on the research field of scholarly references to understand the differences among the research fields. Second, we will consider how to facilitate adding/updating scholarly references to English Wikipedia for editors, such as recommendations of papers for a given article. These tasks are beyond the scope of this study; however, they are important for improving and expanding the process of adding scholarly references to Wikipedia in the future.

Acknowledgments. This work was partially supported by JSPS KAKENHI Grant Numbers JP21K21303, JP22K18147, JP20K12543, and JP21K12592. The authors are deeply grateful to Professor Hideaki Takeda at the National Institute of Informatics (NII), Japan, for valuable suggestions and discussions. We would like to thank Editage (https://www.editage.com/) for the English language editing.

References

1. Day 1 report of Wikimania 2006 - Wikinews, the free news source. https://en.wikinews.org/wiki/Day_1_report_of_Wikimania_2006. Accessed 14 Sept 2022
2. Wikipedia Seigenthaler biography incident - Wikipedia. https://en.wikipedia.org/wiki/Wikipedia_Seigenthaler_biography_incident. Accessed 14 Sept 2022

3. Wikipedia: Core content policies - Wikipedia. https://en.wikipedia.org/wiki/Wikipedia:Core_content_policies. Accessed 14 Sept 2022

4. WikiProject Report: Molecular and Cellular Biology. Wikipedia Signpost. https://en.wikipedia.org/wiki/Wikipedia:Wikipedia_Signpost/2008-01-28/WikiProject_report. Accessed 14 Sept 2022

5. USATODAY.com - A false Wikipedia 'biography' (2005). http://usatoday30.usatoday.com/news/opinion/editorials/2005-11-29-wikipedia-edit_x.htm. Accessed 14 Sept 2022

6. Bilder, G.: Geoffrey Bilder: Strategic Initiatives Update #crossref15. https://www.slideshare.net/CrossRef/geoffrey-bilder-crossref15. Accessed 14 Sept 2022

7. Costas, R., van Leeuwen, T.N., Bordons, M.: Referencing patterns of individual researchers: do top scientists rely on more extensive information sources? J. Am. Soc. Inform. Sci. Technol. **63**(12), 2433–2450 (2012). https://doi.org/10.1002/asi.22662

8. Crossref: Crossref Metadata API JSON Format (2021). https://github.com/CrossRef/rest-api-doc/blob/master/api_format.md

9. Halfaker, A., Taraborelli, D.: Research: Scholarly article citations in Wikipedia - Meta (2019). https://meta.wikimedia.org/wiki/Research:Scholarly_article_citations_in_Wikipedia

10. Halfaker, A., Kittur, A., Riedl, J.: Don't bite the newbies: how reverts affect the quantity and quality of Wikipedia work. In: Proceedings of the 7th International Symposium on Wikis and Open Collaboration, WikiSym 2011, pp. 163–172 (2011)

11. Kikkawa, J., Takaku, M., Yoshikane, F.: DOI links on Wikipedia: analyses of English, Japanese, and Chinese Wikipedias. In: Proceedings of the 18th International Conference on Asia-Pacific Digital Libraries (ICADL 2016), pp. 369-380 (2016). https://doi.org/10.1007/978-3-319-49304-6_40

12. Kikkawa, J., Takaku, M., Yoshikane, F.: A method to identify the edits adding bibliographic references to wikipedia. J. Japan Soc. Inf. Knowl. **30**(3), 370–389 (2020). https://doi.org/10.2964/jsik_2020_033, (in Japanese, English abstract available)

13. Kikkawa, J., Takaku, M., Yoshikane, F.: Analyses of Wikipedia editors adding bibliographic references based on DOI links. J. Jpn. Soc. Inf. Knowl. **30**(1), 21-41 (2020). https://doi.org/10.2964/jsik_004, (in Japanese, English abstract available)

14. Kikkawa, J., Takaku, M., Yoshikane, F.: Dataset of first appearances of the scholarly bibliographic references on English Wikipedia articles as of 1 March 2017 and as of 1 October 2021. Zenodo (2021). https://doi.org/10.5281/zenodo.5595573

15. Kikkawa, J., Takaku, M., Yoshikane, F.: Time-series analyses of the editors and their edits for adding bibliographic references on Wikipedia. J. Japan Soc. Inf. Knowl. **31**(1), 3–19 (2021). https://doi.org/10.2964/jsik_2020_037, (in Japanese, English abstract available)

16. Kikkawa, J., Takaku, M., Yoshikane, F.: Dataset of first appearances of the scholarly bibliographic references on Wikipedia articles. Scientific Data 9, article no. 85, pp. 1–11 (2022). https://doi.org/10.1038/s41597-022-01190-z

17. Kousha, K., Thelwall, M.: Are Wikipedia citations important evidence of the impact of scholarly articles and books? J. Am. Soc. Inf. Sci. **68**(3), 762–779 (2017). https://doi.org/10.1002/asi.23694

18. Larivière, V., Archambault, É., Gingras, Y.: Long-term variations in the aging of scientific literature: From exponential growth to steady-state science (1900–2004). J. Am. Soc. Inf. Sci. Technol. **59**(2), 288–296 (2008). https://doi.org/10.1002/asi.20744

19. Lin, J., Fenner, M.: An analysis of Wikipedia references across PLOS publications. figshare (2014). https://doi.org/10.6084/m9.figshare.1048991.v3

20. Mammalian Gene Collection (MGC) Program Team: Generation and initial analysis of more than 15,000 full-length human and mouse cDNA sequences. Proceedings of the National Academy of Sciences 99(26), 16899–16903 (2002). https://doi.org/10.1073/pnas.242603899
21. Nielsen, F.Å.: Scientific citations in Wikipedia. First Monday 12(8) (2007). https://doi.org/10.5210/fm.v12i8.1997
22. Ota, T., Suzuki, Y., Nishikawa, T., et al.: Complete sequencing and characterization of 21,243 full-length human cDNAs. Nature Genetics 36(1), 40–45 (2003). https://doi.org/10.1038/ng1285
23. Pooladian, A., Borrego, Á.: Methodological issues in measuring citations in Wikipedia: a case study in Library and Information Science. Scientometrics 113(1), 455–464 (2017). https://doi.org/10.1007/s11192-017-2474-z
24. van Raan, A.F.J.: On growth, ageing, and fractal differentiation of science. Scientometrics 47(2), 347–362 (2000). https://doi.org/10.1023/A:1005647328460
25. Teplitskiy, M., Lu, G., Duede, E.: Amplifying the impact of open access: Wikipedia and the diffusion of science. J. Am. Soc. Inf. Sci. 68(9), 2116–2127 (2016). https://doi.org/10.1002/asi.23687
26. Thelwall, M.: Does Astronomy research become too dated for the public? Wikipedia citations to Astronomy and Astrophysics journal articles 1996–2014. El Profesional de la Información 25(6), 893–900 (2016). https://doi.org/10.3145/epi.2016.nov.06
27. Varga, A.: The narrowing of literature use and the restricted mobility of papers in the sciences. Proc. Natl. Acad. Sci. 119(17), e2117488119 (2022). https://doi.org/10.1073/pnas.2117488119
28. Wikimedia Foundation: Editor Trends Study/Results - Strategic Planning. https://strategy.wikimedia.org/wiki/Editor_Trends_Study/Results. Accessed 14 Sept 2022
29. Wikimedia Foundation: Wikimedia Downloads. https://dumps.wikimedia.org/backup-index.html. Accessed 14 Sept 2022
30. Wikipedia: User:ProteinBoxBot - Wikipedia. https://en.wikipedia.org/wiki/User:ProteinBoxBot. Accessed 14 Sept 2022
31. Wikipedia: User: Qbugbot - Wikipedia. https://en.wikipedia.org/wiki/User:Qbugbot. Accessed 14 Sept 2022
32. Zhang, L., Glänzel, W.: A citation-based cross-disciplinary study on literature aging: part I—the synchronous approach. Scientometrics 111(3), 1573–1589 (2017). https://doi.org/10.1007/s11192-017-2289-y

Examining Interest in Open Government Data Through Digital Traces

Caroline Stratton(✉) and Shezin Hussain

Florida State University, Tallahassee, FL, USA
cstratton2@fsu.edu

Abstract. The benefits that open government data (OGD) may hold for society are plentiful, including increased government transparency and economic growth. To realize these benefits, users must access and transform OGD to create value. Yet, the increasingly widespread provision of OGD has not necessarily spurred abundant uses nor has it attracted a multitude of users. To support the expansion of uses and users, research about OGD has turned to examination of data provision and users' intentions to engage with OGD. A complementary approach to characterize actual demand for OGD has received little attention. In our exploratory study, we take a snapshot of the most viewed items on the OGD portals of the fifty most populous US cities to investigate naturalistically the topics and types of items apparently attracting user interest. We draw implications for OGD research and practice from our preliminary analysis of highly viewed items.

Keywords: Open government data · Municipal OGD portals

1 Approaches to the Problem of Limited OGD Use and Variable Interest in Items

OGD initiatives have flourished throughout the world, with potential to benefit individuals, organizations, and society. The motivations associated with the provision of open data range from lofty and abstract, for example, "creating transparency, participation, innovation and economic value" [1, p. 7] to more mundane and managerial, such as increasing the efficiency of government services [2]. Though governments have made many items available to the public (the U.S. Government's data.gov site boasts more than 300,000 datasets, for example), researchers have pointed to a problem of limited use [1, 3–8]. Scholarship recognizes that not everyone will be able to make use of OGD directly, particularly due to individuals' skills and knowledge for working with data [9], but the situation remains concerning for OGD advocates.

Research about OGD suggests at least two approaches to understanding and rectifying limited use. A first approach investigates factors related to data provision. Within this approach, researchers have evaluated content, features, and usability of open data portals [10–15], as well as data quality [16, 17]. A related stream of research about visualization in OGD aims to make data more usable and useful for a broader population [3, 18, 19]. Taken together, studies in the first approach offer directions to mitigate the

I. Sserwanga et al. (Eds.): iConference 2023, LNCS 13972, pp. 439–448, 2023.
https://doi.org/10.1007/978-3-031-28032-0_34

obstacles that users may face when approaching OGD. A second approach examines factors related to users, such as their motivations and perceptions of OGD. Studies have modeled individuals' intentions to use OGD [7, 20] and their activities when using data and participating in OGD events [21–24]. Research adopting the second approach offers lessons for attracting new users and improving the likelihood of data use that leads to beneficial impacts.

These approaches can be complemented by examining demand for OGD, so that its provision might better correspond with the needs and priorities of actual (and potential) users. The literature presents little empirical understanding of the kinds of data are most interesting or useful for actual users or those that would attract new users to OGD. This may be because studying actual users, particularly those outside of the OGD advocacy community, presents multiple challenges for research design. While research has begun to better characterize the heterogeneity of OGD users [23] and potential users' themes of interest [8], representative studies of demand are scarce.

Empirical studies of OGD use primarily reflect the perspectives of easily identifiable users, such as government employees and hackathon attendees [22, 25, 26] or even simulated users, such as students assigned a class project using OGD [27]. Sampling of users in the private sector and among the general population is difficult [28], in part because identifying them for study through actual OGD use (for example, by asking them to register for a user account tied to a real name and verified identity) conflicts to some extent with the principle of openness. In practice, OGD portals typically permit (relatively) anonymous use. While commonly used OGD software platforms have some internal analytics capability or compatibility with external analytics tools, they do not provide detailed insight into users' identities or intentions when visiting OGD portals. Underscoring this point, [26] found that municipal government employees had little idea about who was using their OGD portals and for what purpose.

A small number of studies have examined digital traces of user activity with OGD and users' outputs, with useful directions for characterizing demand and potentially locating the purposes of use. [5] and [16] turned to publicly available data about views and downloads of OGD to study use, while [29] investigated use through dataset citation in scientific publications. An intuitive yet important implication of these studies is that some datasets are more interesting and valuable to users than others. For example, [5] identified that about 80% of datasets on data.uk.gov had never been downloaded. [29] proposed that popular datasets may be the best or only source of data regarding a phenomenon and/or that they may be of great interest locally. For example, they found that a popular demographic dataset from Kenya was highly cited "to describe the study setting for research on poverty in developing countries" [25, p. 9]. We suggest that understanding the kinds of OGD that attract the most interest from users can be instructive 1) for the problem of limited OGD use and 2) for advancing theory about processes of creating value with OGD.

To the first aim, understanding demand will yield insight into the relative interest that users have in interacting with some datasets and ignoring others. It may additionally suggest more nuanced ways of quantifying use, for example, by measuring engagement with a subset of items relevant to a particular user group, rather than global measurement of engagement with all items on OGD portals. To the second aim, advancing theory about value creation with OGD, knowing more about the items that users most often engage with allows for more detailed specification of causal mechanisms leading to specific impacts of OGD [9]. Our premise that some data are of greater interest to users and therefore more likely to be utilized in a process of value creation leads us to an exploratory research question.

RQ: What kinds of items on OGD portals are associated with high levels of interest from users?

2 Methods

To pursue our research question, we examined the items labeled as the most viewed on the OGD portals of the 50 most populous US cities[1], operationalizing high levels of interest through the technical measure of views. The quantity of portals we sampled is similar to other comparative evaluations of municipal OGD [13, 14] and the selection of populous cities is intended to capture those likely to have an OGD portal, under the assumption that governments of these jurisdictions are likely have greater open data capabilities and resources than those of less populous jurisdictions (as such, our findings are characteristic of urban rather than rural areas).

We constructed a dataset from the sampled OGD portals to allow characterization of topic and type of highly viewed items. For each portal, we recorded the titles of the five most viewed items (and made notes about the nature of items where titles were not sufficiently descriptive), their types (e.g., dataset, map, dashboard) as listed on the portal, and their numbers of views as of mid-August 2022. The selection of five items per portal allowed us to closely examine the content and structure of each item in the dataset for this exploratory research.

Table 1 describes the portals for the 50 most populous US cities and their underlying software platforms, which dictated how we found item view counts. Item view counts were available directly on portals for Socrata, by accessing ArcGIS Online, and by querying the CKAN API following the method described by [30]. Information about most viewed items and view counts was unavailable for four portals using alternative software, listed as "other" in Table 1. Additionally, three CKAN portals were not configured for querying view counts and three cities had no portal. Thus, our data collection represents the most viewed items on the OGD portals of 40 cities.[2]

After developing our dataset, we coded items by topic, beginning from the list of 24 content areas in [13]. An iterative coding process led us to refine some topics and combine others, resulting in a final topic list comprised of 22 codes (see Fig. 1 for topic areas). We then prepared visualizations to observe patterns and unique phenomena, informed by prior research that sensitizes us to the potential significance of highly viewed outlier items in OGD.

---

[1] List drawn from the US Census Bureau City and Town Population Totals: 2020–2021 https://www.census.gov/data/tables/time-series/demo/popest/2020s-total-cities-and-towns.html.

[2] We find the relative comparison of item topics and types more meaningful than absolute comparison of view counts. Portals using Socrata and ArcGIS software generally had higher view counts for most viewed items than those using CKAN; however, this likely reflects differing user actions that the software counts as a view.

Table 1. OGD portals for 50 most populous US cities and their software platforms

	N	%
With portal	47	94
ArcGIS	20	
Socrata	15	
CKAN	8	
Other	4	
No portal	3	6
Total	50	

We use the digital trace data of item views as a pragmatic starting point to explore our research question. Examining technical measures such as view counts of an item does not wholly represent users' interest in or the use of OGD [31], as viewing an item on an OGD portal is not indicative of a user's actions or intentions beyond viewing, which may itself be unintentional or even represent a machine's automated action. The digital trace does, though, provide some degree of naturalistic, unobtrusive insight into the kinds of items accessed with the greatest frequency on OGD portals.

3 Findings

3.1 Item Topics

The 200 items of high interest represent a wide range of domains. Figure 1 displays the counts by topic for the items.

The topic with the greatest number of items from our analysis is geographic (n = 32), those items that describe the spatial attributes of places but do not necessarily capture additional attributes of those places. The predominance of items that are geographic is due to the high number of OGD portals in our sample based on the ArcGIS platform (a geographic information system). The items categorized as geographic have broad utility for displaying other items from OGD portals that are geospatial in nature (e.g., public safety incidents at specific addresses). Their high view counts are most likely related to an array of other OGD items that reference them. If we exclude ArcGIS-based portals, the count for the geographic topic drops to just one item. Other topics with relatively high item counts include transportation (n = 24), public safety (n = 22), crime (n = 15), and building permits (n = 13).

Of interest within the transportation topic are datasets describing phenomena that fluctuate frequently over time and for which real-time data may be highly useful (e.g., active traffic accidents, open parking spaces at airports), as well as those with potentially weaker relations among update frequency and utility for users (e.g., a list of vehicles that have an active limousine license, the routes served by municipal snowplows). Drawing these distinctions among items suggests that user interest in OGD items may vary temporally in relation to the social and natural world (i.e., in relation to a season, time of day,

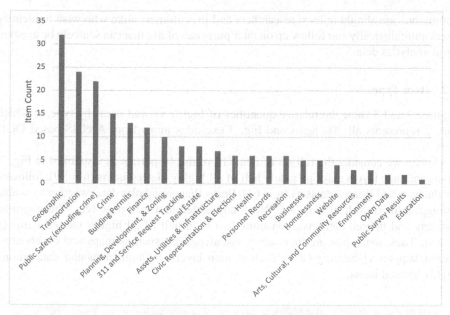

Fig. 1. Highly viewed items by topic

or event) and in relation to the temporal attributes of the data (i.e., in update frequency and recency).

The prevalence of public safety items (pertaining to fire, emergency services, and police activity excluding crime data) and crime items indicates interest around the phenomena of emergencies and municipal responses to them. Combined, the topics of public safety and crime constitute 18.5% of all highly viewed items. The Chicago crime data that [29] found frequently cited in scientific publications using OGD also appeared in our study, represented by three highly viewed items, specifically, a dataset with 7.61 million records of crimes and two visualization products. We note that the highly viewed items in the public safety and crime topics include data associated with known commercial opportunities, such as soliciting people who have experienced an emergency.

Two kinds of notable outliers in our examination of highly viewed items we encountered were those that together point to local applications and to items demonstrating anomalous interest in relation to their content. An example of the first type of outlier, indicative of a topic of local interest, are those related to the phenomena of homelessness in Portland, OR (evidenced in items about public reporting of urban campsites, municipal response to public reports, and locations with public restrooms and hygiene resources). What we identify as anomalous use, a second type of outlier, is a highly viewed item lacking an obvious current application related to its content or update history. Los Angeles' OGD portal offers two examples: a highly viewed dataset of properties foreclosed on in 2014 and a calendar of immigration workshops with a record of events ending in September 2020. To understand why these items are highly viewed, whether for a unique quality, high interest during a time period that has elapsed, general disuse of a portal, or an alternate explanation is beyond the scope of our study; however, items demonstrating anomalous use should interest researchers and practitioners alike who wish to identify users naturalistically and follow up on their purposes of use that can scarcely be guessed from analytics data.

3.2 Item Types

Figures 2 and 3 show the relative quantities of highly viewed items by type, in which Fig. 2 represents all 200 items and Fig. 3 excludes items from ArcGIS-based OGD portals.

When we consider the full set of items from the 40 portals as visualized in Fig. 2, maps and map layers make up nearly half of all highly viewed items (n = 99), followed by datasets and filtered datasets (n = 64). Items that are tabular data, whether viewable through a file download (e.g., a CSV) or embedded in a web page (e.g., those termed datasets and filtered datasets), constitute less than half of all highly viewed items (n = 88). Thus, items that are themselves visualizations, such as maps and dashboards, and/or support visualizing OGD, such as map layers, outnumber tabular data among highly viewed items.

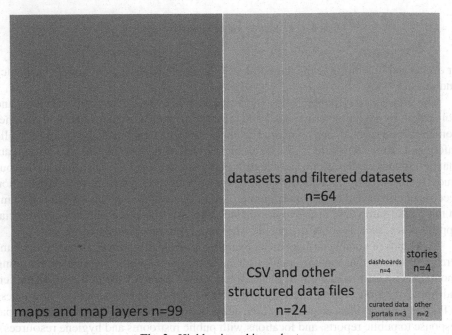

Fig. 2. Highly viewed items by type

If we omit ArcGIS-based portals (recognizing their difference from portal software that is not GIS-based) and their highly viewed items from our dataset, the majority of the remaining 100 highly viewed items are datasets and filtered datasets (n = 61). Tabular data (including CSV and other structured data files) constitutes 75% of highly viewed items on OGD portals that are not GIS-based. In other words, the most viewed items on non-GIS-based OGD portals tend to be structured tabular data, rather than products of data visualization.

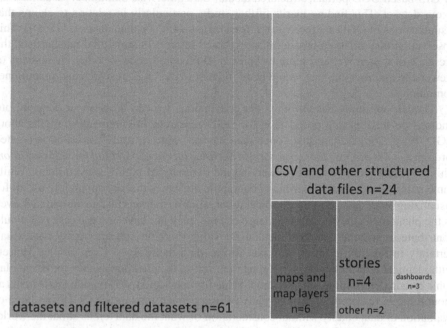

Fig. 3. Highly viewed items by type, excluding items from ArcGIS-based OGD portals

More unusual item types in the dataset include what we term curated data portals (n = 4, called "hub site application" in ArcGIS parlance), unique to ArcGIS-based portals and presenting selected datasets and visualizations related to a specific theme. For example, one curated data portal contains items relating to a ballot measure funding infrastructure projects and services in Long Beach, CA. In general, data visualizations not in map form, such as dashboards displaying multiple charts of related phenomena, were few among the highly viewed items.

4 Discussion and Conclusion

Our analysis of highly viewed items provides some indication of where users' interests may lie when visiting OGD portals, in addition to insight about how the software platforms underlying OGD portals relate to such items. We find broad variety in topics of interest, led by geographic, transportation, public safety, and crime items, and with GIS-based OGD portals reflecting high viewership of geographic items critical for mapping other data. For non-GIS-based portals, our findings are in line with another observation [16] of high viewership of transportation and public safety data. We infer from our examination of items within the transportation, public safety, and crime topics that an item's usefulness to users has a temporal dimension and that OGD items have variable apparent utility for commercial exploitation. Additionally, we observe that visualizations dominate highly viewed items across portals in general, but that this too is driven by GIS-based OGD portals; structured tabular data otherwise outnumber visualizations in our dataset. This finding merits further study, particularly in relation to claims that visualizations of OGD are more useful for a broad audience than datasets [18, 19]. This observation may relate to broader than expected interest in structured tabular data, the presence of a narrower and more technically-skilled audience, or other phenomena of viewership and usership that would be of interest to the OGD research and practitioner community.

Though our study design limits the conclusions we can draw about demand, our findings do lead us to a proposition for OGD research. In enumerating myths about OGD, [9, p. 266] declare that "open data has no value in itself," as value is created through use. *We propose that open data do not have identical potential for value creation.* This proposition emerges from observing the diversity of highly viewed items. While some items, like datasets describing geographic attributes that are apparently useful for visualizing other data geospatially, other items, such as datasets that go un-updated, even as the phenomena they describe undergo change, may not have any use case that would contribute to societal benefit. Potential for value creation appears highly contextual, certainly in relation to users [23], but also to data themselves. Even among datasets with identical interpretability supporting their reuse, the phenomena they represent play some role in determining their potential value for users and use. Treating OGD items as monolithic in research, such as in study of users' intentions to use OGD writ large or evaluation of data quality without consideration of what the data tell us about the world, obscures distinctions that are important for characterizing use and optimizing provision.

Our exploration into the demand-side of OGD suggests that researchers may find it generative to adopt a data-specific approach to OGD use, namely, one in which investigation begins from selecting a subset of items of interest. A subset might be a single item, those with similar characteristics such as real-time utility for residents or identified potential for commercial exploitation, or those related to a particular thematic area, like financial transparency or homelessness. Working with a subset may allow researchers to overcome challenges mentioned earlier regarding research design to locate likely users and to produce studies of use that articulate specific causal mechanisms between use and impact, supported by empirical data. From a practitioner standpoint, pursuing insights about why certain items engage OGD portal users and others do not can contribute to a range of organizational objectives, such as prioritizing resources, improving utilization, and identifying local trends signaled on portals. In closing, our work suggests that additional research about what people currently do (and want to do) with specific OGD will benefit research and practice.

References

1. Gao, Y., Janssen, M., Zhang, C.: Understanding the evolution of open government data research: towards open data sustainability and smartness. Int. Rev. Adm. Sci. (2021). https://doi.org/10.1177/00208523211009955
2. Habib, A., Prybutok, V.R., Philpot, D.: Assessing and building municipal open data capability. Inf. Syst. E-Bus Manag. **20**(1), 1–25 (2021). https://doi.org/10.1007/s10257-021-00539-y

3. Ansari, B., Barati, M., Martin, E.G.: Enhancing the usability and usefulness of open government data: a comprehensive review of the state of open government data visualization research. Gov. Inf. Q. **39**, 101657 (2022). https://doi.org/10.1016/j.giq.2021.101657

4. Attard, J., Orlandi, F., Scerri, S., Auer, S.: A systematic review of open government data initiatives. Gov. Inf. Q. **32**, 399–418 (2015). https://doi.org/10.1016/j.giq.2015.07.006

5. Bright, J., Margetts, H.Z., Wang, N., Hale, S.A.: Explaining usage patterns in open government data: the case of Data.Gov.UK. SSRN Electron. J. (2015). https://doi.org/10.2139/ssrn.2613853

6. Safarov, I., Meijer, A., Grimmelikhuijsen, S.: Utilization of open government data: a systematic literature review of types, conditions, effects and users. Inf. Polity **22**, 1–24 (2017). https://doi.org/10.3233/IP-160012

7. Wirtz, B.W., Weyerer, J.C., Rösch, M.: Open government and citizen participation: an empirical analysis of citizen expectancy towards open government data. Int. Rev. Adm. Sci. **85**, 566–586 (2019). https://doi.org/10.1177/0020852317719996

8. Wang, D., Richards, D., Chen, C.: Connecting users, data and utilization: a demand-side analysis of open government data. In: Taylor, N.G., Christian-Lamb, C., Martin, M.H., Nardi, B. (eds.) iConference 2019. LNCS, vol. 11420, pp. 488–500. Springer, Cham (2019). https://doi.org/10.1007/978-3-030-15742-5_47

9. Janssen, M., Charalabidis, Y., Zuiderwijk, A.: Benefits, adoption barriers and myths of open data and open government. Inf. Syst. Manag. **29**, 258–268 (2012). https://doi.org/10.1080/10580530.2012.716740

10. Lourenço, R.P.: An analysis of open government portals: a perspective of transparency for accountability. Gov. Inf. Q. **32**, 323–332 (2015). https://doi.org/10.1016/j.giq.2015.05.006

11. Nikiforova, A., Lnenicka, M.: A multi-perspective knowledge-driven approach for analysis of the demand side of the Open Government Data portal. Gov. Inf. Q. **38**, 101622 (2021). https://doi.org/10.1016/j.giq.2021.101622

12. Nikiforova, A., McBride, K.: Open government data portal usability: a user-centred usability analysis of 41 open government data portals. Telematics Inform. **58**, 101539 (2021). https://doi.org/10.1016/j.tele.2020.101539

13. Thorsby, J., Stowers, G.N.L., Wolslegel, K., Tumbuan, E.: Understanding the content and features of open data portals in American cities. Gov. Inf. Q. **34**, 53–61 (2017). https://doi.org/10.1016/j.giq.2016.07.001

14. Zhu, X., Freeman, M.A.: An evaluation of U.S. municipal open data portals: a user interaction framework. J. Assoc. Inf. Sci. Technol. **70**, 27–37 (2019). https://doi.org/10.1002/asi.24081

15. Tang, R., Gregg, W., Hirsh, S., Hall, E.: U.S. state and state capital open government data (OGD): a content examination and heuristic evaluation of data processing capabilities of OGD sites. Proc. Assoc. Inf. Sci. Technol. **56**, 255–264 (2019). https://doi.org/10.1002/pra2.20

16. Quarati, A.: Open government data: usage trends and metadata quality. J. Inf. Sci. (2021). https://doi.org/10.1177/01655515211027775

17. Vetrò, A., Canova, L., Torchiano, M., Minotas, C.O., Iemma, R., Morando, F.: Open data quality measurement framework: definition and application to Open Government Data. Gov. Inf. Q. **33**, 325–337 (2016). https://doi.org/10.1016/j.giq.2016.02.001

18. Graves, A., Hendler, J.: Visualization tools for open government data. In: Proceedings of the 14th Annual International Conference on Digital Government Research, Quebec, Canada, pp. 136–145. ACM (2013). https://doi.org/10.1145/2479724.2479746

19. Barcellos, R., Viterbo, J., Miranda, L., Bernardini, F., Maciel, C., Trevisan, D.: Transparency in practice: using visualization to enhance the interpretability of open data. In: Proceedings of the 18th Annual International Conference on Digital Government Research, Staten Island, NY, USA, pp. 139–148. ACM (2017). https://doi.org/10.1145/3085228.3085294

20. de Souza, A.A.C., d'Angelo, M.J., Lima Filho, R.N.: Effects of predictors of citizens' attitudes and intention to use open government data and government 2.0. Gov. Inf. Q. **39**, 101663 (2022). https://doi.org/10.1016/j.giq.2021.101663
21. Crusoe, J.R., Ahlin, K.: Users' activities for using open government data – a process framework. Transforming Gov. People Process Policy **13**, 213–236 (2019). https://doi.org/10.1108/TG-04-2019-0028
22. Hivon, J., Titah, R.: Conceptualizing citizen participation in open data use at the city level. Transforming Gov. People Process Policy **11**, 99–118 (2017). https://doi.org/10.1108/TG-12-2015-0053
23. Lassinantti, J., Ståhlbröst, A., Runardotter, M.: Relevant social groups for open data use and engagement. Gov. Inf. Q. **36**, 98–111 (2019). https://doi.org/10.1016/j.giq.2018.11.001
24. Ruijer, E., Grimmelikhuijsen, S., van den Berg, J., Meijer, A.: Open data work: understanding open data usage from a practice lens. Int. Rev. Adm. Sci. **86**, 3–19 (2020). https://doi.org/10.1177/0020852317753068
25. Robinson, P.J., Johnson, P.A.: Civic hackathons: new terrain for local government-citizen interaction? Urban Plan. **1**, 65–74 (2016). https://doi.org/10.17645/up.v1i2.627
26. Wilson, B., Cong, C.: Beyond the supply side: use and impact of municipal open data in the U.S. Telematics Inform. **58**, 101526 (2021). https://doi.org/10.1016/j.tele.2020.101526
27. Crusoe, J., Simonofski, A., Clarinval, A., Gebka, E.: The impact of impediments on open government data use: insights from users. In: 2019 13th International Conference on Research Challenges in Information Science (RCIS), pp. 1–12 (2019). https://doi.org/10.1109/RCIS.2019.8877055
28. Francey, A., Mettler, T.: The effects of open government data: Some stylised facts. Inf. Polity **26**, 273–288 (2021). https://doi.org/10.3233/IP-200281
29. Yan, A., Weber, N.: Mining open government data used in scientific research. In: Chowdhury, G., McLeod, J., Gillet, V., Willett, P. (eds.) iConference 2018. LNCS, vol. 10766, pp. 303–313. Springer, Cham (2018). https://doi.org/10.1007/978-3-319-78105-1_34
30. Quarati, A., De Martino, M.: Open government data usage: a brief overview. In: Proceedings of the 23rd International Database Applications & Engineering Symposium on - IDEAS 2019, Athens, Greece, pp. 1–8. ACM Press (2019). https://doi.org/10.1145/3331076.3331115
31. Schrock, A., Shaffer, G.: Data ideologies of an interested public: a study of grassroots open government data intermediaries. Big Data Soc. **4** (2017). https://doi.org/10.1177/2053951717690750

"Trapped" by Recommendation Algorithms? A Mixed Methods Study on the Use of Content Recommendation System in Everyday Life in Western China

Pu Yan[1]([✉]), Jieyu Lu[2], Yueyan Zhao[2], and Wenjie Zhou[2]([✉])

[1] Peking University, Beijing, China
puyan@pku.edu.cn
[2] Northwest Normal University, Gansu, China
joshua@nwnu.edu.cn

Abstract. The internet has provided users with informational access and resources. Users, even those living in underdeveloped regions in the Global South countries, have benefited from everyday information available online. However, much of online information is increasingly delivered to users via recommendation systems, which are based on user's online activities (such as previous browsing preferences) or user profiles (such as gender, age, or location). The prevalence of recommendation systems used in mobile APPs such as news aggregators, online shopping platforms, or online video-sharing platforms has led to a heated discussion on the new role of recommendation systems as algorithmic "gatekeepers" that control users' information flow. Yet, few empirical studies have explored how users adopt and adapt to such technologies in everyday life contexts. As recommendation systems increasingly shape the online content consumed by rural internet users, how marginalised users living in rural areas in China perceive and interact with recommendation systems remain unknown to researchers and policymakers. This paper aims to explore how Chinese rural users adapt to recommendation systems in everyday lives, using mixed methods approaches such as face-to-face surveys and in-depth interviews. Findings from this research will inform technology designs of mobile apps that use recommendation systems and will also highlight potential digital divides in how different social groups adapt to digital technologies such as recommendation systems.

Keywords: Recommendation systems · Digital divides · Rural China · Everyday life

1 Introduction and Background

Social media users around the world were shocked when internal documents revealed that one of the biggest social media platforms worldwide, Facebook, designed algorithms to get users hooked on information flows on the social media platform, sometimes even at the cost of spreading harmful or misleading information. As discovered in the leak,

I. Sserwanga et al. (Eds.): iConference 2023, LNCS 13972, pp. 449–472, 2023.
https://doi.org/10.1007/978-3-031-28032-0_35

automated ranking algorithms used by Facebook played a key role in prolonging the time users spent on the social media platform [20]. Researchers are concerned about the untransparent algorithms and the forming of a "black-box society": recommendation algorithms used in content platforms such as search engines (i.e., Google or Baidu in China), video platforms (i.e., YouTube or Douyin in China), or social media platforms (i.e., Twitter or Sina Weibo in China) continue to determine the varied visibility of search results, prioritise some types of information over the others, or define what is "trending" among all public posts.

Internet users nowadays are increasingly used to receiving automatically generated news feed at their fingertips, delivered by super-sticky multi-functional apps such as TikTok, YouTube, Facebook, WeChat, or news Apps. Recommendation systems, such as the ones used by short-video platforms or news apps, are often key features for popular mobile Apps, for example, TikTok (or Douyin in mainland China), Toutiao (a popular news App in China), or Flipboard. Thus, developing countries such as China and India might experience a stronger impact from algorithm-driven recommendation systems than developed countries, as Internet users in the Global South are predominantly dependent on mobile devices for Internet access [18].

Yet investigations that showed how recommendation systems have controlled or even distorted users' information flows warned the public of the potential risks of algorithms gatekeeping everyday information channels. Meanwhile, the algorithmically shaped information flow is generated based on user practice data, for example, users' daily logs of engaging with the platform and content of users' social media posts. It is thus crucial for sociological studies on algorithms to also explore the "multidimensional 'entanglement' between algorithms put into practices and the social tactics of users who take them up" [11]. Internet users, policymakers, and technology companies are reflecting on the question of who should get control over one's information diet. Should all aspects of everyday information, whether it is about social networks, entertainment, e-commerce, or education, be analysed, ranked, and recommended by personalisation algorithms? To what extent do the users need to maintain their agencies in monitoring and gatekeeping their online information flows? Answers to these questions are not only important for understanding the better designs of recommendation systems but also essential for creating a user-friendly information ecology and building a "smart" information system that utilises automation to learn from users' preferences. Nevertheless, an important step to address these questions is to first understand user experiences, attitudes, and practices in an information system shaped and driven by algorithms such as recommendation systems.

Researchers have empirically studied users' perceptions of artificial intelligence in using voice assistants [13], facial recognition technology [17], and self-driving cars [23]. However, very few studies focused on content recommendation algorithms that shape what content is visible on people's news feed, social media interfaces, or short-video streaming list. In this study, we took a mixed-methods approach that combined an offline survey with in-depth interviews, which were conducted in rural China, Gansu Province, to explore digital divides in relation to algorithms such as recommendation systems.

To our knowledge, this is one of the first empirical research on the public perception of artificial intelligence-driven recommendation systems. More importantly, our research is conducted in developing regions and among marginalised social groups in China, which is often neglected by researchers who studied the social impact of algorithms. By linking the literature of digital divides with studies focusing on user experiences in algorithm-rich information systems, the research aims to examine 1) Are there digital divides in the use of artificial intelligence? 2) What are the social and informational barriers to using recommendation systems in rural China? 3) How can internet users be categorised into different groups according to their usage of and attitudes toward recommendation systems?

The Urban-Rural Digital Divides in China

Recent years have witnessed the rapid development of information and communication technology in rural and urban China. On the one hand, top-down informatisation poli-cies have accelerated internet development in rural China, for example, by reimbursing broadband costs of rural internet to improve the internet proliferation rate in the most under-developed areas in China. On the other hand, technologies such as mobile inter-net and multi-functional social media platforms such as WeChat have lower technical barriers for inexperienced internet users to access internet services. By September 2021, the Internet penetration rate in China has reached over 71 per cent, among which more than 99 per cent of Internet users have accessed the Internet via smartphones. Never-theless, China's internet population is disproportionally distributed in rural and urban areas: While urban residents account for around 64 per cent of the population, more than 70 per cent of internet users reside in urban areas [5].

Compared to urban internet users, rural internet users are disadvantaged not only in internet infrastructures, devices, and the quality of internet access but also in internet skills and experiences. A survey of non-users of the internet in China showed that the most important reason for not adopting the internet is the lack of information and internet skills [5]. The prevalence of mobile internet in developing countries such as China and India has also raised concerns over whether mobile Internet users are disadvantaged than PC Internet users in their familiarity with algorithms or lacking experience in utilising the internet for capital-enhancing purposes [18].

A Black-box Society? Public Scrutiny and Government Regulations of AI and Rec-ommendation Systems in China

While the existing rural-urban divides in internet adoption and use has not been miti-gated, new divide has started to emerge in an information ecology where algorithms such as personalisation and recommendation systems shape what people consume every day. As Pasquale warned in his book *The Black Box Society*: "Our own lives are increasingly open books. Everything we do online is recorded; the only question left is to whom the data will be available, and for how long" [21, p3]. An empirical research has suggested that users' skills in interacting with algorithmically driven information systems differ across various user groups [34], the black-box society might yield further information barriers and challenges to the information have-less and information-poor population. The consequences of information flow curated by biased recommendation algorithms are under intense scrutiny from the media and the public.

2 Literature Review

Existing literature on the intersection of technology and society focused extensively on the topic of digital divides, which highlights the group variations in how Internet users, access, adopt and use information and communication technologies in their everyday lives. In this paper, we will start by first reviewing scholarly works, including theories and empirical research, on digital divides, particularly the shift from the first- and second-level divides to the third-level divides. As we will discuss in the following review, there has been an increase in digital divides in how users satisfy or fail to satisfy their information and communication needs in everyday lives. Users' ability to understand, interact, and engage with the algorithmic system is influenced by whether they can benefit from using algorithmic-driven information environments. Meanwhile, the emerging technologies used on social media platforms on the news or short-video platforms, namely recommendation systems, are increasingly shaping how various groups of Internet users consume digital content. The second part of the review will summarise findings from existing empirical studies that focused on social variances in recommendation system use.

2.1 Digital Divides: From Access, Use, to Information and Algorithmic Divides

The proliferation of digital technologies leads to profound social changes and yields a significant impact on individuals' everyday lives. Nevertheless, access, adoption, and use of digital technologies such as the Internet and mobile phones are not equally shared across all social groups. Social science scholars have begun to examine and theorise the issue of digital divides since the early stage of the digital era, when researchers focused on "whether significant differences in Internet usage exist across socioeconomic groupings, such as sex, age, household income, education, and race and ethnicity" [15, p41]. In addition to individual-level socioeconomic and demographic factors, country-level differences, for example, ICT development stages between the Global South and the Global North countries, as well as region-level differences, for instance, rural-urban differences in ICT infrastructures, are also associated with gaps in access to digital technologies [25, 26]. Schroeder [29] used the Weberian approach to understand digital divides and defined digital divides as differences between elites and the people in how they use information technologies in everyday lives. Nevertheless, A Weberian approach to digital divides does not attribute the information inequalities simply to the "economic logic of capitalism" (p. 2822) but widens the scope of research to the realm of everyday life and examines the social and political context of the media system in different countries [29].

The development of the infrastructure of digital technologies increased the availability of the Internet in both developed and developing countries [8]. User groups of digital technologies also include technology savvy users and more general populations in the society. Empirical research on digital divides also gradually shifted from studying variances in *access to* digital technologies to also examining the *uses of* ICTs [7]. Pearce and Rice identified four dimensions of digital divides in their comparative study of mobile and PC Internet users: *access to Internet, use of different devices, extent of usage,* and *engagement in different Internet activities.* They pointed out that although mobile Internet is available for users who are at the lower end of digital divides, mobile internet users are disadvantageous in participating in so-called "capital enhancing" internet activities [22]. Meanwhile, scholars have shown that diversity in information devices is also important for having a more diverse internet activity and better internet use outcomes [30]. Napoli and Obar's [18] literature review on the so-called "mobile-only" internet users, who solely depend on mobile internet as their internet access, suggested that being over-dependent on mobile internet as the only internet device might lead to widened digital gaps between the information haves and have-nots. One of the reasons accounting for the mobile disadvantage is the limited level of user engagement in mobile platforms.

Multi-functional mobile social media Apps such as Facebook or WeChat (in China) have created new information channels that are embedded in social networking platforms and blurred the boundary between information seeking and other online activities such as entertainment and social networking. New digital divides emerge in online information practices [32] or in different stages of internet domestication [28]. Another group of researchers who also examined on *internet use* and *internet activity* divides focused on users' information practices on the internet. The concept of information divides or information inequality focuses on social disparities in the access, use, and possession of information resources. For example, Elfreda Chatman's research focused on information poverty in marginalised social groups such as female prisoners [2–4]. Chatman's work showed the importance of understanding information divides and information poverty within users' life world and everyday contexts. In a similar vein, Savolainen [27] studied two groups of information users (workers and teachers) in his empirical study on everyday information-seeking practices and found that workers relied more heavily and easily accessible information than teachers, and yet availability and accessibility did not necessarily yield high-quality information for the problem-solving information task.

In addition to information haves and have-nots, researchers also studied internet users who are not yet information *rich* but rely on low-end information technologies. Qiu [24] studied the everyday life of "information have-less" groups in China, for example, migrant and laid-off workers or elderly internet users in urban China (See also 34]) empirical study on the information poor in rural and urban China). Compared to digital divides scholars from communication science disciplines who studied digital inequalities and social-economic as well as technology use factors, information scholars incorporated factors beyond social, economic, and technological variables in explaining social disparities in information practices on the Internet. For example, Liangzhi Yu [33] proposed a model to explain the causes of information divides, which includes macro-level (societal factors), middle-level (community factors), and micro-level (individual factors).

Literature review of digital divides and information divides literature has suggested a shift from technology access (first-level) to the use of the internet (second-level) or outcome of using the internet (third-level) [31], as well as the increasing importance of understanding digital inequalities in everyday contexts and within users' life worlds. While artificial intelligence (AI) and recommendation system driven technologies become deeply embedded in everyday life, compared to the literature on digital divides in access, adoption, and use of the Internet, very few empirical research has focused on digital divides in how users of seek information, interact with algorithms, and engaged in tailoring information flow on recommendation systems. The global crisis of the COVID pandemic has led to an overwhelming amount of public health data for governments worldwide; however, researchers pointed out a data gap between developed and developing countries in their capacities to collect, organise, and analyse big data [19].

2.2 User Awareness, Knowledge, and Adaptability of Algorithms

Existing research has explored *whether* people are aware of the role of algorithmics in gatekeeping their information flow online and *what* social, demographic, and technology use variables are associated with users' awareness of algorithms. Hargittai and Micheli included "awareness and understanding" of algorithms as one of the ten essential dimensions of internet skills [14, p144]. Carter et al. [1] reviewed literature centring around digital divides and AI and they highlighted both socio-demographic variables, such as age, and variables related to users' perception of and trust in AI.

Scholars also empirically examined misconceptions about algorithms and social-demographic or information use factors that account for these misconceptions. A large-scale survey concluded on Dutch Internet users showed that demographic variables such as age, gender, and education levels are associated with algorithm misconceptions. Meanwhile, people who do not have information sources to educate themselves about algorithms and people who rely on their families and friends as information sources on algorithms are both disadvantageous in terms of having more misconceptions about algorithms [36]. In addition to the access, affordability, and availability of algorithms, which are included in the theoretical framework of digital divide research, Yu [35] also suggested that *adaptability,* users' capabilities to tame algorithms to their own information needs, should be an important dimension of algorithmic divides.

Search engines and recommendation systems are two AI-driven platforms that are perhaps most commonly used by Internet users in everyday life contexts. Cotter and Reisdorf [6] studied algorithmic knowledge in search engines among American Internet users and found that in addition to socio-demographic variables such as age and education, experiences with search engines, measured by the frequency of using search engines and the diversity of using search engines for various information tasks, is positively associated with users' algorithmic knowledge. Gran et al. [12] studied Norwegian Internet users' attitudes against three algorithms, all related to recommendation systems, algorithm-driven recommendations, such as Spotify, algorithm-driven advertisement, and algorithm-driven content, such as personalised news feed. The study identified education as a key demographic variable in accounting for algorithm awareness. Meanwhile, higher awareness of algorithms is also related to more critical reflections on the role of algorithms in gatekeeping everyday information.

Another group of scholars who have examined public attitudes toward algorithms are researchers from the field of public understanding of science. Chinese public seems to hold a more favourable view against artificial intelligence than people in other countries: A comparative study that compared public perceptions of Facial Recognition Technology in China, Germany, the UK, and the US showed that the acceptance of facial recognition technology is the highest in China. Unlike other countries where the public is concerned about the state or private companies using facial recognition technology for control and surveillance, Chinese respondents see such technologies as beneficial for providing convenience and security [17]. The same study also found that among Chinese survey respondents, younger, more educated and people with higher income are more likely to have higher acceptance of facial recognition technology, suggesting group variances in public trust in emerging technologies.

Nevertheless, very little research has examined how users *adapt to* and *engage with* information flow generated automatically by recommendation algorithms, which are based on user's previous preferences, location information, or demographics. One exception is the in-depth qualitative interviews conducted by Klawitter and Hargittai, in which the researchers investigated algorithmic skills, practices, and strategies in using social media and news feed among entrepreneurs in the US [16]. Such skills are important, as "they help users recognize that actions they take can increase the chances of posted content showing up on relevant people's feeds" (p. 3493). In other words, different levels of algorithmic skills will lead to differentiated levels of content *visibility* that appear on users' content platforms. Klawitter and Hargittai's study showed varied levels of algorithmic knowledge and, accordingly, algorithmic strategies among the interviewees, which often leads to different information-seeking and Internet use outcomes. Eslami and her colleagues explored user awareness of content curation algorithms and users' strategies to modify the algorithmically curated social media news feed. Their work shows that the opaqueness of content curation algorithms, which are commonly used by social media platforms, has led to unawareness and confusion of algorithms among internet users [10]. Despite various theories developed by users to explain why some content is prioritised while others are undermined by the content curation algorithms, users fail to take back the power from algorithms to rearrange content shown on their own news feeds [9]. The findings suggest that when developing algorithms for recommendation systems, the agencies of users as content consumers is largely missing from the technology design. Hence, understanding *if* and *how* users interact with recommendation systems is crucial for developing user-centric information systems.

However, current empirical research on algorithm knowledge and user practices in algorithm-driven platforms has not studied Internet users who are at the lower end of digital divides. However, knowing how algorithms have influenced the everyday lives of information have-not and have-less users is important for the understanding of social disparities in the digital era. Our research will fill the gap in the literature by focusing on an internet population that has been overlooked in empirical research on algorithm use. We focus on the information-poor users in rural China, whose everyday lives have already been profoundly influenced by AI, but their user interactions with algorithms such as recommendation systems are often under-studied by social science researchers.

3 Methods

3.1 Data Collection

Data in this paper was collected between July 15 to 23,2021, from Gansu province, Western China, by a team consisting of ten undergraduate, two graduate student assistants and three researchers. We chose Gansu province as the field site not only because of our familiarity with the local area (two researchers are based in the province) but also because Gansu represents the most under-developed region in China. Gansu ranked as the poorest province in China measured by GDP per capita in 2021.

There are mainly two types of data collected from each participant: a 40-min survey collected via face-to-face interviews, accompanied by interviews with the participants about their everyday internet experience and online information seeking practices. We applied a purposeful sampling approach to recruit survey and interview respondents: The final sample includes a sample that is almost representative of the population living in the region, with the majority of the population based on agriculture as the main income source. While collecting the survey sample, our team also strived to include a diverse range of social groups.

The survey consists of four types of questions: 1) Dependent variables on how users perceive the role of recommendation systems in shaping what they consume on news Apps and how users interact with recommendation systems by providing feedback to the systems. All dependent variables are measured using six Likert-scale items, with 1 representing strongly disagree and 5 strongly agree with the statements. 2) The second group of variables focused on the information skills of users, for example, whether they rely on information brokers for seeking online information, and their self-evaluated skills in using basic or advanced search functions on search engines. Also included in this type of variable is a measurement of the level of critical thinking involved when seeking online information. The higher the score, the more critical views users hold against online information; 3) The third group of variables focus on time spent on different online activities, including but not limited to social media platforms, online video platforms, news aggregators, websites, or gaming. 4) Finally, the fourth type of variables surveyed socio-economic and demographic factors such as age, gender, education, occupation, and income level.

Each survey questionnaire is coded and analysed in STATA, and qualitative interviews are transcribed and analysed in NVivo. The quantitative method is triangulated with the qualitative method via a procedural approach: we started with the survey analysis by testing research hypotheses outlined based on the literature review of empirical studies on how users engage with recommendation systems. After identifying the associations between recommendation system use and attitudes, information skills, and internet users, we then used qualitative data to explore the group variances and nuances of using recommendation systems, particularly differentiated attitudes and uses of recommendation systems across users of various levels of information skills and types of internet usages. The triangulation of quantitative data with qualitative interpretation will together contribute to a comprehensive understanding of how rural Chinese users understand, utilise, and interact with recommendation systems.

3.2 Descriptive Data Analysis

Table 1 provides descriptive data on key socio-economic and demographic variables. The surveyed sample consists of more female correspondents than males, with the majority of respondents being middle-aged and having less than high school education levels. Most of the survey respondents are farmers, but our sample also includes local government officials or professionals such as doctors or teachers. Our respondents spent

Table 1. Descriptive data of socio-economic, demographic, and information skills variables

Variable name	Variable	Levels	Summary statistics Frequency/Mean (SD)	Valid cases
Gender	Gender	Male Female	115 (32.1%) 243 (67.9%)	358 (100%)
Age	Age		48.1 (14)	355 (99.2%)
Occupation	Occupation	Entrepreneur Farmer Government official or professionals Worker Others	52 (14.9%) 179 (51.4%) 42 (12.1%) 60 (17.2%) 15 (4.3%)	348 (97.2%)
Edulevel	Education level	Less than elementary school Elementary school Junior high school High school or over	62 (17.3%) 77 (21.5%) 99 (27.7%) 120 (33.5%)	358 (100%)
Income_3_year_average	Average annual income over the recent three years		38516.6 (65940.8)	343 (95.8%)
Time_internet_mobile	Time spent using mobile phone per day		2.5 (2.3)	358 (100%)

(continued)

Table 1. (*continued*)

Variable name	Variable	Levels	Summary statistics Frequency/Mean (SD)	Valid cases
Info_search_need_broker	Need information brokers to identify online information	Yes No	285 (80.1%) 71 (19.9%)	356 (99.4%)
Info_search_engine_basic	Use basic functions of search engine (i.e., text search)	Yes No	181 (51.0%) 174 (49.0%)	355 (99.2%)
Info_seach_engine_advanced	Use advanced functions of search engine (i.e., advanced search functions, image search etc.)	Yes No	29 (8.2%) 326 (91.8%)	355 (99.2%)
Info_critical	Level of critical views against online information	Completely trust Most likely trust Partially trust Most likely critical	61 (18.3%) 67 (20.1%) 177 (53.0%) 29 (8.7%)	334 (93.3%)

approximately 2.5 h per day using mobile phones. Although over half of the respondents have used basic functions of search engines, such as Baidu or Sogou in China, a considerable proportion of rural internet users (80.1%) need help from information brokers (for example, family members or neighbours) to seek information online.

3.3 Regression and Clustering Analysis

We apply multiple regressions on three dimensions of the use and perception of recommendation systems, using information skills, information trust, internet use, and socio-economic variables in the model (Table 2).

Table 2. Names and wordings of dependent variables

Variable name	Wording	Levels	Valid cases
Recom_diverse_topic	Recommendation systems often feed me with diverse topics	Strongly disagree Somewhat disagree Neither disagree nor agree Somewhat agree Strongly agree	264 (73.74%)
Recom_diverse_view	Recommendation systems often enable me to see diverse perspectives of the same event		260 (72.63%)
Recom_same_topic	Recommendation systems often feed me with the same topics		257 (71.79%)
Recom_same_view	Recommendation systems often provide me articles that share my own view		259 (72.35%)
Recom_reject_irrelavant	I don't click on content provided in recommendation systems that I'm not interested in		263 (73.46%)
Recom_feedback	I will click the "dislike" button in recommendation systems to provide feedback to the algorithm		260 (72.63%)

3.4 Dimensions of Recommendation System Usage

Before running regression analysis on the use and perception of recommendation systems, we first categorise six survey items on the recommendation systems on different online activities in the PCA analysis. Three components were detected using PCA, which account for 68.9% of total variances. Table 3 shows factor loadings of each survey item on different factors. The PCA result suggests that six survey items on recommendation systems can be divided into three dimensions: diversity of recommendation systems in topics and views; relevance of content suggested by recommendation systems; and user engagement with recommendation systems. In the regression analysis to explain what information use and socio-economic factors are associated with the perception of recommendation systems, we will use these three dimensions as dependent variables on recommendation systems.

Table 3. Factor loadings of survey items on recommendation systems

Survey items on recommendation systems	Factor loading		
	1	2	3
Factor 1: Diversity of recommendation systems			
Recom_diverse_topic	−0.0311	0.8837	−0.0096
Recom_diverse_view	0.2212	0.8179	0.1158
Factor 2: Relevance of recommendation systems			
Recom_same_topic	0.7590	0.0810	−0.1444
Recom_same_view	0.7770	0.1107	0.0775
Recom_reject_irrelavant	0.5877	0.0516	0.3940
Factor 3: Engagement with recommendation systems			
Recom_feedback	0.0032	0.0513	0.9412

3.5 Regression and Cluster Analysis

We ran regression analyses on three dimensions of the use and perception of recommendation systems, using variables on information skills, information trust, and internet use. Having explored the information and internet use factors behind the use and perception of recommendation systems, we conducted cluster analysis on all survey respondents based on three identified dimensions of recommendation systems and applied k-means algorithm using the Euclidean Distance to measure the similarities between different clusters of users based on their varied perceptions of recommendation systems. To better understand different types of recommendation system users, the quantitative cluster analysis was supplemented with qualitative analysis of case studies drawing from our fieldwork, which discussed the variances in the user experiences of recommendation systems.

4 Result

4.1 Factors Accounting for Variances in the Use and Perception of Recommendation Systems

To understand what information use, socio-economic or demographic factors are associated with different dimensions of the use and perception of recommendation systems, we run regression analysis in models with different levels of factors. Table 4, Table 5 and Table 6 summarise regression analysis on each dimension. We find that including all four types of factors – information skills, information trust, internet use and socio-economic and demographic variables - increase adjusted R^2 values for all three dimensions. All three full models in the regression analysis are statistically significant.

For the diversity dimension of recommendation systems, we find that users who seek help from other people to use the internet, and those who need internet brokers, experience lower levels of diversity in information courses and viewpoints when using recommendation systems (B $= -1.172, p < 0.05$). People who spend longer time using mobile internet, however, are more likely to benefit from diverse information sources and viewpoints using recommendation systems (B $= 0.210, p < 0.05$). Education level positively correlates with the diversity of information sources and content users received on recommendation systems (B $= 0.162, p < 0.05$).

Meanwhile, we also find that users who receive higher education levels are more likely than those with lower education backgrounds to benefit from receiving the relevant information that is tailored to their needs (B $= 0.125, p < 0.05$).

Very interestingly, we find that when it comes to users' active engagement with recommendation systems, such as providing feedback to the algorithm, the only set of variables that are associated with user engagement is internet use. Mobile internet experience, which is measured by time spent mobile internet daily, is positively correlated with higher engagement levels when using recommendation systems (B $= 0.159, p < 0.05$). Similarly, longer time spent on browsing websites is also associated with higher engagement with recommendation systems (B $= 0.630, p < 0.01$). Both findings are not surprising because many implications of recommendation systems, for example, mobile news or mobile video social platforms such as TikTok and online content providers such as news websites, are based on cutting-edge recommendation algorithms. Users of mobile internet and online content websites are more familiar with recommendation algorithms than internet users who are new to mobile internet or content websites. However, we also find that users who spent longer time using search engines are less likely to provide user feedback to recommendation system (B $= - 0.419, p < 0.05$), possibly because their information needs for complex information search tasks are already met by using search engines.

4.2 Four Types of Recommendation System Users

Using three dimensions of using and perceiving recommendation systems, which include diversity, relevance, and engagement of recommendation systems, we ran cluster analysis based on the three dimensions to identify different types of users. Results suggest that users can be divided into four clusters (see Table 7 and Fig. 1). Qualitative interviews

Table 4. Summary table for regression analysis on the diversity dimension of the use and perception of recommendation system

		Model 1		Model 2		Model 3		Model 4	
		B	SE	B	SE	B	SE	B	SE
Information skill	Need internet broker	−1.152**	−2.90					−1.172*	−2.58
	Basic search engine use	0.337	0.88					0.273	0.65
	Advanced search engine use	0.0148	0.03					0.00615	0.01
Information trust	Critical of online information			0.0676	0.32			0.0516	0.24
Internet use	Time spent on mobile internet					0.278**	2.92	0.210*	2.12
	Time spent on online social					−0.133	−0.73	−0.0802	−0.42
	Time spent on online videos					0.159	0.90	0.157	0.89
	Time spent on online games					−0.150	−0.42	−0.387	−1.02
	Time spent on search engines					−0.212	−0.78	−0.280	−0.97
	Time spent on browsing website					0.646	1.90	0.633	1.87
	Time spent on news applications					0.00280	0.01	−0.00693	−0.03

(continued)

Table 4. (continued)

		Model 1		Model 2		Model 3		Model 4	
		B	SE	B	SE	B	SE	B	SE
Socio-economic and demographic variables	Gender [REFERENCE female]								
	Male	0.254	0.71	0.330	0.92	0.304	0.82	0.427	1.14
	Average income per year	0.00000120	0.09	−0.00000111	−0.09	−0.000000594	−0.05	0.000000102	0.01
	Occupation [REFERENCE farmer]								
	Worker	−0.122	−0.28	0.116	0.27	−0.0496	−0.11	−0.370	−0.81
	Government official or professional	−0.578	−1.07	−0.377	−0.70	−0.442	−0.78	−0.730	−1.25
	Entrepreneur	−0.0987	−0.22	0.0827	0.18	−0.180	−0.38	−0.241	−0.50
	Others	−1.044	−1.42	−0.478	−0.66	−1.058	−1.43	−1.654*	−2.14
	Age	0.000726	0.05	−0.0186	−1.42	0.00191	0.12	0.00434	0.25
	Education level	0.209***	5.13	0.199***	4.48	0.174***	3.94	0.162***	3.38
	Constant	5.762***	6.14	5.715***	6.31	4.375***	4.54	5.275***	4.37
Model summary statistics	N	189		186		179		176	
	Prob > F	0.0000		0.0000		0.0000		0.0001	
	R^2	0.2251		0.1829		0.2402		0.2682	
	Adj R^2	0.1769		0.1411		0.1702		0.1790	
	Root MSE	2.0599		2.0901		2.079		2.0536	

t statistics in parentheses.
* $p < 0.05$, ** $p < 0.01$, *** $p < 0.001$.

Table 5. Summary table for regression analysis on the relevance dimension of the use and perception of recommendation system

		Model 1		Model 2		Model 3		Model 4	
		B	SE	B	SE	B	SE	B	SE
Information skill	Need internet broker	-1.037*	-2.25					-0.940	-1.72
	Basic search engine use	0.213	0.48					0.153	0.31
	Advanced search engine use	-1.002	-1.57					-1.604	-1.89
Information trust	Critical of online information			0.199	0.81			0.306	1.16
Internet use	Time spent on mobile internet					0.146	1.28	0.0980	0.82
	Time spent on online social					-0.0819	-0.37	-0.117	-0.51
	Time spent on online videos					0.0480	0.23	0.0571	0.27
	Time spent on online games					0.289	0.68	0.248	0.54
	Time spent on search engines					-0.171	-0.52	-0.00731	-0.02
	Time spent on browsing website					0.273	0.67	0.324	0.80
	Time spent on news applications					0.00483	0.02	0.157	0.61

(continued)

Table 5. (*continued*)

		Model 1		Model 2		Model 3		Model 4	
		B	SE	B	SE	B	SE	B	SE
Socio-economic and demographic variables	Gender [REFERENCE female]								
	Male	0.589	1.43	0.530	1.27	0.529	1.20	0.688	1.54
	Average income per year	-0.0000108	-0.73	-0.0000109	-0.73	-0.0000102	-0.65	-0.0000107	-0.69
	Occupation [REFERENCE farmer]								
	Worker	0.0646	0.13	0.150	0.30	0.120	0.23	-0.0313	-0.06
	Government official or professional	0.0307	0.05	0.0164	0.03	-0.0700	-0.10	-0.239	-0.34
	Entrepreneur	0.0454	0.09	0.188	0.35	0.00492	0.01	-0.177	-0.30
	Others	-0.732	-0.86	-0.277	-0.33	-0.559	-0.63	-1.036	-1.12
	Age	-0.0125	-0.73	-0.0207	-1.35	-0.00670	-0.36	-0.00649	-0.31
	Education level	0.156**	3.29	0.133*	2.57	0.126*	2.39	0.125*	2.16
	Constant	6.565***	6.03	5.833***	5.52	5.422***	4.70	5.390***	3.72
Model summary statistics	N	189		186		179		176	
	Prob > F	0.0026		0.0101		0.1554		0.0564	
	R^2	0.1461		0.1136		0.1137		0.1652	
	Adj R^2	0.0930		0.0682		0.0322		0.0635	
	Root MSE	2.3911		2.4401		2.4919		2.4691	

t statistics in parentheses.
* $p < 0.05$, ** $p < 0.01$, *** $p < 0.001$.

Table 6. Summary table for regression analysis on the engagement dimension of the use and perception of recommendation system

		Model 1		Model 2		Model 3		Model 4	
		B	SE	B	SE	B	SE	B	SE
Information skill	Need internet broker	−0.555*	−2.05					−0.394	−1.30
	Basic search engine use	−0.353	−1.35					−0.360	−1.30
	Advanced search engine use	0.145	0.38					0.137	0.29
Information trust	Critical of online information			0.298*	2.09			0.217	1.49
Internet use	Time spent on mobile internet					0.180**	2.89	0.159*	2.43
	Time spent on online social					−0.192	−1.60	−0.184	−1.47
	Time spent on online videos					0.0315	0.27	0.0709	0.60
	Time spent on online games					0.606*	2.60	0.450	1.79
	Time spent on search engines					−0.454*	−2.54	−0.419*	−2.18
	Time spent on browsing website					0.632**	2.84	0.630**	2.81
	Time spent on news applications					−0.173	−1.28	−0.159	−1.12

(continued)

Table 6. (continued)

		Model 1		Model 2		Model 3		Model 4	
		B	SE	B	SE	B	SE	B	SE
Socio-economic and demographic variables	Gender [REFERENCE female]								
	Male	0.240	0.98	0.321	1.32	0.230	0.95	0.233	0.94
	Average income per year	−0.00000670	−0.77	−0.00000895	−1.02	−0.000000509	−0.60	−0.00000467	−0.55
	Occupation [REFERENCE farmer]								
	Worker	0.267	0.91	0.336	1.17	0.0855	0.30	−0.0791	−0.26
	Government official or professional	−0.624	−1.68	−0.644	−1.77	−0.536	−1.45	−0.631	−1.63
	Entrepreneur	0.110	0.35	0.123	0.39	0.0588	0.19	−0.0607	−0.19
	Others	−0.269	0.53	−0.211	−0.43	−0.604	−1.24	−0.750	−1.47
	Age	−0.00734	−0.73	−0.00687	−0.77	−0.00527	−0.52	−0.00874	−0.77
	Education level	0.1***	3.6)	0.0746*	2.48	0.0628*	2.18	0.0476	1.50
	Constant	3.160***	4.93	1.868**	3.03	2.462***	3.91	2.806**	3.51
Model summary statistics	N	189		186		179		176	
	Prob > F	0.0018		0.0016		0.0000		0.0000	
	R^2	0.1505		0.1377		0.2484		0.2767	
	Adj R^2	0.0978		0.0936		0.1792		0.1886	
	Root MSE	1.4084		1.4208		1.3605		1.3621	

t statistics in parentheses.
* $p < 0.05$, ** $p < 0.01$, *** $p < 0.001$.

with our survey respondents suggest that education level and age are indeed important social factors behind different uses of recommendation systems.

User type 1 scored second highest on the relevance of recommendation systems but second lowest on providing feedback to recommendation systems. We, therefore, consider this user type as the *lurkers*, those who mainly consume relevant and personalised information provided by recommendation systems but with lower interest in diversified sources of information. Another type of users, user type 4, scored second highest on the functions of recommendation systems in providing diverse information content and diversified views; they do not, however, emphasise the importance of information relevance of recommended content or actively engage with the recommendation systems. We name this user type the *explorers*. We found that the *lurkers* and *explorers,* with the former value relevance of information and the latter diversity of information provided by recommendation systems, share similar socio-economic backgrounds, although the *explorers* receive higher education levels than the *larkers.* An example for the explorers and lurkers is Bo, a 62-year-old retiree, who holds a high-school education background, spends much less time on mobile internet than Ai, is mainly interested in short-video platforms, which is also driven by recommendation systems. Unlike Ai, he relies on subjective decisions to "filter" out content that is not relevant to his information needs. Instead of actively reporting to the system content that is not relevant, he only selectively read articles or what videos that he is interested in. Bo's daily use of search engines is also less diverse than that of Ai; he mostly uses basic search functions on Baidu to solve information-seeking queries.

User type 2 scores the highest on all three dimensions, emphasising diversity, relevance, and engagement of recommendation systems (Table 7). We name this type of user as the *experts* of recommendation systems. The *experts* are the youngest user groups among all four types of users and have the highest education levels among all recommendation system users. An example of expert user is Ai, who is a 21-year-old female primary school teacher with an undergraduate degree. Ai is an experienced user of multiple mobile platforms that are backed up by state-of-the-art recommendation systems, for example, Douyin, Kuai, and several news Apps. Ai's information channels are not only diverse but also highly personalised to her personal interests. For example, she frequently engages with the recommendation systems by clicking the "not interested" button on mobile Apps. Ai's information skill is also higher than most of the respondents surveyed in our study. For example, her choices of search engines for solving everyday information queries are quite diverse, including Baidu, Google, and Sogou.

User type 3 are the most inexperienced users of recommendation systems, as they did not consider themselves benefiting from the diversity or relevance of information fed by recommendation systems. Neither did they interact or engage with the systems. We name this type of user as the *sceptics* due to their lack of interest or user engagement in recommendation systems. The *sceptics*, those who do not find recommendation systems useful in providing relevant or diverse information and who do not engage with recommendation systems are also the most disadvantaged internet users among all four groups. They are often older generation users who receive lower education levels compared to the other three user groups. Cui, a 62-year-old housewife who is a middle-school graduate, exemplifies the user experiences of recommendation systems for the sceptics.

Compared to Ai and Bo, Cui is overwhelmed by house chores and only spends less than 30 min browsing mobile internet. Her online time is mostly spent on WeChat, the social networking platform, and reading e-books on her mobile phone. Platforms such as recommendation algorithms driven short-video platforms or news platforms are not Cui's frequently used mobile Apps. Interestingly, Cui indicates that she has a low interest in consuming text or video content on the internet and seems to hold a rather pessimistic view that content platforms can do no benefit to the improvement of her life world. Cui's information channel beyond recommendation systems is also rather limited; for example, she relied on asking her family members to search for information online for her everyday information needs.

Table 7. Result of cluster analysis on the use and perception of recommendation systems.

User type	Number of users	Centre of the cluster		
		Diversity	Relevance	Engagement
User type 1: Lurkers	44	5.573	8.883	3.737
User type 2: Experts	74	8.876	9.322	3.903
User type 3: Sceptics	25	2.772	3.351	1.942
User type 4: Explorers	90	7.818	5.816	2.981

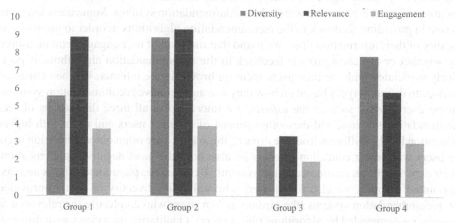

Fig. 1. Visualisation of cluster analysis result

5 Conclusions and Discussions

Content recommendation algorithms shape what people read, listen to, or consume in everyday life. News Apps, short-video platforms, and food delivery services are all examples of recommendation systems that filter, rank, and "push" personalised content to Internet users. Meanwhile, users of recommendation systems are noticing negative influences of the new gatekeepers of information on their information flow. For example, advertisements are recommended as equally important as high-quality news content. Users' personal information, such as age and gender are used by technology companies to push seemingly relevant but often discriminative content. While tech-savvy users of the internet become aware of the algorithmically shaped content, it is unclear whether information poor or information have-less users can also adapt to the new information environment driven by recommendation systems.

Our study focused on the social consequences of algorithmically moderated media platforms; in particular, we are interested in the social group variances in how the marginalised community in China adopt, use, and engage with recommendation systems. We took a mixed methods approach by combining survey and interview datasets, which were both collected from extensive fieldwork in Western China. We found that the use and perception of recommendation systems can be categorised into three dimensions: the diversity of content, the relevance of content, and user engagement level with recommendation systems. Having identified different dimensions of recommendation system usage, we then explored the factors accounting for different use of recommendation systems. Regression analysis suggested that users who rely on information proxies to find information online or users who spend shorter time using mobile internet are more likely to experience the lack of content diversity fed by recommendation systems. In addition to informational factors, we also found users who receive higher education levels are also more likely to enjoy a more diverse media diet when engaging with content recommendation systems. High education level is also associated with a higher likelihood of locating relevant information within the recommendation systems. Some users are more active in providing feedback to the recommendation algorithms in order to improve the quality of their information flow: We found that the level of user engagement, measured by whether or not users provide feedback to the recommendation algorithms, is positively associated with the time users spent on browsing the internet. We then clustered users into different types based on how they use and perceive recommendation systems. Some user groups, such as the *experts,* are interested in all three dimensions of recommendation systems, and they often consist of younger users and users with higher education levels. Different from the *experts*, the *sceptics* are often older generation users or users with lower education levels, who also hold the most negative opinions about their experiences on recommendation systems. Between the passionate experts and disappointed sceptics, we also found users who value the diversity of content provided by recommendation systems (the *explorers*), \ or users who emphasise the relevance of content recommended by algorithms (the *lurkers*). Qualitative interviews with different types of users suggest how user experiences vary across all four types of users.

References

1. Carter, L., Liu, D., Cantrell, C.: Exploring the intersection of the digital divide and artificial intelligence: a hermeneutic literature review. AIS Trans. Human-Comput. Interact. **12**(4), 253–275 (2020). https://doi.org/10.17705/1thci.00138
2. Chatman, E.A.: Life in a small world: applicability of gratification theory to information-seeking behavior. J. Am. Soc. Inform. Sci. Technol. **42**(6), 438–449 (1991)

3. Chatman, E.A.: The impoverished life-world of outsiders. J. Am. Soc. Inform. Sci. Technol. **47**(3), 193–206 (1996)
4. Chatman, E.A.: A theory of life in the round. J. Am. Soc. Inform. Sci. Technol. **50**, 207–217 (1999)
5. CNNIC: 中国互联网络发展状况统计报告 (2021). http://www.cnnic.net.cn/hlwfzyj/hlw xzbg/hlwtjbg/202109/P020210915523670981527.pdf
6. Cotter, K., Reisdorf, B.C.: Algorithmic knowledge gaps: a new dimension of (digital) inequality. Int. J. Commun. **14**, 745–765 (2020). https://ijoc.org/index.php/ijoc/article/view/12450. Date accessed
7. DiMaggio, P., Hargittai, E., Celeste, C., Shafer, S.: Digital inequality: from unequal access to differentiated use. In: Neckerman, K.M. (ed.) Social Inequality, pp. 355–400. Russell Sage Foundation, New York (2004)
8. Donner, J.: After Access: Inclusion, Development, and A More Mobile Internet [still image]. The MIT Press, Cambridge (2015)
9. Eslami, M., et al.: First I "like" it, then I hide it. In: Proceedings of the 2016 CHI Conference on Human Factors in Computing Systems (2016)
10. Eslami, M., et al.: I always assumed that I wasn't really that close to [her]. In: Proceedings of the 33rd Annual ACM Conference on Human Factors in Computing Systems (2015)
11. Gillespie, T.: The relevance of algorithms. In: Media Technologies: Essays on Communication, Materiality, and Society, pp. 167–193. MIT Press (2014)
12. Gran, A.-B., Booth, P., Bucher, T.: To be or not to be algorithm aware: a question of a new digital divide? Inf. Commun. Soc. **24**(12), 1779–1796 (2020). https://doi.org/10.1080/136 9118x.2020.1736124
13. Gruber, J., Hargittai, E., Karaoglu, G., Brombach, L.: Algorithm awareness as an important internet skill: the case of voice assistants. Int. J. Commun. **15**, 1770–1788 (2021). https://ijoc. org/index.php/ijoc/article/view/15941/3412
14. Hargittai, E., Micheli, M.: Internet skills and why they matter. In: Graham, M., Dutton, W.H. (eds.) Society and the Internet: How Networks of Information and Communication are Changing Our Lives, pp. 109–124. Oxford University Press, Oxford (2019)
15. Katz, J.E., Rice, R.E.: Social Consequences of Internet Use: Access, Involvement, and Interaction. MIT, Cambridge (2002)
16. Klawitter, E., Hargittai, E.: "It's like learning a whole other language": the role of algorithmic skills in the curation of creative goods. Int. J. Commun. **12**, 3490–3510 (2018)
17. Kostka, G., Steinacker, L.A., Meck, M.: Between security and convenience: facial recognition technology in the eyes of citizens in China, Germany, the United Kingdom, and the United States. **30**(6), 671–690 (2021). https://doi.org/10.1177/09636625211001555
18. Napoli, P.M., Obar, J.A.: The emerging mobile Internet underclass: a critique of mobile Internet access. Inf. Soc. **30**(5), 323–334 (2014). https://doi.org/10.1080/01972243.2014. 944726
19. Naudé, W., Vinuesa, R.: Data deprivations, data gaps and digital divides: lessons from the COVID-19 pandemic. Big Data Soc. **8**(2) (2021). https://doi.org/10.1177/205395172110 25545
20. Oremus, W.: Why Facebook won't let you control your own news feed (2021). https://www. washingtonpost.com/technology/2021/11/13/facebook-news-feed-algorithm-how-to-turn-it-off/. Accessed 28 Dec 2021
21. Pasquale, F.: The Black Box Society: The Secret Algorithms That Control Money and Information. Harvard University Press, Cambridge (2015)
22. Pearce, K.E., Rice, R.E.: Digital divides from access to activities: comparing mobile and personal computer internet users. J. Commun. **63**(4), 721–744 (2013). https://doi.org/10. 1111/jcom.12045

23. Peng, Y.: The ideological divide in public perceptions of self-driving cars. **29**(4), 436–451 (2020). https://doi.org/10.1177/0963662520917339
24. Qiu, J.L.: Working-Class Network Society: Communication Technology and the Information have-less in Urban China. MIT Press, Cambridge (2009)
25. Robinson, L., et al.: Digital inequalities 2.0: legacy inequalities in the information age. First Monday, **25**(7) (2020). https://doi.org/10.5210/fm.v25i7.10842
26. Robinson, L., et al.: Digital inequalities 3.0: emergent inequalities in the information age. First Monday, **25** (2020). https://doi.org/10.5210/fm.v25i7.10844
27. Savolainen, R.: Everyday life information seeking: approaching information seeking in the context of "way of life." Libr. Inf. Sci. Res. **17**(3), 259–294 (1995). https://doi.org/10.1016/0740-8188(95)90048-9
28. Scheerder, A.J., van Deursen, A.J., van Dijk, J.A.: Internet use in the home: digital inequality from a domestication perspective. New Media Soc. **21**(10), 2099–2118 (2019). https://doi.org/10.1171/1461444819844299
29. Schroeder, R.: A weberian analysis of global digital divides. Int. J. Commun. **9**, 2819–2837 (2015). 1932-8036/20150005
30. van Deursen, A.J., van Dijk, J.A.: The first-level digital divide shifts from inequalities in physical access to inequalities in material access. New Media Soc. **2**(2), 354–375 (2019)
31. van Dijk, J.: The digital divide. Polity (2020)
32. Yan, P., Schroeder, R.: Variations in the adoption and use of mobile social apps in everyday lives in urban and rural China. Mobile Media Commun. **8**(3), 318–341 (2020)
33. Yu, L.Z.: The divided views of the information and digital divides: a call for integrative theories of information inequality. J. Inf. Sci. **37**(6), 660–679 (2011). https://doi.org/10.1177/0165551511426246
34. Yu, L.Z., Zhou, W.J.: Information inequality in contemporary Chinese urban society: the results of a cluster analysis. J. Am. Soc. Inf. Sci. **67**(9), 2246–2262 (2016). https://doi.org/10.1002/asi.23531
35. Yu, P.K.: The algorithmic divide and equality in the age of artificial intelligence. Florida Law Rev. 331 (2020).
36. Zarouali, B., Helberger, N., de Vreese, C.H.: Investigating algorithmic misconceptions in a media context: source of a new digital divide? Media Commun. **9**(4), 134–144 (2021). https://doi.org/10.17645/mac.v9i3.4090

Community Design of a Knowledge Graph to Support Interdisciplinary PhD Students

Stanislava Gardasevic[✉] and Rich Gazan

University of Hawaiʻi at Mānoa, Honolulu, HI 96826, USA
{gardasev,gazan}@hawaii.edu

Abstract. How do PhD students discover the resources and relationships conducive to satisfaction and success in their degree programs? This study proposes a community-grounded, extensible knowledge graph to make explicit and tacit information intuitively discoverable, by capturing and visualizing relationships between people based on their activities and relations to information resources in a particular domain. Students in an interdisciplinary PhD program were engaged through three workshops to provide insights into the dynamics of interactions with others and relevant data categories to be included in the graph data model. Based on these insights we propose a model, serving as a testbed for exploring multiplex graph visualizations and a potential basis of the information system to facilitate information discovery and decision-making. We discovered that some of the tacit knowledge can be explicitly encoded, while the rest of it must stay within the community. The graph-based visualization of the social and knowledge networks can serve as a pointer toward the people having the relevant information, one can reach out to, online or in person.

Keywords: PhD students · Tacit knowledge · Knowledge graph · Data model · Interdisciplinary research

1 Introduction

Pursuing a PhD degree can be both rewarding and stressful. A significant percentage of PhD students are experiencing at least two psychological symptoms and have sought help for anxiety or depression related to their studies [1, 2]. One key factor influencing the overall experience of PhD students during their course of study is the so-called *departmental culture*, encompassing "student/faculty relationships, student involvement in academic life, student satisfaction with programs, student-to-student interactions, institutional financial assistance to students, and dissertation factors" [3]. The issue of navigating departmental cultures becomes even more problematic in interdisciplinary PhD programs, where students reported "feeling disconnected from faculty and peers, having to span boundaries between areas, departments, and knowledge bases" [4]. In this study, we describe the participative development of a knowledge base to support interdisciplinary PhD students to visualize and navigate multiple departmental cultures.

© The Author(s), under exclusive license to Springer Nature Switzerland AG 2023
I. Sserwanga et al. (Eds.): iConference 2023, LNCS 13972, pp. 473–490, 2023.
https://doi.org/10.1007/978-3-031-28032-0_36

Science can be described as a "complex, self-organizing, and evolving network of scholars, projects, papers and ideas" [5]. As Börner [6] noted, researchers and authors can be perceived as nodes in networks of support and influence, while their selection of research topics, collaborators, students, and publication venues influence and shape their place in these networks. In these 'knowledge networks,' actors serve both as keepers of knowledge and as agents that seek out, communicate, and create knowledge [7, 8]. However, information is often not equally available to all actors [4], and the opportunities for "social" information sharing [9] diminished due to the pandemic.

Consequently, we chose a multilayer/multiplex network as the medium to address the raised issues and create a knowledge graph combining information on social and knowledge traces in a community. The aim of building this graph is to facilitate explicit and tacit information discovery and informed decision-making related to the factors identified as meaningful for this population: i) establishing collaboration with faculty [3, 4, 10], ii) information and resources available about research topic of interest [3, 7, 11], and iii) interaction with peers, including community building [3, 4]; while creating a testbed for exploring multiplex network visualization and navigation options [12].

The setting for this case study is the Interdisciplinary PhD Program in Communication and Information Sciences (CIS), at the University of Hawai'i at Mānoa. Students—especially those new to the program who have not been exposed to informal information flows—are considered the main user population of this information discovery system. Following the activity theoretical approach and requirements/milestones for the program, students were engaged in every step of the knowledge graph modeling process.

As noted by Hogan et al. [13], the definition of a knowledge graph remains contentious, but in short, it can be described as "a graph of data intended to accumulate and convey knowledge of the real world, whose nodes represent entities of interest and whose edges represent relations between these entities". Before building the graph, we created the database model to support tacit knowledge exchange-such as first-hand impressions of other students-that have been shown to be of crucial importance for this population [7, 9, 10].

Getting procedural advice or hearing other students' experiences with faculty, classes, and exams usually happens in a serendipitous way, via in-person conversations, but these opportunities for informal information exchange were severely disrupted by COVID-19. Therefore, we propose this data-driven discovery tool that combines topical research representations and tacit interpersonal relations data to identify and support impactful interdisciplinary collaborations [5] and multiple departmental cultures [7] common to iSchools.

The main contribution of this paper is the graph database model developed and presented alongside user-derived needs. We outline some of the data categories and relationships between them (including refining attributes) that can be used to encode both explicit and tacit knowledge, while the affordance of network visualization supports the discovery of people with pertinent information that is not encoded in the knowledge graph.

2 Related Work

The aim of this section is to connect the present study to previous research streams relevant to the challenges of tacit knowledge transfer, representing and supporting interdisciplinary collaborations, and to summarize and justify the affordances of a knowledge graph approach.

2.1 Tacit Knowledge Exchange for PhD Students

Personal networks and peer communities present a vital information source for doctoral students [3, 7]. So-called "insider" knowledge is something perceived as necessary for the success of interdisciplinary PhD students but is available only to students and professors who have been involved in the program for a certain amount of time [4, 7]. This knowledge is often referred to as experiential or tacit knowledge, here operationalized as the values and quality of the resource of interest, as perceived by students [14]. Resources that help students discover appropriate faculty to collaborate with are especially critical for this population [3, 4, 10], as well as information about research topics of interest [3, 7, 11].

Visualizing social networks of people in a shared academic setting could support "social" sharing [9] by providing a better picture of the common links, potentially democratizing access to useful information currently available only to those conveniently located in the social network.

2.2 User Needs for iSchools and Interdisciplinary PhD Programs

The need for a community portal to support students from diverse disciplines has been identified in previous studies as a potentially useful forum for peer information exchange [15], but it remains an elusive goal. The challenge multiplies when interdisciplinary PhD students must select appropriate faculty advisors from a rich pool of multi-disciplinary researchers, which has been a longstanding success factor in PhD student persistence [3, 16].

Choi focuses on the importance of identity formation within iSchools, where students can question dominant research trends, locate their own interests and develop their own research identity [17]. Wiggins and Sawyer propose an analysis of interdisciplinary faculty research output to outline the landscape within which iSchool students might locate their work [18].

Each of these studies distinguishes between research and community relationships but tends to focus on research topics as the basis for connection rather than social relationships. We propose a lightweight, extensible visualization, driven by student focus groups, to capture and represent community interactions and tacit information alongside research connections, so students can view paths and interactions of those who have come before.

2.3 Network-Based Representation and Discovery

Faculty profile pages can be a lightweight data source of potential connections between researchers and students from diverse fields, and community stakeholders [19], and can provide a way to identify one's place in the interdisciplinary community. However, in the case of the program studied here, students reported that faculty profiles are often not up to date, and too numerous to inspect thoroughly [10]. Also, expert finding applications in the scholarly domain are usually based on recommending acclaimed researchers based on their publication history (i.e. [20, 21]). These attempts have traditionally been based on the networks generated from publication data obtained from a single database such as Computer Science Bibliography – DBLP [21–23], Web of Science, Scopus, and PubMed [24]. However, this research, based on a convenience sample, is often addressing only a limited number of relationships, usually pertaining to co-authorship and shared research topics. Our approach aggregates different web resources (including multiple sources indicating researchers' expertise) in a single knowledge graph-since research has shown that the graph-based interface is more practical for finding specific information and simple question-answering tasks, compared to hierarchically organized information [25]. Furthermore, we expand the scope of relationships to represent the interdisciplinary domain, as three dimensions are considered as a minimum to understand the full complexity of social structures [26].

We model interdisciplinary PhD program information as a multiplex network, defined as "networks where the same set of nodes is represented in every layer, although the interaction between nodes might be different in each one. As an example, two nodes might be connected in one layer and might not in other" [27]. Analyzing and visualizing multiplex graphs are considered complex problems, as each additional relation makes the choice of an appropriate layout more challenging, even incomprehensible, as soon as it contains a few dozen nodes [28]. One previous attempt to visualize scholarly domain multiplex networks included a dataset of 61 nodes connected over five layers (work, leisure, coauthor, lunch, and Facebook) [28]. Unlike in this exploratory approach, we are grounding the graph in user needs, answering the necessity to re-frame user needs and data as multilayered networks problems, providing visualization researchers more exposure to the application domain [12].

3   Case Introduction

The CIS PhD Program was established in 1986 and has approximately 30 current students and over 100 alumni. The program is a voluntary and collaborative effort of over 40 faculty from four units housed in three colleges (as of Fall 2022):

- Communications (COM) (College of Social Sciences)
- Library and Information Science (LIS) (College of Social Sciences)
- Information and Computer Sciences (ICS) (College of Natural Sciences)
- Information Technology Management (ITM) (Shidler College of Business).

While the flexible, decentralized structure of the program provides more possible research avenues for PhD students, it also requires students to find and navigate their own path through program requirements [4, 10]. This is especially acute since the selection of a dissertation chair and other faculty mentors is the crucial factor contributing to PhD student retention and satisfaction in general [3, 31]. In addition, CIS students and alumni also serve as valuable information resources, sharing their firsthand experiences and wisdom regarding potential faculty collaborators and the practical mechanics of how to meet program requirements. However, an increasing number of students are not physically present at the university (so-called "off-island" students) and participate in joint activities such as the required weekly interdisciplinary seminar online via Zoom. This part of the population does not have the same opportunity to be part of informal interactions and information flows and gain so-called "insider" knowledge contributing to the success of interdisciplinary PhD students [4], further justifying the need for the remotely accessible technology presented here. These concerns are even more urgent considering the COVID-19 pandemic when all coursework moved online, and at this writing, the two most recent cohorts of students have yet to meet their peers or faculty in person.

Official CIS program milestones and requirements are inscribed in a Policies and Procedures document[1], which formed the basis for developing research instruments, as well as for creating the first iteration of the graph database model, later modified based on CIS student input from the workshops.

The research presented in this paper is the second stage of a larger project. The results of the first stage suggested that information resources and relevant data categories can be formalized and encoded in a form of a knowledge graph and suggested a path to capture/obtain tacit information.

The present study builds on the first, and explores the research question:

What tacit knowledge can be represented and discovered through a knowledge graph, and what can be only indicated?

The final stage of this project will involve the same population in the participatory design of visualizations and seamless visual analytical approach of the multiplex graph, to examine if this artifact has utility compared to current means of information discovery, and if it is worthwhile to develop it further into an information system.

4   Method

Following a Human-Centered Design approach, upon the requirements gathering process that consisted of interviews and a website usability study engaging program students and alumni [10], we conducted three workshops over two years and developed the database model shown in Fig. 1. Students helped identify relevant people, roles, resources, actions, experiences, and relationships, and these were iteratively integrated into the database model, shared back in successive workshops and refined based on feedback. Including the community in the design of a technology to support their interactions helps reveal and unravel the underlying values of both the proposed system and the PhD program itself [29], creating a rationale and platform for further cooperation and community building.

---

[1] CIS Program policies and procedures- https://bit.ly/cis_policy_procedures.

4.1 Positionality and Limitations

Both authors are insiders to the CIS program, with different roles and perspectives, and with access to different kinds of knowledge about the community, which we feel provides a productive tension.

The first author is a CIS PhD candidate and must balance her own experience with those of other students with whom she is engaging in this study, including informal daily interactions. The limitation imposed by this position as a student is that graph design decisions and interpretations may be biased by personal experience. We have attempted to balance this threat to internal validity by including member checks as validation points to incorporate multiple students' perspectives.

The second author is a faculty member and former CIS Chair who teaches one of the three core courses and serves on multiple dissertation, exam, and other program committees. His perspective yields different stories about enablers, barriers, and metrics of student experience and degree progress. This limitation is that students could be understandably hesitant to share their unfiltered observations with someone in a position to evaluate them, due to courtesy bias or other factors. We address this limitation by emphasizing the anonymization component of the data analysis process and creating faculty-free workshops and spaces for data collection.

4.2 Data Collection

This research is framed by *activity theory*, as this approach has been used to inform the ways in which interactive tools should be designed to make a positive impact on human activities [30]. In this case, the overarching goal (activity) of a student is to obtain a PhD degree; to get there, students are motivated to fulfill written program requirements (actions), such as taking certain *courses* and *exams,* but also unwritten requirements such as developing and successfully navigating relationships with faculty and peers. Each step in the research design was informed by activity theory, encompassing formal program requirements and other practical and less tangible aspects of the interdisciplinary PhD student experience to help guide future students.

In the three workshops, current CIS students shared their experiences in a forum environment and reacted to the evolving graph design. Student participation was voluntary, and data was collected without faculty present and analyzed with full confidentiality and anonymity. For that reason, only the first author facilitated workshops and anonymized the raw data, then shared it with the second author in a form that honors the privacy of the participants. All workshops used a visual representation of a graph database model in a then-current version, to communicate the data modeling efforts thus far, to serve as a community member check on the "ontology" of the shared domain, and to identify areas for improvement.

The three workshops took place from December 2019 to April 2022. The first included both face-to-face and online participants, while the other two were fully online via Zoom, and included 18, 15, and 10 students, respectively. The workshops were recorded, transcribed and anonymized by the first author, while the rest of the data was captured as text files created by the participants' chat, and Google documents where students were invited to leave anonymous comments on the topics discussed.

During the first workshop, participants completed a questionnaire[2] designed to validate the findings from the previous study stage, while the poll results were used as a prompt for discussion during the workshop.

The aim of the second workshop was to gather feedback on the draft data collection form, designed with the intention to populate parts of the graph with students' personal information, based on data categories they perceived as relevant. The intent was to hone the questions and structure of the form to get the most useful information when collecting data in the future, negotiate data privacy boundaries, and get feedback and further recommendations on what data would be most relevant for this population. This workshop resulted in an elaborate data collection form[3] created in Qualtrics that was used to collect the data from the students to populate the graph. This form was designed for collecting user-generated information via pre-determined categories, as well as the free text inputs, while all the data collected corresponds with the graph model.

The third workshop invited open discussion on the students' experiences, where participants were distributed in breakout rooms depending on i) program progress stage and ii) preferred methodological approach[4], to discuss and exchange information about what helped and hampered their progress.

4.3 Data Analysis

The data consist of anonymized i) transcription of workshops, ii) Google documents, iii) researcher notes, and iv) pertinent questionnaire/form inputs. The data analysis was conducted iteratively. After each workshop, both authors conducted the first cycle of descriptive coding of student responses, and the categories that emerged in all three workshops were pertinent to 'flow of information in the community', 'lack of opportunities for in-person contact with peers', and 'obtaining information on program requirements'. Upon the discussion about results from this phase, researchers created the utility-driven set of codes, to conduct the structural data coding [31] with the previously elicited and potential new concepts that could be represented via a graph model. Upon the second round of coding, we discussed revisions to the data model based on the data analysis insights as we outline in several examples below. To perform the participant' checks, each workshop started with an overview of the graph model in its current state, to gather further feedback and reflect on the accuracy of data representation for their information needs. Participatory research relies on participant engagement with the data collection and coding processes, which helps create a sense of ownership of the data reflecting their community, a "safe space" where subjects can interact and reflect, and an understanding of how their actions and interactions are represented within the graph [32].

---

[2] Questionnaire with results- https://bit.ly/cis_worskhop_1.
[3] Data collection form - https://bit.ly/student_data_collection_cis.
[4] Breakout room prompts for Workshop 3 https://bit.ly/cis_workshop_3.

5 Results: User-Driven Graph Modeling Decisions

In this section, we discuss the themes that emerged as important for the community during the workshops, and how they influenced the graph modeling and design decisions. In Fig. 1, we presented the CIS domain graph database model in its current iteration and the nodes and relationships between them. The model or its parts can be adapted and reused in other interdisciplinary environments.

Since we use the Neo4J graph database for building this knowledge graph, we utilize the native Cypher language syntax when referring to specific parts of the model, i.e.: (Node)—[RELATIONSHIP]—> (Node); in this case, (Node) represents a class/category in the model, and not pertinent instances.

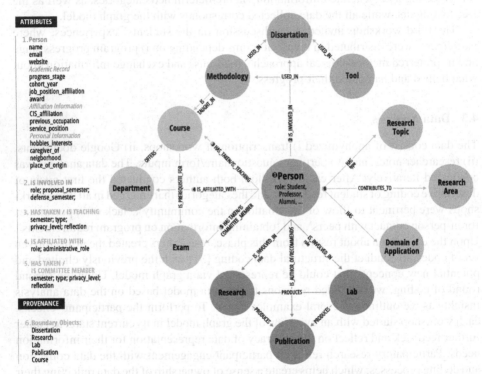

Fig. 1. CIS graph database model (Color figure online)

Considering our aim to facilitate the active exchange of tacit information, (Person) occupies the central place in the model and is connected to most of the surrounding 12 nodes/classes, presented through 4 color-coded groupings. Those nodes present the affiliations (layers) via which the actors in this multiplex network may be connected. The data comprising the graph was gathered from different web locations, normalized and ingested into the Neo4J, and is available for download and reuse[5], while the student-generated data is not included in this dataset. The graph created according to this model

---

[5] The data 'dump' of CIS Neo4J database-https://doi.org/10.6084/m9.figshare.21663401.v2.

represents a picture of a domain, as it is captured in Spring 2022, while the publications in the corpus represent the sample of publishing activity of faculty in the last 10 years. We acknowledge the challenge of maintaining updated data, but we offer this model as a useful snapshot to elicit student reaction and engagement.

Following the activity theory approach, the categories that were initially included by default in the graph were the CIS degree requirements that every student must fulfill to advance to ABD (all but dissertation) status. Those categories are (Course), (Exam), (Dissertation), and (Publication).

5.1   (Person) Node and Its Attributes (Fig. 1, Central Orange Node)

The (Person) node, naturally, has the most attributes, as it is designed to capture information primarily about other students and outline some interesting, relevant, or potentially shared interests and experiences.

There are three subsections of attributes; *Academic Record* attributes representing information such as *cohort_year*, indicating the strength of ties with others that share the same value attribute since participants stated that taking classes together with cohort peers makes them closer, as they can talk about challenges and struggles (noted as pre-COVID practice). In the *Affiliation Information* subsection, we capture the CIS affiliation, with a Boolean value, to distinguish CIS-affiliated people from others (such as co-authors or faculty that left the university). The *Personal Information* section contains categories that capture free-text information that may serve as potential connection points, such as shared hobbies or neighborhoods. This was intended to support community-building, since students reported feeling lonely, especially those at the dissertation research and writing stage and due to pandemic isolation [4, 10].

Another attribute that evolved based on participant suggestions was *caregiver_of*. Initially, the category was named *family_status*, where students could share data such as the ages of their minor children, to potentially connect for play dates. Participants broadened our conception of this category to include other senses of caregiving, which also provided deeper insights into the range of students' life situations:

> *For the number of 'minor children'…some of us have adult children. Also consider changing this to 'are you a caregiver' as some need to care for elderly parents, etc.*

5.2   (Dissertation), (Methodology), (Tool) Nodes (Fig. 1, Top Three Green Nodes)

As mentioned, (Dissertation) is crucial for this population, therefore separated from the (Research) as a category and forms the basis of one of the most important networks—the dissertation mentorship network.

In this program, there are over 40 faculty members from which students can choose i) a dissertation chair, ii) three dissertation committee members (at least two of which must be affiliated with different units (Department) to help ensure an interdisciplinary research approach), and iii) an "external" member, which further increases the disciplinary range of potential collaborators. Based on the inputs from participants, asking to see what faculty served as "external" members in previous committees, we modeled the relationship by adding the *role* of faculty involved in the previous dissertations. Upon applying social network analysis and centrality metric, visualizing this network can quickly show the most active dissertation chairs and committee members; seeing their previous collaborations might help students decide who to invite to serve on their committee. In Fig. 2 we demonstrate a perspective of the dissertation mentorship network, where faculty node colors represent their departmental affiliations (LIS-purple, COM-orange, ITM-yellow, ICS-blue); green nodes are dissertations; while the number of dissertation engagements is shown in node size, and dissertation chairing via red edges.

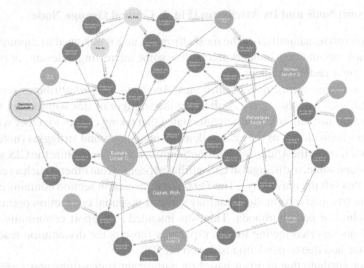

Fig. 2. Dissertation-mentorship network showing collaboration between faculty from different departments. (Color figure online)

Considering the importance of the relationship with the supervisor for the overall PhD experience [3, 31], one workshop participant wrote succinctly and directly about the information they seek from other students:

I would ask them-is your supervisor a good mentor?

This statement demonstrates that some of the most-sought information is not easily encodable, but the graph supports the option to indicate a person that can share it with you, directly.

The (Methodology) node reflects the program requirement of taking a research methods course, and the common but informal practice of including a methodology expert in the dissertation committee. With the information encoded this way, students can get i) a quick overview of faculty who use a certain methodological approach in their research (Fig. 3); and ii) discover appropriate methodology classes based on the comments of other CIS students-a requirement expressed during the first workshop.

The (Methodology) node relates to the (Tool) node, as students are interested in finding out methodology classes that use particular tools. This information was lacking from the current information space and was indicated by study participants at the third workshop as much needed. Students who populated the data collection form indicated tools they used in classes they attended. Furthermore, the graph also contains data on the people who used a tool to perform research, so a student can identify and directly consult that person on the issue.

5.3 (Course), (Department), (Exam) Nodes (Fig. 1, Left Three Blue Nodes)

On the left side of the model, we formalized the departmental affiliation of people, and the attribute named *role* is intended to capture data that would help distinguish/filter actors based on their affiliation to different departments ("Student", "Professor", "Alumni", "TA", etc.). This modeling decision helps students see the interdepartmental collaborations (interdisciplinarity indicator), and current students' graduate assistantship affiliations (insider knowledge indicator).

When it comes to encoding tacit knowledge, some community members were understandably hesitant to leave written traces of their experience with a professor, as opposed to their experience regarding courses and exams taken. During the first workshop, more students expressed support for the latter, both via the questionnaire and discussion. A comment illustrating this point is:

Social rating is toxic.

As a result, we included the space for *reflection* as an attribute of the relationship (Person)—[HAS_TAKEN]—>(Course/Exam), where students can note their experiences if they feel they should share them with their peers, allowing for tacit knowledge encoding and sharing. This way, students can comment on professors if they wish, albeit indirectly. To manage the privacy settings, upon discussion with students, we allowed three options of the public for the reflection *attribute* value: "public," "CIS students", and "private". For those who indicated their observations as "private", we anonymized the data by connecting it to an *Anonymous* person instance-so the comments are still available to other CIS students, without clear implications of who might have left them. Via graph visualization, students will be able to see others who took a course/exam of their interest and reach out to them for a private discussion, if sufficient reflection input is missing.

Some of the reflections left by students for courses are:

This class was meant to prepare us for [a qualifying] exam, but it did not.

Way too much reading.

I enjoyed this class, it helped me write dissertation proposal- without this class I wouldn't be able to write it that fast. It gives you the basic structure and what you can expect from the journey. And I liked the professor- she's very encouraging and inspirational.

5.4 (Research Topic), (Research Area), (Domain of Application) Nodes (Fig. 1, Right Three Yellow Nodes)

Considering the case of an interdisciplinary PhD program, facilitating communication across disciplines [33] is a core aim of this work. The three yellow nodes on the right side of the model, namely (Research Topic), (Research Area), and (Domain of Application) are intended to host vocabularies that will serve as boundary objects, which "inhabit several communities of practice and satisfy the informational requirements of each of them" [34]. With these concepts in mind, we have chosen controlled vocabularies for pertinent nodes that would be understandable across the four constituent disciplinary areas of CIS. This contribution helps bridge gaps in cross-disciplinary understanding among diverse units that have been identified in prior studies (e.g. [35, 36]). As one of the participants stated:

> The program's strength — the cross-discipline nature — is also its weakness. It would be interesting to find the "e Pluribus Unum" that makes the "one from the many," some set of unifying principles to rally around.

Our approach was to involve people educated in the different disciplines encompassed by the program, to serve as translators or mediators, and create vocabularies to improve cross-disciplinary communication [33].

In the first version of the modeling effort, *Discipline* was not included as a separate node in the graph, since it was potentially repetitive with the (Department), and we did not wish to reify disciplinary divisions. However, the workshops again yielded valuable insights from community members, and we introduced a (Research Area) as a node in response to comments in line with:

> I think because there is interdisciplinarity, people tend to gravitate to others who are doing a similar type of research.

Research Area is a loosely defined term, often used to refer to discipline-like structures, yet targeting smaller units that often span disciplinary borders [37]. This term is used throughout the CIS website to describe areas of focus, such as Human-Computer Interaction, Data Science, and Health Informatics, providing a warrant from the community to include the term and node in the model.

We operationalize Research Topic entries as uncontrolled, free-response words and phrases that allow students and researchers to describe their research interests in their own words. Finally, we operationalize the Domain of Application as the particular setting, technology, and/or community with which their research engages.

For the sake of the readability of the model, links from other nodes were omitted but are originating from (Publication), (Dissertation), (Research), (Lab), and (Course) instances. The controlled vocabularies were used to manually index (Publication) and (Dissertation) instances and are subsets of the Australian and New Zealand Standard Research Classification (ANZSRC). Pertinent classification systems were complemented by domain-specific inputs. The same corpus was automatically indexed by Computer Science Ontology [38].

Students consider information about the research nuances of CIS faculty particularly valuable, and a participant in the third workshop expressed their issue as follows:

I talked to [CIS chair] and I was like, who else studies [Topic X]? And l they were like "Oh, well you just have to go through everyone's CV." And I'm like,

"I don't have time to go through how many different CVs to find out potentially someone who might be able to help me!" And maybe it's just because I'm intro- verted too. But I don't know how to start those conversations with professors like, "What do you study? Can you help me?"

Indexing the work of faculty and students with familiar terms would allow not only for quick discovery of potential collaborators, but also provide potential inputs for con- versation starters for students to approach faculty, as they reported a lack of opportunities to communicate with them.

While the boundary object nodes may appear to be similar categories with sub- tle distinctions, within this interdisciplinary environment researchers often have the same Domain of Application, but different lenses for conceptualizing and studying it. For example, "Cybersecurity" might encompass various disciplinary topics such as algorithms, system architecture, policy, or ethics.

Potentially, these nodes could be entry points to which graphs from other departments and programs could be "attached", to help identify shared topics of interest across the university system.

5.5 (Research), (Lab), (Publication) Nodes (Fig. 1, Bottom Three Purple Nodes)

The nodes on the bottom of the model are yet another three categories that indicate valuable affiliation information, allowing for visualization of collaboration networks. The current graph has a corpus of 260 publications that served as a basis for the co- authorship network as well as input for populating the boundary object nodes.

6 Discussion

In this paper, we have proposed a graph model to support interdisciplinary Ph.D. students in their academic journey by encoding both explicit and tacit/experiential knowledge to make 'insider' information crucial for this population [4, 7] available to newcomers. Upon demonstrating the current knowledge graph and querying options, the majority of participants in the third workshop had positive attitudes toward the perspective of this technology being implemented, emphasizing its usefulness for newly admitted students.

We therefore suggest that the approach of engaging community members to iden- tify and help aggregate into a knowledge graph both formal and informal information they find relevant to success in the domain is a promising avenue for other groups and knowledge management applications. Some of the comments on the utility of having data from multiple web locations aggregated in the knowledge graph versus the online search were:

"Direct, in one platform" and *"More easily accessible information"*

6.1 Transfer of Tacit Knowledge

As mentioned, one of the most important factors in PhD student retention is related to their satisfaction with their research supervisor and faculty collaborations [3, 31]. Even though some of the students expressed their hesitance to leave written traces of their experiences with supervisors, the data (encoded in the *reflection* attribute) gathered via the form captured the experience of students who took directed readings courses with two faculty members, clearly indicating the differences in their styles of supervision:

E.g. 1 - Very helpful, because [they] give you exactly what to do, specific advice-tools, websites, etc.

E.g., 2 - They are really hands-off, which can be a problem if you want direction.

The student-provided data support the decision-making process, and upon inspecting *reflections* of students on different exams they have taken, the latest cohort student was able to make a more informed decision when choosing a focus area exam:

Reading through what you've collected from students was helpful. I'm all for data-driven decisions:).

At the same time, the graph-based technology allows for recording the collaborations of current students with faculty, and better possibility to exchange tacit knowledge and student reflections upon establishing relationships with peers. However, for the proposed approach to be successfully implemented, some of the motivators (e.g. self-efficacy, self-enjoyment, reciprocity, and rewards) [39] need to be enacted, within the system or the program policy, to entice the continuity in knowledge sharing practices among peers.

Finally, the format of workshops to discuss these issues was also proven to make a difference as the community building effort, considering they reported lack of opportunities to exchange information with peers [10]. Participating students labeled the experience as "insightful" and "enlightening".

6.2 Affordances of Graph Modeled Approach

The graph supports both specific curiosity (e.g. Fig. 3) as well as exploratory search [40] this user population considers useful.

The current iteration of the created knowledge graph has 5,365 node instances (about 122 are CIS-affiliated people) and 6,116 relationships among them, making it a small-scale but rich-in-context dataset, created to explore visualization and navigation options. This dataset has double the layers and sample size of the graph created by [28] and the model was designed by researchers immersed in the domain created with the end users' involvement - all of which are considered necessary to tackle the complex problem of multiplex visualizations [12] - issue that will be addressed in the future participatory design workshops. We provided this dataset to other researchers who are interested in examining the stated problem.

Aside from serving the PhD student population, this research aims to tackle challenges encountered by iSchools faculty involved in interdisciplinary research [36] with a domain analytical angle to build the vocabularies and capture disciplinary norms via

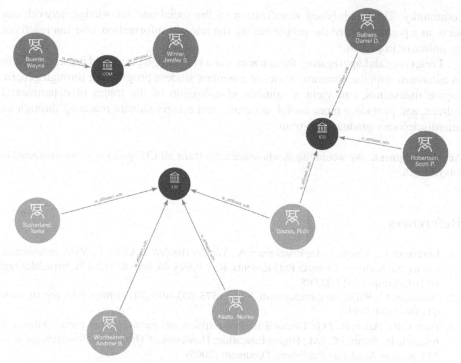

Fig. 3. Example query showing faculty from different departments conducting qualitative research

'boundary object' nodes, and possibly facilitate the collaboration of researchers with different disciplinary traditions looking at the same domain of application.

7 Conclusion

Anyone who remembers their first days in a graduate program can appreciate the inadequacy of relying solely on formal program documentation as a guide to the overall experience. By engaging students through iterative workshops, we propose a network-based visualization and discovery tool that integrates topical research data, degree requirements, and the tacit knowledge by which a program's culture–and its members' lived experiences–are communicated.

With it, students can capture their progress, plan/project future steps and collaborations, and see themselves as part of the community, subcommunity, and/or an invisible college, while providing valuable information and tacit knowledge traces for the other students.

This approach emphasizes an active role for both information seekers and sharers, by putting the people within the community in the center of the information retrieval loop, to allow a direct exchange of trusted tacit information. We discovered that some of the tacit knowledge can be explicitly encoded, while most of it must stay within the community. The graph-based visualization of the social and knowledge network can serve as a pointer toward the people having the relevant information, one can reach out to, online or in person.

Preserving and aggregating these traces via a knowledge graph and presenting them as a contrast with the common model of a generic student progressing through generic degree milestones, can yield a valuable visualization of the traces of departmental culture, and provide a more useful, accurate, and compassionate roadmap through an interdisciplinary graduate program.

Acknowledgment. We would like to wholeheartedly thank all CIS students who participated in this research.

References

1. Levecque, K., Anseel, F., De Beuckelaer, A., Van der Heyden, J., Gisle, L.: Work organization and mental health problems in PhD students. Res. Policy **46**, 868–879 (2017). https://doi.org/10.1016/j.respol.2017.02.008
2. Woolston, C.: PhDs: the tortuous truth. Nature **575**, 403–406 (2019). https://doi.org/10.1038/d41586-019-03459-7
3. Bair, C.R., Haworth, J.G.: Doctoral student attrition and persistence: a meta-synthesis of research. In: Smart, J.C. (ed.) Higher Education: Handbook of Theory and Research, pp. 481–534. Kluwer Academic Publishers, Dordrecht (2005)
4. Gardner, S.K.: 'A Jack-of-All-Trades and a Master of Some of Them': successful students in interdisciplinary PhD programs. Issues Integr. Stud. **29**, 84–117 (2011). http://hdl.handle.net/10323/4465
5. Fortunato, S.: Science of science. Science. **359**, 6379 (2018). https://doi.org/10.1126/science.aao0185
6. Börner, K.: Atlas of Science: Visualizing What We Know. MIT Press, Cambridge (2010)
7. Boden, D., Borrego, M., Newswander, L.K.: Student socialization in interdisciplinary doctoral education. High Educ. **62**, 741–755 (2011). https://doi.org/10.1007/s10734-011-9415-1
8. Phelps, C., Heidl, R., Wadhwa, A.: Knowledge, networks, and knowledge networks: a review and research agenda. J. Manag. **38**, 1115–1166 (2012). https://doi.org/10.1177/0149206311432640
9. Talja, S.: Information sharing in academic communities: types and levels of collaboration in information seeking and use. New Rev. Inf. Behav. Res. **3**, 143–160 (2002)
10. Gardasevic, S.: User-driven efforts in creating knowledge graph information system. Digit. Libr. Perspect. **36**(2), 97–111 (2020). https://doi.org/10.1108/DLP-12-2019-0043
11. Catalano, A.: Patterns of graduate students' information seeking behavior: a meta-synthesis of the literature. J. Documentation **69**, 243–274 (2013). https://doi.org/10.1108/00220411311300066
12. McGee, F., Ghoniem, M., Melançon, G., Otjacques, B., Pinaud, B.: The state of the art in multilayer network visualization. Comput. Graph. Forum **38**, 125–149 (2019). https://doi.org/10.1111/cgf.13610
13. Hogan, A., Blomqvist, E., Cochez, M., d'Amato, C., de Melo, G., Gutierrez, C., et al.: Knowledge graphs: a comprehensive introduction. arXiv:2003.02320 [cs] (2020)
14. Seufert, A., von Krogh, G., Back, A.: Towards knowledge networking. In: Österle, H., Back, A., Winter, R., Brenner, W. (eds.) Business Engineering — Die ersten 15 Jahre, pp. 289–308. Springer, Heidelberg (2004). https://doi.org/10.1007/978-3-642-18542-7_14

15. Naughton, R., Hall, C., Zhao, H., Lin, X.: PhD portal: developing an online iSchool doctoral student community. In: iConference, Urbana-Champaign, IL, USA (2010)

16. van Rooij, E., Fokkens-Bruinsma, M., Jansen, E.: Factors that influence PhD candidates' success: the importance of PhD project characteristics. Stud. Contin. Educ. **43**, 48–67 (2021). https://doi.org/10.1080/0158037X.2019.1652158

17. Choi, H.: An academic nomad? Identity formation of iSchool students. In: iConference, Newport Beach, CA, USA (2015). https://www.ideals.illinois.edu/items/73928

18. Wiggins, A., Sawyer, S.: Intellectual diversity and the faculty composition of iSchools. J. Am. Soc. Inf. Sci. **63**, 8–21 (2012). https://doi.org/10.1002/asi.21619

19. Archer, M., Zytko, D.: Social matching systems for research collaboration: a profile page design for university faculty. In: Conference Companion Publication of the 2019 on Computer Supported Cooperative Work and Social Computing, pp. 146–150. ACM, Austin, TX, USA (2019)

20. Javed, M., Payette, S., Blake, J., Worrall, T.: Viz–vivo: towards visualizations-driven linked data navigation (2016). https://doi.org/10.6084/M9.FIGSHARE.3545663.V1

21. Osborne, F., Motta, E., Mulholland, P.: Exploring scholarly data with rexplore. In: Alani, H., et al. (eds.) ISWC 2013. LNCS, vol. 8218, pp. 460–477. Springer, Heidelberg (2013). https://doi.org/10.1007/978-3-642-41335-3_29

22. Cabanac, G.: Accuracy of inter-researcher similarity measures based on topical and social clues. Scientometrics **87**, 597–620 (2011). https://doi.org/10.1007/s11192-011-0358-1

23. Chen, S., Arsenault, C., Gingras, Y., Larivière, V.: Exploring the interdisciplinary evolution of a discipline: the case of biochemistry and molecular biology. Scientometrics **102**(2), 1307–1323 (2014). https://doi.org/10.1007/s11192-014-1457-6

24. Liu, J., Tang, T., Wang, W., Xu, B., Kong, X., Xia, F.: A survey of scholarly data visualization. IEEE Access. **6**, 19205–19221 (2018). https://doi.org/10.1109/ACCESS.2018.2815030

25. Sarrafzadeh, B., Vtyurina, A., Lank, E., Vechtomova, O.: Knowledge graphs versus hierarchies: an analysis of user behaviours and perspectives in information seeking. In: Proceedings of the 2016 ACM on Conference on Human Information Interaction and Retrieval - CHIIR 2016, pp. 91–100. ACM Press, Carrboro, North Carolina, USA (2016)

26. Dickison, M.E., Magnani, M., Rossi, L.: Multilayer Social Networks. Cambridge University Press, New York (2016)

27. Aleta, A., Moreno, Y.: Multilayer networks in a nutshell. Annu. Rev. Condens. Matter Phys **10**, 45–62 (2019). https://doi.org/10.1146/annurev-conmatphys-031218-013259

28. Rossi, L., Magnani, M.: Towards effective visual analytics on multiplex and multilayer networks. Chaos, Solitons Fractals **72**, 68–76 (2015). https://doi.org/10.1016/j.chaos.2014.12.022

29. Carroll, J.M., Rosson, M.B.: Wild at home: the neighborhood as a living laboratory for HCI. ACM Trans. Computer-Human Interact. **20**, 1–28 (2013). https://doi.org/10.1145/2491500.24915042

30. Kaptelinin, V., Nardi, B.: Activity Theory in HCI: Fundamentals and Reflections. Morgan & Claypool Publishers, San Rafael (2012)

31. MacQueen, K., McLellan-Lemal, E., Bartholow, K., Milstein, B.: Team-based codebook development: structure, process, and agreement. In: Handbook for Team-Based Qualitative Research, pp. 119–135 (2008)

32. Bergold, J., Thomas, S.: Participatory research methods: a methodological approach in motion. Forum Qualitative Sozialforschung/Forum: Qual. Soc. Res. **13**, 191–222 (2012). https://doi.org/10.17169/fqs-13.1.1801

33. Schummer, J.: Science Communication Across Disciplines. Practising Science Communication in the Information Age: Theorising Professional Practices, pp. 53–66. Oxford University Press, Oxford (2008)

34. Star, S.L., Griesemer, J.R.: Institutional ecology, 'translations' and boundary objects: amateurs and professionals in Berkeley's museum of vertebrate zoology, 1907–1939. Soc. Stud. Sci. **19**, 387–420 (1989). https://doi.org/10.1177/030631289019003001
35. Firpo, D., Zhang, S., Olfman, L., Sirisaengtaksin, K., Roberts, J.: System design for an online social networking app with a notification and recommender system to build social capital in a university setting. In: Proceedings of the 52nd Hawaii International Conference on System Sciences (2019)
36. Luo, L.: Being interdisciplinary : a look into the background and experiences of iSchool faculty members. LIBRES **23**(2), 1–20 (2013). https://doi.org/10.32655/LIBRES.2013.2.3
37. Hammarfelt, B.: Discipline. In: Hjørland, B., Gnoli, C. (eds.) Encyclopedia of Knowledge Organization. ISKO (2016)
38. Salatino, A.A., Thanapalasingam, T., Mannocci, A., Osborne, F., Motta, E.: The computer science ontology: a large-scale taxonomy of research areas. In: Vrandečić, D., et al. (eds.) ISWC 2018. LNCS, vol. 11137, pp. 187–205. Springer, Cham (2018). https://doi.org/10.1007/978-3-030-00668-6_12
39. Nguyen, M., Malik, A., Sharma, P.: How to motivate employees to engage in online knowledge sharing? Differences between posters and lurkers. J. Knowl. Manag. **25**(7), 1811–1831 (2021). https://doi.org/10.1108/JKM-08-2020-0649
40. Sarrafzadeh, B., Vechtomova, O., Jokic, V.: Exploring knowledge graphs for exploratory search. In: Proceedings of the 5th Information Interaction in Context Symposium on - IIiX 2014, pp. 135–144. ACM Press, Regensburg, Germany (2014)

Potential of Participatory Geographic Information System to Build Environmental Information Ecosystem and Claim Environmental Justice: A Research Agenda for Fisherfolk Community in Bangladesh

Md Khalid Hossain(✉) ⑩ and Misita Anwar ⑩

Monash University, Melbourne, VIC 3800, Australia
{md.khalid.hossain,misita.anwar}@monash.edu

Abstract. A participatory geographic information system (GIS) is a process through which disadvantaged groups can access geospatial information technologies and techniques to enhance their capacity to generate, manage, analyze, and communicate different spatial information. Environmental information regarding climate change impacts, natural disasters, access to natural resources, and ecological degradation are significant for nature-dependent disadvantaged groups in developing climate-vulnerable countries, making participatory GIS relevant. These groups can also use such information to claim environmental justice at local, national, and global levels since their marginalization is due to unequal exploitation of ecological resources by more powerful groups. The fisherfolk community in Bangladesh is a nature-dependent disadvantaged, unorganized working group where participatory GIS could be relevant to build an environmental information ecosystem for them to claim environmental justice. However, since fisherfolks lack participation in the policymaking process due to a lack of information, motivation, organization, and digital inclusion impacted by their socio-economic status, participatory GIS may not work without understanding the enabling socio-economic factors. Therefore, this short research paper aims to set a research agenda for participatory action research by exploring the potential of a participatory geographic information system since academic literature has not adequately focused on this issue.

Keywords: Participatory GIS · Environmental information · Environmental justice · Fisherfolk · Bangladesh

1 Background: GIS and Participatory GIS

As a computer system, the geographic information system (GIS) has been prevalent and useful for different disciplines beyond geography like agriculture, business, and environmental management to understand spatial patterns and relationships for decision-making through geographic data [1, 10, 18, 29]. GIS as a system can create and manage

I. Sserwanga et al. (Eds.): iConference 2023, LNCS 13972, pp. 491–499, 2023.
https://doi.org/10.1007/978-3-031-28032-0_37

geographic data and analyze and visualize that data, making it a powerful evidence-based tool to influence decision-makers [22]. Among the different methods, due to the advancement of satellite technology and the precision of real-time satellite data, remote sensing is widely used to integrate the data collected from other earth objects through remote sensors [31]. However, supplementary data are also gathered from the site to analyze contextual knowledge through community engagement to link the remote sensing data to ground reality [11].

Participatory GIS fundamentally differs from expert-driven GIS, where GIS experts remain in the driving seat and use community participation to generate supplementary ground-truthing data. Participatory GIS promotes the idea that spatial technologies will be available to disadvantaged communities [8]. They will be able to use those technologies in community involvement in the production and use of geographic data to influence the decision-making process at different levels. Therefore, it is considered a more socially aware system with legitimacy gained from the local and indigenous spatial knowledge at the outset of any process [12]. However, participatory GIS has challenges due to the ideas and methods. Participation of disadvantaged communities depends on power dynamics in a particular context and the ability and enabling environment for using any specific technology or system [16]. Participatory GIS has content and methodological limitations and may not ensure representation, equity and access by default [5]. Moreover, participatory GIS needs facilitation by the community geographer which is highly challenging [24]. Therefore, understanding the socio-economic factors is highly significant while promoting participatory GIS in a particular context [20, 32].

In this regard, a research partnership between Monash University in Australia and Oxfam in Bangladesh has found that participatory GIS could be a valuable tool for nature-dependent fisherfolks in Bangladesh. Fisherfolks face climate change impacts, natural disasters, and ecological degradation and suffer from inequitable access to natural resources. Power inequality plays a significant role in Bangladesh. The fisherfolks face intense competition with more powerful groups to access natural resources and are affected by government conservation measures while accessing natural resources without adequate compensatory support. They are also the victims of global climate change impacts and local environmental degradation caused by powerful countries and groups. Besides, they are primarily unorganized and do not work together as a group to claim their rights as workers in the fishing supply chain and the citizens in need of social services from the state due to their socio-economic status. However, in this context, academic research and development interventions have not explored whether participatory GIS can play a role in building the fisherfolk's environmental information ecosystem so that they can claim environmental justice considering different socio-economic factors. Consequently, this short research paper proposes a research agenda for participatory action research with an initial research co-design for academic institutions and development organizations to explore the potential of a participatory geographic information system (PGIS).

2   Environmental Information Ecosystem and Environmental Justice

In describing the information ecosystem, Harris and Kirby-Straker [14] have used the definition provided by Internews, which works as a media development organization focusing on sustainability-related challenges faced by marginalized and vulnerable communities, including environmental challenges. The Information Ecosystem for Resilience framework designed by Internews indicates that information is the foundation of an information ecosystem. Still, overall, it is a complex adaptive system with the inclusion of 'information infrastructure, tools, media, producers, consumers, curators, and sharers' being organized in complex and dynamic social relationships [14, p 342]. Although the information is the base of an information ecosystem, how it will move and transform inflows ultimately depend on the socio-ecological, socio-economic, and socio-political relationships in an information ecosystem. Tools and media in an information ecosystem like records, geographic information systems, or social media are within one set of components. They do not necessarily represent the whole information ecosystem by disregarding social relationships.

Similarly, the Environmental Information Ecosystem can be considered as a branch of the Information Ecosystem that mainly deals with Environmental Information by considering socio-ecological, socio-economic, and socio-political relationships in a particular context. These relationships in a particular context may have influence on generation, sharing and management of environmental information. Powerful countries as well as powerful groups in a society that are engaged in inequitable natural resource extraction and hazardous waste generation by harming the less powerful countries and groups may try to restrict the flow of environmental information. Consequently, the discussion of facilitating a favorable Environmental Information Ecosystem for the disadvantaged groups is highly relevant in the discussion of claiming environmental justice by the affected countries and groups.

In this regard, Mohai et al. [21, p 407] referred to the definition of environmental justice provided by the U.S. Environmental Protection Agency (EPA) as 'The fair treatment and meaningful involvement of all people regardless of race, color, national origin, or income with respect to the development, implementation, and enforcement of environmental laws, regulations, and policies'. The definition argues that fair treatment can be ensured when no population will have to bear a disproportionate share of the negative human health or environmental impacts of pollution caused by the execution of federal, state, local and tribal programs and policies that facilitate harmful industrial, municipal, and commercial operations [21]. Since environmental injustice is the result from a combination of historic political, social, and economic interactions rather than a single event, claiming environmental justice is not a one-off process and may require a long-time through a planned advocacy process [28]. Secondly, environmental injustice is sometimes the result of actions that were once considered as justified by all the parties and stakeholders [13]. Therefore, claiming environmental justice may not be entertained when significant changes happened over time with changed circumstances. The groups claiming environmental justice needs to be pragmatic while advocating for environmental justice. Finally, the advocacy for environmental justice needs to have a life cycle perspective to understand who benefitted the most and who suffered the most over time and space due to hazard production and consumption [28]. Therefore, any tool (like participatory GIS) to be used in an environmental information ecosystem aimed to claim environmental justice has to consider the realities associated with environmental justice along with the socio-ecological, socio-economic, and socio-political relationships discussed earlier.

3   Fisherfolk Community in Bangladesh: Research Relevance

The Intergovernmental Panel on Climate Change (IPCC) has reiterated in their sixth Assessment Report published in 2021 that human influence has warmed the atmosphere, ocean, and land. The scale of recent climate change is unprecedented over many centuries and thousands of years [15]. According to the Climate Risk Index published by Germanwatch yearly, Bangladesh is one of the twenty most vulnerable countries considering human fatalities and economic losses due to climate change over the years [7]. Although countries such as Bangladesh do not contribute hugely to the global emissions causing climate change, the country is, unfortunately, highly vulnerable to devastations caused by climate change. The nature-dependent communities such as fisherfolks are the ones who have been suffering the most due to these [27]. Minimizing the adverse effects through climate action and natural resource management by the community is therefore urgent and considered a priority.

Besides, in Bangladesh, artisanal fisherfolks are one of the significant disadvantaged groups due to lower access to and availability of natural resources resulting from climate change impacts [27]. They also have reduced access and availability of fish because of intense competition with powerful groups and random conservation measures (without rolling out technology-based research) like a ban on fishing or declaration of a marine protected area, without adequate compensatory support [3, 6] According to the definition of environmental justice, fisherfolks are, therefore, sufferers of severe environmental injustice. Therefore, claiming environmental justice is highly relevant for Bangladesh as a country, and fisherfolks in Bangladesh in particular as an affected group, at local, national and global scales by conducting research on the potential of a tool within an environmental information ecosystem while looking at different social relationships.

In this scenario, spatial prioritization based on the targeted conserving species and resource extraction by marginal fisherfolk communities is absent due to a lack of spatial information about species habitat and resource accessed areas [25]. These issues impact their potential to take climate action and adequately manage natural resources. However, artisanal fisherfolks are primarily unorganized and do not work together as a group to claim their rights and take any collective action [30]. Consequently, the decision-making and policy-making processes often exclude them from participation in co-designing policy and programs. The overall situation makes it challenging to achieve SDG 13 to take urgent action to combat climate change and its impacts on the fisherfolks, and SDG 14 to conserve and sustainably use the oceans, seas, and marine resources for sustainable development by engaging fisherfolks [26]. Since there is a potential to avoid conflict of interest between conservation decisions and natural resource rights through Earth Observation-based inclusive natural resources management [17], the above-mentioned challenges can be addressed by exploring the potential of the participatory geographic information system (GIS) with integrated Earth Observation (EO) techniques as a tool of the environmental information ecosystem to advocate for environmental justice by fisherfolks in Bangladesh.

4 PGIS for Fisherfolks: A Research Agenda and Design

For impactful research, after determining the applicability of the research for fisherfolks in Bangladesh, the research agenda initially needs to consider a partner in the ground considering the research to be led by an academic institution. The researchers need to be engaged with the fisherfolks in Bangladesh through the project of an agency that works to empower the fisherfolks through digital inclusion by addressing different challenges. The main aim of the research partnership will be to conduct action research with large research grants on participatory GIS for the fisherfolks to observe how it can assist their empowerment through digital inclusion. For this reason, the initial socio-economic feasibility study on participatory GIS needs to be conducted, considering the associated challenges of participatory GIS. Therefore, the initial research through multi-disciplinary collaboration will use the qualitative research method for collecting data through interviewing experts and organizing focus group discussions with the fisherfolks.

After the feasibility study, with a strong awareness on social relationships while using participatory GIS as a tool of the environmental information ecosystem, the researchers will explore the potential of participatory GIS as an environmental justice advocacy tool for climate action and accessing natural resources by fisherfolks in Bangladesh. GIS as a system can create and manage the geographic data and analyze and visualize that data, making it a powerful evidence-based decision support tool to influence and facilitate decision-makers. However, the researchers will gather supplementary data from the site through a participatory process for analyzing contextual knowledge through community engagement to link the satellite based remote sensing data to ground reality and formulate a geospatial database. The community will keep and update this data as a record to observe and monitor climate and natural resource access changes and advocate for supportive actions.

In terms of academic contribution, the proposed research will engage with other studies about digital inclusion, particularly the literature from ICT for development (like [4, 19]). The socio-economic., socio-political and socio-ecological perspectives of participatory GIS coming out from the research will demonstrate whether or not participatory digital technologies result in desirable outcomes when different factors interplay (considering other academic works like [2, 23]). The research will also use theory behind agency, participation and empowerment (like [9]) to understand positive and unwanted outcomes of participatory GIS.

Through participatory GIS to be explored in the proposed research, fisherfolks and local institutions will have the capacity to produce and use geographic data related to climate change, habitats, resource abundance, natural resources access changes, and associated actions to influence the decision-making process at different levels. In this regard, the researchers will organize participatory mapping workshops focused on climate change impacts, climate actions, challenges in accessing natural resources, and community-based natural resources management practices. Besides, the research would attempt to link the participatory inputs with earth observation data to validate the evidence created from satellite-based exercise. A semi-structured focus-group technique will be followed in these workshops with men and women from the fisherfolk community using printed satellite images or interpreted maps at a 1:25,000 scale to discuss and map the issues related to climate change and natural resources. The participatory maps (for printed ones) will be scanned and georeferenced, or the inputs will be updated directly on the geospatial platforms to document the features associated with climate change and natural resources as a digitized geospatial database.

Using participatory GIS as an advocacy tool for climate action and accessing natural resources is a unique application of existing information technology. Doing so will require human-centric approaches in designing sustainable IT solutions that include participatory processes and mechanisms to foreground fisherfolk communities' needs.

This research needs to enhance the capacity of disadvantaged communities 1) by increasing the ability of nature-dependent fisherfolk communities to produce and use geographic data related to climate change and natural resources access changes which envisage portraying their accessibility-based needs, and 2) by advocating for their well-being and development of evidence-based findings for use in recommendations to policy makers. The benefits will be realized by working together with beneficiaries to develop some measurable outputs.

One of the outputs could be a practice guide on the potential of participatory GIS as an advocacy tool for nature-dependent communities to claim environmental justice. The guide will be based on research findings, mainly showcasing the preliminary participatory maps created during the workshops and basic data acquired from satellite image interpretation. A conceptual framework to design appropriate participatory GIS tools and linking with earth observation grounded in nature-dependent communities' values and preferences: The framework needs to be based on the methodology followed in the research project and the actual participation of the community in the research project. This conceptual framework should be the base of the larger project planned to develop and test the solution.

Another output could be a training outline for building capacity of nature-dependent communities on participatory GIS. The outline will be based on the capacity-building needs identified during the research project implementation. The outline will consider the needs of nature-dependent communities, local government institutions, and local NGOs working with the communities. With larger funding, later, training for the local level decision-makers on how they can use the participatory geospatial data in their decision loops needs to be organized.

The research needs to be designed to significantly enhance the impact of research for users and beneficiaries outside the academic research community. The researchers need to aim to improve how research is conducted and communicated through extensive and tailored engagement with grassroots communities, local institutions, policymakers, and the wider stakeholder community.

The researchers need to disseminate the proposed framework of applying participatory GIS and cloud-based earth observation techniques (e.g., Google Earth, Google Earth Engine) to take climate action and manage natural resources so that different agencies can design their related initiatives. The dissemination of the training outline will also assist in developing a capacity-building program on participatory GIS.

The researchers need to further disseminate the practice guide to the broader community and local institutions on the potential of participatory GIS as an advocacy tool for nature-dependent communities. The dissemination may build awareness and motivate different organizations to promote advocacy and management by nature-dependent communities around climate action and natural resources management. The path based on capacity building, awareness, program implementation, and advocacy will generate desired outcomes around climate justice and natural resource rights by the use of participatory GIS.

The short-term (6 months) output of the research needs to be prototypes of co-designed digital tools for the nature-dependent disadvantaged communities. The preliminary research aims to better understand the economic and social aspects of sustainability that will guide research to achieve sustainable development goals (SDGs). Within this timeframe, representative participants need to be recruited from the fisherfolk communities in Bangladesh for participatory research and conduct co-design sessions with non-digital tools to develop prototypes of digital tools.

In the longer term, the outputs need to be fully working digital tools (e.g., Spatial Decision Support System - SDSS) through integrating earth observation and participatory geographic information system (GIS) to aid advocacy for climate action and natural resource management by nature-dependent disadvantaged communities in multiple countries. Focusing on two or more climate vulnerable and nature-dependent developing countries in the Asia-Pacific will enable researchers to develop fully working digital tools later with more significant funding.

5 Conclusion

The primary beneficiaries and users of the research agenda highlighted in this paper would be the disadvantaged communities themselves. These include climate-vulnerable communities such as artisanal fisherfolks, subsistence farmers, forest-dependent people, and so on in Bangladesh initially, who have also continuously struggled to access natural resources. The use of participatory GIS will benefit them to keep a record, monitor changes, and advocate for equitable climate actions and natural resource management. The use of a participatory GIS-based geospatial database will also be helpful for respective local government organizations and local NGOs of the countries of concern in promoting and contributing to community-based climate action and natural resources management as a part of implementing the Local Adaptation Plan of Action (LAPA). With larger resources in the future, based on the geospatial database, the researchers can aim to develop the Spatial Decision Support System that can help policymakers, and managers of ecosystems/Protected Areas to take appropriate decisions based on priority needs without compromising the resource rights of the marginal community (e.g., fisherfolks).

References

1. Aziz, M., et al.: Mapping of agricultural drought in Bangladesh using geographic information system (GIS). Earth Syst. Environ. **6**(3), 657–667 (2022). https://doi.org/10.1007/s41748-021-00231-8
2. Barrett, M., Sahay, S., Walsham, G.: Information technology and social transformation: GIS for forestry management in India. Inf. Soc. **17**(1), 5–20 (2001)
3. Bhowmik, J., Selim, S.A., Irfanullah, H.M., Shuchi, J.S., Sultana, R., Ahmed, S.G.: Resilience of small-scale marine fishers of Bangladesh against the COVID-19 pandemic and the 65-day fishing ban. Mar. Policy **134**, 104794 (2021)
4. Chipidza, W., Leidner, D.: A review of the ICT-enabled development literature: towards a power parity theory of ICT4D. J. Strateg. Inf. Syst. **28**(2), 145–174 (2019)
5. Cho, M.A., Mutanga, O.: Understanding participatory GIS application in rangeland use planning: a review of PGIS practice in Africa. J. Land Use Sci. **16**(2), 174–187 (2021)
6. Deb, A.K., Haque, C.E.: 'Sufferings start from the mothers' womb': vulnerabilities and livelihood war of the small-scale fishers of Bangladesh. Sustainability **3**(12), 2500–2527 (2011)
7. Eckstein, D., Künzel, V., Schäfer, L., Winges, M.: Global climate risk index 2020. Germanwatch, Bonn (2019)
8. Elwood, S.: Critical issues in participatory GIS: deconstructions, reconstructions, and new research directions. Trans. GIS **10**(5), 693–708 (2006)
9. Emirbayer, M., Mische, A.: What is agency? Am. J. Sociol. **103**(4), 962–1023 (1998)
10. Estaville, L.: GIS and colleges of business: a curricular exploration. J. Real Estate Lit. **15**(3), 441–448 (2007)
11. Flügel, W.A., Märker, M., Moretti, S., Rodolfi, G., Sidrochuk, A.: Integrating geographical information systems, remote sensing, ground truthing and modelling approaches for regional erosion classification of semi-arid catchments in South Africa. Hydrol. Process. **17**(5), 929–942 (2003)
12. Green, D.R.: The role of public participatory geographical information systems (PPGIS) in coastal decision-making processes: an example from Scotland, UK. Ocean Coast. Manag. **53**(12), 816–821 (2010)
13. Grove, M., et al.: The legacy effect: understanding how segregation and environmental injustice unfold over time in Baltimore. Ann. Am. Assoc. Geogr. **108**(2), 524–537 (2018)
14. Harris, U.S., Kirby-Straker, R.: Participatory environmental communication: toward enhanced collaboration and dialogue in caribbean and pacific communities. In: Takahashi, B., Metag, J., Thaker, J., Comfort, S.E. (eds.) The Handbook of International Trends in Environmental Communication, pp. 339–356. Routledge, New York (2021)
15. IPCC: Climate Change 2022: Impacts, Adaptation, and Vulnerability. In: Pörtner, H.-O., et al. (eds.) Contribution of Working Group II to the Sixth Assessment Report of the Intergovernmental Panel on Climate Change. Cambridge University Press, Cambridge (2022)
16. Kwaku Kyem, P.A.: Power, participation, and inflexible institutions: an examination of the challenges to community empowerment in participatory GIS applications. Cartographica: Int. J. Geogr. Inf. Geovisual. **38**(3–4), 5–17 (2001)
17. Lavaysse, C., Roudier, P., Venkatachalam, V., Klooster, J.V.T., Clerici, M.: On the use of the eStation developed in the GMES & Africa EU project: results from the user survey. Atmosphere **12**(2), 258 (2021)
18. Lü, G., Batty, M., Strobl, J., Lin, H., Zhu, A.X., Chen, M.: Reflections and speculations on the progress in Geographic Information Systems (GIS): a geographic perspective. Int. J. Geogr. Inf. Sci. **33**(2), 346–367 (2019)

19. Mehra, B.: Toward an impact-driven framework to operationalize social justice and implement ICT4D in the field of information. J. Assoc. Inf. Sci. Technol (2022). https://doi.org/10.1002/asi.24693

20. Mekonnen, A.D., Gorsevski, P.V.: A web-based participatory GIS (PGIS) for offshore wind farm suitability within Lake Erie, Ohio. Renew. Sustain. Energy Rev. **41**, 162–177 (2015)

21. Mohai, P., Pellow, D., Roberts, J.T.: Environmental justice. Annu. Rev. Environ. Resour. **34**, 405–430 (2009)

22. Nykiforuk, C.I., Flaman, L.M.: Geographic information systems (GIS) for health promotion and public health: a review. Health Promot. Pract. **12**(1), 63–73 (2011)

23. Puri, S.K., Sahay, S.: The politics of knowledge in using GIS for land management in India. In: Kaplan, B., Truex, D.P., David Wastell, A., Wood-Harper, T., DeGross, J.I. (eds.) Information Systems Research. IIFIP, vol. 143, pp. 597–614. Springer, Boston, MA (2004). https://doi.org/10.1007/1-4020-8095-6_32

24. Robinson, J.A., Block, D., Rees, A.: Community geography: addressing barriers in public participation GIS. Cartogr. J. **54**(1), 5–13 (2017)

25. Roy, S., Hossain, M.S., Badhon, M.K., Chowdhury, S.U., Sumaiya, N., Depellegrin, D.: Development and analysis of a geospatial database for maritime spatial planning in Bangladesh. J. Environ. Manage. **317**, 115495 (2022)

26. Saputra, D.K., et al.: Characteristics of mangrove fisheries in essential ecosystem area Ujungpangkah, Indonesia. J. Environ. Manag. Tour. **13**(3), 812–820 (2022)

27. Sharifuzzaman, S.M., Hossain, M.S., Chowdhury, S.R., Sarker, S., Chowdhury, M.N., Chowdhury, M.Z.R.: Elements of fishing community resilience to climate change in the coastal zone of Bangladesh. J. Coast. Conserv. **22**(6), 1167–1176 (2018). https://doi.org/10.1007/s11852-018-0626-9

28. Sze, J., London, J.K.: Environmental justice at the crossroads. Sociol. Compass **2**(4), 1331–1354 (2008)

29. Tsihrintzis, V.A., Hamid, R., Fuentes, H.R.: Use of geographic information systems (GIS) in water resources: a review. Water Resour. Manage **10**(4), 251–277 (1996). https://doi.org/10.1007/BF00508896

30. Uddin, M.M., et al.: Impacts, diversity, and resilience of a coastal water small-scale fisheries nexus during COVID-19: a case study in Bangladesh. Water **14**(8), 1269 (2022)

31. Weng, Q.: A remote sensing? GIS evaluation of urban expansion and its impact on surface temperature in the Zhujiang Delta, China. Int. J. Remote Sens. **22**(10), 1999–2014 (2001)

32. Ziadat, F., et al.: A participatory GIS approach for assessing land suitability for rainwater harvesting in an arid rangeland environment. Arid Land Res. Manag. **26**(4), 297–311 (2012)

Caring for People, Caring for Their Data: Data Stewardship and Collaborative Care in Social Service Provision for People Experiencing Homelessness

Stephen C. Slota[1]([⊠]) [iD], Kenneth R. Fleischmann[1] [iD], and Sherri R. Greenberg[2]

[1] School of Information, University of Texas at Austin, Austin, TX 78712, USA
stephen.slota@austin.utexas.edu
[2] LBJ School of Public Affairs, University of Texas at Austin, Austin, TX 78712, USA

Abstract. This paper reports findings from a study on service provision for people experiencing homelessness in the Austin/Travis County region. Drawing on 39 interviews with stakeholders in service provision and 137 open-ended surveys with service users, we explore how 'matters of care' Baker & Karasti, [1] become central when collecting and using data describing this vulnerable population. We propose that collaborative care structures clients' and social workers' interactions around data, and that attention to matters of care serves to both reduce harm and improve data quality and coverage.

Keywords: Homelessness · Collaborative care · Social services provision

1 Introduction

Every day, we encounter decisions that implicitly ask us to balance how much personal information we disclose to access the systems, social networks, and services that require that information. While such disclosures are often needed to use a particular digital platform, the stakes are raised significantly when a person experiencing homelessness encounters this trade-off while seeking access to social services. In this paper, we consider the disclosure of information with significant consequences for health, safety, and equity through a study of service provision for people experiencing homelessness in the Austin/Travis County region. Drawing on 39 interviews with government and non-profit service providers and other stakeholders in homelessness services, alongside 137 open-ended surveys conducted with people experiencing homelessness, we consider the careful balance of disclosure and protection of personal information when that information is needed to gain access to vital social services. In this paper, we explore how service providers and service users balance data completeness and accuracy versus the privacy and care for sensitive personal information.

We begin by considering the ethical responsibilities that service providers have toward care, in terms of both providing services and care to people experiencing homelessness, as well as in caring for their data. Then, we describe the qualitative data collection and analysis methods that we use in this study, drawing upon critical incident

I. Sserwanga et al. (Eds.): iConference 2023, LNCS 13972, pp. 500–513, 2023.
https://doi.org/10.1007/978-3-031-28032-0_38

technique and thematic analysis. Key themes emerging from the 39 interviews and 137 open-ended surveys include the importance of data stewardship and the critical role of collaborative care. We explore the care tensions inherent in social service provision, particularly in the era of big data. Finally, we discuss the implications of this research for theory and for practice, concluding that people need to be empowered to make their own decisions about when and how to make trade-offs between information disclosure and information privacy.

2 Background

We define 'care', following Martin et al. [13], as a "mode of attention that directs action, affection, or concern" (p. 635). However, the definition of care, and where care is valued, are significantly contested and political. Care can provoke attention to fragilities and vulnerabilities in socio-technical systems [6], and brings to light the necessary work of maintenance and repair, both in the technical and in the social aspects of the system. Murphy [15] cautions against leaning too far into the positive aspects of care, and characterizing it only as affection and nurturing, and calls for a focus on unsettling care, which can direct attention to harmful and unwanted stratifications and inequities. "Adequate care requires knowledge and curiosity regarding the needs of an 'other' – human or not – and these become possible through relating, through refusing objectification" [18, p 98]. Puig de la Bellacasa argues for a transformative ethos of care, one that considers caring itself as a living technology to be applied differently in various spaces. Drawing on this transformative ethos, Baker and Karasti [1] explore how 'matters of care' provide a lens towards better understanding local data practice, refining data needs, and understanding the implications of data processes. It is through the perspective of this transformative ethos of care that we consider how social service providers work with, and through, both their colleagues and their clients in stewarding clients' personally identifiable information and data.

Data, information, and knowledge about homelessness is increasingly fundamental to how it is addressed nation-wide and beyond. Even well-coordinated care models are limited by the availability of resources, especially in terms of affordable housing, temporary housing, shelters, and permanent supportive housing [24]. While knowledge-oriented solutions seek to more effectively use these limited resources, visibility of homeless populations and an accurate understanding of the scope of homelessness both regionally and nationally can be powerful drivers towards increasing this support. 'Missingness' and misclassification of homelessness through data remains a significant area of need [3], and obtaining even accurate counts of people experiencing homelessness in a given region is a significant data and managerial challenge. People experiencing homelessness, however, are often not in a position, due to circumstance or capacity, to effectively advocate for themselves or ensure their own visibility. Social workers in various roles are commonly in a position to advocate for their clients, but themselves are frequently in an asymmetric power relationship with their clients, serving as gatekeepers to information about services and access to those services. Hence, the ethical and professional commitments of social workers are vital interlocutions between the client and social worker, requiring that the relationship between client and social worker – which might be compared to a fiduciary responsibility given its focus on the interests of the client [8, 11] – be grounded in trust.

Effective stewardship of personal data is a part of the National Association for Social Work's Code of Ethics [16], but the specifics on how to achieve these goals are particular to the systems, data collection regimes, and technologies being used at that site. In a new standard added in 2021, the Code of Ethics calls for Social Workers, "When using electronic technology to facilitate evaluation or research, [to]... Ensure that participants provide informed consent for the use of such technology... [and to] assess whether participants are able to use the technology and, when appropriate, offer reasonable alternatives to participate in the evaluation or research." (Section 5.02 (f)). As such, the delicate balancing act between privacy, capacity, and necessary information can be informed by socio-technical analysis and a client-centered perspective.

However, social workers are not expected to be data experts, nor are their clients. Buse et al. [4], in their heuristic reconsideration of the materialities of social care, argue that 'spaces of care' are often materialized by those thought to be outside of that space; "those who shape care at a distance, designers, architects, and planners can orchestrate the texture of environments where care may take place with intended and unintended consequences" (p. 253). Similarly, the specific information that social workers are expected to collect as part of their work is often externally imposed, oriented towards tracking of information determined by funders and government, and might not correspond well to the immediate needs of service users. Even in the healthcare context, there is reason to believe that the perceived information needs of users significantly differ from what providers believe patients need to know [26] - and in social work those needs, for both providers and users, can be more situational, more nebulous, and more heterogeneous.

Müller and Pihl-Thingvad [14] identify three categories of how users can be involved in social work innovation: user-centered, co-produced, and citizen-driven. Across all of these, they address the need for awareness of the role of social workers, for a well-organized system, and for user empowerment. In short, the thorny landscape of personal data and care for people experiencing homelessness calls out for a socio-technical perspective on care. A socio-technical perspective on social work enables designers to, "prioritize practice over process, seeking solutions that augment autonomy, retaining the local flexibility" [25]. In managing data, Jackson and Baker [9] emphasize 'thick heterogeneity' to account for those differences that should be preserved and identify collaborative care as a key means for doing so. They argue that collaboration itself is a key means of addressing 'matters of care', and that "the grounding for this ethical model is to be found ultimately in the relations of trust and care that grow from the experience of collaboration itself." (p. 66).

In this paper, we apply a socio-technical perspective to social work undertaken to aid people experiencing homelessness in the Austin/Travis County region, addressing two primary research questions:

1. How do service providers think about matters of care in the context of social service delivery and data?
2. How do social service users think about social service delivery and data in the context of care?

3 Methods

This study reports some initial findings from 39 interviews and 137 open-ended surveys, conducted as part of a program evaluation of a social service provider operating in the Austin/Travis County region. Interview participants were drawn from the evaluated social service provider, as well as collaborating service providers and stakeholders in the region. As the program evaluation is still underway, we refer to the service provider being evaluated as "primary" and contracted collaborators as "secondary" service providers. This does not reflect their importance or position in the social service ecosystem, but rather our own attention in directing this work. Our team has previously published findings [20–23, 27] from an earlier study involving 32 interviews with social service providers in the Austin/Travis County area, but this is the first paper to report findings from these two new datasets; importantly, the 39 interviews reported in this paper are an entirely new corpus from the 32 interviews from the prior study.

Of the 39 hour-long interviews conducted, 21 were drawn from the primary service provider, and 18 from secondary service providers. Participants were initially selected through the interlocution of key informants, then further developed through snowball sampling [17]. Interviews were structured according to critical incident technique [7], and participants were asked to relate three recent cases, experiences, or projects: one that was as yet unresolved, one that resolved in a positive or successful fashion, and one that resolved in a frustrating or unsuccessful fashion. For each incident, participants were asked about information needs, collaborations, and barriers to completing their goals. All participants were asked about how they collect and use data, and about how the success of their work is evaluated.

We drew survey participants from three distinct groups of people on the homelessness continuum. We conducted twelve surveys with community leaders participating in a local advisory council who either were currently experiencing homelessness or had previously experienced homelessness. We conducted another 75 surveys with people currently experiencing homelessness, who were recruited through the primary service provider. Finally, we conducted 50 surveys with people currently in permanent supportive housing (PSH) who had previously experienced homelessness and were recruited through the PSH community where they resided at the time. Each survey included twelve open-ended questions, and participants were compensated for their time in completing the survey. The surveys asked participants to relate their information needs and resources, their engagements with local service providers, and how the resources available to them aligned with their needs and values.

We coded and analyzed the surveys and interview according to thematic analysis techniques [5]. Initial open coding by the lead author inductively identified themes, which were presented to the full research team for refinement, before additional rounds of coding were conducted to develop those themes, two of which are reported in this paper.

4 Findings

Considering the vulnerability and social situation of the population being served, data itself must be treated with the utmost care to avoid the potential harms of information sharing. Across these interviews, it was clear that social service providers were expected to care for the personal data of their users across the entire 'data lifecycle', from ensuring accurate collection, to the role of case managers as a key point of mediation between clients and systems, and to observing and accounting for those data are used in analyses and arguments for future policy and funding. As both the collector and primary user of data about their clients, the fiduciary aspects of this relationship were brought to the forefront, and ethical commitments to the effective care of clients underpinned interview responses. Thematic analysis revealed two related themes related to information sharing and data collection. The first considers how service providers understood the utility of data, and gaps in its collection. The second theme, closely related to the first, revolves around the notion of collaborative care, and explores how trust, collaboration, and agency inform how data are collected from service users, and to what extent those data become useful.

4.1 Data Stewardship

Across the interviews we conducted, we found that service providers use a number of formal and informal criteria to determine eligibility for their services, most tied to personal characteristics or history of people being served. Through formal coordinated assessment, formal instruments, and informal data collection, services access is prioritized, individual service users are tracked as they progress through different service providers, and necessary information for obtaining future services is recorded and tracked. A key step in this process is coordinated assessment, a required step in homelessness service provision for regions making use of federal funding. However, coordinated assessment tools are imperfect, as argued by a secondary service provider:

> "so in my experience, administering it, folks still tend to score pretty low… they added a section to address racial disparities, which is great, but now that's what the assessment is like. You get the most points from that section. And I have patients that are literally dying of stage four cancer on the street, and they score extremely low, and I have patients in full psychosis, like [they] cannot manage their own needs, they score extremely low, right, they're never going to be picked for a program. So I think that it's still very fluid… And folks with severe and persistent mental illness are not prioritized, either."

Service users receive a single score through coordinated assessment, and access to certain resources is gated behind certain assessment scores, making this assessment a particularly consequential point of data collection and serving as entry into the system. However, many service providers have additional criteria for eligibility, varying according to their specific missions and pragmatically according to their capabilities, as recalled by the following stakeholder in leadership of the primary service provider:

> "The way [prioritization is] generally done is through the coordinated entry process. And, you know, each agency sets their criteria for the or the eligibility for their program and, you know, an agency can define their eligibility requirements, however, however, is most appropriate for them."

Data needs tended to be related to what was necessary to gain access to specific services, according to the criteria of specific service providers. Nonetheless, the role of coordinated assessment as a formal intake into the services clustered under the CoC maintained its role as both the de facto data collection instrument and prioritization mechanism. This, however, introduced tensions related to the lived experience of service users themselves. Coordinated assessment can take between 40 min and 1 h, and ask questions that can be challenging, embarrassing, or otherwise very personal, such as questions about mental health, self-harm behavior, or substance use. Due to both the length of and sensitive information collected through the instrument, coordinated assessment could actually serve as a barrier to gaining access to services for some users.

"either some individuals just refuse to take [it]… and that means that individual will never be served… Some of these individuals are just so severe that they just refuse to take that assessment. And then, you know, when the individuals do take it, sometimes their acuity skews their responses. And so it's challenging…"

As stated by the above participant in a leadership role in the primary service provider, many individuals are not in a position to participate in self-assessment. This comes before assessments conducted by service providers for their own intake criteria, which can add hours of assessment and information collection to the process, as relayed by the following participant working as a case manager for our primary service provider in describing a collaborative organization.

"their intakes [are] extremely lengthy - about two to two and a half hours and very repetitive - which has been really problematic for clients that I work with… there's a window of tolerance there that our clients have, and understandably so, especially when they're being asked to answer, you know, some pretty invasive questions at times as well. It can be really problematic. I've had a lot of clients blow up in the middle of those intakes and leave and because, yes, they have exceeded that window of tolerance and, and then that results in them not getting the care that they need. So it's sort of this vicious cycle."

Service providers, both primary and secondary, noted similar resistance to sharing sensitive personal information, even where the client knows that these are important steps. As a service user, who had undergone significant trauma prior to their experience of homelessness, wrote: "I have [a case manager] but [it is] hard to talk [to] him." Other service users found the repeated assessments and data collection following the initial coordinated assessment (often a new assessment for each service provider according to their specific criteria) to be burdensome: "There could be sharing of info automatically with all the agencies". However, not just service access, but also funding, is determined by personal data collected through formal and informal assessments. Funding can be targeted to certain demographic or other groups as well as for general use, and accounting for those groups provides broader access to funding sources where specialization of efforts is possible. Similarly, accurate counts of people experiencing homelessness in the region aids in creating a case for further funding, and accurate counts of specific needs such as mental health or prescription drug support are vital to ensuring access to that funding. As related by a secondary service provider:

"With our outreach screening, assessment, and risk lobbying, the state [are] gate-keepers of state funds. People who don't have insurance have to have [an] assessment to see if the State will pay for their treatment and suffer before they go anywhere else."

The need for better, more complete, and more accurate data, however, was balanced by, and occasionally in tension with, the desire to support the agency and recovery of clients. In some cases, this took the form of a lighter hand in conducting assessments and collecting personal information, in others, it took the form of a more collaborative arrangement, where a case manager would serve as both a gauge of what is normal and as an interlocutor to service providers and systems. As relayed by the below case manager working for our primary service provider, the lived experience of service users can affect the sense of what is normal, making self-assessment especially challenging.

"because when you're in crisis, you lose perspective of what is a crisis… so if you're in a chronic crisis, which is what we're evaluating, with chronic homelessness, a self-assessment tool, in my personal opinion, and my professional opinion [is] not an effective tool, because you're going to ask somebody, is this a crisis? And they're gonna say no, because they have to live in it, you know, so. So, there's issues with it regardless. But they did transition away from that."

This support was seen as valuable to many service users who completed surveys, as with the below participant:

"Having a case manager to be kind of like an advocate for me has kept me from not giving up for the most part and also the very kind people of Austin who have helped me get by on a daily basis with their support and charity."

At the intersection of the need for personal information to navigate systems and services, and the commitment to supporting agency and recovery, we observed the development of care collaborations between service providers, users, and their data and information systems.

4.2 Collaborative Care

The quantity and type of personal information that had to be shared by people experiencing homelessness before they could access services was considered problematic by many interviewees, from both the primary provider and among the secondary provider stakeholder groups. Coordinated assessment, even though still somewhat problematic, was seen as a significant step forward in protecting personal information, as related below by a participant from a secondary service provider.

"I've kind of almost become radicalized with how much people experiencing homelessness are asked to decide to divulge their information… Coordinated entry was a response to that, as opposed to having done an intake at every possible agency, you're doing one. I think that's an improvement, because the way it used to be pre 2014… You would have to repeat your story of being homeless three or four times. So is it good that it collects all that information? Probably not. But I think ultimately, over time, it protects clients information better than how we did it pre coordinated entry. I wish there was a way that it could be better integrated into other programs, including RS systems."

Service users prioritized a sense of humanity, which we broadly understood as a combination of both how they were treated by the general public and their sense of agency within supportive systems. As one service user responded, "[I] Need housing and want to be to live in my own place again. Be independent again, feel like I'm someone, and [feel like] a part of the movement in the community." The desire for independence as expressed through these surveys can be understood as a desire for personal agency, and living independently was a priority for many respondents, "Hopefully, I can, within the next few months, get a reasonably priced home. No group home. I would like to live by myself." Service users often found themselves, despite having ongoing engagement with case managers, not meeting their personal goals for recovery or housing, "Yes I work with a couple of case managers, one with the City of Austin and one with the VA. And they are bending over backwards to help me – but I have been that horse that is led to water but has not taken a drink yet. Lol."

When barriers to recovery exist as part of information systems, it is necessary to negotiate and manage not only the recovery process, but also, the information practices themselves - something we saw service providers doing regularly. Interviews revealed numerous 'side-channels,' or parallel services, that can be navigated by a knowledgeable representative to find access to services even where they might be ineligible. In cases managed by the primary service provider, clients are assisted with a very broad range of activities, from obtaining ID, to accessing insurance benefits, receiving mental health treatment, and even support in grocery shopping and similar life skills.

Clients, in their surveys, regularly emphasized how basic needs structured their lives and information practices. The vast majority listed food and shelter access, with many adding health and mental health care access, as being information they most needed in their daily lives.

"Yes, I have considered family, food, housing, transportation just everything that makes life go is what a human being needs. Also just to be treated like another human being just in a general sense not some inhuman animal or something."

Among those who referenced having a case worker, that case worker was usually the primary point of information access, with cell phones and word of mouth consistently referenced as well. It is in this dynamic that we see case managers entering into a collaborative care relationship with their clients, oriented towards finding housing but first seeking to meet basic needs - in interviews, many case managers across the service provision landscape mentioned supporting transportation as well: "it kind of comes back to anything that is creating a barrier to their wellbeing, their mental health, their, you know, their ability to be housed, we are going to try to support in any way we can".

Case managers had to address certain needs before others could meaningfully be approached. Clients who had no access to a cell phone, nor a consistent address, could often be difficult to find, and had trouble arriving on time to scheduled meetings (which were quite often assessments in their own right), as related by the case manager below.

"It's just difficult with communication a lot of times... part of that is just the nature of being unsheltered. Things go missing and cell phone bills become a low priority, and... making a meeting with your case manager is lower priority. Sometimes when you have to decide [to] find someone to let you stay on the couch... or you can't get a ride or something. So I'm, like, totally empathetic, and like I get in, it's no, I'm not like frustrated, like, in that way about it. It just does make things longer."

As the above case manager for the primary service provider expressed, the nature of being unsheltered itself served as a barrier to participating in a system that relies on organizational time frames and its attendant information needs. Perhaps, then, it is unsurprising that among the case managers and others working directly with service users, that empathy and understanding become imbricated in organizational and information processes. Collaborative arrangements between service providers, through both informal and personal channels, and central information repositories, aid in finding missing clients, in coordinating services, and in sharing necessary information.

In addition to asking for humanity and personal agency as overall goals, some clients still wished for more care in how they were treated, as very clearly stated by the following participant. "[Secondary Service Provider's] case management could be more informative about their services provided. They could also express more care and understanding. I would like my case manager to be more available and communicate more." While in some facets of the system we saw the emergence of collaborations of care in both data collection and navigation of the service provision ecosystem, client surveys revealed that this is not an across-the-board change. There remains in this system significant opportunity to collaborate more closely, coordinate more coherently, and otherwise build on the positive collaborative dynamics being developed. "If I had the information I have now sooner I wouldn't have had to experience homeless[ness] as long."

5 Discussion

Throughout these interviews, we saw a tension between information needs. Systemic information needs were in tension with a sense of personal agency, and often capacity. Information about services available as mediated through social workers was often frustrating or did not meet the more immediate needs of clients. It thus becomes a significant challenge to get someone to focus on root causes if they are dealing with blisters from not having work boots, or if they don't have glasses in their prescription. What was revealed here was a need to understand and address the whole person as they experience life, an understanding that often failed to correspond well with coordinated and other formal or informal assessments.

While much of what we discussed here seems remote to the apparently lower-stakes exchanges of information that characterize other types of disclosure, like through the use of social media, we argue that many of the same values and vulnerabilities are at stake. In this study, we focused on people whose vulnerability is more visible, and the consequences of protection of personal information versus its disclosure more immediately present, than the more diffuse and indirect forms of disclosure present in nearly all online interactions. However, issues of agency over data, over valuing personal privacy, and the stigmas of social shame and embarrassment, all remain present across these platforms. While the population we studied was actively interested in addressing issues of equity such as racial disparities in outcomes of formal assessments, those issues are less visible, less immediate, and more pervasive in areas less directly oriented towards social service. Algorithmic assessment of credit-worthiness, for example [10], can have significant and lifelong consequences, and become all the more troubling for their opaque processes and data collection practices.

What is being done in these assessments can be a model for more just collection of personal data: service providers are aware of problematic outcomes and actively seek to circumvent them; data collection is often done in a transparent fashion, with a knowledgeable interlocutor assuring accuracy and consistency even in times of personal crisis, the mental state and capacity of people who are being asked to share data are considered throughout the collection and use of that data, and the well-being of clients is consistently prioritized. In line with the arguments of Buse et al. [4], we found that information requirements and systems were developed with significant influence from 'outside', emphasizing the vital mediating role of social workers in ensuring just and empathetic collection of data.

Findings here echo Marathe & Toyama [12], who demonstrate the 'situated, relational, and evolving' ways that data can be interpreted by doctors trying to get their patients the care they believe they need. Similarly, Slota, Fleischmann, et al. [20] describe how case managers demonstrate a 'feeling for the data', negotiating information systems and how data are collected and represented to pursue client goals. This 'feeling for the data' characterized both formal and informal collaborations around data and showed how client interest structured data collection activities of service providers.

Considering social service provision work in terms of its socio-technical aspects calls attention not only to the lived experience of social service users, but also to the dynamics of data as informing policy action and resource availability for this vulnerable population. Accurate representation of the needs and situation of clients must be balanced against the harms that might come from the often-uncomfortable disclosure. "Because ultimately thinking with the notion of care does illuminate the affective aspects of knowledge politics. The tensions of care are present in its very etymology that includes notions of both 'anxiety, sorrow and grief' and of 'serious mental attention'." [19, p. 212]. The affective experience of clients, mediated by social workers, preconfigures the quality, scope, and completeness of data being collected, and reminds us that to care, in this sense, is to collaborate to ensure client agency, even at stages of early data collection and through secondary uses.

Findings from this study invoke Murphy's [15] notion of unsettling care, or care that lacks positive affect. Formal information collection generates some level of emotional distance, and the collaborations of care formed among service providers and their clients call attention to histories of trauma, inequity, and inhumanity among people experiencing homelessness. In forming these collaborations of care, the unsettling must be considered alongside the positive as drivers of potential change, and the means by which inequity and stratification might, if not be fully resolved, at least be considered for their social and political consequences.

Hence, establishing collaborations of care is not solely a technological intervention, but, in true socio-technical manner, must also consider the organizational arrangements, policies, and personal relationships that heterogeneously contribute to the ecology of service provision. As argued by Bennett and Rosner [2], "When designers focus on the practical and achievable qualities of a task... they may gloss over a wider history of disability, activism, affective understanding, and personal capacity that they could meaningfully draw upon." (pg. 10). Visibility only through data excludes the capacity of a self-reporter in effectively representing themselves, often fails to account for unwillingness to share information, and otherwise provides a limited, occluded, view of the needs and dynamics of service users.

Ultimately, though this work focused on a single site, it raises the question: what would other regimes of data collection look like if we start from a position of caring and collaboration? Participants in these interviews began from a position of care for their clients and built collaborations of care that address a wide range of informational activities, from disclosure to use, in support of that position. Findings from this study are applicable to data collection regimes and use describing populations that are less immediately vulnerable, where harms can be more broadly distributed. The tension between privacy and disclosure, in this work, was mediated by trust, interpersonal relationships, and an ethical commitment to care. The delicate balance of information disclosure and personal security of information pivots on affect. Considering data collection more broadly as a collaboration of care has the potential to redirect our attention in productive ways in creating technologies that serve social good.

5.1 Limitations and Future Directions

As this study reports initial findings from this data set, further analysis of both interviews and survey responses is warranted. Initial analysis of both surveys and interviews focused on commonalities across participating stakeholders. In future work, we will conduct a more comparative analysis, to explore how and where stakeholders differ in addition to where they agree. More work is needed to explore the socio-technical aspects of care, especially as they are imbricated in other disciplines. Future work will explore how a focus on matters of care might structure policy framing, scientific communication, or the design of social media and other information systems oriented around the collection and representation of personal data. While we sought to represent the lived experience of social service users experiencing homelessness through surveys, more participatory approaches can bring that experience to the design of systems and data collection instruments, ensuring more just information regimes.

6   Conclusion

Informed consent, algorithmic transparency, and even the right to be forgotten are important, but can be insufficient given how much of life is barricaded behind personal information disclosure. Sometimes, that disclosure is absolutely necessary and vital. In spaces where personal information disclosure is necessary for engagement with a system, we should not be solely attentive to how information can be restricted or controlled, but instead should be engaged in producing systems that can reduce the harm of disclosure. A key factor in this reduction of harm were back- and side- channels, where individuals or their representatives can advocate for themselves outside of formal mechanisms. Contesting, seeking remediation, and similar activities require a transparent system and, in many cases, a knowledgeable interlocutor, and building these possibilities into an organizational structure requires a perspective founded on client care.

We argue here that collaborations of care are a vital means by which apparent values tensions in information systems might be effectively resolved. Vulnerable users benefit from systems that are sensitive to their capacities, lived experience, and personal situation. To better serve vulnerable users, care, and the affective experience of data, must be centered in systems design and across the lifecycle of data. To adopt a user-centered approach is, at least implicitly, to center matters of care in the design and implementation of information systems. If we expect data to inform our policies, our use of limited resources, and our approaches to solving significant social problems, caring for the user becomes not just a redirection of attention, but the center of future work.

Acknowledgement. This study was funded by the City of Austin #2021–01-UT-DACC. We would like to thank Min Kyung Lee, Robert Kingham, Raeesa Khan, David Cruz, Varshinee Sreekanth, Apoorva Gondimalla, Vasudha Singh, and Takayuki Suzuki for their collaboration and contributions to recruitment, study design, and data collection. Thank you to Rachel Tunis for your comments on early drafts. We also thank all of our participants for their intellectual contributions to this study.

References

1. Baker, K.S., Karasti, H.:. Data care and its politics: designing for local collective data management as a neglected thing. In: Proceedings of the 15th Participatory Design Conference: Full Papers. vol. 1, pp. 1–12, Article 10. Association for Computing Machinery (2018). https://doi.org/10.1145/3210586.3210587

2. Bennett, C.L., Rosner, D.K.: The promise of empathy: Design, disability, and knowing the "other". In: Proceedings of the 2019 CHI Conference on Human Factors in Computing Systems (CHI '19). Paper 298, pp. 1–13. Association for Computing Machinery (2019). https://doi.org/10.1145/3290605.3300528

3. Bensken, W.P.: How do we define homelessness in large health care data? Identifying variation in composition and comorbidities. Health Serv. Outcomes Res. Method. 21(1), 145–166 (2020). https://doi.org/10.1007/s10742-020-00225-5

4. Buse, C., Martin, D., Nettleton, S.: Conceptualising 'materialities of care': making visible mundane material culture in health and social care contexts. Sociol. Health Illn. 40(2), 243–255 (2018). https://doi.org/10.1111/1467-9566.12663

5. Clarke, V., Braun, V., Hayfield, N.: Thematic analysis. In: Smith, J. (ed.) Qualitative Psychology: A Practical Guide to Research Methods, pp. 222–248. Sage, Thousand Oaks (2015)
6. Denis, J., Pontille, D.: Material ordering and the care of things. Sci. Technol. Human Values **40**(3), 338–367 (2015). https://doi.org/10.1177/0162243914553129
7. Flanagan, J.C.: The critical incident technique. Psychol. Bull. **51**(4), 327–358 (1954). https://psycnet.apa.org/doi/10.1037/h0061470
8. Guttmann, D.: Trust in client-social worker relationships. In: Ethics in Social Work: A Context of Caring. Routledge (2013)
9. Jackson, S.J., Baker, K.S.: Ecological design, collaborative care, and ocean informatics. In: PDC-04 Proceedings of the Participatory Design Conference, Toronto, Canada, vol. 2, pp. 64–67 (2004)
10. Kear, M.: Playing the credit score game: Algorithms, 'positive' data, and the personification of financial objects. Econ. Soc. **46**(3–4), 346–368 (2017). https://doi.org/10.1080/03085147.2017.1412642
11. Levy, C.S.: Social Work Ethics. Human Sciences Press, New York (1976)
12. Marathe, M., Toyama, K.: The situated, relational, and evolving nature of epilepsy diagnosis. In: Proceedings of the ACM on Human-Computer Interaction, vol. 4, no. CSCW3, pp. 1–18 (2021). https://doi.org/10.1145/3432916
13. Martin, A., Myers, N., Viseu, A.: The politics of care in technoscience. Soc. Stud. Sci. **45**(5), 625–641 (2015). https://doi.org/10.1177/0306312715602073
14. Müller, M., Pihl-Thingvad, S.: User involvement in social work innovation: a systematic and narrative review. J. Soc. Work. **20**(6), 730–750 (2020). https://doi.org/10.1177/1468017319837519
15. Murphy, M.: Unsettling care: troubling transnational itineraries of care in feminist health practices. Soc. Stud. Sci. **45**(5), 717–737 (2015). https://doi.org/10.1177/0306312715589136
16. NASW: 5. Social workers' ethical responsibilities to the social work profession. NASW Code of Ethics (2021). https://www.socialworkers.org/About/Ethics/Code-of-Ethics/Code-of-Ethics-English/Social-Workers-Ethical-Responsibilities-to-Clients. Accessed 18 Sept 2021
17. Noy, C.: Sampling knowledge: the hermeneutics of snowball sampling in qualitative research. Int. J. Soc. Res. Methodol. **11**(4), 327–344 (2008). https://doi.org/10.1080/13645570701401305
18. Puig de La Bellacasa, M.: Matters of care in technoscience: assembling neglected things. Soc. Stud. Sci. **41**(1), 85–106 (2011). https://doi.org/10.1177/0306312710380301
19. Puig de La Bellacasa, M.: 'Nothing comes without its world': thinking with care. Sociol. Rev. **60**(2), 197–216 (2012). https://doi.org/10.1111/j.1467-954X.2012.02070.x
20. Slota, S.C., et al.: A feeling for the data: How government and nonprofit stakeholders negotiate value conflicts in data science approaches to ending homelessness. J. Assoc. Inf. Sci. Technol. Online Pre-release (2022). https://doi.org/10.1002/asi.24715
21. Slota, S.C., Fleischmann, K.R., Greenberg, S.R.: A brief typology of time: temporal structuring and dissonance in service provision for people experiencing homelessness. In: Smits, M. (ed.) Information for a Better World: Shaping the Global Future, pp. 211–224. Springer, Cham (2022). https://doi.org/10.1007/978-3-030-96957-8_19
22. Slota, S.C., Nigam, I., Fleischmann, K.R., Greenberg, S.R., Cruz, D.: From communities of practice to smart and connected communities: information sharing practices among social service providers. Proc. Assoc. Inf. Sci. Technol. **59**(1), 287–298 (2022). https://doi.org/10.1002/pra2.753
23. Slota, S.C., et al.: Just infrastructure? Field research on a standardized assessment tool for a continuum of care for people experiencing homelessness. Proc. Assoc. Inf. Sci. Technol. **58**(1), 327–336 (2021). https://doi.org/10.1002/pra2.460

24. Velasquez, D.E., Mecklai, K., Plevyak, S., Eappen, B., Koh, K.A., Martin, A.F.: Health system-based housing navigation for patients experiencing homelessness: a new care coordination framework. Healthcare **10**(1), 100608 (2022). https://doi.org/10.1016/j.hjdsi.2021.100608

25. Wastell, D., White, S.: Beyond bureaucracy: emerging trends in social care informatics. Health Informatics J. **20**(3), 213–219 (2014). https://doi.org/10.1177/1460458213487535

26. Xie, B.: Older adults' health information wants in the internet age: implications for patient–provider relationships. J. Health Commun. **14**(6), 510–524 (2009). https://doi.org/10.1080/10810730903089614

27. Zimmerman, T., Slota, S.C., Fleischmann, K.R., Greenberg, S., Snow, J., Rodriguez, S.: Socio-technical collaboration to end homelessness: a case study of perspectives on the value of interorganizational cooperation for data sharing. In: TMS Proceedings (2021). https://doi.org/10.1037/tms0000117

Is There a Scientific Digital Divide? Information Seeking in the International Context of Astronomy Research

Gretchen Renee Stahlman(✉)

Rutgers University, New Brunswick, NJ 08901, USA
gretchen.stahlman@rutgers.edu

Abstract. Access to informational research resources is critical to successful scientific work across disciplines. This study leverages a previously conducted survey of corresponding authors of a sample astronomy journal articles to investigate the existence and nature of a global "scientific digital divide". Variables from the survey are operationalized, including GDP of respondent, whether the paper was produced through international collaboration, whether the author collected original observational data, and whether the author located data through accessing the literature. For exploratory purposes, Pearson's and Spearman's rank correlation coefficients were calculated to test possible relationships between variables, and some preliminary evidence is presented in support of a scientific digital divide in astronomy. International collaboration is more common for respondents in lower-GDP countries; collecting observational data is more common with international collaboration; paper citation is impacted for respondents who do not collaborate internationally; and respondents from lower GDP countries do not discover data through the scholarly literature less frequently. The study concludes that collaborative networks may be key to mitigating information seeking challenges in astronomy. These dynamics should be investigated through further research.

Keywords: Digital divide · Information seeking · Information access · Astronomy

1 Introduction

For scholars across disciplines, having sufficient access to research-related information such as journal articles and data is fundamental for success. Many academics around the globe are nonetheless underprivileged with respect to access to critical information and technology to conduct their work. Santoro Lamelas & Belli [1] identify a "scientific digital divide" that contributes to a systemic "lack of scientific production and sharing of knowledge" (p. 20) through reduced access to digital resources such as scholarly literature databases, data, and software. Challenges related to this academic digital divide may be experienced acutely in fields such as astronomy that depend on observational and experimental data generated by costly instruments and facilities. On the other hand, researchers that do depend on large-scale instrumentation including telescopes

© The Author(s), under exclusive license to Springer Nature Switzerland AG 2023
I. Sserwanga et al. (Eds.): iConference 2023, LNCS 13972, pp. 514–523, 2023.
https://doi.org/10.1007/978-3-031-28032-0_39

collaborate in unique ways, both to leverage elite institutional status [2] and to encourage communality within a "moral economy" of research resources [3, 4]. Information behavior scholarship has explored the information seeking and sharing practices of academics [5–9]. However, researchers' strategies for seeking and accessing specialized scientific information such as literature and data in a global context represent an area for further investigation. This paper leverages an international survey of astronomers that was previously designed and conducted to understand astronomy data management issues and practices [10, 11]. This new analysis of existing data provides an opportunity and empirical lens for exploratory inquiry into the possible existence and nature of a "scientific digital divide" in astronomy. While a single discipline is represented and analyzed as a case study, broader implications for academic information seeking and access across disciplines and nations are considered, including the role of information professionals and institutions in mitigating global inequalities.

2 Background

Astronomy research has traditionally relied on celestial observations collected by telescopes. In more recent decades, the discipline has evolved towards construction of large-scale ground- and space-based telescopes as well as computational modeling and data science to understand complex phenomena [12, 13]. These technological dynamics have led to the growth of unique social and technical infrastructures to manage data and knowledge production [14]. Astronomy is a relatively intimate discipline overall - Forbes [15] estimated approximately a decade ago that there were only around 10,000 practicing astronomers in the world, with a majority based in the United States. International cooperation is common to navigate the political and fiscal challenges of instrumentation construction, typically with rewards of competitive telescope time and data for partner institutions and nations. Meanwhile, astronomy has a reputation for relative openness and democratization of data and literature, with the Astrophysics Data System (ADS) literature index and arXiv preprint server exemplifying disciplinary norms of sharing information publicly [16, 17]. As a case study for exploring the "scientific digital divide", astronomy may seem to be a privileged discipline with respect to scholarly information access. The analysis presented here examines this assumption and illuminates some challenges and adaptive strategies of astronomers as they seek information resources to contribute to the global intellectual community.

Astronomy and other domains have seen a shift in recent years towards more inclusive and equitable research practices throughout the scholarly career pipeline. Areas of focus include addressing gender disparities, underrepresented and vulnerable populations, hiring, retention and promotion, and COVID-19 pandemic impacts, among others [18]. As an example of a shifting disciplinary culture in astronomy, the Astronomy & Astrophysics Decadal Survey – which establishes consensual priorities for the next decade of astronomical research in United States – included a panel on the "State of the Profession and Societal Impacts" for the first time since the survey's inception sixty years ago [19]. This panel issued a variety of recommendations in alignment with the broader astronomy community's "inclusion revolution" [20, 21], including a call for democratizing science through enhanced data access [22]. Nevertheless, the discipline itself is structurally and geographically organized around historically elite institutions and hubs of influence. The work of Chang & Huang [2] illuminates the distribution of astronomy research resources internationally, finding that network centrality is important for institutions, while resource-rich institutions are especially influential in the international collaboration network. However, the authors also find that institutional research resources do not necessarily lead to preferential collaboration, and that institutions tend to prefer partnering with neighboring countries. Taken together, these findings point to a complex global ecosystem of localized affordances, cultures, and practices in which institutional access to research resources does not inherently determine success.

This paper adopts Santoro Lamelas and Belli's [1] definition of a global "scientific digital divide", attributed to marginalized access to research resources such as literature, computational tools, and publishing opportunities. Similarly, Arunachalam [23] explains that scientists in developing countries tend to be sidelined by the high cost of journals and databases, biases in peer review, and difficulty accessing literature including pre-print archives due to poor Internet connectivity. Over time, these challenges have severely impacted scientific work globally [24, 25], and despite technological and organizational advances the same challenges may persist to some extent for practicing scientists throughout the world. It is a key motivation of the open science movement to address information access disparities [26, 27], and academics across disciplines now enjoy more options for locating and sharing data and other information resources through public online databases [28, 29]. Much exploration has been conducted into the different ways contemporary scientists seek and utilize data [30–34] and scholarly literature [35, 36]. However, researchers of journal publication patterns have revealed alarming effects of national wealth on research attention and success [37–42], indicating that the international context is an important consideration for scientific information behavior research, data studies and inclusivity initiatives.

3 Methodology and Research Questions

An online survey of corresponding authors of astronomy journal articles was conducted between May and June 2019, with 211 recorded responses [10, 11]. The survey focused on understanding the characteristics and accessibility of astronomical data used and generated throughout the research processes corresponding to a sample of individual published journal articles. Survey responses provided insight into information processes in relation to specific papers and authors. A high number of respondents indicated non-U.S. nationalities (n = 86), and a total of 27 countries are represented, as shown in Fig. 1 and Table 1.

The survey has been repurposed through the present study as a preliminary investigation into potential indicators of international astronomers' information seeking and access needs and satisfaction of those needs. Variables captured by the survey that are informative about these dynamics include 1) whether the respondent utilized new observational data that they collected or collaborated in collecting to produce the sampled paper; 2) whether the respondent utilized data that they discovered through a published journal article to produce the sampled paper; and 3) whether the respondent participated

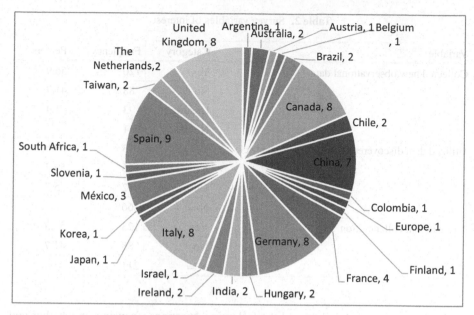

Fig. 1. Nationalities of non-U.S. survey respondents

Table 1. Nationalities of respondents (U.S. versus non-U.S.)

Variable	Category	Frequency	Percent
Nationality	United States citizen	117	55.7
	Not a United States citizen	86	41.0
	Prefer not to respond	7	3.3
	N =	210	

in international collaboration to author the sampled paper (measured through institutional affiliation recorded in Web of Science bibliographic records). These variables and descriptive statistics are shown in Table 2.

The study considers the possibility that research progress may be impeded by limited access to important informational research resources (operationalized here as observational data and literature access) for researchers from less privileged countries (measured using Gross Domestic Product based on purchasing power parity (GDP (PPP)) of respondents' nations). Such constraints may also lead to increased international collaboration for the purpose of accessing astronomical data and gaining publishing advantages and research attention. Per capita GDP (PPP) of respondents' nations in 2017 was recorded where it was possible to ascertain this information from survey responses (n = 200 total; n = 76 for non-US respondents). GDP was retrieved from https://www.worldometers.info/gdp/gdp-per-capita/.

Table 2. Survey variables of interest

Variable	Category	Frequency	Percent
Collected new observational data	Yes	120	56.9
	No	88	41.7
	Unsure	3	1.4
	N =	211	
Utilized data discovered through a journal article	Yes	73	34.6
	No	126	59.7
	Unsure	12	5.7
	N =	166	
International collaboration	Yes	123	58.3
	No	88	41.7
	N =	211	

Analysis was structured around the following questions, focusing on whether and how astronomers from less privileged countries mitigate barriers to their information needs through collaboration:

- RQ1: Do astronomers from less wealthy countries engage more in international collaboration?
- RQ2: Does international collaboration lead to increased research attention for astronomers from less wealthy countries?
- RQ3: Do astronomers from less wealthy countries experience reduced access to secondary data discovered via published scholarly literature?

Survey data was analyzed using R, and results are presented and discussed below. For this exploratory analysis with repurposed questionnaire data, simple bivariate tests were conducted including Spearman's rho for ordinal variables and Pearson r for interval variables [43]. Statistical significance was determined at a .05 alpha level.

4   Results

4.1   RQ1: GDP and International Collaboration

Spearman's rank correlation coefficients were calculated to assess the relationships between GDP (PPP) and international collaboration, and between international collaboration and whether original observational data were utilized for the sampled journal article. There is a significant negative correlation between GDP (PPP) of respondent and international collaboration ($r(198) = -.30$, $p = .000$). This result is interpreted as a potential indicator that researchers from higher-GDP countries engage less in international collaboration. At the same time, utilizing original observational data – which would occur in this context through telescope usage - correlates positively with international collaboration (r(206) = .19, p = .006). Taken together, the results provide some support for the notion that astronomers from less privileged countries may collaborate internationally to gain access to telescope data. On the other hand, given that many telescopes are international facilities, the latter finding alone is not compelling.

4.2 RQ2: International Collaboration and Research Attention

Research attention was operationalized as Normalized Citation Impact (NCI), which is calculated as the ratio of actual (c) to expected (e) citations for a particular discipline at a particular time (t) since paper publication:

$$NCI = \frac{c}{e_t}$$

Pearson correlation coefficients were calculated to assess the linear relationship between NCI and GDP (PPP). Among respondents who did not collaborate internationally, there is a significant positive relationship between log normalized NCI and GDP (PPP) of the respondent's nation (r(69) = .347, p = .003); this effect does not exist within the group of astronomers who do collaborate internationally (r(90) = .056, p = .593). These findings may indicate that astronomers from lower-GDP countries can be more highly cited by collaborating internationally, while those who are unable to collaborate may be more susceptible to the financial stability of their nations in terms of research attention. Future work should examine the collaborations in more detail to further understand the role of GDP in international collaboration and in relation to research attention.

4.3 RQ3: GDP and Access to Secondary Data via the Scholarly Literature

Spearman's rank correlation coefficient was calculated to assess the relationship between GDP (PPP) and whether the respondent utilized secondary data discovered through the literature, and a significant relationship was not found (r (197) = .00, p = .981). This does not support the notion that international astronomers may experience reduced access to the scholarly literature, at least for the purpose of locating data. Considering astronomy's widespread use of preprint databases and the openly available Astrophysics Data System (ADS) index of literature, the result is not surprising.

5 Discussion and Conclusions

This preliminary study has investigated a potential "scientific digital divide" in astronomy by utilizing a questionnaire that was collected for another purpose. As a result of this repurposing of a research instrument, a robust set of variables to address the research questions was not available. However, through exploratory analysis of survey respondents' national GDP, observational data collection behavior, engagement in international collaboration, and literature use, this analysis points to potential information seeking and access challenges for researchers in lower-GDP countries in the international context of astronomy. First, international collaboration appears to be more common for survey respondents from lower-GDP countries. Meanwhile, collecting original telescope data seems to be more common where international collaboration occurs. The results also suggest that if an astronomer does not collaborate internationally, GDP could impact the number of citations a paper receives. Finally, respondents from lower GDP countries do not appear to use the scholarly literature as a gateway to locate data for reuse less frequently, which suggests functional access to the literature for the purpose of finding data.

The exploratory findings presented here suggest that international collaborative networks may provide key affordances for gaining access to valuable research tools, data, and information to mitigate disparities. Individual and institutional networks in astronomy are complex and structured around the unique facilities that astronomers require, as shown by Chang & Huang [2] and McCray [12]. Considering astronomy's relative technological wealth as a discipline and its reputation for information and data democratization and openness (as discussed in the Introduction), potential information-related disparities are likely to be present to a greater degree in other less privileged and less well-networked disciplines and contexts than astronomy. This topic represents an area for further research and for development of targeted information and library services internationally, where facilitating enhanced collaboration and resource sharing opportunities across the sciences could help to mitigate effects of reduced access.

Furthermore, the international context is an important area for further work in information science and information behavior research. Recent academic discourse has highlighted relevant barriers with respect to scholarly literature access and output [44, 45] and visibility of scholarship [46, 47]. At the same time, the information science community has acknowledged substantial challenges associated with international studies [48]. Future qualitative and quantitative research should consider these perspectives and build upon related efforts to further uncover academic information seeking, access and collaboration dynamics specifically related to the international "scientific digital divide". For example, while Santoro Lamelas and Belli [1] focus their work on Latin America, broader explorations of unmet information needs of researchers globally from an information science perspective would be beneficial. Possible questions to guide such work may include: a) What are the similarities and differences across disciplines and research contexts, and are there opportunities for tools, infrastructures and other mitigation strategies that span disciplines and nations? b) What are the mechanisms through which researchers across disciplines establish connections internationally to acquire information needed for success? c) What are the roles of social media, conferences, societies, and other scholarly communication channels in brokering these connections? and d) What roles should libraries and international librarianship communities play? A larger-scale and focused study would be ideal for these questions, and for developing a more nuanced and informed theoretical framework to better understand this unique information seeking context.

Acknowledgements. I gratefully acknowledge Attila Varga for methodological advice and assistance with calculating Normalized Citation Impact. I am also thankful to the survey respondents for sharing their insights, and to the reviewers for providing helpful suggestions to clarify the manuscript.

References

1. Santoro Lamelas, V.S., Belli, S.: Comunicación digital en las prácticas científicas: Limitaciones y posibilidades para la equidad. Revista Prisma Soc. 316–332 (2018)
2. Chang, H.-W., Huang, M.-H.: The effects of research resources on international collaboration in the astronomy community. J. Am. Soc. Inf. Sci. **67**, 2489–2510 (2016). https://doi.org/10.1002/asi.23592
3. McCray, W.P.: Large telescopes and the moral economy of recent astronomy. Soc Stud Sci. **30**, 685–711 (2000). https://doi.org/10.1177/030631200030005002
4. McCray, W.P.: How astronomers digitized the sky. Technol. Cult. **55**, 908–944 (2014)
5. Ellis, D.: Modeling the information-seeking patterns of academic researchers: a grounded theory approach. Libr. Q. **63**, 469–486 (1993). https://doi.org/10.1086/602622
6. Talja, S.: Information sharing in academic communities: types and levels of collaboration in information seeking and use. New Rev. Inf. Behav. Res. **3**, 143–159 (2003)
7. Haines, L.L., Light, J., O'Malley, D., Delwiche, F.A.: Information-seeking behavior of basic science researchers: implications for library services. J. Med. Libr. Assoc. **98**, 73–81 (2010). https://doi.org/10.3163/1536-5050.98.1.019
8. Haeussler, C.: Information-sharing in academia and the industry: a comparative study. Res. Policy **40**, 105–122 (2011). https://doi.org/10.1016/j.respol.2010.08.007
9. Gordon, I.D., Meindl, P., White, M., Szigeti, K.: Information seeking behaviors, attitudes, and choices of academic chemists. Sci. Technol. Libr. **37**, 130–151 (2018). https://doi.org/10.1080/0194262X.2018.1445063
10. Stahlman, G.R.: Exploring the long tail of astronomy: a mixed-methods approach to searching for dark data (2020). https://www.proquest.com/docview/2435763825/abstract/8BE120032D894021PQ/1
11. Stahlman, G.: Evaluating the (in)accessibility of data behind papers in astronomy (2022). http://arxiv.org/abs/2209.04543
12. McCray, W.P.: Giant Telescopes: Astronomical Ambition and the Promise of Technology. Harvard University Press, Harvard (2006)
13. Bell, G., Hey, T., Szalay, A.: Beyond the data deluge. Science **323**, 1297–1298 (2009). https://doi.org/10.1126/science.1170411
14. Borgman, C.L., Wofford, M.F.: From data processes to data products: knowledge infrastructures in astronomy. Harvard Data Sci. Rev. **3** (2021). https://doi.org/10.1162/99608f92.4e792052
15. Forbes, D.A.: So you want to be a professional astronomer! (2008). http://arxiv.org/abs/0805.2624
16. Henneken, E.A., et al.: E-prints and journal articles in astronomy: a productive co-existence. Learn. Publish. **20**, 16–22 (2007). https://doi.org/10.1087/095315107779490661
17. Sahu, H.K., Nath Singh, S.: Information seeking behaviour of astronomy/astrophysics scientists. ASLIB Proc. **65**, 109–142 (2013). https://doi.org/10.1108/00012531311313961
18. American Finance Association: DEI in Academia: A Literature Review - Academic Female Finance Committee. https://afajof.org/affect/dei-in-academia/
19. National Academies: Pathways to discovery in astronomy and astrophysics for the 2020s. The National Academies Press (2021). https://nap.nationalacademies.org/catalog/26141/pathways-to-discovery-in-astronomy-and-astrophysics-for-the-2020s
20. Norman, D.J.: The inclusion revolution. Bulletin of the AAS **52** (2020)
21. Bauer, A.E., et al.: Petabytes to science (2019). http://arxiv.org/abs/1905.05116
22. Peek, J.E.G., et al.: Robust archives maximize scientific accessibility (2019). http://arxiv.org/abs/1907.06234

23. Arunachalam, S.: Information and knowledge in the age of electronic communication: a developing country perspective. J. Inf. Sci. 25, 465–476 (1999). https://doi.org/10.1177/016555159902500603

24. Newhall, T.: The global digital divide and its effect on women scientists worldwide. AWIS Mag. 29 (2000)

25. Cerdeira, H., Cottrell, R.L.A., Fonda, C., Canessa, E.: Developing countries and the global science web. https://cerncourier.com/a/developing-countries-and-the-global-science-web/

26. Ahmed, A.: Open access towards bridging the digital divide–policies and strategies for developing countries. Inf. Technol. Dev. 13, 337–361 (2007)

27. Belli, S., Cardenas, R., Vélez Falconí, M., Rivera, A., Santoro Lamelas, V.: Open science and open access, a scientific practice for sharing knowledge, pp. 156–167 (2019)

28. Nosek, B.A., et al.: Promoting an open research culture. Science 348, 1422–1425 (2015). https://doi.org/10.1126/science.aab2374

29. Wilkinson, M.D., et al.: The FAIR guiding principles for scientific data management and stewardship. Sci Data. 3, 160018 (2016). https://doi.org/10.1038/sdata.2016.18

30. Tenopir, C., et al.: Data sharing by scientists: practices and perceptions. PLoS ONE 6, e21101 (2011). https://doi.org/10.1371/journal.pone.0021101

31. Bishop, B.W., Hank, C., Webster, J., Howard, R.: Scientists' data discovery and reuse behavior: (Meta)data fitness for use and the FAIR data principles. Proc. Assoc. Inf. Sci. Technol. 56, 21–31 (2019). https://doi.org/10.1002/pra2.4

32. Gregory, K., Groth, P., Cousijn, H., Scharnhorst, A., Wyatt, S.: Searching data: a review of observational data retrieval practices in selected disciplines. J. Am. Soc. Inf. Sci. 70, 419–432 (2019). https://doi.org/10.1002/asi.24165

33. Gregory, K.M., Cousijn, H., Groth, P., Scharnhorst, A., Wyatt, S.: Understanding data search as a socio-technical practice. J. Inf. Sci. 46, 459–475 (2020). https://doi.org/10.1177/0165551519837182

34. Gregory, K., Groth, P., Scharnhorst, A., Wyatt, S.: Lost or found? Discovering data needed for research. Harvard Data Sci. Rev. 2 (2020). https://doi.org/10.1162/99608f92.e38165eb

35. Nicholas, D., Huntington, P., Jamali, H.R., Watkinson, A.: The information seeking behaviour of the users of digital scholarly journals. Inf. Process. Manag. 42, 1345–1365 (2006). https://doi.org/10.1016/j.ipm.2006.02.001

36. Nicholas, D., Williams, P., Rowlands, I., Jamali, H.R.: Researchers' e-journal use and information seeking behaviour. J. Inf. Sci. 36, 494–516 (2010). https://doi.org/10.1177/0165551510371883

37. May, R.M.: The scientific wealth of nations. Science 275, 793–796 (1997)

38. Salager-Meyer, F.: Scientific publishing in developing countries: challenges for the future. J. Engl. Acad. Purp. 7, 121–132 (2008). https://doi.org/10.1016/j.jeap.2008.03.009

39. Miranda, L.C.M., Lima, C.A.S.: On trends and rhythms in scientific and technological knowledge evolution: a quantitative analysis. Int. J. Technol. Intell. Plan. 6, 76–109 (2010). https://doi.org/10.1504/IJTIP.2010.033925

40. Bornmann, L., Stefaner, M., de Moya Anegón, F., Mutz, R.: What is the effect of country-specific characteristics on the research performance of scientific institutions? Using multi-level statistical models to rank and map universities and research-focused institutions worldwide. J. Informet. 8, 581–593 (2014). https://doi.org/10.1016/j.joi.2014.04.008

41. Harzing, A.-W., Giroud, A.: The competitive advantage of nations: an application to academia. J. Informet. 8, 29–42 (2014). https://doi.org/10.1016/j.joi.2013.10.007

42. Smith, M.J., Weinberger, C., Bruna, E.M., Allesina, S.: The scientific impact of nations: journal placement and citation performance. PLoS ONE 9, e109195 (2014). https://doi.org/10.1371/journal.pone.0109195

43. Nardi, P.M.: Doing Survey Research: A Guide to Quantitative Methods. Routledge, New York (2018)

44. Ford, A., Alemneh, D.: Scholars experiencing epistemic injustice due to management of scholarly outputs. Proc. Assoc. Inf. Sci. Technol. **59**, 67–75 (2022). https://doi.org/10.1002/pra2.605

45. Nguyen, B.X.: The effects of collaborative country and discipline on an international research collaboration indicator: the case of the United States. Proc. Assoc. Inf. Sci. Technol. **59**, 767–769 (2022). https://doi.org/10.1002/pra2.720

46. Islam, M., Howlader, A.I., Roy, P.: Google scholar metrics: assessing LIS researchers' scholarship in a developing country. Proc. Assoc. Inf. Sci. Technol. **59**, 712–714 (2022). https://doi.org/10.1002/pra2.699

47. Obinyan, O.O., Tella, A.: Nigerian LIS academic and scholarly publishing experience: challenges and the way forward. Proc. Assoc. Inf. Sci. Technol. **59**, 235–241 (2022). https://doi.org/10.1002/pra2.619

48. Matusiak, K.K., Bright, K., Colón-Aguirre, M., Schachter, D., Tammaro, A.M., VanScoy, A.: Re-imagining international research: challenges and approaches. Proc. Assoc. Inf. Sci. Technol. **59**, 583–587 (2022). https://doi.org/10.1002/pra2.632

Digital Information Infrastructures

The Conceptualization of Digital Inclusion in Government Policy: A Qualitative Content Analysis

Kaitlin Wiley and Anne Goulding

Victoria University of Wellington, Wellington, New Zealand
anne.goulding@vuw.ac.nz

Abstract. Governments globally are committed to closing the gap between citizens who are digitally engaged and those who are not. Digital inclusion is a government policy response aimed at addressing factors associated with digital inequities. States across the globe have developed digital inclusion policies and strategies to try to reduce inequalities within their societies but there is little research that conceptualizes digital inclusion policy at an inter-country level. This study examines how digital inclusion is represented within the government policies of five different jurisdictions. The five digital inclusion policies were coded and analyzed through qualitative content analysis. Deductive and inductive coding identified five main areas of concern across the policies: core pillars of digital inclusion; goals of digital inclusion policies; groups targeted by digital inclusion policies; drivers of digital inclusion policies; and responsibility for change. Within these, the evidence suggests that government policies are concerned mainly with access and attitudes and there is an emphasis on skills development in the workplace and throughout the education system. Collaboration and partnerships between governments and commercial partners are positioned as fundamental to achieving change and supporting the digital inclusion of those currently disengaged.

Keywords: Digital inclusion · Government policy · Qualitative content analysis · Digital equity · Digital inclusion policy

1 Introduction

For many of us, the COVID-19 pandemic meant that our lives became mainly online. Working and studying from home became the norm, our interactions with services such as health and financial services were carried out through digital technology, and even our leisure activities and socializing with friends and family became virtual. People with good access to digital devices and connectivity and appropriate skills were able to adjust to this new way of life but COVID-19 also revealed the extent of inequities in access to digital technologies and connectivity [1]. While interventions to tackle digital inequality had been widespread before the pandemic, governments around the world took additional actions to address shortfalls in access to devices and internet connections when the impact of COVID-19 and the preventative measures to address it became evident. In

I. Sserwanga et al. (Eds.): iConference 2023, LNCS 13972, pp. 527–543, 2023.
https://doi.org/10.1007/978-3-031-28032-0_40

Aotearoa New Zealand, for example, the Ministry of Education installed copper, fiber and satellite connections in areas where there were many unconnected homes, worked with internet service providers to remove data caps, and distributed devices to school students who lacked one [2]. These initiatives, and other similar activities internationally, can be considered the continuation of a long-standing drive by governments to improve digital capability and support digital inclusion.

Governments play a prominent role in supporting digital inclusion. As public administrations at all levels undergo digital transformation and deliver more and more information and services to citizens via the internet [3], they have a responsibility and vested interest in ensuring that people are able to access and use digital services. More generally, there is a clear link between digital access and the ability of individuals to actively participate in society and fulfil essential needs [4], so much so that digital skills and access have been identified as basic human rights [5]. In response, governments around the world have adopted digital inclusion policies and strategies to try to address inequalities in engagement with digital technologies within their populations [6]. Although the phenomenon of digital inclusion has become a strong focus for many governments and has held the attention of researchers globally for around three decades [7], there is a lack of studies that analyze the overarching themes across multiple digital inclusion approaches. This gap indicates the lack of a solid understanding about what drives digital inclusion policy, limiting our ability to identify what makes policies successful and inhibiting the dissemination of effective practice from an inter-country perspective. To address this and guided by Helsper's [6] conceptualization of digital inclusion, this research investigated the focus of government digital inclusion policies across five different jurisdictions through qualitative content analysis, guided by the following research question:

RQ: How is digital inclusion conceptualized in government policy?

Within this broad research question, the objectives of the research were to:

- Define the core pillars of each country's digital inclusion policy.
- Understand what drives digital inclusion policies.
- Determine the goals of digital inclusion policies.
- Identify whether any specific groups within society are targeted by digital inclusion policies.
- Assess how governments propose to support change through strategies and initiatives that promote digital inclusion.

The findings of the analysis will provide a better understanding of how digital inclusion is understood and governed across different countries, highlighting common themes and differences with the aim of providing insight into the key drivers, strategies and priorities for digital inclusion internationally.

2 Literature Review

While information and communication technologies are now an integral part of many people's lives around the globe, there are those who do not have the resources, ability or motivation to go online. Originally termed the "digital divide" [8], newer terms such as digital inclusion, digital equality and digital equity are now used to try to disrupt deficit discourses that position non-users as a problem to be fixed [9], with researchers focusing increasingly on what it means for societies to be digitally inclusive [10]. Digital inclusion is perceived as more than just being able to access the internet but also covers concepts of use and skills that facilitate successful integration into society [11]. Many researchers have aimed to create frameworks that encapsulate the aspects considered most impactful on digital inclusion. Although they have different titles, the meanings behind the most influential frameworks have many similarities. For example, Bradbrook and Fisher's 5 C's focus on connectivity, capability, content, confidence and continuity [12], whereas others highlight just four main elements, e.g. van Dijk's usage, digital skills, physical/material access and motivation [13]. Helsper, whose framework incorporates use, access, skills and attitudes, developed these further to include subcategories that segment these overarching themes, creating a richer understanding of the concepts [6]:

- Use – or digital engagement.

  - Nature of engagement: the range of ways people use technologies.
  - Extent of engagement: the time people spend using different ICTs.

- Access – where and how people use ICTs.

  - Location: where a person has access to the internet.
  - Quality: broadband, wireless or dial-up access.
  - Platforms: media richness or variety of platforms available.

- Skills – the ability to use ICTs.

  - Transferable skills – general skills that allow people to participate in a digital context.
  - Self-efficacy – a person's evaluation of their own ability to use ICTs.

- Attitudes – ideas about the usefulness and dangers of ICTs.

  - General ICTs attitudes – a person's evaluation of the impact of ICTs on themselves or society.
  - Regulation – a person's evaluation of the opportunities and risks of digital engagement.
  - Importance of ICTs – a person's evaluation of the importance of ICTs to their everyday life.

Another feature of the literature in this area is a focus on how minority and disadvantaged groups engage with technology [4], thus combining social inclusion with digital inclusion. Factors such as race, gender, education and age have been identified as influential determinants of digital inclusion [14] with many researchers agreeing that access and use are no longer the main concerns and that external socio-economic influences better define digital inclusion [15–17]. Nevertheless, there is still a place in the literature for considering how factors like access and use affect how citizens from underserved groups are able or unable to engage and participate within today's information society [7] and to what extent they become digitally excluded as a result of prior inequities [18]. By refocusing digital inclusion to consider its linkages with social inclusion, the role of government policy in addressing digital inequalities assumes greater importance [19]. Digital inclusion policies thus become a mechanism to address the digital divide [10].

Governments around the world have developed policies and strategies that aim to limit inequality in digital engagement as way of addressing wider societal inequalities, therefore. Digital inclusion initiatives have focused on improving physical access, digital skills and attitudes towards ICTs [16]. Moreover, as the consequences of low digital engagement were highlighted and became a driver for government intervention, digital inclusion research on government policies became abundant with a focus on outcomes, effectiveness and possible future focus of digital policies and initiatives [18, 20, 21]. Analyses of the outcomes and impact of government digital inclusion initiatives is limited in the academic literature although there is evidence of some success of initiatives aimed at specific groups such as SeniorNet in Aotearoa New Zealand [22] and digital skills courses for older people in Europe [23]. Government initiatives aimed at ensuring widespread access to overcome first level divides are also common, e.g. NBN (National Broadband Network) in Australia [24] or infrastructure investments in Korea [25], and are generally considered to have been successful [21, 26].

To summarize, previous research has identified that vulnerable and disadvantaged groups are more likely to be negatively impacted by lack of access to digital technologies, exacerbating their social exclusion [21]. Analyses have identified many factors, including age, income and education that may cause individuals to be digitally excluded [27]. Government policy and digital inclusion are closely interlinked as the primary purpose of government policy in this area is to overcome exclusion caused by the digital divide [28]. There is, however, a lack of research into how digital inclusion is governed through policy and how digital inclusion is conceptualized and enacted. This research aimed to address this gap by highlighting similarities and differences across countries' digital inclusion policies and exploring how key drivers of digital inclusion are prioritized and conceptualized.

3   Methodology

The research adopted qualitative content analysis (QCA) as the most appropriate strategy for identifying key concepts within documents [29] and for presenting a holistic and factual description of phenomena [30]. Research that uses QCA differs from other forms of documentary analysis because it focuses on understanding the language used alongside the contextual meaning within which it sits [31]. Hecker et al.'s study of citizen science policies from a range of countries demonstrated the effectiveness of QCA for analyzing policy documents as well as its use within an emerging field and it was felt that the approach would be similarly effective in a study of digital inclusion policies [29]. In this research, QCA enabled a comparative analysis of policies and initiatives through a grouping of common themes between documents [32]. It facilitated a deductive approach while also allowing for the emergence of additional themes through inductive analysis. Helsper's [6] framework guided the deductive coding through the application of the categories and sub-categories of the conceptualization of digital inclusion detailed in Sect. 2. Additional codes emerged from the analysis inductively.

Within QCA, the choice of sampling strategy is important because it relies heavily on the researcher's judgement as they must be sure that their collection of documents will provide the knowledge sought [33]. Purposive sampling is the most common strategy used and includes considering factors such as unit of analysis [34]. While this gives some freedom to the researcher to decide the form, nature and extent of the sample, the decisions made about the sample must be explained to ensure trustworthiness [35]. For this research, the selection was restricted to government policy on digital inclusion with the following criteria:

- Countries with a government published policy or section of their digital strategy that directly relates to and promotes digital inclusion as the focal point.
- There must be enough available information on the strategy to ensure analysis is viable, i.e. well-saturated data sources [36].
- Strategies are available in English (limitation set by the researcher).
- Open access via the internet.

The policies that met these criteria were: Aotearoa New Zealand[1]; Australia[2]; UK[3]; Scotland[4]; Wales[5]. Digital policies from other countries were considered but were removed when it was found that they did not have sections specifically targeting digital inclusion. Note that while there is a strategy covering the whole of the UK, Scotland and Wales have devolved governing bodies to develop strategies targeted to their specific needs and have developed policies that feature distinct elements representative of their contexts.

Specifying the unit of analysis and coding processes within QCA ensures transparency and reliability [37]. The unit of analysis refers to how the document will be fragmented. This should be large enough to be considered a saturated source but small enough to be focused closely on the research questions [32]. Government policy layout and content differ significantly making it difficult to compare. Because of this, analysis included only main sections within policies which had a clear and direct relationship to digital inclusion or digital skills. Helsper's conceptualization of digital inclusion was used as the foundation framework for the analysis due to its focus on understanding the

---

[1] https://www.digital.govt.nz/assets/Documents/113Digital-Inclusion-BlueprintTe-Mahere-mo-te-Whakaurunga-Matihiko.pdf.

[2] https://www.industry.gov.au/sites/default/files/2018-12/australias-tech-future.pdf.

[3] https://www.gov.uk/government/publications/uk-digital-strategy/uk-digital-strategy.

[4] https://www.gov.scot/binaries/content/documents/govscot/publications/strategy-plan/2021/03/a-changing-nation-how-scotland-will-thrive-in-A-digital-world/documents/a-changing-nation-pdf-version/a-changing-nation-pdf-version/govscot%3Adocument/DigiStrategy.FINAL.APR21.pdf?forceDownload=true.

[5] https://gov.wales/sites/default/files/pdf-versions/2022/3/4/1646322827/digital-strategy-wales.pdf.

links between social disadvantage and digital exclusion and Helsper's comments on the implications of these links for policy [6]. It was decided that Helsper's framework had the closest relationship to public policy of the different frameworks considered and so the policies were coded using the key themes of: use, access, attitudes and skills.

A coding frame was developed using concept-driven codes developed deductively, and relating to the research objectives:

- Core pillars of digital inclusion: use, access, attitudes, and skills.
- Motivators behind digital inclusion.
- Drivers of change.
- Types of initiatives.
- Groups impacted by digital inclusion

Within QCA the most common approach to coding is to combine deductive and inductive practices [32] and that was the approach taken for this research. As well as the deductive concept-driven codes listed above, inductive data-driven codes were also developed. To establish these, any ideas that did not fit into the concept-driven codes were grouped into similar themes during the initial reading, assigned a name and included in the code book from where they were applied to the texts during subsequent close readings. Eight main categories and 28 deductive sub-codes were derived deductively from previous literature. An additional three main categories and 37 sub-codes were derived inductively (see Figs. 1, 2, 3, 4 and 5).

As QCA has a high level of subjective interpretation, the reliability and validity of the method is often questioned [36]. To minimize the impact of this, inter-coder reliability was applied where the coding frame and relevant examples were reviewed by a third-party. It was established that the meanings did not overlap, that the examples were relevant to the codes, and that the codes were relevant to the body of literature and the research question and objectives.

4 Analysis

Returning to the objectives of the study, the analysis showed that the deductive codes related primarily to:

- Core pillars of digital inclusion.
- Groups impacted by digital inclusion.

The inductive codes facilitated a better understanding of how the following are represented within policy:

- Drivers behind digital inclusion.
- Goals of digital inclusion policies.
- Drivers of change relating to digital inclusion.
- Responsibility for driving change.
- Types of initiatives implemented to overcome digital inclusion.

The last three of these are considered together because, collectively, they are connected with how change occurs in the digital inclusion context. The remainder of this section will focus on selected findings of particular interest emerging from the analysis.

4.1 Core Pillars of Digital Inclusion

The *Core Pillars of Digital Inclusion* were framed across four main categories: use, access, attitudes and skills, all of which were concept-driven. All showed significant presence across the policies analyzed, with access being the most prominent. Figure 1 presents the four pillars and their sub-categories including those inductively derived from the data.

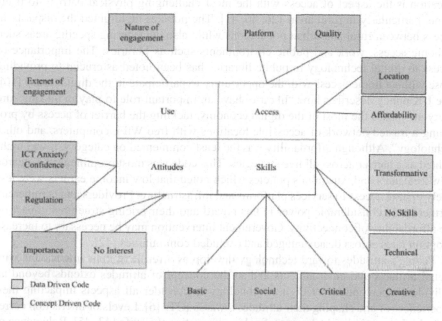

Fig. 1. Core pillars of digital inclusion

The core pillars of use, access, attitudes and skills were foundational in the development of the policies and were mentioned 368 times, almost double that of any other groupings of codes. In the policy documents, use was concerned with the extent of engagement and nature of engagement, defined in the digital inclusion discourse as the nature, way or content of engagements between an individual and technology [6, 38]. In this sample of documents, nature of engagement featured more prominently, discussing why individuals use ICTs, and defining their relationship, underlying needs and purpose of use. There was a strong focus on employment and the workplace, emphasising the digital nature of work and job opportunities. The Australian policy, for example, recognizes the importance of "creating a modern workforce that builds rewarding career paths", highlighting the increase in tech-related work and the comparatively low employment rates of women and older people in the sector. Similarly, the UK policy highlights the need for the workforce to be prepared for significant changes to skills required in the workplace, citing predictions that 90% of jobs will require elements of technical skills in 20 years' time. The other key focus of the nature of engagement was an individual's ability to participate fully in society through the use of online services. The Welsh policy emphasizes the importance of "managing household finances, shopping online, accessing public services and keeping in touch with loved ones".

Academic research has highlighted the need to move the focus of digital inclusion beyond access towards skills and use [39] but this study demonstrates that access remains at the core of government policy. Access is a foundational aspect of the first level divide and one of the most well-researched areas in the literature [7]. Access is a multifaceted phenomenon that encompasses factors of platform, location, quality and affordability. Location is the aspect of access with the most challenging physical barriers to overcome, particularly in rural areas [26, 40, 41]. The policies highlighted the disparity in access between rural and urban populations while also considering specific areas such as home access, work and public environments such as libraries. The importance of access to digital technology in public libraries has been noted as crucial to providing those without home access with the opportunity to participate in the digital space [10]. The UK policy describes how "libraries have an important role to play in making sure everyone makes the most of the digital economy, tackling the barrier of access by providing a trusted network of accessible locations with free WiFi, computers, and other technology". Although affordability was the least commented on category, it was highlighted as a barrier across all five strategies. This code was most prominent in Aotearoa New Zealand's and Australia's policies which noted that low income earners were less likely to have access to services platforms and infrastructure. Providers and commercial partners hold considerable power in this regard and their pricing structures impact on the affordability of connectivity. Government intervention may be necessary to increase adoption rates across disadvantaged and excluded communities [42].

People's attitudes toward technology develop as a result of their interactions with digital artifacts and environments and so the concept of attitudes extends beyond an individual's perceptions of digital technology to consider all aspects impacting their experiences of and shaping their attitudes towards ICTs [6]. Levels of interaction correlate with how an individual sees technology impacting their life [43–45]. Reluctance or lack of confidence with technology was reflected across the policies with the Welsh and UK policies highlighting confidence as the most influential factor, as noted by previous research [6, 12, 38]. The role of socio-economic factors and their impact on confidence and anxiety was also acknowledged.

Digital skills have been widely researched in relation to digital inclusion and are strongly related to the second level of the digital divide [6]. Basic and technical skills were most prominently discussed in the policies. The Welsh and Scottish policies link basic skills with confidence, indicating that supporting the development of basic skills would enable individual to participate and fulfil their essential needs online. Technical skills were defined as the ability to undertake work related tasks using technology, Both the Australian and UK policies had a strong workforce focus which drove the development of this inductive code.

Overall, all four pillars of digital inclusion were conceptualized within the policies but use and access were more prominent, no doubt due to their relationship with economic value [16, 46]. Use has been heavily researched [47] and in these policies was related closely to jobs and workplaces. Access continues to be a focal point of both academic research and policy on digital inclusion although the evidence suggests that the focus is shifting from locational access to quality, affordability and platforms, probably due to the implementation of broadband initiatives and diminishing location-based barriers [21, 26]. While research into skills and attitudes has developed [48], these pillars were highlighted less within the policies analyzed although it is recognized that they are linked and must be addressed to encourage excluded individuals to engage digitally.

4.2 Drivers of Digital Inclusion

Across *Drivers of Digital Inclusion* as presented in the documents, social inclusion and economic value were the only concept-drive codes with the other six data-driven codes derived inductively from the texts where they featured prominently as influencing the need for or development of digital inclusion strategies (Fig. 2).

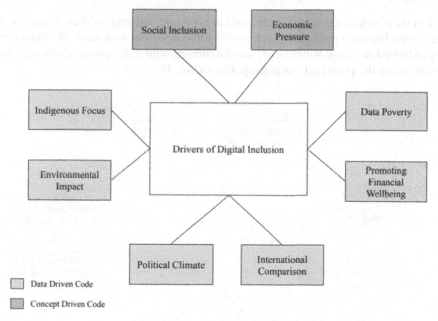

Fig. 2. Drivers of digital inclusion

Academic literature positions social inclusion as an influential driver behind digital inclusion policy and strategy [4] and the findings support this with social inclusion mentioned more than double the times of every other concept except for economic value. The Australian policy emphasizes the relationship, highlighting that, "exclusion from the digital world exacerbates any other form of social inclusion." Academic research also notes that a digitally inclusive society has a positive impact on economies [46] and this is picked up in Aotearoa New Zealand's policy that discusses the positive relationship between digital inclusion and economic value, estimating a $1 billion boost to the economy through support for digital inclusion. Thus, although social inclusion is the apparent foundational driver for the policies considered, the economic benefits of digital inclusion also feature strongly. Of the five policies, Aotearoa New Zealand's and Australia's were the only ones to mention the impact that an indigenous focus has on policy development with the former devoting a section to "Digital inclusion through a Māori lens" and the latter referencing the importance of developing culturally inclusive and appropriate technologies. Turning to environmental concerns, there is little academic research on the relationship between environmental impact and digital inclusion. Positive change can occur through developing infrastructure and platforms to address climate change although mass supply chains often result in overconsumption [49]. Scotland's policy was the only one to highlight this aspect, aiming to replace, reduce and streamline unnecessary digital infrastructure and practices, stating that digitally inclusive landscapes must also be environmentally conscious.

4.3 Digital Inclusion Policy Goals

Each of the policies established future goals or proposed outcomes of their strategies. As noted in the literature review, research on this topic is scarce. As a result, the main category of *Digital Inclusion Policy Goals* was data driven, with eight inductive subcategories encompassing the goals laid out in the policies (Fig. 3).

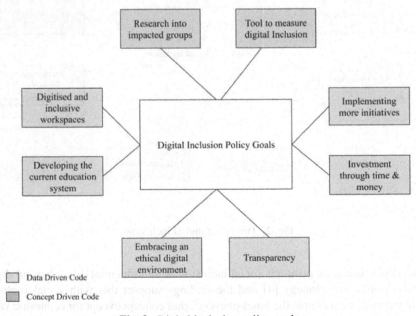

Fig. 3. Digital inclusion policy goals

The policies focused heavily on the goals they aimed to achieve through creating a more digitally inclusive environment. Creating a transformative education system is a goal commonly mentioned, most prominently in the UK and Australian policies. The policies outline goals to ensure that digital skills are a key part of education systems, taught at every level and promoting collaboration between schools and commercial partners to support their aims. Developing frameworks that support the upskilling of the workforce was another key goal across the policies. As noted, the UK and Australian policies focused heavily on the economic impact of digital inclusion and it is therefore unsurprising that they also discussed workplace initiatives to support this goal. For example, the Australian policy advocates supporting workers through the automation of workplaces, ensuring their skills are up to date and addressing shortages around technical skills. The need to upskill the current workforce is recognised in the literature [50] and acknowledged extensively in the policies analyzed.

How to assess success and the extent to which the goals outlined are achieved also features prominently in the policies. Goals around creating measurement tools and scaling up the number of initiatives and investment in digital inclusion were common across the policies, driven by the need to ensure that citizens can see how policies and funding are having a positive impact. This links to investment as the governments are keen to see a return on money committed to digital inclusion. Investment is defined broadly in the documents and includes money, time, effort and understanding, and the policies discuss priorities for future investment in this area. In Australia, for example, the need to invest in talent retention is discussed, recognizing that investing in digital skills training will keep more people economically active and create more job opportunities.

4.4 Groups Impacted by Digital Exclusion

The study of *Groups Impacted by Digital Exclusion* is an established research area and similarities in this regard were found across the policies analyzed. Some of the groups had been identified through the literature search and had deductive codes applied while others emerged from the coding process (Fig. 4). Previous literature has highlighted rural communities [26, 40, 41], women [14], seniors [51], children [19, 52], low socio-economic areas [10, 14, 53], and indigenous peoples [26, 54, 55] as disadvantaged groups in relation to digital technologies. The needs of small business, students and the unemployed are highlighted increasingly, though, due to widening disparities between those digitally included and excluded due to external factors such as COVID-19. The need to adapt and digitize quickly in response to crises such as the pandemic means that more and different groups are being prioritized as crises like this demonstrate the importance of digital inclusion [56]. The Australian policy highlights small businesses, specifically in relation to developing skills surrounding technologies, focusing on the negative impact on small businesses of a failure to develop and harness digital skills, as digitized environments become the norm throughout employment sectors. Alongside this, both the Australia and UK policies focus on students as an emerging group impacted by digital exclusion. The UK policy showcases this by discussing initiatives to ensure programmes and scholarships are put in place to give students the opportunity and accessibility to continually develop their digital skills, thus ensuring they will be able to participate and engage within evolving digital workplaces. Policy has also started to acknowledge unemployed people as disproportionally digitally excluded. In Australia, for example, the policy discusses how individuals risk becoming unemployed or underemployed if they lack the appropriate digital skills as technological change become inevitable.

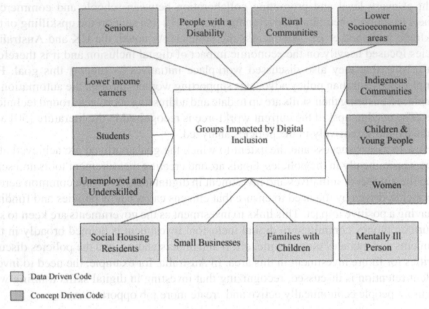

Fig. 4. Groups impacted by digital inclusion

4.5 How Change Occurs

Finally, the research aimed to understand how the policies represented a changing digital landscape and their representation of *How Change Occurs*. Four principal codes were developed inductively with the majority of sub-codes also developed inductively (Fig. 5).

The most common driver of change was collaboration, mentioned over three times more than any other code, acknowledging the need for governments to work with other groups to support digital inclusion. The groups mentioned included communities, businesses, libraries and charities, working with or alongside government to move policy into action that delivers results. This leads into consideration of who is responsible for driving digital inclusion. As expected, governments were mentioned most often but commercial partners were also highlighted as key players who bear a large degree of responsibility for employment, infrastructure, access and affordability. A range of initiatives were mentioned in the policies to demonstrate where and how change was occurring. Across all five policies, the initiatives noted focused on either the communities or groups impacted or the pillars of digital inclusion they aimed to address with access and skills being the most prominent. Skills-focused initiatives were most common and often directed at individuals with the aim of improving knowledge and providing support. Access initiatives, on the other hand, were primarily focused on improving the infrastructure for communities,

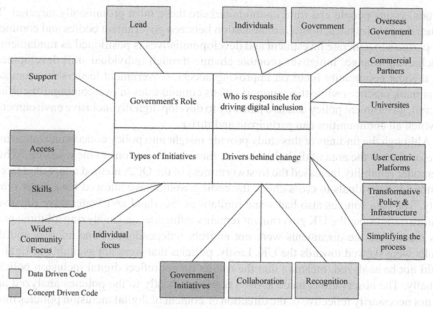

Fig. 5. How change occurs

through 4G roll-out, for example. Previous research suggests that community-targeted initiatives meet their intended outcomes more successfully that individual-focused initiatives [57], although now access is arguably less of an issue due to initiatives such as the NBN [24], the emphasis may shift to improve skills at an individual level with programs targeted at specific excluded groups.

The coding process identified the role of government as both supporter and leader of digital inclusion approaches. Support was mentioned twice as often as leadership, was prominent across all five policies analyzed and refers to how governments can communicate and be a key support system within the digital inclusion context by, for example, providing funding or other types of support to organizations promoting digital engagement. As leaders, governments across the globe are moving services online and must ensure that their processes, policies, content, and services are appropriate for a digitally inclusive environment.

5   Conclusion

In response to the research question guiding this study, digital inclusion is conceptualized within the government policies analyzed through five key facets: the core pillars; drivers of policy; goals; groups targeted; and drivers of change. Digital inclusion is most prominently characterised through its relationship to the core pillars and mainly concerned with the impact of access and attitudes. An emphasis on the need to address technological change in workplaces and education settings accentuates the relationship between digital inclusion and economic value and social inclusion. Action on social inclusion and economic value strongly underpin the development of the digital inclusion policies and women, young people and rural communities are those most prominently targeted. To ensure the policies are actioned, collaboration between government bodies and commercial partners to generate investment and develop initiatives is positioned as fundamental to achieving change. Initiatives promote change through individual skill development and a wider community focus on improving access. Government leadership promotes benchmark practices while their support assists communities in overcoming difficulties. Overall, government policy acts as a pathway to develop digitally inclusive environments in which all communities can participate and thrive.

Although the findings of this study provide insight into policy conceptualization and development in the area of digital inclusion, there are limitations to the research. While intercoder reliability increased the trustworthiness of the QCA method adopted, a larger number of individuals to cross-check the coding would have allowed for greater reliability. The data sources also had some limitations. Scotland and Wales have devolved administrations but the UK government remains influential and analyzing all three policies meant that the documents were not entirely independent of one another and the results were skewed towards the UK. Lastly, policies that were not available in English could not be analyzed, meaning that the results do not reflect digital inclusion policies globally. The observations made above relate specifically to the policies analyzed and are not necessarily reflective of the direction or content of digital inclusion policies more generally. The government policies analyzed were all from wealthy, developed, western nations and the priorities of governments in other regions or different profiles will no doubt diverge from those identified here.

Despite these limitations, this research contributes to our understanding of how digital inclusion is conceptualized in policy. Further research on how initiatives arising from policy positively impact individuals and communities would be valuable. Analysis of the extent to which the goals of the polices are achieved and, if so, which groups benefit most, would be a useful addition for scholars researching this area and policy implementation.

References

1. Nguyen, M.H., Hargittai, E., Marler, W.: Digital inequality in communication during a time of physical distancing: the case of COVID-19. Comput. Hum. Behav. **120**, 106717 (2021)
2. New Zealand Government, Tackling the digital divide during COVID-19. https://www.dig ital.govt.nz/showcase/tackling-the-digital-divide-during-covid-19/. Accessed 10 Sept 2022
3. Gong, Y., Yang, J., Shi, X.: Towards a comprehensive understanding of digital transformation in government: analysis of flexibility and enterprise architecture. Gov. Inf. Q, **37**(3), 101487 (2020)
4. Warschauer, M.: Technology and Social Inclusion: Rethinking the Digital Divide. MIT Press, Cambridge, MA (2004)
5. Economist Intelligence Unit Ltd: The inclusive internet index 2018. https://theinclusive internet.eiu.com/assets/external/downloads/3i-executive-summary.pdf/. Accessed 5 March 2022
6. Helsper, E.: Digital inclusion: an analysis of social disadvantage and the information society. Department for Communities and Local Government. http://eprints.lse.ac.uk/26938/. Accessed 15 Sept 2022

7. Adam, I.O., Alhassan, M.D.: Bridging the global digital divide through digital inclusion: the role of ICT access and ICT use. Transform. Govern. People, Process Policy **15**(4), 580–596 (2021)

8. Katz, J., Aspden, P.: Motivations for and barriers to Internet usage: results of a national public opinion survey. Internet Res. **7**(3), 170–188 (1997)

9. Honan, E.: Deficit discourses within the digital divide. English Aust. **41**(3), 36–43 (2006)

10. Jaeger, P.T., Bertot, J.C., Thompson, K.M., Katz, S.M., DeCoster, E.J.: The intersection of public policy and public access: digital divides, digital literacy, digital inclusion, and public libraries. Public Libr. Q. **31**(1), 1–20 (2012)

11. Crandall, M., Fisher, K.E.: Digital Inclusion: Measuring the Impact of Information and Community Technology. Information Today Inc, Medford, NJ (2009)

12. Bradbrook, G., Fisher, J.: Digital Equality: Reviewing Digital Inclusion Activity and Mapping the Way Forwards. CitizensOnline, London (2004)

13. van Dijk, J.A.: The Deepening Divide: Inequality in the Information Society. Sage Publications, New York, NY (2005)

14. Parsons, C., Hick, S.F.: Moving from the digital divide to digital inclusion. Curr. Scholarship Hum. Serv. **7**(2) (2008). https://journalhosting.ucalgary.ca/index.php/currents/article/view/15892. Accessed 15 Sept 2022

15. Codagnone, C. (ed): Vienna study on inclusive innovation for growth and cohesion: modelling and demonstrating the impact of e-inclusion. European Commission, Brussels, Belgium. https://air.unimi.it/bitstream/2434/171480/2/eco_report.pdf. Accessed 15 Sept 2022

16. Borg, K., Smith, L.: Digital inclusion and online behaviour: five typologies of Australian internet users. Behav. Inform. Technol. **37**(4), 367–380 (2018)

17. Kumar, R., Subramaniam, C., Zhao, K.: Special issue on digital inclusion. ISEB 1–4 (2021). https://doi.org/10.1007/s10257-021-00531-6

18. Klecun, E.: Bringing lost sheep into the fold: questioning the discourse of the digital divide. Inf. Technol. People **21**(3), 267–282 (2008)

19. Livingstone, S., Helsper, E.: Gradations in digital inclusion: children, young people and the digital divide. New Media Soc **9**(4), 671–696 (2007)

20. Aziz, A.: Digital inclusion challenges in Bangladesh: the case of the National ICT Policy. Contemp. South Asia **28**(3), 304–319 (2020)

21. Helsper, E.: The emergence of a digital underclass: digital policies in the UK and evidence for inclusion. LSE, London (2011). http://eprints.lse.ac.uk/38615/1/LSEMPPBrief3.pdf. Accessed 15 Sept 2022

22. Craig, B.: From digital divides to digital inclusion: promoting the benefits of participation in the digital world. In: 14th CIRN (Community Informatics Research Network) Prato Conference 2017, 25–27 October 2017@ Monash University Centre, Prato, Italy Special Stream: Art as Archive: Archive as Art & The Imagined Archive, p. 49 (2017)

23. Blažič, B.J., Blažič, A.J.: Overcoming the digital divide with a modern approach to learning digital skills for the elderly adults. Educ. Inf. Technol. **25**(1), 259–279 (2019). https://doi.org/10.1007/s10639-019-09961-9

24. Walton, P., Kop, T., Spriggs, D., Fitzgerald, B.: A digital inclusion: empowering all Australians. J. Telecommun. Dig. Econ. **1**(1), [9–1]–[9–17] (2013)

25. Curran, N.M.: A reflection on South Korea's broadband success. Media Cult. Soc. **41**(3), 385–396 (2019)

26. Grimes, A., White, D.: Digital inclusion and wellbeing in New Zealand. Available at SSRN 3492833 (2019)

27. van Deursen, A.J., van Dijk, J.A.: Internet skills and the digital divide. New Media Soc. **13**(6), 893–911 (2011)

28. Hache, A., Cullen, J.: ICT and youth at risk: how ICT-driven initiatives can contribute to their socio-economic inclusion and how to measure it. Luxembourg (Luxembourg), Publications Office of the European Union (2010). https://publications.jrc.ec.europa.eu/repository/handle/JRC58427. Accessed 15 Sept 2022

29. Hecker, S., Wicke, N., Haklay, M., Bonn, A.: How does policy conceptualise citizen science? A qualitative content analysis of international policy documents. Citizen Sci. Theory Practice 4(1), 32 (2019)

30. Eriksson, P., Kovalainen, A.: Qualitative Methods in Business Research, 2nd edn. SAGE Publications, London (2016)

31. Hsieh, H.F., Shannon, S.E.: Three approaches to qualitative content analysis. Qual. Health Res. 15(9), 1277–1288 (2005)

32. Elo, S., Kyngäs, H.: The qualitative content analysis process. J. Adv. Nurs. 62(1), 107–115 (2008)

33. Etikan, I., Musa, S.A., Alkassim, R.S.: Comparison of convenience sampling and purposive sampling. Am. J. Theor. Appl. Stat. 5(1), 1–4 (2016)

34. Cho, J.Y., Lee, E.H.: Reducing confusion about grounded theory and qualitative content analysis: similarities and differences. Qual. Rep. 19(32) (2014)

35. Creswell, J.W.: Research Design: Qualitative, Quantitative, and Mixed Methods Approaches, 4th edn. SAGE Publications, London (2014)

36. Elo, S., Kääriäinen, M., Kanste, O., Pölkki, T., Utriainen, K., Kyngäs, H.: Qualitative content analysis: a focus on trustworthiness. SAGE Open 4(1) (2014)

37. Mayring, P.: Qualitative content analysis: theoretical foundation, basic procedures and software solution. Klagenfurt (2014). https://nbn-resolving.org/urn:nbn:de:0168-ssoar-395173. Accessed 15 Sept 2022

38. van Dijk, J.A.G.M.: The evolution of the digital divide: The digital divide turns to inequality of skills and usage. In: Bus, J., Crompton, M., Hildebrandt, M., Metakides, G. (eds.) Digital enlightenment yearbook, 2012, pp. 57–75. IOS Press, Amsterdam (2012)

39. Hargittai, E.: Second-level digital divide: mapping differences in people's online skills. arXiv preprint cs/0109068 (2001)

40. Townsend, L., Sathiaseelan, A., Fairhurst, G., Wallace, C.: Enhanced broadband access as a solution to the social and economic problems of the rural digital divide. Local Econ. 28(6), 580–595 (2013)

41. Marshall, A., Dezuanni, M., Burgess, J., Thomas, J., Wilson, C.K.: Australian farmers left behind in the digital economy–insights from the Australian Digital Inclusion Index. J Rural Stud 80, 195–210 (2020)

42. Glass, V., Stefanova, S.K.: An empirical study of broadband diffusion in rural America. J. Regul. Econ. 38(1), 70–85 (2010)

43. Harris, R.W.: Attitudes towards end-user computing: a structural equation model. Behav. Inf. Technol. 18(2), 109–125 (1999)

44. Durndell, A., Haag, Z.: Computer self efficacy, computer anxiety, attitudes towards the internet and reported experience with the internet, by gender, in an East European sample. Comput. Hum. Behav. 18(5), 521–536 (2002)

45. Yang, B., Lester, D.: Liaw's scales to measure attitudes toward computers and the internet. Percept Motor Skill 97(2), 384–394 (2003)

46. Broadbent, R., Papadopoulos, T.: Bridging the digital divide – an Australian story. Behav. Inf. Technol. 32(1), 4–13 (2011)

47. Cushman, M., McLean, R.: Exclusion, inclusion and changing the face of information systems research. Inf. Technol. People. 21(3), 213–221 (2008)

48. Díaz Andrade, A., Techatassanasoontorn, A.A.: Digital enforcement: rethinking the pursuit of a digitally-enabled society. Inf. Syst. J. 31(1), 184–197 (2021)

49. Souter, D.: ICTs, the internet and sustainability: a discussion paper. International Institute for Sustainable Development. http://citeseerx.ist.psu.edu/viewdoc/download?doi=10.1.1.362.8336&rep=rep1&type=pdf#page=57. Accessed 15 Sept 2022

50. Peinado, I., de Lera, E., Usero, J., Clark, C., Treviranus, J., Vanderheiden, G.: Digital inclusion at the workplace post Covid19. In: Proceedings of the 13th International Joint Conference on Computational Intelligence - SmartWork (2021). https://doi.org/10.5220/0010722900003063. Accessed 15 Sept 2022

51. Lips, M., Eppel, E., Craig, B., Struthers, S.: Understanding, explaining, and self-evaluating digital inclusion and exclusion among senior citizens. Victoria University of Wellington (2020). https://www.wgtn.ac.nz/__data/assets/pdf_file/0009/1866672/2020-digital-inclusion-among-senior-citizens.pdf. Accessed 15 Sept 2022

52. Hartnett, M., Fields, A.: Digital inclusion in New Zealand. J. Open Flexible Distance Learn. **23**(2), 1 (2019)

53. Blank, G., Lutz, C.: Benefits and harms from internet use: a differentiated analysis of Great Britain. New Media Soc. **20**(2), 618–640 (2018)

54. Carew, M., Green, J., Kral, I., Nordlinger, R., Singer, R.: Getting in touch: language and digital inclusion in Australian indigenous communities. Lang. Document. Conserv. **9**, 307–323 (2015)

55. McMahon, R.: From digital divides to the first mile: Indigenous peoples and the network society in Canada. Int. J. Commun. **8**, 25 (2014)

56. Reisdorf, B., Rhinesmith, C.: Digital Inclusion as a Core Component of Social Inclusion. Soc. Incl. **8**(2), 132–137 (2020)

57. Greenfield, E.A., Oberlink, M., Scharlach, A.E., Neal, M.B., Stafford, P.B.: Age-Friendly Community Initiatives: conceptual Issues and Key Questions. Gerontologist **55**(2), 191–198 (2015)

Dublin Core Metadata Created by Kuwaiti Students: Exploration of Quality in Context

Saleh Aljalahmah[1] and Oksana L. Zavalina[2]

[1] Basic Education College, The Public Authority for Applied Education and Training (PAAET),
Adailiyah, Kuwait
sh.aljalahmah@paaet.edu.kw
[2] College of Information, University of North Texas, Denton, TX 76203, USA
oksana.zavalina@unt.edu

Abstract. Metadata education is evolving in the Arabian Gulf region. To ensure the effective instruction and skill-building, empirical data is needed on the outcomes of these early metadata instruction efforts. This paper is the first one to address this need and provide such data from one of the countries in the region. It reports results of the examination of metadata records for Arabic-language eBooks. The records were created by novice metadata creators as part of the undergraduate coursework at a Kuwaiti university in one of the classroom assignments over three semesters. Analysis focused on two important criteria of metadata quality: accuracy and completeness. The results are presented in-context, after introducing the metadata teaching practices at this undergraduate program, and the major Dublin Core skill-building assignment. Discussion of results is followed by discussion of future research.

Keywords: Metadata evaluation · Metadata instruction · Dublin core · Kuwait

1 Introduction and Brief Review of Relevant Literature

In Western countries, since the emergence (in early 2000s) and rapid development of digital library initiatives, libraries are interested in hiring employees who are not only proficient in Machine Readable Cataloging standard (MARC) but also have a working knowledge of non-MARC metadata standards used in digital collections: mainly Dublin Core. To respond to this demand, courses that focus on digital library metadata are now taught in most of the library degree programs. These academic programs also often include basic non-MARC metadata content in other existing relevant courses beyond the metadata-focused ones.

In the Middle East, the situation is different. Despite strong digital library developments in the past decade, these are largely happening at the national libraries and major academic libraries, with most other libraries not participating yet. Many libraries only engage in traditional MARC cataloging and some still rely on card catalogs to provide access to their collections. With much weaker employers' demand for digital library metadata skills, the librarianship degree programs do not consistently offer specialized metadata courses.

Traditional library cataloging courses have been offered to students in the Arabian Gulf countries since late 1980s or 1990s. Regional universities are taking different approaches with library cataloging courses: many of them focus on card cataloging, while providing students with training in the machine-readable cataloging using MARC standard is less common. Several studies looked at cataloging education in some of the Middle East countries (e.g., [1, 2, 5, 8–11]). One of them [5] comparatively analyzed cataloging course offerings at 11 universities in Egypt. Reported findings of existing studies however do not allow to conclude that digital library metadata is covered in cataloging education.

In the Arabian Gulf countries, development of digital repositories has been ongoing since 2012, yet only one study so far analyzed the quality of metadata in a digital repository [3]. Likewise, there is a gap in literature on metadata education in the region. The only reports on metadata education in Arabian Gulf were published either before the creation of the first digital libraries there ([8, 9]) or soon after [2]. Thus, the existing reports could not capture the reflection of these then very recent developments in the education domain. While reports focusing on Oman and Saudi Arabia ([2, 8, 9]) exist, no studies have been published about education of metadata creators in the other 4 countries in the region. This includes Kuwait where until recently, digital library metadata courses were rarely offered – mostly because of the shortage of qualified instructors and lack of Arabic-language academic materials to support such teaching. However, new faculty of Kuwaiti library schools do have the necessary preparation and are starting to address this gap.

Although metadata courses are taught in the librarianship degree programs in the Western countries for the last 20 years or so, there is only one published report on the quality of student-created metadata. That study [12] examined – with the focus on accuracy, completeness, and consistency criteria of metadata quality   DCTERMS Dublin Core metadata records created by the United States university's graduate students to represent born-digital textual works. No studies so far have examined the quality of student-created metadata that uses the most widely applied in the world simple version of Dublin Core: Metadata Element Set 1.1.

In this paper, we provide a brief overview of the metadata instruction in the librarianship undergraduate program at a Kuwaiti university (including the required core course and a new specialized elective course), report results of the analysis of accuracy and completeness of student-created metadata records, and discuss the implications for improving the outcomes of this instruction in relation to the preparedness of this program graduates to provide access to resources in digital repositories by creating high-quality Dublin Core metadata.

2 Metadata Instruction Overview

At the Basic Education College of The Public Authority for Applied Education and Training (PAAET), the undergraduate specialized metadata course was offered occasionally between 2018 and 2020, whenever the institution had a qualified instructor available.

Since the summer of 2021, when a new faculty member trained in metadata at the United States' Masters' and Ph.D. programs joined the PAAET faculty, the undergraduate metadata course developed by this professor – the first author of this paper – is offered to students in the librarianship degree program every semester. This is an elective course that students usually take in their third academic year. To enroll in it, students must pass a prerequisite – a core course that introduces basic concepts of cataloging, subject headings, thesauri, and other controlled vocabularies, and MARC cataloging. At the end of that prerequisite course, students also receive a brief introduction to metadata beyond the traditional library cataloging and are encouraged to take the metadata-focused elective.

Students in the core course usually complete exercises that include creating bibliographic records for information resources, as well as finding controlled vocabulary terms (subject headings) for the list of given work titles.

In the elective metadata course, students learn about digital library metadata in the context of the history of cataloging. The new Arabic-language textbook written by the course instructor and published in 2021 has been used as a required reading since the beginning of 2021–2022 academic year. The textbook introduces students to metadata concepts, practices, and standards. Students learn about Dublin Core standard (both simple and qualified), MARC and MODS (Metadata Object Description Schema). However, the bulk of this course content focuses on the simple Dublin Core (DCMES 1.1). In the required face-to-face class meetings held twice a week in long semesters and 4 times a week in summer semesters, all students are provided with the detailed description of each of the 15 metadata fields in the DCMES 1.1 standard over the course of 6–8 class meetings.

Likewise, the practical assignments of the specialized metadata course focus on the DCMES 1.1 standard. After several in-class non-graded practice exercises, and a graded group assignment, students work individually on the written assignment (roughly equivalent to a midterm exam) in which they are allowed to use their notes and textbook in creating a DCMES 1.1 metadata record for an Arabic-language eBook in a PDF document accessible online. The assigned eBook for this assessment changes every semester and is different from the one in the team project. Students are instructed to use controlled vocabularies – introduced in the course textbook – for two metadata fields: Language and Type. Because of the limited availability of non-subscription-based Arabic-language interfaces for searching controlled vocabularies for names and subjects, students are instructed to simply invert the names in Creator and/or Contributor fields the way this is done in major standard name authority files and to provide at least 3 free-text keywords in the Subject field. In the end-of-semester oral exam which covers the entire range of course topics, some of the questions focus on Dublin Core.

3   Method: Evaluation of Student-Created Metadata

In this study, we chose as evaluation target the DCMES 1.1 metadata records representing eBooks. These records were created as part of the open-book written exam-like assignment (described above) as this allows to evaluate the skill-building outcomes of the metadata course most meaningfully. The data were collected from three semesters of 2021–2022 academic year: Fall, Spring, and Summer. The students had the same experiences in class meetings, learning materials, and exercises leading to this test-like assignment, as well as in the way the test was administered. However, in Fall 2021, students completed some of their non-graded practice exercises online due to Covid-19-related restrictions. Almost 90% of students who took this course so far are females. To exclude the possibility of gender-related effect on the quality of student work, only the submissions from female students were selected for analysis, with a total of 137 metadata records. The data was collected unobtrusively, and students were not aware that the quality of their records is examined for purposes other than grading.

The questions we sought to answer were:

1. How accurate are the metadata records created by students in the PAAET specialized undergraduate metadata course?
2. How complete are the metadata records by students in the PAAET specialized undergraduate metadata course?
3. What are the patterns of application of DCMES 1.1 metadata fields in student-created records?
   a. In which metadata fields do students make accuracy errors more often or less often? What types of accuracy errors are observed?
   b. In which metadata fields do students make completeness errors more often or less often? What types of completeness errors are observed?

The study utilized a quantitative comparative content analysis method. The data was analyzed using a version of the tool (a spreadsheet) that was developed and tested in the DCTERMS metadata analysis [12]. For this study, it was adjusted for DCMES 1.1 simpler version of Dublin Core https://www.dublincore.org/specifications/dublin-core/dces/ which includes 15 metadata elements: Coverage, Creator, Contributor, Date, Description, Format, Identifier, Language, Publisher, Relation, Rights, Source, Subject, and Type. The analysis instrument was also adjusted for the choice of metadata quality criteria as this study focused on the two of the three major criteria of metadata quality: accuracy and completeness defined by Bruce and Hillmann [4] and used in multiple studies of metadata quality. Because the application of controlled vocabularies in this undergraduate course is limited as described above, and because each student creates a single DCMES 1.1 record, evaluation of metadata consistency – the third major criterion of metadata quality – was outside of the scope of our research project.

4 Results and Discussion

In the 137 records analyzed, a total of 519 errors were found: 413 accuracy errors (an average of 3.01 per record) and 106 completeness errors (an average of 0.77 per record). The errors were found in 25% of the total instances of metadata fields in the dataset. Most of them were accuracy errors (appeared in 20% of all field instances in student-created records). Completeness errors were found in 5% of all field instances.

Out of 413 accuracy errors, 342 were the situations when the student included wrong data value in a field (for example, used the publisher's name in the Source field, or the

Creator field for translator's name that belongs to Contributor field). In 71 cases, the data was formatted incorrectly. The examples included creator or contributor name parts not inverted as explained above, using the term instead of the code in the Language field, etc.

Among the 106 completeness errors, in 32 cases students left the applicable field empty. In 74 remaining cases, the entered data value was insufficient. Typically, a student only provided 2 terms in Subject field when instructed to include at least 3, or the Description field had too short of a data value that did not adequately represent the resource. The latter included unfinished sentences (e.g., *"This book is ..."* in the Description field).

The distribution of metadata errors by field is shown in Fig. 1. Five DCMES 1.1 metadata fields most prone to metadata quality issues of any kind were Rights, Format, Contributor, and Source, with 30% or more of student records containing mistakes in these fields. Previous research on Dublin Core metadata quality suggests the vague definition of Source metadata element causes a high level of errors in this field, and disambiguation between Creator and Contributor roles might be tricky for novice metadata creators. However, the finding that the Format element was one of the most error-prone, is unexpected.

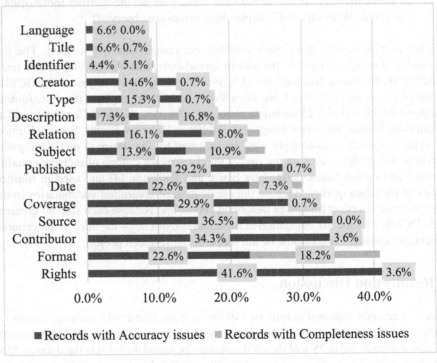

Fig. 1. Distribution of metadata quality errors among 15 DCMES 1.1 metadata fields

Analysis revealed metadata fields with lowest and highest levels of accuracy and completeness errors. Accuracy errors were observed the most often in Rights (41.6% of all metadata records analyzed), Source (36.5%), Contributor (34.3%) and Coverage (29.9%) metadata fields. On the other hand, the fields with the lowest level of accuracy errors were Identifier, Language, Title, and Description. The following metadata fields contained the highest number of completeness errors: Format (18% of all metadata records analyzed), Description (16%), Subject (10%), and Relation (8%). The lowest level of completeness errors was detected in Language, Source, Coverage, Type, Publisher, Creator and Title.

No published reports exist so far that examine the DCMES 1.1 student-created records to offer direct comparisons to the findings of this study. However, since both DCMES 1.1 and DCTERMS are versions of Dublin Core, results of this study can and should be compared to available results of DCTERMS student-created metadata evaluation. The prevalence of accuracy errors over completeness errors discovered in this study of eBook DCMES 1.1 Arabic-language metadata records created by Kuwaiti undergraduate students is similar to overall findings of the examination of metadata quality in DCTERMS records created by the US graduate students enrolled in the introductory metadata course to represent digital text resources (conference proceedings papers, journal articles, etc.) [12].

Similar patterns were observed in the two studies in question regarding some of the most error-prone Dublin Core metadata fields. Rights and Format fields exhibited errors in almost 46% and 41% of student-created records respectively in this study. This is very similar to almost 44% and over 38% respectively observed for these two fields in Zavalina & Burke's study [12]. Both studies also found that Title field presents the least difficulty to beginning metadata creators as evidenced by the fewest number of completeness or accuracy errors in this field. However, substantial differences were observed too. The DCMES 1.1 Creator field was one of the fields with the fewer errors in the records created by Kuwaiti undergraduate metadata students (15% of records) while in the previous DCTERMS student-created records analysis, Creator was one the metadata fields that contained a high level of quality problems (45.2%). It is worth noting here though that most of these kinds of mistakes were categorized as consistency (mainly controlled vocabulary application) errors in the previous US-student-created DCTERMS metadata study and this metadata quality criterion was not used in the present study focusing on DCMES 1.1 student-created metadata quality in Kuwait.

5   Conclusions, Limitations, and Future Research

This study provides the first benchmark assessment of student-created Dublin Core metadata using an Arabian Gulf country data. These findings allow to make informed decisions regarding the areas that need enhancement in teaching metadata in the region. For example, the prevalence of accuracy issues some of which seem to stem from confusion of the definitions of Dublin Core metadata elements points to the need to revise the course materials to place more emphasis on metadata accuracy, and to provide students with examples of common Dublin Core metadata accuracy errors made by beginning metadata creators.

This exploratory study has some limitations that might affect generalizability of its results to diverse types of information resources represented by metadata and to broader population of metadata students in the region. This study focused on eBooks DCMES 1.1 metadata created by female undergraduate students, so it is possible that the outcomes might be somewhat different for graduate students of both genders, for resource types other than eBooks, and/or for other metadata schemes that define metadata elements in a more specific and straightforward way than Dublin Core.

To address these limitations, future studies are needed that will examine the metadata for different types of information resources such as video recordings, audio recordings, images, etc. Also, future research should include different widely used metadata standards beyond Dublin Core: MARC 21 or MODS. The studies that compare the metadata instruction and metadata-creation related outcomes of this instruction between two or more universities from different countries in and outside the Arabian Gulf region would help develop better understanding of the best practices and future directions.

Comprehensive examination of digital library metadata curriculum in Kuwait and other Arabian Gulf countries, similar to the studies of cataloging education in Egypt by Hady and Shaker [5] and in North America by Joudrey and McGinnis [7] and Hudon [6], is needed. Specifically, as the use of controlled vocabularies is vital for access to information by providing collocation and disambiguation of search results, we believe that investigations of the use of cataloging tools (e.g., Arabic-language subject headings, as well as regional name authority files and genre authority files) in teaching metadata and cataloging courses in the Middle East are essential. Also, the implementation of FAIR principles (https://www.go-fair.org/fair-principles/) that aim to optimize the reuse of data with the help of findable, accessible, interoperable, and reusable metadata, in Arabic databases is an important topic for future exploration.

References

1. Al Hijji, K.Z.: Cataloguing and classification education in Gulf Cooperation Council (GCC) countries. Catalog. Classific. Quar. 50(4), 276–292 (2012). https://doi.org/10.1080/01639374.2011.653873
2. Al Hijji, K.Z., Fadlallah, O.S.: Theory versus practice in cataloging education in Oman: students' perspectives. Catalog. Classific. Quar. 51(8), 929–944 (2013). https://doi.org/10.1080/01639374.2013.832456
3. Aljalahmah, S., Zavalina, O.L.: A case study of information representation in a Kuwaiti archive. Presentation at the iConference 2021. http://hdl.handle.net/2142/109683
4. Bruce, T.R., Hillman, D.I.: The continuum of metadata quality: defining, expressing, exploiting. In: Hillman, D., Westbrook, L. (eds.) Metadata in Practice, pp. 238–256. American Library Association, Chicago (2004)
5. Hady, M.F.A., Shaker, A.K.: Cataloging and classification education in Egypt: stressing the fundamentals while moving toward automated applications. Catalog. Classific. Quar. 43(3/4), 407–429 (2006). https://doi.org/10.1300/J104v41n03_11
6. Hudon, M.: The status of knowledge organization in library and information science master's programs. Catalog. Classific. Quar. 52(5), 506–550 (2021). https://doi.org/10.1080/01639374.2021.1934766
7. Joudrey, D., McGinnis, R.: Graduate education for information organization, cataloging, and metadata. Catalog. Classific. Quar. 59(6), 576–596 (2014). https://doi.org/10.1080/01639374.2014.911236

8. Khurshid, Z.: Preparing catalogers for the electronic environment: an analysis of cataloging and related courses in the Arabian Gulf region. J. Educ. Library Inform. Sci. **39**(1), 2–13 (1998). https://www.jstor.org/stable/40324175

9. Khurshid, Z.: Continuing education for catalogers in Saudi Arabia. Catalog. Classific. Quar. **43**(3/4), 461–470 (2006). https://doi.org/10.1300/J104v41n03_14

10. Kokabi, M.: An account of cataloging and classification education in Iranian universities. Catalog. Classific. Quar. **43**(3/4), 431–441 (2006). https://doi.org/10.1300/J104v41n03_12

11. Shoham, S.: Cataloging instruction in Israel. Catalog. Classific. Quar. **43**(3/4), 443–460 (2006). https://doi.org/10.1300/J104v41n03_13

12. Zavalina, O.L., Burke, M.: Assessing skill building in metadata instruction: quality evaluation of Dublin Core metadata records created by graduate students. J. Educ. Libr. Inf. Sci. **62**(4), 423–442 (2021). https://doi.org/10.3138/jelis.62-4-2020-0083

Trustworthy Digital Repository Certification: A Longitudinal Study

Devan Ray Donaldson[✉][iD] and Samuel Vodicka Russell[iD]

Indiana University, Bloomington, USA
drdonald@indiana.edu

Abstract. Increasingly, government policies are directing federal agencies to make the results of federally funded scientific research publicly available in data repositories. Additionally, academic journal policies are progressively recommending that researchers deposit the data upon which they base their articles in repositories to ensure their long-term preservation and access. Unfortunately, having the necessary technical, legal, financial, and organizational resources for digital preservation is a significant challenge for some repositories. Repositories that become certified as Trustworthy Digital Repositories (TDRs) demonstrate to their stakeholders (e.g., users, funders) that an authoritative third party has evaluated them and verified their trustworthiness. To understand the impact of certification on repositories' infrastructure, processes, and services, we analyzed a sample of publicly available TDR audit reports (n = 175) from the Data Seal of Approval (DSA) and Core Trust Seal (CTS) certification programs. This first longitudinal study of TDR certification over a ten-year period (from 2010 to 2020) found that many repositories either maintain a relatively high standard of trustworthiness in terms of their compliance with guidelines in DSA or CTS standards or improve their trustworthiness by raising their compliance levels with these guidelines each time they get recertified. Although preparing for audit and certification adds to repository staff's dockets of responsibilities, our study suggests that certification can be beneficial. Therefore, we advocate for more specific policies that encourage certification and the use of TDRs.

Keywords: Trustworthy Digital Repositories · Certification · Core Trust Seal

1 Introduction

Increasingly, government policies are directing federal agencies to make the results of federally funded scientific research publicly available in repositories that provide stewardship and access to data without charge while also requiring researchers to better account for and manage these data [11,13,19,20]. Additionally, whether data result from federally funded research or not, academic journal policies are progressively recommending that researchers deposit the data upon

I. Sserwanga et al. (Eds.): iConference 2023, LNCS 13972, pp. 552–562, 2023.
https://doi.org/10.1007/978-3-031-28032-0_42

which they base their articles in repositories to ensure their long-term preservation and access [3,7,25]. Unfortunately, having the necessary technical, legal, financial, and organizational resources for digital preservation is a significant challenge for some repositories [1]. Repositories that become certified as Trustworthy Digital Repositories (TDRs), "demonstrate to both their users and their funders that an independent authority has evaluated them and endorsed their trustworthiness" [5].

To understand the impact of certification on repositories' infrastructure, processes, and services, we analyzed a sample of TDR audit reports from the Data Seal of Approval (DSA) and Core Trust Seal (CTS) TDR certification programs, as they represent the most widely adopted certification programs worldwide, and they make their audit reports publicly available in English. This first longitudinal study of TDR certification over a ten-year period (from 2010 to 2020) found that many repositories either maintain a relatively high standard of trustworthiness in terms of their compliance with guidelines in DSA and CTS standards or improve their trustworthiness by raising their compliance levels with these guidelines each time they get recertified. Although preparing for audit and certification adds to repository staff's dockets of responsibilities, our study suggests that certification can be beneficial. Therefore, we advocate for more specific policies that encourage certification and the use of TDRs.

Although there are currently over 2,400 scientific data repositories covering a broad range of disciplines [22], only a few hundred are certified as TDRs. Some suggest that presently there are not enough policies in place that require certification and use of TDRs to close this gap [16]. While some government policies and academic journal policies require or recommend that researchers make data publicly available [13,19,23], few of these mention TDR standards, certification, and the use of TDRs specifically (c.f., [3]). This is important because data sharing infrastructure networks such as the Common Language Resources and Technology Infrastructure (known as CLARIN), the Consortium of European Social Science Data Archives (CESSDA), and the European Research Infrastructure Consortium for the Arts and Humanities (known as DARIAH) all provide evidence of the power of policy to drive increases in certification as becoming a TDR is a prerequisite for inclusion in and financial support from these networks, and consequently TDR standards such as the Core Trust Seal (CTS) have seen recent increases in applications from repositories, archives, and data centers that wish to join these networks [17].

Besides the benefits of membership in data sharing infrastructure networks and complying with government and academic journal data policies, prior research has explored the benefits that repositories seek via certification. These include: stakeholder confidence, where repositories' funders, the people who deposit data in repositories, and those who use those data will be more confident in repositories' protection and management of the data because they are certified as TDRs; improvements in processes, where conducting self-assessment and audit stimulates repositories to improve their processes and procedures and move to a higher level of professionalism, with an incentive to improve their operations over time; and transparency, where certification is designed to provide an open statement of repositories' evidence enabling anyone to evaluate repositories' operations and policies [8,9,17]. In contrast, studying the long-term benefits of certification including recertification may prove useful for spurring more repositories to become certified and provoking the development of more policies that require certification and the use of TDRs.

2   Methods

To assess the impact of certification on TDRs, we analyzed 175 audit reports of 127 repositories, 36 of whom got recertified either once or twice. The repositories span five continents and over 26 countries. We selected these repositories because they were certified by the Data Seal of Approval (DSA) and/or its successor, the CTS, the two most widely adopted TDR standards. Both certification programs require a self-audit report that is later reviewed and approved by the standards' representatives. Each audit report describes a repository's level of compliance with a set of 16 guidelines covering a repository's background information, organisational infrastructure (e.g., mission, licenses, continuity of access, sustainability, confidentiality/ethics, skills and guidance), digital object management (e.g., integrity, authenticity, appraisal, storage, preservation, quality, workflows, discovery, identifiers, re-use) and technology (e.g., technical infrastructure and security). We processed all of these documents as a dataset to obtain findings for the measurement of document similarity between recertifications, and to compute term frequency-inverse document frequency (TF-IDF) weights for keyword and topic discovery. Because our focus was on the effects of recertification, we compared the audit reports of all repositories that got recertified, examining the following features: changes in cumulative compliance scores; the number of recertifications; document similarity; and vocabulary terms added and deleted from successive documents.

2.1   Study Design

The purpose of this study was to detect and interpret the significance of changes between chronologically subsequent documents belonging to particular data repositories and their improvement or maintenance of compliance to TDR standards. Natural language processing and topic modeling techniques were employed for two reasons. First, to establish whether changes in documents reflected changes in repositories' overall level of compliance. Second, to extract information, represented as topics (i.e., vectors of tokens), about what changes were being implemented by these repositories.

2.2   Nature of Corpus

The corpus is the entire set of self-assessment audit documents from the DSA and CTS certification programs as of October 2020. All the documents in the corpus follow the same format of a numerical score and narrative description of a repository's compliance with each of the 16 guidelines. Although both have 16 scored sections, the guidelines for the earlier DSA and more recent CTS certification programs differ in the thematic arrangement of subtopics per section.

The changes in document structure over time led us to pursue methods that would facilitate topic discovery and document similarity comparison on the basis of a "document" being defined as each audit report. However, our acquisition and preprocessing of the dataset allowed us to retain reference to the section-by-section text and numerical scores of each document to facilitate the discovery of clusters of topics that demonstrate different rates of change and stability across the 2–4–year intervals between recertifications.

The size of the corpus was relatively small (n = 175) though each document contained at least 1,000 words.

2.3   Data Acquisition

Audit reports were obtained from two sources. First, we acquired all DSA and early CTS audit reports from a MySQL database archived and made accessible in DANS EASY [6]. Second, we acquired more recent CTS audit reports from the list of certified repositories on the CTS website [4].

We migrated and extracted the audit reports and their metadata from both sources into a file-based SQLite database that would serve as inputs for analysis. Our database [10] includes the section-by-section text and numerical scores of each repository's audit reports, along with information used to identify repositories.

To arrive at our sample, we filtered raw data based on three criteria. First, to only include audit reports that had both a numerical score and a response text entry for each of the guidelines. Second, we de-duplicated the audit reports so that each repository had either zero or one audit report for each certification period. Third, to identify the subset of repositories that recertified either once or twice between 2010 and 2020, we ran queries on our database.

2.4   Models and Data Analysis Techniques (Feature Selection)

To process and analyze the data derived from raw text, we used multiple techniques: rule-based systems for text-preprocessing; a pre-trained vector space model for word embedding to compute document similarity comparisons; term-frequency inverse document-frequency (TF-IDF) to refine token collections; and latent Dirichlet allocation (LDA) to produce a topic model.

We used the Python NLP library SpaCy [14] to provide a suitable word vector model and utilities for preprocessing. We used the large English language model package [24] obtained from SpaCy's pre-trained model download script. This model package implements methods for part-of-speech parsing, named entity recognition, and lemmatization based on a convolutional neural net trained on

OntoNotes 5.0 dataset. Also included in this package is the Common Crawl-trained GloVe word vector model which we used to analyze document content quantitatively.

The baselines of average improvement and/or maintenance of compliance for comparison against the results of our topic analysis were established by obtaining descriptive statistics for the sum of the compliance level scores (ranging from 0 to 4) reported for each section within each TDR audit report. We also found the slope of the least-squares linear regression for these cumulative compliance level scores for repositories that recertified at least once.

To quantitatively compare document text and to prepare the dataset for topic modeling, we used Python scripts to read the document string data from the SQLite database into the SpaCy language processing pipeline. To quantify the degree of differences between documents, we computed similarity scores, which represent cosine similarity, obtained by finding the Euclidean distance of the L2 vector norm applied to the dot product of each document's tokens. We also created lists of uniquely added and removed terms for all cases of recertification by finding the set difference of the lemmatized form of sets composed of each token from the earlier and later documents. These lists were combined with contextual information identifying the repository, the report, the token's vector norm, document similarity, cumulative score, etc. to aggregate the relevant tabular data in a single flat file.

After constructing our comprehensive table of document changes, we created histograms to visualize the extent to which changes in content reflect changes in TDRs' cumulative compliance level scores.

2.5   Topic Discovery Techniques

In addition to cumulative score and document similarity, we examined whether these changes coincided with topics discussed in the documents. We used part-of-speech, regular expressions, and other rule-based utilities provided by Python and SpaCy to filter out "noisy" tokens.

We also used the Python libraries Matplotlib [15] and SciKit-Learn [21] to visualize word distances of terms frequently added or removed from the documents. We used the Principal Component Analysis (PCA) algorithm supplied by SciKit-Learn to decompose the representative 300-element word vector of each term into a 2-dimensional point, along with the k-means clustering algorithm provided by SciKit-Learn to examine how the terms group together. To select input values for PCA, we sorted the list of words by their TF-IDF weight into three categories: highly specific terms (high-weight); an intermediate group; and broadly general terms (low-weight). For these TF-IDF categories, we selected the 20 most frequently occurring terms. We then used the LDA model from SciKit-Learn to generate a representation of changes in document content derived directly from our corpus.

The parameters required for LDA include: number of topics; number of passes and iterations to be performed; and the alpha and beta parameters for expected topic-document density and topic-word density [2, 12]. Because we did not have any prior expectations about the topic-document density and topic-word density, we used the default arguments of 1/number of topics (n = 8) for the priors. Sentences associated with terms that changed were loaded into a sparse matrix and transformed by the LDA model into a distribution of topics represented in the sentence. We selected the top three proportionally most representative topics for each sentence. For both groups–terms classified by PCA and k-means, and terms classified by LDA–we found the mean rate of change in cumulative compliance score by referencing the rows in our document changes table that contained those tokens. We also used the terms changed data as an aid for finding examples of improvements as demonstrated by text added and text deleted for a repository whose cumulative compliance level score significantly improved after recertification.

3   Findings

3.1   Cumulative Compliance Scores

Analysis of descriptive statistics for the TDRs' compliance level scores shows that repositories that recertify commonly report both increases, and to a lesser extent decreases in their compliance, with the mode amount of change being +2.5. Performing a least-squares linear regression on the scores of repositories that recertify shows a slope of 0.08, bearing a slightly positive trend (see Fig. 1). We observed a ceiling effect where most of the TDRs' cumulative compliance scores cluster near 64, the top of the graph and the maximum cumulative compliance level for these TDRs (see Fig. 2). Additionally, analysis of the data along the x-axis demonstrates that most of the repositories' scores change minimally, that is, no more than a gain or loss of five points between certifications.

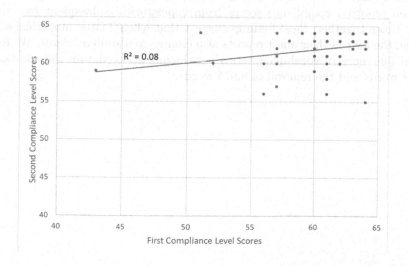

Fig. 1. Changes in TDRs' compliance level scores.

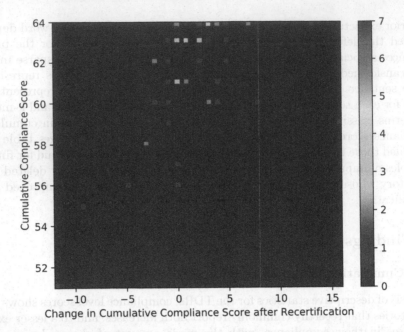

Fig. 2. Changes in compliance with TDR standards. This heatmap shows changes in repositories' compliance with TDR standards each time they recertify. The colors reflect how many repositories had similar compliance level score changes (n = 36).

3.2 Document Similarity Comparisons

As shown in Fig. 3, we found a correlation between the document similarity comparisons obtained with word vector modeling and the amount of change observed between reported compliance scores from repositories' subsequent recertifications. Taken together, these findings suggest that when TDRs' numerical scores change, the text in their audit reports also change to a similar degree. We found the set difference of vocabulary terms per document to contain the addition of 36,328 words and the removal of 8,675 words.

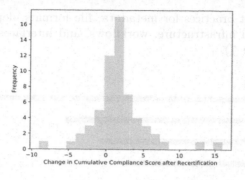

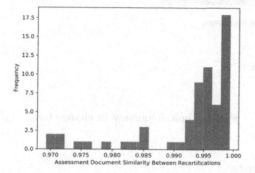

Fig. 3. Histograms comparing TDRs' audit reports. These comparisons consider consecutive recertification (e.g., comparing 2010 certification to 2014 recertification or 2014 certification to 2017 recertification) and non-consecutive recertification (e.g., comparing 2010 certification to 2017 recertification) for repositories that got recertified twice between 2010 and 2020 (n = 36). The top histogram compares cumulative compliance level scores of repositories showing that repositories' change in score based on recertification typically ranges from −2 to +4, with a tail extending to both extremes (from 0 to +16). The bottom histogram compares document similarity of audit reports from consecutive and non-consecutive recertifications showing a concentration around a small degree of difference with a tail extending towards 0, which contains both negative and positive extremes of the difference in scores between certifications (from 0.96 to 0.99).

3.3 Topic Modeling

As shown in Fig. 4, the results of transforming passages of changed text with a topic model show that most of the changes to audit reports when repositories recertified correspond to five of our topics: governance, organizational networks and expertise (Topic 3); fitness-for-use of data by researcher communities (Topic 2); security and recovery planning (Topic 6); licensing and ethics (Topic 4); and discovery and reuse of data by end-users (Topic 1). The topics less likely to be the subject of textual changes were associated with our remaining three topics: versioning, integrity, description, and metadata harvesting (Topic 0), requirements, standards, and best practices for metadata, file formats, deposit, and submission (Topic 5); and infrastructure, workflows, and interfaces for data lifecycle management (Topic 7).

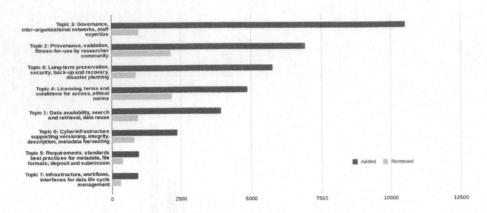

Fig. 4. Topic frequency in change text.

3.4 Improvements

For repositories whose cumulative compliance scores changed the most between certifications (i.e., scores improved by 10 or more points), we identified improvements to their storage, quality control processes, codes of conduct, workflows, cyberinfrastructure, and their adoption of other relevant repository standards. For example, one repository reported no evidence of compliance in multiple areas the first time they certified, and in contrast, reported full compliance for those guidelines when they recertified.

The finding that text associated with depositor requirements was poorly represented among changes in document vocabulary may indicate greater sophistication of both computational and human systems for accessioning data of increased variety in quality and formats for TDRs over time. Although, at the surface level, it might seem counterintuitive to associate accessioning data, including those that range in quality, with improvement, in reality, if a repository can preserve data of less-than-perfect quality, it is better than the data not being preserved at all. Furthermore, preserving data of varying levels of quality requires a metadata strategy capable of reliable data quality representation. Standards and requirements for deposit continue to be important for digital preservation, but an increased focus on data description and quality assessment implies an improvement for different classes of stakeholders, for example, with more flexibility for data producers and greater assurance for data consumers.

In sum, our analysis of ten years of repositories' DSA and CTS audit reports suggests that these TDRs are discussing exactly the types of topics that are vital for data management and sharing. Our findings demonstrate that these repositories expanded their purview in response to digital preservation challenges beyond bit-level fixity with strategies for long-term organizational sustainability to focus on maximizing their holdings' accessibility and usefulness for researchers. Moreover, our results show that many of these TDRs have either maintained a standard of excellence or have improved in their stewardship capabilities as a result of recertification. Topic frequency in changed text was more distinct among words added than words removed, suggesting that improvement is expressed by developing new services and strategies for continued access and preservation, while less drastic revisions are evidence of maintenance of existing capacity.

4   Recommendations

We found that repositories in our sample either maintained or increased their compliance with DSA or CTS TDR standards over time. Since attaining certification involves third-party evaluation of a repository's capacity and commitment to preserving and making data publicly available [18], we offer the following recommendations based on our results. First, we recommend that policymakers who mandate open access to the results of federally funded scientific research revise and expand their directives to include explicit verbiage about certification and the use of TDRs. Specifically, funders should require data repositories to undergo audit and attain certification by CTS or some other certifying body. And funders should require or recommend that their grantees deposit data in TDRs. Second, we recommend that more journal policymakers update their data policies to require authors to deposit their data in TDRs. Even though we are starting to see these trends [3,11], more policy needs to be developed in this area.

References

1. Austin, C.C., Brown, S., Fong, N., Humphrey, C., Leahey, A., Webster, P.: Research data repositories: review of current features, gap analysis, and recommendations for minimum requirements. IQ **39**, 24–38 (2016)
2. Blei, D.M., Ng, A.Y., Jordan, M.I.: Latent Dirichlet allocation. JMLR **3**, 993–1022 (2003). https://www.jmlr.org/papers/volume3/blei03a/blei03a.pdf
3. Coalition for Publishing Data in the Earth and Space Sciences (COPDESS) - Author Guidelines. http://www.copdess.org/enabling-fair-data-project/author-guidelines. Accessed 16 Sept 2022
4. CoreTrustSeal, Core Certified Repositories. https://www.coretrustseal.org/why-certification/certified-repositories/. Accessed 12 Aug 2022
5. CoreTrustSeal Standards And Certification Board: CoreTrustSeal Trustworthy Data Repositories Requirements 2020–2022 (2019). https://doi.org/10.5281/ZENODO.3638211
6. Data Seal of Approval (DSA) - EASY. https://easy.dans.knaw.nl/ui/datasets/id/easy-dataset:116038/tab/2. Accessed 12 Aug 2022

7. Data Policies|Scientific Data. https://www.nature.com/sdata/policies/data-policies. Accessed 16 Sept 2022

8. Dillo, I., De Leeuw, L.: Ten years back, five years forward: the data seal of approval. IJDC **10**, 230–239 (2015). https://doi.org/10.2218/ijdc.v10i1.363

9. Donaldson, D.R., Dillo, I., Downs, R., Ramdeen, S.: The perceived value of acquiring data seals of approval. IJDC **12**, 130–151 (2017). https://doi.org/10.2218/ijdc.v12i1.481

10. Donaldson, D.R., Russell, S.V.: Replication Data for: "Trustworthy Digital Repository Certification: A Longitudinal Study", Harvard Dataverse (2022). https://doi.org/10.7910/DVN/TDX2J8

11. European Commission, Directorate-General for Research and Innovation: Guidelines on FAIR data management in Horizon 2020 (2016)

12. Hoffman, M.D., Blei, D.M., Wang, C., Paisley, J.: Stochastic variational inference. JMLR **14**, 1303–1347 (2013). https://www.jmlr.org/papers/volume14/hoffman13a/hoffman13a.pdf

13. Holdren, J.P.: Increasing access to the results of federally funded scientific research. Executive Office of the President, Office of Science and Technology Policy, Washington, D.C. (2013)

14. Honnibal, M., Montani, I.: spaCy 2: natural language understanding with Bloom embeddings, convolutional neural networks and incremental parsing (2017)

15. Hunter, J.D.: Matplotlib: a 2D graphics environment. Comput. Sci. Eng. **9**, 90–95 (2007). https://doi.org/10.1109/MCSE.2007.55

16. Husen, S., de Wilde, Z., de Waard, A., Cousijn, H.: Recommended versus Certified Repositories: Mind the Gap, https://papers.ssrn.com/abstract=3020994, (2017). DOI: https://doi.org/10.2139/ssrn.3020994

17. L'Hours, H., Kleemola, M., De Leeuw, L.: CoreTrustSeal: from academic collaboration to sustainable services. IQ **43**, 1–17 (2019). https://doi.org/10.29173/iq936

18. Lin, D., et al.: The TRUST principles for digital repositories. Sci Data. **7**, 144 (2020). https://doi.org/10.1038/s41597-020-0486-7

19. Marcum, C.S., Donohue, R.: Breakthroughs for all: delivering equitable access to America's research. https://www.whitehouse.gov/ostp/news-updates/2022/08/25/breakthroughs-for-alldelivering-equitable-access-to-americas-research. Accessed 16 Sept 2022

20. Obama, B.: Executive Order - Making Open and Machine Readable the New Default for Government Information. https://obamawhitehouse.archives.gov/the-press-office/2013/05/09/executive-order-making-open-and-machine-readable-new-default-government-. Accessed 16 Sept 2022

21. Pedregosa, F., et al.: Scikit-learn: machine learning in python. JMLR **12**, 2825–2830 (2011)

22. Re3data.org. https://www.re3data.org. Accessed 19 Sept 2022

23. Research Data - Elsevier. https://www.elsevier.com/about/policies/research-data. Accessed 16 Sept 2022

24. spaCy Models Documentation. https://spacy.io/models/en. Accessed 12 Aug 2022

25. Understanding and using data repositories. https://authorservices.taylorandfrancis.com/data-sharing/share-your-data/repositories. Accessed 16 Sept 2022

Design Principles for Background Knowledge to Enhance Learning in Citizen Science

Kevin Crowston[1]([⊠])[iD], Corey Jackson[2][iD], Isabella Corieri[1][iD],
and Carsten Østerlund[1][iD]

[1] Syracuse University, Syracuse, NY 13244, USA
{crowston,ilcorier,costerlu}@syr.edu
[2] University of Wisconsin, Madison, WI 53706, USA
cbjackson2@wisc.edu

Abstract. Citizen scientists make valuable contributions to science but need to learn about the data they are working with to be able to perform more advanced tasks. We present a set of design principles for identifying the kinds of background knowledge that are important to support learning at different stages of engagement, drawn from a study of how free/libre open source software developers are guided to create and use documents. Specifically, we suggest that newcomers require help understanding the purpose, form and content of the documents they engage with, while more advanced developers add understanding of information provenance and the boundaries, relevant participants and work processes. We apply those principles in two separate but related studies. In study 1, we analyze the background knowledge presented to volunteers in the Gravity Spy citizen-science project, mapping the resources to the framework and identifying kinds of knowledge that were not initially provided. In study 2, we use the principles proactively to develop design suggestions for Gravity Spy 2.0, which will involve volunteers in analyzing more diverse sources of data. This new project extends the application of the principles by seeking to use them to support understanding of the relationships between documents, not just the documents individually. We conclude by discussing future work, including a planned evaluation of Gravity Spy 2.0 that will provide a further test of the design principles.

Keywords: Citizen science · Document genre · Boundary objects · Provenance

1 Introduction

The increasing use of automated data-collection instruments has led to an explosion in the amount and diversity of data collected in many settings, from the sciences and medicine to engineering and manufacturing. Making sense of this data deluge requires human perspectives. An increasingly powerful source of human insight at scale is the crowd. A variety of scientific projects currently benefit from engaging volunteers in data analysis—e.g., classifying galaxy shapes

I. Sserwanga et al. (Eds.): iConference 2023, LNCS 13972, pp. 563–580, 2023.
https://doi.org/10.1007/978-3-031-28032-0_43

in the Galaxy Zoo project or identifying exoplanet transits in Planet Hunters—a form of public participation in science referred to as citizen science. Recruiting volunteers to assist with data analysis benefits science from the application of human abilities at a large scale. For instance, Galaxy Zoo data have supported at least 67 publications and Planet Hunters volunteers discovered 120 candidate exoplanets that were not identified by the science team[1]. Volunteers may also benefit by learning about science, provided the opportunity.

Furthermore, we have evidence that with the right support volunteers are capable of more advanced scientific analyses. For instance, Galaxy Zoo volunteers serendipitously discovered a novel kind of galaxy, nicknamed Green Peas [6]. Research on involving volunteers in advanced scientific work suggests that many are both motivated and capable, but need a structured task to be able to contribute [11]. As well, scientific analysis often requires specialized understanding of the nature of the data to effectively navigate and interpret them [13]. Without the proper expertise and knowledge about a dataset and its provenance, volunteers and other less-expert individuals can do little even with large datasets, often being restricted instead to basic analysis.

To address the challenge of enabling crowd members to perform useful and interesting scientific analyses, we aim to develop our understanding of the support they need to collaboratively engage in scientific work. We propose that providing relevant background knowledge will enable even novices to contribute to research. In this paper, we 1) describe the theoretical foundation that guides our search for relevant background knowledge, 2) analyze a citizen-science project to document the ways in which background knowledge is presented to volunteers and 3) use the results of 1 and 2 to develop design ideas about how knowledge should be presented in the follow-on version of the project. The contribution of the paper is to show how the design principles about background knowledge apply in a new setting and how they can be used proactively for design.

2   Theory Development

Past work on citizen science has explored how volunteers learn the task of classifying data. For instance, Jackson et al. [18] found that it benefits volunteer learning and engagement to introduce types of data to be classified gradually rather than all at once. More recent work has shown that as volunteers continue their engagement with a project, the type of learning resource that improves their performance changes: volunteers initially benefit from authoritative resources provided by the science team but later from tools that support their own exploration of the data and interaction with other volunteers [19]. These findings provide a theoretical basis for the current project, but are limited in at least two ways. First, no work has at yet theorized and tested in detail *the nature of the resources* to be provided to support the volunteers. And second, much of the work to date on learning has focused on the basic task of classifying, not the *more advanced work* we seek to support in our project.

---

[1] https://blog.planethunters.org/2018/11/26/planet-hunters-a-new-beginning/.

To develop principles about the kind of support that will be useful for non-experts to contribute to a project, we draw on research that examines the documents created and used in the process of work [25]. For many collaborators, documents constitute the primary (or even sole) means for knowledge sharing and exchange and form a material instantiation of the work practices. However, to be useful, documents need to be more or less explicit depending on the background knowledge of the intended user [15,20]. Newcomers might need detailed documentation of the work, while an expert can make do with a few bullet points. The latter group holds a shared and practical understanding of the work context that the newcomer lacks. To support the newcomer, a document would have to explicate this knowledge.

To elucidate more precisely the nature of the knowledge needed, we draw on work by Østerlund and Crowston [23], who explored the relationship between free/libre open source software (FLOSS) developers' stock of knowledge and their need for explanations of how to use different documents (e.g., source code, system documentation, project procedures and policies). Participants in FLOSS projects range from core developers with extensive knowledge about the software and software development to peripheral users with limited knowledge. Østerlund and Crowston [23] identified three bodies of theory that speak to the information needs of collaborations that involve such heterogeneous participants: genre theory [3,31,32], boundary objects [29,30] and provenance [14,24]. Each theory addresses the relation between users' stocks of knowledge and their information needs but brings attention to different aspects of the documents that are important.

First, genre theory focuses on the common knowledge people have about documents that they work with. Genre is defined as socially recognized regularities of form and purpose by [32] (e.g., a conference review with a specified form that covers specific topics to inform a publication decision). Members of a relevant community can recognize that a document is of a particular genre, and so know what the expected uses are, but those who do not share that knowledge will need the use, form and expected content spelled out.

Second, the notion of a boundary object addresses how artifacts can bridge between people with few shared points of reference by indicating coincidence boundaries, ideal types or standardized forms [29]. We interpret coincidence boundaries as indicating the value of commonly recognized temporal or participatory boundaries that situate different uses of a document. Ideal types are documents such as diagrams, atlases, or other descriptions that provide an exemplary instance of a document without precisely describing the details of any particular locality, thing, or activity. Finally, standardized forms offers a uniform way to index communicative content and form.

Third, provenance studies speak to how people preserve the history and genealogy of information to alleviate a lack of shared reference points and knowledge that would otherwise impede understanding. For instance, knowing who wrote a document and when can be important to understand its relevance to a current problem.

Combining these three perspectives, Østerlund and Crowston [23] found that documents intended for use by less-knowledgeable members of the community were more likely to be accompanied by explicit statements about:

1. the purpose of the document.
2. the expected form and content of the document. These might even be specified as a standardized form or an ideal type that demarcates specific elements or organization.
3. the context of the document, including the appropriate participants, times and places of the work and the boundaries of the work.
4. the provenance of the document, including the origins of the data and genealogy of its development and use.

In addition to elements suggested by prior theory, Østerlund and Crowston [23] found that documents for novices also expressed a fifth element: the process expectations about the work at hand, that is, what happens to a particular document once it is created.

Of further significance to our project, the study found that FLOSS developers' need for support changed over their engagement with a project. Newcomers required more help understanding the purpose, form and content requirements compared to more advanced participants. As developers gained understanding of the work, they need to understand the boundaries and relevant participants involved in the work (i.e., context), and the information provenance and the process of the information work. This finding suggests directing volunteers to different kinds of background knowledge at different stages rather than simply presenting everything all at once.

Navigating and learning from large scientific datasets comes with unique challenges that differ from learning to contribute to software development processes. FLOSS participants deal with bug reports and source code changes while work with large scientific datasets involves understanding questions like the configuration of instruments and modes of data collection. Nevertheless, generalizing from documents to presentations of data, we believe that providing the identified elements of background knowledge about components of a dataset will support less-expert users in being able to make sense of the data, enabling them to contribute to more advanced analysis.

Based on the review above, we developed the following research questions to address in this paper:

1. What kinds of background knowledge about a dataset are useful for non-experts to be able to understand and work with the data?
2. How does the required knowledge change as volunteers gain experience?
3. What do these findings about background knowledge suggest for the design of future citizen projects?

The first study presented in this paper addresses the first two questions. The second study builds on those results to address the third question.

3   Study 1: Presentation of Background Knowledge

In the first study, we address the first two research questions by carrying out a study of the presentation of background knowledge resources in an existing citizen-science project called Gravity Spy[2] [33].

3.1   Methods

The research uses virtual ethnography [16]. Virtual ethnography adapts traditional ethnographic methods, such as participant observation and in-person interviews, to studying online communities like Gravity Spy. To enhance our understanding of how volunteers in Gravity Spy use background knowledge, we (the authors and other members of the research team) first engaged in Gravity Spy as participant-observers. As participants, we created user accounts, completed requisite training, made classifications, and contributed to project discussions over the course of the first year of the activity, with a lower engagement since then. A first task for all new members of the research team is to go through the same process of initial engagement. We used our position as observers to build knowledge about how volunteers engage with background knowledge on the platform, e.g., what background knowledge resources the system currently provides to volunteers at different stages of engagement and how participants use background information to learn about the project throughout their interaction. We analyzed the resources we identified to determine how they mapped to the categories in the theoretical framework.

We also conducted fifteen interviews, three with members of the Gravity Spy science team and the rest with Gravity Spy volunteers and moderators. Each interview lasted approximately one hour, and was recorded and transcribed. The interviews with scientists focused on how Gravity Spy scientists use data, tools, and other materials to make inferences about relationships between glitches and the auxiliary channels (the task we hope to facilitate in the next version of Gravity Spy). Interviews with volunteers and moderators focused on current background knowledge used to develop insights about the relationships among glitches. Although the inference task is not yet supported, volunteers have attempted to make inferences by linking external materials such as research articles and summary descriptions of detector observation notes on Gravity Spy discussion boards. We also asked moderators questions about how new forms of work (i.e., making inferences) could be supported in a new Gravity Spy interface.

3.2   Setting: Gravity Spy

The Gravity Spy citizen science project [33] incorporated advances in machine learning and new approaches to citizen science to support the Laser Interferometer Gravitational-Wave Observatory (LIGO), a dramatic example of large-scale scientific data collection. LIGO's goal is to detect gravitational waves (GWs),

---

[2] https://gravityspy.org/.

extremely faint distortions in the fabric of space created by astronomical events such as merging black holes. A challenge for LIGO scientists is that the detectors (one in Hanford, Washington and one in Livingston, Louisiana USA) need to be extremely sensitive to be able to detect GWs, but as a result, they also record orders of magnitude more noise events (referred to as glitches) caused by terrestrial interference or by internal faults or interactions in the detectors. Glitches can obscure or even masquerade as GW signals, so identifying and eliminating their causes is a key activity to improve the detectors [8,12]. These efforts to understand and mitigate these sources of noise, both in the instrument and the data, are collectively referred to as "detector characterization". Gravity Spy supports this work by recruiting volunteers to sort observed glitches into different classes, known or thought to have a common cause. LIGO scientists use the Gravity Spy purified collections to guide their search for the underlying cause of a particular class of glitch, with the goal of eliminating them. We briefly describe the current Gravity Spy project and the volunteers' work to provide context for the discussion of the needed background knowledge.

Classification Work. The Gravity Spy project uses data from the main GW channel from LIGO, a 16 kHz stream of samples [2]. The data-import pipeline extracts two seconds of data around each observed event with a high signal-to-noise ratio, signalling a potential glitch. The data are processed for presentation to humans as spectrograms, specifically, Omega scans [9], a visual representation of the glitch with time on the horizontal axis, frequency on the vertical axis, and intensity of the signal represented by the color from blue to yellow (Fig. 1).

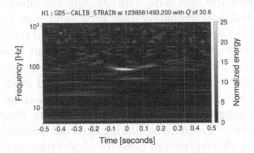

H1 : GDS−CALIB_STRAIN at 1236561493.200 with Q of 30.6

Fig. 1. Spectrogram of a Whistle glitch in the main GW channel

The spectrograms are imported to the Gravity Spy project on the Zooniverse platform [26], where they are presented to volunteers for classification. The classification interface was created using the Zooniverse project builder[3], which enables a Zooniverse project to be created with a few mouse clicks and data uploads. Volunteers label each glitch as being of a known class (23 currently) or "None of the above". To scaffold learning, volunteers progress through

---

[3] https://www.zooniverse.org/lab.

a series of levels in which they have an increasing number of options for classifying. Newcomers to the project start in level 1 where they given a choice of only Whistle and Blip glitches, which are easy to recognize and distinguish, plus None of the above. Machine learning (ML) supports this process [10]. In initial levels, volunteers are shown only glitches classified by a ML system as being quite likely to be of the classes included in the level. Volunteers also have the option of "None of the above" in case the ML is wrong, meaning that even beginners are doing useful work checking the ML. As volunteers classify and gain experience with glitches, they are promoted to higher levels with more choices, increasing eventually to all 23 classes. At level 5, their attention is focused on glitches that the ML was unable to classify.

Novel Glitch Identification Work. Assigning glitches to the predefined set of glitch classes represents the lion's share of the work done in Gravity Spy. However, some glitches do not fit any known class and so may be examples of as-yet undescribed classes of glitches. If new classes of commonly-occurring glitches were better understood, their causes might be addressed to improve the detectors [28]. Experienced Gravity Spy volunteers identify new classes of glitches by creating and describing collections of "None of the above" glitches with similar novel appearance (collections are a feature of the Zooniverse platform). This work is supported by tools to search for glitches similar to a given glitch and to retrieve metadata for the glitches in a collection. Volunteers can work independently but often collaborate with other volunteers in describing novel classes. Cooperation among volunteers takes place using the Zooniverse platform's Talk forum [17]. Descriptions of suggested new glitch classes are provided to LIGO scientists and if the class is common, volunteers can create a formal proposal that the new glitch be added to the Gravity Spy classification interface. Six new classes have been added to date and many more candidates have been proposed.

3.3 Findings: Background Knowledge in Gravity Spy

In this section, we describe background knowledge resources needed to understand glitches in the LIGO detectors in the current Gravity Spy project, based on our own observation and use of the site. We map these resources to the identified design principles that suggest which will be useful at different stages of engagement with the project. We draw on interviews with active developers to identify background knowledge resources that were not provided by the project developers but that the volunteers identified as helpful.

A Zooniverse project includes multiple venues for presenting background knowledge: the project description and "About this project" pages, a tutorial that is presented to volunteers when they start classifying, a mini-course whose pages are presented interspersed with the classification work, a field guide that can be referenced during the task, a description panel that pops up when a classification is selected, and Talk pages for discussion among volunteers and with the science team. We expect that the About pages and tutorial address the background knowledge needs of newcomers, the mini-course, field guide and detail panels, more experienced volunteers (those over the immediate hurdle of learning how to contribute), and the Talk pages, advanced volunteers. This progression shows a transition from authoritative to collaborative resources [19].

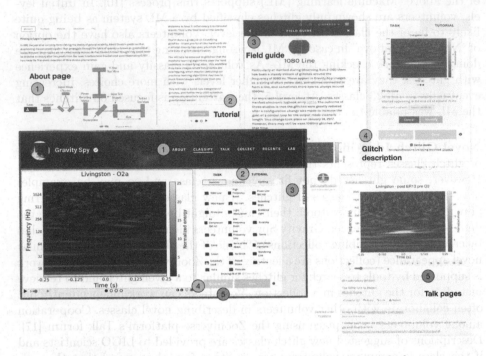

Fig. 2. The Gravity Spy classification interface is on the lower left, with the spectogram of the glitch to be classified on the left and the possible classes on the right. The numbered circles indicate the background knowledge resources provided, with examples above and to the right.

For the classification task in Gravity Spy, the documents that volunteers need to understand are the spectograms that they classify (shown on the left side at the lower left in Fig. 2). In the current Gravity Spy, the "About" pages (1 in Fig. 2) present the goals of LIGO, how the detectors work, what glitches are, the goals of the Gravity Spy project and the research team. The pages also provide links to published papers about Gravity Spy and to other reading about LIGO and the detector. Each level has its own tutorial (2 in Fig. 2) to introduce features added at that level. The tutorial is automatically shown the first time a volunteer starts a level and is available afterwards on demand. The level 1 tutorial, shown to newcomers to the project, explains what a spectogram is, how to perform a classification using the Zooniverse interface and how volunteers are promoted to advanced levels. The mini-course (not shown) presents information about LIGO, as much to keep volunteers' interest than because of its immediate relevance to the task. The field guide (3 in Fig. 2) describes each of the 23 known classes of glitch with examples of their appearance, as do the popups that appear when a class is selected for a glitch (4 in Fig. 2). Finally, the Talk pages (5 in Fig. 2) includes boards to chat, ask for help, report bugs, comment on specific glitches or to discuss the science behind the project. Additional boards were created later to discuss and propose potential new glitch classes discovered by the volunteers. Some experienced volunteers act as moderators for the Talk pages and often answer questions from other volunteers.

The design principles developed above suggest that newcomers require help understanding the purpose of documents and their form and content. Reflecting this ordering, the current Gravity Spy About pages and tutorial describe the purpose of a spectogram, i.e., to show a glitch in a human readable format, its form and what content it contains, namely a glitch. More established users need to understand the boundaries and relevant participants involved in the work, that is, how the work they are doing connects with other tasks and other participants. The Gravity Spy project initially did not provide this information. However, advanced Gravity Spy volunteers have posted a range of potentially useful information to the Talk pages, an example of collaboratively-created background knowledge resources [19]. These include discussions of how the spectograms are created and links to LIGO aLogs[4], which record work done on the detectors, linking the work of the LIGO scientists to the work of the volunteers.

As noted above, the advanced work in Gravity Spy consists of collecting examples of potential new glitch classes and describing some of these classes in a glitch proposal document. This work introduces two new kinds of documents that must be understood, specifically collections and glitch class proposals. Volunteers often collaborate to create these documents. Gravity Spy at present does not explicitly describe this work nor provide relevant background knowledge beyond the knowledge needed to do the initial classification task. Again, the volunteers have created Talk posts that explicate the process. The project scientists did create a template for a glitch class proposal, consistent with Østerlund and Crowston [23]'s finding that such standard forms are used to regulate communicate between groups with different levels of background knowledge, in this case volunteers and science team members. Accepted glitch class proposals also constitute a kind of ideal type for creating new proposals. In summary, the framework seems to capture the kinds of background knowledge provided in Gravity Spy as well as identifying lacunae (RQ1), and how these resources change as volunteers gain experience (RQ2).

4   Study 2: Theory-Driven System Design

In this section, we present the second study, which seeks to use the design principles developed above to proactively guide the design of a system to address a novel problem (RQ3). We describe the novel problem, how that problem is handled by experts and the suggestions from the principles about how to present necessary background knowledge to enable volunteers to take on the task.

---

[4] https://alog.ligo-la.caltech.edu/aLOG/.

As noted above, a finding of our study is that the current Gravity Spy system does not provide authoritative resources to support the advanced work of identifying new glitch classes but that volunteers have created some. Still, volunteers face challenges identifying and describing new glitch classes in a useful way. The hope is that glitches in a new class have a common cause that can be addressed. However, at present volunteers have limited knowledge about the underlying mechanisms within the detectors that generate glitches, nor can they explore those mechanisms. As a result, new glitch class identification is done phenomenologically, i.e., by grouping glitches with similar appearance (witness the fact that volunteer-identified glitch classes are named by shape, e.g., Helix or Crown, in contrast to most LIGO-identified classes that are named by cause, e.g., Whistle or Scattered Light). This approach has been effective in identifying new glitch classes. However, the essential next step of identifying causes requires the attention of the overloaded LIGO science team. In this section, we describe how we are using what we have learned about background knowledge to design a new citizen-science project that will enable volunteers to take on some of this analysis work, addressing our third research question.

4.1   Methods

To identify what resources would be useful to support this task, we carried out interviews with experts as described above for Study 1. These interviews gave us an understanding of the task to be supported and background knowledge resources that might be useful. The resources identified by the experts were sorted by the categories in the theory and to modes of delivery in the project.

4.2   Data-Centred Approaches to Glitch Analysis

We start by describing how professional LIGO scientists address the task. To explore the cause of glitches (i.e., what is happening in the detector or the environment that causes particular classes of glitches), LIGO scientists carry out studies using what are called auxiliary channel (AC) data. Along with GWs, the LIGO detectors record more than 200,000 channels of data per detector from a diverse set of sensors that continuously measure every aspect of the detectors and their environment (e.g., equipment functioning, activation of components, seismic activity or weather) [21,22]. This dataset holds clues to the cause of glitches, but the large volume of data demands ways to transform this massive volume of data from disparate sources into useful information.

Currently LIGO uses a number of algorithms (e.g., hVeto [27], iDQ [4], Karoo GP [8]) that identify statistically-significant correlations between a loud event occurring in the main GW channel (a likely glitch) and an event in one of the other channels. Since different classes of glitches are created by different mechanisms, they are correlated with diverse ACs. As useful as these tools are for providing clues to the causes of glitches, statistical correlations represent an incomplete picture and do not clearly point to causality. Some channels experience loud events frequently, so the fact that they correlate with a glitch might not be informative. Channels have complicated interdependencies (e.g., because of being in the same location or actually dependent on each other through feedback loops), so many channels can show correlation with the same glitch. As a result, a channel may be a statistically-significant witness for a class of glitch even though it is not actually close to the root cause. A further issue is that only some of the mechanisms connecting parts of the detector are well understood. Mechanisms can be complex and non-linear, may involve complicated interactions (e.g., between environmental conditions and detector functioning) and some are yet to be discovered. Much work is needed to determine if highly-correlated events in the ACs point to the root cause of the glitch.

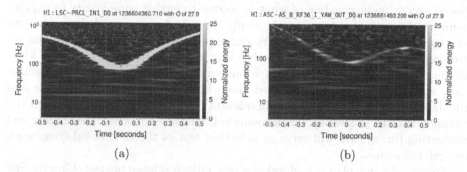

(a)   (b)

Fig. 3. Spectrograms of two auxiliary channels related to the glitch in Fig. 1, (a) power recycling cavity length (PRCL) and (cb alignment control channel (ASC).

Figure 3 illustrates the exploration process as currently performed by LIGO scientists. Simply looking at a spectrogram of a glitch from the main GW channel (Fig. 1 above) does not show a very obvious morphology. The slight change in frequency hints at the type of glitch, a Whistle, but information from auxiliary channels is needed to understand its cause. A first step in the exploration is a closer comparison of the morphology of the glitch and correlated channels. For our Whistle, looking at the power recycling cavity length (PRCL) channel (Fig. 3a) one finds an event that looks like a louder version of the Whistle glitch; the same shape is present in the GW channel (Fig. 1), but at a much lower amplitude, largely obscured by noise. Other channels may show similar patterns-e.g., Fig. 3b, an alignment control channel (ASC)-but not as strongly as PRCL. Understanding the layout of the detectors and the provenance of the dataset helps to make sense of the root cause of the Whistle: the GW and the PRCL channel (among others) witness radio frequencies; different radio frequency oscillators move closer and farther apart in frequency, creating a varying beat note that is the Whistles' unique pattern.

Whistles provide a particularly clear example of a connection between glitches and events in other channels. More challenging classes of glitches require exploring correlations between multiple manifestations of the class and relevant ACs over longer periods of time to develop a full picture. Looking through spectrograms comparable to those in Figs. 1 and 3 (but for hundreds of ACs) over many different glitches can provide hints to the root cause of the glitch, as the same pattern of channels reappear in association with the same kinds of glitches. However, interpreting these patterns requires understanding likely mechanisms of glitch creation.

4.3 Enabling Volunteers to Engage in Glitch Analysis

At the moment, the analysis of novel glitches described above is done only by the LIGO scientists, and their analyses are limited by the time they have available. Based on our understanding of what is needed to enable non-experts to explore complex datasets, developed in the study described above, we believe that we can enable citizen scientists to carry out some of the time-consuming analysis required for the novel classes of glitches that they are already involved in identifying. To do this, we will provide volunteers with access to auxiliary channel data and, more importantly, support them in learning about the detector and the data it records, e.g., by providing relevant background information about the channels and the process by which channels influence each other. Developing and evaluating this system will serve as a further test of the theoretical framework articulated above.

Specifically, our plan is to develop a new citizen-science project, Gravity Spy 2.0. Volunteers will move through different tasks as they contribute to the analysis and build their knowledge, as shown in Fig. 4. In the first task, knowledge will be built while examining individual glitches and vetting their relation to activity in the various ACs. We have identified a subset of several hundred channels that are most informative to use in the project. This task will be performed in a Zooniverse project-builder project. As in the current Gravity Spy system, we plan to introduce glitches and ACs gradually so volunteers have time to learn the nature of that set of glitches or channels. This staging will be supported by

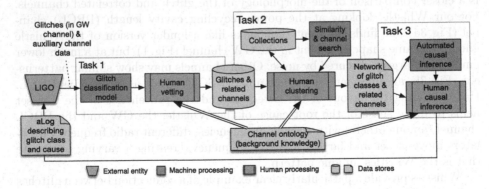

Fig. 4. Flow of data through volunteer and ML processing for Gravity Spy 2.0.

doing an initial sort of glitches using the ML glitch classification models created for Gravity Spy.

In the second task, volunteers will examine collections of glitches and the ACs identified as related in the first stage to identify recurring patterns of connections for a particular class of glitch, and ultimately (in the third task) to deduce which ACs are the causes of those glitches. Both tasks will be supported by additional ML processing, to search for glitches with similar appearance and pattern of related ACs or to draw causal inferences from the connections.

4.4 Background Knowledge to Support Gravity Spy 2.0

In this section, we present our ideas for designing background knowledge for Gravity Spy 2.0, considering primarily Task 1, our current design focus. As with the original Gravity Spy, we expect newcomers to first need to understand the form and content of the documents, through material presented in the About pages and tutorial. Much of the background knowledge material developed for Gravity Spy is still applicable. Indeed, it would likely be beneficial for volunteers to have experience with Gravity Spy 1.0 before engaging with 2.0. However, for Task 1, the materials will also need to explain how the spectograms present information from different ACs and what those are.

The design principles suggest that more established volunteers need help understanding information provenance and the process of the work. Provenance information for LIGO AC data includes what kind of detector collected them (e.g., a seismometer vs. a magnetometer), which is necessary for understanding their implications for glitch formation. To understand provenance, a basic understanding of the parts of the detector will be necessary. One resource is published descriptions of the detector and its subsystems, e.g., [1,5], along with papers describing glitches and how they are characterized, o.g., [2,12,21,22]. These papers might be linked directly or summarized. A list of acronyms[5] will also be helpful for decoding the detector descriptions and the channel names.

A key element in the system will be an ontology of the ACs that presents the background knowledge needed to understand each channel. We are currently building an initial ontology from existing LIGO documentation, with input from LIGO experts. For instance, LIGO maintains a public website[6] that describes the physical and environmental monitoring sensors and a private website describing the instrumental channels. The ontology will be refined throughout our project. A limitation of the Zooniverse project builder is that the field guide is a simple list, making it unusable for presenting information about hundreds of channels. To get around this limitation, we will present the information on a Wiki. Part of the Wiki page will be populated from structured data about each channel (see Fig. 5 for a prototype of a channel page). The Wiki will also allow description and exploration of clusters of related channels, e.g., those in the same subsystem or at the same physical location in the detector (the links in the breakdown of

---

[5] https://dcc.ligo.org/M080375/public.
[6] http://pem.ligo.org/.

the component name). A key benefit of presenting the information on a Wiki is that volunteers will be able to add to it, thus supporting individual exploration and collaborative background knowledge creation in a structured way.

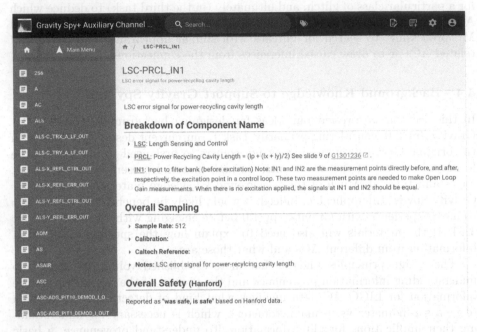

Fig. 5. Prototype Wiki page for the channel shown in Fig. 3a.

4.5   Background Knowledge for Understanding Related Documents

The design principles presented above describe the kinds of background knowledge need to understand single documents. A needed extension to the model is that, in addition to understanding documents individually, we also want the volunteers to understand possible relations between documents, i.e., how a glitch recorded in the GW channel relates to a signal in one of the ACs. We believe that the design principles developed above also apply to describing the background knowledge needed to understand these relations.

Specifically, we believe that newcomers to the task will first need to understand the purpose of the relations and their form and content. The purpose will be described in the About pages, namely, to identify which channels may be part of the processes creating glitches. Form and content in this case refers to how the two spectograms are related. As noted above, glitches do not simply appear in the same form in different ACs, so volunteers will need to learn the form of the relation (i.e., what a Whistle glitch looks like in other channels). We plan to add information about relationships to the AC ontology, e.g., information showing the form of a relationship between channels as it is discovered. As it would be impractical to capture all combinations of hundreds of channels, we will focus on describing how a signal in the AC affects the GW channel for a particular kind of glitch. For instance, the page shown in Fig. 5 could describe for which glitch classes it has been observed to be active; a page for a particular glitch class, the seemingly related channels, perhaps with examples. However, it could be that some other combinations are interesting and worth describing, e.g., channels that seem to be frequently active in combination. An advantage of presenting the information on a Wiki is that the volunteers will be able to extend the channel information as they discover interesting relations.

A major complication is that we lack training material for most combinations of glitches and ACs. To fill this lacuna, we will use the volunteers' contributions to identify relations. To do so, we need to develop a way of describing the relations between spectograms in a few basic terms (e.g., "identical", "same shape, reduced intensity", "truncated", "no relation") that volunteers can reliably identify. In task 2, volunteers will examine collections of glitches to identify which ACs are reliably related and in what way. This identification can then feedback to support the volunteers working on task 1 and eventually to train ML systems.

Once volunteers are past the initial hurdle of learning how to interpret the form and content of related channels, we expect that they will need information about provenance and process. In this setting, provenance means understanding the origin of the relation between the GW and ACs, that is, what about the detector causes those channels to interact? The plan is to provide a description of the detector functioning that should support volunteers in understanding these connections. Finally, to support the most advanced users, we need to present information about the context of the work, specifically, how identifying relationships will support further work with this dataset. Such information can be presented in the Talk discussions or added to the Wiki.

5   Conclusion

We are currently building the system described above. The Zooniverse project builder makes it straightforward to present spectograms to volunteers and to collect their judgements about the relationships. The difficult part in building the initial phase of the project is determining what kinds of background knowledge volunteers need to make sense of the images being presented and to understand whether there is or is not a relationship. By drawing design principles from the theories presented above, we have developed a starting set of ideas about what kinds of background knowledge are important and are now developing materials to populate the site (e.g., the Wiki pages shown in Fig. 5). We are also investigating the contribution of ML processing, e.g., to pick glitches of a particular class to show a volunteer or to cluster channels with a similar relationship to a glitch.

We are currently conducting focus groups with advanced volunteers to refine the design. Participants have suggested additional resources that they have found helpful that we are including in the design. For instance, one volunteer pointed us to a Ph.D. thesis [7] describing the control system for the Virgo detector, which operates on a similar principle to LIGO. A few volunteers will be interested in such resources, while more may benefit from excerpts or summaries on the Wiki.

In future studies, we will evaluate the usefulness of identified elements of background knowledge by analyzing system log data which contains information about elements that volunteers interact with. Through this analysis, we hope to uncover which knowledge (e.g., form and content, purpose, etc.) about glitches and ACs is important in supporting less-expert users in being able to make sense of the data. We will also evaluate learning enhancements by correlating use of background knowledge with volunteers' performance and engagement. Since we expect background knowledge will enhance learning, we can identify whether volunteers who used certain resources produced more advanced analysis. We can also test whether the framework applies to understanding document relationships, as well as documents individually.

Overall, we expect our ongoing research to provide useful and novel insights about the kinds of background knowledge that are effective in enhancing the abilities of non-experts to conduct advanced data analysis. We expect our results to be informative in the many settings where less expert users want to be able to contribute to a complex on-going project. The design principles articulated in Sect. 2 describe the kinds of background knowledge that should be supplied and how these should be ordered. For instance, in a biodiversity project like Snapshot Serengeti[7], we expect newcomers to benefit from explanations of the purpose, form and content of the documents they will encounter (e.g., the photographs and descriptions of the species). Information about the context of the work or provenance of the images might be deferred until those elements are mastered. Our experience in building and operating Gravity Spy 2.0 will provide a needed test and perhaps update of these principles. Armed with these results, future project developers will be better able to scaffold the introduction of relevant background knowledge to smooth volunteers' entry into and progression through their projects.

Acknowledgments. Partially funded by grants from the US National Science Foundation, INSPIRE 15–47880 and HCC 21–06865. The authors thank the Gravity Spy volunteers who participated in this research. Without their contribution, the project would not exist.

References

1. Aasi, J., et al.: Advanced LIGO. Class. Quantum Gravity **32**(7), 074001 (2015)
2. Abbott, B.P., et al.: A guide to LIGO-Virgo detector noise and extraction of transient gravitational-wave signals. Class. Quantum Gravity **37**(5), 055002 (2020)
3. Bazerman, C.: Systems of genres and the enactment of social intentions. In: Freedman, A., Medway, P. (eds.) Genre and the New Rhetoric, pp. 79–101. Taylor and Francis (1995)

---

[7] https://www.zooniverse.org/projects/zooniverse/snapshot-serengeti.

4. Biswas, R., et al.: Application of machine learning algorithms to the study of noise artifacts in gravitational-wave data. Phys. Rev. D **88**(6), 062003 (2013). arXiv: 1303.6984
5. Buikema, A., et al.: Sensitivity and performance of the advanced LIGO detectors in the third observing run. Phys. Rev. D **102**(6), September 2020
6. Cardamone, C., et al.: Galaxy zoo green peas: discovery of a class of compact extremely star-forming galaxies. Mon. Not. R. Astron. Soc. **399**(3), 1191–1205 (2009)
7. Casanueva Diaz, J.: Control of the gravitational wave interferometric detector Advanced Virgo. Ph.D. thesis, Université Paris-Saclay (ComUE) (2017)
8. Cavaglia, M., Staats, K., Gill, T.: Finding the origin of noise transients in LIGO data with machine learning. Commun. Comput. Phys. **25**(4) (2019). arXiv: 1812.05225
9. Chatterji, S., Blackburn, L., Martin, G., Katsavounidis, E.: Multiresolution techniques for the detection of gravitational-wave bursts. Class. Quantum Gravity **21**(20), S1809–S1818 (2004)
10. Coughlin, S., et al.: Classifying the unknown: discovering novel gravitational-wave detector glitches using similarity learning. Phys. Rev. D **99**(8), 082002 (2019)
11. Crowston, K., Mitchell, E., Østerlund, C.: Coordinating advanced crowd work: Extending citizen science. Citizen Science: Theory and Practice 4(1) (2019)
12. Davis, D., et al.: LIGO detector characterization in the second and third observing runs. Class. Quantum Gravity **38**(13), 135014 (2021)
13. Finholt, T.A., Olson, G.M.: From laboratories to collaboratories: a new organizational form for scientific collaboration. Psychol. Sci. **8**(1), 28–36 (1997)
14. Gilliland-Swetland, A.: Electronic records management. Ann. Rev. Inf. Sci. Technol. **39**(1), 219–253 (2005)
15. Harper, R.: Inside the IMF. Routledge (2009)
16. Hine, C.: Virtual Ethnography. SAGE Publications Ltd, SAGE Publications Ltd, Apr 2000
17. Jackson, C., Crowston, K., Østerlund, C., Harandi, M.: Folksonomies to support coordination and coordination of folksonomies. Comput. Supported Cooperative Work (CSCW) **27**(3–6), 647–678 (2018)
18. Jackson, C.B., et al.: Teaching citizen scientists to categorize glitches using machine-learning-guided training. Computers in Human Behavior 105 (2020)
19. Jackson, C.B., Østerlund, C., Harandi, M., Crowston, K., Trouille, L.: Shifting forms of engagement: Volunteer learning in online citizen science. In: Proceedings of the ACM on Human-Computer Interaction 4(CWCW), 36 (2020)
20. Latour, B.: Pandora's Hope: Essays on the Reality of Science Studies. Harvard University Press (1999)
21. Nguyen, P., Schofield, R.M.S., Effler, A., Austin, C., Adya, V., Ball, M., Banagiri, S., Banowetz, K., Billman, C., Blair, C.D., et al.: Environmental noise in advanced LIGO detectors. Class. Quantum Gravity **38**(14), 145001 (2021)
22. Nuttall, L.K.: Characterizing transient noise in the LIGO detectors. Philosophical Trans. Roy. Soc. A Math. Phys. Eng. Sci. **376**(2120), 20170286 (2018)
23. Østerlund, C., Crowston, K.: Documentation and access to knowledge in online communities: know your audience and write appropriately? J. Am. Soc. Inform. Sci. Technol. **70**, 619–633 (2019)
24. Ram, S., Liu, J.: A semantic foundation for provenance management. J. Data Semant. **1**(1), 11–17 (2012)
25. Shankar, K., Hakken, D., Østerlund, C.: Rethinking documents. In: The Handbook of Science and Technology Studies, 4 edn., pp. 59–86. MIT Press, Cambridge (2017)

26. Simpson, R., Page, K.R., De Roure, D.: Zooniverse: observing the world's largest citizen science platform. In: Proceedings of the 23rd International Conference on World Wide Web, pp. 1049–1054. ACM (2014)
27. Smith, J.R., et al.: A hierarchical method for vetoing noise transients in gravitational-wave detectors. Class. Quantum Gravity 28(23), 235005 (2011). arXiv: 1107.2948
28. Soni, S., et al.: Discovering features in gravitational-wave data through detector characterization, citizen science and machine learning. Class. Quantum Gravity 38(19), 195016 (2021)
29. Star, S.L.: The structure of ill-structured solutions: boundary objects and heterogeneous distributed problem solving. In: Gasser, L., Huhns, M.N. (eds.) Distributed Artificial Intelligence, vol. 2, p. 37–54. Morgan Kaufmann (1989)
30. Star, S.L., Griesemer, J.R.: Institutional ecology, 'translations' and boundary objects: amateurs and professionals in Berkeley's Museum of Vertebrate Zoology, 1907–39. In: Social Studies of Science, vol. 19, pp. 387–420. Sage (1989)
31. Swales, J.M.: Genre Analysis: English in Academic and Research Settings. Cambridge University Press (1990)
32. Yates, J., Orlikowski, W.J.: Genres of organizational communication: a structurational approach to studying communications and media. Acad. Manag. Rev. 17(2), 299–326 (1992)
33. Zevin, M., et al.: Gravity spy: integrating advanced LIGO detector characterization, machine learning, and citizen science. Class. Quantum Gravity 34(6), 064003 (2017)

"We Avoid PDFs": Improving Notation Access for Blind and Visually Impaired Musicians

William Payne(✉) 🄳 and Amy Hurst 🄳

New York University, New York, NY 10014, USA
{william.payne,amyhurst}@nyu.edu

Abstract. While music notation can be represented across modalities, it is typically only available visually (in standard print) resulting in access barriers for Blind and Visually Impaired (BVI) musicians. Automated conversion tools and common formats such as MusicXML have enabled new workflows where a print score is transcribed (copied) and made into large print and/or braille music. However, many musicians are unable to acquire music in a format legible to them as transcriptions require time, expertise, and specialized software to produce. Drawing upon the experiences and suggestions of 11 adult BVI musicians with varying vision ability and musical backgrounds, we outline a path to improving access to music notation. To this end, we describe opportunities for utilizing automation and crowd workers, make recommendations for customizing music in print, braille, and audio, and identify open challenges and research directions for creating, storing, and sharing music across formats.

Keywords: Blindness · Vision impairment · Music notation · Accessibility

1 Introduction

Fig. 1. Three music excerpts shown in standard western notation (left), MusicXML data (center), and braille music (right). Transcribers leverage automated technologies and specialized tools to convert between mediums, but many musicians do not have access to scores they can read.

Music notation is any system of instructions depicting what sounds to make and how and when to make them. Conventional western notation appears as printed

© The Author(s), under exclusive license to Springer Nature Switzerland AG 2023
I. Sserwanga et al. (Eds.): iConference 2023, LNCS 13972, pp. 581–597, 2023.
https://doi.org/10.1007/978-3-031-28032-0_44

dots and symbols arranged spatially on lines indicating pitch, rhythm, and other stylistic information (Fig. 1). Music notation is more prevalent in some traditions like classical music, e.g. orchestral and choral composition, than others, e.g. pop songwriting [43]. While the ability to read notation is not a prerequisite to make music or pursue it professionally, it is telling that many notable blind musicians across American history like Stevie Wonder did not read music and instead learned "by ear" [37]. Blind and Visually Impaired (BVI) musicians face significant barriers if they wish to learn notation or pursue a style of music where notation skill remains mandatory.

There is a huge backlog of music that is only available visually. Visual music notation, engraved on scores in standard print/PDF formats, follows typical distribution of media and can be obtained from libraries, online repositories [33], and publishers. BVI people cannot access PDF scores with their screen readers, assistive technologies that speak the contents of a digital screen [4]. Perpetuating this environment of visual-only music, commercial software pervasively use graphic, "what-you-see-is-what-you-get" interfaces geared towards print scores [3,31,32], while most publishers only sell new music in print and do not sell source files, such as MusicXML, to create accessible formats due to copyright concerns. As a result, small but dedicated teams across the world transcribe (manually copy) visual music and convert it accessible formats.

The goals of this research are rooted in the social model of disability [23] in which we believe that the problem of inaccessible notation arises out of systems and infrastructures oriented towards producing visual-only music. We set out to understand the experiences of BVI musicians accessing the scores they need, and propose systemic solutions to increase access. We first give an overview of music notation in Related Work (Sect. 2) in which we describe the braille music and large print formats read by BVI musicians, identify organizations and structures that make accessible notation available, and detail processes for transcribing print music. We then present our Methodology (Sect. 3) to understand how 11 BVI musicians use notation. In Findings (Sect. 4), we depict participant experiences with transcription, customization, and music repositories. Finally, we discuss recommendations (Sect. 5) drawn from participant suggestions and past work to make accessible music notation more widely available.

2   Related Work

We describe accessible alternatives to standard print (braille and large print), identify popular organizations and resources that produce or share alternative notation, and outline the transcription processes for copying and converting print scores into these alternative formats.

2.1   Alternative Notation: Braille and Large Print

Braille and large print notation are currently the two most common alternatives to visual music. Many BVI musicians learn and read music using braille or large print but their preference depends on vision ability, training, and interest.

Braille Music. Braille music uses the same six-dot cells as in other forms of braille [20]. Unlike print notation, where notes are arranged spatially and markings can iconically represent their sounds, braille music is linear and symbolic. Braille scores tend to be longer than their print counterparts and the rules and conventions governing the format of scores are well defined [40]. Physical braille music scores are made with embossers while digital files can be accessed on refreshable braille displays.

Many prior studies have depicted the experiences of braille music readers, learners, and educators e.g. [2,3,17,30,35]. In a large UK study, 100 of 191 BVI musicians surveyed said they read braille music, though the authors acknowledge that the word "read" constitutes a wide range of skill. While blind musicians have discussed alternatives to making music without formal notation [32] and argued for and against its relevance, braille music expertise is perceived necessary for some practices, especially high-level classical performance [3]. Park and Kim argue that learning braille music is more difficult than print while braille music readers use scores differently and leverage audio recordings frequently in practice/memorization [30]. We suggest multimodal tools and workflows for learning and discuss alternatives to conventional braille music.

Large Print Notation. Large print scores, also referred to as Modified Stave Notation [3], feature enlarged elements and paper, increased spacing and thickness, adjusted color, and other alterations making them more legible for people with low vision. There is little research on large print notation and fewer BVI musicians appear to read it compared with braille. One study reported that only 20 out of 191 BVI musicians read large print notation, yet this small group reported varied vision abilities and score preferences [3]. Large print readers used different layouts, some preferred print while others preferred digital copies, and one described fatigue after extended use. As our paper discusses, a single magnified version may not support all users given such diversity.

2.2 Software for Notating Music

Most mainstream music notation tools, e.g. Finale [22] and Sibelius [1] feature a graphic user interface in which a digital score is manipulated via mouse and keyboard. While they do not export music in braille, some support large print scores. Since these systems are often inaccessible or difficult to use, many BVI musicians combine commercial and custom tools [3,32,39]. Past research [3,32] has shown one common alternative is Lime Aloud, developed by Dancing Dots, a company led by a blind developer [8]. Lime Aloud supports screen readers and braille displays, and as discussed below, comes bundled with software that aids transcription. However, Lime Aloud is expensive and only available on Windows.

Text-based systems, in which print notation is generated from plain text, can be more immediately accessible to BVI musicians because text is directly interpreted by screen readers [31,41]. For example, ABC is a human-readable syntax widely used to notate folk tunes [45] while LilyPond is an advanced engraving language akin to LaTeX for music [13]. While many editing environments and command line tools only create print notation, the SoundCells system, co-developed by researchers and blind musicians, converts ABC into braille music and large print music within an accessible, web interface [31]. Additional tools dedicated to braille include the Braille Music Editor [10] and Braille Music Notator [38]. General-purpose braille editing software, like Duxbury [9], is viable because braille music uses the same underlying system as other forms of braille.

2.3   Braille and Large Print Music Repositories and Distribution

BVI musicians have a few avenues for acquiring braille and large print music, but the collections available are smaller than collections of standard PDF scores. In the United States, the National Library Service (NLS) collection of braille music transcriptions emphasizes piano, vocal, and choral music composed between the 18th and 20th centuries [27]. The collection also includes large print scores in one standard layout, and other educational and audio materials. Furthermore, the NLS maintains a list of certified, professional transcribers who produce braille scores as a service [26]. Other national organizations across the world [12] like ONCE in Spain, and local community organizations such as the Filomen M. D'Agostino Greenberg School in New York [11], also hold collections and may provide transcription services. However, their contents are not always shared publicly and may not be available outside the local population/community. To address the scattering of materials and expertise, the DAISY Music Braille project, an international consortium of blind-serving organizations, schools, and companies [42], has begun an initiative for sharing scores and transcription work between organizations. Additionally, the Marrakesh Treaty simplifies sending musical materials across countries who have signed the treaty through limitations and exceptions to traditional copyright law [46].

BVI musicians are at a disadvantage both when purchasing new scores and when acquiring free scores in the public domain. While we do not discuss the legalities of copying and sharing music under copyright, laws such as the Effective Communication Clause in the Americans with Disabilities Act (ADA) [44], protects services that provide accessible materials, like braille and large print, to BVI people. Music publishers only sell one version of a score in standard print or PDF format and do not usually share MusicXML files due to the ease with which they can be copied, edited, and otherwise misused. Thus, BVI musicians can pay twice, first for the score and second for the transcription service.

Alternatively, there is a vast collection of free music in the public domain that can be shared in any format. The International Music Score Library Project (IMSLP) [33], is the largest online catalogue containing more than 650,000 (inaccessible) PDF scores dwarfing the NLS collection of instructional music materials and scores, about 25,000 braille, large print, and audio files [27]. Another large online collection, MuseScore, holds hundreds of thousands scores that can be downloaded in MusicXML and accessed within an interface that supports audio playback and resizing [25]. MuseScore's collection consists of original works and transcriptions posted by users rather than professional publishers or transcribers.

While scores can be filtered by user rating and copyright, this repository has not been evaluated in research as a resource for acquiring music in braille/large print.

2.4   Transcription Processes

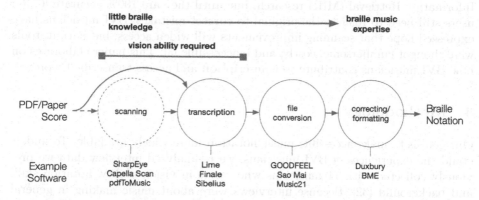

Fig. 2. Overview of braille music transcription process to convert from PDF/paper score to braille notation depicted with corresponding software. Early steps require vision ability while later steps require braille expertise.

Transcriptions can made by certified, sighted experts [26], or sighted/non-sighted pairs in which the former reads from a score while the latter notates braille [16]. In this paper, we focus on processes that distribute work across a team with the use of software to help convert from print to braille. Conversion tools include GOODFEEL bundled with Lime Aloud [8], Sao Mai Braille available for free on Windows [34], music21 an open source Python library [7], and other systems developed by researchers [14, 15, 21]. Typically, these programs import MusicXML, a standard music source file supported by all music notation software, and generate a braille file. Unfortunately, a MusicXML file is not often available and conversion programs are imperfect [3].

When a MusicXML source file is unavailable, a collaborative transcription process consists of multiple stages (depicted in Fig. 2 and detailed in [31]). First, one or more sighted people transcribe (copy) a PDF or print score into notation software. One approach is to manually copy all musical elements, – notes, markings, lyrics, etc. – a time-consuming and expensive task for a professional. An alternative to manual copying is to use score scanning or Optical Music Recognition (OMR) software, such as SharpEye bundled with Lime Aloud [8]. Then, once a score has been manually transcribed or scanned, it can be exported to MusicXML and then converted to braille with one of the aforementioned programs. Because this automatically generated score may contain mistakes and inconsistencies, it is usually sent to a braille music expert to make corrections and improvements to layout and style [18].

Human and technological efforts to improve the quantity and quality of transcriptions have been pursued. The OpenScore project has explored crowd-sourcing, or distributing transcription labor across volunteers [28] with mixed success. One effort resulted in the completion of hundreds of *lieder*, short songs for voice and piano, while another effort to transcribe 100 complicated orchestral works remains largely incomplete. Scanning systems are being pursued in Music Information Retrieval (MIR) research, but until they are 100% accurate [6,36], users still need to refer to the original to correct mistakes. BVI musicians have expressed hope that scanning improvements will widen access, but current tools were thought cumbersome, costly, and inaccessible [3]. This paper elaborates on how BVI musicians contribute to transcription and access transcribed scores.

3   Methodology

Our goal is to make accessible music notation more widely available. To under-stand the experiences of BVI musicians, we re-analyzed interview data we pre-viously collected with 11 musicians who range in vision ability, notation skill, and background [32]. Because interviews were about music making in general and our earlier publication highlighted technology-mediated practices that do not use notation, like music production, significant portions of the data had yet to be considered.

3.1   Interview Protocol

We ran remote interviews via Zoom with 11 BVI adults who had at least one prior experience making original music with technology. Participants shared an example of their work before the interview so we could discuss it and understand their musical practice. Further details about the interview protocol are published in [32].

3.2   Evaluation

We conducted a thematic analysis on the interviews recorded and transcribed verbatim [5]. We used an inductive coding approach and did not incorporate themes from that prior analysis. The lead author read each interview and high-lighted responses referring to specific music notation, e.g. a braille or print score, or notation in general. Prior evaluation focused on how participants wrote and produced original work with music technology. Here, we include participant expe-riences, strategies, and anecdotes about acquiring, memorizing, and practicing with notation. Following two iterations and discussions within the research team, we finalized tags organized by the main themes, "Modality," "Notation," "Tran-scription," and "Curb Cut Effect" referring to speculation about broad impacts of novel systems or approaches. As this report is solution-oriented, we orga-nize Findings (Sect. 4) by challenges and address each challenge in order in the Discussion (Sect. 5).

3.3   Participants

Participants, listed in Table 1, possess diverse music backgrounds. Three (P6, P9, and P11) do not actively read and/or write notation because they do not use it in styles rooted in popular music and jazz. Four (P2, P4, P5, and P7) have worked professionally as transcribers producing braille or large print music for themselves and others. Additionally, three (P3, P8, P10) have worked to prepare braille, standard, or large print scores for themselves and/or their collaborators. Two (P1 and P8) discussed a changing relationship with notation corresponding with a gradual decline in visual ability over many years. P1 read music expanded on an iPad, but had not written notation in years, while P8 preferred learning by ear and improvising though she could read braille and has prepared scores for others. All but P1, P2, and P5 are older than 50, and only P8 identifies as female while the others identify as male.

Table 1. Participants

ID	Training	Music format	Computer access*
P1	Master in Composition	Large print	MM
P2	Master in Jazz	Large print	MM
P3	School for the Blind	Braille	SK
P4	School for the Blind	Braille	SK
P5	Bachelor in Composition	Braille	SK
P6	Lessons/Self Taught	None	SK
P7	BM Jazz	Braille	SK
P8	Lessons	Braille	SK
P9	Audio Production Diploma	Large print	MM
P10	School for the Blind	Braille	SK
P11	Bachelor in Audio Engineering	Braille	SK

*MM = Magnification/Mouse, SK = Screen Reader/Keyboard

4   Findings

We report experiences making music notation accessible through transcription, customizing scores to improve usefulness and legibility, and finally accessing scores found in online repositories.

4.1   Transcription Experiences

Participants shared how they acquired music or contributed to a transcription, and explained how humans address constraints of automation.

Possibilities and Pitfalls of Automated Transcription. Participants had experience with two stages of an automated transcription process (Fig. 2): scanning a PDF score, and conversion from a transcribed score to a braille file. While scanning provides an alternative to manual copying, P7, who used the commercial software SharpEye [8], told us that scanning is "wonderful" when it works, but when it does not work, mistakes cannot be corrected without vision ability: "If you're blind, you're kind of dead in the water with music scanning if there are errors because in order to correct them you need two things: You need to be able to use these applications, which by nature aren't very accessible. But even more basic you need to be able to refer back to the original score."

Conversion scripts that generate braille from a source file were used widely among participants (P2, P3, P4, P5, P7, and P10). Describing his workflow, P4 said, "I'll write in Lime and then pass the Lime to GOODFEEL which turns Lime's printed notation into braille." When a MusicXML file is already available, automated conversion enables independent access and can negate need for professional transcription. P7 reflected, GOODFEEL is "great for piano sonatas, string quartets, individual vocal parts. Somebody sent me recently a MusicXML file of the first movement of Mozart's 40th symphony, and it imports great, plays back great, transcribes the braille." However, some outlined how complicated music and edge cases led to limitations and errors. P7 acknowledged that "GOOD-FEEL is not a tool for some pretty complicated things like page directions." Furthermore, P5 reported that GOODFEEL supports advanced notation like quarter tone accidentals (notes in between notes), but describing a non-western scale, told us "I think for any custom accidental beyond that, a symbol will have to be defined by the transcriber."

When Humans in the Loop Are Helpful. While automation has increased speed and accuracy, participants found human input important to improve formatting and legibility. P2, P3, P4, P5, and P7 all had experience notating music for sighted people and needed sighted aid in the final stages making print scores they could not read. For example, P2 said, "it's actually quite difficult to prepare regular sheet music because everything is scaled down to normal size and so I had some assistance just to get everything nice and presentable," and P3 estimated, "90% or 95% of the arrangement, I can do by myself." P4 identified common issues, "I'll send the PDF and they'll tell me, 'It needs to be spaced a little differently' or 'you forgot a double bar' and I'll fix it. Probably the biggest problem is clashes of text." Like print, automatically generated braille scores rarely follow formatting best practices. P5 described how the formatting of GOODFEEL can be "crude" because, "braille music rules with formatting are harder to implement than some other ones specifically about symbols being used in certain places." P5 manually formats scores with Duxbury [9].

Manual formatting was not always thought necessary. For example, P8 described her process creating parts for her chorus without sighted aid, "I discovered that I could use ABC and create an ASCII text file that could then generate actual printed music. I never got good at actually putting the words located correctly underneath each staff. But ABC will also do a quick and dirty version where you have several notes and then the words below. It's a little harder for singers, but still achievable." Furthermore, in order to get parts to musicians quickly, P4 requested that transcribers "not worry about GF [GOOD-FEEL] processing and braille proofing" because P4 owns the software to make corrections if/when they come up.

4.2   Barriers to Customizing Scores

Best summed up by P4 who told us succinctly, "We avoid PDFs," participants described how standard print alternatives aid learning, memorization, and performance.

Experiences with Large Print Music. When only standard print was available, participants used other access strategies, but sometimes these complicated their ability to learn. For example, P3 and P8 read print music as students but did not have a means to acquire large print scores. P3 said, "my father used to write it bigger. My father doesn't know anything about music, but he just copied it, I guess." P8 said, "I had to literally bend over the piano keyboard, get my nose up into the book, and see just a portion of the score." She eventually "rebuilt the music rack on the piano" to position the music closer to her face, but this required P8 to practice uncomfortably with her "hands crammed in the stomach." The difficulty reading led her to memorize music very quickly and make predictions, which she sometimes got wrong. P8 joked, "needless to say, it was easier to learn Mozart than Beethoven or Scriabin."

Digital scores increased music access for large print readers. P1 initially faced difficulty in a musical theater class in which students were expected to sight read print handouts. He said, "it's possible for me to read something on a piece of paper with no backlighting, it just takes a long time and I lose my place easily." He requested digital copies be provided in advance enabling him to read with the aid of iPad settings, like zoom and color contrast, and become familiarized with key sections before class. Of those we spoke to, P2 was most experienced making large print scores for himself and others by fine tuning layouts within the commercial notation software Finale [22] in which he adjusts "very specific engraving things," such as "lines needing to be darker or lighter, measures per system, how many pages, where are rehearsal marks, where are dynamics..." To initially determine vision ability for musicians, P2 uses an eye chart with music notation instead of letters, and he maintains a spreadsheet with musicians' preferences. Other requirements, such as whether a score will be read in performance or memorized beforehand, also determine layout.

Braille Customization for Learning and Navigation. Braille scores tend to be longer than print counterparts, and navigation can be tedious due to braille notation density. P6, who decided not to pursue braille music said, "this teacher was trying to teach me braille music and it was just too complicated." Others fluent in braille music discussed their approaches to learning new scores. Instrumental musicians memorize music in advance. For example, P5 described his process on piano, "I learn measure by measure, part by part and then I have to build it up and commit everything to memory." Singers, in contrast, may read braille during rehearsal or performance because their hands are not occupied, but they may not need or want the entire score. P7 said, "I'm much better remembering tunes than words so I would get my own lyrics to have when I perform. I like to read it just to keep on track."

Some read non-standard braille notations or invented their own. P4 and P8 used the text-based notation ABC [45], while P4 and P10 explained idiosyncratic notations: P4 wrote orchestral scores in his own reduced format, "I used my own notation, but it's still conventional enough... I often would do each orchestral part as a group, almost like a piano reduction. So the winds had their own section, the strings had their own section, the brass had their own section – unless there was a solo and I worked out ways to do that. I even took little shortcuts." P10 remembered a sighted teacher who refused to transcribe music into braille and instead "came up with his own text-based method of showing the note and the duration. He used a spatial layout where equal signs and dashes sort of represented where notes were placed in the measure." More recently, P10 and a collaborator invented a notation (discussed again below) that only depicts chord charts and is much simpler than conventional braille music: "People get tripped up with braille music when it comes to actual music notation. The way the code works really throws people off at first... What we're doing is just giving access to chord charts."

Advantages of Audio Playback for Learning and Memorization. Many participants described the use of synthesized audio, sound generated in software, as part of their learning/practice routine. Four participants, who cannot read large print and often choose not to use braille (P6, P8, P9, and P11), preferred to learn through sound. P6, P9, and P11 do not find braille useful because they perform popular styles without notation. For example, P6 said "you know for rock or folk it's not that important." P8 finds braille uncomfortable, "after several minutes of trying, literally my fingers don't like to move across it anymore - it starts to irritate." As a result, she modified her piano performance style and believes that "if you are a reasonably good musician, the ears are arguably faster than braille." That said, she admits that the audio channel is limited especially for advanced musicians, "Braille is probably still good to really validate... What you don't have (from audio) is all the ancillary data, you know the staccato mark, that other stuff. I'm not sure how you get that... Why not work with a teacher if you're working at that level?"

P3, P4, P7, and P10 combined braille and audio playback to learn music. For example, P4's chorus consists of BVI musicians with access to braille and large print, but P4 works with the music production software Sonar [8] to create additional "audio learning material" including isolated parts with synthesized voice (e.g. soprano, alto) and recordings of spoken lyrics. P10 additionally created audio files that he felt enhanced learning guitar songs: "As a blind person playing the guitar, I have to have both hands on my instrument... So I came up with a super simple scheme to learn a song more quickly than stopping and referring back and stopping. Talking about low-tech, I will get a metronome going and then I literally make a recording of me in time saying, 'A minor seven', 'D seven'... And then like faster counts... I felt I can learn the tune in a fraction of the time."

4.3 Limitations of Existing Notation Collections

Participants found limitations in existing resources and catalogs in regards to genre, file type, and quality. For example, P10 said, "While I do have access, you know in a very limited form, to some jazz and popular music, there's really not a lot out there." Participants have sought out alternative collections with mixed success. For example, P8 downloaded scores in LilyPond and ABC texts, formats accessible via screen reader, but despite prior programming experience, she found LilyPond extremely challenging. P10 attempted to download MusicXML files from MuseScore [25] but found the results unsatisfactory when imported into Lime: "MuseScore and other repositories out there have a bunch of transcriptions. But right now for me, it isn't quite worth printing that stuff out. There's a little too much guesswork going on until it [Lime's MusicXML importer] makes those corrections." Alternatively, P10 found a more reliable collection in the iReal Pro guitar tablature application, "I downloaded a jazz playlist, like hundreds of jazz standards. I listened to some and the controls for playing and stopping, and using the mixer, and changing the key and the tempo - that was all accessible." P10's subsequent effort to convert this library to custom braille chord notation provides, as he envisions, "access to charts that sighted users have that blind folks never had before. The comparison would be if I gave you access to a home library and then suddenly gave you an internet connection."

Music source files, if accurate, enabled some to navigate music within accessible software across modalities. P8 discussed the Android SM music player app [34]: "It'll take either a MIDI file or a MusicXML file and allow you to play it at any tempo in any key, to play the left hand parts within the left speaker, the right hand part through the right speaker, set your beginning and end points here and play over and over again." Finally, P7 discussed how importing MusicXML into Lime Aloud supports a range of people: "A sighted user and a blind user can use the same thing pretty much on the same level. They can get the job done and get the information in the format that's most helpful to them, even two or three formats."

5 Discussion

Connecting our findings with related work, we share our vision to 1) increase the quantity of transcribed music, 2) make music notation customizable across multiple versions and 3) distribute music files in an accessible manner. When relevant, we include participant suggestions and ideas.

5.1 Efficiently Incorporate Crowd Sourcing in Transcription

While automation will become more accurate, including humans in the loop will usually improve a transcription. Human input can be most effective in the transcription stages of initial score input and final braille score editing (Sect. 4.1). Because score input can be completed by sighted non-specialists with a variety of commercial and free software, we see the largest opportunity for crowd sourcing, or as P7 proposed "recruit people who aren't specialists, as far as braille, who can actually function as transcribers and can do the vast majority of the meat and potatoes stuff." The OpenScore project, a prior crowd-sourced effort to transcribe and digitize "significant works," offers lessons for future approaches [28]. As of this writing, only 14 of 100 tasks have been completed and posted to the OpenScore repository [29]. OpenScore suggested that the complexity of selected works intimidated volunteers [28] because a separate effort to transcribe 250 shorter, simpler works was completed in four months. We propose partnering with local blind-service organizations. In our experience as transcribers, complex, massive works beyond 100 pages are rarely needed. Usually, musicians request excerpts or individual parts. Furthermore, scores selected to meet immediate need may increase volunteer motivation. We also propose recruiting high school and college students studying music who are required to learn notation software in their coursework and are often assigned practice transcriptions. Open questions are how accurate volunteer input will be, whether accuracy increases with experience, and how many workers are ideal to contribute to a single score. Researchers should test workflows that incorporate automated score scanning and even utilize manually-corrected results to improve data sets given that current Optical Music Recognition systems are trained via machine learning [6].

The final stage of a braille transcription process, improvements to accuracy, formatting, and legibility, requires expertise. As this is skill uncommon and can take years to cultivate and become certified [26], braille music editing is unlikely to be a task easily adaptable to crowd labor. However, high quality MusicXML files appear to yield sufficient braille scores (Sect. 4.1) rendering a professional unnecessary at times, e.g. when one needs immediate access, does not want to pay extra for professional work, or can proofread and format on their own. In instances when automated braille conversion is insufficient for a particular score or it prioritizes choices that may be open to interpretation, limitations, warnings, and errors should be communicated to an end user. Platforms that provide MusicXML files (e.g. MuseScore [25]) could direct end-users to professional service providers, whose work remains unmatched despite software advances and alternate workflows.

5.2   Design for Customization in Scores in Notation Tools

There is no one-size-fits-all solution for music notation as evidenced by the range
of formats, mediums, and notations used by participants. In this section we list
specific customization requirements including page size, notation size, layout,
and density across modalities. The following characteristics are technically mod-
ifiable in music notation and braille editing software, but they require navigating
menus and knowing which settings to tweak (e.g. line spacing and thickness, note
size, font size, etc.) to achieve a desired effect.

Large Print Music. When customizing a large print score, end users should be
presented with general settings and optional details that may be tweaked. The
main features to determine are paper size (e.g. 8.5×11, 11×17), orientation,
and systems per page which is more relatable to print readers than magnification
percentage. The user should be made aware of page count given its relevance
to performance, e.g. two 8.5×11 sheets can lie on a typical music stand at
a time. Other parameters that have been explored by P2 and cited in prior
research [3] include font selection, paper color, removal of repeated information
like clef/meter symbols to reduce clutter, and breaking pages across rests, which
can enable page turns during performance at the expense of longer page counts.
An open question is whether there are generic large print formats that could
be made available as PDFs, or whether each large print reader needs a unique
version.

Braille Music. Automated braille conversion tools already provide settings
both for formatting scores, e.g. paper size, cells per line, arrangement of parts or
voices, and presenting content, e.g. chord notation. Further customization would
support other use cases, e.g. isolating lyrics to support P7's choral performance
practice (Sect. 4.2). P4 envisioned a system that can "present only the parts of
the music that you want to see. For instance, if you have a vocal score, it can
show you only the lyrics or only the music. You can have it jump to rehearsal
marks. You can have it filter out dynamics and things just so that you can
see the notes." Given that MusicXML files are structured and labelled, and
music theory researchers already use tools like music21 [7] to filter and sort
score content, we see research opportunities to apply existing techniques to aid
braille music learning and memorization.

Synthesized Audio. Participants described using synthesized audio, making
audio recordings, and using accessible software for music playback (Sect. 4.2).
While there do not exist guidelines for generating effective audio learning materials in this context, we suggest options to alter tempo, isolate parts, and loop
specific sections. P8 described the difficulty of navigating audio files and suggested drawing inspiration from NLS talking books: "You can skip forward, not
by time offset, but to the next chapter. You can then set the navigation granularity and skip to the next chapter and the next subsection of the same chapter."

An additional approach used by P10 is reading music notation out loud. While P10 used his own voice, solutions that use text-to-speech have been proposed as "talking scores" [3]. While researchers have not studied text-to-speech music learning, recently a free system called Talking Scores has been made available online that generates a web page from MusicXML with notation described in English that can be voiced by screen readers [24]. Research that evaluates talking score features, including content, granularity, and speed, could have broader impacts for other audio descriptions of materials.

5.3   Storage and Distribution: Support Multiple Types of Notation

Future libraries and repositories of music notation can no longer include scores in only one standard PDF version. Collections should include quality MusicXML source files, but as these are not human readable or editable, they are not immediately useful without other software. Instead, each score should contain a mix of source and output files. Source files include languages like MusicXML, software-specific files (e.g. .mus for Finale), and ABC/LilyPond for editing a score using ASCII text. Output files should capture each modality including print/large print, braille, and MIDI (audio). Braille files that have not been proofed may be included, but flagged as potentially containing limitations and errors. Ideally, the customization options listed above should be incorporated directly into repositories preventing the need to download and learn additional software.

Including multiple file types supports more individuals and environments with diverse needs and equipment. As P10 notes, with a braille score alone, "it is presumed that the user has not only some proficiency in braille, but also has access by way of a braille display or an embosser." We further reflect on custom notations created by P4 and P10 (Sect. 4.2). While non-standard notations, such as these, are unlikely to be found in libraries like the NLS, we think they should be shared and made publicly available (with reading instructions). Drawing inspiration from performers like Molly Joyce and Jerron Herman who emphasize their disabilities in their work and infuse dance and music performances with accessible media, like audio description and American Sign Language [19], music collections should include rather than exclude readers, and scores should transcend a single modality or notation.

6   Limitations and Future Work

We interviewed a small population of experienced, BVI musicians who were recruited without demographic targets. Most of the notation referenced and discussed by participants can be labelled as "western classical." As we showed, "mainstream," western scores are hardly made accessible, but scores from other traditions are considered even less. It is important that accessible music collections promote diversity, and few of the approaches discussed above – automation, crowd-sourcing, standard customization options – are likely to be effective at broadening access to non-western styles. Future research should incorporate the perspectives of non-western, BVI musicians. Additionally, our participants were mostly older with established musical practices. Engaging with younger BVI musicians, for whom access to notation could meaningfully impact relationship with music performance and composition, will likely result in additional requirements and research opportunities. Ahead, our team will continue designing systems that export music across formats, pilot a initiative to pair volunteers with a local organization that serves BVI musicians, and work with composers and BVI musicians to make and perform using original tactile notations.

7   Conclusion

In this paper, we depicted difficulties BVI people face when accessing music notation made in a format they can't read. Our recommendations are intended to address a significant backlog of visual-only music: Using crowd workers could make music source files more quickly available, while supporting score customization could include more diverse needs. Our collections of music in the future need to incorporate more than standard PDFs.

Acknowledgement. We thank Alex (Yixuan) Xu, Fabiha Ahmed, and Lisa Ye for their contributions and the NYU Ability Project for its support.

References

1. Avid: Music Notation Software - Sibelius (2021). https://www.avid.com/sibelius
2. Baker, D.: Visually impaired musicians' insights: Narratives of childhood, lifelong learning and musical participation. Br. J. Music Educ. **31**(2), 113–135 (2014). https://doi.org/10.1017/S0265051714000072
3. Baker, D., Green, L.: Insights in sound: visually impaired Musicians' lives and learning. Routledge (2017)
4. American Federation of the Blind: Screen readers (2022). https://www.afb.org/blindness-and-low-vision/using-technology/assistive-technology-products/screen-readers
5. Braun, V., Clarke, V.: Using thematic analysis in psychology. Qualitative Res. Psychol. **3**(2), 77–101 (2006). https://doi.org/10.1191/1478088706qp063oa. http://www.tandfonline.com/doi/abs/10.1191/1478088706qp063oa
6. Calvo-Zaragoza, J., Jr., J.H., Pacha, A.: Understanding optical music recognition. ACM Comput. Surv. **53**(4), July 2020. https://doi.org/10.1145/3397499
7. Cuthbert, Michael Scott: music21 Braille Translate (2021). https://web.mit.edu/music21/doc/moduleReference/moduleBrailleTranslate.html
8. Dancing Dots: Dancing dots: Accessible music technology for blind and low vision performers since 1992 (2020). https://www.dancingdots.com/
9. Duxbury Systems: Duxbury DBT: Braille Translation Software (2021). https://www.duxburysystems.com
10. Associazione Giuseppe Paccini ETS: Braille Music Editor (2021). https://braillemusiceditor.com/
11. Filomen M. D'Agostino Greenberg Music School: Fmdg school: Fostering education, access, and inclusion for people of all ages with vision loss (2021). https://fmdgmusicschool.org

12. Firman, R.: International braille music: a worldwide listing of organisations producing and loaning braille music (2021). https://www.golden-chord.com/braille-music-organisations.php
13. GNU Project: LilyPond (2021). https://lilypond.org
14. Goto, D., Gotoh, T., Minamikawa-Tachino, R., Tamura, N.: A transcription system from MusicXML format to braille music notation. EURASIP J. Adv. Signal Process. **2007**(1), 1–9 (2007). https://doi.org/10.1155/2007/42498
15. Gotoh, T., Minamikawa-Tachino, R., Tamura, N.: A web-based braille translation for digital music scores. In: Proceedings of the 10th International ACM SIGACCESS Conference on Computers and Accessibility, Assets 2008, pp. 259–260. Association for Computing Machinery, New York (2008). https://doi.org/10.1145/1414471.1414527
16. Howell, J.: Innovation in braille music translation: processes and transcription practices to produce more music. In: 7th General Assembly of the International Council on English Braille, ICEB 2020, International Council on English Braille (2020). http://www.iceb.org/GA20.html
17. Jacko, V.A., Choi, J.H., Carballo, A., Charlson, B., Moore, J.E.: A new synthesis of sound and tactile music code instruction in a pilot online braille music curriculum. J. Visual Impairment Blindness **109**(2), 153–157 (2015). https://doi.org/10.1177/0145482X1510900212
18. Jessel, N.: Access to musical information for blind people. In: International Conference on Technologies for Music Notation and Representation, pp. 232–237. Institut de Recherche en Musicologie (IReMus) (2015)
19. Joyce, M.: Moving and thriving alongside the physicality of disability: The work of jerron herman, August 2020. https://disabilityarts.online/magazine/opinion/moving-and-thriving-alongside-the-physicality-of-disability-the-work-of-jerron-herman/
20. Kersten, F.: The history and development of braille music methodology. Bull. Hist. Res. Music. Educ. **18**(2), 106–125 (1997)
21. Leopold, M.: Hodder-a fully automatic braille note production system. In: International Conference on Computers for Handicapped Persons, pp. 6–11. Springer (2006)
22. makemusic: finale music notation software (2021). https://www.finalemusic.com
23. Mankoff, J., Hayes, G.R., Kasnitz, D.: Disability studies as a source of critical inquiry for the field of assistive technology. In: Proceedings of the 12th International ACM SIGACCESS Conference on Computers and Accessibility, ASSETS 2010, pp. 3–10. Association for Computing Machinery, New York (2010). https://doi.org/10.1145/1878803.1878807
24. Marchant, P.: Talking Scores Beta (2022). https://www.talkingscores.org
25. MuseScore BV: MuseScore (2022). https://musescore.com/
26. National Library Service for the Blind and Print Disabled: Music Braille Transcribing (2021). https://www.loc.gov/nls/braille-audio-reading-materials/music-materials/circular-no-4-braille-music-transcribers/
27. National Library Service for the Blind and Print Disabled: Music Instructional Materials and Scores (2021). https://www.loc.gov/nls/about/services/music-instructional-materials-scores/
28. OpenScore: OpenScore: One Year On (2018). https://openscore.cc/blog/2018/8/20/openscore-one-year-on
29. OpenScore: OpenScore Sheet Music (2022). https://musescore.com/user/13033246/sheetmusic

30. Park, H.Y., Kim, M.J.: Affordance of braille music as a mediational means: significance and limitations. Br. J. Music Educ. **31**(2), 137–155 (2014). https://doi.org/10.1017/S0265051714000138

31. Payne, W., Ahmed, F., Gardell, M., DuBois, R.L., Hurst, A.: Soundcells: Designing a browser-based music technology for braille and print notation. In: 19th Web for All Conference, W4A 2022. Association for Computing Machinery, New York, May 2022. https://doi.org/10.1145/3493612.3520462

32. Payne, W.C., Xu, A.Y., Ahmed, F., Ye, L., Hurst, A.: How blind and visually impaired composers, producers, and songwriters leverage and adapt music technology. In: The 22nd International ACM SIGACCESS Conference on Computers and Accessibility, pp. 1–12 (2020). https://doi.org/10.1145/3373625.3417002

33. Petrucci Music Library: IMSLP: Sharing the world's public domain music (2021). https://imslp.org/

34. Phuc, D.H.: Sao mai braille (2022). https://www.saomaicenter.org/en/smsoft/smb

35. Pino, A., Viladot, L.: Teaching-learning resources and supports in the music classroom: Key aspects for the inclusion of visually impaired students. British J. Visual Impairment **37**(1), 17–28 (2019). https://doi.org/10.1177/0264619618795199

36. Rebelo, A., Fujinaga, I., Paszkiewicz, F., Marcal, A.R., Guedes, C., Cardoso, J.S.: Optical music recognition: state-of-the-art and open issues. Int. J. Multimed. Inf. Retrieval **1**(3), 173–190 (2012)

37. Rowden, T.: The Songs of Blind Folk. University of Michigan Press (2009). https://doi.org/10.3998/mpub.232221

38. Rush, T.W.: Braille Music Notator (2019). https://tobyrush.com/braillemusic/notator/

39. Saha, A., Piper, A.M.: Understanding audio production practices of people with vision impairments. In: The 22nd International ACM SIGACCESS Conference on Computers and Accessibility, pp. 1–13 (2020)

40. Smith, L.R., Auckenthaler, K., Busch, G., Gearreald, K., Geminder, D., McKenney, B., Miller, H., Ridgeway, T.: Braille Music Code. American Printing House for the Blind, Louisville, Kentucky (2015)

41. Payne, T., et al.: Empowering blind musicians to compose and notate music with soundcells. In: The 24th International ACM SIGACCESS Conference on Computers and Accessibility, ASSETS 2022. Association for Computing Machinery, New York, October 2022. https://doi.org/10.1145/3517428.3544825

42. The DAISY Consortium: Music Braille (2021). https://daisy.org/activities/projects/music-braille/

43. Tobias, E.S.: Composing, songwriting, and producing: informing popular music pedagogy. Res. Stud. Music Educ. **35**(2), 213–237 (2013). https://doi.org/10.1177/1321103X13487466. http://journals.sagepub.com/doi/10.1177/1321103X13487466

44. U.S. Department of Justice: Effective communication (2022). https://www.ada.gov/effective-comm.htm

45. Walshaw, C.: abc notation (2021). https://abcnotation.com/

46. World Intellectual Property Organization: The marrakesh treaty (2022). https://www.wipo.int/marrakesh_treaty/en

The Rural Informatization Policies in China: The Power Dynamics and Policy Instruments

Xiaoqian Zhang[1]($\boxtimes$) (iD), Feng Yang[2] (iD), and Yi Wan[3] (iD)

[1] McGill University, Montreal, Quebec H3A1X1, Canada
xiaoqian.zhang@mail.mcgill.ca
[2] Sichuan University, Chengdu 610065, Sichuan, China
[3] University of South Carolina, Columbia, SC 29208, USA

Abstract. Rural informatization in China has developed rapidly in recent years. However, there are still significant differences in the rate of informatization of rural and urban areas resulting from the historical resources imbalance. Existing research is limited in studying the text of China's rural informatization policies. To understand the power dynamics and instruments in policies, content analysis and frequency counts were used in this study. Research results find that the Ministry of Agriculture and Rural Affairs is China's leading rural informatization policymaker, but contributions are also made by other government agencies. Policy implementation is led by government departments with the assistance of non-governmental stakeholders. The adopted policy instruments have evolved from supply-side and environmental considerations to form a coordinated combination of supply-, environmental-, and demand-side instruments. These findings provide an understanding of the underlying power dynamics of current policy and assist the formulation of future policy. Moreover, these findings provide new perspectives that can improve the efficiency of policy implementation and maximize policy benefits.

Keywords: Rural informatization · Policy analysis · Policymakers · Policy implementers · Policy instruments

1 Introduction

The development of information infrastructure can considerably improve a country's economy and people's life quality [1]. However, positive changes created by information and communication technologies (ICTs) might not always be equal between urban and rural regions in China. Rural informatization is "the process of using modern technology to improve agricultural production capacity, rural management level, and farmers' quality of life in rural areas" [2]. It could narrow the urban-rural developing gap in China caused by digital disparities [3]. Rural informatization would empower rural regions by 1) providing relevant, reliable, and high-quality information for agriculture development, 2) facilitating agriculture based on new technologies, 3) restructuring the economic framework, and 4) improving the sustainability of agriculture [4–6]. Correspondingly,

I. Sserwanga et al. (Eds.): iConference 2023, LNCS 13972, pp. 598–613, 2023.
https://doi.org/10.1007/978-3-031-28032-0_45

the Chinese government issued various long-term, medium-term, and industry-specific informatization policies [6], such as the "Rural Revitalization Strategy," "Cyber Power Strategy," "National Big Data Strategy," "Internet+ Action," and "National Informatization Development Strategy." The information infrastructure saw significant growth in rural China with these policies. At the end of 2018, the rates of China's rural fiber-optical and 4G network coverage and telephone and Internet penetration were 96%, 95%, 99.7%, and 38.4%, respectively. Moreover, information technologies such as the Internet of Things, big data, and spatial information have been applied for online monitoring, precision operations, and the digital management of agricultural production [7].

Given the critical role of policies in rural informatization, researchers paid increasing attention to this topic. The existing literature on rural informatization in China has primarily focused on recommendations for policy making. For example, researchers indicated that China's national broadband strategy should focus on users' demands [8], the policy system should encourage ICTs application in agricultural and rural areas [9], and rural informatization policies should empower farmers by improving their information literacy [10]. The methods used by previous researchers to analyze China's rural informatization include the data envelopment analysis method [11], the improved fuzzy analytic hierarchy process [12], and the catastrophe progression method [13].

Though various studies are conducted to increase the understanding of rural informatization policies, the research of current policy texts seems to be inadequate. Analyzing policy texts can effectively present facts and meanings contained in policies. All policies require legalization and implementation by the corresponding individuals and institutions. The interests and abilities of policymakers directly affect the formation of policies. Implementers directly determine the effectiveness of policy implementation and the achievement of policy goals. Policy instruments are specific means and methods used to solve social problems and achieve policy goals; they can explain the intentions of policymakers and predict policy continuity [14]. However, few studies have analyzed the subject and context of China's rural informatization policies. Therefore, this study tends to fill the gap by addressing the following research questions:

1) Who issues China's rural informatization policies, and what are their roles?
2) Who is responsible for policy implementation, and what are their roles?
3) What instruments are used in these policies?

By shedding light on the above characteristics of rural informatization policies in China, this study aims to reveal the underlying power dynamics and instruments in policies and provide suggestions for rural information policymaking in the future.

2   Methodology

2.1   Data Collection

We collected 41 Chinese policies related to rural informatization. The dataset spans 20 years (from 1999 to 2019). We searched for the policies from various sources, including popular law databases in China, such as Beida Fabao, the Laws and Regulations Database of Wanfang, the China Laws & Regulations Database, the China

Political News Bulletin and Periodical Literature Database, and the relevant government departments' portals, such as the Ministry of Agriculture and Rural Affairs of the People's Republic of China and the Ministry of Industry and Information Technology. We searched the above channels with multiple keywords, including "nongcun xinxi hua (rural informatization)," "nongye xinxi hua (agricultural informatization)," "nongmin xinxi (farmer information)," "nongye xinxi (agricultural information)," "san nong xinxi (information on agriculture, farmers, and rural areas)," "nongcun xinxi (rural informatization)," "xinxi ziyuan gongxiang gongcheng (information resources sharing project)," and "nongjia shuwu (farmer's library)."

We refined the search results with the following criteria: (1) duplicate policies were removed; (2) less relevant policies were removed, including those with a low frequency of keywords and limited association with rural informatization (e.g., Notice of the Ministry of Agriculture and Rural Affairs, the Ministry of Industry and Information Technology, and the Ministry of Public Security on Printing and Distributing the "Key Points on National Fight Against and Supervision Over Agricultural Supplies Counterfeiting (2018)"); (3) given that policies in China issued by the local government tend to be detailed and localized extensions of state policies, they duplicate the content of those issued by the state government; therefore, local policies were eliminated from the analysis.

2.2 Data Analysis

We analyzed the 41 rural informatization policies using content analysis and frequency counts. The content analysis uncovers characteristics (e.g., intention, focus, and patterns) of messages. Frequency counts are one of the most straightforward ways to discover the number of occurrences of particular units in particular contexts. The combination would help us balance subjectivity and objectivity and understand the common features and trends of these policies.

We first developed the etic codes based on our research questions and the existing literature. The top-level codes, echoing the research questions, are policymakers, policy implementers, and policy instruments. Further, we divided policy instruments into the supply side, the environmental side, and the demand side [15]. Supply-side instruments refer to the resources, equipment, services, human resources, and other material and non-material government investments to promote rural informatization. Environmental instruments aim to create a favorable social context for rural informatization through making changes by the government at institutional, legislative, academic, and cultural levels. Demand-side instruments empower stakeholders by engaging them in government decision-making procedures. Commonly used demand-side instruments include pilot projects, evaluations and assessments, and public bidding.

The authors then read through the materials and created emic codes. The issuing departments of the policies were coded into policymakers. The policy implementers mentioned in the text include government departments, scientific research institutions, enterprises, and individuals. In terms of policy instruments, we first inductively identified potential codes from policy text (Table 1). These codes then were integrated into the coding hierarchy mentioned above (Table 2).

Table 1. Policy excerpts and their responding codes

Policy excerpts	Codes
"… to establish comprehensive information systems related to agricultural science and technology at different levels to provide agricultural resource information…"	Resource Management, Facility Construction, Technological Support
"… to coordinate the construction of agricultural information platforms, agriculture call centers, and information service stations (points) to improve the utilization of information facilities and equipment…"	Facility Construction, Service Guarantee
"… focusing on strengthening the training of leading enterprises in agricultural industrialization, economic farmer cooperatives, information service personnel of intermediary organizations, large and specialized family agricultural businesses, and rural brokers…"	Talent Support, Service Guarantee
"… training new farmers with informatization…"; "… fully utilizing educational resources of agricultural radio and television educational institutions… Strengthening the training on agricultural and occupational skills of farmers and using modern information technology to cultivate new farmers with corresponding knowledge, technique, and operational skills."	Education and Training, Technological Support
"… strengthening the integrated application and presentation of modern information technology, conducting pilot tests, mature applications, and transformation of various modern technologies to comprehensively improve agricultural information technology…"	Technological Support, Project Sponsorship
"… actively promote the project under the unified leadership of the local government and participation of other relevant departments…" "… reinforcing the guidance of the pilot unit; and creating favorable conditions and the active support needed to ensure the sustainable development of demonstration projects…"	Organization and Leadership, Service Guarantee

(*continued*)

Table 1. (*continued*)

Policy excerpts	Codes
"… the agricultural departments at all levels should work together with relevant departments to actively promulgate supporting policies, simplify administrative procedures, and decentralize powers… for providing a sound and relaxed development environment for agricultural and rural informatization…"	Laws and Regulations
"… pilot provinces (autonomous regions and municipalities) and pilot counties (municipalities and districts) are expected to attach great importance to [the projects], effectively reinforcing the organization and leadership of the project and accelerating the formulation of implementation plans and provisions of supporting funds…."	Organization and Leadership, Financial Support
"… all local relevant units should utilize various media and channels to display and report the progress and achievements of demonstration projects… to further create a favorable atmosphere for the development of rural informatization…"	Promotion and Propagation
"… exchange progress and achievements of pilot projects of new rural informatization… focusing on the driving mechanisms and sustainable development…"	Project Sponsorship, Theoretical Research
"…to implement the requirements of the Central Conference on Rural Work… Accelerate the promotion of agricultural and rural informatization,… the ministry has decided to initiate the accreditation of the 2015 national agricultural and rural informatization demonstration base…"	Project Sponsorship
"…to strengthen the assessment and management of the national agricultural and rural informatization demonstration bases… an evaluation and assessment of national agricultural and rural informatization demonstration bases accredited in 2013 will be conducted this year…"	Evaluation and Assessment, Project Sponsorship

(*continued*)

Table 1. (*continued*)

Policy excerpts	Codes
"…in accordance with the relevant requirements of the Ministry of Industry and Information Technology and the Ministry of Finance and corresponding agreement template, [our department] has entrusted procurement agencies to use public bidding to select enterprises in each pilot area for the provision of universal telecommunication services…"	Public Bidding

Table 2. Analysis framework for policy instruments and corresponding definitions

Policy instrument		Elaboration
Supply Side	Resource Management	Emphasizes the increase in the supply, sharing, and management of information resources related to subjects such as agriculture, modern technology, production management, and policy and regulations during rural informatization
	Facility Construction	Emphasizes the promotion of information projects such as combining online stores, post offices, and e-commerce services into one system; the construction of information service stations; and the development of information network systems, agricultural information systems, and decision support systems
	Service Guarantee	Underscores the optimization of an information service system and improvement of information service capabilities to ensure that farmers and related social organizations can access convenient and efficient information services in production and life
	Talent Support	Based on the training of agricultural informatization practitioners in rural areas, such as IT personnel and researchers of related fields, to provide intellectual support for rural informatization

(*continued*)

Table 2. (*continued*)

Policy instrument		Elaboration
	Education and Training	Calls for attention to the strengthening of the education and training of informatization technology (IT) personnel and farmers and enhancing their information awareness, literacy, and skills to transform IT into productivity
	Technological Support	Focuses on the supporting role of information technology in the development of rural informatization, exerting its driving role for rural and agricultural development, and strengthening the innovation, research, and development of information technology
Environmental Side	Organization and Leadership	Stresses that government departments should attach importance to rural informatization and coordinate various parties and tasks
	Laws and Regulations	Government departments should improve standards, rules, and operational systems required for rural informatization and provide appropriate political preferences for corresponding projects and programs
	Financial Support	The government should provide financial support for rural informatization, such as increasing capital investment in rural informatization and providing tax incentives to information enterprises
	Promotion and Propagation	Demonstration units, demonstration projects, advanced experiences, and the application of technology based on the publication, exchange, and propagation of rural informatization policies
	Theoretical Research	Focuses on theoretical research on rural informatization issues such as development stages, models, difficulties and challenges, and experiences of other nations

(continued)

Table 2. (*continued*)

Policy instrument		Elaboration
Demand Side	Project Sponsorship	Encourages relevant departments, enterprises, and institutions to apply to pilot projects
	Evaluation and Assessment	Emphasizes the investigation of existing projects and tasks through evaluation, assessment, work summary, and questionnaire surveys to better understand the progress of rural informatization and guide future implementation
	Public Bidding	Aims to attract enterprises and social organizations to participate in the construction of rural information infrastructure and other informatization projects through public bidding

3 Results and Discussions

3.1 Policymakers

Policymakers are expected to coordinate with stakeholders and introduce relevant policies to guide social action that alleviates social problems. Table 3 summarized the policymakers specialized in rural informatization in China. The primary policymakers were the Ministry of Agriculture and Rural Affairs, the Ministry of Finance, the Ministry of Industry and Information Technology, the Ministry of Science and Technology, and the State Council. Overall, most policies were issued by a single department and other departments formulated and issued follow-up policies correspondingly, which indicates limited cross-departmental coordination in policy making.

The Ministry of Agriculture and Rural Affairs played a leading role in making rural informatization policies. It issued 78.05% (32) policies. The centralization might enhance the stability and consistency of rural informatization.

The Ministry of Industry and Information Technology also played a key role in issuing rural informatization policies (17.07%). Its missions include (1) guiding and promoting informatization across all sectors, (2) coordinating major issues during informatization, and (3) promoting major informatization projects. These missions decided its high engagement in rural informatization policies.

Financial support is a prerequisite of rural informatization, especially for the construction of information infrastructure. Therefore, the Ministry of Finance was crucial to rural informatization. In particular, the Ministry of Finance primarily cooperated with the Ministry of Industry and Information Technology to formulate policies to engage information technology (IT) companies and other social sectors in funding pilot projects for telecommunication services in rural areas.

Table 3. Descriptive analysis of policymakers

	Total policies issued	%	Number of policies issued jointly with other department(s)	Number of policies issued individually
Ministry of Agriculture and Rural Affairs	32	78.05	0	32
Ministry of Industry and Information Technology	7	17.07	2	5
Ministry of Finance	2	4.88	2	0
Ministry of Science and Technology	1	2.44	0	1
State Council	1	2.44	0	1

Rural informatization also needs technological support. Therefore, the Ministry of Science and Technology was responsible for formulating innovation-driven strategies and coordinating the construction of an innovation system and the scientific and technological system revolution.

The State Council, the highest administrative agency in China, stipulates the missions of ministries and manages rural construction. Therefore, the policies issued by the State Council clarified that government departments' responsibilities were developing a rural information industry, promoting modern agriculture featured with "Internet+," and reinforcing the establishment of a national-level digital system for agriculture and rural areas.

Rural informatization is closely associated with various aspects of society, such as technology, economy, culture, and education. The process requires the joint efforts of different departments to establish relevant regulatory and legal frameworks [16]. The participation of multiple departments in policy formulation can effectively avoid duplicated and contradictory policies, integrate the functions of different departments, and improve policy's effectiveness [17, 18]. The Ministry of Agriculture and Rural Affairs, the most responsible department for works related to agriculture, rural areas, and farmers, can continue its leading role in rural informatization policy making. The participation and coordination of other departments are also essential. For example, the "2019 Digital Agricultural and Rural Development Evaluation Report at the County Level" revealed that "the development of rural informatization is strongly and positively correlated with regional economic development." According to the report, the development of agricultural digitalization in eastern, middle, and western China was 36%, 33%, and 30% respectively, and counties ranking higher in digital agriculture rate showed higher economic performance. These results indicate that the roles of the Ministry of Industry and Information Technology, Ministry of Finance, and Ministry of Science and Technology should not be neglected.

3.2 Policy Implementers

The policy implementers mentioned in the 41 rural informatization policies were government departments, enterprises, social organizations, scientific research institutions, IT professionals, and farmers (Table 4). Government departments were leaders and the primary policy implementers. All investigated policies clarified different government departments' responsibilities. Meanwhile, enterprises, social organizations (e.g., academic associations and farmer cooperatives), and scientific research institutions were core institutions of policy implementation and were mentioned in 31, 22, and 21 policies, respectively. Some policies also mentioned individual-level policy implementers like IT professionals and farmers since they were stakeholders of rural informatization.

Table 4. Descriptive analysis of policy implementers

Executor	Frequency	Frequency %
Government Departments	41	100.00%
Enterprises	31	75.61%
Social Organizations	22	53.66%
Scientific Research Institutions	21	51.22%
IT Professionals	15	36.59%
Farmers	12	29.27%

Local governments were responsible for formulating relevant standards, providing finance supports, and strengthening the organization and leadership of relevant enterprises, institutions, and other policy implementers. Government departments are key players in informatization. Therefore, policymakers should define their responsibilities in the process in detail, which can be found in the existing informatization policies.

The general statements in the current policies about the roles of scientific research institutions, IT professionals, and enterprises, three stakeholders with high power originated from their possessions of resources and expertise, might be problematic. Enterprises (such as IT and agricultural companies) are the objects of rural informatization services and are engaged in the public bidding processes. The role of social organizations in rural informatization was ambiguous in the investigated documents. There were only general descriptions in the policies such as "encouraging the participation of social forces" and "encouraging and supporting the operations of farmer cooperatives." Scientific research institutions mainly focused on theoretical issues, such as strategic models, evaluating the rural informatization progresses, and reflecting current rural informatization policies. They are key to the innovation, promotion, and application of agricultural and informatization technology.

Policymakers should clarify their connections to the informatization process and define their power boundary in policy implementation. In addition to define every stakeholder's role in detail, the efficient implementation of public policies requires collaboration among the public sector, private sector, non-profits, and civil society [19]. The cooperation can effectively reduce costs, meet service demands, and improve service efficiency [20]. Rural informatization requires the collaborative participation of various aspects under the leadership of the local government to motivate the interests of the market, farmers, and other stakeholders and form a "multi-level and comprehensive" driving force.

Creating the resources and conditions for informatization policy should also involve both institutional- and individual-level efforts. One problem facing rural informatization in China is "the contradictions of farmers' growing demand for information services and the inadequate development of IT" [21]. Farmers and IT professionals are essential in the rural informatization process. Farmers usually acquire information from personal experiences, family members, and outreach staff [4]. Therefore, IT professionals should enhance their understanding of farmers' information needs and actively outreach rural areas. Moreover, the active participation of farmers is critical for achieving rural informatization.

3.3 Policy Instruments

As shown in Table 5, supply-side and environmental instruments were more frequently used than demand-side instruments. Among supply-side instruments, many policies emphasized the construction of infrastructure (60.98%) since the infrastructure is a prerequisite and basis for implementing agricultural informatization. Further, service guarantee (58.53%) and resource management (51.22%) were frequently found in this category, whereas policies related to technology support (46.34%), talent support

Table 5. Descriptive analysis of policy instruments

	Policy instrument	Frequency	%
Supply side	Resource Management	21	51.22
	Facility Construction	25	60.98
	Service Guarantee	24	58.53
	Talent Support	18	43.90
	Education and Training	18	43.90
	Technological Support	19	46.34
Environmental side	Organization and Leadership	31	75.61
	Laws and Regulations	23	56.1
	Financial Support	19	46.34
	Promotion and Propagation	33	80.49
	Theoretical Research	15	36.59
Demand side	Demonstration Project	15	36.59
	Evaluation and Assessment	17	41.46
	Public Bidding	2	4.88

(43.90%), and education and training (43.90%) were less mentioned. As to environmental instruments, more attention was given to propagation and promotion (80.49%) and organization and leadership (75.61%), while laws and regulations (56.10%), financial support (46.34%) and theoretical research (36.59%) were subordinated. The application of demand-side instruments was limited. Assessment and evaluation (41.46%) and demonstration project (36.59%) were typical demand-side instruments adopted by policymakers; public bidding, however, was only adopted in two policies.

The development of rural informatization policies can be divided into four stages, as shown in Fig. 1. The numbers in the figure represent the number of policy tools used each year. For example, two policies adopted resource management in 2006.

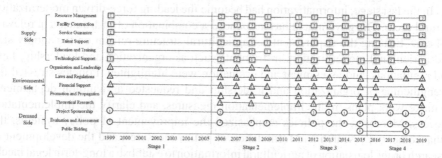

Fig. 1. Policy instruments adopted in different stages

In the first stage (1999–2005), the policies primarily applied supply-side instruments. The Chinese government issued the first national informatization plan, which emphasized national economic development and social informatization development policies and underlined the importance of strengthening modern information infrastructure. The plan promoted the application of information technology and accelerated electronic product manufacturing. To answer the call of the Central Committee of the Communist Party of China (CPC) and the State Council, the Ministry of Agriculture launched the "Information Service Action Plan" to facilitate the construction of information systems and services in the rural market. To fundamentally change the underdeveloped market of information services in rural areas, measurements in this stage included (1) establishing an information service network connecting villages within three to five years, (2) strengthening the dissemination of information in rural markets, (3) establishing a team of rural information workers, and (4) improving the information transmission networks at the township (town) and village levels.

The second stage (2006–2010) was crucial to the construction of rural informatization as rural informatization became a major task in economic and social development. Supply-side instruments still dominated policies in this stage; however, the number of environmental and demand-side instruments increased significantly. In addition to emphasizing the requirement of the complete implementation of key projects to drive rural informatization, such as full radio and television coverage ("Cun Tong [Connecting to All Villages]") with telephone systems ("Cun Tong Gongcheng [Connecting Village Project]" and "Jin Nong Gongcheng [Golden Agriculture Project]") across all villages, the government also emphasized attracting social funds into rural informatization construction and diversifying financing system and a mechanism that can satisfy the development requirements of a socialist market economy.

In 2011, rural informatization entered a new development stage. The efforts in previous years significantly improved the informatization infrastructure in rural areas, including more diverse information resources, the wide use of ICTs, and the advanced information system. In addition to the increased demand for modern agriculture through the ICT application, agricultural and rural informatization shifted from a government-driven phase to a demand-driven development stage [22]. Thus, one feature of rural informatization policies at the stage was the soaring use of demand-side instruments, and the specific strategy was to launch demonstration projects across the country.

In the last stage, informatization had become the leading force-driven modernization in rural areas. The government has introduced a combination of instruments in relevant policies. Echoing the requirements of agricultural structure reform on the supply side and agricultural modernization, instruments such as organization and leadership, laws and regulations, and assessment and evaluation were highlighted. Policies stressed the strengthening of organization and leadership and requested agricultural departments to make work plans, refine implementation measures, and clarify the implementation process. Moreover, the policies emphasized the improvement of policy systems, the enhancement of research and formulation of policy measures, and the development of research on the legislation of agricultural information to establish a long-term legal mechanism to promote agricultural and rural informatization. Finally, the policies focused on improving the evaluation system for agricultural informatization and integrating agricultural and rural informatization in the evaluation indicators of economic and social informatization development.

Using multiple types of policy instruments in policymaking is crucial in developing rural informatization as the comprehensive use of various policy instruments can achieve policy goals more effectively than a single policy instrument [23–25]. Firstly, supply-side instruments can be emphasized (1) to provide resources, facilities, services, talent, skills, and technologies required for rural informatization; (2) to synchronize agricultural, agroeconomic, technological, and service resources; (3) to improve the education and training provided to farmers and professional personnel; and (4) to reinforce the research, development, promotion, and application of advanced technologies. Secondly, it is crucial to create an environment that engages social forces in rural informatization through environmental instruments. The available approaches include: (1) Government departments should include and underline rural informatization in laws, regulations, and system standards. (2) Government departments should provide financial supports to related enterprises and institutions, such as reducing tax, telecommunications tariffs, and rental of spaces and equipment. (3) Since researching rural informatization can anticipate and incorporate initiatives for project implementation and problem-solving in the future, more studies (e.g., basic theories, barriers in the implementation of rural informatization, and development trends) can be done on rural informatization research. Finally, the demand-side instruments are the attractive force exerted by the government on the market and are manifested in demonstration projects, evaluation and assessment mechanisms, and public bids. However, few policies have stimulated the instruments.

Future policies can explore the use of new demand-side instruments such as international cooperation, market shaping, and trade management.

4   Conclusions

Rural informatization in China has developed rapidly in recent years. However, significant differences in the rate of informatization of rural and urban areas existed as a result of the historical resources imbalance. To resolve this problem and to respond to the Chinese strategies of "developing China as a Cyber Power" and "constructing new socialist rural areas," the government has introduced various policies to drive economic and social development in rural areas through informatization. In this study, we employed content analysis and frequency counts to analyze the policymakers, implementers, and instruments of the corresponding policies issued by the government. The results showed that the Ministry of Agriculture and Rural Affairs was the leading policymaker. However, the Ministry of Industry and Information Technology, the Ministry of Finance, and the Ministry of Science and Technology should increase their involvement in the formulation of the corresponding policies to promote the coordinated development of informatization. The local government is the key player in implementing the policies, with various related stakeholders playing active roles. This pattern was prominent throughout the development and should remain in place in future policy implementation trends. Further development will require the leadership and coordination of government departments and the participation of scientific research institutions, social organizations, enterprises, farmers, IT professionals, and other social forces. The results also show that the application of policy instruments was consistent with the social and economic background of the corresponding stages, which shifted from the dominant position of supply-side and environmental instruments in policies to a coordinated use of supply-side, environmental, and demand-side measures.

The findings of this study can be used to examine the effectiveness of the formulation and implementation of existing policies. The findings related to policymakers reveal issues related to power distribution and indicate problems regarding the ways in which power is coordinated and distributed among different functional departments in policy formation. Meanwhile, the findings related to policy implementers provide a reference to improve the implementation of rural informatization policies and promote their influence. Policy instruments can help review the implementation of existing policies and priorities for improving the organization and the feasibility of future policies. In summary, the research results not only objectively presented the implicit rules of current policies but also inspired the future formulation of relevant policies and provided a textual approach to improving policy implementation efficiency and maximizing policy benefits.

This study has certain limitations. As the focus of the research was national-level policies, regulations issued by local governments were not included. Future research may include local regulations in the analysis to identify the characteristics of local rural informatization. In addition, although this study analyzed policymakers, implementers, and the instruments of the investigated policies, the relationship among the three categories was not explored. Future studies can further investigate these relationships (e.g., policymakers' preferences for certain instruments and implementers).

References

1. Parker, E.: Appropriate telecommunications for economic development. Telecommun. Policy 8(3), 173–177 (1984). https://doi.org/10.1016/0308-5961(84)90002-8
2. Yu, Y., Xiangyang, Q., Lidong, Z.: Development status of rural informatization in Beijing, China. Int. J. Agric. Biol. Eng. 4(4), 59–65 (2011). http://www.ijabe.org/index.php/ijabe/article/view/546
3. Huang, H.: The strategy, model and culture sense of informatization during the process of new rural construction. China Commun. 6(3), 47–51 (2009)
4. Phiri, A., Chipeta, G.T., Chawinga, W.D.: Information needs and barriers of rural smallholder farmers in developing countries: a case study of rural smallholder farmers in Malawi. Inf. Dev. 35(3), 421–434 (2019). https://doi.org/10.1177/0266666918755222
5. Li, M.J., Wang, J., Chen, Y.II.: Evaluation and influencing factors of sustainable development capability of agriculture in countries along the belt and road route. Sustainability 11(7), 1–28 (2019). https://doi.org/10.3390/su11072004
6. Atkinson, R.D.: ICT innovation policy in China: a review. The Information Technology & Innovation Foundation (2014). http://www2.itif.org/2014-china-ict.pdf
7. MOA: China digital village development report (2019). http://www.moa.gov.cn/xw/bmdt/201911/t20191119_6332027.htm
8. Liu, C., Wang, L.: Does national broadband plan narrow regional digital divide? Evidence from China. Chin. J. Commun. 12(4), 449–466 (2019). https://doi.org/10.1080/17544750.2019.1609539
9. Qu, D.Y., Wang, X.B., Kang, C.P., Liu, Y.: Promoting agricultural and rural modernization through application of information and communication technologies in China. Int. J. Agric. Biol. Eng. 11(6), 1–4 (2018). http://www.ijabe.org/index.php/ijabe/article/view/4428
10. Deng, R., Ran, G.H., Zheng, Q., Wu, X.J.: The nonlinear effect of agricultural informatization on agricultural total factor productivity in China: A threshold test approach. Custos E Agronegocio on Line 14(2), 213–236 (2018). http://www.custoseagronegocioonline.com.br/numero2v14/OK%2011%20informatization.pdf
11. Xu, X., Luan, J: Measuring the efficiency of rural informatization in China 2007–2009: an application of data envelopment analysis. In: Pacific-Asia Conference on Knowledge Engineering and Software Engineering, vol. 115, pp. 451–458 (2012). https://doi.org/10.1007/978-3-642-25349-2_60
12. Lei, Y., Fang, C., Huang, C., et al.: Evaluation of the rural informatization in China under the background of the construction of new socialist countryside. In: 3rd International Conference on Wireless Communication and Sensor Networks (WCSN), pp. 405–410 (2016). https://doi.org/10.2991/icwcsn-16.2017.86
13. Zhang, L., Liu, X., Fu, Z., Li, D.: Evaluation of the rural informatization level in central china based on catastrophe progression method. In: Li, D., Liu, Y., Chen, Y. (eds.) CCTA 2010. IAICT, vol. 347, pp. 672–679. Springer, Heidelberg (2011). https://doi.org/10.1007/978-3-642-18369-0_80
14. Shroff, M.R., Jones, S.J., Frongillo, E.A., Howlett, M.: Policy instruments used by states seeking to improve school food environments. Am. J. Public Health 102(2), 222–229 (2012). https://doi.org/10.2105/AJPH.2011.300338
15. Rothwell, R., Zegveld, W.: Industrial Innovation and Public Policy: Preparing for the 1980s and 1990s. Frances Printer. London, UK (1981)
16. World Bank. Information and communication technologies for rural development: issues and options. https://openknowledge.worldbank.org/handle/10986/8316 License: CC BY 3.0 IGO
17. Feiock, R.: The institutional collective action framework. Policy Stud. J. 41, 397–425 (2013). https://doi.org/10.1111/psj.12023

18. Gemma, C., Bradley, C.: What works in joined-up government? An evidence synthesis. Int. J. Public Adm. **18**, 1 (2015). https://doi.org/10.1080/01900692.2014.982292
19. Rosenbaum, A.: Cooperative delivery of public services: reflections on the dynamics of public sector – Private Sector – Civil Society collaboration on governmental service delivery. In: The Fourth Global Forum on Reinventing Government: Capacity Development Workshops, Marrakech, Morocco (2002). https://pdfs.semanticscholar.org/0a94/5a447c24f5cec1d9e4f07 53ca0a8bdce84a7.pdf
20. Hilvert, C., Swindell, D.: Collaborative service delivery: what every local government manager should know? State Local Govern. Rev. **45**(4), 240–254 (2013). https://doi.org/10.1177/ 0160323X135139
21. Li, Q., Yang, K., Hu, J. Current situation and countermeasures of rural information construction. In: 1st International Forum on Studies of Rural Areas and Peasants (IFSRAP), pp. 1–6 (2013). https://www.shs-conferences.org/articles/shsconf/pdf/2014/03/shsconf_ifsr 2013_01005.pdf
22. MOA: The "Twelfth Five-Year Plan" for the development of national agricultural and rural informatization. http://www.moa.gov.cn/ztzl/sewgh/sew/201112/t20111207_2424551.htm
23. Meissner, D., Kergroach, S.: Innovation policy mix: mapping and measurement. J. Technol. Transf. 1–26 (2019). https://doi.org/10.1007/s10961-019-09767-4
24. OECD: Instrument mixes for environmental policy. OECD, Paris. (2007). https://doi.org/10. 1787/9789264018419-en
25. Li, L., Taeihagh, A.: An in-depth analysis of the evolution of the policy mix for the sustainable energy transition in China from 1981 to 2020. Appl. Energy **263**, 114611 (2020). https://www. sciencedirect.com/science/article/pii/S0306261920301239#s0010

Author Index

Printed in the United States
by Baker & Taylor Publisher Services

Printed in the United States
by Baker & Taylor Publisher Services